Sir John Fisher's Naval Revolution

STUDIES IN MARITIME HISTORY
William N. Still, Jr., Series Editor

Sir John Fisher's Naval Revolution

Nicholas A. Lambert

University of South Carolina Press

© 1999 University of South Carolina

Published in Columbia, South Carolina, by the
University of South Carolina Press

Manufactured in the United States of America

First paperback printing 2002

06 05 04 03 02   5 4 3 2 1

The Library of Congress has cataloged the cloth edition as follows:

Lambert, Nicholas A., 1967–
    Sir John Fisher's naval revolution / Nicholas A. Lambert.
       p. cm. — (Studies in maritime history)
    Includes bibliographical references and index.
    ISBN 1-57003-492-3 (paperback)
    1. Fisher, John Arbuthnot Fisher, Baron, 1841–1920.   2. Great
Britain—History, Naval—20th century.   3. Great Britain—History,
Naval—19th century.   4. Great Britain. Royal Navy—History.
I. Title. II. Series.
DA89.1.F5 L36   1999
359'.0092—dc21
  [B]   99-6012

To Jenny, my wife
—Who Bid Highest . . .

Contents

Illustrations

Maps

Acknowledgments

Over the years I have received help and encouragement from a great many people. Among my most valued supporters I am privileged to count the late John Dottridge and the late "Gus" Britton. Both saw a great deal of active service with the Royal Navy—the former held the rank of lieutenant (RNVR) and the latter that of ordinary signalman. Both did their best to provide me with a sense of perspective toward the documents I have read. And both were friends. I also owe a debt of thanks to my grandfather, the late Lt.-Commander Douglas Lambert DSC*, who served in submarines from 1937 to 1950. His name opened many doors for me and served as a letter of introduction to former submarine officers, old comrades, and their families.

I am particularly grateful to Professor George Baer, David Brown, Professor James Campbell, Jock Gardner, Professor Paul Halpern, Brian Head, Professor Sir Michael Howard MC, Professor Paul Kennedy, Jan Morris, the late Rear Admiral David Dunbar-Nasmith DSC, Professor Robert O'Neill, Mrs. Kathleen Nicholson, Professor Keith Neilson, Mrs. Frances Read, Captain Jeremy Read RN, Professor Jon Sumida (my coconspirator), Professor Russell Weigley, and Jenny Wraight. I am obliged to Tim and Bahija Dottridge, Professor Daniel E. Rogers, and Wyatt and Jennifer Rushton.

Thanks are also due to the following: Miss Pat Andrews (Cabinet Office Historical Section), Anne-Louise Antonoff, Miss Elizabeth Bennett and Carolyn Lye (Churchill Archives Centre), Mr. Edward Cadwallender, Dr. Evelyn Cherpak (U.S. Naval War College), Mr. Peregrine Churchill, Mme. Edith Colli (French Naval Archives, Vincennes); Mr. Richard von Dornberg (U.S. National Archives); Captain James Goldrick RAN, Miss Caroline Humphreys (Hampshire Records Office), Dr. Charles Fairbanks, Dr. Norman Friedman, Dr. G. Andrew Gordon, Capitaine de Vasseau Claude Huan, Martin Jones, Mrs. Jill Kelsey (Royal Archives), Mr. G. H. Le May, Mr. David Lyon (National Maritime Museum), George Malcolmson, Mrs. Jan Martin, Commander Richard Percival-Maxwell RN ret., Professor David Rosenberg, Commander Mark Ruddle RN ret., Dr. Mark Shulman, Miss Bridget Spiers (MoD Naval Library), Anthony

Simmonds, Lt.-Commander David Stevens RAN ret., Dr. Rodderick Sudderby (Imperial War Museum), Commander Jeff Tall RN ret. (RN Submarine Museum), Bob Todd (Brass Foundry, National Maritime Museum), Lt.-Commander Brian Witts RN ret. (HMS Excellent RN Gunnery Museum), and Dr. Christopher Woolgar (Southampton University Library).

Three institutions contributed generously towards my research expenses. A postdoctoral fellowship from the Olin Foundation under the auspices of the International Security Program at Yale University gave me the opportunity to read and think for more than a year. It was during this time that I became convinced I must stop rewriting my dissertation and instead begin the present book. A Charter fellowship at Wolfson College, Oxford, and a Hartley research fellowship at Southampton University enabled me to complete my research and (nearly) finish writing the manuscript.

⋙◆⋘

Extracts from the Royal Archives are quoted with the gracious permission of Her Majesty Queen Elizabeth II; crown copyright material at the Public Records Office and on deposit at various other archives is quoted by permission of the Controller of Her Majesty's Stationary Office. For permission to quote extracts from the various manuscript collections I have used, I thank the Admiralty Librarian (collections held by the Ministry of Defence Admiralty Library); the Bodleian Library; the trustees of the National Maritime Museum (collections held by the National Maritime Museum); the trustees of the British Museum (collections held at the British Library); Mr. Nigel Arnold-Forster (H. Oakley Arnold-Forster papers); the Royal Navy Submarine Museum (Rear-Admiral Frank D. Arnold-Forster papers); Jane Bonham-Carter (H. H. Asquith papers); Mrs. Margret Sinclair (Sir Henry Campbell-Bannerman papers); the trustees of the Broadlands archive and Dr. Christopher Woolgar (Admiral Prince Louis of Battenberg papers and Sir Edward Cassel papers); Winston Churchill (Sir Winston S. Churchill papers); the Lord Esher (Viscount Lord Esher papers); the masters and fellows of Churchill College Cambridge (Admiral of the Fleet Lord Fisher papers); Gloucestershire County Records Office (Sir Michael E. Hicks Beach papers); the Hon. Mrs. Ann Gascoigne and Mr. Andrew Dixon (Lewis Harcourt papers); the Rt. Hon. The earl Jellicoe (Admiral of the Fleet Lord Jellicoe papers); Lord Keyes (Admiral of the Fleet Lord Keyes papers); Mr. David McKenna (Reginald McKenna papers); the late Rear Admiral David Dunbar-Nasmith (Admiral Sir Martin E. Dunbar-Nasmith papers); Mr. J. Edward Sandars (John S. Sandars papers); the earl of Selborne (the 2d Earl of Selborne papers); Mr. Thomas Troubridge (Admiral Ernest Troubridge papers); the late Mr. John Dottridge and Mrs. Anne Lankton (Admiral Sir Reginald Tupper papers); the Bedford Estate Office (Arnold White papers).

Abbreviations

AP	Armour Piercing (shell)
APC	Capped Armour Piercing (shell)
ART	Annual Report of the Torpedo School (volumes held at Ministry of Defence Admiralty Library)
BEF	British Expeditionary Force
Captain (D)	Senior Captain commanding destroyer flotilla or flotillas
Captain (S)	Inspecting Captain of Submarines
CHART	Winston S. Churchill Papers, Chartwell Trust Collection held at Churchill College, Cambridge.
Commodore (S)	Commodore (second class) commanding submarine service
CID	Committee of Imperial Defence
DNC	Director of Naval Construction
DNI	Director of Naval Intelligence
DNM	Director of Naval Mobilisation
DNO	Director of Naval Ordnance
a/DNO	Assistant Director of Naval Ordnance
DID	Director of Intelligence Division, Naval Staff (after 1912)
DOD	Director of Operations Division, Naval Staff (after 1912)
DMD	Director of Mobilisation Division, Naval Staff (after 1912)
FDSF	*From the Dreadnought to Scapa Flow,* Arthur J. Marder (5 vols.)
FGDN	*Fear God and Dread Nought,* Arthur J. Marder, ed. (3 vols.)
FISR	Fisher Papers held at Churchill College Cambridge
FLM	First Lord's Minutes (1911–1915)(volumes held at Ministry of Defence Admiralty Library)
F.P.1.	*Fisher Papers Volume 1,* Peter Kemp, ed. (Naval Records Society: 1960)

F.P.2.	*Fisher Papers Volume 2,* Peter Kemp, ed. (Naval Records Society: 1964)
HMS	His Majesty's Ship
IQDNO (or PQ)	Important Questions dealt with by the Director of Naval Ordnance (volumes held at Ministry of Defence Admiralty Library)
NID	Naval Intelligence Division
NMM	National Maritime Museum (Greenwich)
PQ (or IQDNO)	Principal Questions dealt with by the Director of Naval Ordnance (volumes held at Ministry of Defence Admiralty Library)
PRO	Public Record Office, Kew
RE	Royal Engineers (Army)
RN	Royal Navy
RNAS	Royal Naval Air Service
RNVR	Royal Naval Volunteer Reserve
YS, c2	*Winston S. Churchill: Young Statesman,* companion volume 2, Randolph S. Churchill, ed. (London, 1967–69)
YS, c3	*Winston S. Churchill: Young Statesman,* companion volume 3, Randolph S. Churchill, ed. (London, 1967–69)

Sir John Fisher's Naval Revolution

Introduction

Mr. Churchill: "I must say again that it would be a very good thing when we have got our report that we should agree upon what papers should be kept and burn all the rest. It is a great pity that there should be a great quantity of documents of all kinds dealing with different aspects of professional views. They all ought to be surrendered."
The prime minister: "Certainly. The larger the holocaust the better in my opinion."

Testimony of the first lord of the Admiralty before the Invasion Subcommittee of Imperial Defense, 3 December 1913.

The formulation of British naval policy in the decade or so prior to the beginning of the First World War is usually explained in terms of great power rivalry in Europe. The received opinion is that by about 1902 the British government realized that the expansion of the High Sea Fleet was intended by German statesmen to gain diplomatic leverage over Great Britain by threatening the Royal Navy's command of the narrow European seas. Once recognized, the lords commissioners of the Admiralty responded by implementing a series of overdue reforms designed to improve the navy's fighting efficiency. As the competition intensified, however, Britain was obliged to concentrate a steadily larger proportion of her fleet at home in order to ensure her continued dominance of northern waters. Beginning in December 1904 the Board of Admiralty began recalling warships from the periphery toward the center of the empire.[1] As the legions returned, the security of imperial interests in the outer marches became increasingly more dependent upon diplomacy than naval deterrence. This notion that British defense policy was driven by an anti German imperative is simple, suits the standard political and diplomatic accounts of the period, and favors the predisposition of many to view the period as a lead up to the outbreak of the First World War.[2]

This book is founded upon the premise that from the beginning of the twentieth century the overriding problem for British defense planners was the insufficiency of central government finance. This is not a novel argument. It features prominently in the works of those historians who

1

have studied the decline of the British empire as a world power.[3] Financial limitation, they argue, was symptomatic of Britain's relative decline as an economic and industrial power, and "in the final three or four decades of the nineteenth century its [Britain's] position as an *industrial* power of the first order—indeed in a class of its own—shrank rapidly as other nations overtook it in various fields of industry and technology, which are, after all, the foundations of modern military strength." Britain's continued predominance in the financial and commercial world, they further insist, was no substitute for industrial might. Any British involvement in a major conflict would inevitably destabilize the global trading system upon which the prosperity of the nation's increasingly service-based economy depended.[4]

Of course, at the time, Britain's leaders did not comprehend their problems in exactly these terms. Those serving at the Board of Admiralty in particular would certainly not have entertained such notions. Before 1914 the naval lords (the professional members of the Board of Admiralty) could see no insoluble industrial or technological obstacles to the continued maintenance of a supreme war fleet and, thus, global maritime supremacy. Britain's naval-armaments industry was the largest, most innovative, best organized, and most profitable in the world. Warships built in British yards generally were qualitatively superior and cost less than foreign-built craft. The Admiralty maintained close links with armaments firms in the private sector and kept a close eye of the health of the navy's principal suppliers. On the eve of the First World War, firms such as Vickers, Maxim, & Son Ltd.; Armstrong-Whitworth; and John Brown Ltd. still dominated the world's warship-building industry and, unlike most of their European rivals, were all reported to be in good financial shape. It is often forgotten, furthermore, that the Board of Admiralty itself was responsible for the management of perhaps one of the largest manufacturing concerns in the country. The Royal Dockyards employed upwards of 30,000 artisans and workmen in the United Kingdom alone, more than any other shipbuilding organization in the world.

Not only was Great Britain relatively well endowed with the industrial assets required to produce naval armaments, but the Board of Admiralty could also draw upon all the resources of the largest and wealthiest maritime empire in the world. The Royal Navy either owned or had access to an unrivaled network of naval bases at strategic locations around the globe. British companies dominated the world's merchant marine, controlled most of the wireless and cable communication networks, and, perhaps most importantly, possessed an effective monopoly on the supply of steam coal outside European waters and the east coast of the United States. Without access to coal and colliers, fleets simply could not move. Ultimately, of course, naval mastery depended upon the size and efficiency of the imperial war fleet. During the quarter of a century prior to the outbreak of war, the Royal Navy maintained a larger battleship fleet than the second- and third-ranking naval powers combined and possessed more cruisers than the four largest naval powers. For the most part, moreover, the fleet was comprised of up-to-date warships. As one authority has noted, "the numerical, material and strategical superiority of the Royal Navy was a cold, hard reality, as the French nation found to its dismay at the end of 1898 when faced with a Britain ready to go to war over the [control of the] Upper Nile."[5] For good reasons, therefore, the Admiralty had no major worries at the turn of the nineteenth century about the ability of British industry to meet the navy's matériel requirements. The board was also broadly satisfied with the existing stock of modern warships and the condition of the fleet-support infrastructure.

What did perturb the naval lords, however, was the willingness of Parliament to fund an adequate warship replacement program. In every era of history the costs associated with building and maintaining modern, up-to-date fleets have been enormous and beyond the means of all but the richest states. For much of the nineteenth century, Britain had possessed the largest and most efficient navy in the world, and at little cost to the nation's taxpayers, largely because the other great powers lacked either the industrial base or willingness to mount a sustained challenge. From the mid-1880s, however, as European powers turned outward and began to develop their maritime strengths, the price of global naval supremacy started to climb. This upward trend in British naval expenditure was accelerated by an unparalleled growth in the cost and complexity of warships. Between 1889 and 1904 the price of a modern battleship more than doubled and that of a first-class cruiser quintupled.[6] Meanwhile, largely because the pace of technological change was so rapid, the combat-effective life of a warship dropped to fifteen years or less. As the predominant naval power determined to maintain the largest stock of modern warships in the world, Britain obviously suffered the most from the effects of capital depreciation. Indeed, the declining relative strength of the Royal Navy over this period was due much more to the ravages of capital depreciation than the increased building programs of rival powers. The financial consequences of rapid technological progress were severe; between 1889 and 1904 the relative strength of the British Navy remained fairly constant but overall naval expenditures more than doubled. Over the same period capital expenditure (on construction and major improvements to warships and dockyards) soared from £4.9 million per year—representing 44 percent of the total budget—to £26.9 million or 64 percent of gross annual naval expenditure.[7]

As the Admiralty demanded more and more money to meet its commitments, Treasury opposition mounted. By the end of the last decade of the nineteenth century, British naval expenditure was running into the limits of what many financial experts believed the state could afford. For a variety of reasons they believed that taxation could not be increased significantly without endangering the city of London's primary position in the world financial system or jeopardizing the state's ability to borrow large sums in an emergency. And as Capt. Alfred Mahan observed: "Money, credit, is the life of war; lessen it and vigour flags; destroy it and resistance dies."[8] Successive British governments had long recognized that the security of the empire depended upon the maintenance of sound finance no less than on a credible naval deterrence. Opinions in Westminster may have varied on the relative importance of economic prosperity and naval supremacy; indeed, some defense experts argued that these alone were insufficient and demanded in addition the creation of a large army. Yet by the turn of the twentieth century, most leading politicians of the day accepted that Britain could no longer have sound money and at the same time afford towering naval supremacy—let alone create a continental-sized army as well.

From about the beginning of 1902, historians have agreed, Britain statesmen instructed the armed forces to lower their strategic horizon. The Board of Admiralty at once complied by jettisoning commitments in the less vital regions of the globe and concentrating the fleet at home.[9] In the process the Royal Navy abandoned its hundred-year-old pretensions to global naval supremacy. The naval lords willingly embraced strategic retrenchment, it is argued, because the steady growth of the German High Sea Fleet threatened the Royal Navy's command of the seas that washed the British Isles.[10] The only way to meet this challenge was to reinforce the battle fleet in home waters, and, given the unwillingness of the politicians to pay for more new battleships, the only way this could be achieved was by recalling vessels then stationed abroad. The subsequent reorganization of the fleet was accomplished under the direction of Adm. Sir John "Jacky" Fisher, who in October 1904 was appointed the senior naval lord and remained the senior professional member of the Board of Admiralty until early 1910. It is generally accepted that during his administration the Royal Navy was transformed from "a drowsy, inefficient, moth-eaten organism" into a formidable fighting machine fully prepared for war against Germany.[11] Meanwhile, the overseas dockyards were allowed to run down, the traditional system of overseas station fleets was abolished, and their ships redeployed in European waters; fleets were trained for war instead of peace-time operation, and crews were drilled relentlessly in the techniques of modern gunnery, which were developed by Adm. Percy Scott.

The Fisher era was truly a time of profound change for the Royal Navy, and not just in organizational and administrative terms. Fisher initiated a virtual revolution in naval matériel during his five years in office. Outdated ironclads and gunboats were scrapped en masse and replaced with modern dreadnoughts, submarines, and aircraft. Muzzle loading guns and sail training were finally abolished; turbine machinery, wireless-telegraphy sets, and analog fire-control computers were introduced. Yet, most historians maintain, technological change had no real impact upon the formulation of naval policy. Fisher and his colleagues rationalized their multitude of new weapon systems within a more or less static strategical and tactical framework. That is to say, while the Royal Navy equipped itself with modern weaponry, naval leaders retained their old theories on the application of naval force. "That the primary duty of the Navy was battle at sea and the destruction of the enemy's battle fleet was the opinion of successive Boards of Admiralty," it is asserted.[12] Tactical thinking was equally retarded, it is assumed.

Even today, almost a century after the occurrence of these events, it is still not generally recognized that the core histories of the pre-1914 Royal Navy were written without recourse to systematic examination of financial, economic, technological, administrative, or personnel records. Or that when writing these narratives their authors placed theory ahead of fact and description. That is to say, they interpreted events using the theory of naval warfare rather than making a proper analysis of the background decision-making process. As a consequence, these core histories are still widely regarded as being, if not definitive, close to it. But even those who do accept that there are deficiencies in the currently accepted narratives believe that further investigation would result in no more than detail improvement. To most historians, Fisher's motives and goals seemed straightforward, unproblematic, and even obvious: his aim was to prepare the Royal Navy for the inevitable war with Germany.

The main conclusion of this book is that when Fisher became first sea lord in 1904, he was not unduly concerned by the growth of the German High Sea Fleet. It will be shown that not only did he conceive most of the elements of his reform program at a time when France and Russia were regarded as the main threat to Britain's interests, but that the shifts in European diplomatic alignments and the various changes in the direction of British foreign policy that occurred after he took office had surprisingly little impact upon his strategical thinking. Furthermore, Sir John Fisher was not convinced, in 1904, that the age of Pax Britannica had passed. Throughout his term as first sea lord, he remained committed to the ideal of global naval supremacy and sought to build a fleet powerful enough to protect Britain's imperial interests against all comers.[13] More specifically, Fisher wanted what his predecessors in office had sought—namely a navy capable of defeating any combination of (two) maritime powers. That being said, however, he recognized that Britain could not much longer afford to continue modernizing and expanding the existing fleet in response to each new invention or every naval expansion by rival powers. He understood that the cost of maintaining a superabundant fleet of modern battleships and cruisers would soon become fiscally prohibitive.

Fisher proposed that the Royal Navy could overcome this financial limitation by giving up the old policy of relying upon an overwhelming numerical superiority to achieve supremacy, and instead exploit new technologies to build specific force capabilities to meet the most probable threats to imperial interests. Or put another way, he wanted to build a new model navy capable of containing specific threats to British interests, instead of maintaining a conventional fleet organized primarily for battleship engagements and designed to intimidate potential enemies from even challenging the supremacy of the Royal Navy. Fisher believed that new inventions and developments in engineering permitted the creation of new types of warships and enabled the adoption of new radical methods of applying naval force. He further believed that naval supremacy and effective deterrence demanded capability rather than universal presence; in other words, the navy did not need to be deployed in force everywhere at once—that was the dream of only the most extreme jingoists. In the case of oceanic trade protection, for example, Fisher argued that the development of wireless telegraphy coupled with the exploitation of naval intelligence allowed the navy to replace the numerous assortment of cruisers scattered around the globe with a centrally located force of modern long-range, high-speed vessels that could be vectored toward any commerce raiders at large.[14]

It will also be argued that the existing narratives of pre-1914 Royal Navy policy are fundamentally flawed because their authors approached their subject with a series of mistaken presumptions.[15] For one thing, the change in the diplomatic climate during the prewar decade was not nearly so coherent nor as comprehensive as it appears with hindsight. British policy makers never focused upon the German menace to the exclusion of all others potential threats.[16] For another, the naval historians responsible for the core histories failed to consider that the Admiralty was just one of several departments of government competing for limited resources. Their narratives also failed to appraise a myriad of "internal" influences upon the formulation of "naval policy," such as the prevailing climate of financial limitation, institutional or personal ambitions, or the impact of interservice rivalry, not to mention the confusion generated by the rapid technological change. In short, they forgot that naval policy was not a function of Cabinet policy or strategic principles, but the product of individuals belonging to a bureaucratized institution and operating within a dynamic environment. For much of the period 1904–1914, it will be shown, many important strategic decisions previously thought to have been taken in response to external considerations such as foreign naval rivalry were in fact determined more by internal domestic concerns, especially money and service politics.[17] But undoubtedly the most serious misperception is that Fisher's overriding aim was to reorganize the navy (by redistributing the battleship fleet) to conform with a change in international climate (i.e., the object of British naval policy switched from providing imperial defense to meeting the German threat). Or to put it another way, the ends of naval policy changed but the means remained the same. In fact, Fisher sought to achieve exactly the opposite. With his eyes fixed upon maintaining an effective system of imperial defense, at an affordable price, he reconceptualized the theory of applying naval force.

One major reason why historians have so misunderstood Fisher's aims and motivations is that for most of his administration he felt compelled to mislead the nation's political executive as to the true direction of naval policy. Whereas the Conservative Party leadership shared his commitment to the principle of naval supremacy and took seriously the responsibility for imperial defense, the other major British political party, the Liberals, were ambivalent toward the former and essentially avoided discussing the latter. From the end of 1905 until 1915, moreover, the Liberals remained the party of government. The Liberals took office determined to cut naval expenditure by slashing the new construction budget and compelling the navy to live off its existing capital. This shift in naval policy was inspired mainly by financial considerations—although ideology also had a part to play. The Liberals needed to find large savings in government expenditure in order to pay for their expensive program of social reform, and the fastest way of achieving this was to shrink the naval budget by cutting off capital investment. Liberal ministers justified these proposed cuts by insisting that the Royal Navy was far stronger than was necessary to safeguard the country from invasion; that diplomacy rather than naval deterrence should be the primary means of protecting British interests in distant seas; and that the self-governing dominions should relieve the British taxpayer of a large proportion of the defense burden by shouldering responsibility for their own defense. They declared themselves satisfied with the largest fleet in European waters, which from 1905 meant a fleet capable of overmatching the German navy and no more.

From one perspective the Liberal administration proved highly successful. Between 1905 and 1914, British defense spending as a proportion of total state expenditure fell steadily from more than 50 to less than 40 percent. But such statistics are misleading. The ministers who took office in 1905 intended to achieve their goals without raising any significant additional state revenues. Though naval expenditure did fall, the Liberals failed to cut as deeply into the navy's budget as they had first hoped—or needed to. The traditional explanation is that the Admiralty was able to point to the aggressive intent behind the expansion of the German navy. This, however, was only part of the reason. Notwithstanding the German "threat," for many years after 1905 the Royal Navy remained three or four times stronger than the High Sea Fleet. British capital ship construction, in other words, could safely have been cut almost to zero as the Liberals had originally demanded. What really prevented them from doing so was Admiral Fisher's ability to exaggerate the magnitude of the German naval menace, blur the true strength of the Royal Navy and conceal the real direction of British naval policy. As we shall see, one of his most successful maneuvers was to propound the concept of a "dreadnought revolution" in capital ship design. This allowed the Admiralty to discount the Royal Navy's huge superiority in "pre-dreadnought" warships and thereby justify continued high levels of new capital ship construction. Fisher, it must be understood, was not interested in building a fleet just for fighting in European waters. He was aiming rather to create an effective imperial defense force with global reach. For a variety of reasons, moreover, Fisher was especially anxious to preserve the construction budget. Of course he wanted to equip the Royal Navy with up-to-date warships, but also, as we shall see, to maintain warship building capacity. While appearing to cooperate with the wishes of his political masters, therefore, Fisher worked to create a new model fleet that was not only far stronger than necessary to ensure control of home waters but also was designed primarily for imperial defense. By controlling the world's oceans and, thus, the ability to trade overseas, Fisher believed the Royal Navy could simultaneously insulate the British economy from the worst effects of conflict while inflicting massive damage on the enemy. For Britain, at least, business would continue as usual.

Thanks largely to Fisher's efforts, between 1906 and 1909 the navy was able to retain a much larger share of the national budget than the government intended. As a consequence the pace of social reform was slower and the Liberal's ability to implement their domestic agenda was undermined. Fisher's ability to preserve the naval budget from significant cuts ultimately compelled the Liberal chancellor in 1909, David Lloyd George, to take a huge electoral gamble by massively increasing the level of personal taxation. As it happened that gamble succeeded, and at the 1910 general election the Liberals were returned to power albeit with a reduced majority in the House of Commons. Over the next four years state revenues increased by a third from £151 million to £209 million—partially the result of the new levies and partially due to a fortuitous surge in yields from existing taxes—thus allowing the government to pay for both social reform and (at least until 1913) easily meet the Admiralty's demands for increases in naval expenditure.

Fisher's successful duplicity was largely the result of his ability to exploit the technological illiteracy of the politicians, thereby misleading them on the real reasons for his various reforms, the purpose of the warships he was building, and the true strength of the fleet. The best documented example has been provided recently by Prof. Jon Sumida.[18] His analysis of Fisher's capital ship policy has explained how and why all previous historians have completely misunderstood the so-called "dreadnought revolution." Far from encouraging the development of the *Dreadnought* (as he publicly claimed), Fisher was actually in favor of a cessation in battleship construction. His opposition to the building of all-big-gun battleships notwithstanding, however, Fisher indeed intended a "revolution" in capital ship design. He wanted the Royal Navy to build a new type of armored warship, the battle cruiser, a heavily armed yet lightly armored warship designed to be swift enough and powerful enough to overwhelm enemy cruisers preying on British oceanic commerce and capable of exploiting their speed advantage to bring enemy battleships to action at relatively long ranges where their state-of-the-art fire control equipment and all-big-gun battery would allow them to hit without being hit in return. Before Fisher developed his battle cruiser, the Royal Navy planned to use its small protected cruisers to fight the enemy's protected cruisers, big armored cruisers to fight armored cruisers, and battleships to fight battleships. By giving the battle cruiser the capability to fight a battleship successfully, and making it fast enough to catch and overwhelm all classes of smaller cruisers, Fisher sought to make one type of ship perform the work previously done by three. Had his policy been fully implemented, it would have resulted in the liberation of vast amounts of money and scarce manpower. "In all history," as another scholar has observed, "there have been few proposals for such radical changes in force structure."[19] But opposition from within the service to Fisher's radical theories obliged him to compromise his capital ship policy and to continue building conventional (albeit dreadnought type) battleships.

This book will show that Fisher's battle cruiser concept was just one component of his radical vision and that the mechanized gunnery fire-control system was just one of the inventions he proposed to exploit. As head of the navy, Fisher invested large sums in the development of submarines, long-range torpedoes, wireless telegraphy, the intelligence services, and a range of other projects. The full measure of Fisher's "revolution in naval affairs," however, can only be taken in by considering the characteristics of his program as a whole. Fisher recognized that new technologies lent themselves to potentially revolutionary adaptation and thus proposed to reorganize the entire naval force structure so as better to exploit new weapon systems. Instead of continuing to build a fleet comprised largely of battleships and cruisers, he attempted to create a navy built around the battle cruiser and the newly developed submarine. The battle cruiser, of course, was to serve as the blue water multi-role surface warship for imperial defense. Submarines were to form the cornerstone of Britain's naval defense against invasion. To this end, Fisher developed a new theory of sea power—the concept of "flotilla defense." This was a sea denial strategy intended to protect the British Isles from the possibility of invasion in the absence of the main fleet, thus restoring to the Royal Navy the ability to project naval force into distant waters without fear of a "bolt from the blue" from another European power while the surface fleet was on foreign service. Fisher hoped that his new system would enable Britain to maintain if not enhance its naval strength relative to other great powers in spite of financial weakness. In modern parlance, Fisher conceived a military—or naval—technological revolution.

Fisher's theories were not confined to paper. During his administration he introduced most of the elements of his program under the guise of necessary reforms. The system of flotilla defense, for instance, was in place by 1907. And by 1909 the Royal Navy had its first squadron of battle cruisers. Although Fisher was not immediately able to convince all his professional colleagues of his naval revolution, he was able, nevertheless, to push through much of his program by relying upon a core of supporters within the service to implement the necessary changes and by ruthlessly suppressing all internal dissent. And even though Fisher's immediate successors at the Admiralty abandoned flotilla defense and altered much of his strategic policy after his retirement in 1910, within two years worsening financial problems led to them being resurrected by a dynamic new civilian head of the Admiralty—Winston S. Churchill. By 1913, the majority of Britain's naval leaders had been persuaded that Fisher's strategy theory was sound, and early the following year the Board of Admiralty (civilian and professional) endorsed the change in policy and prepared to implement his naval revolution.

＝▷◆◁＝

This book has three parts. Each consists of three chapters. Part one serves as an introduction to the Fisher era proper. The first chapter explores the origins of financial limitation and its impact upon the navy. Chapter two looks at the Admiralty's policy with regard to submarines before the appointment of Fisher as first sea lord, and explodes the myth that the Royal Navy ignored the invention of the submarine and was opposed to their incorporation into the fleet. The third chapter studies the evolution of Fisher's radical theories and shows how his reaction to important innovations (such as the perfection of the submarine) or his appreciation of key events was more often than not fundamentally different from those of his contemporaries. The responses he advocated, accordingly, were also different. Part two covers the Fisher administration. These three chapters examine his true motives and intentions, how he implemented his theories, how he misled the government over the purposes of his reforms, how further technical progress modified his vision, and how he was deflected from his course by a range of political, financial, administrative factors, culminating in his battle for control of naval policy with Adm. Lord Charles Beresford and then the Liberal prime minister, H. H. Asquith. The final three chapters look at how Fisher's strategic vision was perverted by his successors. It will be shown, for example, that the ponderous Grand Fleet of Battle system employed by the Royal Navy throughout the First World War—a large integrated fleet of dreadnoughts, cruisers, destroyers, and even submarines that prowled the North Sea in the hope of catching and annihilating the German fleet at sea—which all historians have thought represented the embodiment of all strategic and tactical thinking for at least twenty years before the war, was in fact created as an experiment during the period 1910–13. The book closes with an analysis of why Churchill's administration ultimately decided to revive Fisher's strategy, and the reasons why the change in policy was kept so secret.

PART I

PART I

CHAPTER 1

The Price of Naval Supremacy

The maintenance of naval supremacy is our whole foundation. Upon it stands not the empire only, not merely the commercial property of our people, not merely a fine place in the world's affairs; upon our naval supremacy stands our lives and the freedom we have guarded for nearly a thousand years.

Winston S. Churchill, first lord of the Admiralty, 10 November 1911

British naval supremacy has always been a difficult concept to define. Although the term was commonplace in the language of politicians and statesmen of the late-nineteenth and early-twentieth centuries, and the notion was already deeply engraved into the national consciousness long before Capt. Alfred Mahan expounded his theory of the influence of sea power upon history, for much of this period a precise definition was regarded as neither necessary nor desirable. The art of naval warfare was a highly complex and technical subject about which politicians knew little and cared less. Statesmen thought of navies and sea power in terms of deterrence and prestige rather than fighting capability; this was just as true in 1914 as it was in 1880. From this perspective numbers of warships (and their cost) were more important than combat effectiveness.

Throughout this period the British government expected the Royal Navy to perform three main tasks: first, and foremost, the navy was to dominate the narrow seas and approaches to the British Isles and so prevent invasion;[1] second, the navy was to secure communications with the colonies, and particularly the route through the Mediterranean to India; and third, the navy was held responsible for the preservation and security of the global trading system upon which the prosperity of the nation depended. This involved patrolling the ocean trade routes, charting and surveying, suppressing piracy, and generally protecting British and imperial trade from interference. In return, it was always understood that the Royal Navy would be provided with ample forces to ensure a maritime predominance over any reasonable combination of other European great powers.[2] This meant sufficient line-of-battle ships to be

15

sure of a decisive victory in engagements against enemy main fleets, enough cruising vessels to protect maritime trade from interference,[3] and a supply of flotilla craft (chiefly gunboats) for imperial constabulary duties and to perform the minor operations of war.

It was the responsibility of the lords commissioners for executing the office of the lord high admiral (collectively known as the Board of Admiralty) to articulate the Royal Navy's requirements. At the head of this board, or committee, sat the first lord. This post was a ministerial portfolio carrying senior rank in the Cabinet of ministers, the political executive, and during the period covered by this survey was always held by a civilian. His chief assistants were two junior members of Parliament, who held the offices of financial secretary and parliamentary secretary; usually the same man held both. The two most senior civil servants in the department (again civilians) were also members of the Board of Admiralty. They occupied the posts of civil lord (from 1912 there were two civil lords) and that of permanent secretary. Three naval lords, the controller, and the naval secretary represented professional naval officers. The controller, who sometimes was also referred to as third naval lord, held responsibility for all aspects of naval matériel. He supervised the Royal Dockyards, the Corps of Naval Constructors, the Contracts Department, and the Directorates of Naval Ordnance and Torpedoes. The controller, in effect, was the managing director of the navy's substantial manufacturing concerns. The naval secretary generally served as administrative assistant to the first lord and oversaw the promotions and appointments of naval officers. Before 1904 the naval lords proper held joint responsibility for the general running of the navy. After this date their labor was divided: the senior or first took charge of operational and strategic policy; the second, naval personnel; and the junior or fourth naval lord was given responsibility for stores, supply, and the transport service. Although it was the first lord who was accountable to Cabinet and Parliament for the navy and thus the man who held ultimate authority, the other members of the Board were not his assistants. Power to take decisions was vested in the Board: without support of the naval lords the first lord could not act.

For most of the nineteenth century, Great Britain lacked a great power competitor capable of mounting a serious and sustained challenge at sea. She was, consequently, able to preserve her "naval mastery" at little cost, with a fleet comprised of old ships as well as new ones. Thus, the construction budget was low. Although the numerical strength of the active British fleet—comprised of line-of-battle ships—was perhaps only one-third more than that of its principal rival, the Marine Française, the Royal Navy possessed an enormous reserve stock of wooden warships that could, in an emergency, be swiftly recommissioned and manned by crews drawn from the largest merchant marine in the world. Nor was Britain's naval position seriously challenged during the transition from sail-driven to steam-propelled warships. When it came to building ironclads, the Royal Navy was able to rely upon Britain's huge financial and industrial strength to build warships both faster and cheaper than any other power. As late as 1880, for instance, Britain's output of coal, pig-iron, and steel was more than twice that of any Continental power.[4] In 1914 the British naval armaments industry could still build more warships per year than all the other great naval powers combined.

During the 1880s there grew within the country a perception that the Royal Navy was losing its naval mastery, Great Britain's still commanding lead in naval technologies and unrivaled manufacturing strength notwithstanding. Not only had other powers begun to invest in naval power, but, more ominously, Britain's economic lead was seen to be slipping to countries with better endowed and more flexible economies. War scares in 1884 and 1885 against Russia and again in 1888 against France incited a public clamor in Britain for naval expansion. But the government's response was equivocal. Increases in naval estimates in 1885 and 1886 were followed by cuts in naval expenditure the next two years. Both political parties were reluctant to raise taxes to fund a permanent increase in the naval establishment. The question of whether late-Victorian Britain retained her naval mastery was immensely difficult to prove or disprove. The crude quantitative measures of naval strength that had served in the age of sail were meaningless in a period of rapid technological innovation, and it was virtually impossible to add a sufficiently flexible qualitative element to the equation. Battleships under construction at the beginning of the decade were already obsolescent by the time they had been launched and within ten years were unfit to lie in the line of battle, being no match for more modern vessels. That being said, however, until the development during the late 1890s of the American navies, and especially the Japanese navy, such warships were capable of rendering service in distant waters. "In the China Sea, on the west coast of South America, in every harbour remote from Europe," as Sir Thomas Brassey, a prominent naval authority, noted in 1882, "our flag will be shown with credit for years to come in ironclads, condemned as obsolete for a commission in the Channel and Mediterranean."[5] In peacetime anyway. The value of these semi-obsolete vessels in wartime was more debatable.

Britain's naval leaders deliberately made little effort to educate their political masters on the true workings of sea power. For the Admiralty there was some advantage in using "vague and insubstantial" language whenever the first lord was obliged to ask Parliament for more money. A spectrum of political interest groups could be persuaded to ensure the provision of additional money needed to uphold "naval supremacy" without having to agree how the new appropriation would be spent or what exactly it would buy. The growing complexity of ironclad warships reinforced this tendency to leave all details to the experts. Whereas in the age of sail, laymen could estimate the relative strength of a fleet, in the age of industrial navies, especially during an age of rapid technological change, estimates of the fighting value of warships were highly subjective, and, thus, only professional naval officers were in a position to say with any authority how many ships were required to uphold naval supremacy—if such a number existed. So long as the Admiralty's demands upon the Treasury were moderate, and dissatisfied naval officers did not try to stir up public support for more ships by issuing sensational revelations (as occurred in 1884),[6] the Cabinet seldom challenged the Admiralty's authority.

Once the navy estimates began to climb, however, the government began demanding justification for further increases in expenditure. The question as to whether or not Britannia still ruled the waves became a political matter of growing importance. By the end of the 1880s, this and other naval issues grabbed the public attention "in a way that would have been unthinkable" ten years before.[7] During the winter of 1888, the government came under attack for failing to provide adequate funding for the navy at a time when rival powers were increasing their maritime capabilities. The unfairness of these accusations, based as they were upon subjective measures of naval power, persuaded the first lord of the Admiralty, Lord George Hamilton, that the government could avoid much of the arbitrary criticism of naval policy by publishing a yardstick by which its commitment to upholding British naval supremacy could be visibly measured. In cooperation with the naval lords of the Admiralty, Hamilton set himself the task of calculating the navy's matériel requirements in a modern war. On 7 March 1889, the first lord explained his new formula to Parliament.

> I have endeavoured to study the speeches of those who in previous years have held my position and that of Prime Minister, so as to ascertain what was the paramount idea underlying their utterances when they spoke of the standard at which our naval establishment should be maintained. I think I am correct in saying that the leading idea has been that our establishment should be on such a scale that it should at least be equal to the naval strength of any two other countries.[8]

By "our establishment," Hamilton meant the number of modern battle-ships. "Supremacy at sea," he observed, "must, after all, be measured by the number of battleships we can put into the line."[9] Elsewhere in his speech, the first lord insisted that only up-to-date types would be count-ed toward the new standard; this was a very significant departure from established practice and represented a concession to those who had argued that older battleships would be of little use in a real war. Deleting older vessels also provided justification for new construction.

As to how he intended to calculate his "two-Power standard," as it became known, Hamilton remained deliberately vague. At the very least it meant a modern British battleship force numerically equal to the com-bined battleship fleets of the next two strongest naval powers; at the most it provided for a fleet certain of containing the combined fleets of the next two strongest naval powers or, in quantitative terms, a British battle fleet approximately 10 to 15 percent larger than that of her poten-tial opponents.[10] Equality plus a margin, in other words. When later that March Hamilton announced a huge naval construction program that clearly exceeded his new two-power formula, the confusion was exacer-bated.[11] Without explaining his calculations, Hamilton fixed the estab-lishment of the British fleet at forty-seven battleships. This gave the Royal Navy a margin of six units over the combined battle fleets of France and Italy—the then second- and third-ranking naval powers. Over the next five years, Hamilton revealed to Parliament, seventy new warships would be added to the navy's list, including ten capital units that were much superior to all previous battleships. The total cost of the Naval Defense Act was projected at twenty-one million for warships plus an additional five million to pay for improvements in fleet-support infra-structure. Hamilton maintained that this construction program would provide the navy with ample warships, "adequate not only to our imme-diate, but also our future wants." In the process he explained that the Board hoped the magnitude of the sum to be spent under the Naval Defense Act would discourage the naval aspirations of rival powers.[12]

All interested groups quickly accepted the "two-Power standard" as the literal definition of British naval supremacy; in other words public and parliamentary opinion remained satisfied that Britain was still supreme at sea so long as the Royal Navy possessed as many battleships as the second and third naval powers combined. In 1890, the standard was endorsed by the Liberal Party. In the House of Commons, the issue of naval spending faded in importance. One reason why the new stan-dard appealed to the politicians was that its definition was so flexible. No amendments were required when Russia assumed the rank of third naval power, or when France and Russia announced their formal alliance a year later. Whereas originally the standard was intended to establish the minimum level of naval strength consistent with upholding naval supremacy, it quickly became regarded as a maximum level. After further increases in foreign naval programs during the 1890s, there was informal agreement between the political parties that the British tax-payer would not be asked to assume the full burden of matching the increases in the French and Russian fleets ship for ship. By the middle of the decade, Hamilton's "margin of superiority" in battleships had been eroded to zero, much to the dismay of the professional members of the Board of Admiralty.

While the two-power formula may have simplified the politics of naval finance, it nevertheless did not satisfy the navy's material require-ments. What most historians have failed to realize is that essentially it was always a political rather than a military standard. It was useful to the Board of Admiralty insofar as it served as a guarantee that the naval establishment would not fall below a minimum level. But it certainly did not reflect either the direction of naval strategic thinking or the funda-mentals of naval doctrine. Nor was it based upon any theoretical principles of naval warfare. Most senior naval officers in fact, felt that two-power parity in numbers of battleships was insufficient. Sir Frederick Richards, for example, who served as senior naval lord from 1893 until 1899, frequently complained that "at every turn we feel the inconvenience of the policy of being content with equality in battleships with France and Russia."[13] For "a power which lives by the sea," he felt, "the only true policy lies in *unquestioned* superiority."[14] Adm. Lord Walter Kerr, who succeeded him entirely agreed and throughout his term constantly pressed for the restoration of the "safety margin." Nevertheless, both appreciated that, in the prevailing political and financial climate, their aspirations were impracticable.

Britain's naval leaders held more serious—and much more legiti-mate—concerns at the available number of modern cruisers suitable for protecting the empire's oceanic trade. In a scheme for the defense of trade prepared during the 1885 war scare, the naval intelligence depart-ment calculated on the Royal Navy being able to augment its force of eighty-three trade protection vessels with at least seventy-five armed merchant ships. By 1892, however, the Admiralty had recognized that an auxiliary cruiser would be no match for a modern warship, and the plan to use armed merchant ships as cruisers was consequently shelved. There was no alternative, the naval lords argued, other than to build more cruisers. The Admiralty estimated that to provide adequate pro-tection to British trade in time of war, the Royal Navy would require at least twice as many cruisers as its prospective opponents. In other words, twice as many as those possessed by the Franco-Russian combination. In number of battleships, it will be noted, the Admiralty accepted (albeit reluctantly) temporary equality with the combined French and Russian fleets. The concern at the shortage of cruisers in time of war was to a certain extent allayed by the announcement in 1894 of the Spencer program, which added to the naval establishment another seven battleships, twenty large cruisers, and over one hundred flotilla craft (notably torpedo boat destroyers). But soon the naval lords found themselves confronted by a quite different and much more serious threat to their preparations for the defense of maritime trade.

The Armored Cruiser Threat

In 1896, the French navy laid down a new model cruiser named *Jeanne d'Arc*. She was a large, high-speed, long-range, armored cruiser that was purposely designed for raiding commerce on the high seas. In theory the great length of the hull coupled with a huge coal capacity would enable her to outpace and outdistance any more powerful adversary. But the most remarkable feature of this warship was the provision of an armored belt along the complete length of the hull. Previous generations of "first-class" cruisers had not received this degree of protection, because it was simply not possible to armor a large enough area of the hull without prohibitive sacrifices in either speed or endurance or both. Instead, large cruisers had been given an armored deck located at the waterline covering the machinery spaces and the magazines, which were further protected by coal bunkers located along the ship's sides.[15] With the development in the early 1890s of face-hardened armor, however, it became practicable to mount armor plates of sufficient thickness to stop projectiles from medium caliber (up to 6–inch) weapons. This meant that the hull of the *Jeanne d'Arc*, and all subsequent French side-armored cruisers, was virtually shotproof against the armor piercing shells fired from the 6-inch guns that composed the main batteries of the British cruisers with the speed to catch them.[16] Their own battery of quick-firing guns, moreover, was sufficient to overwhelm even the more powerfully armed (yet slow steaming and slow shooting) old British ironclads relegated to station duties in distant waters.

At first the British paid little attention to the French development of the side-armored cruiser, questioning the accuracy of their intelligence reports. The ordering of two similar vessels at the beginning of 1897 also drew no response. Not until April that year, after the French parliament voted a supplementary estimate providing for another four armored cruisers protected by the newly perfected Krupp face-hardened armor, did the Admiralty finally react.[17] The Board now realized with some concern that these powerful vessels outclassed even the newest British cruisers and, in effect, rendered obsolete the Royal Navy's entire stock of trade protection vessels. It was quickly agreed that the only appropriate response was for the Royal Navy to build armored cruisers of its own and in greater numbers. On 23 July 1897, accordingly, the first lord of the Admiralty, George Goschen, informed Chancellor of the Exchequer Michael Hicks-Beech that "in view of the extra exertions made by France specially in respect of very fast cruisers" the navy required money to lay down immediately four (later increased to six) large cruisers with the necessary speed to run down the French vessels.[18] Three days later the House of Commons voted the necessary sum.[19] Toward the end of that year, the Admiralty learned that the French intended to lay down yet more armored cruisers early the following year. The Board rightly interpreted this as a direct challenge to British naval supremacy. The naval lords in London were not alone in expressing their alarm at this "new and formidable development."[20] In February 1898 the commander in chief of Britain's premier Mediterranean squadron expressed strong doubts as to the ability of the cruising vessels then in his fleet to contain the new generation of fast armored cruisers.[21]

Later that month Goschen explained the seriousness of the situation to the Cabinet:

> The French, so far as their policy can be gauged, have begun to recognise that it is by cruisers rather than battleships that they can damage us most. What their efforts on battleships have been had been seen from the facts which I have described, but in the new and vast program which is now awaiting the sanction of the Chamber there is only one new battleship to be laid down in 1898. Their first class cruiser program, on the other hand, is most formidable.[22]

In early 1898, the Admiralty laid down the Royal Navy's first batch of armored cruisers. The six *Cressy* class were big ships. They carried a powerful main armament of 9.2-inch guns capable of piercing Krupp armor plate and a numerous battery of quick-firing 6-inch guns. In the opinion of the then director of naval construction, such vessels would be able to engage a battleship with some prospect of success and thus be of use in wars against powers other than France.[23] The second naval lord and the controller agreed that "they would be quite capable of dealing with many of the foreign battleships if they caught them singly."[24] Although the hulls of armored cruisers were actually larger than those of contemporary battleships, because they carried less armor their displacement was not so great and they thus did not cost so much to build. But because of the large number of stokers needed to feed the boilers when driving them at high speeds, armored cruisers required larger crews than battleships and, as a consequence, were more expensive to maintain. The dimensions of the Royal Navy's second batch of four armored cruisers, ordered in May 1898, were even larger.[25] At 14,000 tons, the four vessels of the *Drake* class displaced just 350 tons less than the *London* class battleships ordered under the same program and, at £1.05 million apiece, cost virtually the same.[26] To proceed at top speed, these craft required a complement of almost nine hundred men—no fewer than one hundred and fifty more than a battleship. On first reading these figures, the senior naval lord immediately labeled the *Drake*s as "man eating" vessels.[27] Goschen, too, hesitated to authorize their construction, being concerned not so much with their price as their "vast pull on our manning resources."[28] It was no coincidence that in 1898 the Admiralty raised an additional 6,300 active service ratings.[29]

No sooner had the Admiralty finished responding to the French armored cruiser program, than they were compelled to react to an unexpectedly large increase in the Russian navy.[30] The first indications that the Russians were planning to increase their fleet reached London in early February 1898. The British attaché in St. Petersburg informed the Admiralty that a senior Russian admiral had "left for the United States with discretionary power to buy warships."[31] A month later, Tsar Nicholas announced a six-year naval construction program but refused to disclose exactly how much money he intended to spend on his navy. In London, Goschen hesitated to act until the Naval Intelligence Division could obtain a clearer sense of the Russian intentions.[32] In the meantime, nevertheless, he obtained Cabinet approval for "the proposition that we must meet the Russian program whatever it might be."[33] In effect, he was given a blank check. Several months later even the Admiralty was taken aback when it was learned that the Russians intended to borrow £27,560,000 to build a new fleet to be stationed in the Far East at the recently acquired naval base at Port Arthur.[34] "The Russian government has inaugurated a gigantic program of shipbuilding," Goschen reported to the Cabinet on 6 June, "which is to be carried out in addition to the construction provided for in the regular Russian annual budgets."[35] To meet this challenge, the Admiralty requested an immediate supplementary appropriation to pay for four battleships and four armored cruisers (costing approximately £9 million).[36] More would be required the following year.

It was now apparent to the Admiralty that Britain was racing neck to neck with the second- and third-ranking naval powers and that substantial additional funds would have to be provided for the Royal Navy if the security of the trade routes was to be insured. "In view of the programs of France and Russia" Goschen hastened to warn the chancellor in a private letter dated 21 July 1898, "we must resolutely face the necessity of our having to *add considerably to ours in next years ordinary program.* I mention this now, so that there be no misunderstanding as to what we may have to do. What I am proposing now is *not* in alleviation of next years' estimates."[37] Hicks-Beech was aghast. The following day Goschen assured him that the navy's demands were modest. The battleships were required to maintain the two-power standard, while the addition of just four extra cruisers left the Royal Navy with no margin of superiority. Later that day the first lord reminded the chancellor of the Exchequer that the Admiralty had always maintained that "we must have many more than our enemies if our trade routes and food supplies are to be protected."[38] The only concession that Goschen was prepared to make was to overrule objections from his advisors to the purchase of smaller armored cruisers, the *Kent* class, which cost just £750,000 apiece and which required only half the crew of the *Drake* class.[39] In time they proved to be a false economy.[40] In August 1898, and again in December, the first lord badgered Hicks-Beech to sanction the purchase of yet more fast cruisers, but without success.[41]

A nationwide strike by the engineering unions in 1899 resulted in a shortage of armor plate, which prevented the Royal Navy from ordering as many armored cruisers as it wanted that year. The Admiralty, however, wasted little time in notifying the Treasury that, as a consequence, no fewer than seven would have to be laid down the following year.[42] For the first time, moreover, cruisers ordered under the 1900 program would be given priority over the construction of battleships. Increasingly loud complaints from Hicks-Beech at the magnitude of the sums already spent on armored cruisers failed to discourage the Admiralty. "Every day brings further proof of the kind of cruiser war we shall have to face, if we have war at all," Goschen replied in February 1899.[43] Yet it can hardly be denied that the Admiralty's approach to meeting the Franco-Russian challenge by maintaining a numerically superior fleet of battleships and cruisers was, by the turn of the century, running into the limits of the British state's willingness or ability to pay.

Asymmetrical Force Structures

The Board of Admiralty had good reason to doubt whether the French threat to British trade could be contained by a naval strategy based upon the maintenance of a large fleet of battleships. In 1896 François Fournier, a highly respected French admiral, postulated that recent advances in technology allowed navies to build new types of warships and even adopt new force structures. With an eye on confounding "perfidious Albion," he suggested that France should build a new fleet comprised of fast, long-range armored cruisers. Fournier advised that these vessels must always strive to exploit their greater speed to avoid fighting with superior British forces. He also argued that deliberately seeking combat with a more numerous enemy fleet made little sense when the opponent's vital interests could be more effectively attacked by other means. Rather than attempting to contest command of the sea, Fournier believed that the easiest and cheapest way France could strike at Great Britain would be to wage a systematic *guerre industrielle*. This "industrial war" was to take the form of an attack on the global trading system. The French hoped that sinking British merchant ships would disrupt the London financial markets by driving up the price of insurance and interest rates to politically unacceptable levels. The supposed vulnerability of Britain's financial system, according to Fournier, made the actual material severing of Britain's trade arteries unnecessary.[44] Steadily worsening economic disruption would eventually force the city of London to demand the government make peace.

Fournier insisted that the implementation of his strategy was practicable and that the commerce raiders could inflict sufficient damage on Britain's oceanic trade to bring about the necessary conditions for economic collapse. Anticipating those critics who argued that the French had unsuccessfully employed a similar strategy against Britain one hundred years before, Fournier explained that the previous attempts to wage a *guerre de course* by encouraging civilian privateering had failed for two main reasons: first, French attacks on British trade had been haphazard and uncoordinated; and second, the Royal Navy had successfully contained much of the French effort by mounting an effective blockade over French home ports, thus, preventing warships free egress to the open seas. The admiral further insisted that the economic system at the end of the nineteenth century was far more complex and, thus, more vulnerable than had existed a century before. In addition, the navy of the Third Republic would be better equipped. Fournier argued that whereas previously the Marine Française had lacked reach, it now possessed a global network of defended bases from which to operate purpose-built corsairs in distant waters where British trade was most vulnerable. But the most important reason Fournier cited in support of his *guerre industrielle* strategy was the widespread belief that close blockade of French ports was no longer practicable.[45]

The French admiral's faith in the ability of the armored cruisers to evade the blockade was based upon the belief that the French navy's already sizeable force of torpedo boats was capable of driving back the British observation squadrons whenever necessary. Since 1886 the

Marine Française had been investing heavily in torpedo craft.[46] Originally their function had been to render all French territorial waters permanently unsafe for hostile warships and thereby keeping ports open to trade. During the 1880s, torpedoes were still relatively primitive weapons with an effective range of perhaps 600 yards. Nevertheless they conferred "battle power" on the flotilla—in other words a small cheap torpedo boat had the power to sink the largest most expensive warship in the world. But after the perfection in 1888 of quick-firing artillery and high-explosive shells, most naval experts believed the torpedo threat had been contained. Armed with a battery of quick firers a battleship could throw out a "hail of fire" capable of sinking its assailant before it could approach to within torpedo range—at least in the hours of daylight. At night, torpedo boats were still a formidable weapon against any hostile warship that ventured too close to their base. Until Fournier suggested that the armored cruisers should endeavor to exploit this situation by entering and leaving port only at night, the night-fighting potential of the French flotilla appeared to be of little use. From the late 1890s, however, the French torpedo boats practiced at night driving back hostile warships lurking in their territorial waters.

Fournier's vision was of a force structure different from that of all other fleets. Traditional navies, organized for combat and to contest the command of the sea, comprised three general categories of warships: battleships, cruisers, and flotilla craft. In wartime, battleships would fight other battleships, cruisers and scouts would be expected to face other cruisers and scouts, and so forth. Except for torpedo craft, warships were not intended to fight outside their own class. Battle power, therefore, could not be improvised. Numbers of battleships would prove decisive. Instead of continuing to build a conventional or symmetrical fleet, matching the force structures of rival navies, Fournier urged his peers to adopt a different structure and build new-model warships that did not compare with conventional vessels. The armored cruiser was the perfect example of the intermediate type. These craft were fast enough to evade hostile battleships, yet possessed sufficient fighting power to overwhelm trade-protection cruisers. He also advised that France should not build any more expensive battleships. Fournier's idea of a navy built upon a fleet of corsairs found considerable support in the French parliament, particularly from the colonial lobby.[47] Fournier's theory of an "asymmetrical force structure" also caught the imagination of Edouard Lockroy, the chairman of the parliamentary naval committee who had also served a short term as minister of marine.[48] Lockroy recognized that his nation lacked the financial strength to compete with Britain and other powers in maintaining large battle fleets. He nevertheless saw an opportunity in Fournier's strategy for France to keep her rank as a first-class maritime power. In addition, the notion that France could employ a more sophisticated form of warfare than the British, and the idea that the demand for technologically sophisticated naval equipment would help boost the nation's flailing industries, also appealed.[49]

British suspicions that the French navy had actually adopted the *guerre industrielle* strategy appeared to be substantiated by Founier's appointment at the end of 1897 to command the French main fleet based in the Mediterranean. The impression was considerably boosted early the following year when Lockroy was returned to the office of minister of marine. One of his first acts, moreover, was to drop a battleship from the published French construction program and use the money thus saved to fund an acceleration in the armored cruiser program, and to pay for improvements in the fortifications protecting overseas bases. Successive reports from the British naval attaché in Paris noted an upsurge of interest in radical theories of naval war among politicians, the press, and especially among junior naval officers. Important technological breakthroughs by French naval engineers in other areas of naval weaponry further strengthened the credibility of the new-look French navy. From 1898 the effective range of all torpedoes was effectively doubled overnight by the application of the gyroscope to their guidance mechanism. Even more significant, however, was news of the French navy's successful experiments with submarine torpedo boats.[50]

On 19 November 1898, Lockroy personally charged the commanding officer of the experimental submarine *Gustave-Zédé*, Lt. Lucian Mottez, with the task of finding ways to demonstrate the military value of his craft.[51] For whose benefit he did not say. With the connivance of Vice Adm. François Fournier, another submarine enthusiast, the *Gustave-Zédé* was granted permission to participate in the forthcoming Mediterranean Fleet exercises. In the first week of December, Mottez navigated his craft the forty miles from Toulon to the Isles d'Hyères whereupon he twice torpedoed the gunnery training ship *Magenta;* the first time when the battleship was at anchor, the second while she was under way.[52] The significance of this achievement was enormous. The submarine had demonstrated for the first time that it was no longer an engineer's toy but capable of performing deadly acts of war. This was the first time a submerged submarine had successfully fired a torpedo at a surface target. Early in the new year (1899) Mottez repeated his achievement for the benefit of Lockroy and the world's press. But most foreign naval analysts, notably the head of the British naval intelligence department, dismissed the event by claiming that the exercises had been staged for political reasons.[53] Their skepticism seemed justified. On board *Magenta* to witness the attack were Lockroy, his wife, Fournier, his wife and daughter, the port admiral, and several other notables and selected members of the press. Their presence undoubtedly encouraged a theatrical atmosphere.[54] Although the second *Gustave-Zédé* trials might not have been actually stage-managed, Lockroy was not slow in exploiting their success for political capital, thereby appearing to confirm the allegations and suspicions of his foreign critics. In a speech introducing the forthcoming estimates to the Chamber of Deputies given in March 1899, for instance, Lockroy claimed that the perfection of the submarine heralded a renaissance in the fortunes of the French navy.[55] And he was not backward in claiming for himself much of the credit by reminding his audience that it had been he who had initiated the submarine program back in 1896. Lockroy was rewarded with the congratulations of the chamber and a large appropriation to build more submarines. For his part, Mottez received an accelerated promotion. Thanks largely to Lockroy's efforts, by the time he left office in late 1899, the French navy possessed two submarines in commission with another ten under construction. The British response to the French submarine program is the subject of the next chapter.

When viewed in the light of the new *guerre industrielle* strategy, the development of the armored cruiser, the torpedo, and the submarine posed a credible threat to Britain's system of trade defense. Even before the advent of the submarine, which made any permanent blockade untenable, senior naval officers had reached the conclusion that "a close blockade of an enemy's port hardly seems advisable in these days of Torpedo Warfare."[56] It would be safer, instead, for the Royal Navy to impose a looser "observational" blockade. But the drawback to greater safety by taking station further out to sea was obvious—without the provision of more warships the net surrounding the blockaded port would have to be thinner, thus giving commerce raiders more chance to escape undetected, especially at night. Papers the Admiralty submitted to the Cabinet to justify the huge sums required to build expensive armored cruisers in addition to the requisite number of battleships, show that the Admiralty was truly afraid of the *guerre industrielle*. The most lucid explanation of the situation was provided in a Cabinet memorandum circulated in January 1901.

> The French coast of the Channel is now studded with torpedo-boat stations, and this development of what is known as the "Défense Mobile" has for its object to make it impossible for British battleships to blockade any of the French naval ports owing to the danger to which they would be exposed by torpedo-boats and submarines. The blockade of the French

ports by a British fleet being thus rendered, in their view impracticable, the idea of the French strategists is that from these ports could issue by night their powerful fast new armored cruisers, which would then proceed to place themselves upon our trade routes and do great damage to our mercantile marine. None of the large fleet of unarmored cruisers which are allocated for the protection of our commerce on the various trade routes would be capable of meeting any of these new armored cruisers, but as the preceding tables will have shown, we have already begun to build the ships that could do so, though not yet in sufficient numbers.[57]

By this time, however, the Admiralty was becoming increasingly aware of the specter of state financial limitation that was casting a lengthening shadow over the achievement of naval sufficiency.[58] The cost of building armored cruisers "in sufficient numbers" to protect British trade, while at the same time building sufficient battleships to preserve naval supremacy, was threatening to strain British state finances to the point of collapse.

Financing the Navy

At the end of the nineteenth century, the spiraling trend in naval expenditure was a major worry for most British politicians, who were still unwilling to alienate the electorate by raising taxation to pay for a larger navy. To avoid this the government resorted to borrowing. While paying for current expenditure by adding to the national debt was always politically out of the question, since 1895 Parliament had relaxed this "principle of national finance" by passing an act that allowed improvements in naval works to be paid for by the issue of thirty-year bonds.[59] The government of the day had justified this controversial step by claiming that improvements to dockyard facilities could legitimately be regarded as a capital investment project to meet the navy's long-term requirements, in which case there was no reason why the entire cost should fall entirely upon the current generation of taxpayers. As a gesture towards fiscal orthodoxy, though, the interest payable on these bonds was deducted from the naval estimates account. This practice of paying for naval works by money raised on the capital markets rather than out of current revenue was continued until 1904, when the parliamentary finance committee protested it must stop. Notwithstanding the passage of successive naval works acts, paying for warships by long-term borrowing was never an option for any British government.

The crisis in naval spending came suddenly. In 1889, funding the Naval Defense Act had not been a problem for the Treasury. A year earlier, the chancellor of the Exchequer had introduced a debt conversion scheme that substantially reduced the cost of annual debt servicing, thereby releasing money to pay for the fleet expansion. Similarly, in 1894 the government had been able to respond generously to the navy's request for more warships, because the introduction of graduated scale of death-duties that year subsequently provided the state with an additional three million pounds a year.[60] Between 1896 and 1898, moreover, the upward trend in state revenues was sustained by an economic boom. The bountiful revenues from existing taxes allowed the Conservative government not only to pay for the large increases in defense expenditure but also to buy some political popularity with its supporters by easing the burden of land tax.[61] Even if some political leaders doubted "that the junction of Russia and France in a maritime war is at all a probable contingency," additional money was always provided whenever the Admiralty asked.[62]

Indications that the British government might encounter difficulties in meeting all the Admiralty's future requirements first emerged in the summer of 1898. Treasury forecasters had for several months been aware of an impending surge in state expenditure, largely due to the unprecedented size of the 1898–99 naval construction program. The Admiralty had ordered no fewer than seven battleships and eight armored cruisers. Initially, the Treasury was confident of finding the necessary extra funds if the Cabinet sanctioned the expenditure. The economy was booming and, because most of these vessels would not be laid down until late in the year, the financial burden would not be felt until the following fiscal year. In the autumn of 1898, however, while preparing for the forthcoming budget, Sir Michael Hicks-Beech discovered that the growth of the state's revenue was no longer keeping pace with projected expenditures. On 12 October 1898, he cautioned the prime minister, Lord Salisbury, that the level of duty on "Beer and Spirits" had inexplicably reached a point of diminishing returns and that, consequently, in the following year net revenue was projected to fall.[63] This was serious because excise duties contributed over 40 percent of Treasury revenue, and Hicks-Beech had been relying upon an anticipated increase in revenue from this source to help pay for the naval increase.[64] Over the next few months, the chancellor became increasingly gloomy at the fiscal outlook. "I am sorry to tell you," he informed the prime minister at the end of January 1899, "that the prospect is very disagreeable."[65] Revenues had already begun to fall, and the Treasury now anticipated a sizeable budget deficit of at least four million pounds: "mainly, of course, due to the Army and Navy."[66]

At first the prime minister disputed his chancellor's economic predictions and refused to let taxes be raised. "An increase of taxation—I suppose a penny on the income tax and something on tea and wine—will require justification because it is clearly an alarmist budget," he replied. "Though I cannot say there is *no* danger," he added, "I do not see any danger justifying such a step."[67] Salisbury insisted that the fiscal deficit must be the result of a "temporary" shortfall in excise revenues and could legitimately be covered by borrowing.[68] Hicks-Beech strongly disagreed. "This is no temporary emergency," he wrote back, "it is the result of a continuous increase of expenditure which will grow rather than diminish in future years."[69] The Admiralty, he again protested, was continuing to ignore the Treasury's requests for economy.[70] But the prime minister remained unmoved. While Salisbury agreed with Hicks-Beech that Goschen's Board of Admiralty had become "insatiable," and acknowledged that fiscal difficulties existed, he refused to allow the Treasury to impose a ceiling on the navy estimates.[71] He did not, however, forbid Hicks-Beech from canvassing his other Cabinet colleagues for support over the issue.

British state finances received a mauling during the South African colonial war that lasted from October 1899 until mid-1902. Although the Treasury quickly raised taxes to meet the necessary increase in military expenditure, the unexpectedly long duration of the Boer War obliged the government to borrow on a large scale. The Cabinet's reluctance to upset the voters at the general election at the end of 1900 further encouraged the preference to pay for the war mainly through loans rather than higher taxes. As a result, between October 1899 and the end of 1903, the national debt grew by more than a quarter. More importantly, from a fiscal standpoint, the annual debt service charges grew by almost a third, from £25.9 million to £32.2 million.[72] Over the same period, the peacetime level of naval expenditure continued to rise. Gross spending on the navy rose from £22.5 million in 1897–98 to £41.7 million in 1904–5 (or by more than 80 percent). And the trend was still upwards.[73] To put these figures in perspective, over the same period total government expenditure rose from £103 million to £142 million (or by only 40 percent). Furthermore, as Hicks-Beech had predicted, the yields from the prewar levels of taxation did not keep pace with expenditure.

Of course the impending fiscal crisis did not immediately become apparent to the British government. At the beginning of the Boer War, Hicks-Beech was still exhibiting more concern at the inexorable rise in naval expenditure than the cost of military operations in South Africa and the impact the war was having upon the debt repayment account. In January 1900, for instance, he protested to the prime minister that the Admiralty, rather than trimming their expenditure as requested, had yet again submitted inflated estimates. This time the Admiralty demanded that no fewer than nine large armored warships be added to the construction program. It is significant that the chancellor did not quibble at construction of the two battleships included. He focused his anger rather at the Admiralty's cruiser policy, questioning the wisdom of ordering seven armored cruisers en bloc during a period of rapid technological change.[74] Cruisers were supposed to have an effective life of twenty years, but vessels less than half this age were already being classified by the Admiralty as obsolete. "It may very well be that we want more *fast* cruisers," Hicks-Beech moaned to Salisbury, "we have built an enormous number of cruisers in the last ten years [but] I fear much of the money has been comparatively wasted, because we are in too much in a hurry."[75]

Hicks-Beech's case had merit. In the eight years between the passage of the Naval Defense Act in 1889 and the advent of the armored cruiser in 1896, the Royal Navy had spent £18.8 million on new battleships and just £7.3 million on first-class cruisers. Over the next eight years, between 1897 and 1904, expenditure on construction rose to £29.6 million for battleships and £26.9 million for armored cruisers. Several more millions had been spent on smaller cruisers in addition. The cost of responding to the French armored cruiser program, moreover, was not limited to the price of the warships. The dimensions of these vessels (it will be recalled that the hull of an armored cruiser was larger than that of a battleship) compelled the Royal Navy to spend considerable sums on rebuilding all its dockyards to accommodate them. In the eight years prior to 1896, total spending on naval works came to £5.1 million, whereas over the second period expenditure on naval works totaled £24.8 million.[76]

George Goschen's decision to retire from politics at the general election called in November 1900 afforded the chancellor a rare opportunity to bring naval spending under control.[77] A week before the election, moreover, Salisbury assured Beach that for some time he too had been "most anxious" to see the Board of Admiralty address "the question about naval expenditure," adding that he had thought it "useless" to press the matter while Goschen remained first lord.[78] The desire to exert tighter financial control over the navy may partially explain why the prime minister awarded the prized Admiralty portfolio to the earl of Selborne. Selborne was a much younger and less experienced man than his predecessor and was in addition Salisbury's own son-in-law. After the election, Hicks-Beech greeted the new first lord with a letter requesting a conference to go through the sketch navy estimates page by page looking for possible cuts.[79] Selborne, however, refused to be hustled into making concessions and declined the invitation. His resolve to proceed cautiously was bolstered by the senior naval lord, Adm. Lord Walter Kerr, who was equally determined to secure an increase in the naval budget. Kerr wasted no time in remonstrating to his new master that the British government was failing to uphold the two-power standard. The Royal Navy, he complained, was only just clinging to numerical equality over France and Russia by counting eight old battleships armed with obsolete muzzle-loading guns.[80] The Treasury had already been warned that these units would shortly have to be replaced and two years earlier had agreed in principle to fund their replacements.[81] But since then no money had been forthcoming. Kerr, in fact, demanded even more; he wanted the restoration of the traditional "margins of superiority" for battleships and first-class cruisers. By his calculations, over the next five years the Royal Navy should be augmented by at least eleven battleships and no fewer than nineteen armored cruisers.[82]

Selborne was sold.[83] At the end of December 1900 he replied to the chancellor that a reduction in naval spending was impossible and that some increase was necessary. "Leaving out of account the rapidly increasing navies of Germany, Japan and the U.S.," he explained, "we must keep at least equal to France and Russia combined." Selborne agreed that a three-power standard was beyond the financial means of the state, but, he added, "I am inclined to think that we shall be liable to be blackmailed by our 'friends' if we give ourselves no margin."[84] Selborne's "margin" translated into a request for naval spending to be raised by approximately £2.75 million.[85] The first lord of the Admiralty's idea of restoring the "margin" was put before the Cabinet on 17 January 1901.[86] At the meeting Selborne justified the proposal by pointing out that the recent inventions of the gyroscopically controlled torpedo and the submarine-boat had "materially increased" the chances of a British battle squadron being successfully ambushed. "The loss of a few battleships by us after starting with an exact equality of numbers," he observed, "might make just the difference between the possibility and impossibility of an invasion of England."[87] Selborne's costly request, however, received short shrift from the Cabinet. Much to the naval lords' chagrin, indeed, the new first lord failed to prevent his political colleagues from trimming a battleship and an armored cruiser from the building program "for reasons of state."[88] In March 1901 Walter Kerr privately confessed to a friend his exasperation at the "difficulty of getting through anything on account of the Treasury."[89]

Pressure on the Admiralty to curb their expenditures was renewed toward the end of the year. In October 1901, partially in response to ominous reports from his advisers on the fiscal outlook and partially because of the rapidly mounting national debt due to the war in South Africa,[90] Hicks-Beech issued to the Cabinet an "appeal for economy in the estimates."[91] In his memorandum, the chancellor explained that revenue generated from existing taxes was forecast to remain more or less constant for many years. Consequently, a return to balanced budgets and politically desirable levels of direct taxation after the war would not be possible unless "the growth of the normal expenditure, which of recent years has shewn a tendency to advance at an ever increasing rate" could be contained or ideally reversed. Failure to do so, he warned, would lead "straight to financial ruin."[92] Hicks-Beech went on in his memorandum to single out the Admiralty as the worst offender and to suggest possible areas in naval expenditure where economies might be found.[93] But any hopes the chancellor might have entertained of winning Cabinet approval for reductions in the navy estimates were quickly dashed by the reply several weeks later of Lord Selborne.[94] The first lord skillfully persuaded the majority of ministers that "the efforts of France and Russia to establish a naval superiority over this country" was a more immediate and pressing threat to the future of the empire than the possibility of national bankruptcy.[95] While privately the prime minister "sympathised deeply" with Hicks-Beech's position, he explained that he could not impose a ceiling on naval expenditure or even endorse the chancellor's appeal for economies without risk of breaking up the Cabinet.[96]

Twelve months later, in October 1902, the Cabinet inexplicably endorsed the Admiralty's policy of equality plus a margin. Selborne was authorized to build up during the next five years a margin above the two-power standard of six battleships and fourteen armored cruisers—at a cost to the Treasury of another £3 million per year.[97] The navy was also allowed to build a brand new dockyard at Rosyth on the Firth of Forth, which was projected to cost ten million pounds. Previously, historians have used the decision to establish a dockyard on the North Sea as evidence to support the argument that as early as 1902 the Admiralty was responding to the growth of the German High Sea Fleet. This was not so. The recommendation to build a dockyard in the north of Britain came from a committee set up to investigate the shortage of berthing and repair facilities at existing naval ports. The committee chose to site the new dockyard at Rosyth because of its proximity to existing shipbuilding facilities in Scotland.[98] No mention was made of its potential utility in case of a war with Germany. "Any strategical points in favor of the Firth of Forth," as Kerr explained in a private letter to Selborne dated 28 April 1902, "are secondary to the necessary expansion for repairs and berthing."[99] In any case, shortage of funds resulted in construction work being postponed until late 1909.

In view of the long-term financial outlook in 1902, the Cabinet's willingness to raise the naval standard was, to say the least, surprising. The decision to give Selborne his naval margin is largely explained by the fact that over the previous twelve months the political balance within the Conservative Party had shifted. At the beginning of July 1902, Lord Salisbury retired as prime minister and had been succeeded by Arthur Balfour, his nephew, who for many years had held a keen interest in defense matters. During the transition of power, Selborne had intimated to Balfour that the price of his loyalty was a promise to endorse his margin.[100] The first lord's prospects were boosted later that month after his nemesis, Hicks-Beech, announced his intention to follow Salisbury into retirement. The former chancellor complained to the new prime minister that he was tired of the Admiralty constantly wrecking his budget forecasts.[101] Selborne could scarcely contain his glee at the news. "Matters had got to the point between him and me," he observed in a letter to his friend the secretary of state for India, "that one of us had to go."[102] With his most troublesome critic out of the way, the first lord proceeded to convince the rest of the Cabinet to give the Royal Navy the measure of superiority he wanted.

Lord Selborne's victory was short-lived.[103] At the end of 1902, the Treasury reported that Britain's economic boom was over and that the fiscal outlook was dire; though it was difficult to say just how bad the situation was. Military expenditure was still at an inflated level because of the ongoing war in South Africa, and the government was still borrowing large sums to meet all its financial requirements. The Treasury warned, however, that even after the army had been demobilized and expenditure returned to peace-time levels, a sizeable budget deficit could be expected. The government would then be confronted by stark fiscal alternatives. They could either abandon certain defense commitments to allow a cut in defense spending or court electoral disaster by maintaining a high level of income tax. Both alternatives carried severe political price tags—though whether the latter policy was at all practicable was doubtful. Many politicians and financial experts believed that the electorate simply would not accept a larger burden of taxation.[104] Some within the Conservative Cabinet, notably the colonial secretary, Joseph Chamberlain, believed there was an alternative way of raising additional revenue while at the same time keep within the bounds of internationally accepted sound financial methods, and that was to levy a tariff on imports. But this idea was vehemently opposed by a large group of Cabinet ministers who refused to countenance any move away from the principle of free trade.[105] While there may have been argument over the long-term trends in British state finances, it was clear to everyone that a fiscal revolution could not be accomplished overnight and that consequently some retrenchment would be necessary, at least in the medium-term. Given that cuts in expenditure on Ireland, education, and the civil service were politically out of the question, the obvious target was the defense budget.

It was in anticipation of the need to reduce the defense budget that in December 1902 Arthur Balfour formed a defense committee of the Cabinet to assist him in reviewing the military requirements for the empire.[106] His aim was to define Britain's essential defense requirements and thence to calculate the lowest possible level of defense expenditure. While the status and reputation of the navy stood considerably higher than that of the army, especially in Balfour's eyes, and the Cabinet had recently authorized a further increase in the navy estimates for the next financial year while at the same time demanding large cuts in military expenditure, the Admiralty could not take it for granted that the service would automatically retain the Cabinet's favor. In February 1903 Selborne began urging the naval lords to look for possible economies, directing them to take:

> finance to their fireside to sit beside efficiency and not leave the derelict orphan to my sole charge. Further they must reverse their mental process. They must cease to say "This is the ideal plan; how can we get money enough to carry it out?" They must say instead "Here is a sovereign; how much can we squeeze out of it that will really count for victory in a Naval war?"[107]

In the meantime, the Cabinet Defense Committee fixed its attention on evaluating the possibility of serious invasion. As both services claimed the primary role in home defense, there were strong grounds for thinking that there was duplication of effort and that savings would be found. Here as well the Admiralty could not afford complacency. There was always a possibility that the committee would side with the army, in which case the axe would fall on the naval budget.[108]

Although much has been written about the Edwardian fiscal crisis and the subsequent tariff reform controversy, historians have scarcely appreciated the extent of its impact upon the navy.[109] The level of naval expenditure and thus, indirectly, the direction of naval policy, became increasingly determined by fiscal rather than strategical considerations. Maintaining a supreme battleship and cruiser fleet threatened to become prohibitively expensive. This was especially so after the two-power standard was revised upwards in 1902. There were serious doubts as to whether the state could support a superabundant fleet of modern warships. Selborne may have believed initially that internal reform coupled to "a change in attitude and approach" could yield significant additional fighting strength at no extra cost to the taxpayers; but the events of 1903 had disabused him. Foreign navies were continuing to grow while the British state was rapidly running out of money. Sooner rather than later, it seemed, the Board of Admiralty would have to surrender its claim to global naval supremacy and withdraw its protection to nonessential British interests in distant waters.[110] The pervasive assumption, that Edwardian Britain was confronted by acute and long-term deficiencies in the management of state finances, forms the backdrop to the revolution in British naval policy that follows.

CHAPTER 2

Complexity and Duplicity: The Admiralty and the Submarine, 1898–1904

[T]he main duty of the navy will be, not to remain in or off the harbours, which form the bases of our naval operations, but to blockade the enemy in his own ports, and cruise at sea in search of any squadrons which may have set forth to attack our colonies or to interrupt our communications. Smaller vessels are needed, as will hereafter be shown, as auxiliaries to the powerful ships on which our efforts should be mainly concentrated: but the fighting fleet should be adapted primarily for the time of battle. No success in secondary enterprises can be set in the balance against defeat in the decisive struggles.

Sir Thomas Brassey, The British Navy

Naval historians have frequently condemned Britain's naval leadership for its consistent hostility toward the development of the submarine during the late nineteenth and early twentieth centuries. This negative disposition, it is often argued, was typical of the Victorian navy's attitude toward "progress" in naval armaments. But in this particular case such criticism seems neither fair nor justified. After all, when primitive submarine boats first began to appear during the last quarter of the nineteenth century, the Royal Navy possessed the largest and best equipped fleet of ironclad warships in the world. Furthermore, the very foundations of British naval strategy rested upon the continued maintenance of that crushing naval preponderance. History taught the Board of Admiralty that the power which possessed the strongest line of battle could invariably rely upon this superiority to intimidate weaker enemy battle fleets; they would remain in port, thus leaving the stronger power with effective command of the sea. Once this "moral superiority" had been established, the stronger power could then deploy its cruisers and flotilla craft off the enemy coast. These "inshore squadrons" could watch enemy ship movements, interdict the enemy's overseas trade, guard against the possibility of an invasion fleet putting to sea, and intercept commerce raiders. All the while, the squadrons of battleships would remain close by ready to inflict a crushing blow on the enemy main fleet when the opportunity arose. This strategy had been repeatedly proven effective during the age of sail, and at the end of the nineteenth century the Board of Admiralty could see no reason to abandon it for another.

Why then should the late-nineteenth-century Royal Navy have wanted to develop submarine boats? And how would it have employed them if it had? The experimental craft then available possessed neither the range nor the endurance to operate in open waters with, or against, a main fleet. Nor, for that matter, did they carry weapons capable of inflicting serious damage upon a battleship. Torpedo tubes were not fitted to the experimental craft before 1892 and, as we have seen, the first successful attempt to fire a torpedo underwater was not made until 1898. Even assuming that a submarine could have crossed the Channel to blockade the enemy coast, a surface vessel that could be built at less cost could perform that duty for a much longer period and considerably more efficiently. Submarines, in other words, were of little use to the Royal Navy. In the hands of "a maritime power on the defensive," on the other hand, submarines would obviously prove more useful. They might just have the range to prove troublesome to the enemy inshore squadrons, thus forcing them to take station further to seaward and thereby loosening the blockade. But until the very end of the nineteenth century no submarine in existence could reliably perform even this limited mission.

Throughout the nineteenth century, the Board of Admiralty kept itself well informed about the capabilities of the experimental submarine boats. Beginning in 1856 with the vessel designed by Charles Fox and the prominent naval architect John Russell, Royal Navy officers discreetly inspected all the submarine craft built in Britain by civilian inventors. In 1879, for example, the Admiralty sent observers to watch the trials of Rev. George Garrett's *Resurgam*. In 1886 naval officers inspected Charles Waddington's *Porpoise,* and in 1888 they tested Thorsten Nordenfelt's *Nordenfelt IV* before it was sold to the Russian government. The Admiralty archives show that successive naval ministries recognized that one day the submarine would be perfected as a weapon of war.[1] But they also saw this could not be achieved without a sustained effort and the expenditure of considerable sums of money. Only a large organization, such as a rival navy or a British naval armaments firm, it was felt, possessed sufficient resources and engineering know-how to complete such a project. So long as the development of underwater craft remained in the hands of amateur inventors, therefore, the pace of progress would continue to be very slow.

For almost one hundred years, the Board of Admiralty's policy toward submarines rested upon the premise that the Royal Navy must not do anything to "justify or encourage" rival navies from sponsoring their development. As Adm. Sir Edmund Freemantle recorded in his memoirs at the beginning of the twentieth century,

> the natural attitude of the naval mind towards the submarine is the same now as that expressed by Lord St.Vincent [in 1805] . . . Fulton has been trying some [submarine] experiments before [Prime Minister William] Pitt, who favored the project, to which Lord St. Vincent, the First Lord of the Admiralty, was strongly opposed, and he bluntly stated that, "Pitt was the greatest fool that ever existed, to encourage a mode of war which they who commanded the seas did not want, and which, if successful, would deprive them of it."[2]

Throughout the remainder of the nineteenth century, British naval leaders expressed similar sentiments.[3] Often, indeed, they went further than necessary. There are numerous anecdotes of senior officers having publicly scoffed at all talk of submarine warfare, ridiculed any suggestions that submarine boats might pose a major threat to British supremacy, and having dismissed all civilian inventors who built such craft as eccentrics.[4] With Admiralty officers this posturing was probably deliberate. When, in 1901, the Royal Navy finally decided to acquire its first submarines, the then controller of the navy explained to a new colleague on the Board that every previous type of underwater craft built in Britain "has been carefully examined and sufficient experiment has been made in each case to ascertain its probable value. It has then been quietly dropped with the result of delaying the development of the submarine boat for about twenty years."[5]

Without attracting attention the Admiralty also managed to keep a watchful eye on submarine progress abroad. In 1866, British officers conducted clandestine inspections of the *Intelligent Whale* built by the American Oscar Halstead, and John Holland's *Fenian Ram* in 1881.[6] The Admiralty's ability to gauge the rate of progress overseas was improved after February 1887 with the expansion of the Foreign Intelligence Committee into the Naval Intelligence Division (NID) of the Admiralty. The NID was established especially to pierce the thickening veils of secrecy surrounding foreign-warship development and to collate information gathered by naval attachés and other agents on foreign progress in naval technologies. As the pace of technological innovation accelerated during the 1880s, so up-to-date naval and industrial intelligence became increasingly important to the Royal Navy. Progress at this time could be dramatic. By exploiting a breakthrough in, say, metallurgy or engineering, it was perfectly possible for a foreign power to create a new model battleship possessing significantly greater fighting capabilities than any British warship. Alternatively, that rival navy could develop a completely new weapon system, such as the torpedo or the submarine.

In 1887 the Marine Française became the first major navy to sponsor the development of the submarine. Early success with a fifty-ton experimental boat, *Gymnote*, encouraged the French to lay down in 1892 a much larger two-hundred-and-seventy-ton vessel christened *Gustave-Zédé*. This craft was built at Toulon Dockyard under great secrecy and took four years to complete. The British response to news that the French had commenced a submarine development program was to order their naval attaché in Paris to collect as much relevant information as he could find.[7] Although the NID subsequently received some excellent intelligence on the progress of experiments with *Gustave-Zédé*, the quality of the data was not always appreciated and often was buried within a mass of contradictory reports. Not having had practical experience of submarines themselves, moreover, officers serving in the NID could not, understandably, judge the relative value of the intelligence reports they received. None of the officers serving in the department had any special interest in the subject nor were any given incentive to develop such an expertise. Analysis of intelligence on submarine development received only a low priority, and besides, until 1896 there was little to evaluate. It is therefore hardly surprising that the Admiralty misjudged how quickly the French were progressing.[8]

Before the setting up of the naval secret service, the best source for information on the French navy was the British naval attaché in Paris. Much, of course, depended upon the energy and enthusiasm of the officer chosen for this post. Between 1896 and 1899, the NID was most fortunate to have the services of Capt. Henry Jackson, a scientifically minded officer who was a rival of Signor Marconi in pioneering the development of wireless telegraphy. Jackson supplied the Admiralty with a number of particularly informative reports. In February 1898, for example, he witnessed the first trials of a privately sponsored submarine boat *Le Goubet*—a tiny vessel displacing only eleven tons designed to be carried aboard a surface warship. The attaché was excited by the demonstration and immediately informed London that such a craft might be of use to the Royal Navy.[9] The director of the Naval Intelligence Division at once passed the (from his perspective) dispiriting report to Sir William White, the director of naval construction, who was widely regarded as the preeminent authority in the country on warship design.[10] From behind his desk at Whitehall, however, White dismissed Jackson's appraisal of the craft as "estimates and not the result of actual trials."

White assured the DNI that submarines were not yet practical weapons of war.[11] The Admiralty relaxed.

In January 1899 Captain Jackson notified Whitehall that during recent French naval maneuvers, the *Gustave-Zédé* had reportedly launched a torpedo at the battleship *Magenta*. To Jackson the implications of this achievement were serious: "These submersible vessels have reached a practical stage in modern warfare," he concluded, "and will have to be reckoned with, and met, in a future European war." In a most unusual step, the British ambassador endorsed Jackson's report and warned the Admiralty that "belief in the success in this invention is likely to encourage Frenchmen to regard their naval inferiority to England as by no means so great."[12] The opinions of a diplomat, however, did not interest the Admiralty. Nor, it seems, were they much impressed with Jackson's report.[13] Only the director of Naval Ordnance, Capt. Edmund Jeffreys, exhibited any real interest. Though he was less concerned with finding out more about French progress than with establishing whether submarines "if their development continues, might not be of great value for offensive purposes against an enemy's fleet in their ports"—in which case they might be of use to the Royal Navy. "As we could convoy or tow them across to within a short distance I am of the opinion that they might be used most effectively," he speculated.[14]

Although George Goschen, the first lord of the Admiralty, and the other members of the board considered Jeffreys's suggestion, they were reluctant to do more.[15] Their hesitation appeared to be vindicated a few weeks later after a second report on the torpedoing of *Magenta* arrived at Whitehall and was judged "much less favorable to the *Gustave-Zédé* than that given by Captain Jackson."[16] Just who wrote this second report is not known. In the covering docket, the author was referred to only as "a most reliable source." Yet it is interesting to note that the director of Naval Intelligence, Capt. Reginald Custance, placed far more weight upon the views of this anonymous agent than he did upon the opinion of the British naval attaché. Summarizing the papers for the naval lords, Custance curtly dismissed the *Gustave-Zédé* as "a failure," insisting that "her ever coming back from Marseilles after her recent trip was very problematical."[17] "*For political reasons,*" he explained to the board, the *Gustave-Zédé* "was bound to succeed and they said she did so, but she is not worth much."[18] To support his assessment, Custance drew attention to a speech delivered in the French Chamber of Deputies on 17 March 1899, in which the minister of marine had somewhat theatrically described the recent success of the *Gustave-Zédé* as heralding a renaissance in the fortunes of the Marine Française.[19] After William White cast further doubts on the credibility of Jackson's assessments, labeling him as an "enthusiast," the Admiralty subsequently dismissed his claim that the *Gustave-Zédé* had proved the submarine to be a weapon of war and rejected as unsubstantiated his warning that the French had secretly ordered between eight and twelve more submarines.[20] Again the board concluded that no action was necessary.

In January 1900 the short-sightedness of this decision was brought home to the Admiralty after the Naval Intelligence Division was literally flooded with reports indicating that submarine development was now rapidly progressing. First to arrive was a dispatch from the naval attaché in Washington, D.C., with news of "a rumour that the United States government are about to purchase" the submarine-boat designed by John Holland. Enclosed with the report from Capt. Charles Ottley were confidential reports on the performance of the boat written by the United States Navy's Board of Inspection and Survey, complete with blueprints.[21] Pressure on the Admiralty to take action intensified three weeks later after the new naval attaché in Paris, Capt. Douglas Gamble, reported that his predecessor had not been exaggerating French progress. "Submarine-boats of the *Gustave-Zédé* type are considered to be a real success," he confirmed, "and the extremely difficult problem of submerged navigation is looked upon as practically solved after ten years of laborious experiment."[22] This latest assessment, from a new man who could not be dismissed as an enthusiast, was impossible to ignore. "The French seem to be overcoming the difficulties of the submarine boat," noted the new senior naval lord, Adm. Lord Walter Kerr, and "we cannot altogether afford to disregard them and their increased proficiency."[23] The Naval Intelligence Division was directed to gather all available intelligence on submarines for submission to the board, and at the same time prepare a confidential print for issue to senior fleet officers.[24]

While the papers were being recovered from the files at the record office, in February 1900 the Admiralty received an urgent despatch from Adm. Sir John Fisher (commander in chief, Mediterranean, 1899–1902) requesting advice on how best to protect warships at anchor from the threat of submarine attack. In the dispatch, Fisher expressed his opinion that the easiest solution would be to plant a protective barrier of contact mines around his anchorage.[25] This suggestion was disingenuous. Fisher knew full well that since 1895 it had been Admiralty policy not to use or even experiment with contact mines so as not to "justify and encourage" the efforts of other powers.[26] Predictably, therefore, the board's initial reaction was to refuse; that is until the imaginative Captain Jeffreys pointed out that "foreign nations, especially France and Russia, have not waited for our 'justifying and encouraging them' but have [already] adopted them [contact mines] on an extensive scale."[27]

Meanwhile, the submarine boat, he added, "appears to be rapidly approaching a defined position as a new instrument of warfare," and it seemed likely that very soon British warships would find themselves confronted with underwater craft. Jeffreys insisted that the Admiralty was compelled to address the issue. So far, he wrote, "the only practical way to stop these boats, or frighten them so much as to keep them at home, seems to be by blockade mines."[28] If so, he concluded, the ban on using contact mines ought to be lifted.

The Admiralty was initially uncomfortable with this logic.[29] "It can hardly be accepted that the blockade mine is the only practical way to meet the submerged boat," Custance responded. An observation with which Kerr at first agreed. But upon further reflection the senior naval lord changed his mind. "The march of events," he conceded at the end of April, "now calls for some response on our part to the action taken by foreign powers in their construction of submarine boats."[30] On 4 May Kerr declared that "the success of the French submarine boats appears to be sufficiently assured to make it necessary now to meet them."[31] A fortnight later, orders were sent to the navy's torpedo schools at Portsmouth and Devonport to organize in secret a program of experiments to discover "the best means of dealing with submarine boats and destroying them when discovered."[32] Barely a week after issuing orders to begin antisubmarine experiments, the Admiralty learnt that the United States Navy was now sponsoring a program of submarine development after Fleet Adm. George Dewey, the "hero of Manila bay," strongly advised Congress to purchase John Holland's submarine boat.[33] The American decision seems to have had a profound impact upon the collective mind of the British naval establishment. As Lord Charles Beresford, a rear admiral in the Mediterranean Fleet, observed: "when a common sense level headed nation like that of the United States has tried and adopted submarine boats, it would appear probable that such craft must have some value in warlike operations."[34]

Kerr was likewise impressed. His first act was to authorize the dispatch of contact mines to the Mediterranean Fleet. Next, he advised the first lord that "that the matter of submarine boats cannot be ignored and will have to be taken up by us—our first want is a design."[35] Almost certainly Kerr had been convinced to take this "drastic" step by the pleas of the controller, Rear Adm. Arthur Knyvett-Wilson *VC*, who was most anxious to develop counter measures against the submarine.[36] Wilson was no submarine enthusiast; but he had been persuaded by Capt. Charles Robinson, in charge of the torpedo school at Portsmouth, that until someone could explain to him and his staff something of what a submarine could do he could hardly be expected to advise "the best means of avoiding and destroying them."[37] Accordingly, he had asked the board to authorize the purchase of a submarine "for the purpose of ascertaining for ourselves the limits of the powers of these vessels and the best means of avoiding and destroying them."[38] The logic was irrefutable. "I have read the whole of the papers very carefully," Goschen gloomily noted on the file, "they are not pleasant reading—for clearly great progress is gradually being made with submarine boats."[39] Reluctantly, the first lord granted permission to buy a submarine and entrusted the task of finding a suitable design to Wilson.

Acquiring a practicable submarine design for the Royal Navy was never going to be easy. Except for the Naval Construction Company (since taken over by Vickers Ltd.) which had built the Nordenfelt boats in the late 1880s, no shipbuilding firm in Britain had experience in building such craft. Unable to find a suitable design at home, ultimately the Admiralty turned to the United States. The story has often been told of how the Royal Navy ended up buying John Holland's submarine boat, an Irish-American inventor who devoted his life to perfecting his craft out of hatred for the British, and so need not be recounted here.[40] Suffice it to say that in August 1900, Wilson approached the Holland Torpedo Boat Company to find out "whether they are in a position to supply a boat or furnish us with drawings."[41] After Sir William White (the DNC) grudgingly conceded that "the Holland type seems to afford the best opening," formal discussions were opened between the Admiralty and Isaac Rice, president of the Electric Boat Company, which had recently purchased the Holland patents.[42] Within weeks an arrangement was reached whereby Electric Boat would license Messrs. Vickers Ltd. of Barrow-in-Furness to build submarines for the Royal Navy.[43] And shortly afterwards the Admiralty placed an order for five boats. This was reckoned to be the smallest number that would be required for a program of antisubmarine experiments—"one to be attached to the 'Vernon,' one to the 'Defiance' and the other three allocated one to each port to be used in connection with the destroyer flotillas in practising methods of meeting their attacks."[44] This was not regarded as a one-off purchase. All parties understood that if the Holland boats proved successful, then Vickers would receive further contracts to supply the Royal Navy with submarines.

On 23 October 1900 Wilson drafted a letter to the Treasury requesting a secret appropriation to enable the Admiralty to order the submarines at once and submitted it to the first lord for approval. To his undoubted surprise, the draft provoked a sharp debate among the members of the board over what exactly the Royal Navy would do with the submarines after they had been delivered. In Wilson's opinion, for instance, the craft were needed to find some method "of meeting attacks of submarine boats which are now building in considerable numbers in France." In other words, they were required solely as antisubmarine targets.[45] His colleagues, however, disagreed. Commenting on the draft letter Goschen scribbled:

> I do not think we should confine ourselves so absolutely to the doctrine that it is only in order to ascertain the best means of meeting foreign submarine boats that we wish to buy five boats from the United States. They may be useful to us in many places, like torpedo boats: e.g. Hong Kong, and other ports we might wish to defend in absence of our men of war.[46]

Goschen added he was under the impression that other members of the board shared his viewpoint. Two days later, on 26 October, Kerr confessed that while he accepted the principal use of the submarine boats at the present stage is to work out, if possible, some plan for meeting hostile submarines, he too was prepared to see the vessels exploited "for any purpose to which they can be adapted"—even "as an intimidation to large vessels menacing our ports."[47] Kerr, it should be added, was also intrigued by the possibility of developing the submarine as an offensive weapon.[48] Normally, these comments would have provoked a debate on the subject. But all discussion was suspended at the beginning of November 1900, after the prime minister called a snap general election. The Board agreed that the request for the appropriation should be sent immediately. Goschen was not inclined to press his objections to the wording of the letter because he had already decided to stand down at the election and quit politics.

The new first lord of the Admiralty, the earl of Selborne, was a man with no previous interest or experience in naval affairs. But it should be noted that the prime minister nominated his own son-in-law for the vacant portfolio only on the understanding that he "submit" to accepting Hugh Oakley Arnold-Forster as the parliamentary secretary in the House of Commons.[49] Arnold-Forster's peers regarded him as something of an expert on defense matters. As a journalist and as a member of Parliament, he had made his reputation amplifying complaints about the inadequate strength of the armed forces made by various interest groups. His selection promised the jingoes of the party a voice in naval policy making. More importantly for this story, he had a long-time interest in submarines.

Before Arnold-Forster joined the government, he had tried to entice Goschen into providing Parliament with an explanation for the Admiralty's apparent lack of concern at the development of the submarine.[50] Throughout 1900 Goschen had not been allowed to rest in peace. Although Arnold-Forster did not succeed in his original object, during one verbal exchange in the Commons he did succeed in drawing the aged first lord into carelessly describing the submarine as "the weapon of the weaker power." "I have no doubt whatsoever," the young M.P. had retorted, "that this argument about the weapon of the inferior power seems absolutely meaningless."[51] Goschen had been made to look foolish and his department reactionary. Shortly before Arnold-Forster joined the new Board of Admiralty in December 1900, he mentioned to his nephew, a lieutenant in the navy, that he was "anxious that we should start building submarine boats as a reply to the French."[52] He must, therefore, have been surprised to learn on taking office that the Admiralty had already secretly negotiated the purchase of five Holland boats (contract dated 18 December 1900); yet Arnold-Forster was not satisfied. After the Christmas recess, he petitioned the new first lord to abandon the pretense that the Admiralty was not interested in submarines and also to adopt a more ambitious construction program.

Selborne did indeed begin to pay more attention after he learned on 29 December 1900 that the French parliament had recently voted "no less a sum" than £4,750,000 for new flotilla craft. "This means nearly 150 torpedo-boats and submarines," the first lord exclaimed in a letter to the chancellor of the Exchequer![53] After reviewing the British response thus far to the French submarine program, Selborne began echoing Arnold-Forster's complaints. "I do not think," he remarked to his Cabinet colleagues on 17 January 1901, that the decision to buy the Holland boats "has been taken a day too soon."[54] Later that week Selborne expressed dissatisfaction to the naval lords that the first Holland boat would not be delivered before the end of October, thus allowing the French another nine months to extend their already considerable lead in submarine development.[55] It also concerned him that the American craft might not be as sophisticated as the French boats.[56] For these reasons the first lord subsequently ordered his parliamentary secretary to reexamine the possibilities of obtaining "workable boats at an earlier date than now anticipated."[57] Selborne was quickly informed that the prospects were nil. Nevertheless, Arnold-Forster added, it might anyway be a good idea for the Admiralty to approach several "well known firms" in order "to encourage British Constructors" to develop submarines for the Royal Navy and so more quickly catch up with the French.[58] The first lord, seeing no objections to the idea, passed the parliamentary secretary's paper onto the naval lords.[59]

Arnold-Forster's suggestion did not find favor with the service members of the Board. At this stage the naval lords were still uncomfortable with the idea of so blatantly "encouraging" the development of the submarine. Vice Adm. Archibald Douglas, for instance, the second naval lord, felt it would be most unwise "to use the inventive powers of the country to develop and advance submarine warfare," and declared himself "averse to doing anything more than is at present contemplated."[60] Douglas maintained that the secret contract with Vickers still conformed with the old principle of doing nothing to "justify and encourage" submarines. Rear Adm. Sir Arthur Wilson was even more outspoken in his rejection of Arnold-Forster's recommendation "to abandon the policy of discouragement and to adopt one of unostentatious progress."[61] Many historians have claimed that Wilson "disliked submarines so intensely that he suggested that the board should publicly announce that, in time of war, the crews of all submarines captured would be treated as pirates and hanged."[62] Various writers have charged, moreover, that this statement typified "the orthodox naval view" held by late-Victorian naval officers.[63] The evidence for these assertions is a memorandum Wilson wrote on 21 January 1901. Though often cited by historians, the paper has seldom been read in its original format—which must explain why Wilson's views have been so badly misrepresented. When read in the proper context, the views expressed therein were perfectly logical, if obscured by a poor style.

Wilson began his paper with an acknowledgment that the French policy of developing submarines was perfectly sound, "but this does not imply that our best policy would be to meet it by submarines of our own as suggested." Wilson could see no point in keeping pace with French submarine construction as the Royal Navy would have no use for such craft. "It may be thought that if French submarines are a danger to our ships our boats would be an equal danger to theirs," he reasoned, "but this would only come to be the case if our Fleet was so weakened that the French were able to attempt a blockade of our ports." Wilson recognized that as yet French submarines were not capable of crossing the Channel, but, he predicted, when such craft became available both Britain and France would find their warships and merchant fleets bottled up in port. For Wilson this was the crux of the matter. While it was essential for Britain to keep her overseas trade flowing, "it is not so important for them to maintain free access for their own ships." Thus:

> The development of submarine warfare must be detrimental to a nation depending on navigation at the surface for its supplies of food and the necessaries of life. We cannot stop invention in this direction [and] we cannot delay its introduction any longer, *but we should still avoid doing anything to assist in its improvement in order that our means of trapping and destroying it may develop at a greater rate than the submarine boats themselves.* [To this end,] politicians should take all favorable opportuni-

ties of enlisting the moral sense of nations against this method of warfare, and above all avoid saying anything to prevent the sternest measures being adopted in war against the crews of submarine boats when caught in the act of using them.[64] [my italics]

The reprisals Wilson advocated may have been open to question, but his sentiments were cogent. What is more, the other three professional members of the board endorsed the broad thrust of Wilson's remarks. Even the progressive Walter Kerr, who favored the Royal Navy exploiting submarines, found himself concurring with "the argument he brings forward." His only objection to Wilson's remarks was that they were "perhaps too forcible."[65] Evidently Selborne thought so too, for in March 1901 Wilson was dismissed from the post of controller for his "obstinate" manner and banished to a sea-going command.[66]

With the four professional members of the Board of Admiralty unanimously opposed to the motion calling for the Royal Navy to adopt a more openly progressive submarine policy, the motion put forward by the parliamentary secretary seemed defeated. But having served alongside Arnold-Forster for less than three months, the naval lords had yet to learn that he rarely took "no" for an answer. Arnold-Forster's goal was made a good deal easier at the end of February 1901, after a Glasgow newspaper revealed what was really under construction inside the covered "yacht shed" at Vickers yard at Barrow-in-Furness.[67] On 1 March the Admiralty confirmed the story. Everyone now knew that Britain was building submarines—even if it was not yet clear for what purpose they were being built. Over the next few months, Arnold-Forster subjected his naval colleagues to a sustained verbal attack supported by a well-directed barrage of memoranda.[68] In March, for instance, he protested that "if the French were by this time next year to have a squadron of twenty perfected submarines it is impossible to doubt that our [merchant] shipping in the narrow waters of the Channel would be exposed to serious danger."[69] Whether or not members of the Board believed in submarines (which they all clearly did) surely, he pleaded, it was sensible to keep pace with the French over numbers of submarines completed? "It seems to me," he urged Selborne in July, "that it may be a good plan to have no submarines, or to have a great many, but there can't be much advantage in having six only."[70] In August 1901 Arnold-Forster developed a new line of attack. That month he circulated a memorandum suggesting that Admiralty could use submarines to safeguard the British Isles from invasion. At the time, most of the army was away fighting in South Africa, and there was widespread concern in the country at the possibility of a French invasion. As usual his argument was well presented and logical. "Provided we are as well equipped in the matter of submarines as our neighbours," he speculated,

> the introduction of this new weapon, so far from being a disadvantage to us, will strengthen our position. We have no desire to invade any other country; it's important that we ourselves are not invaded. If the submarine proves as formidable as some authorities think is likely to be the case, the bombardment of our ports, and the landing of troops on our shores will become absolutely impossible.[71]

Although the first lord still refused to overrule the advice of his professional advisers on submarine policy, personally he had been persuaded. In a paper circulated to the Cabinet in November 1901, Selborne placed on record his "conviction that the submarine is a vessel to be seriously reckoned with."[72] He also concurred that, the "submarine is an answer to submarine in order that whatever value the submarine may prove to have in war in the future it may be an asset on our side as well as to our opponents, and whatever damage they may be able to work upon us by its means, we may be able to retaliate upon them."[73] Still, when it came to projecting the navy's requirements for the next seven years, the first lord requested money for no more than twenty submarines.[74] It is likely that three vessels per annum were probably the minimum number Vickers demanded to keep them interested in manufacturing submarines. Meanwhile, Selborne urged Arnold-Forster to be patient. He assured him that after "a year or two" the numbers would be "subject to reconsideration."[75] Although hindsight may show that Arnold-Forster was right to have pressed the Admiralty to move faster, readers should note that at this stage, November 1901, the Royal Navy had yet to commission its first submarine. Without practical experience with these craft, the decision to proceed with caution was understandable.

Experiments and Prototypes

The single most important reason why the Royal Navy adopted the American Holland boat was to obtain as quickly as possible a proven underwater craft for trials. It did not matter that their performance was well below that of French submarines already in service. Submerged, the Holland boats were capable of running just twenty miles at five knots, or less than a third the range of French boats. The Admiralty's first priority was to master the principles of submarine navigation. The naval lords soon discovered, however, they had greatly underestimated the difficulties of actually constructing submarines. It was not, as William White had assured them, simply a matter of the contractors, Vickers Ltd., "following" the plans provided by the Electric Boat Company. There was, as a result, a considerable delay in delivery. Though to be fair it must be said that Vickers were not sold the designs of the original *Holland* but an improved experimental design known in the United States as *Fulton*. This version was somewhat larger than the prototype, displacing one hundred six tons and measuring sixty-three feet and ten inches in length as opposed to fifty-three feet and only sixty-five tons. The British built boats had also been given a much more powerful but as yet untested 180 hp. gasoline engine for surface propulsion. Teething problems took time to rectify and further contributed to the delay.[76] As a result, HM submarine torpedo boat "number 1" which was supposed to have been ready by October 1901, did not make her first dive at sea until 6 April 1902.[77]

Readers will recall that in January 1901, Lord Selborne had queried the naval lords as to whether they still thought that the purchase of the Holland boats from Vickers arranged by his predecessor was the best course. By this time, it will also be remembered, the Admiralty no longer regarded submarines simply as antisubmarine targets but as prototypes for future development. At that time, however, no one in the service was really capable of making an informed judgement on this question. Because the Admiralty were reluctant to depend upon Vickers for technical advice, in May 1901 Capt. Reginald Bacon was appointed to the controller's department with the title of inspecting captain of submarines. He was charged to acquaint himself with all aspects of submarine boats and to oversee their construction and trials. In other words he was ordered to become the navy's resident expert on submarine warfare. There was no obvious reason for Bacon's selection. He was a promising young captain with what might be termed a technical bent, trained as a torpedo officer and greatly experienced with surface torpedo boats. But the Royal Navy possessed several equally well-qualified and much less prickly officers.

After seeing the plans of the Holland boats, Bacon informed the new controller, Rear Adm. William May, of his doubts that the performance of the American craft would match the French submersible *Narval*, which had been reported to be "capable of steering along the surface of the water for a distance at least sufficient to cross the Channel, and then of submerging itself and acting as a submarine-boat."[78] Bacon acknowledged that doubtless the Holland boats could operate safely underwater, but his experience with surface torpedo boats led him to question their seagoing capabilities.[79] He rightly suspected the Holland boats would be "fair weather craft"—too small to operate in anything but the calmest of weather.[80] Bacon thus suggested that before the fourth and fifth Holland boats were laid down their lines could be modified to enhance their sea-keeping abilities.[81] But the Admiralty contracts department refused to allow any alterations to be made; the "sea-lawyers" feared that "any interference [by the navy] with the plans of the Holland Company must result in that company disclaiming responsibility should any mishap occur."[82] Bacon's arguments that the commercially designed Holland boats would not accurately reflect the capabilities of a French submarine was too persuasive to ignore, however. So the following month, the Board of Admiralty authorized the construction of a sixth submarine to be built to "Admiralty design" and incorporating the improvements suggested by Captain Bacon.[83] The new model vessel, the "number six boat" or "A1" as she was known, was laid down two days after *Holland 1* was finally completed in February 1902.[84] She was significantly larger than the Holland boats, displacing 203 tons, and propelled by a 500 hp. engine. By far the most important improvement was the building of a "conning" tower on top of the deck that greatly improved sea-keeping in poor weather. Also by raising the ventilation intakes sixteen feet above the water, the main engine could be operated on the surface in a seaway without the danger of water flooding down the hatches and into the boat.[85]

Shortly after *Holland 1* was commissioned into the Royal Navy in 1902, she was "borrowed" by the Torpedo School at Portsmouth and employed as an antisubmarine target.[86] Over the preceding two years the staff at the "Vernon" had achieved little success in their quest to develop a workable antisubmarine weapon. It had been hoped that an antidote would be found in the use of high explosive bombs.[87] In 1901, trials had been conducted using a torpedo as the submarine. Beforehand, the experts at the "Vernon" had expected the target to be destroyed by a 168 lb. guncotton charge detonated at nine hundred feet. It was, therefore, a considerable shock to discover "that the torpedo was only damaged, at eighty-four to ninety feet instead of 900 as calculated."[88] Further experiments conducted in October 1901, at closer ranges and with bigger (250 lbs. and 500 lbs.) charges had proved equally unsuccessful.[89] In November 1902, the experiments were repeated against the brand new *Holland 1* in the hope that a nearby explosion might incapacitate the crew. But no damage was caused to the submarine—or the crew—by a charge detonated at only fifty yards.[90]

At the end of 1902, Bacon confidentially informed the controller that he believed continuing the experiments was futile because of the near impossibility of dropping a charge sufficiently close to the submarine to do any damage.[91] He advised that first it was necessary to devise some means to locate the approximate position of a submerged vessel.[92] Shortly afterwards Bacon initiated attempts to detect the presence of submarines by using a primitive hydrophone to listen for underwater machinery noises.[93] But the results were discouraging and only served to reinforce his conviction that submarines were effectively "unattackable." Yet despite Bacon's insistence that further attempts to develop an explosive antisubmarine weapon were a waste of time, the controller ordered the officers at the "Vernon" to persevere. The Torpedo School spent the next eighteen months trying to develop a bomb that could be dropped from a destroyer, towed to the position where the submarine periscope was last seen, and then detonated. But as Bacon had predicted, it was found impossible to ascertain when or where to fire the charge. Further "live" experiments with a Holland boat confirmed that at a range of "eighty yards the submarine would suffer no inconvenience from the explosion of 200lbs of gun cotton."[94] It was not until the controller was warned that the towed explosive charge was more likely to blow the stern off a destroyer than sink a hostile submarine, that the program was finally abandoned.[95] Another reason for dropping the idea was reluctance of the senior naval lord "to lumber up" destroyers with equipment that hindered them from performing their primary role as torpedo boat destroyers.[96] At that time destroyers displaced less than six hundred tons and were thus too small to carry more than a couple of these explosive bombs without endangering their stability and reducing their speed.[97]

In February 1903, with the completion and delivery of the remaining Holland boats, Bacon commenced a program of tactical maneuvers between surface ships and his submarines. The early trials off Portsmouth were undertaken, supposedly, "not so much with the view of establishing the actual value of the Holland boat, as to arrive at general conclusions as to the visibility of the boats, the errors they would make in attack, and to practice them in the correction of these and at the same time to indicate general rules for ships to avoid these craft."[98] It must be said though, that Bacon and his lieutenants exhibited far more interest in perfecting submarine tactics than in trying to work out suitable evasive maneuvers for surface vessels. In any case, after only three months Bacon started to campaign openly for the navy to spend less time trying to destroy submarines and more on developing them as torpedo boats. In May 1903, the inspecting captain of submarines proclaimed that "sufficient experience has been obtained with these boats to assign them a definite role in the armaments of the Navy."[99] A group of just three to five submarines, he advised the Admiralty, would pose an insurmountable obstacle to a squadron attempting to operate in the vicinity of a port where submarines were based. "The risks of allowing a large ship to approach such a port are so great that I unhesitatingly affirm that in war time it should never be allowed," he thought.[100] Bacon closed his report with a recommendation that the Admiralty consider emulating the French network of "défenses mobiles" by relying upon submarines and torpedo boats for coastal defense rather than mines. Submarines, he advised, were a far better deterrence to intruding hostile warships than mines because being mobile, "the possibility of their being encountered near any part of the coast, is a fact that an enemy cannot disregard."[101]

According to one prominent historian, Captain Bacon's report of May 1903 was instrumental in persuading the Board of Admiralty to take "very seriously" the advent of the submarine.[102] Largely because of Bacon's report, he argued, in the autumn of 1903 the Board of Admiralty created a "defence system" involving the allocation of "a few boats at each of the principal [naval] bases."[103] Surprisingly, however, the historian passed no comment on what amounted to a fundamental departure from the prevailing doctrine that "defensive" warships were of no use to the Royal Navy. The significance of this point cannot be overstated. For instance, in 1902 the Admiralty insisted that in papers circulated at the Colonial Defense Conference, "the word 'defense' [must] not appear. It is omitted advisedly, because the primary object of the British navy is not to defend anything but to attack the fleet of the enemy . . . this is the ultimate aim."[104] Even Lord Selborne had been infected by this dogmatism.[105] In view of the entrenched hostility within the service towards any "defensive" craft, therefore, it is inconceivable that a junior post-captain armed with a single report could have changed the collective mind of the Board of Admiralty virtually overnight. Furthermore, in making his report Bacon knew full well that his proposals would collide with the principles of "blue water" doctrine. "Considerable prejudice has always existed against England developing torpedo craft," he had observed in his report, "chiefly on account of the seductive formula stating that torpedo craft were 'the arm of the weaker power.'"[106]

In fact, documents show that some five months before Captain Bacon began his tactical trials with the Holland boats, and almost a year before his "epoch making" report reached Whitehall, the Admiralty had already found sufficient reason to give submarines "a definite role in the armaments of the navy." Sometime between July and October 1902, the first lord agreed to commit the navy to purchase ten submarines a year for the next four years, these in addition to the nine already built and building. The earliest reference to this decision is a memorandum by Selborne dated 10 October 1902.[107] The proposal involved the expenditure of approximately £500,000 per annum, or roughly one-third of the price of a new battleship. The importance now attached to underwater craft may be gauged from the Admiralty's willingness to fund their construction by cutting a proportionate number of surface flotilla vessels from the projected naval estimates.[108] Four months later, in February 1903, the Admiralty awarded Vickers a contract for the first batch of ten vessels. That was before Vickers had delivered the last of the Holland boats to the Royal Navy.[109] There is some evidence that the navy would have liked to have ordered even more than ten craft annually but ten "was the largest number that Vickers could turn out."[110]

There is no obvious explanation for why the decision to order submarines in large numbers was taken when it was. It is true that since the summer of 1902 the navy had been "playing" with its first submarine boat. But clear ideas on submarine tactics or capabilities had yet to emerge and the advent of the submarine had not produced a discernible impact upon naval opinion.[111] In July, Arnold-Forster was still complaining that the Admiralty was not yet taking submarines seriously.[112] Although serious doubts had begun to emerge over the practicality of enforcing a close blockade of French ports, these stemmed more from concern at the dramatic improvement in the effectiveness of torpedoes after being fitted with gyroscopes. Nor had intelligence uncovered any new revelations about the French program.[113] In the absence of concrete documentary evidence, therefore, the only credible explanation for the Admiralty's change in policy is that majority opinion on the Board had shifted in favor of Arnold-Forster's proposal to keep pace with French construction. Such a change at Whitehall is plausible.[114] Since Arnold-Forster's idea had been first rejected in early 1901, two new men had joined the Board. In March 1901, Capt. William May had succeeded Wilson as controller. And in July 1902, the energetic Adm. Sir John Fisher took office as second naval lord in place of Admiral Douglas. As we shall see, both officers soon became powerful and consistent supporters of the submarine.[115]

Fighting for Supremacy:
The Army, the Navy, and Home Defense

Strange as it may seem, much of the credit for encouraging the Admiralty to give submarines "a definite role in the armaments of the Navy" belongs to the British army. It is essential to understand that the change in policy at Whitehall during the winter of 1902 took place against a background of heightened interservice rivalry over the demarcation of responsibility for the defense of naval bases throughout the Empire. The details of this squabble are important. For many years the Admiralty had tried to avoid being drawn into disputes with the War Office over this question. Successive naval administrations had acted upon the principle that the safest course was always to leave the entire responsibility in the hands of the army. This stance had been reaffirmed most recently in December 1900, at a joint-services conference held to "consider the strategical considerations governing the coast defense of the United Kingdom."[116] On that occasion the attending naval representative, Rear Adm. Custance, advised the War Office that "in order that the Navy may not be hampered in its primary functions, the Admiralty decline in any way to be responsible for coastal defenses beyond giving advice on matters that directly or indirectly effect the navy. It follows therefore, that the Military authorities are alone responsible for the same."[117] In short, the navy did not really care what the War Office did provided their defensive preparations did not interfere with shipping leaving or entering port. There was not an admiral on the flag list who did not earnestly believe that all talk about the possibility of an invasion of the United Kingdom was balderdash.[118]

During the second half of 1902, the Admiralty was given good reason to reconsider its approach. The preceding twelve months had seen a deepening crisis in government finances, a renewed invasion scare in the press, and the Admiralty had also come under renewed pressure from the Treasury to find savings in their budget. More ominously, the War Office, desperate to justify inflated military estimates in the aftermath of the army's dismal performance in the Boer War, began claiming the need for a large peace-time army to protect the country from invasion. At the end of 1902, Prime Minister Arthur Balfour ordered the newly established Cabinet Defense Committee to investigate the possibility of an invasion of the British Isles. At the beginning of 1903, service chiefs were asked to submit their assessments of the likelihood of the French capturing a port on the south coast to facilitate an invasion of the British Isles.[119] Seeing the fiscal axe poised to strike, the Admirals saw advantage in quietly abandoning their usual position. When the finished papers were distributed for comment, the War Office was dismayed to find that "the Admiralty now contend that the Navy will entirely suffice to protect the United Kingdom from any attack or invasion," other than the occasional minor raid.[120]

The Admiralty now claimed that history taught "an attack on a first-class defended home port, such as Portsmouth, involving not only bombardment by a squadron of armored ships, but the landing of a field force with heavy artillery for the purpose of capturing the place from the land side, [was] impossible . . . while the fleet remains undefeated."[121] Even if the main battle fleet suffered a reverse or was temporarily absent from home waters, the naval representatives contended, there would still be sufficient older battleships and cruisers to form a respectable force. This fleet could be bolstered by the navy's large flotilla of torpedo craft, including the submarines.[122] In the Admiralty's opinion the role of the army in home defense was simply to provide coastal defense batteries to guard the approaches to important naval bases and other valuable maritime targets such as in the naval shipbuilding yards on the Tyne.[123] "Land fortifications," it was admitted, were "a better form of local defense, as a rule, than stationary ships."[124] In addition, a small field force was required to deal with enemy raids. While the enemy fleet remained in being, the Admiralty advised, "we cannot make sure of preventing a small force, say 5000 men, being landed somewhere in the three Kingdoms."[125]

In the ensuing (and animated) discussion, the Admiralty comprehensively demolished the War Office arguments for a large field army for home defense. The politicians were persuaded that invasion was indeed impossible so long as the Royal Navy remained supreme at sea. The generals were left to pick at minor inconsistencies in the navy's case. Their only line of attack was to query the "admission" that the navy could not ensure the interception of all raiding forces.[126] If the army was supposed to have sole responsibility for coastal defense, insisted the generals, then they should be allowed to fix the appropriate level of protection at each port. The War Office then proceeded to demand of a force of 350,000 men to defend the British coasts from minor raids![127] Of these, 229,000 would be locked up in thirty-seven defended ports to man the coast defense artillery, garrison the fortresses, and maintain the sea mines sown in the vicinity of those ports.[128] The remainder would form a mobile field army. When it was suggested that perhaps the size of this force was a little big to deal with enemy raids by no more than 5,000 men, the soldiers retorted they had understood from Admiral Custance that a strong home army was essential to "unshackle" the navy from the British coastline to conduct the offensive operations prescribed by its "blue water" doctrine, and anyway the proper size of the army was a technical matter which only the War Office was qualified to judge.[129]

From the navy's perspective, the most disturbing aspect of the War Office defense scheme for the defense of Home Ports was the role assigned to the Royal Engineers Corps of Submarine Miners. This volunteer formation had been established during the 1870s, at a time when coast defense artillery consisted of slow firing muzzle loaders which were incapable of being trained and fired quickly enough to prevent steam propelled warships from closing to ranges where they could bombard the port facilities behind the guns. The function of the mines was to serve as an obstacle to ships: the duty of the coastal defense gunners was to prevent the mines from being removed.[130] The mines employed, it should be noted, were the old "observation" type. In other words they did not explode when struck by a ship: only an observer on shore could detonate them. This was not much consolation to the navy. Most of the observers were reservists, and, as had been frequently shown in maneuvers, could not tell a friendly ship from a foe.[131] In fact, the Admiralty only tolerated the Royal Engineers Corps of Miners after the Board recognized in 1893 that already too much capital—political as well as financial—had been sunk into the organization.[132] In return for the navy's silence the Royal Engineers had agreed to consult the local port admiral before sowing any mines.[133] Cynics like Col. Sir George Clarke, a former engineers officer and a noted defense expert, felt sure that "most of the mines at naval ports will never be used anyway because the Royal Navy don't want them obstructing channels!"[134]

In January 1903, the secretary of state for war, St. John Brodrick, notified the Admiralty that his department was preparing to reorganize and reequip the Corps of Submarine Miners and build a new training school at Sheerness.[135] On the list of intended reforms was a proposal to replace the relatively harmless observation mines with indiscriminatory contact mines. Before embarking on such an expensive program Brodrick asked the Admiralty for their opinion on "the general question of the future functions of submarine mines in Naval Warfare."[136] Capt. George Egerton, in charge of the torpedo and mine-warfare school, was the first naval officer to comment. His view was unequivocal. Egerton shuddered at the thought of allowing part-time soldiers to sow contact mines off British ports. "It would be cheaper to the country and *more reliable* from a naval point of view," he advised, "if the floating defences of the chief arsenals in home waters were turned over to the Navy." Egerton went on to suggest the Admiralty should consider whether "submarines and torpedo-boats could take the place of submarine mines"?[137] Capt. Henry Jackson, formerly the naval attaché in Paris and now serving at Whitehall as assistant to the DNO, echoed Egerton's assessment. Somewhat more diplomatically, however, he stressed that:

> the increased range of modern guns has in most cases reduced the value of the minefields, as the observation mines could not be laid and effectively fired, at distances beyond which effective attack by artillery fire could not be easily carried out by the attacking ships on the guns defending the minefield, and possibly on the main objective such as a dockyard in rear.[138]

"Nothing," Jackson admitted, "can well replace a suitably placed observation mine." But off many ports the water was too deep for observation mines to be employed effectively which was why the army were now proposing to lay contact mines. Jackson was adamant that the Board of Admiralty must oppose this proposal. If improved port defense were deemed necessary, Jackson agreed with Egerton, then in many cases submarine boats might well prove safer and more reliable than contact mines.[139]

The new director of Naval Intelligence, Capt. the Prince Louis of Battenberg, was less happy with the idea of detailing submarines for the defense of ports in lieu of mines. He agreed that "the submarine could in the near future be relied upon to do all that a minefield does now and probably a good deal more."[140] Indeed, at a meeting of the CID on 14 February, Battenberg referred to the embryonic submarine flotilla as "probably the most formidable obstacle of all" to a successful French amphibious raid on the south coast.[141] But the DNI recognized that nominating submarines for port defense duties would have wider implications. On 26 February he reminded the naval lords that for years the army had been trying to foist upon the Admiralty the responsibility for the defense of the navy's coaling stations scattered around the world.[142] The last attempt had been made just twelve months earlier. "One of the chief reasons why the War Office has so persistently endeavoured to throw on to the Admiralty the duty of providing garrisons for certain colonial ports," the DNI suspected, "is that many of these places are unhealthy [and] the duties irksome in time of peace."[143] Battenberg feared an admission by the Admiralty that submarines could protect naval ports more effectively and also probably at less cost than mines, might well induce the soldiers to petition the government to give navy the responsibility for all imperial ports. This eventuality, he reminded his superiors, would add considerably to the expense and complexity of naval strategic policy.[144] In his opinion, such an unpleasant possibility was to be avoided:

> The arrangement by which the War Office defends our ports leaving us free to do our duty at sea, is the basis of our War Policy. It is not a question, as some naval officers contend, that we could do it better than the army. Probably we could. The point is that if we were to undertake it, a portion of the strength which we are now able to develop at sea, would be absorbed by local defenses.[145]

The first lord refused to allow such a stance. "If the submarines can do more effectively and economically the work done by the larger submarine mining organisation of the Army," he told the naval lords on 4 March, "then submarine boats must replace submarine mines whether controlled by the Army or the Navy."[146] Fortunately Selborne was persuaded to suspend judgement until after a joint services committee had been given a chance to investigate the merits of idea. Brodrick's agreement to the formation of such a committee allowed the matter to be shelved until the end of the year. This, however, did not stop the naval lords from trying to prejudice the Admiralty's case. The naval representatives appointed to the joint service committee were briefed not to make any statement that could be (mis)interpreted as an admission of naval responsibility to defend ports. If pressed to give an estimate of the relative value of mines and submarines, they were ordered to reply that while there could never be any question of submarines replacing mines the Admiralty would prefer the army not to plant mines close to naval bases, such as Portsmouth, because they would "interfere with the freedom of action of the [submarine] boats."[147]

Aside from the political reasons for not assuming responsibility for port defenses, the Admiralty must have held some genuine doubts as to the wisdom of taking such a course. The latest reports from Captain Bacon (dated February 1903) indicated that numerous minor technical problems still had to be overcome before submarines could be relied upon for combat duties. In mid-March, Lord Selborne, Lord Kerr, and William May all visited Portsmouth to witness for themselves the submarine boat trials in the Solent—possibly with the view to giving further consideration to the idea of relying upon them for port defense.[148] Unfortunately the weather that week was exceptionally poor, and the Holland boats failed to live up to Captain Bacon's boasts. The unfavorable impact this demonstration had upon the Board was measurable. At the next meeting of the Cabinet Defense Committee, when Battenberg was asked by the War Office to outline the Admiralty's thoughts on the utility of submarines, his reply was much more cautious than before. "We are not at present in possession of sufficient evidence," he advised,

> to be able to form an exact estimate of the value of submarines in war. This much, however, we do know, that the main difficulty they experience in attacking is to keep a good view of the enemy and when the latter is on the move it seems probable that this difficulty will be so great as to seriously militate against their value. Their radius of action is also very limited.[149]

Besides the political and technical objections to submarines acting as the main defense of ports, there must have been some concern inside Whitehall at the probable reaction from many flag officers to news that the Admiralty intended to purchase submarines for defensive purposes. Allocating naval resources to the defense was bound to antagonize men like Adms. Hedworth Lambton or Reginald Custance. The latter was particularly opposed to the navy assuming a defensive "attitude of mind" and loudly condemned all those who wished to develop the submarine as a defensive vessel. "The most effective method of defending our ports and preventing invasion," he blustered, "is a rigorous offensive against the floating force of the enemy, and that the submarine should be developed with that in view—as an offensive and not defensive weapon. [Otherwise] large sums of money will be diverted from the offensive to the defensive. . . . The fact is that naval opinion is and has been for years saturated with the ideas of defense not withstanding the efforts of a small minority to counteract them."[150]

The Possibility of Invasion: A Role in Imperial Defense

In the fall of 1903, Prime Minister Arthur Balfour came under renewed pressure to find a solution to the on-going military reform issue. In March, the House of Commons had rejected as too expensive the latest War Office proposal to reorganize the British army into six European style army corps: yet six months later the secretary of state for war confessed he was unable to put forward a cheaper and more flexible scheme.[151] The administration of the War Office had recently been subject to further criticism by the independent commission appointed under the chairmanship of Lord Elgin to investigate the abysmal performance of the army during the South African war. The generals, however, had chosen to ignore the commission's report. Finally, the chancellor of the Exchequer warned that he could not deliver a politically significant cut in the rate of income tax until after defense spending had been brought under control. Here again, the blame lay at the door to the War Office administration. The generals were obstructing all attempts by the Cabinet Defense Committee to calculate the military requirements of the empire in order to fix the establishment of the army at a realistic and affordable level. Balfour, recognized he had "to do something" about the army and the War Office bureaucracy in order to bring down military expenditure and so rally his supporters in the Commons.[152] But what exactly he did not yet know.

The urgency of finding a solution was underlined in September 1903, after the Cabinet disintegrated over the question of whether or not the Conservative Party should try to overcome its fiscal constraints by renouncing Britain's commitment to free trade and adopting an empire wide system of tariffs on imports. It was desperation rather than conviction that drove most MPs to call for imperial preference.[153] During the Cabinet reshuffle that followed, Balfour was able without comment to rotate the discredited Brodrick out of Pall Mall and into the India Office. To replace him, the prime minister first turned to the highly respected and politically neutral Lord Esher; but Esher declined to do more than chair a small committee of independent experts to investigate the internal organization of the War Office. Balfour subsequently offered the post of secretary of state for war to ten other statesmen before eventually handing the "poisoned chalice" to Oakley Arnold-Forster, the parliamentary secretary to the Admiralty. Personally, Balfour did not like Arnold-Forster, sharing the widely held view that he was an "uncompromising personality whose dogmatism and self assertiveness went beyond all limits."[154] Nevertheless, the prime minister recognized Arnold-Forster possessed "great ability" and a "burning zeal" for military reform.[155] He was, moreover, a tariff reformer. But perhaps most importantly, he shared Balfour's view "of the War Office's gross exaggeration of its importance in the defense of the empire."[156]

Arnold-Forster took office as secretary of state for war on 5 October 1903, charged with the task of defining precisely the role of the army in imperial defense, thus permitting the Cabinet Defense Committee to fix the level of its permanent strength.[157] The former defense correspondent set to work with some very clear ideas on army reform.[158] Within two months Arnold-Forster had sketched a new organization for the army which at first glance appeared to be much more suitable for imperial defense purposes than Brodrick's army corps plan. Basically, the scheme called for massive reductions in military garrisons at home and overseas in order to free men and money for the creation of a large rapid deployment force. As a bonus, he promised to deliver substantial savings in military expenditure. Of course there were a number of drawbacks to his scheme. For example, the new minister demanded the jettisoning of several important military commitments without considering the political or diplomatic repercussions. But, as we shall see, Arnold-Forster's biggest mistake was the methods he employed to achieve his goals. Not only did he not bother obtaining the support of the senior military advisors who would have to implement the proposed reforms, but in pursuing his objective he was devious and underhanded.

Arnold-Forster began looking for savings by scrutinizing the large number of auxiliary and volunteer units organized for home defense. In view of his penchant for submarines and his recent experience at the Admiralty, it was hardly surprising that within a month of taking office he decided to take an axe to the Royal Engineers Corps of Submarine Miners.[159] He was undoubtedly encouraged to pursue this course after discovering on 30 October that his old colleague the senior naval lord had recently become more favorably inclined to the idea of allocating submarines for port defense duties.[160] After reading Captain Bacon's "epoch making" report on tactical trials with submarines, Kerr admitted to having second thoughts over the Board's refusal to have anything to do with port defenses.[161] Arnold-Forster had also known, of course, that the previous March, the first lord had been uncomfortable with Battenberg's suggestions that the Admiralty should deliberately mislead the government over the practicability of using submarines in this role.[162] He had reasons to believe, therefore, that Selborne would help him overcome any lingering resistance from the armed forces. Thus after consulting the army's commander in chief on the subject of the disbandment of the Royal Corps of Miners,[163] on 2 November Arnold-Forster wrote unofficially to Selborne asking for his support in abolishing the "military aquatics." "The mining," his letter began,

> is undertaken with the object of protecting maritime ports against attack from the sea; in other words with the object of denying access to foreign men of war. I have frequently heard it said that in the opinion of Naval officers, much of the work done by these submarine miners is useless, or superfluous, as far as the Navy is concerned. I remember that there have frequently been complaints during the maneuvers of the difficulties caused by the want of harmony between land and sea forces, respectively.[164]

"If on the other hand," suggested Arnold-Forster, "the Navy thinks that submarine mines are necessary," then in order to eliminate confusion in the command and control of seaward defenses, "the Navy itself should undertake the service which they are particularly qualified to perform." To sweeten the pill he offered to transfer the £556,000 spent annually on the "aquatics" from the army to the navy estimates.[165] By approaching Selborne unofficially, the war minister clearly hoped to entice the first lord to overrule the politically inspired objections to a formal transfer.

Despite the loss of the original copy of the aforementioned "Bacon report" and the all-important minute sheets with the remarks of the naval lords, it is possible to reconstruct the docket from the sizeable extracts quoted by Arthur Marder in his book *The Anatomy of British Sea Power*. In addition, there are among Selborne's private papers a number of documents on the subject. According to Marder, "the Admiralty found the report most instructive" and "it was agreed after full discussion that Bacon's experience had proved that submarines were a very effective 'défense mobile' for the naval harbours."[166] This is unquestionable. The Board decided that "submarines should gradually replace minefields in the defense system, a few boats each at each of the principal naval bases—Portsmouth, Sheerness, Plymouth, Malta, Hong Kong, Queenstown, Pembroke. Some were [also] to be stationed at Dover and Gibraltar where their presence would make passage of the straits very hazardous for any hostile ships." Even Battenberg, it seems, endorsed the scheme.[167] There is no doubting Kerr's change of heart. In a private letter to Selborne dated 4 November, the senior naval lord credited Bacon with having persuaded him that "not only are submarine boats more effective in themselves," but "we may well accept in principle, that wherever we have submarine boats, the mines may go."[168] Commenting on the former parliamentary secretary's offer to transfer or abolish the "military aquatics," Kerr responded with cautious enthusiasm.[169] Accordingly on 14 November Selborne informally replied to Arnold-Forster that:

> If the War Office ask the Admiralty to relieve them of the responsibility for submarine mines, the Admiralty will reply that, so far as the Naval Ports are concerned, they are willing to have that responsibility transferred to them as submarines become available. We could, I think, begin with the [three] Home Ports at once. But in respect of the eighteen ports in which there is now a submarine mining organisation but which are not naval ports, the Admiralty would not be prepared to accept responsibility.

Though eventually, he added, "submarines might be stationed at these non-naval ports in charge of the R.N.V.R." (Royal Navy Volunteer Reserve).[170] The Admiralty were considering a proposal to store the unwanted experimental submarines on land to prevent deterioration, which would be commissioned during wartime by crews of reservists.[171] But it would be many years, Selborne emphasized, before such a scheme could be implemented.

That the Admiralty was greatly impressed by Captain Bacon's report cannot entirely explain the newfound willingness to employ submarines as adjuncts to port defenses. It will be recalled that when the Admiralty had discussed this question earlier in 1903, few officers had doubted that submarines would provide a better defense than mines. Much more serious concerns had been expressed over the "political," financial, and strategic ramifications of the navy taking responsibility for the defense of naval bases. Selborne's senior professional advisors had all been vehemently opposed to the idea. So why then six months later did the Board suddenly overcome these fears? The reason is almost certainly attributable to the increasingly bitter debate in the Cabinet Defense Committee over the allocation of limited defense resources. Minutes by Battenberg dated October 1903, makes it clear that it was with their eyes focused on the War Office rather than the French, that the Admiralty agreed to tie submarines to the defense of naval bases. "The establishment of submarine stations along the South Coast of England," Battenberg remarked,

> ought to go a long way towards dispelling the ever-recurring fears of invasion so dear to the "old women of both sexes" mentioned by Lord St.Vincent. To these (a few live in the War Office) it may be pointed out that the French in all their utterances on the subject—be they Ministerial speeches or press articles—point out with pride that the existence of submarines as part of the defense mobile [sic] makes any attempt at invasion of French territory the act of lunacy. *They are quite right and the argument cuts both ways.*[172]

The Admiralty's motives are not hard to understand. By the end of 1903, the thoroughness with which the Cabinet Defense Committee was studying Britain's imperial strategic policy had convinced the naval lords that the government was determined to make deep cuts in the defense budget. And it was obvious that as the pool of defense resources shrank, either the Royal Navy would have to abandon its claim to naval supremacy or fight the army for a greater share of the defense budget. As we have seen, at the beginning of 1903 the Admiralty chose the latter policy by disputing War Office claims for the need to retain a large army for home defense. Their subsequent decision to take responsibility for the defense of naval bases, therefore, was no more than another step along this road. Whether the Admiralty really believed that submarines were needed to defend ports from possible invasion or raids by hostile cruisers was not the point: the argument justified the claim that the navy could protect the country at less cost and more efficiently than the army and that the navy should thus receive priority in the allocation of the limited defense resources.[173]

The Admiralty had another reason to propose giving submarines an important role in home defense. Since taking over the chairmanship of the Cabinet Defense Committee in mid-1903, Prime Minister Arthur Balfour had developed a keen interest in the submarine. Very quickly, this enthusiasm had grown into a conviction that the submarine offered the only affordable solution to Britain's chronic defense problems. In November, Balfour drafted a memorandum outlining his thoughts on the possibility of "Serious Invasion" which subsequently was adopted as the Defense Committee's final report on the subject. In it the prime minister sided unequivocally with the Admiralty. So long as the Royal Navy retained command of the sea in home waters, he concurred, "the chief military problem which this country has to face is that of Indian, rather than of Home defense."[174] Explaining his rejection of the War Office case, Balfour argued that the invasion question had been "profoundly modified to our advantage by the progress of invention." During "the old wars" in the age of sail, he explained, it had not always been possible for the Royal Navy to concentrate a superior force at the threatened point. But in the age of technology, steam power enabled warships to move independently of the wind direction, and wireless telegraphy permitted an admiral to summon his ships from over the horizon.[175] "It is not too much to say," he concluded, "that the whole problem of landing large bodies of troops on a hostile shore has been revolutionised by the invention of the torpedo and the submarine."[176]

Developing this theme, Balfour agreed with the Admiralty that even if the British battle fleet was absent from home waters, the Royal Navy's ample force of cruisers and flotilla craft would still provide an effective deterrent to invasion. He based his reasoning not upon the continued existence of a sizeable reserve fleet (as the Admiralty had done) but rather upon the assumption that neither an invasion convoy nor a covering battle fleet would dare "long remain within reach of the torpedo and the submarine."

> History has no record of what would happen to an army of 70,000 men closely packed in improvised transports if even two or three torpedo-boats got in amongst them—to say nothing of a whole flotilla. That the confusion the destruction and the horror would exceed anything which we can easily imagine in cold blood is certain.[177]

Balfour reasoned that because battleships could not sweep the sea of the Royal Navy's much larger fleet of torpedo boats, and because "the submarine cannot be driven from the sea at all," invasion across a narrow stretch of water such as the English Channel would thus be impossible.[178] The first lord of the Admiralty moved quickly to endorse Balfour's assumptions.[179]

At a meeting of the Defense Committee held on 25 November, Balfour explored the possibility of further extending the role of submarines to imperial defense. During a discussion on the appropriate scale of defenses for the naval base at Bermuda,[180] the prime minister asked the naval and military representatives to consider "whether the island might not be made almost impregnable at a small cost by strengthening the naval defenses, and whether, in this case, the existing garrison might not be reduced"?[181] What exactly Balfour had meant emerges from the written reply submitted by the War Office. This document shows that the phrase "strengthening naval defenses" meant "the addition of submarine-boats and more torpedo-boats to the local naval force."[182] Very properly the generals had replied that "this is a matter for the naval authorities to determine"—then with a parting shot added several reasons why the Army did not believe the idea practicable.[183] Although this time the Admiralty was much slower to endorse the prime minister's idea, it seems that Selborne at once assured Balfour in private that his department would look favorably on the idea.[184] In January 1904, the prime minister wrote to another submarine enthusiast, Adm. Sir John Fisher, that "some of the things you recommend have, I think, been already practically agreed upon by the defense Committee and the Cabinet, e.g. the substitution of submarines for mines, and the defense of places like Malta, Gibraltar and Bermuda by submarines."[185]

Balfour was not the only one to be excited by the thought of using submarines for imperial defense. The political members of the Cabinet

Defense Committee, including Arnold-Forster, Selborne, Esher and Austen Chamberlain (the chancellor of the Exchequer) were all mesmerized by the possibilities offered of building twenty or thirty submarines for the price of a single battleship. In one highly imaginative paper distributed at this time, Lord Esher prophesied that "submarine boats, coupled with a system of rapid communications by W/T, will not impossibly alter the scheme of defense for our coaling stations all over the world."[186] Another advantage of relying upon submarines, Balfour thought, was that their military value would depreciate much more slowly than conventional surface ships because enemy transports would always be vulnerable to even the oldest and slowest submarine boats. This idea came from Admiral Fisher.[187] In early 1904, the Prime Minister wrote to Selborne:

> I wish we had more submarines. Would it not be possible to induce some new firm to build us a few? They are, after all, cheap, and their peculiarity is that, inasmuch as they cannot be attacked by other submarines, the type does not get antiquated;—in other words, however much submarines may be improved in the future, existing submarines will never become obsolete as against the types of vessels with which they are intended to fight.[188]

Adopting a high technology approach to national defense seemed to offer a realistic chance to cut the Gordian Knot that had been dogging British defense planners for more than twenty years—how to provide effective defense of imperial maritime interests at a time of "imperial overstretch." Or to put it another way, exploiting high technology appeared to offer the government a way of meeting defense commitments at a time when costs were spiraling and financial resources were either static or diminishing. But as we shall see, ordinary naval officers greeted this vision with skepticism.

—————≫◆≪—————

At the end of November 1903, Selborne arranged with Arnold-Forster for Captain Bacon to tour all the army mining establishments at the three Home Ports to inspect their suitability for conversion into submarine bases.[189] On 14 December 1903, Kerr circulated Bacon's favorable appraisal to the other naval Lords along with a request for them to endorse the plan.[190] In his minute, the senior naval lord hinted that taking responsibility for the three naval bases would only be the first step. "Commercial and other naval ports in the United Kingdom will have to be considered in the future," he noted, "but the commercial ports in any case must be left until our *foreign* naval bases have been provided."[191] Much to Kerr's and Selborne's surprise, however, both Vice Adm. Charles Drury (who in September had replaced Fisher as second naval lord) and Rear Adm. John Durnford (the junior lord), replied that they were "unable to agree to this far reaching proposal."[192] To better understand their objections, the first lord called upon Drury and Durnford to submit their views in writing.

Rear Adm. John Durnford was particularly forceful in his condemnation of the proposal. Substituting naval submarines for army mines, he anticipated, would be

> a great and additional burden to the Navy in men and materiel, the Navy Estimates must bear it: these are and must be limited, and do what you will, Vote 8 [the construction budget] is the loser. A large and well trained personnel will be required sooner or later. . . . I think the acceptation [*sic*] of the principle as regards the Home Ports will in the end involve taking over a great deal, including probably the coaling stations abroad, a proposition that has been always strongly resisted, as involving the Navy in local defense and making him responsible for the safety of localities, thus hampering his liberty and freedom of action with the fleet at sea.[193]

Drury concurred. "This is a principle of defense that their Lordships have up to the present time never admitted as part of the duties of the Royal Navy [and] if this principle is now adopted the Admiralty must be prepared to appropriate a large number of Submarine boats and personnel as "*fixed defenses.*"[194] Both admirals also expressed their doubts on the efficiency of submarines. Durnford insisted on first seeing a demonstration. So did Drury. "As far as I know," wrote the former,

> no *practical* experiment has been made by us in this direction. Our submarines have never run a torpedo at a ship underway or at anchor for that matter, and I strongly urge that more practical experiments be undertaken, as for instance in attempting to prevent ships of the home Fleet entering the Solent . . . we are in no sense ready for the transfer. Captain Bacon with his eyes fixed on the success of submarines has become an enthusiast(!).[195]

Drury's and Durnford's memoranda indicate just how secret the submarine experimental program had been kept. They also indicate how deeply embedded among naval officers was the notion that the Admiralty should have nothing to do with defensive preparations—for political reasons. Rear Admiral Durnford's memorandum indicates he was unaware that the "practical trials" he demanded had already been carried out. Considering this officer's rank and position, not to mention his experience as a torpedo officer, it seems remarkable. Yet the fact is confirmed in minutes attached to the file by Rear Admiral May, the controller. "I am afraid," he wrote, "neither the Second nor Junior Naval Lords has had the benefit of seeing the reports of tactical exercises that have already been carried out by submarines."[196] And on 6 January 1904, Kerr added: "the Second and Junior Naval Lord's can hardly be aware of the extent of the experience already gained."[197] Kerr also dismissed the fear that by agreeing to provide the seaward defense of the Home Ports the navy might later be compelled to accept the full responsibility for the defense of "our principal Naval Ports and our coaling stations."[198] On 7 January 1904, Selborne endorsed this view. "I cannot agree," he wrote, "that the question raised in these papers has any connection with that of the garrisons of the coaling stations or Home Ports."[199] Days later, however, Selborne and Kerr learned they had been mistaken.

Three weeks earlier, and unbeknown to Selborne, Arnold-Forster had outlined his army reform scheme to the prime minister.[200] The secretary of state for war's memorandum posited that Britain's requirements for imperial defense could be met with a regular army of 190,000 strong—always assuming "that a successful invasion of the UK by a large force need not be contemplated under present conditions." Out of this total, one hundred thousand men would be organized into a rapid reaction force and the remainder forming permanent garrisons around the globe.[201] Arnold-Forster further informed Balfour that he still anticipated an overall saving in the army budget, mainly realized by cutting the militia, the volunteers and the auxiliary reserves such as the Corps of Miners, but the need to retain so many regulars for garrison duties meant that the overall reduction in the military budget could not be as large as he originally had promised.[202] But, he deviously offered,

> it is possible that an additional reduction of the Army might be effected by a change of policy with respect to the defense of naval bases at home and abroad. It would be no doubt advantageous to the Army if the duties of maintaining garrisons and fixed defenses of all naval bases and coaling stations abroad, except Gibraltar, Malta, Aden, Indian defended ports, and the Cape were transferred to the Admiralty. To avoid an undue proportion of foreign service thus being thrown upon the Royal Marines, the entire defenses of the Naval bases at Plymouth, Portsmouth, and the Medway, might also be handed over to the Navy.[203]

Arnold-Forster must have known that the Board of Admiralty would never approve such an idea.[204] It is also difficult to believe that he could have interpreted Selborne's agreement to take charge of the defenses for the three Home Ports for an endorsement of the principle that the navy should take full responsibility for all imperial naval bases. Selborne's letter had been emphatic on this point. Nevertheless, notes in Arnold-

Forster's private papers suggest that he actually intended to exploit Selborne's concession to compel "the Admiralty to undertake the entire maritime defense" of naval bases and coaling stations by the navy,[205] a duty which he had convinced himself the War Office "ought not to have."[206] By thus foisting upon the Admiralty the entire responsibility for the defense of all imperial naval bases and coaling stations, the secretary of state for war hoped to achieve his goal of affecting a dramatic reduction in the War Office budget and freeing men for his expeditionary force. It is not clear when exactly the Admiralty discovered the plan, but it was certainly not well received.

If possible, the generals were even more outraged. By working through the Defense Committee rather than the machinery of the War Office, Arnold-Forster had hoped to gain Cabinet approval for his scheme before revealing his intentions to the army high command. He justified such behavior by arguing (probably quite rightly) that as soon as the service chiefs learned of any government plan to impose large cuts, resistance would quickly solidify.[207] Indeed he was quickly proved right. When in the last week of December 1903, the War Office administrators discovered their minister's intention to abolish the Royal Corps of Miners, they immediately tried to brake the secretary of state by informing him he could not act before the joint service committee on the function of mines in war had reported.[208] This did not work for long. On 7 January, Arnold-Forster acquired a draft copy of the report and forwarded it to Selborne with a covering note informing him that he had already taken steps to disband the "aquatics" at the three Home Ports. Would the Admiralty endorse the abolition of mining stations at any other ports, he innocently inquired?

On 13 January 1904, Selborne convened a special meeting of the Board of Admiralty to consider the question.[209] The minutes show that everyone present agreed that submarines would be "effective aids in the defense of a port" and that a flotilla should be stationed at each major naval base.[210] Within two years sufficient craft would be available to defend the six naval bases in home waters.[211] By now, however, the naval lords were more wary of Arnold-Forster and resolved to proceed more cautiously in their negotiations with the War Office.[212] It was established that henceforth the Admiralty would resist any attempt to link "their" submarines to a reappraisal of the strength of military garrisons.[213] Accordingly, the Board wrote to Arnold-Forster expressing their thanks for removing the minefields from the Home Ports "as they were bound to hamper the movements and curtail the effectiveness" of submarines operating from them.[214] Then in the next sentence the Admiralty politely insisted that the "sole responsibility for the defense of Portsmouth,

Devonport, and the Medway, will henceforward as heretofore rest with the War Office."[215] Replying to Arnold-Forster's personal communication, Selborne explained that at present his advisors were "not disposed" to press for the abolition of minefields at any other ports, although they were prepared to see the formation of yet another joint service committee to consider the matter.[216]

Any counterattack that Arnold-Forster might have contemplated making against the Admiralty was unavoidably postponed in February 1904, after Japan commenced hostilities against Russia by launching a surprise torpedo attack on the enemy fleet stationed at Port Arthur. As both departments were keen to observe the effectiveness of modern weapon systems in action before committing to any policy decisions, it was agreed that further discussion on the substitution of mines for submarines would be suspended.[217] The files were not reopened until July 1904.[218] During this interlude, meanwhile, as the generals learned the true scale of Arnold-Forster's proposed scheme for military retrenchment, opposition to any changes in policy solidified inside the War Office.[219] Led by the director-general of military intelligence, Lt. Gen. Sir William Nicholson, the soldiers fought "tenaciously" to retain their claim for a role in home defense. Their first action was to try to stop the disbandment of the Royal Engineers Corps of Miners. In February 1904, the members of the newly established army council announced themselves "at variance" with the secretary of state for war over the plans to disband the corps, and "inclined to question the wisdom of definitively abolishing the mines in favor of the [submarine] boats."[220] As opinions hardened, resistance gave way to open defiance.[221] In May, the army council informed the Defense Committee that military opinion was "opposed to any reduction in the overall garrison requirements of the Empire, in view of the Admiralty's refusal to take responsibility for the defense of overseas bases."[222]

Arnold-Forster also encountered unexpectedly stiff opposition from within the Cabinet to his plans to abolish the militia. Two ministers were honorary colonels of their local regiments; and a third was the brother of the army's chief of staff. It was clear that Arnold-Forster had badly misjudged his support.[223] This was characteristic of the man. After a similar misunderstanding later that year, Balfour remarked to Lord Esher that Arnold-Forster often "believes after he has talked with someone that they always agree."[224] Similarly, any sympathy Selborne might have had for the proposal to transfer imperial naval bases to Admiralty control had evaporated after Arnold-Forster's duplicity. Notwithstanding the strength of opposition to his ideas for military reform, Arnold-Forster remained confident that as the fiscal position continued to deteriorate the logic of his arguments would eventually prevail. In June 1904, he succeeded in placing the question of whether to abolish the "Aquatics" high on the agenda for discussion by the newly formed Committee of Imperial Defense. He was confident that a change in attitude at Whitehall was likely with the imminent appointment of Sir John Fisher to the post of senior naval lord.[225] After one particularly frustrating meeting of the Cabinet, Arnold-Forster recording in his diary:

> we discussed the reduction of Colonial garrisons at some length, and I made considerable progress in getting my principles admitted. When Fisher comes to the Admiralty, I do not doubt that some of the battalions at which my friends now boggle will be brought home and out of their present useless garrisons at short order.[226]

Arnold-Forster knew that he and Admiral Fisher shared a similar strategic outlook. They had worked closely when both served on the Board of Admiralty in 1902, and more recently while Fisher had been serving as a member of the War Office Reconstitution Committee. As we shall see in the next chapter, the admiral was fully aware of the political importance to the government of securing reductions in the military estimates. Indeed his appointment to succeed Kerr had been the result of his promise that he could find the government substantial savings in the naval estimates which would enable the Conservative Party to make tax cuts, thereby improving its chances of reelection. Fisher was determined that any further reductions in defense expenditure should be imposed on the army rather than the Royal Navy.

CHAPTER 3

Radical Jack Fisher, 1899–1904

> I am perfectly certain I am right in what I tell you and I am perfectly con-
> vinced I could carry out all the proposals I make, but ten years' experi-
> ence at the Admiralty as Director of Naval Ordnance and Controller of the
> Navy in very troublesome times has taught me that unless one has the
> actual carrying out of reforms and innovations, with ruthless and relent-
> less removal of all obstructionists, it is usually a waste of time and only
> causes friction . . .
>
> *Sir John Fisher to Selborne, 19 December 1900*

The naval career of John Arbuthnot Fisher already has been the subject of three major and two minor biographies, a "caprice," plus numerous
other books, articles, and essays.[1] More biographies are in the process of
being written: countless others have been aborted.[2] In addition, there have
been published no fewer than five volumes of Fisher's private and official
correspondence. Despite this huge volume of output, however, the magnitude and exact nature of Jacky's achievements have been scarcely recognized. Partially this is because Fisher's biographers blindly accepted the
old assumptions as to his motives, his intentions, and the direction of his
naval policy. And partly it is because his biographers and naval historians
have slanted their efforts away from analyzing his naval policy in favor of
trying to capture Jacky's personality; ignoring warnings from those who
knew him well that "no writer, however capable a judge of character . . .
can make 'Jacky Fisher' as he really was to live again for the benefit of
those who never saw or knew him."[3] "It is difficult enough to describe a
man who differs but little from the normal run of mankind," wrote Fisher's
first biographer and former naval assistant, Reginald Bacon:

> How can success be achieved when portraying one of whom a close
> observer wrote: "I have known personally a dozen men who have been in
> my time among the most remarkable and famous men in the world; Lord
> Fisher was the most fascinating of them all, and the least like any other
> man." Since it is impossible to describe personality in mere words, the
> more abnormal the person the more difficult the description becomes.[4]

Something of Fisher's character can of course be recovered by examining his private correspondence, but it should not be forgotten that the Admiral communicated most of his ideas verbally rather than on paper. Those who knew and worked alongside Fisher remembered him mainly as a "demonic" and mesmerizing conversationalist rather than as "a great letter writer."[5] That Fisher generally provoked violently contrasting emotions in people also makes it hard to draw a balanced picture. As Jan Morris discovered while gathering material for her "caprice", "Fisher, it seemed, was a Great Englishman, a disgrace to his uniform, a manipulator, a hobgoblin, a damned Socialist, a crook, a paragon of kindness, a parvenu, a cad, a genius, a fraud, a delight. Only one thing all were agreed upon: he had a marvellous face."[6]

Fisher is more easily measured by his deeds. Entering the Royal Navy in 1854, "penniless" and "forlorn," he rose to the top of his profession on his own merit and in spite of the widespread jealousy and mistrust he inspired among his peers. "I won't hide from you that I am called a 'Radical enthusiast,' 'Gambetta,' and several other names indicating a very bad opinion of me," he admitted to prospective allies.[7] Fisher never once received an accelerated promotion. He was thus sixty-one-years old when he was at last promoted admiral and just three months short of his sixty-fourth birthday when he was appointed senior naval lord. Throughout his career, Fisher retained the reputation for being a progressive officer with a keen interest in new technologies. He was an expert in gunnery and also a pioneer in torpedo warfare. But it was as a Whitehall administrator that Jacky was to leave his mark upon the service. In 1886, Fisher was appointed to the Admiralty as director of Naval Ordnance, remaining there for the unusually long period of five years. After a brief spell as superintendent of Portsmouth Dockyard overseeing the construction of HMS *Royal Sovereign*—the "dreadnought" of her day and lead ship of the Naval Defense Act—Fisher returned to the Admiralty as controller of the navy in 1892. Here again he served a double term: this time an unprecedented five-and-a-half years. In 1897, after fifteen years away from the sea, Fisher left the Admiralty to take command of the North America and West Indies Station, a maritime backwater that was normally allocated to passed over flag officers as a sinecure. Half way through this commission, however, in March 1899, George Goschen telegraphed Sir John Fisher informing his that the Cabinet had selected him to attend the forthcoming Hague Peace Conference as the British naval delegate and that afterwards he would be given the command of the Mediterranean Fleet—which at that time was "*the* tip-top appointment of the service."[8] Both honors were unexpected; the latter particularly so because Fisher had no reputation of being a "fighting admiral" and in making the appointment the first lord had passed over several more senior and arguably better qualified men.[9] Why exactly Goschen picked Fisher for the job, thereby reviving his flagging career, is still not clear.

Fisher's ideas on the application of naval force underwent a dramatic modification while serving in the Mediterranean between September 1899 and June 1902. Having spent most of his recent career developing new weapon systems and overseeing their development and eventual procurement, he had found little time to consider properly the implications of the veritable revolution in naval matériel that had occurred with the introduction during the 1890s of armored cruisers, destroyers, and submarines, not to mention wireless telegraphy, smokeless powder, and quick-firing guns.[10] But, to be fair, nor had anyone else. As the man who had been mainly responsible for introducing the new equipment into service, Fisher was perhaps thought to be the best qualified admiral to develop ideas for means of using them. In the Mediterranean, the prospect that in the event of war he would be commanding Britain's premier fleet encouraged Fisher to think very carefully about how he would employ his forces. He was undoubtedly encouraged to do so by the knowledge that in recent years the French Mediterranean fleet had been worked up to a high level of efficiency, first by Adm. Albert Gervais and then by Adm. François Fournier.[11] Fournier, moreover, was highly regarded as a tactician and known to favor radical theories on force deployment.

All Fisher's contemporaries and naval historians have agreed that the admiral injected a new spirit and sense of purpose into the Mediterranean Fleet.[12] "It is difficult for anyone who had not lived under the previous regime to realise what a change Fisher brought about," Lord Hankey, then a captain in the marines, recalled in his memoirs.

> Naval personnel was, and always will be, keen and full of enthusiasm. In the pre-Fisher era, however, this keenness was often wasted on comparatively unworthy objects. Before his arrival the topics and arguments of the officers' messes . . . were mainly confined to such matters as the cleaning of paint and brasswork, the getting out of torpedo nets and anchors, and similar trivialities. After a year of Fisher's regime these were forgotten and were replaced by incessant controversies on tactics, strategy, gunnery, torpedo warfare, blockade etc. It was a veritable renaissance and affected every officer in the fleet.[13]

Scholars have also recognized that it was while commanding the Mediterranean Fleet that Fisher formulated the new theory of capital ship design he tried to introduce after becoming senior naval lord.[14] But few commentators have realized the profound changes that occurred in his thinking during this period on the more fundamental question of how future wars would and should be fought.

It was also while serving in the Mediterranean that Fisher developed his interest in submarine warfare. As his appointment coincided with the acceleration in the French submarine program, and their main testing ground was off Toulon, it was small wonder that Fisher was the first British fleet commander to take the underwater threat seriously. As early as February 1900, it has been shown, Fisher was pressing the Admiralty to revoke their ban on contact mines in order that some might be sent out to the Mediterranean to protect the fleet when at anchor.[15] Except for his second in command, Rear Adm. Lord Charles Beresford, no other British admiral chose to take this possibility seriously.[16] In the meantime Fisher kept himself informed about further developments in France.[17] Reading the French newspapers paid dividends, as did employing consular officials to spy on French naval maneuvers or establishing an informal intelligence network that spanned the Mediterranean region.[18] Fisher's private letters to Lord Selborne show that he very quickly became fascinated with submarine-boats.[19] Yet the significance of this enthusiasm should not be overstated. At this time Fisher's apprehension of submarines was overshadowed by his greater concern over the French surface fleet.

Fisher was particularly haunted by the specter of the newly developed side-armored cruiser. Although congestion in the French arsenals delayed the completion of most of these vessels till after Fisher left the Mediterranean, the few that had already entered service were a source of great concern.[20] None of the ships attached to the Mediterranean Fleet for scouting duties, Fisher complained, were of "such calibre as not to cause an admiral grave concern if allowed to wander from the protection of larger ships."[21] Rather than use the third-class cruisers and gunboats with which he had been provided, therefore, Fisher preferred to employ torpedo-boat destroyers to scout for the fleet. If these craft did not have the endurance or seakeeping qualities for proper cruiser work, at least they had the speed to escape trouble. Fisher anticipated the French armored cruisers would prove even more dangerous and difficult to contain if deployed independently as commerce raiders.[22] "It can be incontestably shewn," he wrote, "that unarmored cruisers can be rendered powerless and be captured one after another by swifter armored cruisers no matter how great may be the preponderance in numbers of unarmored cruisers."[23] Fisher's concerns were widely shared. Both Selborne and Kerr accepted that the "armored cruiser will brook no rival in war."[24]

Fisher was concerned also about the threat to his fleet posed by surface torpedo boats. By 1901, the French flotilla in the western Mediterranean had grown to ninety-five vessels, though only forty-six were reckoned to be effective beyond inshore waters.[25] Coping with the numerous French torpedo flotillas was always going to be a major headache for any British observation squadron cruising the Gulf of Lyons in wartime. Attrition was expected to be high. In February 1902, Fisher confessed his doubts whether the Mediterranean Fleet would be able to keep an effective watch over Toulon.[26] But after reading of the aggressive deployment of torpedo craft during the French naval maneuvers in 1900 and 1901, Fisher became much more concerned that larger French torpedo boats might simply ignore the inshore squadron and attack more valuable targets lying further out to sea.[27] Still more alarming was the possibility that the French flotilla operating in conjunction with their numerically weak battle squadron might be a potent match for the British fleet. For many years the French had been practicing their torpedo boats to launch mass attacks against enemy battle squadrons. Hitherto the Royal Navy had dismissed the threat—at least during the hours of daylight—trusting to the numerous quick-firing guns mounted on their ships to throw out an impenetrable "hail of shot" which would sink the enemy torpedo craft before they reached firing range.

By the beginning of the twentieth century, however, the relative difference between the effective range of naval artillery and the torpedo narrowed considerably. The addition of a gyroscope to the torpedo guidance mechanism in 1896, an invention perfected by 1900, overnight transformed the existing torpedo from a weapon accurate only at ranges up to six hundred yards into one that could hit at three times this distance. "Whereas a year ago 600 yards was considered a maximum range at which a torpedo could be relied on," noted Capt. George Egerton in a report that was widely circulated within the fleet during 1900,

> now 1,000 or even 2,000 can be relied on; and whilst at that time running from a stern tube was quite unreliable, now it is as good as from any other tube, even with the ship under extreme helm. That being so, its effects on the tactics of a fleet requires full consideration, and I would point out that the French, who, we know, advocate the use of torpedo boats in fleet actions, will derive from the adoption of the gyroscope so much advantage that we can no-longer afford to look on these boats merely as an encumbrance to the fleet to which they are attached . . . The prospect of destroying a torpedo boat at, say, 1,200 yards during a fleet action is very much less than the chances of destroying one at 600 yards range, and the chances of the torpedo hitting at 1,200 yards is greater now than it was formerly at 600 yards.[28]

By early 1901, most senior naval leaders, including Admirals Fisher, Lord Charles Beresford, Sir Harry Rawson and Arthur Wilson, agreed that with increasing range and accuracy, the torpedo was becoming a significant factor in fleet tactics.[29] "It is no exaggeration to say that the perfecting of this application, which is now an accomplished fact," acknowledged the first lord of the Admiralty in January 1901, "has made the torpedo a four-fold more dangerous weapon of offence than it has previously been."[30]

It was mainly out of fear for the torpedo that British fleet commanders began encouraging their battle squadrons to practice long-range gunnery.[31] At the beginning of 1900, the effective range of naval guns was generally held to be less than 2,000 yards.[32] But the year after, following a series of fleet exercises, Vice Adm. Sir Arthur Wilson, then commander in chief of the Channel Squadron, was persuaded of "the respect in which the gyroscopic torpedo must be held in a modern naval action, and it would appear that, even with the present torpedo (18-inch Mark IV), it is unsafe to approach within 2,000 yards." Wilson concluded: "This points to the all-importance of long range fire."[33] Fisher was yet more cautious. He insisted that it must be a cardinal point of fleet tactics "not to get inside 4,000 yards of the enemy (even though we are suffering from want of accuracy in gunfire due to want of velocity), because, as sure as you do so, the torpedo will get in."[34] As early as June 1900, Fisher was authorizing gunnery officer to conduct practice shoots with medium caliber quick-firing guns (which then were regarded as a battleship's long-range weapons) at the then unprecedented range of 6,000 yards.[35] Following the lead from the Mediterranean Fleet, the Admiralty next year directed that all fleets should practice at that range at least once a year. These impossibly high standards were modified after very disappointing results. Not until 1905, with the introduction of better sight-setting instruments and more sophisticated fire control techniques, did the Royal Navy again strive to master long-range gunnery.[36]

Lack of confidence in long-range naval gunnery, meanwhile, led Fisher and Wilson to attach torpedo-boat destroyers to their battle squadrons. Both believed that especially during the hours of darkness, destroyers would protect the line of battle from torpedo attack far more reliably than battleship gunfire. "It will be simply suicidal," Fisher lectured his subordinate captains, "for any battleship squadron to cruise without an attendant destroyer flotilla."[37] A series of fleet exercises were held to demonstrate the point.[38] When Fisher arrived in the Mediterranean, he was given only sixteen destroyers and thereafter was constantly complaining that the force at his disposal was insufficient for his needs.[39] According to his own committee of experts at least sixty were required. The Admiralty, however, were unsympathetic to his demands.[40] "Both Fisher and Wilson," Lord Walter Kerr protested to Selborne in August 1901, "have used their destroyers for purposes which they were not intended."[41] "Destroyers were not intended to accompany a fleet at sea," Kerr explained on another paper, "but were designed to operate from bases against the torpedo boats of the enemy also operating from a base"; instead of employing destroyers as scouts, Kerr declared, fleet commanders should use the third-class cruisers and gunboats with which they had been provided.[42] The senior naval lord was encouraged to stand firm on this point by the DNI Rear Adm. Reginald Custance, who was convinced that using destroyers to screen a fleet rather than deploying them to seek out and destroy enemy torpedo craft was unsound. "The mind of the Commander in Chief leans largely to a defensive policy," he sneered, "and that [worse] he has to some extent indoctrinated those about him with the same views."[43] In official minutes to the Board, Custance accused Fisher of promulgating pusillanimous doctrine—a serious charge. Kerr was inclined to agree.[44] Both men, however, underestimated the torpedo threat, and neither offered an alternative method of protecting a fleet from torpedo attack.[45]

After Fisher left the Mediterranean in June 1902, he became increasingly convinced that the danger from torpedoes would soon inhibit the Royal Navy from regularly deploying its armored warships within range of hostile torpedo craft.[46] To the consternation of naval officers such as Rear Adm. William May, the controller, the plausibility of this notion strengthened as the range of the torpedo continued to lengthen.[47] "Soon it will be 5,000 yards," Fisher exclaimed to his flag captain in January 1904, "and then where is your gunnery going to be?"[48] Later that year, furthermore, the Royal Navy began experimenting with a device that heated the compressed air used to drive the torpedo's engine.[49] "Heaters" threatened to extend the range of torpedoes well beyond the maximum range at which naval artillery could then be fired with effect.[50] Another reason to take torpedoes seriously was that its warhead was much more destructive than a shell fired by the biggest gun. It was generally accepted that "one shot getting home from a torpedo tube is worth thirty from a gun."[51] The magnitude of the danger from torpedoes was brought home to the Admiralty in 1903 after practical trials revealed that existing armored warships were even more vulnerable to underwater damage than had previously been presumed.[52] The most dramatic confirmation of this fact took place in September. This involved the old cruiser HMS *Belleisle* that had been specially modified to withstand a hit from a torpedo. So confident were the experts of the "Vernon" that they had made the ship unsinkable that the experiment was conducted inside

Portsmouth Harbor; to everyone's embarrassment the ship sank at her mooring inside seven minutes. "I regret very much," afterwards wrote Admiral May, "but I fear we must accept that with our present knowledge it is not possible to make a ship invulnerable against attacks of the 18-inch Whitehead, without going to prohibitive size."[53] Subsequently, a private salvage company was hired to remove the wreck from the middle of the harbor.[54]

In the autumn of 1902, Admiral Fisher was unexpectedly recalled to Whitehall as second naval lord.[55] Although recognizing that Sir John was too senior to be "playing second fiddle," Selborne had overruled Kerr's objections and insisted upon recruiting Fisher's unrivaled administrative skills to help sort out the navy's critical personnel problems. Among Fisher's duties as second naval lord was the responsibility for providing crews to man the armada of new submarines under construction.[56] This allowed him special access to the dockets on submarine policy, which until then had been given a limited circulation even within Whitehall. It also brought him into contact with Capt. Reginald Bacon, the inspecting captain of submarines, who proceeded to educate him on the tactical possibilities with submarines. Until then Fisher's notions had been simplistic, lacking in detailed knowledge of their technical limitations and actual capabilities. Before he became second naval lord, for instance, Fisher had envisaged the Royal Navy using submarines to "flush out like rabbits" reluctant enemy warships sheltering in port.[57] Capt. Edmond Jeffreys, the DNO, Capt. Henry Jackson, the former naval attaché in Paris, and Adm. Lord Walter Kerr had all expressed similar ideas.[58] Thanks to Bacon, Fisher was disabused of such impracticable ideas and left Whitehall with a thorough grasp of the true tactical possibilities of submarines.[59]

Much more difficult to gauge is the extent to which Bacon might have contributed to the radicalization of Fisher's thinking on naval strategy. Many historians have assumed Bacon's influence upon the admiral was great: but as their private correspondence has not survived this impossible to prove. Nevertheless, it is perhaps significant to note that Bacon did not complete his report on the role of the submarine until 31 May 1903, and that it did not arrive in Whitehall until October—or several months after Fisher quit the Board.[60] Yet in a speech to the Royal Academy delivered on 14 May 1903, Fisher was already asking the audience to consider:

> the submarine-boat and wireless telegraphy. When they are perfected we do not know what a revolution will come about. In their inception they were weapons of the weak. Now they loom large as weapons of the strong.

Will any fleet be able to be in narrow waters? Is there the slightest fear of invasion with them, even for the most extreme pessimist?[61]

This early demonstration of Fisher's vision notwithstanding, it was not until after he became commander in chief at Portsmouth, in September 1903, that he began to talk of this "revolution" being already under-way. Nor should the extent of Fisher's influence upon British subma-rine policy at this stage be overstated. "The submarine," one former inspecting captain of submarines asserted in his memoirs, "was Fisher's child, and his dynamic energy overrode all naval and depart-mental obstruction and gave it a good start in life."[62] But, although "Radical Jack" did lend his "irresistible" drive to Captain Bacon's cam-paign in the spring of 1903 "to give the submarine a definite role in the armaments of the navy," his support was indirect and his influence lim-ited. As we have seen, Fisher's "zealous support" simply was not a fac-tor in the Admiralty's decision to accept the submarine as an adjunct to the defense of naval ports.

As commander in chief at Portsmouth, the submarine service came under Fisher's direct command. He was thus in a position to watch closely the development of the embryonic Holland boats. Possibly Fisher was alluding to his own conversion when he wrote in November 1903, that "only those who have seen a flotilla of submarine-boats (as at Portsmouth) working out in the open sea can form the right conception of the revolution they have caused."[63] The Admiral subsequently took and created every opportunity to bring influential politicians down to Portsmouth to see the submarines for themselves. In one instance, recalled one young submariner, "Jackie Fisher took a lot of MP's from Portsmouth to Osborne in [HMS] *Volcano* to inspect new training college [on the Isle of White]." During the crossing "submarines attacked the tug and showed off at Spithead."[64] Fisher was on hand to provide a running commentary of the display, and to distribute programs outlining the chief points of interest covered by the tour. "Submarines have made impossible what was formally perhaps just feasible as regards invasion, and will be productive of such War Office economies as will bring down income tax to 3d in the £," he claimed in these booklets: "but as Mr. Rudyard Kipling says, 'that's another story.'"[65] On special occasions Fisher allowed selected journalists to make unauthorized visits inside submarines in return for favorable publicity.[66]

Some historians have alleged that Fisher assigned abilities to the submarine that it did not possess.[67] This was not so. Most if not all of his ideas on the tactical possibilities with submarines came from Reginald Bacon. As second naval lord, Jacky had deliberately cultivated the notoriously "prickly" inspecting captain of submarines, in order to keep his own emerging thoughts on the strategic implications of submarines within the bounds of technical and tactical practicability. After he became commander in chief at Portsmouth, the two developed an even closer working relationship. When Fisher was appointed senior naval lord in October 1904, indeed, he invited Bacon to become his assistant. It is also relevant to note that in early 1904, Bacon too was accused of exaggerating the capabilities of submarines. His response had been to "insist that my experience as to the performance of the boats is greater than that of many critics who have never seen an attack made, or a boat submerged."[68] Bacon always maintained that only a handful of persons were really qualified to make assessments of the value of submarines.[69] Few officers, he declared, realized just how rapidly submarine were developing. With hindsight it is possible to see that Bacon was justified in his claims. As early as January 1904, Bacon began planning exercises "far out in the [English] Channel."[70] Once the **A** class submarines began entering service in the middle of that year, Bacon conducted "extended maneuvers" on the French side of the Channel "over towards the Channel Islands."[71] Also in early 1904, the Admiralty endorsed Bacon's plans for a 300-ton submarine with a radius of action of 800 miles designed to operate anywhere in the Channel for up to a week.[72] One of the ten **A** class submarines projected under the 1903–4 estimates was replaced by an experimental (**B** type) vessel. By 1906, after just three years service, the original Holland boats were classified as obsolete by the Royal Navy and judged unsuitable even for training duties.[73]

At Portsmouth, Fisher spent a great deal of time contemplating the impact submarines would have upon traditional methods of conducting war at sea. Fisher, for instance, read Bacon's report on the possibilities of submarines more carefully than Kerr, and reflected upon about the more "fantastic" predictions it contained. "He was particularly impressed with the fact that the submarine was no answer to the submarine," recalled Captain Bacon, "here was a new invention, to combat which some new method, some new appliance, perhaps some new vessel, would have to be invented."[74] For the foreseeable future, Fisher was persuaded, submarines would remain "absolutely unattackable." To Fisher, this was "the pith and marrow of the whole matter."[75] If correct, he reasoned, then it was difficult to imagine how large armored vessels could exercise command of seas in the face of submarines.[76] In May 1903, Bacon had suggested that the Dover Straits "might, and should be easily held and controlled by torpedo craft without risking large ships at sea, wasting coal and exposed to attack in such narrow waters."[77] By January 1904 Fisher had already gone further and was speculating that improved torpedo craft would be able to control the "narrow seas" and other key strategic waters: he predicted that "in the course of a few years no fleet will be able to remain in the [western] Mediterranean or in the English Channel!"[78]

A number of letters written by Fisher in the first half of 1904, show in unambiguous language that he envisaged the submarine playing a central role in the next war. "My beloved submarines," he wrote to a friend in March, are "going to magnify the naval power of England seven times more than present."[79] "It's astounding to me, *perfectly astounding*, how the very best amongst us absolutely fail to realise the vast impending revolution in naval warfare and naval strategy that the submarine will accomplish," he exclaimed to Admiral May. "In all seriousness I don't think it is even *faintly* realised—*the immense impending revolution which the submarines will effect as offensive weapons of war*," he added, before going on to suggest that, "when you calmly sit down and work out what will happen in the narrow waters of the Channel and the Mediterranean, how totally the submarines will alter the effects of Gibraltar, Port Said, Lemnos and Malta, it makes one's hair stand on end!"[80]

Submarines and Fleet Maneuvers

On 13 January 1904, the Admiralty instructed Sir Arthur Wilson to arrange a series of exercises off Portsmouth between Bacon's submarines and his Channel Squadron.[81] These orders were prompted by concerns expressed at Whitehall by the second and junior naval lords at the wisdom of abolishing the observation minefields at naval bases, examined in the last chapter.[82] The maneuvers were set for March; their object was "to ascertain as far as possible the extent of the danger which threatens a fleet compelled by strategic exigencies to move within the radius of action of a strong hostile torpedo craft flotilla, but having the advantage of superiority of force."[83] Wilson arrived at Portsmouth at the end of February 1904, however, with a very different agenda in mind. Since his departure from the Admiralty some three years before, he had been frequently urging "a commencement being made in the work for which these [submarines] were originally purchased—namely, the investigation of the best methods of destroying them or of frustrating their attacks."[84] "You know," Wilson privately reminded Lord Selborne shortly before the exercises commenced, "I attach great importance to developing the means of destroying submarines boats, while all efforts hitherto have been made on the side of improving them."[85]

By insisting upon framing the program of events himself and at the same time appointing himself commander of the attacking fleet, Sir Arthur succeeded in altering the intended character of the exercises to serve his ends. Instead of organizing a "wargame" as the Admiralty had wanted, Wilson arranged a series of set-piece maneuvers to test the practicability of several antisubmarine weapons he and his staff had devised. Although none of the devices proved successful, in his official report Wilson consoled himself with the thought that "the result of the maneuvers has been to establish the great value of destroyers as a guard to a fleet in waters supposed to be infested with submarines."[86] The exercises, he informed the Admiralty at the end of March, showed that destroyers could easily intimidate submarines from putting to sea by steering directly for their periscopes.[87] The validity of this conclusion appeared to have been demonstrated by the accidental loss with all hands of the brand new submarine HMS *A1*. She had been run into and sunk by a mail steamer passing through the area.[88] The loss deeply shook Bacon and prompted Wilson to cut short the remainder of his program of maneuvers.[89]

Wilson's report provoked bitter argument among other officers who had been witness to the maneuvers. Fisher, for instance, thought they had been so "unrealistic" as to have made them a complete waste of time. In a letter to Lord Esher he condemned the set-piece tactical scenarios devised by Wilson as being "the most misleading set of circumstances that the mind of man could have evolved!"[90] In any case, "we ought to have 5 times as many submarines against such a large force as the Home Fleet and 3 flotillas of destroyers," Fisher explained to the King's private secretary, Lord Knollys.[91] Other commentators complained that Wilson had been too preoccupied with tactical issues and had consequently missed the strategical lessons taught by the exercises. Bacon, for example, argued that the most important lesson of the maneuvers was the "extraordinary restraining influence" exercised by his submarines "on the operations of the Home Fleet."[92] As he and Fisher had predicted, Bacon pointed out, the submarines had successfully intimidated the Channel Squadron. Wilson had kept his battleships well out to sea—out of harm's way—where they were in no position to bombard the dockyard they were supposed to have "attacked." Capt. Robert Arbuthnot, the chief umpire, also observed that the submarines had "introduced a restraining care and vigilance on the fleet." In his report, he told the Admiralty that not only had the maneuvers shown the capabilities of the submarine to be "very great," but more fundamentally "the fear of what it can do renders its strength still greater."[93] Characteristically, it was Fisher who best summed up the results. "The six submarines we have here of the original type," he declared, "succeeded in the recent maneuvers in sinking millions of £'s of battleships and cruisers and established such a 'funk' as to keep the Home Fleet miles away from Portsmouth."[94]

In May 1904, Fisher organized a second series of maneuvers to settle the argument over "the relative value of the destroyer and the submarine boat when opposed to each other."[95] In contrast to Wilson, Fisher remained aloof from conducting the trials and sensibly delegated all responsibility for writing the official report to Edward Charlton (captain of destroyers at Portsmouth) and Reginald Bacon (inspecting captain of submarines). The admiral's trust was not misplaced. His subordinates concluded after three weeks of trials that "the balance of power to inflict damage lies with the submarine." While they conceded that escorting destroyers could distract submarines from larger targets, "the destroyers however incur considerable danger in thus protecting a ship." For destroyers "to remain in such waters without any objective other than the attack of S.M. boats, we consider decidedly hazardous," and likely to prove more danger to the hunter than the hunted. Bacon and Charlton closed their report by reminding their superiors that "no method by which destroyers can inflict injury on s.m. boats *with certainty*, has yet been devised."[96]

Fisher held up this report as a vindication of his idea on the deterrent value of submarines, but in London the naval lords were less sure.[97] While conceding that the submarines certainly "had the best of it," Kerr found it "not easy to imagine struggles between s.m. and destroyers unless they were forming a cover to battleships operating against a port."[98] In which case, May agreed, "when submarines are harassed by a well organised combination of small boats or vessels, their attention must be taken off the primary object viz:—the battleships."[99] Admiral Wilson was similarly unconvinced. Returning his copy of the report to the Admiralty, the commander in chief insisted that it did "not throw any additional light on the important question of the risks that destroyers would really incur from the torpedoes of submarines."[100] He felt that this question could not really be settled "except by actual trials" with the submarines firing real torpedoes fitted with collision heads. The only problem with this apparently sensible suggestion was that even without a warhead, a half ton (1,326 lb.) torpedo proceeding at thirty-one knots could seriously damage or even sink a lightly plated destroyer.[101] Nonetheless, Wilson thought the loss of a couple of destroyers would be worth the experience.[102]

In August 1904, a third series of maneuvers were held in the Irish Sea involving eight submarines and one hundred and six destroyers, plus several fleet units from the Channel Squadron. Once again there were too few submarines to patrol or "infest" the waters around their base, thus compelling the submariners to improvise new tactics for the occasion. Bacon subsequently chose to confound his opponents by instructing the Holland boats to operate on the surface at night. "The result was in every way satisfactory," he afterwards gloated, "five destroyers were attacked at close range, and in no case was a submarine seen." With their low silhouettes the craft were found to be virtually invisible at night.[103] Though these tactics worked they were dangerous, and for this reason were prohibited in all subsequent fleet maneuvers before 1914. With the three larger more seaworthy **A** class vessels Bacon had hoped to "strike a blow at the battle fleet." But the opportunity never arose. Wilson's fleet seemed content "merely to steam up and down the manoeuvre area with as little loss as possible."[104] Although frustrated from actually engaging the Channel Squadron, the submarines were again judged by neutral umpires to have exerted a decisive "moral influence" over its movements. "The existence of submarines made the close blockade of Milford Haven more difficult, and the fact of their presence inspired fear," judged chief umpire Rear Adm. Hugh Grenfell. Although "they were repeatedly being reported off Queenstown [they] never left the precincts of Milford Haven."[105] Begging to differ with Wilson, Rear Adm. Charles Robinson reported that "battleships and cruisers are *not* safe within the radius of action of hostile torpedo craft, even though protected by a larger force of destroyers than is possessed by their enemy."[106] This exercise killed dead any lingering thoughts of imposing a close blockade against a port defended by submarines.[107] The Irish Sea maneuvers also provided yet another endorsement of Bacon's and Fisher's axiom that "ship will not risk themselves in narrow waters known to contain submarine boats. The risk is out of all proportion to the gain."[108]

National Strategic Policy

As commander in chief, Portsmouth, Adm. Sir John Fisher was in a marvelous position to watch the extraordinarily rapid progress being made by the navy in exploiting several recent inventions and improve the effectiveness of naval armaments. Letters passed through his office en route to the Admiralty from HMS *Excellent* (overseeing the development of long range gunnery); HMS *Vernon* (the torpedo and mine warfare school, which had also been given the responsibility for wireless telegraphy); and of course HMS *Mercury* (head quarters of the submarine section). Fisher was well placed to consult with the heads of these establishments when he needed clarification of certain points. In addition, with the entertainment facilities of Admiralty House at his disposal, he was able to cultivate a wide range of political and industrial leaders and most importantly cement his friendship with King Edward

VII and his satellites.[109] But undoubtedly the most valuable experience he acquired at Portsmouth was the insight he gained into the difficulties with formulating national defense policy, through his close association with two of the most influential defense authorities of the day—Reginald Viscount Esher and Arthur James Balfour.

Shortly after being sent to Portsmouth, Fisher was invited first by the king and then by the prime minister to join "The War Office Reconstitution Committee" chaired by Lord Esher. Despite fierce objections from the Admiralty that he would be fully occupied with routine administrative duties, Fisher was able to accept the post after Balfour silenced Selborne's protests by arranging for the committee to assemble at Admiralty House, Portsmouth, rather than in London.[110] The third member of the committee was Col. Sir George Clarke, a retired soldier turned colonial governor. The prime minister's determination that Fisher would be one of the triumvirate is an indication of the confidence he had in the latter's abilities. During 1903, the two had often met while both were in attendance at the royal palaces. In their conversations, Fisher convinced Balfour that he understood the government's financial difficulties, and let it be known he accepted that for political reasons defense cuts were inevitable. "The time is coming when the cry will be heard for "retrenchment and reform," he chimed. "It is well to face the inevitable reaction of public sentiment, and, if possible, to anticipate it by wise economies."[111] Fisher willingness to accept Balfour's invitation to reform the War Office was not motivated entirely by personal ambition. Having served so recently as second naval lord, Fisher was also aware of the wrangling within the Cabinet Defense Committee over the army's role in home defense. And he recognized that a seat on the Esher committee would afford chances to undermine the War Office case for a large home army. After his appointment was finally confirmed, Fisher informed the nervous Lord Selborne of his intention to exploit every such opportunity![112] He justified this aggressive stance by claiming that securing the necessary funds to uphold Britain's naval supremacy was more important than treading carefully to avoid the "ill-feeling and bitterness amongst the soldiers" which would result from such an aggressive posture.[113]

As soon as the inquiry got underway, Admiral Fisher urged Lord Esher and Sir George Clarke first to consider the broad picture. "We cannot reform the Army administration," he argued, "until it is laid down what the administration is going to administer."[114] Furthermore,

> It has to be put in the forefront that the organisation of the War Office is intimately associated with our naval superiority. Who has yet stated what we want the British Army to do? No one! . . . what would be the good of a

British Army as big as that of Germany if the Navy was insufficient to keep command of the sea?[115]

To counter the standard War Office retort that a home defense army served as an "insurance policy" against a naval disaster, Fisher pointed out that if Britain lost her naval supremacy the nation would be confronted not with invasion but starvation.[116]

Follow this for a moment:—In the month of May England has three days food in the country—in the month of September (on account of the in-gathering of the English harvest) there is three weeks food. Stop the incoming food for a week or two: what can the Army do? The country must capitulate! As the French Admiral said, "an empty belly is more powerful than patriotism![117]

Of course Sir John Fisher was a fervent navalist: but this does not mean his attempts to gain financial priority for the navy were motivated, as some historians have suggested, by a "childish" sense of interservice rivalry. When he wrote "every penny spent on the Army is a penny taken from the Navy," at a time of acute financial limitation, he was right.[118] Nevertheless, when Fisher first began to grapple with the problems of national defense he demonstrated that his vision extended far beyond the limited horizon of the "Blue Water School" of naval strategists. Shortly before the Esher Committee convened, the Admiral raised the possibility with King Edward VII and Arthur Balfour of reorganizing Britain's armed forces into a single service under a supreme minister of defense—provided, of course, the army was subordinated to the navy.[119] "I've got a new big scheme hatching next year which I think will put everything in the shade which has been done in the past. I am interesting some very influential people in it," he wrote to his son at the end of September. "My idea for 23 millions only for the Army, 37 millions for the Navy, and three penny income tax. [T]he Army will be a Lord Lieutenant's army, each county providing its own military force à la militia and a small expeditionary army for extraneous purposes."[120] Jacky soon learned that revolutionary schemes—even when put forward by a senior admiral—did not appeal to established interests. Most of Britain's political and military leaders, he found, did not understand benefits of maritime strategy well enough to see that the navy must be given financial priority ahead of the Army. They always tried to steer a middle course. Fisher discovered that he made more headway in arguments by emphasizing and attacking military profligacy instead of arguing the merits of his own case.

During his tenure on the Esher Committee, Fisher deliberately steered the inquiry towards the broader questions of military policy and the organization of the field. After opening this door he surreptitiously campaigned to have the War Office relieved of "unnecessary" responsibilities that entitled the generals to claim a share of the defense budget. For example, he was quite prepared to see the Admiralty assume the burden of manning the coastal defense batteries at home and overseas.[121] Fisher gave and was given considerable support in his endeavors by Oakley Arnold-Forster, the secretary of state for war, who was an old acquaintance and shared many of his views.[122] It is no coincidence that Arnold-Forster drafted the outline of his scheme of Army reform while he was staying with Fisher at Portsmouth during the weekend of 5–6 December 1903.[123]

In November 1903, Fisher was asked to appraise a draft copy of the prime minister's report on "The Possibility of Serious Invasion." Balfour had written that even if the navy's battle fleet was absent from home waters, he had been convinced that the Royal Navy's superiority in cruisers and flotilla craft would be sufficient to deter any French attempt at invasion.[124] Fisher appreciated the emphasis on the implications of the torpedo armed flotilla. The paper was returned with his favorable comments, and an endorsement of the basic premise that:

> A raid on the sea coast is all that is possible with a fleet or a squadron backing up the landing force and ready to re-embark it, but serious invasion (as defined in this paper) is absolutely now beyond the conception of the pessimists however extreme because as stated (though hardly in forceful enough terms) in this paper the development of the submarine-boat has absolutely precluded the idea of a mass of transports approaching any position where the landing of troops is feasible.[125]

At the end of December, Balfour invited Fisher to expand upon his arguments. The admiral enthusiastically complied. In a paper entitled "Invasion and Submarines," Fisher contended that a successful "surprise" invasion of the British Isles would depend upon the enemy capturing a port to facilitate the landing of heavy equipment and supplies. "No rational commander," he asserted, "would rely on landing on an open beach." Fisher went on to plead that if the Royal Navy provided, say, three submarines for the defense of each port on the south coast, the enemy would be intimidated from launching an amphibious assault until first the submarines had been neutralized. "The word intimidate is used since the history of the world points to intimidation being the greatest safeguard against hostile operations."[126] Not only was this rationale well argued, being essentially the same that the War Office had always used to justify the siting of observation mines at all major ports, it was also calculated to leave the soldiers unable to respond.

The memorandum on "Invasion and Submarines" was not the product of Fisher's desire to draw attention to the possibilities with submarines, as has often been assumed. It was not a particularly good example of his vision in anticipating the dominance of the submarine in the war at sea.[127] Most of the ideas employed were not original. Balfour certainly did not regard the paper as at all controversial. "It is unnecessary to tell you," he replied to Fisher, "how heartily I am in sympathy with your observations on the relations between submarines and invasion."[128] So self-evident did he regard the connection, indeed, that he did not bother to spell it out. Actually, "Invasion and Submarines" was intended to serve as a political document. It was drafted to provide ammunition against recalcitrant generals and their supporters in Cabinet.[129] Fisher actually wrote in his covering letter to Jack Sanders, the prime minister's private secretary: "I got out the invasion print from our War Office committee to show the futility of invasion and the six Army corps and the mismanagement of the Woolwich arsenal."[130] The timing of its circulation is equally significant. It almost certainly was no coincidence that Fisher circulated his paper shortly after Arnold-Forster launched his campaign to replace the army's observation mines guarding the navy's ports with submarine boats.[131]

Gratified by the favorable reception given to his paper by Balfour, Fisher immediately aired his much more radical idea that very soon submarines, in conjunction with surface torpedo craft, would be able to control key strategic waters, which he referred to as "narrow seas."[132] "Even Satan disguised as the Angel of Light," he told the prime minister, "wouldn't persuade any late colleagues at the Admiralty that in the course of a few years no fleet will be able to remain in the Mediterranean or the English Channel."[133] In another letter, also written in January 1904, this time addressed to Rear Adm. Francis Bridgeman, Fisher predicted that:

a) The submarine is coming into play in ocean warfare almost immediately.
b) Associated with a Whitehead torpedo eighteen feet in length it will displace the gun and absolutely revolutionise naval tactics.
c) No single submarine ever built or building will ever be obsolete.

"I stake my reputation on the absolute reliability of these three statements," Fisher proclaimed. "The deduction is:—'drop a battleship out of the program' (if it be necessary on account of financial necessities) but at any cost double the output of submarines."[134]

Qualifications as Senior Naval Lord

In May 1904, Sir John Fisher was formally invited to become senior naval lord from October, following the retirement of Lord Walter Kerr.

Contrary to general belief, before then his appointment was far from being a certainty even though the field of selection was very narrow.[135] Fisher's proven talents as an administrator might have made him the obvious choice but he was almost sixty-four years old. Furthermore, "Radical Jack" was highly unpopular among his peers and generally distrusted.[136] Among his fiercest critics was Lord Walter Kerr.[137] Indeed it had been growing friction between the two, caused by the Kerr's refusal to endorse Fisher's ideas to alleviate the strain on the naval budget, that had caused the latter's early departure from the office of second naval lord in the summer of 1903.[138] "My dear Walker," Fisher had remarked to his private secretary after one particularly heated Board meeting, "I did not think admirals could have been so rude to one another!"[139] According to Rear Adm. George King-Hall, who was then serving in Whitehall and who knew both men well, Kerr and Fisher made no attempt to conceal their dislike for each other.[140] Selborne's habitual reluctance to ignore professional naval opinion, caused him to hesitate appointing Fisher as senior naval lord. What eventually compelled him to relent was intensifying pressure from the Cabinet to reduce the navy estimates, and recognition that Fisher was the only admiral on the flag list willing (and able) to find economies in naval expenditure. "In his heart of hearts," Capt. Louis Battenberg wrote to Fisher, shortly before he was finally offered the top post, Lord Selborne "knows you are the directing brain and mainspring of the 'Selborne Administration.' Before you joined the Board and since you left it, he has accomplished nothing [though] he would rather die than admit this to others. . . ."[141]

In 1904, Britain still based her naval supremacy upon a conventional fleet comprised of battleships and cruisers, that was numerically stronger than the second- and third-ranking naval powers. Naval strategy was based upon the theory of deterrence. For this to work, the Royal Navy required sufficient battleships to guarantee victory in any fleet action, and a large force of cruisers to ensure the defense of trade. To maintain the Royal Navy's relative strength, the Admiralty was committed to build (on average) three new battleships and four armored cruisers per annum plus smaller craft. For a series of complex financial reasons, already explained, by 1900 this approach to naval supremacy was becoming difficult to sustain. By 1904 it had become impossible. The price of each battleship had risen to £1.6 million, and cruisers cost £1.4 million apiece,[142] pushing the construction budget above £12 million—representing a 30 percent increase since the turn of the century.[143] Meanwhile, the Treasury was demanding a significant cut in naval expenditure.

Fisher was undoubtedly an imaginative and gifted administrator, historians have agreed. But what they have failed to appreciate is that

Fisher's ability in 1904 to offer significant economies in naval expenditure stemmed mainly from his radically different vision of future naval warfare. During the early months of 1904, in anticipation of his promotion to senior naval lord, Fisher began outlining his ideas for reform on paper and circulating them to trusted friends for comment.[144] Those relating to the distribution of the fleet and the warship construction program, in particular, were based upon a fundamentally different understanding of naval strategy. Fisher, moreover, was acutely aware of the controversy his ideas would provoke, which is why he deliberately withheld them from Selborne until after he was safely established in Whitehall.[145] "I'm not such a born idiot as to tell those chaps at the Admiralty what I'm going to do before I go there," he once let slip to his flag captain.[146] Although these papers have been widely available for many years, naval historians have dismissed Fisher's assaults on conventional naval theory, such as his suggestion to abandon the construction of battleships, as speculative rhetoric.

In fact, abandoning the construction of battleships was fundamental to Fisher's vision of future war at sea and central to his plans to affect large cuts in naval expenditure. "In approaching the important question of ship design the first essential is to divest our minds totally of the idea that a single type of ship as now built is necessary," Fisher declared in a carefully reasoned paper written in early 1904, entitled "The Fighting Characteristics of Vessel of War."[147] "STRATEGY," he wrote, not tradition, "should govern the types of ships to be designed."[148] Fisher, it must be understood, thought of strategy in terms of capability rather than deterrence. He believed that the Royal Navy's principal duties were to prevent invasion of the United Kingdom and to protect sea communications with the empire. Fisher, incidentally, also believed that a *guerre industrielle* waged against British commerce would be much more difficult to contain than most naval officers realized.[149] Recognizing that battleships were vulnerable to torpedo attack in the "narrow waters" of the English Channel, and lacked the endurance and speed to catch commerce raiding armored cruisers on the high seas, led Fisher to query the utility of battleships. "Here," Fisher postulated,

> there is good ground for enquiry whether the naval supremacy of a country can any longer be assessed by its battleships. To build battleships merely to fight an enemy's battleships, so long as cheaper craft can destroy them, and prevent them of themselves protecting sea operations, is merely to breed Kilkenny cats unable to catch rats or mice. For fighting purposes they would be excellent, but for gaining practical results they would be useless.

Fisher continued:

> Of what use is a battle fleet to a country called (A) at war with a country called (B) possessing no battleships, but having fast armored cruisers and clouds of fast torpedo craft? What damage would (A's) battleships do to (B)? Would (B) wish for a few battleships or for more armored cruisers? Would not (A) willingly exchange a few battleships for more fast armored cruisers? In such a case, neither side wanting battleships is presumptive evidence that they are not of much value.[150]

Although Fisher closed his paper by conceding that "*naval experience is not sufficiently ripe to abolish totally the building of battleships*" he was being deliberately disingenuous. In another paper written at about the same time he noted that "no one can draw the line where the armored cruiser becomes a battleship any more than when a kitten becomes a cat!"[151] As Professor Jon Sumida has shown, once Fisher was safely installed in the chair of the senior naval lord he began openly pressing for the battleship to be replaced by the "super" armored cruiser—later known as the battle cruiser—a large armored vessel with the speed and endurance to perform trade protection duties, yet with the gun armament to engage battleships when necessary.[152] Building a single dual purpose armored warship instead of two types offered enormous potential saving in both money and manpower.

Fisher's "battle cruiser concept" becomes more comprehensible once it is understood that by the time he was appointed senior naval lord, he was convinced that in the face of hostile torpedo craft and submarines, large armored ships could not be regularly deployed in the "narrow seas." No one was more aware that Fisher really believed that such a revolution in naval warfare had occurred than the first lord of the Admiralty, the earl of Selborne. On leaving the Admiralty to become governor of South Africa in early 1905, he warned Balfour of what he regarded as Fisher's eccentric viewpoint. "I always said," Selborne wrote,

> that the battleship held the field, that the battleship counted for more than anything else, and that no number of cruisers could be substitutes for them. Fisher did not believe this when I left the Admiralty, though he believed it before all other opinions when he was Commander-in-Chief in the Mediterranean. Fisher believed that the torpedo as used by torpedo-boats and the submarine was going to make the narrow seas (they widely interpreted) impossible for battleships, that the torpedo was going to be the lord and master of the narrow seas under all conditions. I never believed anything of the kind.[153]

Instead of relying upon the battle fleet to deter invasion and raids against the British Isles, Fisher proposed to give this task to the Royal Navy's own torpedo armed flotilla. Not only would "flotilla defense" prove more effective, he argued, but a mosquito fleet could be built and maintained and considerably less cost than a battle fleet. Such a revolution in naval strategy, of course, left no role for the traditional battleship. This then was the logic behind Fisher's attempts to reorientate the Royal Navy's surface fleet away from being organized primarily to win decisive battle fleet actions, towards combating the threat to oceanic communications. In the next chapter we shall expand on Fisher's theory of "flotilla defense," follow the evolution of this idea into a coherent strategy, and examine its implementation in the wider context.

PART II

Chapter 4

Necessary Reforms, 1904–1905

It is impossible, without confusion of narrative, to deal chronologically
with Sir John Fisher's work as First Sea Lord. His many activities ran
concurrently during the whole period that he held office.
Adm. Reginald Bacon, The Life of Lord Fisher

On 20 October 1904, Adm. Sir John Fisher joined the Board of
Admiralty as senior naval lord.[1] His first business was to change the title
of his office. The next day (Trafalgar Day) Jacky—as he was popularly
known—was proclaimed first sea lord.[2] Since learning of his appointment the previous May, Fisher had been working on a policy manifesto
outlining his intended course of action. For most of the summer he
"steadfastly declined to say a word or write a line" about his plans until
safely installed in his chair at Whitehall.[3] The admiral made Lord
Selborne wait until the third week of August before showing him just an
outline of his proposed administrative reforms.[4] Although Radical Jack
refused to divulge his thoughts to anyone, even to his future colleagues,
several persons anticipated he was contemplating "revolutionary
schemes."[5] When on the very eve of his appointment Sir John finally
unveiled his grand "scheme" to the first lord, this proved to be the case.[6]

Early in November the first sea lord bound together a selection of his
prints, some of which included the marginal comments written by
Selborne on the October drafts, and circulated them to selected naval
officers under the title of "Naval Necessities."[7] Included in this volume
were thirty-four essays, thirteen sets of tables, plus nine appendices. The
size of this document and the range of subjects it covered not only reveal
Fisher's "boundless energy and relentless enthusiasm," it also stands as
a testament to his organizational skills and professional competence.[8]
The scope of Fisher's vision was extraordinary. "Naval Necessities" represented a blueprint for tackling simultaneously all the major problems
which had been plaguing the navy for at least twenty years. In a pream-
ble to the manuscript, Fisher insisted that *the scheme herein shadowed
forth must be adopted as a whole!* Simply because all portions of it are

absolutely essential—and it is all so interlaced that any tampering will be fatal!"[9] This was no hyperbole. The reforms could not be introduced in part or in series because they were interdependent rather than interrelated. How this was the case will become clearer below.

After the Board of Admiralty endorsed the broad outlines of Fisher's crusade of reform, Selborne immediately appointed a committee of Whitehall administrators under the chairmanship of the Director of Naval Intelligence, Prince Louis of Battenberg, to appraise the scheme in more detail and make the necessary preparations.[10] The first lord also promised Fisher that in due course his new armored warship designs would be examined by a special "Committee on Designs" and considered in light of recently received evaluations of naval matériel tested under combat conditions supplied by the Japanese navy.[11] Instead of allowing Fisher to oversee the DNI's committee, Selborne put him to work as chairman of a finance committee charged to scrutinize every vote of the naval estimates looking for possible economies. This task occupied nearly all his time. In the meantime, towards the end of November, the Battenberg steering committee reported that all arrangements were complete and the reforms ready to be implemented.

On 6 December 1904 Selborne proclaimed to the Cabinet, "the Board of Admiralty have decided to make certain changes in the distribution of the fleet, and in the arrangements for its mobilization, the nature and reason of which I desire to explain."[12] "The principles, on which the present peace distribution of His Majesty's ships and the arrangement of their stations are based," the first lord began, "date from a period when the electric telegraph did not exist and when wind was the motive power." Over the preceding thirty years the emergence of new first-class naval powers around the globe had totally changed the strategic environment in which the Royal Navy operated. In addition the development and application of new technologies during this period had dramatically improved the fighting capabilities, range, and endurance of warships. "In the British Navy all the older battleships have been replaced by modern ones, so that it may now be said that all the battle fleets in commission are composed of modern battleships," he reported, "but still more significant and far reaching in its consequences is the fact that this country is now rapidly becoming possessed of a number of modern armored cruisers."[13] Over the past four years this new type of warship had been added to rival navies in considerable numbers.

> The features in these ships, that differentiate them from anything that has preceded them, are their great speed . . . their armour . . . and their armament, which in some cases is as powerful as that of the older battleships.

With such ships even the best protected cruisers would engage at a considerable disadvantage, and the slower or smaller protected cruisers and
all unprotected cruisers would be hopelessly outmatched; their only
chance would be flight, and they could not flee because they have not the
speed.[14]

In their wake, Selborne thus concluded, the armored cruiser has brought
"a revolution in respect of the composition of our cruiser squadrons."[15]

Selborne next outlined the plans to rationalize the strategic command and control for the numerous gunboats and cruising vessels scattered around the globe into three geographical commands. In essence,
he opened, various station fleets were to be merged and warships "too
old to fight and too slow to run away" withdrawn from service. To support the colonial station fleets, the Royal Navy presently maintained four
main fighting fleets. In home waters there were the Channel Squadron,
composed of eight battleships, and the Home Fleet, with another eight
plus a "flying squadron" of six armored cruisers. Overseas, the navy
maintained twelve battleships in the Mediterranean and five in China.[16]
Included within each fleet was also a "fast-division" of two or more
armored cruisers.[17] Selborne announced that from 1 January 1905, the
existing Channel Squadron would be shifted to Gibraltar and thenceforth
known as the Atlantic Fleet; the Home Fleet would be renamed the
Channel Fleet and its strength increased from eight to twelve battleships
by recalling four units from the Mediterranean.[18] A decision on the future
of the China battle squadron would be deferred until the end of the
Russo-Japanese War.[19] In addition, armored cruisers would henceforward be separated from battleship commands and grouped into three
independent flying squadrons "ready to go anywhere."[20] Although techni-
cally these squadrons would be affiliated to the fighting fleets in
European waters, this was done more for administrative than tactical
reasons. Their primary role was not to support the battleships but when
necessary to defend the trade routes or rapidly reinforce the outer
marches of the empire.[21]

In conjunction with the redistribution of the fleet, Selborne continued, the Admiralty planned to reform the arrangements for manning of
the fleet. Under the old system, warships based in home waters were
kept permanently in commission. Every six months or so, a quarter of
each crew was rotated out of the fleet into training schools or was posted overseas, with "fresh entries from the depots, generally the youngest
and last entered seamen, taking their place."[22] This constant shifting of
complements undermined the fighting efficiency, interfered with training, and caused resentment among the lower deck. Even more unpopu-

lar with the ratings was the prospect of spending up to six years abroad if their ship commissioned for service overseas. Under the new scheme the Admiralty intended that all ships would be commissioned for a fixed period of two years. "No officer or man will be removed from her except by promotion, sickness or death." After spending two years at sea men would be allowed to spend one year "at home" crewing a ship in reserve.[23]

A reorganization of the fleet reserve was also announced.[24] Hitherto, warships without permanent crews but still on the effective list were scattered up various creeks and their machinery was looked after by care and maintenance parties. These were drawn from a pool of seamen kept in barracks at each of the Home Ports, "who went backwards and forwards daily to the ships to which they were told off."[25] In a period of emergency these ships would be commissioned with a mixture of active service ratings from the training schools and reservists. In case of full mobilization, additional crews would be formed by diluting the crews of ships already in commission. This meant the captain of a warship could expect to lose up to a quarter of his trained men at the beginning of a war.[26] The disadvantages of this system were obvious. It took months, sometimes years, for scratch crews to reach peak efficiency.[27] Most importantly, "gunnery was daily becoming more and more the business of experts; and to obtain really efficient shooting, the officers and men had to be trained [constantly] in their own ships."[28] A newly commissioned ship, critics of the system pointed out, was no match for an enemy craft manned by an experienced crew.

Under the new scheme, promulgated in January 1905, the best warships in reserve were grouped together into homogenous squadrons and each given a permanent "nucleus crew" of two-fifths of their war complements. Essentially this was equivalent to a full crew less the unskilled men, such as stokers and ammunition handlers—men who were only really needed when the ship was on active service. A nucleus crew could drill normally and periodically take their ship to sea for gunnery and tactical exercises. The main advantage of this new arrangement was that by keeping together the teams of principal officers and skilled ratings, the fighting efficiency of the warship could be maintained at almost the level of a fully commissioned warship yet at a fraction of the cost (and manpower). It took a matter of hours to draft balance crews from the local training schools.

The first lord closed his address to Cabinet by quietly admitting that "in order to provide the personnel for the above mentioned purposes a certain number of ships of comparatively small fighting value have been or will be withdrawn from commission."[29] What he did not say was that the Admiralty planned to strike off no fewer than 154 ships from the navy list. This decision, Lord Selborne knew, would be greeted with a storm of protest—which is probably why he omitted to print any figures in his memorandum. For many years, pressed by Arnold-Forster, he had been trying to reduce the numbers of dilapidated gunboats in commission but had been always thwarted by protests against such a reform by other departments of government, and by the refusal of Lord Walter Kerr to disregard their wishes. The former senior naval lord had maintained that "the Foreign Office, Colonial Office and India Office are largely responsible both for the present distribution and also for the present composition of those squadrons."[30] And he had insisted that the navy was obliged to provide the numbers of gunboats requested. Kerr's reluctance to endorse retrenchment had been reinforced by his personal conviction that "if we do not show the flag we shall lose prestige" overseas.[31] Selborne, believing "disruption of the Board was a greater evil" than the retention of these obsolete craft, had always refused to overrule Kerr.[32] Or so he claimed.

Fisher's perspective of imperial defense and of the navy's obligations to the other departments was quite different. He held that the Admiralty's first duty was to ensure the fighting efficiency of the main fleet. Since the end of 1901, if not earlier, Fisher had been urging Selborne to replace isolated gunboats scattered across the globe with centrally located cruiser squadrons.[33] "The Navy is being fleeced in every direction by every department of the state" he protested in one letter to the first lord. "We ought to absolutely decline any work for our ships and men that unfits them for fighting."[34] More than half seriously, Fisher suggested that "police duties" might be performed just as well by a retired officer in a converted merchant ship armed with a machine gun![35] Incidentally, when in December 1904 Kerr wrote to congratulate the first lord on the new "scheme," he acknowledged that "the key" to the reforms was the policy of scrapping the gunboats—"which as you may remember," he conceded, "I was always a bit shy about not on the Admiralty so much as the Foreign Office account."[36]

Motives and Intentions

Historians have uncritically attributed the "rearrangement of naval forces" and related reforms announced by Selborne at the end of 1904 to a desire by the Admiralty to concentrate the fleet against the "German navy menace."[37] Arthur Marder, for instance, insisted that Fisher persuaded the rest of the Board to distribute warships "to meet strategical '(and not sentimental)' requirements." The first sea lord's motives and intentions were "to concentrate the cream of the fleet where it belonged—in home waters."[38] To achieve this primary goal, he further argued, Fisher sacrificed the Royal Navy's ability to protect British lives and interests in distant waters. And the scrapping policy, the reorganization of the fleet reserve, and the introduction of nucleus crews were similarly explained by him as intended simply to improve the war readiness of ships in reserve.[39] By placing a larger proportion of the fleet in reserve, Marder declared, Great Britain was steadily (and subtly) able to concentrate the fleet in home waters "without unduly straining the international political situation" or offending sensitive public opinion. Thus, he reasoned, "Fisher concentrated the most powerful battleships in the North Sea before the Germans were aware of what was happening."[40] With the benefit of hindsight there is much logical appeal to this explanation. And it conforms with most of the standard political and diplomatic accounts of this period.[41]

Until recently, most historians of this period have agreed that between 1902 and 1906, a fundamental shift occurred in the direction of British diplomacy. Henceforward London regarded Germany rather than the Franco-Russian alliance as the most dangerous threat to British interests.[42] Lately, however, a group of scholars have protested the importance placed on the Anglo-German antagonism in the formulation of British foreign policy.[43] While not denying that a deterioration in relations did occur between Germany and Great Britain during this period, they argue that imperial considerations continued to have a major influence upon foreign policy decision making. Britain, after all, was not simply a European state but rather an imperial power. This school insists, that for most of the decade before the outbreak of war in 1914, Russia, not Germany, was regarded as the greatest long-term threat to Britain and her empire.[44] While it is not intended to enter this debate here, it is pertinent, nevertheless, to question the widespread notion that the Admiralty, and specifically Fisher, was among the first to recognize the German threat and that this is what induced him in 1904 to press for a redistribution of the fleet. As we shall see later, there are many reasons to doubt whether the Admiralty was as preoccupied with the German threat at this time as has so often been asserted. New evidence has been found, moreover, to show that Fisher possessed a more imperialist perspective than has been generally realized.[45]

Many historians have overstated the strength of the German navy in 1904. At that time, Germany was still only the fourth- or fifth-ranking naval power—depending on how one counts the strength of the United States Navy. In numbers of battleships, the High Sea Fleet was a quarter the strength of the Royal Navy, and in cruisers and flotilla craft the Germans were even weaker. Ships for ship, moreover, German vessels were qualitatively inferior to British ones. Although Germany had a published naval program that provided eventually for the provision of a "home fleet" consisting of nineteen modern battleships, many of these warships had not yet been built and it was by no means certain that the German legislature was prepared to endorse an ongoing replacement program to ensure that the fleet was always provided with up-to-date warships.[46] In addition, until the beginning of 1905 the Admiralty was not yet aware of the seriousness of Russia's naval losses in the Far East, and nobody predicted that the Russian Second Pacific Squadron, then en route for Port Arthur, would be intercepted and annihilated at the Straits of Tsushima at the end of May. The few internal planning documents from this period that have survived suggest that if the Admiralty were concerned about the High Sea Fleet at the end of 1904, then it was in the context of the German fleet joining a triple alliance against Britain. "The worst case which can befall us under present conditions is for Germany to throw her weight against us in the middle of a still undecided war between [us and] France and Russia in alliance," noted Selborne on 21 November 1904.[47]

Whether or not British foreign policy underwent a fundamental shift in response to the growing Anglo-German antagonism, no one can deny that throughout the winter of 1904—while the Admiralty was preparing to adopt Fisher's scheme—all eyes in London were focused on the war in the Far East between Russia and Japan.[48] With justification. France was allied to Russia. And since 1902, Britain and Japan had been allies. Hitherto, the Western powers had avoided entanglement in the conflict, being able to do so because the two antagonists were so evenly matched. But there was real concern both in London and Paris that if one of the belligerents gained the upper hand in the conflict, the other might demand military assistance from their ally, which could well precipitate a global war.[49] The Admiralty certainly took this eventuality seriously. While Selborne's memorandum was being printed for distribution to the Cabinet on 6 December, the Admiralty was ordering large stocks of coal to be deposited at Aden and Hong Kong, and the British Mediterranean Fleet was standing by to proceed east of Suez.[50] Even so, the Russo-Japanese War had little impact upon the Admiralty's deliberations in the winter of 1904 upon the redistribution of the fleet. Selborne's memorandum to Cabinet makes it clear that while fixing the strengths of the various squadrons the Admiralty were looking beyond the war in the Far East.

The notion that an anti-German imperative spurred the Admiralty into initiating wholesale reform was first challenged by the author of Fisher's most authoritative biography, Ruddock Mackay. He noted that there was little evidence to support the view that in 1904 Britain's naval leadership sought deliberately to concentrate the fleet in home waters against the growing German navy. Mackay subsequently argued that the 1904 redistribution was not directed against any single great power. Rather, "the Admiralty's view of the strategic probabilities remained flexible."[51] If any concentration of naval force took place, he suggested, then it was at Gibraltar. A new Atlantic fleet was created, to use Fisher's own words, which comprised "our best and fastest battleships and cruisers and our best admirals," poised on the flank, "always instantly ready to turn the scale (at the highest speed of any fleet in the world) in the North Sea or the Mediterranean."[52] Admittedly, Selborne did refer to the new German fleet in his memorandum to a Cabinet as "a navy of the most efficient type" and also noted it was "fortunately circumstanced [*sic*] that it is able to concentrate almost the whole of its fleet and including all its battleships at its home ports." But, as Mackay warned, historians should not make too much out of a single remark and should be careful to "leave the sentence in its context."[53] In the same paragraph the first lord referred to each of the great naval powers. And Selborne's observation therein, that "the French navy stands, as always, in the forefront," can scarcely be classified as "innocuous"—as Marder did.[54] Finally, and perhaps most conclusively, documents show that Fisher's ideas on how the fleet should be redistributed can be traced back to the beginning of 1902 when there was very little concern about the German fleet. In February that year, Fisher submitted a paper to Selborne calling for the replacement of the station fleets with cruiser squadrons and for the Channel Squadron to be moved to Gibraltar. The proposed distribution and organization were almost identical to those made in 1904.[55]

For various reasons the idea of a traditionally "flexible" or "Gibraltar-based" strategy designed to protect British imperial interests against all comers never achieved widespread acceptance among historians. The thesis was most recently dismissed, if not actually ignored, by Aaron Friedberg. He found that it did not fit into his analysis of Britain's relative decline between 1895 and 1905, one of the central arguments of which was that at the end of this ten-year period the Admiralty "acquiesced in the loss of its long-standing control of the world's oceans" in order to ensure "supremacy in home waters."[56] Although he admitted in a footnote that maybe, "in their early formulations, Fisher's redistribution schemes were driven by a concern over the balance of forces in the Mediterranean—in other words they were essentially anti-French," he went on to assert that "there seems little doubt that by the beginning of 1905 Germany had emerged as Britain's number one enemy at sea."[57] In the main text he took as given that "the intention and eventual result of the scheme that Selborne announced [in December 1904] was to permit a permanent strengthening of British naval power in European waters at the expense of the Far East and the Western hemisphere. This became evident in the following year after five battleships were withdrawn from the China station and assigned to the Channel fleet."[58] (No mention was made of the enhanced military effectiveness of the numerically smaller British "station" fleets after the reorganization.) To reinforce this argument he cited evidence which showed that even before Fisher's arrival at Whitehall, several more open-minded officers at the Admiralty, notably Capt. Louis Battenberg (the DNI) had already recognized the inevitable and had been pressing Selborne to recall battleships from distant waters to face Germany.[59]

A closer examination of Battenberg's correspondence with Selborne, however, reveals some confusion over precisely what the DNI was asking for and why. It is true that he wanted to recall "the China B[attle] Ships," and did argue that the deployment of these ships in the Far East was "misplaced power."[60] Other documents dating from this period cast his words in quite a different light. For one thing, when Battenberg asked the China battleships be brought home, he was not proposing (as implied) to reinforce the numbers of battleships in commission in home waters. This is made clear in a subsequent letter the DNI penned to Selborne: "I wish we could get two *Oceans* [class battleships] home from China and with the two [*Oceans*] in reserve, replace the four *Royal Sovereigns* in the Home Fleet."[61] Four days later he further clarified his thoughts. Battenberg argued that he wanted the newer battleships home from China because he was afraid that in wartime the older *Royal Sovereigns* would handicap the rest of the Home Fleet. Battenberg felt they belonged in reserve. "It is merely a matter of degree," he explained: "they are undoubtedly very powerful ships and fit to lie in our line for a good many years to come. Still in protection, armament and speed they stand now at the bottom of the list of our completed first class ships to the number of forty . . . and the difference in speed is serious."[62] Paying off the *Royal Sovereigns* and transferring the *Oceans* to the Home Fleet would have resulted in a net reduction of battleships in full commission.[63]

Similarly, when in early October 1904 Battenberg asked for "the four Mediterranean *Duncan*" class battleships to be brought home, he did not want them to face the German High Sea Fleet. At this time the Royal Navy already had sixteen modern battleships in home waters. Rather, he wanted them "to match and cover" the five remaining battleships of the Russian Baltic Fleet.[64] On this occasion the DNI was worried about the possibility of an alliance between Russia and Germany, who "have now between Kiel and Libau seventeen first class battleships in commission (5+12)."[65] As unlikely as such a combination seemed, even Kerr admitted "one cannot shut ones' eyes to the possibility of a Russo-German combination someday."[66] Though on this occasion Lord Walter Kerr advised Selborne that he and Adm. William May (the controller) believed the DNI was being overcautious. The sixteen battleships of the Channel Squadron and Home Fleet (which unit for unit were more powerful than foreign ships) would be quite sufficient force for the purposes of home defense.[67] If the Home Fleet needed reinforcing, he added, "I am much more concerned in getting more destroyers in commission, an object we have for some time had in view but unable to meet from want of personnel."[68] These additional destroyers, moreover, were needed for service in the Mediterranean rather than the North Sea. Ultimately, Kerr did nothing.

Most historians continue to believe that the weight of evidence points to the 1904 naval reforms being inspired mainly by strategic (or diplomatic) considerations and were aimed, Mackay's observations notwithstanding, at Germany. Preconceived notions about the character of war at sea have also helped obscure the picture of what really happened at the end of 1904. So long as naval warfare is believed to have been mainly an affair of battleships and that the object of the 1904 redistribution was to recall all capital units to European waters, then the argument that the Admiralty was attempting to affect a concentration of force against Germany seems incontrovertible. That being said, however, it is often forgotten that the redistribution actually resulted in an overall reduction in the numbers of British battleships in full commission. Whereas in October 1904 the Royal Navy had thirty-five fully manned battleships, a year later this figure stood at only thirty-two. Perhaps even more significant is the fact that the number of fully commissioned battleships kept in home waters also fell. Although four battleships were recalled from the Mediterranean Fleet at the end of 1904, as Battenberg had requested, simultaneously eight newer units (*King Edward* class) were dispatched to Gibraltar—two days steaming from Malta and four away from the North Sea. Expressed in crude numbers, this move left the Royal Navy with only the twelve battleships of the Channel Fleet in home waters, albeit supported by fourteen older vessels manned by nucleus crews, to match the twelve newest battleships of the High Sea Fleet. Although the British fleet in home waters was certainly stronger after 1904 than it had been before, this was largely the result of providing warships in reserve with nucleus crews, thereby making them almost as efficient as units in full commission. The fighting efficiency of the fleet in home waters was increased, in other words, through reorganization of existing resources rather than through an increase in absolute numbers. Indeed, the total of battleships in the active and reserve fleets actually fell. The issue of distribution of naval personnel will be considered later.

While trying to fathom the complex strategic intentions behind the 1904 reforms, historians have allowed themselves to be mesmerized by the marching and counter marching of battleships. A closer look at the evidence shows that in 1904 Britain's naval leaders were at least, and perhaps more, concerned with the numbers and redistribution of armored cruisers. In the last chapter it was shown that historians have been certainly wrong in thinking that Sir John Fisher measured naval strength by numbers of battleships. There is ample evidence that he attached more importance to armored cruisers. While Fisher was serving as commander in chief, Mediterranean, for example, he postulated in one of his lectures to fleet officers that in the next war admirals would fly their flags in armored cruisers rather than battleships and use their cruiser squadrons as the principle striking force.[69] In February 1902, when Fisher first aired his ideas on a large-scale redistribution of the fleet, he proposed that an "elite" Atlantic fleet based at Gibraltar should be formed of twelve armored cruisers.[70] More tangibly, in October 1904 Fisher handed Lord Selborne a paper that claimed "there is good ground for enquiry whether the naval supremacy of a country can any longer be assessed by its battleships."[71] Although he went on to anticipate objections to this proposal and conceded that maybe giving up battleship construction was not yet practicable, he was, personally, convinced that his new-model "super" armored cruisers could better protect Britain's far flung empire than battleships. Jacky went on to suggest that the navy should measure its relative strength by numbers of armored cruisers and torpedo craft rather than battleships.[72]

> The battleship of the olden days was necessary because it was the one and only vessel that nothing could sink except another battleship. Now every battleship is open to attack by fast torpedo-craft and submarines. Formerly, transports or military operations could be covered by a fleet of battle-ships with the certainty that nothing could attack them without first being crushed by the covering fleet! now all this has been absolutely altered! A battle-fleet is no protection to anything, or any operation during dark hours, and in certain waters no protection in daytime because of the submarine. Hence what is the use of battleships as we have hitherto known them? None! Their one and only function—that of ultimate security of defense is gone—lost! No one would seriously advocate building battleships merely to fight other battleships—since if battleships have no function that the first class armored cruiser cannot fulfil, then they are useless to an enemy and do not need to be fought.[73]

Fisher's paper did not convince the first lord of the Admiralty.[74] Nor did he manage to persuade him to cancel the two battleships authorized but not yet laid down under the 1904–5 program. The maxim "from which I will never depart," Selborne replied, is to "lay down battleships every year."[75] The only concession he was prepared to make was to agree generally with Fisher's observation that "the battleship type and the armored cruiser type are merging into each other."[76]

Barely months later, in early 1905, Fisher issued repeated appeals to the Committee on Designs to endorse his call for the Royal Navy to abandon the construction of battleships. He requested his chosen experts to set aside the turbine driven all-big-gun battleship in favor of the faster, less well-protected "armored cruiser" version.[77] With one exception they refused: but agreed to reconsider the proposal at a latter date. Ultimately the Board of Admiralty ordered under the 1905–6 program four (later reduced to three) "Indomitable" type big-gun armored cruisers plus HMS *Dreadnought*. Still, however, Fisher did not give up. After Selborne's departure from the board in March 1905, the first sea lord launched his third attempt to persuade the rest of the Admiralty to give up the construction of battleships in favor of battle cruisers.[78] This time he approached his goal obliquely. He disingenuously tried to persuade his colleagues that overall savings would accrue from adopting a single, qualitatively superior, "multi-role" armored warship-type instead of continuing to build both battleships and armored cruisers. Unfortunately, his so-called "fusion design" projected for the 1906–7 program was rejected by his second (hand-picked) Committee on Designs. In the committee's opinion, the recent cementing of the Anglo-French understanding coupled to the annihilation of the Russian fleet at Tsushima, had significantly diminished the likelihood that the Royal Navy would have to fight the global cruiser war for which the battle cruiser had been primarily designed. It was felt that "whatever armored cruiser peril still remained could be met by existing vessels."[79] Instead, to Fisher's chagrin, the design committee recommended the construction of more battleships or "dreadnoughts" as they were becoming known.

Fisher was not the only senior policy maker in Whitehall at this time with a high regard for the armored cruiser. Even before Jacky's appointment as first sea lord had been confirmed, Battenberg had been petitioning Selborne that the imminent completion of the large number of armored cruisers then under construction must drastically "affect the foreign stations—beyond the Mediterranean."[80] Battenberg's correspondence with Selborne shows that he shared much, if not all, of Fisher's concern of the armored cruiser threat. In May 1904 the DNI had urged the first lord to overrule Kerr's opposition and go ahead with the formation of a second "flying" squadron "ready to go anywhere." But "nothing that I can say," he afterwards lamented to Fisher, "will make Selborne give way. He is as obstinate as a mule."[81] Later in November, Battenberg counseled the first lord to switch all funds earmarked for new battle-ships under the 1905–6 program to buy "five armored cruisers of the new type"—in other words five battle cruisers.[82] It is no coincidence, fur-thermore, that when Prince Louis left Whitehall in February 1905, he was promoted to command the First Cruiser Squadron based at Gibraltar. The importance Battenberg attached to the armored cruiser—incidentally—sheds important new light on his attempts as DNI to bring home the battleships from China. It has already been shown that when he first made this suggestion he had not envisaged increasing the num-ber of battleships in home waters; he had wanted to substitute them for two *Royal Sovereigns* which he thought belonged in reserve. It is now clear that he wanted to pay off these ships in order to free personnel to man a couple of new armored cruisers.[83] Thus when Battenberg referred to the battleships in China as being "misplaced power," what he really meant was that capital ships were not the appropriate vessels to protect British interests east of Suez where the main threat to British interests was directed at seaborne commerce.[84] Or put another way, the battle-ships were locking up valuable personnel that might better be employed in new cruisers—a view that mirrored exactly the opinion of the first sea lord.[85] The views of Fisher and Battenberg on the importance of armored cruisers belie the notion that Britain's naval leaders thought about naval strategy only in terms of battleships.

Motives and Intentions—Part 2

There is too often a tendency by naval historians to stress the role of armed forces in the context of a particular country's external securi-ty at the expense of considering the influence upon policy of domestic considerations.[86] The argument that the 1904 naval reforms were inspired solely or mainly by external factors such as the change in the European diplomatic climate or a growing perception of a threat to British interests posed by an expansionist German empire is based on thin evidence. It also takes no account of the many administrative prob-lems confronting the Admiralty at this time and the interrelatedness of the strategic and administrative reforms. For example, it has been recently demonstrated that while the Board of Admiralty was consider-ing Fisher's "scheme," uppermost in everyone's mind at Whitehall was the strict limits imposed by the Cabinet on all plans for future naval spending.[87] Indeed, Fisher was appointed first sea lord largely on the understanding that he would make the significant reduction in naval esti-mates that the Balfour government so desperately required. When Selborne first offered him the post on 14 May 1904, he made it "abundantly clear" to the admiral that "economy" must be "the essential basis of Admiralty policy."[88]

> It is quite certain that the Navy Estimates have for the present reached their maximum in the present year. In 1905–06 not only can there be no possible increase, but it is necessary, for the influence of the Admiralty over the House of Commons and for the stability of the national finances, that we should show a substantial decrease.[89]

The first lord added that he envisaged most of savings would come from a reduction in the construction program and the postponement of necessary expenditure on other votes. At his stage, of course, Selborne had yet to hear Fisher's ideas on warship redistribution.[90]

Most writers have either failed to appreciate the paramount importance of financial limitation as a motive for naval reform during the winter of 1904, or they have misunderstood how the money issue influenced decision making. In one sense it is true that "economy and efficiency" were the principal motives behind Fisher's "scheme," as some historians have argued. But it is wrong to say that Jacky was inspired to volunteer economies purely for the sake of efficiency.[91] They were not volunteered. Similarly, Fisher cannot fairly be condemned for displaying an "administrative rather than strategic way of thinking" in the formulation of his scheme.[92] Nor can he be criticized for possessing an "evident lack of interest in strategic analysis, both in this and later variants of his scheme," or for showing an "overriding concern" for solving "organisational or technical problems."[93] Such accusations ignore the overwhelming evidence that Fisher was brought into the Admiralty specifically to implement retrenchment and solve the consequent administrative problems. He was not appointed first sea lord in order to execute a shift in the Royal Navy's strategic orientation.[94] This must always be remembered.

Lest Fisher forget this, just three days before he took office, Selborne again hammered home the order of priorities: "the *first* thing we must do after you have taken your seat on the Board on October 20 is to establish the framework of the estimates for [19]05/6. When once we have done that *then* the departments of the Admiralty will be able to go on filling up the details and we shall be free for the consideration of the multifarious subjects we desire to deal with."[95] At the same time, he cautioned Fisher that the financial climate was forecast to deteriorate still further and it was likely that even deeper cuts would have to be made in the navy estimates. "Revenue is dropping so fast that it looks like a deficit on the estimated revenue of the current year of two millions and on that of next year of [even more]!!!"[96] In early November, the chancellor of the Exchequer reminded Selborne that "the whole character of the budget, vile or passable" depended upon the magnitude of the savings offered by the Board of Admiralty. "Nothing but millions would really help."[97] Accordingly, there can be little doubt that Fisher's proposals for the redistribution of the fleet were accepted by Selborne not because they better suited "strategical requirements," though they did, but primarily because the new organization he was offering was very much cheaper to maintain.

Another "domestic" concern worrying Selborne in 1904 was the acute shortage of trained personnel.[98] For many years the navy had seen this as its worst long-term problem.[99] It is not generally appreciated that the Royal Navy did not keep its entire fleet in full commission. In peacetime, at least one-third of naval personnel were billeted ashore in training schools and almost half the "War Fleet" was in reserve. To develop its full two-power strength, therefore, the Royal Navy had to mobilize the reserve. With the high degree of probability that Britain would be facing two, if not three, other great powers in the next war, it was essential that her fleet could be made ready for action as quickly as possible. In his memorandum to Cabinet dated 6 December 1904, the first lord stated that one of the Admiralty's main objectives in proposing the fleet reorganization was "to overcome certain difficulties with which they have been long confronted in matters of mobilization."[100] For at least fifteen years the navy had been unable to keep more than a handful of ships of the fleet reserve in good mechanical condition because of a shortage of personnel.[101] This further exacerbated the inefficiency of the newly commissioned warships manned at the outbreak of hostilities by scratch crews.[102] The introduction of the nucleus crew system was intended to eliminate these problems.[103] Just how seriously the first lord regarded the personnel issue is revealed in a memorandum sent by Selborne to Lord Knollys, King Edward VII's personal secretary. The first lord intimated that the manning difficulty was in fact the main reason for reform:

> The Board for some years past have had no greater anxiety than in respect of the condition of the ships in the Fleet reserve on mobilization for war. . . . there never has been a time in recent years when there were enough officers and men at home to provide proper care and maintenance parties for the ships in the Fleet reserve, and the Board have come to the decision that the only way to cure this evil is to provide a sufficient number of officers and men for the purpose of keeping these ships in proper order. These officers and men could only be provided in one way and that is by reducing the number of ships in commission.[104]

Understanding the personnel question, which has been mostly ignored by naval historians, is essential to comprehending the distribution of the

Royal Navy's warships not just in 1904, but throughout the entire period before 1914 and beyond. Between 1889 and 1904, fleet manpower had more than doubled to 131,100. Despite the huge expansion, over the same period increases in the number and size of ships in commission had "more than swallowed the increases in personnel" voted by Parliament.[105] In other words the shortage of personnel was even more pressing in 1904 than it had been in 1889. The explanation was simple. Over these fifteen years "practically no vessels were being discarded from the Navy as old, out of date, and, therefore, not worth their upkeep. Hence no relief was obtained, as might reasonably have been expected, in the amount of personnel required, by getting rid of the oldest ships as the new ones were built."[106] In 1904 the navy had an abundance of modern ships. But, as an Admiralty memorandum on this subject explained, "to have supplied all ships of the Navy with crews, even nucleus crews, would have been impossible unless the numbers of the navy were largely increased, or unless the whole of the training establishments were broken up."[107] Clearly the naval organization that existed in 1904 was not only financially expensive to maintain but also wasteful of manpower. The introduction of the "scheme" in 1905, and the subsequent scrapping of 154 old ships, was later calculated to have released no fewer than 950 officers and 11,000 men.[108] To put this into perspective, the entire naval establishment at this time (including 5,000 coastguardsmen who were not available to man warships in peacetime and the 30,000 odd personnel billeted ashore at training depots) stood at about 130,000 men. Yet even after scrapping this many old vessels, the navy still did not have enough men to provide crews for all its modern warships.[109]

For mainly financial reasons, continuing to expand "the numbers of the navy" was no longer an option after 1904.[110] Three years earlier Lord Selborne had begun expressing alarm at the projected growth in "ancillary" votes—wages, victuals, and pensions—resulting from expansion in the numbers of active service personnel.[111] As early as June 1901, he tried unsuccessfully to apply the brakes to the growth in numbers, warning the naval lords that if steps were not taken in this direction then the Cabinet might take matters into their own hands and appoint a royal commission.[112] His entreaties at that time, however, went unheeded. Kerr's reluctance to address the worsening personnel crisis subsequently led the first lord, at the end of 1901, to insist on the appointment of Fisher as second naval lord. Fisher was charged with the task of untangling the personnel mess so that the Admiralty might better optimize their existing manpower resources. This step had unfortunately backfired on Selborne. Towards the end of 1902, Fisher uncovered serious miscalculations in his predecessors' estimates for the number of men required to man the "war fleet" fixed for completion by the end of 1905.[113] The result had been a further expansion in prospective naval personnel requirements. When Fisher became first sea lord, the Royal Navy was already paying almost a million a year in pensions and related charges. According to calculations made by Fisher at the end of 1905, even if the establishment of the navy could be held constant at 131,000 men, this sum was set to double within a matter of years as the additional ratings recruited during the 1890s began retiring from the service.[114]

The Admiralty had other compelling reasons, besides finance, to stem the flow of recruits into the navy. There was, as Selborne put it in 1902, "a definite limit to the rate at which additional men can be added to the personnel of the Navy." Not only was the supply of high-quality volunteers limited, but "the complements of our ships are even now too young and I should deplore the rate of addition being further forced."[115] In 1904, sixty percent of naval personnel were under twenty-five years of age.[116] At first glance it is difficult to see why the first lord was quite so concerned. On paper, the numbers borne by the Royal Navy increased between 1900 and 1904 by only 19,100 from 110,978 to 130,078—a 16 percent increase over the space of four years. These figures, however, do not include the numbers enlisted to replace the "natural wastage" of men leaving the navy once their term of engagement had expired. If these are included, the total number of men recruited by the navy over these four years reached 58,892.[117] Perhaps as many as 40 percent of ratings serving at the end of 1904, therefore, may have been in the navy for less than four years. For a professional service, this was an unacceptably high proportion. The entry of large numbers of recruits, moreover, brought with them a host of administrative problems.[118] Most importantly, British warships were increasingly being fitted with sophisticated labor-saving equipment designed to be operated by skilled ratings.[119] As many as three-quarters of the seamen ratings in *Invincible* (1906-design battle cruiser) were supposed to hold higher rates as compared with only one-third of the seamen complement manning the armored cruiser *Drake* designed only four years earlier.[120] The crux of the problem was that it took the navy not less than six years to qualify a suitable ordinary seaman as a specialist gunnery or torpedo rating.[121] Or twice as long as it took to build a large ship. And to keep its warships at a high level of battle efficiency, the Royal Navy needed experienced long service ratings.

Further examination of the redistribution of personnel at the end of 1904 brings to light more evidence to contradict the notion that the naval reforms were motivated primarily by an anti-German imperative. Between 1902 and 1909, effective fleet manpower remained level at between 85,000 and 90,000.[122] The other 30,000-odd men were billeted ashore. A close examination of the shifts in distribution of personnel between October 1904 and April 1907 confirms that large numbers of seamen did flow, as planned, into ships in reserve.[123] In October 1904, the number of men formed into nucleus crews stood at 2,357; a year later the number had jumped to 12,507 and reached no fewer than 14,335 men by January 1907. But there was absolutely no increase in the number of personnel afloat in home waters. In fact numbers fell. In October 1904 there were 42,915 men allocated to ships in home waters. Twelve months later this number had dipped to just 42,001 (these figures include all men allocated to ships in reserve, in nucleus crews readiness, and in full commission).[124] During the same period the total number of personnel allocated to battleships (again including both ships in commission and in reserve) actually fell by over a thousand.[125] In other words, the men freed by the scrapping of overseas cruising vessels were not transferred to man battleships or, for that matter, any other warships in home waters. They actually went to Gibraltar. The number of men allocated to the Atlantic Fleet rose dramatically from almost zero in October 1904, to 13,351 the following year. The Gibraltar Squadron, moreover, was four days steaming away from Scapa Flow yet just two days from Malta. If Germany was really regarded as a major threat it would have made more sense to station them closer to home, perhaps at Queenstown on the south coast of Ireland, rather than at the entrance to the Mediterranean. In any case, not until early 1906 did the number of men crewing ships in home waters reach the level before Fisher took office.[126] And not until the beginning of 1907 did "the legions" begin arriving home in any numbers.[127] By this time, as we shall see, conditions and circumstances had considerably changed. These figures seriously undermine assertions that Fisher's Board of Admiralty was pursuing a policy of concentration in the North Sea, and tend to corroborate Mackay's thesis of a more flexible strategic deployment.

Given that in Fisher's mind armored cruisers were more important than battleships, and after taking into consideration the actual changes in the distribution of naval personnel, the evidence suggests that what Jacky actually intended to accomplish was the creation of a more flexible system for protecting Britain's overseas territorial and trade interests. In essence, Fisher devised his scheme to facilitate a change in the method by which the Admiralty employed naval force, not to concentrate the fleet in home waters. The Royal Navy's primary strategical mission was intended to remain the same. If this does not seem obvious in retrospect it is because his plan for the redistribution of the fleet was not fully implemented. A closer examination of Fisher's original proposals, as set out in "Naval Necessities," shows that after paying off the old gunboats and cruising vessels in distant waters he anticipated sending the crews back out in armored cruisers.[128] For example, the number of cruisers on station in the Pacific was originally scheduled to rise from nineteen to twenty-eight. As a first step, after scrapping the old cruising vessels, Fisher was able in 1905 to commission a half-dozen brand-new armored cruisers that had been sitting in reserve for want of crews.[129] Fisher hoped that station fleets would eventually be made up solely of these vessels.[130] He had first considered this ideal while serving in the Mediterranean.[131] Looking further ahead he had hoped to commission another thirty armored cruisers.[132] The first sea lord proposed to find the necessary crews by further pruning the number of old protected cruisers on the navy list and, more controversially, by cutting the number of men allocated to the battle fleet. In "Naval Necessities," Fisher originally proposed to cut the number of battleships in full commission from thirty-five to twenty-eight.[133] This recommendation, however, was not implemented.

The new distribution of the fleet, as announced on 1 January 1905, was actually the product of a compromise reached between Fisher, Selborne, and a small Admiralty committee headed by Battenberg.[134] In order to secure unanimous support for his scheme, the first sea lord was obliged to make a number of concessions. Consequently, the change in the pattern of warship distribution was not as pronounced as he had originally intended. Largely in order to save money, Selborne directed that more ships be retained in home waters. Most importantly, Fisher's attempt to increase the numbers of armored cruisers available for imperial defense duties was compromised by Selborne's stubborn faith in battleships. Initially the first lord refused to recall the five battleships from China.[135] When, in the spring of 1905 Fisher was at last permitted to order them home, it was on the proviso that four remain in full commission. Two battleships would be added to the Channel Fleet, and one each to the Atlantic and Mediterranean Squadrons.[136] Selborne also insisted on keeping in reserve eleven obsolete battleships the first sea lord had earmarked for scrap.[137] Needless to say, all these battleships continued to absorb scarce manpower. As a result, in October 1905, there were still warships on Fisher's original "List A" of "Fighting Ships" in reserve for want of crews, including six armored cruisers, twelve first-class protected cruisers, and sixteen destroyers.[138] Even if Fisher had been prevented by Selborne from fully implementing his original plans, nevertheless, the Royal Navy's fighting efficiency had certainly been increased, the worst administrative problems had been solved, and over three and a half million had been shaved from the naval estimates.

The Tory Leadership and the 1904 Invasion Enquiry

By the time Sir John Fisher arrived at Whitehall in October 1904, he no longer believed that a fleet centered on battleships was the best force structure for protecting British imperial interests. Nor was he convinced that seeking out the enemy fleet in the blue water was any longer the best strategic policy. We have seen that for several years before he became first sea lord, Fisher had privately believed the navy should abandon the construction of battleships in favor of super armored cruisers, better suited for oceanic imperial defense missions. In the previous chapter it was shown that Fisher was also convinced that large armored warships could not safely be employed in the narrow seas around the British Isles. Based upon this supposition, he developed a theory that home defense could instead be provided by a "mosquito" fleet of submarines and surface torpedo craft. We now return to the evolution and implementation of this concept of "flotilla defense."

Few naval officers would have questioned Sir John Fisher's assertion that in wartime the Royal Navy had just two principal missions to perform: defending the country from invasion, and protecting the trade routes. But whereas most believed that the simplest method of achieving these goals was to bring the enemy warships to action and sink them, for a variety of reasons Fisher believed this would not be practicable. He feared that a British battle squadron patrolling the narrow seas, endeavoring to seek out an enemy fleet or deter an invasion convoy from putting to sea, would be vulnerable to torpedo attack.[139] Since his association with Capt. Reginald Bacon while both were serving at Portsmouth, moreover, he had been persuaded that for the foreseeable future there would be no defense against submarines. This led him to postulate that, henceforth, "the defense of the 'Narrow Seas'—we deal here principally with the English Channel and the western basin of the Mediterranean"— should be dealt with as "a question quite apart and separate from the working of the main fighting fleets."[140] The Royal Navy must rely upon its torpedo flotilla to patrol the narrow seas.

The idea that destroyers, torpedo boats and submarines (backed by units of the reserve fleet) might by capable of deterring invasion independently from the battle fleet was not new. In 1903, it will be recalled, the Admiralty had put forward a similar argument to rebut claims by the War Office that invasion was possible whenever the battle fleet was absent from home waters or if the navy suffered a temporary setback. This argument had been accepted as plausible by the Cabinet Defense Committee.[141] And the concept of "torpedo armed flotilla" had subsequently been incorporated in the prime minister's paper on the possibility of serious invasion.[142] Furthermore, the first lord of the Admiralty had endorsed Balfour's conclusions.[143] "Our fleet of torpedo craft," Selborne wrote in 1904, "play an immense part in the naval protection of this country against invasion. It has really been on the superiority of our fleet of torpedo craft in all possible naval contingencies that the Committee of Imperial Defense has felt able to advise that the strength of the home Army may be calculated apart from any fear of serious invasion."[144] Fisher, however, was the first British admiral to suggest the Royal Navy should deliberately rely upon the torpedo flotilla rather than the battle fleet to act as the main instrument of strategic deterrence.

In "Naval Necessities" Fisher proposed to organize four "défense mobile" groups, comprising each of one flotilla of twenty-four destroyers and one section of twelve submarines, and station them along the south coast.[145] Selborne agreed.[146] The advantages of using torpedo craft to defend naval ports, Fisher claimed, had long been recognized by most naval officers. A torpedo armed flotilla not only provided a port with a more efficient defense than existing mines and guns, but their mobility allowed them to be moved according to strategic requirements. The problem was that up to this time naval officers had always been reluctant to admit this "for fear the Admiralty in any way accepting a part responsibility in the local defences."[147] In consequence, the defense of naval ports had been left in the hands of the army who, it was widely felt, "have never attempted seriously to make their officers in charge of guns or minefields acquainted with the typical differences between British and foreign warships."[148] One naval authority, Battenberg, once described the army's understanding of their role in coast defense as "childish—there is no other word for it."[149] The time had come, Fisher agreed in 1904, for "a reconsideration of the whole question of control" and the "establishment of floating local defences."[150] If this entailed the navy assuming full responsibility for port defenses—then so be it.

Readers will recall that for some months before Fisher was appointed first sea lord, there had been muted War Office calls for the navy to take some responsibility for port defenses. Oakley Arnold-Forster, the ambitious secretary of state for war, had been for some time "not only willing but anxious" for the lines of demarcation to be redrawn.[151] But the generals and admirals both had shied away from picking up what might turn out to be a double-edged sword. Arnold-Forster's insistent pressure, however, persuaded Balfour that this matter ought to be considered by the Committee of Imperial Defense. Discussions over whether or not the Corps of Submarine Miners should be transferred from army to navy control were scheduled for the autumn of 1904. Predictably, the Admiralty's first position paper written that summer opposed the idea unequivocally.[152] After Fisher took over from Walter Kerr, however, the Admiralty changed their tune.[153] Instead of arguing about which service should control the mines, the first sea lord successfully refocused attention onto the more fundamental question of whether or not these mines were of any use and should be employed at all.

The military value of observation mines was formally discussed by the CID during a heated three hour meeting held on 22 November 1904. Unlike his predecessor, Fisher did not temper his aggressiveness in the presence of Cabinet ministers. Although the War Office representatives certainly knew that the first sea lord was a forceful character, they were caught totally off guard by his violent language and brutally direct line of argument.[154] Observation mines, Jacky thundered, would "far more likely to be a hindrance than a protection" to most ports, and anyway most were "insufficient in extent" to provide effective protection. Obviously they should be abolished forthwith. This was not the language of government. Fisher's bellicosity startled even Arnold-Forster.[155] That night he noted in his diary that the Admiral had made "very exaggerated statements" by insisting that the minefields were "more dangerous to friend than foe."[156] The first sea lord's breezy self-confidence, moreover, had proved contagious. Despite knowing "nothing about the matter,"[157] Austen Chamberlain, the chancellor of the Exchequer, had waded into the discussions to demand a "root and branch abolition" of observation mines.[158] Arnold-Forster reflected upon the irony of recent events:

> The abandonment of submarine mining: An odd situation. I, who originally started the idea, in November 1903, and was rebuffed by the Admiralty, now appear as the councillor of moderation, begging the Admiralty representatives not to go too fast, even towards so desirable an end. They are going too fast![159]

The following day the war minister was partially mollified after Fisher privately admitted to him that he had "laid it on with rather a thick brush." He justified his language as being necessary to bolster the resolve of the civilian committee members to over rule the military "experts." Throughout the meeting, apparently, the generals had been muttering "dire consequences" if the CID ignored their advice and endorsed the recommendation for abolition.[160] If Arnold-Forster disapproved of Fisher's methods, he certainly sympathized with his motives. The war minister often confessed in his diary that he was equally exasperated by the uncooperativeness of his military advisors, and there is no doubt that part of him had been exhilarated at the sight of Fisher steamrollering the generals. Arnold-Forster, indeed, had already written to the first member of the army council, Gen. Neville Lyttleton, a terse letter demanding action. "In pursuance to the decision arrived at today at the C.I.D.," he wrote, "*I presume you will now take action* with regard to the question of submarine defense. It was, I think, practically agreed that submarine mining in naval ports should cease forthwith and that the establishment should be broken up."[161]

Direct instructions from the secretary of state for war proved to carry little weight with the army council. Arnold-Forster was roundly disliked and distrusted by his subordinates. The generals had been stung by Fisher's criticisms and had resented being portrayed as a bunch of reactionaries clinging to an obsolete weapon system. They were also not a little afraid of the wider repercussions if they surrendered control of the mines. Two days after the fifty-eighth meeting of the CID, the soldiers demanded a stay of execution, claiming that the Admiralty had "misled" the committee. They continued to insist that observation mines were a cheap and valuable adjunct to coastal defences.[162] The next day, 25 November, the CID was reconvened. At this second meeting, Fisher cleverly changed tack. Instead of complaining about the uselessness of the mines he instead revealed that the navy now believed submarine boats could prove more efficient than mines for the port defense. The first sea lord went on to request the CID direct all "submarine mining establishments" be "handed over to the Admiralty, who would arrange to station submarine boats in lieu."[163] Anticipating the army's objections, he declared that the navy was ready to guarantee that submarines would protect all ports against raids. Fisher was just about to ask the CID to give the Admiralty the full responsibility for all naval ports, maritime fortresses, and coastal batteries, when a nervous Lord Selborne reigned in his first sea lord. Already, however, Fisher's bold maneuvering had again caught the War Office off balance and left the generals spluttering. Throughout the meeting the first sea lord received strong backing from Col. George Clarke, now serving as permanent secretary to the CID. The language he had used to describe the military value of observation mines was reported to have been as colorful as Fisher's![164] Clarke's opinion probably carried more weight with the prime minister. He was widely regarded as an expert on mine warfare.[165] But before any conclusions were reached the meeting was adjourned.[166]

Despite continued opposition to the scheme from the generals and lingering doubts that events were moving too quickly, on 30 November Arnold-Forster assured Balfour that he regarded the original decision to abolish the mines at naval ports "as binding on the War Office and have already taken the necessary steps to give effect to it."[167] At the next meeting of the CID, on 2 December, the prime minister ruled that all mining establishments at the main naval bases should be "at once" transferred "to Admiralty charge."[168] The abolition of mines at the other ports took a little longer to resolve. Balfour felt that commercial ports, which were not directly protected by warships, were more likely to be raided than the navy was willing to admit.[169] For this reason he instructed the formation of a joint service committee to consider whether or not coastal batteries alone could adequately protect commercial ports.[170] But, importantly, he also stipulated that the Admiralty would be "the sole authority for advising as to what classes of hostile ships may reasonably be expected to enter certain waters."[171] Even so, it was another three months before the CID finally endorsed the dismantling of mining stations at commercial ports.[172]

Much to Arnold-Forster's annoyance the CID did not go on to make the "clear pronouncement" he had wanted "as to the future responsibility of the army in connection with the non-naval ports."[173] The committee had apparently lost sight of the question: who would be held accountable if a commercial port were bombarded? Yet it seems that Selborne had urged Balfour not to investigate these questions too closely. To this end he informally assured the prime minister that "my naval colleagues as well as myself look forward to stationing submarine boats at these ports, to be manned, as I believe, by officers and men of the R.N.V.R."[174] Ignoring the whole question was certainly the easiest solution. From Sir John Fisher's perspective, however, this was no more than detail. The principle of relying upon submarines had already been endorsed, and thus the door was now open to the navy setting up a chain of submarine bases and adopting the strategy of flotilla defense.[175] The navy, moreover, had struck a major blow at the army's case for a role in home defense. In light of the still deteriorating fiscal climate, the significance of this should not be underestimated.

In March 1905, the Admiralty scored a decisive victory against the War Office in the battle over the question of responsibility for home defense.[176] After listening to a fine-polished presentation by Fisher and the new DNI, Capt. Charles Ottley, the CID at last "affirmed the doctrine that the maximum strength of the army raid against which we need provide, could not exceed 5,000 men."[177] This decision gave the navy clear priority in the allocation of defense resources for the task of home defense and relegated the army to little more than a minor supporting role. The generals were dismayed. Arnold-Forster, on the other hand, at once capitalized upon this decision by resuming his campaign for reductions in "the absolutely useless force of 375,000 men in peacetime additional to the regular Army and Navy, all tied to this country."[178] Reform of the militia was now given top priority.[179] Arnold-Forster also succeeded in forcing the prime minister to publish, on 12 May 1905, an outline of the conclusions reached so far by the CID. The war minister hoped this would divert some of the "flood of uninformed public opinion in favour of maintaining [these] useless forces."[180] It is quite clear, therefore, that by the spring of 1905, the Admiralty's dominance in matters concerning imperial defense policy had reached a new high. Yet, with one exception, this fact has been overlooked by most historians.[181]

Fisher's Theory of Flotilla Defense

Adm. Sir John Fisher seldom explained his radical strategic theories in writing. Fortunately, however, two documents have survived in which Fisher set out his concept of "flotilla defense." Both date from early 1905. These show that Fisher intended that the aforementioned mobile defense groups would not be restricted to harbor or coastal defense missions. They would be deployed well forward into the middle waters with orders to prevent enemy transports and large warships from cruising on the narrow seas without incurring serious risk of being torpedoed. The object was explained in a "rough paper" sent to Balfour on 24 January entitled "Submarines Used Offensively."[182] The Royal Navy's latest submarines, Fisher began, the **B** type, were seaworthy enough to operate at a considerable distance from their bases and in most weather. They were quite capable of patrolling the straits at Dover and Gibraltar. Others could be positioned off enemy ports ready to attack large ships as they came out. In fact, Fisher claimed, submarines could be used anywhere "within the limits of their radius of action."[183] Their range could be supplemented, moreover, by towing them out to sea with surface ships.

Fisher's strategic objective, however, was fundamentally different from that of conventional naval strategists. He postulated that "offensive strategy must be held to include the circumspection of the free movements of the enemy, any activity that limits their free movement is an action of offence."[184] Simply "denying" the sea to an enemy was a completely new way of thinking. He was also aware that the French too had submarine boats that could also operate more or less anywhere in the channel. Consequently:

> The position in the Channel is the same to France and us when opposed to one another. *The submarine is the only answer to the submarine* (!) since they should be able to elude all craft and no one particular vessel can be built which can be relied upon to destroy them. This being so, by the use of these craft it maybe made impossible to keep large units in the Channel, or other confined waters. If *we* cannot do so but the enemy can, then invasion is a certainty; hence the necessity for the provision of these craft on our sea frontiers. But having them for this purpose they become instantly

available for further extended use . . . before many years navigation [by armored vessels] in the western basin of the Mediterranean in wartime (equally with the English Channel) will become a very dangerous undertaking owing to the offensive action of this class of boat.[185]

In other words if the ability to deploy formations of large surface ships in the narrow seas was denied to both sides, then neither France nor Britain would be able to convoy an expeditionary force across the channel. Strategically, mutual sea denial would be much more advantageous to Britain because it left the Royal Navy free to protect the trade routes and to defend distant colonies with armored ships that would otherwise have been tied to home waters.

The principle of flotilla defense seems not to have been finally adopted until after Lord Selborne had left the Board of Admiralty. On 2 March 1905, he was posted to the governorship of South Africa and his portfolio handed to the earl of Cawdor (formerly chairman of the Great Western Railway).[186] The new first lord was quickly convinced by Fisher that the advent of the submarine heralded a revolution in the conduct of war at sea. In March 1905, Cawdor and Fisher prepared a memorandum for Cabinet entitled "Submarine-boats," which was intended to give some indication of the "general uses these vessels may be put in wartime."[187] This paper was a remarkably detailed presentation of the navy's secret "flotilla defense" strategy, and included a section on Fisher's new theory of mutual sea denial. So explicit was it, indeed, that there must be some question whether Cawdor actually circulated it to the full Cabinet. Copies do not exist in any private papers of leading Cabinet ministers deposited at national archive centers.[188]

This paper provides the historian with the clearest exposition of the concept of flotilla defense and more generally a statement of the Admiralty's views at this time on the military value of submarines. "Their main attribute," emphasized Lord Cawdor, "is their invisibility." This "invests them with a subtle power of producing great uncertainty and apprehension in the minds of officers and crews of vessels working in certain waters."[189] Also,

> Their use in "expectant" blockade cannot be denied, whether this watching is in the offing of an enemy's harbour or in confined waters within reach of the boats' bases. We must also not neglect the possibility of certain waters being denied to large ships, from the danger of being attacked in daylight by submarine boats, and at night by torpedo craft. The only way, at present, of meeting such an investment is by following suit, and denying the waters in turn to the enemy, *thereby neutralising these areas for offensive operations.* Such a case may be far, at present, from actual

realisation: but affairs move quickly in these days, and we must be ready to forestall any dangerous contingencies.[190] [my italics.]

The message was unmistakable. Confronted by "unattackable" submarines by day and "invisible" small craft at night, the Royal Navy's fighting fleets could not possibly remain in the narrow seas without incurring serious risks. In a letter to a journalist friend written at the end of March 1905, Fisher stated that not even the *Dreadnought* would be able to cruise the English Channel in the presence of submarines.[191] "I won't weary you with technicalities," promised Fisher in another letter addressed to Lord Cromer and dated 22 April 1905, "but suffice to say that within three or four years of this date (and you might keep this letter for curiosity!) the English Channel and the western basin of the Mediterranean will not be habitable by a fleet or squadrons in wartime."[192]

How practical was the concept of flotilla defense at this time? Certainly the submarines available to the Royal Navy in 1905 were relatively primitive compared to the vessels employed ten years later during the First World War. But readers should note that at this time Fisher was talking about submarine operations in the narrow waters of the English Channel and the Mediterranean. The sea conditions in these areas were much less severe than the prevailing weather in, say, the western approaches or the Heligoland Bight. The many practical experiments with these early craft suggest their range and endurance was sufficient.[193] In January 1904, the Inspecting captain of submarines expressed confidence that the **A** class could operate as far away as the Channel Islands.[194] He also thought that the new **B** and **C** classes (which were essentially the same), due to enter service towards the end of that year, would be much more seaworthy and capable of navigating anywhere in the English Channel for up to a week.[195] With such positive assessments by the experts, therefore, Fisher had every reason to believe that the submarines available in 1905 were capable of performing the missions he envisaged. Finally, readers should note that ten years later these same craft performed creditably on patrols in the eastern Mediterranean Sea, the Adriatic Sea, and the North Sea.

If there was any doubt over the practicability of flotilla defense, it stemmed from the relative shortage of submarines. Fisher always admitted that the strategy was going to depend upon "swarms" of flotilla craft "infesting" or "saturating" the narrow seas.[196] He once estimated the navy would require close to one hundred submarines and an equal number of torpedo boats.[197] In 1904, however, there were fewer than twenty submarines available. Two years later the total stood at just thirty-three.

The Royal Navy was slightly better equipped with surface torpedo craft. In 1905 there were about forty vessels in commission in home waters plus another eighty or so in reserve. In December 1904, Fisher coveted the forty destroyers in the Mediterranean but wisely abandoned the idea of withdrawing them to home waters.[198] If he had tried to recall these vessels he would certainly have been condemned for hypocrisy; when he had been commander in chief, Mediterranean, he had bullied the Admiralty into sending out more destroyers.

Beginning in February 1905, Sir John Fisher took a number of steps to boost the number of flotilla craft in home waters. His first act was to issue an order directing that "every effective torpedo vessel in reserve [be] now and henceforth commissioned with a crew of two fifths full strength."[199] At the same time, port admirals were warned that "very substantial improvements and extensions of the former organisation should be anticipated."[200] A report on the new organization of flotilla craft written several months later by the DNI clearly stated it was intended that their primary role in wartime would be to cover all "foreign torpedo craft" stationed across the channel "distributed all along the Continental coast from Brest to the Elbe."[201] In other words, flotilla defense was intended to control all the waters between the British Isles and the Continent, thereby shielding the country from any possible "bolt from the blue."

The most tangible evidence that the concept of flotilla defense was actually ratified by the Board of Admiralty lies in the change in the allocation of construction resources after Fisher took office. During his administration, spending on the purchase of new flotilla craft rocketed from one to over two million pounds.[202] This is made all the more significant because over the same period the total construction budget dropped by two million—almost 20 percent. Put another way: when Fisher arrived at Whitehall, less than 10 percent of the construction budget was allocated to the flotilla. By 1909 the proportion had grown to over 20 percent, of which submarines took a third.[203] Had the Conservative government remained in power after 1905, the change in the pattern of naval expenditure would have been quicker and even more pronounced.[204] At the first meeting of the naval estimates committee on 20 July 1905, Fisher directed that "nine and a half millions a year should be spent on new construction." Spending on the flotilla would absorb over 30 percent of that sum.[205] The sketch estimates for 1906 called for twenty coastal destroyers, five fleet destroyers, one "destroyer special" (*Swift*), and twenty submarines to be laid down in addition to the four armored vessels.[206] The following year the flotilla program was scheduled to have been even larger.[207] This program deserves the most careful consideration as being the expression of Fisher's ideal force structure and as an indication of the point to which his radical conception of naval warfare had already reached.

Fisher's desperation to expand the flotilla as quickly as possible can be seen also in his decision to order small and cheap vessels in preference to larger types.[208] Immediately after taking office he canceled a contract for thirteen *River* class destroyers.[209] In their place he ordered vessels he called coastal destroyers.[210] These short-range yet highly seaworthy craft were designed for operations in the channel and could be delivered at half the price of a *River*.[211] Hitherto, no historian has offered any explanation as to why between 1905 and 1907 the navy ordered thirty-six coastal destroyers and only twelve fleet destroyers. The navy also experimented with even smaller craft. In 1906, Fisher accompanied the king and queen to witness the official trials of the Alfred Yarrow–designed motor torpedo boat; the craft displaced no more than eight tons and was propelled by twin napier gasoline engines, giving a surface speed of over twenty-five knots.[212] These craft were not adopted before 1914, however. Again, naval historians have provided no rational explanation for Fisher's willingness to continue ordering large numbers of small but again relatively cheap C class submarines after 1906, when larger, more efficient craft could have been built. The answer was simple. According to Capt. Sydney Hall, who had been closely involved in their design and who in 1906 was appointed inspecting captain of submarines, "this was merely a question of money policy— [the] Admiralty said they preferred to have twelve single screw rather than eight or nine twin screw" submarines.[213]

The switch to flotilla defense enabled the Admiralty to scrap a fairly sizable fleet of obsolete armored warships kept in reserve at anchorages around the country, whose sole function was to be mobilized in war to assist in home defense.[214] This produced overall savings in the navy estimates, which, of course, was the Admiralty's single most important goal during this period. A force of submarines and torpedo boats provided not only a more effective and flexible deterrent against invasion, but it was also cheaper to build and maintain than old armored warships. Relieving the estimates of the cost of repairing and maintaining these vessels saved an estimated £845,000 a year.[215] Further savings were accrued by rendering unnecessary projected increases in personnel and works. Historians have argued these savings were made possible by improvements in the efficiency of the battle fleet.[216] This study, however, has shown that much of the reserve fleet was supplanted, at lesser cost, by the expansion of the flotilla.

Choosing to rely mainly on the torpedo and the flotilla to deter invasion was unquestionably a fundamental shift in strategic thinking by the

Admiralty. But it must be understood that flotilla defense represented a change in method rather than strategic objective. It also represented a switch towards an essentially "reactive" form of naval warfare. The idea of mutual sea denial did not conform to any previously recognized theory of naval strategy. It was fundamentally at odds with the idea of using the battle fleet offensively to enforce command of the sea by seeking out and destroying the enemy fleet in the blue water. And it undercut the notion of the superior battle fleet acting primarily as an instrument of strategic deterrence by intimidating the weaker fleet.[217] Fisher did not expect the flotilla to sink every enemy ship in the narrow seas. A fast-moving ship was a difficult target to torpedo, but cruisers steaming at economic speed or lumbering transports would be much easier targets to hit. The presence of the flotilla was intended to prevent armored warships from "exercising" or "enforcing" command of the sea. And, as we shall see, the ability to rely upon the flotilla to deter invasion was intended to allow the Admiralty unprecedented flexibility in wartime to deploy armored squadrons to reinforce the outer marches of the empire. It also provided justification for adopting the battle cruiser type of capital ship. These fast, powerfully armed, long-range warships were far better suited for imperial defense missions than battleships. Without doubt, Fisher's strategy of flotilla defense in conjunction with the battle cruiser concept, marked a complete turn around in the traditional strategic ethos of the British Admiralty.[218]

Five years of British submarine development: the *Holland 3* (1901 vintage) out-board from HMS D1 (1906 vintage) alongside the depot ship HMS *Dolphin* moored inside Portsmouth Harbour, circa 1909. *Courtesy of Royal Navy Submarine Museum and HMS* Alliance, *Gosport, England.*

Holland and the warrior: the submarine *Holland 2* being refitted at Vickers, Maxim & Sons Ltd., Barrow-in-Furness, September 1906. In the background is a nearly complete warrior-class armored cruiser. *Courtesy of Royal Navy Submarine Museum and HMS* Alliance, *Gosport, England.*

The fleet submarine experiment: the Messrs Scott built the steam-powered craft
HMS *Swordfish*. Seen here undergoing her trial, 1916. *Courtesy of Royal Navy
Submarine Museum and HMS* Alliance, *Gosport, England.*

An admiral with common sense: the vastly underrated Admiral Sir George Callaghan, commander in chief, Home Fleets, 1911–1914. *Courtesy of Ministry of Defense Admiralty Library, London.*

Old "Ard" Art: Admiral of the Fleet Sir Arthur Knyvett-Wilson VC, first sea lord, 1910–1911. *Courtesy of Ministry of Defense Admiralty Library, London.*

Fueling at an advanced base: a flotilla of C-class submarines taking on gasoline along-side the coaling wharf at Imming-ham, 1909 or 1910. *Courtesy of Royal Navy Submarine Museum and HMS* Alliance, *Gosport, England.*

Young Winston: First Lord of the Admiralty Winston Churchill boarding an RNAS seaplane, 1914. *Courtesy of Ministry of Defense Admiralty Library, London.*

VISITOR "BY THE WAY. I SUPPOSE YOU'VE GOT SOME SORT OF SERGEANT JOHNNY WHO UNDERSTANDS ALL ABOUT THESE THING'UMIES, WHAT!"

Gadgets: a perplexed cavalry officer talking to a professional on board what appears to be and E-class submarine. *Courtesy of Royal Navy Submarine Museum and HMS* Alliance, *Gosport, England.*

Rapid shipbuilding I: HMS *Dreadnought* under construction at Portsmouth Dockyard, 13 October 1905. *Courtesy of Ministry of Defense Admiralty Library, London.*

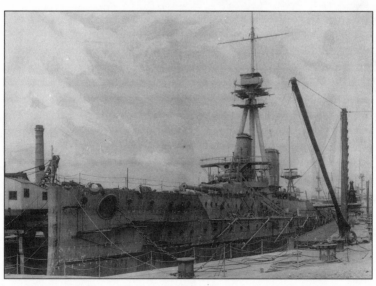

Rapid shipbuilding II: HMS *Dreadnought* fitting out at Portsmouth Dockyard, 16 June 1906. *Courtesy of Ministry of Defense Admiralty Library, London.*

Smoke could be a problem: the battle-cruiser HMS *Inflexible at Speed* and a battle-cruiser squadron curing at sea. *Courtesy of Ministry of Defense Admiralty Library, London.*

"Jackie": Admiral of the Fleet Sir John Fisher, first sea lord, 1904–1910 and 1914–1915. *Courtesy of John Fisher Papers, Master and Fellows of Churchill College, Cambridge.*

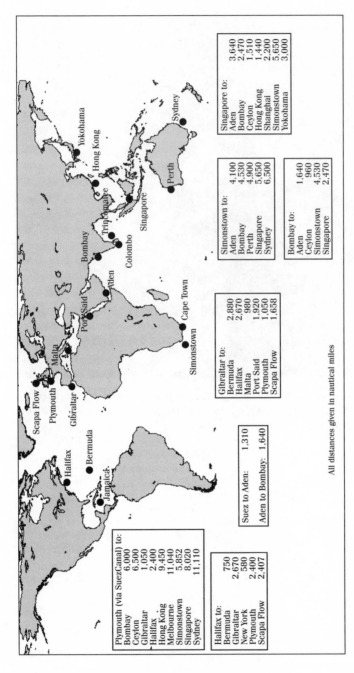

Plymouth (via Suez Canal) to:	
Bombay	6,000
Ceylon	6,500
Gibraltar	1,050
Halifax	2,400
Hong Kong	9,450
Melbourne	11,040
Simonstown	5,852
Singapore	8,020
Sydney	11,110

Halifax to:	
Bermuda	750
Gibraltar	2,670
New York	580
Plymouth	2,400
Scapa Flow	2,407

Suez to Aden:	1,310
Aden to Bombay:	1,640

Gibraltar to:	
Bermuda	2,880
Halifax	2,670
Malta	980
Port Said	1,920
Plymouth	1,050
Scapa Flow	1,658

Simonstown to:	
Aden	4,100
Bombay	4,530
Perth	4,900
Singapore	5,650
Sydney	6,500

Bombay to:	
Aden	1,640
Ceylon	960
Simonstown	4,530
Singapore	2,470

Singapore to:	
Aden	3,640
Bombay	2,470
Ceylon	1,510
Hong Kong	1,440
Shanghai	2,200
Simonstown	5,650
Yokohama	3,000

All distances given in nautical miles

World bases.

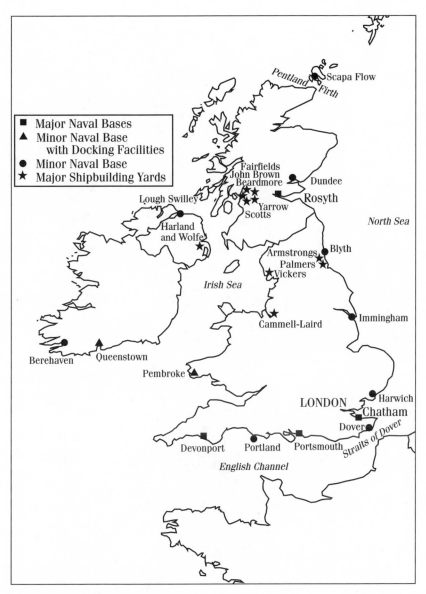

Pentland Firth

Scapa Flow

Fairfields
John Brown
Beardmore

Dundee

Rosyth

Yarrow
Scotts

North Sea

Lough Swilley

Harland
and Wolfe

Armstrongs
Palmers
Vickers

Blyth

Irish Sea

Cammell-Laird

Immingham

Berehaven

Queenstown

Pembroke

LONDON

Harwich

Chatham

Dover

Devonport

Portland

Portsmouth

Straits of Dover

English Channel

■ Major Naval Bases
▲ Minor Naval Base
   with Docking Facilities
● Minor Naval Base
★ Major Shipbuilding Yards

British home waters.

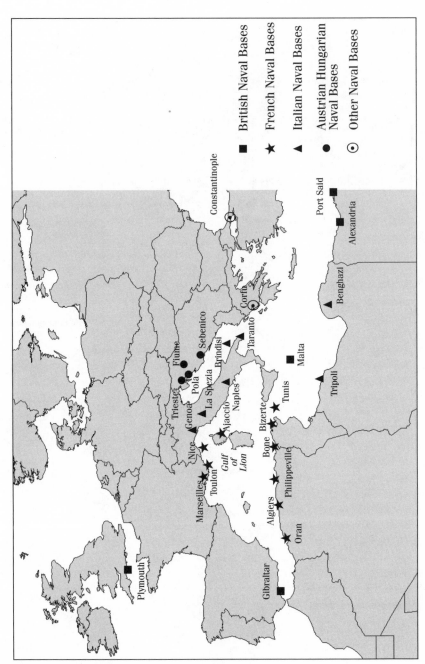

British Naval Bases ■

French Naval Bases ★

Italian Naval Bases ▲

Austrian Hungarian
Naval Bases ●

Other Naval Bases ⊙

Constantinople

Port Said

Alexandria

Benghazi

Fiume

Sebenico

Trieste

Pola

La Spezia

Genoa

Brindisi

Taranto

Corfu

Malta

Naples

Tripoli

Nice

Ajaccio

Tunis

Bizerte

Bone

Marseilles

Toulon

Gulf
of
Lion

Algiers

Philippeville

Oran

Plymouth

Gibraltar

Mediterranean bases.

CHAPTER 5

Defending British Naval Supremacy, 1905–1908

When I was Controller of the Navy I had an excellent secretary. Whenever I asked him for facts, he always asked me what I wanted to prove! There is no doubt that facts are most misleading.

Adm. Sir John Fisher, 1904

On 4 December 1905, Balfour resigned as prime minister bringing to a close ten years of Conservative administration. He surrendered the reins of power to the Liberal leader Sir Henry Campbell-Bannerman. By taking the unusual step of resigning from office rather than seeking dissolution of Parliament, Balfour compelled his successor to form a government before being allowed to appeal to the country. This was a political ploy designed to test the "brittle unity" of the opposition. He believed there was still a visible rift between the so-called "Liberal Imperialist" MPs, who had supported the war in South Africa, and the mainstream "pro-Boer" members of the Liberal Party. In addition, Campbell-Bannerman had in orbit around him an uncertain coalition of social radicals, nonconformists, trade unionists, and Irish nationalists, all of who could be expected to demand a price for their allegiance. Balfour took sly pleasure in thus forcing his opponents to parade "a decade's dirty linen" in front of the voters before the forthcoming general election.[1] It is also possible that along with Joseph Chamberlain, the leading Tory advocate for "tariff reform," the Conservative leader hoped that a brief period in opposition might help unify his party and purge it of free traders.[2] In January 1906, however, the Liberal coalition won the election overwhelmingly, gaining a majority in the House of Commons of 358. The Tories, consequently, were facing a long period out of office and, more importantly, found themselves powerless to stop even drastic changes in policy.[3]

Campbell-Bannerman's platform during the election was built upon pledges to reallocate government funds for social reform, and of course to maintain free trade. From a fiscal standpoint, however, his two key policies were contradictory. Implementing the former would involve the expenditure of a great deal of money, whereas the latter policy denied the Treasury the only conceivable new source of revenue. The experts, moreover, did not anticipate that the yields from existing taxes would rise significantly, and if anything they expected them to keep falling.[4] At this stage, neither Campbell-Bannerman nor H. H. Asquith, his chancellor of the Exchequer, were prepared to contemplate radical solutions to the financial problem. Instead, they intended to finance all welfare programs by making reductions in defense expenditure to pay off the unfunded debt incurred during the Boer War and apply the savings from debt service to increasing social welfare. This policy won over the radicals in Parliament who were ideologically opposed to spending money on armaments.

Senior Liberal Party politicians gave little if any thought to the organization of the armed forces before they assumed power. During the Boer War, and ever since, discussions of military and imperial issues had proved highly divisive for the party. After 1903, the party leadership agreed that such questions were best left alone.[5] Most Liberals were only too pleased. Many potential ministers regarded the entire subject as a "distasteful" distraction from more important domestic issues.[6] As one historian has noted, the Liberal front benches "cleared magically" whenever service matters were debated in the House.[7] When the Liberals at last gained power, indeed, Campbell-Bannerman encountered great difficulty in filling all the administrative posts at the Admiralty and the War Office. It took him no less than three weeks to find someone willing to serve as parliamentary secretary for the Admiralty. Few political commentators would have disagreed with the observation made by the secretary of the Committee of Imperial Defense, Sir George Clarke, "that in matters of national defense, a Liberal Government would not—on taking office—command great confidence."[8] Defense issues, nevertheless, had to be addressed if for no better reason than the fiscal implications of military expenditure. The implementation of social reforms depended upon the effective management of the armed forces. While the new prime minister personally favored drastic cuts in the military, he realized that any journey along this road must be a slow one so as not to frighten his "Liberal imperialist" passengers who believed in strong defences. On the other hand, he could not proceed so slowly as to risk upsetting the more numerous "progressive" wing of his government which was impatient for social reform, or the "radicals" who were zealously keen to attack what they regarded as the "bloated" level of armaments.[9] In the end, Campbell-

Bannerman found the simplest course of action was again to evade the issues. By promising to send official representatives to the international conference on multilateral disarmament scheduled to be held at the Hague in early 1907, he succeeded in postponing any immediate confrontation between his multifarious supporters. Even so, during their first year of office he and his ministers remained constantly wary of their unpredictable radical tail.

Welfare or Warfare: Naval Finance and the Liberal Government

Because the Liberals took office at the end of the financial year they were more or less compelled to pass the defense estimates drawn up by the previous Conservative administration. They were also given little option but to allow Sir John Fisher to continue at the Admiralty as first sea lord after Balfour specially arranged for him to be promoted admiral of the fleet. This final step in rank allowed Fisher to remain on the active list for another five years—without which he would have been obliged to retire upon reaching his sixty-fifth birthday on 25 January 1906. Surprisingly little controversy resulted from this last-minute promotion. The Liberals were delighted to find that the estimates prepared by Fisher and Lord Cawdor provided for a respectable cut in naval expenditure of one and a half million. Toward the end of January 1906, Sir John Fisher reported back to the former Conservative first lord that although the Liberal Cabinet would inevitably demand further retrenchment later in the year, he was confident his "new colleagues" would stand up for the Admiralty. The radical parliamentary secretary, Edmund Robertson, had been tamed—while the new first lord, Earl Tweedmouth, "shows such a nice spirit as to make me very happy."[10] Confident in Fisher's abilities as steward, Cawdor and Balfour subsequently agreed not to quibble with any modest cuts in the naval budget he might endorse so as not to provoke the Liberals into dismissing him and then imposing draconian reductions. From a Liberal perspective, the situation at the War Office was brighter. Richard Haldane took office as war minister determined to make deep cuts in military expenditure. Immediately upon learning of his appointment, indeed, Haldane had promised Asquith, his close friend, that before the end of the year he would somehow trim two million from his budget.[11] Confident that Haldane and Tweedmouth were committed to seeking out further economies within their departments, therefore, Asquith devoted his time during the first few months of 1906 to preparing his first budget.

In early May 1906, the chancellor of the Exchequer resolved to scrutinize the naval budget, it having become evident that Tweedmouth had no intention of offering the Treasury further savings. At first neither the Admiralty nor the Conservative leaderships were unduly alarmed by the news. They all expected Asquith would be lenient. Not only was he identified as a "liberal imperialist" but he was also a professed admirer of Sir John Fisher. At the beginning of the month, moreover, Asquith had assured Lord Tweedmouth that he was pleased with the effort of his "most able and prudent Board."[12] The Admiralty soon discovered, however, that the faith in Asquith was misplaced.[13] The Chancellor's demeanor towards Whitehall cooled noticeably after Tweedmouth explained to him that unless the Admiralty was allowed to continue paying for naval works (improvements to port facilities) by raising loans, the annual estimates for the following year (1907–8) would have to rise sharply.[14] Asquith was not pleased. A "new naval works loan bill—even confined to provision of completing existing works—is quite out of the question," he replied on 23 May. "To propose such a bill would be altogether inconsistent with the position which we took up in the House of Commons in 1905."[15] In order that the Treasury might achieve its fiscal targets, Asquith insisted, a way must be found to reduce naval expenditure. "Nothing," he declared, could change his mind.[16] The chancellor's intransigence prompted Sir John Fisher to convene a special meeting of the board at which the sea lords concluded that the best they could do was to hold the 1907 navy estimates at the 1906 level.[17] This could be achieved by deferring planned improvements to Portsmouth dockyard, reducing the number of ships in full commission, and canceling the battle cruiser authorized under the 1906–7 program and another projected under the 1907–8 estimates.

Asquith rejected the compromise, confident that he could extract much more from the Admiralty on the grounds that any further heavy ship construction appeared unnecessary in the immediate future. According to his calculations, the present strength of the British navy "far exceeds the two-Power standard."[18] This contention was supported by figures contained in an internal Admiralty memorandum that somehow had fallen into his hands.[19] Asquith, therefore, saw little reason to negotiate. At the end of June, Tweedmouth endeavored to side-step his department's antagonist by appealing directly to the Cabinet. Although the arguments he presented were sound, the memorandum he circulated among his colleagues was confused and poorly written. The first lord opened his case by pointing out that over the past two years the Admiralty had reduced their expenditure by five million (13 percent), and had already offered to cut a further million from their next budget. While candidly admitting that in terms of numbers of battleships completed "the present position of the Royal Navy is very powerful," he went on to argue that some capital ship construction was necessary because the fighting value of battleships rapidly depreciated. Tweedmouth explained to his colleagues that "the life of a modern battleship is brief—not more than fifteen years in the first class."[20] In 1908, for instance, an entire class of six battleships presently in commission would be declared obsolete en bloc; and in 1911 the Royal Navy would lose another six. All the while, the relative strength of the British fleet would be further eroded as other maritime powers continued to update and increase of their navies. Thus, Tweedmouth explained, "for us to fold our hands and allow a serious gap in the continuity of our construction of the newest type of battleships would be a rash experiment, and likely to lead to future disaster."[21] This case, which amounted to an appeal for the government to sacrifice their current spending plans by insuring against an invisible threat to national security—that might materialize after their term of office had expired—was unlikely to succeed.

The crudeness of the arguments employed in the Admiralty memorandum enabled Asquith swiftly to undermine any latent support for the navy within the Cabinet. "The upshot of Lord Tweedmouth's forecast of the Navy Estimates for 1907–1908," he warned on 9 July, "is that there will be a net increase on the current year's expenditure of 750,000[£]" at a time of "profound peace."[22] The chancellor revealed to his surprised colleagues that although overall naval expenditure would indeed fall the next year as the Admiralty memorandum claimed the navy estimates the "headline" figure would in fact rise. The first lord, Asquith pointed out, had neglected to mention that from next year money to pay for naval works would no longer be borrowed but instead charged to the navy estimates account. Asquith then proceeded to set out his own thoughts on the subject.

> The governing factor in naval expenditure (at any rate, under present conditions) is the cost of new construction; just as in the case of the Army it is the number of men to be maintained on the establishment. But naval expenditure lends itself much more easily to retrenchment, because the amount of new construction to be put in hand is entirely within the discretion of the Government.[23]

The construction budget, Asquith declared, must never be treated as "a question in which the Admiralty is alone, or even primarily, concerned; though for many years past the tendency has been to allow naval opinion to exercise a predominant, and even a decisive, influence in the matter." Rather it should be seen as "a question of policy which ought to be decided by the Cabinet as a whole."[24] He then went on to explain why he believed the navy did not really need the three battleships they had requested.[25]

It was Asquith's contention that since the signing of the Entente with France and the annihilation of the Russian fleet in the Russo-Japanese War, Britain's two-power naval standard was no longer an appropriate yardstick by which to measure the strength of the Royal Navy and thus needed to be "revised."[26] He was careful not to propose an outright renunciation of the standard. The chancellor realized that plotting such a course would involve political dangers. "In the first instance," he therefore advised, the Cabinet should ask the Committee of Imperial Defense to consider "what our standard of naval strength should be."[27] The essence of Asquith's argument for revision was that a naval standard, which required Britain to build against "the two most powerful navies in the world," was too rigid. He acknowledged that when France and Russia had been the second- and third-ranking naval powers the standard had made sense. Since Germany's promotion to the rank of third-ranking naval power in May 1905, however, the Royal Navy had been striving to overmatch the battle fleets of France and Germany.[28] "Is it reasonable," the chancellor asked of his colleagues, "to expect us to build a combination of that character—in the whole sphere of speculative politics by far the most improbable that can be conceived?" Even if it was, he observed, there seemed no need for Britain to lay down more battleships for some years. According to Tweedmouth's own figures the Royal Navy already possessed "47 completed battleships less than fifteen years old against 29 in France and Germany." As for the potential future threat, Asquith continued, "a great deal of the Admiralty argument" on the need to lay down more capital ships "rests on the effective fulfilment by other powers of the paper programs [which] are to a great extent part of the game of 'bluff,' which the Continental Powers seem to be bent on playing."[29] On this point the chancellor was adamant. "The French program," he reiterated in a letter to Tweedmouth the following day, "exists and will in the main continue to exist on paper and no-where else." And "in Germany, the Kaiser encounters great and ever increasing difficulties in getting his way with the Reichstag."[30] There did not appear to be any visible justification, therefore, for Britain to lay down any more new battleships for the foreseeable future.

Tweedmouth, who was regarded by his colleagues as a weak minister, was no match for Asquith's formidable debating skills.[31] The chancellor of the Exchequer argued his case against the Admiralty so convincingly that by the end of Cabinet deliberations on 9 July, not even the liberal imperialists were prepared to stand by the first lord. Richard Haldane, indeed, seemed more anxious to buy himself more time to find sufficient economies at the War Office by pushing the navy further into the Treasury's line of fire. After the meeting, he joined those who were pressing Campbell-Bannerman to impose drastic cuts in the naval shipbuilding budget.[32] But surely the most remarkable aspect of this story was the attitude of Asquith himself. As a liberal imperialist he was supposed to be protecting the Royal Navy—not leading the charge against that institution. Any analysis of Asquith's motives, of course, must remain speculative. He may well have genuinely believed that under the prevailing diplomatic climate a drastic naval retrenchment was safe. But it should not be forgotten that as chancellor of the Exchequer he was at this time under intense pressure from the backbenchers to find money to pay for social reform. Put bluntly, he knew he would be blamed if the party's social program stalled for lack of funds. In addition, Asquith was an ambitious man who hoped one day to become prime minister. As chancellor he took care to groom himself as a "progressive" and actively sought the support of the radical and Labor members of Parliament. In his memorandum to Cabinet of 9 July, for example, Asquith made a transparent bid for radical support when he suggested that "a reduction in our shipbuilding program would be the best earnest we could give to the world" to demonstrate our willingness to disarm.[33] This sentence cannot be interpreted as anything else.

Asquith's idea of revising the naval standard appealed to the Cabinet. Adopting his formula of superiority over any "reasonable combination" of foreign powers promised to allow the government, at its own discretion, to reduce naval spending below the onerous "irreducible minimum" prescribed by the two-power standard. The first hurdle to cross was the Board of Admiralty. But the sea lords were determined to fight. Ignoring the Treasury directive, they obstinately refused to delete more than a token three destroyers and four submarines from the published building program. Replying to Asquith's claim that presently there was no justification for building more battleships, the Board resorted to the somewhat weak argument that it was a "necessity" to lay down three more "dreadnoughts" in 1906 in order to complete a tactical unit of four.[34] It nevertheless sufficed. More controversially they also refused point blank to drop any more armored ships from the next (1907–8) program.[35] Here the Board could offer nothing more than its original argument. "We cannot build for the moment," Fisher pleaded:

> The ships we lay down this year may have their influence on the international situation twenty years hence, when Germany—or whoever our most likely antagonist may be then—may have the co-operation (even if only temporary) of another great naval power. Hence a two-Power standard, rationally interpreted, is by no means out of date.[36]

It is important to note that the Admiralty did not try to justify further construction by pointing to the growth of the German navy. To have tried to do so would have invited ridicule, given the huge disparity in the relative strengths of the two navies. Besides which, the Admiralty wanted much more than a fleet capable of overmatching the largest rival European fleet and thus guaranteeing control of home waters. The effective defense of Britain's empire required a very much larger force, one at least equal to the combined strength of the second- and third-strongest naval powers. And it was global naval supremacy that the Admiralty wished to maintain.

Confident in its belief that their case was just, Tweedmouth and the Board continued to defy the Cabinet. This left Campbell-Bannerman with two alternatives: restrain Asquith or force out Tweedmouth and risk a mass resignation by the sea lords. Having no wish to test his fragile coalition after only six months in power, the prime minister not surprisingly chose the politically safer route and backed the Admiralty. Three capital ships, accordingly, were laid down under the 1906–7 program. On 10 July, Asquith intimated to the first lord that for the next financial year (1907–8) he was now willing to accept a compromise proposed by Haldane. "Is it not possible to bring everyone in to line," he enquired, "by announcing as the program for 1907/8 two certain dreadnoughts (or whatever you chose to call them) and a third contingent on the [results] of the Hague conference to be held next March? [T]his seems to offer a bridge over which we can all pass without sacrifice of conviction."[37] Two days later the prime minister persuaded the still recalcitrant Board of Admiralty to accept the deal.[38]

Asquith's willingness to back off at this stage probably reflected his confidence that the proposed CID investigation into naval policy would vindicate his demands for the two-power standard to be revised. During the recent estimates debate, Sir George Clarke, the permanent secretary of the CID, had been privately feeding Asquith assurances that "if we lay down one battleship this year, a margin of superiority against the improbable combination of France and Germany will be absolutely assured."[39] Meanwhile, Clarke had been pressing Campbell-Bannerman "to appoint a committee to reconsider the whole question of building policy."[40] Colonel Clarke objected not only to the number of capital ships the Admiralty wished to build but also, as we shall see, he was opposed to the all-big-gun type. Just why he chose this moment to exceed his authority and intervene in naval affairs is not clear. Possibly he was frustrated at having been denied by Haldane a voice in the latest schemes for army reform.[41] In any case, Tweedmouth fortuitously discovered Clarke's "meddling" before the prime minister had time to refer the question of the naval standard formally to the CID.[42] Fisher was beside himself with anger on learning of the attempt to usurp the Admiralty's authority. "The sooner we send Clarke to die of yellow fever as Governor of some West Indian island," he fumed in a letter to Tweedmouth, "the better!"[43] The sea lords, he warned, would ferociously resist any further attempts to refer future naval construction to the Committee of Imperial Defense.[44]

Before proceeding, it is worth noting that several historians have noticed that from 1906 Sir John Fisher became increasingly reluctant to cooperate with any CID investigation that touched on naval affairs.[45] Clarke's maneuvering during the summer of 1906 indicate that the Admiral was not paranoid—as some have suggested—rather he justifiably concerned that the organization he had helped to father had been corrupted.[46] When Balfour had been in the chair, the CID had instinctively sided with the navy on every issue "which the two [service] departments held opposite views."[47] The senior Liberal politicians, by contrast, were less inclined to favor the Admiralty case. Meanwhile Fisher found himself on the horns of a dilemma. On the one hand he had Asquith, encouraged by Sir George Clarke, pressing to annihilate the capital-ship construction budget. On the other, he faced growing criticism of his administration from officers who disapproved of his increasingly radical reforms. Revealing to the Cabinet the true direction of his naval policy, in other words, necessarily meant inviting further and potentially disastrous criticism from within the service. It is little wonder that Fisher became reluctant to hold frank discussions of naval policy with outsiders. From mid-1906, moreover, he started to conceal the Admiralty's true thoughts on naval subjects and instead sought to employ arguments that were designed to justify the current levels of naval expenditure. For this deception to work, it was thus essential to avoid naval policy being scrutinized by outside experts, such as Clarke, especially if they were predisposed to be hostile. Between 1906 and 1910, the relationship between the Liberal Cabinet and the Board of Admiralty became increasingly characterized by mutual distrust and suspicion.

To resume: The Admiralty's first response to their disastrous performance in the estimates debate of July 1906, was to find a different— and more effective—argument with which to block Cabinet demands for a cessation in the construction of armored warships.[48] Thereafter, the Board began to claim that:

> until recently although each succeeding type of battleships were an
> improvement on their predecessors, the advance in fighting efficiency from

one type to another was comparatively small, whereas—with the introduction of the Dreadnoughts—a leap forward of 200% in fighting power
has been effected, so that *as compared with the dreadnought designs,* all
existing types of battleships are more or less out of date.[49]

Certainly there was justification in the Admiralty's claim that all-big-gun
ships would have a considerable gunnery advantage over predreadnoughts.[50] On the other hand for the Board to suggest in July 1906 that
their gunnery superiority would render all existing battleships obsolete
was more open to question.[51] It is perhaps significant that, the Admiralty
made no such claims immediately after the launch of HMS *Dreadnought*
in February 1906.[52] Furthermore, the results of squadron battle practices conducted that year suggested that under certain conditions, in
engagements fought in rough seas or misty weather, battleships armed
with a secondary battery of quick-firing guns might have the edge over
all-big-gun ships.[53] For many years afterwards, a "large number of competent officers" continued to insist that the superiority of dreadnoughts
over older battleships was exaggerated.[54] Even senior Admiralty administrators privately confessed (though not to politicians) that calculating
the relative value of each type was "one of extreme complexity."[55] In public, however, the Admiralty maintained that in future naval engagements
"only dreadnoughts would matter."[56] Furthermore, even though Fisher
was personally opposed to the building of "dreadnought" battleships
(preferring the battle cruiser), outside Whitehall he presented himself as
an uncompromising defender of the type, branding anyone who contradicted the official line as a heretic. Another argument Fisher started
using to justify building the *Dreadnought* was that the Admiralty had
been driven to building all-big-gun battleships by intelligence that foreign navies were already moving in this direction.[57] The evidence to support this argument, however, is thin.[58] But whether or not the claims
made for dreadnoughts were true or not misses the point. What really
mattered to Fisher and the Admiralty was the preservation of the construction budget. This will become clearer below.

Lacking the technical knowledge to refute the Admiralty's claims for
the new model warships,[59] in September 1906 Sir George Clarke was
described by one neutral observer as having become "all agog against
dreadnoughts."[60] Henceforth he encouraged Liberal ministers to believe
that the decision to build the *Dreadnought* and "the three monster
armored cruisers" was the "worst mistake ever" made by a Board of
Admiralty.[61] After other naval powers also started to build "dreadnoughts," Fisher was accused of "throwing away" Britain's huge numerical advantage in conventional battleships. For obvious reasons the tone

of his remarks struck a chord with many in the Cabinet.[62] This impression was reinforced towards the end of 1906, by a series of articles in the press questioning the wisdom of the Admiralty's "dreadnought policy" authored by the former DNI Rear Adm. Reginald Custance, the highly respected naval theorist and tactician, Sir William White, the ex-DNC, and Adm. Sir Frederick Richards, the former senior naval lord.[63] What it is important to realize, nevertheless, and what these distinguished officers did not realize, was the adoption of the dreadnought type battleships proved to be the Admiralty's best justification for the continued construction of big-ships during the Liberal administration; without the concept of a "dreadnought revolution" it is difficult to see how Fisher could have persuaded the Cabinet between 1906 and, say, 1909, to ignore the protests of their radical tail and continue building large armored warships.

It was no coincidence that at the beginning of 1907, several Cabinet ministers began openly to question Fisher's claims for the overwhelming superiority of the all-big-gun armored vessel over predreadnought types. Others, David Lloyd George for example, complained publically that the dreadnought policy was a "piece of wanton and profligate ostentation"— whatever that meant.[64] In January, Campbell-Bannerman admitted to Asquith that he too resented having to pay the costs associated with the development and construction of "experimentally large ships which no other power possesses."[65] Growing skepticism over the Admiralty's claims of a "dreadnought revolution" may explain why, that month, the Cabinet refused to allow the Admiralty to sell two predreadnoughts to the Brazilian navy and use the proceeds to build "another *Dreadnought* or *Invincible.*"[66] Of course the politicians may simply have felt that for diplomatic and deterrence purposes, two old battleships carried more weight than one new one.[67] But judging from the tone of Asquith's correspondence on the subject this does not seem likely.

In early 1907 doubts over the direction of Admiralty construction policy had become sufficiently widespread for Fisher to recruit the historian Julian Corbett to help rebut criticism of his construction policy.[68] To this end, the first sea lord provided Corbett with several confidential papers including the one entitled "The Strategic Aspects of our Building Program."[69] In cooperation with Charles Ottley, the DNI,[70] Corbett subsequently produced an impressive, if partisan, defense of the dreadnought type that succeeded in dampening criticism of the type which earned him the gratitude of the first sea lord and an invitation to write further propaganda articles on behalf of the Admiralty.[71] The historian cautiously agreed and later that summer produced two further papers in support of recent naval reforms.[72] While Corbett's articles silenced the

Admiralty's loudest critics they did not convince their most dangerous foe. Chancellor Asquith, who in April 1908 would become prime minister, remained "sceptical" (in the matter of shipbuilding) as to the whole "dreadnought" policy for many more years. One of Asquith's first acts as prime minister, indeed, would be to dismiss Tweedmouth as first lord and replace him with the chief secretary from the Treasury. "I don't want to press you," an impatient Asquith wrote to the new first lord of the Admiralty in July 1908, for example, "but as you have now surveyed the whole situation from the inside, I should be very glad to know if you have come to any conclusion of your own as to the lines upon which construction ought to proceed for the next few years. There is much money in it—and more than money. . . ."[73]

Fisher's ability from the end of 1906 to always provide a plausible answer as to why more cuts should not be made in the naval construction budget made him extremely unpopular with his political masters. "I confess that after a year's experience," Asquith wrote to Campbell-Bannerman,

> I have very little confidence in the present lot of Sea Lords who chop and change as the whim suits them. Our naval supremacy is so completely assured having regard to the sketchy paper program and inferior ship-building resources of the other powers that there is no possible reason for allowing ourselves to be hastily rushed into these nebulous and ambitious developments.[74]

Campbell-Bannerman "entirely" shared Asquith's "dislike and suspicions of the Navy."[75] Unfortunately at a time when the international naval situation was so confused it was impossible to disregard the expert advice from the Board of Admiralty. "There is desperately little sound standing ground in all this," sighed Campbell-Bannerman.[76] This uncertainty, however, did not discourage him from again trying (unsuccessfully) to coax Tweedmouth into endorsing a change in the definition of the two-power standard.[77] "I think it will be sadly misunderstood if you were to throw over its validity at the present time," the first lord had replied. "All governments for at least twenty-one years have accepted and acted up to the Two Power Standard and it is not to be lightly abandoned now."[78] The public had identified it as the very definition of national security. He did not need to add that any attempt to dilute the standard was bound to be used against the government with potentially serious effect.

From the beginning of 1907 the Cabinet and Treasury became resigned to do no more than hold the line on the Admiralty's spending. This uneasy truce between the departments lasted for almost a year, until the Liberal Party's radical tail began to twitch restlessly.[79] On 4 November, one hundred and thirty-eight backbencher MP's submitted a petition to the prime minister calling for massive cuts in defense spending.[80] After gauging the strength of feeling within the party, on 20 November the Chief Whip reported to the Cabinet that "unless some substantial reduction is made in the combined total of naval and military expenditure, the Government may be exposed to a serious attack by a considerable section of their own followers."[81] Before the Cabinet had time to react to this potential threat, however, the very next day indeed, Asquith was "aghast" to learn from Tweedmouth that the Admiralty intended to ask for an increase in their budget next year of between one and two million.[82] The increase was the result of the Admiralty having now to pay for works out of the annual navy estimates rather than borrow the money as they had been doing since 1895. "I need hardly tell you," the Chancellor at once wrote back, "that I cannot and will not be responsible for submitting such estimates to the House of Commons."[83] This time Asquith's reply was not simply an expression of personal ideology or symptomatic of his desire to remain friendly with the radicals for political reasons. He was committed (and becoming increasingly desperate) to find money to pay for the Old Age Pensions Bill due to be introduced before Parliament early the following year.[84] Yet this time Asquith could hardly accuse the Admiralty of profligacy. The building program for 1908–9 was modest; consisting of just one capital ship—a battleship—and a new model armored cruiser (armed with eight 9.2-inch guns) plus the usual number of flotilla craft.[85] Had the Admiralty not been obliged to provide for naval works, indeed, the navy estimates would actually shown a slight fall. Finding economies elsewhere in the naval budget was unlikely. Tweedmouth warned that after the recent announcement of another expansion of the German fleet, it was not possible to reduce the numbers of ships in commission or delete obsolete vessels from the reserve.

On 26 November, the Cabinet peremptorily informed the Admiralty that their estimates "must be completely revised with the view of securing that the estimated expenditure on the Navy for 1908/09 shall not exceed the figures of last year."[86] Moreover, "the Cabinet have decided that no estimate for a new Dreadnought need be included in the estimates for 1908–09."[87] Unable to persuade Tweedmouth to stand firm, Fisher offered to compromise.[88] By delaying payments on outstanding contracts and postponing the calling of tenders until the end of the financial year, he suggested, the necessary increase might be restricted to just £500,000.[89] These measures, however, would have only deferred expenditure. In the meantime, the Treasury would still have to cough up an extra half million. Five days later, however, the Admiralty withdrew this offer and instead resubmitted the original demand for an extra 1.4 million. Thanks to the sea lords the first lord had found a new resolve. On 3 December 1907, they presented Tweedmouth with a signed document protesting at the Cabinet's diktat.[90] Along with the memorandum went a verbal threat of mass resignation.[91] At the beginning of the New Year the Treasury and the Admiralty were still "at daggers drawn."[92] Tweedmouth's performance must have been convincing because the prime minister, according to his private secretary, was bracing himself to accept resignation of the entire Board of Admiralty.[93]

In an attempt to head off this possible disaster and defuse tensions, Campbell-Bannerman sent Sir Edward Grey, the foreign secretary, into Whitehall with a small committee to ferret out economies. He was chosen because both sides regarded him as neutral. Grey, however, found nothing. And shortly afterwards, sometime during the first week of January 1908, the prime minister overruled the Treasury's objections and agreed to endorse the Admiralty's spending plans.[94] But before Tweedmouth had time to lay the navy estimates before the House of Commons, Campbell-Bannerman suffered a major heart attack. Political commentators knew his resignation or death was only a matter of time.[95] In the meantime Asquith was appointed deputy leader, thus shifting the balance of power within the Cabinet. At the beginning of February, accordingly, Campbell-Bannerman's deal with the Admiralty was declared void. Sir John Fisher was summoned to an assembly of ministers where he was told that the Cabinet "had unanimously determined to reduce the Navy Estimates by £1,340,000, so as to bring them below last year's figure."[96] Withdrawing the concessions already made to the Admiralty and refusing to allow any increase in the navy estimates whatsoever was a clear act of provocation. Afterwards, Fisher remarked to his DNI that he suspected "there were wheels within wheels and that there is a strong party in the Cabinet who want to eject Lord Tweedmouth." He now believed that "the crisis on the estimates has been largely manufactured with this object in view."[97] Fisher also had to contend with the increasingly unpredictable not to say eccentric behavior of Lord Tweedmouth.[98] Polite commentators noted that the first lord's "mental powers had lately shown alarming signs of decay."[99] Others said he had gone mad.

At the end of January, the first sea lord resolved to counterattack.[100] Throughout his career he had always maintained close links with journalists and newspaper editors. Since at least 1884, he had used the press to overcome politicians.[101] In 1908, Fisher's closest confidant in Fleet Street was James L. Garvin—the editor of the *Observer*.[102] Thus it was with

Garvin's help that Fisher connived to embarrass Asquith and the Liberal government by leaking information to the public that contradicted repeated ministerial denials of an estimates "crisis." On 9 February, the *Observer* published an "official" letter received from the first sea lord, deliberately composed to stir up public opinion, that pompously demanded to know who had passed the newspaper confidential papers on naval policy—thereby implying that the editorials were accurate![103] Garvin's biographer concluded that the operation was brilliantly successful and "undoubtedly" did much "to force the Radicals in the Cabinet to modify their demands."[104] In essence this is correct, though it does requires qualification.

On 12 February 1908, the Cabinet called the Admiralty's bluff by granting an increase in navy estimates of just under £900,000 and then declaring the subject closed.[105] It worked. Tweedmouth capitulated. He refused to resign over his department being thus short-changed, although he was furious at "the very cavalier manner" in which he had been treated by his political colleagues. That being said, however, he only conceded after making it clear that the Admiralty expected to be granted a supplementary appropriation later in the autumn. Tweedmouth requested from Asquith that a written "assurance should be given to me [now] that a[ny] proposal for a supplementary estimate will not be received with 'surprise' nor blank opposition."[106] Whether this thinly veiled ultimatum achieved his end or merely precipitated his dismissal from the Cabinet several weeks later is debatable. In any case, at the beginning of April 1908, upon formally succeeding Campbell-Bannerman as prime minister, Asquith replaced Lord Tweedmouth with the much trustworthier Reginald McKenna, after Winston Churchill refused the post.[107] McKenna had previously served as Asquith's chief assistant at the Treasury. It is significant that both candidates Asquith considered for the post were leading members of the "economist" wing of the party, avowedly bent on securing reductions in armaments.[108] Shortly after his dismissal, Tweedmouth sent Asquith a bitter letter reminding him that during his two years at the Admiralty he had repeatedly compromised his own convictions and acted in the Party's interest by refusing to stand by his sea lords. "I ought to have resigned when the Cabinet again and again cut down my estimates," he reflected, "I did not do so because it would have involved the resignation of the whole Board sea and civil and that would have been a terrible thing."[109]

Fisher won another point for the Admiralty in March when, during a debate on the navy in the House of Commons, Asquith mistakenly described the second armored vessel projected under the 1908–9 program as a "battle-cruiser."[110] Fisher gleefully exploited this slip of the tongue and after hastily preparing a new design, surreptitiously upgraded the projected 15,500-ton "armored cruiser" armed with eight 9.2-inch guns into a full-sized 19,000-ton 12-inch gunned battle cruiser.[111] The difference in price more than made up for the quarter of a million pounds the Cabinet had arbitrarily trimmed from the estimates back in February. After the prime minister had informed Parliament that the government would be ordering a "battle cruiser" he could do nothing.

The Naval Industrial Complex

The extraordinary lengths to which Fisher went to defend the battleship standard, his refusal to endorse a redefinition of the two-power standard, and his aggressive defense of the dreadnought program appear to contradict the arguments put forward in previous chapters that he no longer believed that a supreme battleship fleet was the best force structure for defending British imperial interests.[112] Yet at the same time that Fisher was demanding more capital ships, he was privately assuring his closest friends and allies that "our present margin of superiority over Germany (our only possible foe for years) is so great as to render it absurd in the extreme to talk of anything endangering our naval supremacy, *even if we stopped all shipbuilding altogether!!!*"[113] In a letter to King Edward dated October 1907, the first sea lord claimed "the English Navy is *now* four times stronger than the German Navy,"

> but we don't want to parade all this, because if so we shall have Parliamentary trouble. Sir John Brunner MP, and 150 Members of the House of Commons who are Sir Henry Campbell-Bannerman's warmest supporters and have been his steadfast friends in adversity, have sent him quite recently one of the best papers I have read, convincingly showing that we don't want to lay down any new ships at all—*we are so strong*. It is quite true![114]

If such statements are to be believed then why did the Admiralty insist upon ordering more battleships? Much of the confusion over the evidence stems from the pervasive assumption in most historical narratives that Fisher volunteered economies simply for the sake of efficiency.[115] This simply was not the case. Furthermore, it is often forgotten that Balfour's government commanded the largest cuts in naval expenditure. As we have seen, Fisher was appointed first sea lord by the Conservative administration on the understanding that he would effect a significant cut in the navy estimates. He agreed because he realized that government had to "repair and rebuild the structure of British financial credit so rudely shaken by the South African war."[116] There had, however, been a pay off—and this is the key—in return for cleansing the "Augean" waste from the naval budget, Fisher had been allowed to keep the naval construction budget more or less intact. This enabled him to build the ships he desired to effect his naval revolution. In July 1905, the first sea lord informed the Naval Estimates Committee that for the next four years the construction budget would be sustained at "nine and half million a year."[117] With this sum, he had hoped to lay down annually four new model battle cruisers and make "large increases" in the numbers of "submarines and torpedo craft."[118] Assuming the navy estimates did not rise above 33 million, this would have pushed up the naval construction budget to a shade under 30 percent of total navy estimates.[119] Arthur Balfour not only knew about Fisher's aspirations—he endorsed them. One of his last acts as prime minister was to issue a parliamentary paper committing his party to consolidating the Fisher revolution. The memorandum also served to announce that if the Conservatives were returned to power, the navy would be given approximately nine and a half million per annum for new construction.[120]

Historians have made a great deal of confusion over the purpose of the so-called "Cawdor Memorandum." When Balfour authorized its publication his intention had been to convince the electorate that the Conservatives at last had naval expenditure under control, and that if reelected would spend no more than nine and a half million on naval construction annually. Four large armored vessels a year, in other words, was supposed to have been a *maximum* program.[121] The Liberal Party, however, along with most historians, were not privy to the informal understanding between Balfour and Fisher. They, consequently, regarded the Cawdor Memorandum as a thinly disguised attempt to convince the public that four large armored vessels a year was the *minimum* number that had to be laid down annually in order to maintain British naval supremacy.[122] The document, in other words, was seen as another political ploy designed to restrict the Liberals' fiscal freedom of action after taking power.[123] Fisher, who actually drafted the memorandum, insisted in his memoirs that both these interpretations were wrong.[124] He maintained that the prescribed four ships a year building policy represented the *average* number of warships required to be laid down over the five-year period, the actual number of contracts awarded each year depending upon a range of factors. Fisher explained:

> [Great Britain] builds simply and solely to maintain the command of the sea against other Powers. For this end the Admiralty must have its hands free to determine from year to year what the shipbuilding requirements are. But, again, this does not mean that our efforts must be spasmodic, that because foreign Powers lay down six ships one year and none the next, therefore we must do the same. For administrative reasons, which

should be obvious, and which in any case this is not the place to dilate upon, it is very necessary that shipbuilding should approximate year by year, so far as practicable, to some normal figure, and that increases or decreases, when they become necessary, should be made gradually. This double principle, of determining the program from year to year, and yet averaging the number of ships built over a number of years, has to be firmly grasped by anyone who desires to understand the Admiralty ship-building policy.[125]

The Cawdor program, in short, was no more than an assurance that over the next five years new construction would average at four ships a year.[126] The importance of averaging construction will be explained below.

Fisher's aggressive defense of the construction budget is only partially explained by his desire to build the new model ships he required to effect his naval revolution. As we have seen, by January 1906 his "fusion" armored warship project had been rejected by majority opinion within Whitehall; though it is true that within nine months Jacky's hopes that it would be reconsidered were revived after the sophisticated electrical-mechanical fire control computer designed by Arthur Pollen was brought to his attention.[127] He had not, therefore, given up all hope of affecting his revolution in capital ship design. To properly understand why Sir John Fisher fought so hard between 1906 and 1908 to preserve the construction of "dreadnought" battleships it is necessary to look closer at the Admiralty's shipbuilding policy, and more particularly to examine the increasingly complex links between the Royal Navy and the warship building industry.

Historically, the crown had always retained the prerogative to supply armaments to the Royal Navy. In the age of sail, the Admiralty was content to design and build its own ships-of-the-line in the Royal Dockyards, and arm them with guns produced by the Royal Ordnance. Private resources were exploited only to build smaller ships such as frigates and sloops.[128] Outwardly, the pattern of procurement did not change significantly after the introduction of warships built of steel, propelled by steam driven screws mounting breech-loading guns capable of firing high explosive shells. The Admiralty retained the Dockyards as the sole supplier of armored warships to the Royal Navy armed with guns manufactured at the Woolwich Arsenal. Private firms built nothing larger than torpedo boats and destroyers.[129] This apparent continuity, however, reflected in the allocation of contracts for large armored warships, masked important shifts in the pattern of naval procurement. From the mid-1880s the Royal Dockyards relied increasingly upon trade to supply sophisticated heavy engineering. Private firms supplied a steadily larger proportion (by value) of the components that made up a warship. This included the rifled breech-loading guns and marine engines, plus all complex hydraulic and electrical equipment.

After the passage of the 1889 Naval Defense Act and the subsequent rapid expansion of the fleet, the Royal Dockyards proved incapable of meeting all the navy's requirements for large warships. Because a large proportion of dockyards personnel and facilities were permanently preoccupied in refitting older warships, the Admiralty was compelled to give a significant proportion of large-ship contracts to private sector yards. Though the Royal Dockyards always received priority, as the decade progressed, steadily worsening congestion and underinvestment in these yards forced the Admiralty to channel a steadily larger share of contracts towards the private firms.[130] The Royal Dockyards' majority hold on the building of large warships was finally broken in the mid-1890s. In 1897, the Board of Admiralty was compelled by a shortage of large building slips in the state-owned shipbuilding yards to order all six (12,000 ton) armored cruisers of the *Cressy* class from trade.[131] Thereafter, between 1897 and 1904, more than half of the sixty-two large warships ordered for the navy were built in private yards. Over this seven year period the capacity of the private warship construction industry in Britain multiplied. By 1904, there were at least fourteen major companies "listed" as having the necessary facilities and experience to build the hulls of large armored ships; some firms could build more than one at a time.[132] This meant, in theory, sufficient capacity existed in the country to out-build all the major naval powers in the world. Contemporary politicians (and historians alike) subsequently assumed that in the last resort Britain could easily out-build any challenger that threatened her naval supremacy.[133] As we shall see the reality was different.

In late 1904, when the financial horizon seemed likely to remain darkly clouded for some years to come, the Admiralty recognized that with the number of large armored ships laid down annually set to fall sharply, existing warship building capacity could not possibly be kept fully employed. It was inevitable that many "great shipbuilding firms" would find themselves starved of "Admiralty custom."[134] In January 1905, Fisher, as first sea lord, initiated a review of the navy's shipbuilding policy and appointed himself as chairman of the committee established to consider this matter. For reasons that will be explained below, the naval administration was also anxious to establish a stable—and sustainable—working partnership between the navy and the private armaments firms. Fisher was certainly the officer best qualified to understand the dynamics of this relationship. Over the previous twenty years he had built up an unrivaled knowledge of naval technology and munitions procurement. Between 1883 and 1897 he served consecutively in the posts of captain of the Gunnery School, director of Naval Ordnance, superintendent of Portsmouth Dockyard, and controller of the navy. He had served in this last post for an unparalleled two consecutive terms, that is six years. That office, however, had not been senior enough for him to make fundamental changes in the ways the Royal Navy "conducted business." Unusually for a naval officer, Fisher also maintained very close relationships with the leading industrialists of the day, notably Sir Josiah Vavasseur and Sir Andrew Noble—both of whom were senior directors of Armstrong. On his death, indeed, Vavasseur bequeathed most of his considerable estate to Fisher's son. Sir John Fisher's remarkable management skills and grasp of his subject were widely acknowledged; between 1887 and 1913 he was constantly being tempted by offers of fabulous salaries (up to £20,000 p.a.—more than five times his stipend as head of the navy) to become "dictator" of a leading armaments firm.[135]

Fisher's small "shipbuilding industry committee"—for want of a better label—worked closely with the famous 1905 Committee on Designs appointed by Lord Selborne to consider the practicability of all-big-gun armored warships. Armed with the endorsement of these two councils, the first sea lord managed to persuade the Board of Admiralty that "considerable advantages" would result from the navy taking delivery of its new warships within sixteen months as opposed to the normal three and a half or more years.[136] "We are enabled by rapid construction," Fisher explained, "to get vessels into the fighting line with practically all the latest improvements embodied in them."[137] Until then most warships joined the fleet with equipment that was inferior to the latest available models. Not only did this reduce their fighting efficiency, but the need subsequently to refit them was costly.[138]

Amazing at it may seem, halving the time it took to construct a large armored warships proved to be attainable. Reforming labor practices in the dockyards, and ordering critical path components, such as big-gun mountings and turbine engines, several months before placing the contract for the hull, did the most to reduce completion times.[139] In January 1905, the Board of Admiralty resolved to develop Britain's comparative advantage in rapid construction "to the utmost."[140] The only drawback to "rapid shipbuilding" was that "we can only afford to build a few every year."[141] This was because shortening completion times had the effect of accelerating naval spending; whereas previously the payment for a new ship was spread over four or more years, with rapid building the full burden fell upon just two or three fiscal years. Prior to 1905, the Admiralty had envisaged its long-term construction program to average out at three battleships and four armored cruisers per annum. In order to adopt rapid building, therefore, without increasing expenditure, the Admiralty was forced to cut the size of this program. But as the Admiralty was already under pressure to do so anyway this was viewed as desirable. From Fisher's perspective the priority was to feed the ship-building industry with enough money each year to keep it solvent, not to maximize the numbers of warships to be laid down each year.

At a meeting held on 6 January 1905, the Admiralty decreed that henceforth contracts for two capital ships would be reserved for Royal Dockyards at Portsmouth and Devonport, thus leaving two others for the private sector.[142] It was also agreed that "any abnormal increase in building can, it is hoped, be met by private yards."[143] The immediate result of the decision to adopt this two-two formula resulted in discharge of over 8,000 redundant state-employed dockyard workers.[144] Actually the Royal Dockyards could easily have supplied four ships a year. However, for the navy to have relied exclusively upon the state sector to provide large warships would have been "simply ruinous to the private shipbuilding trade of this country."[145] Already many armaments firms had been left struggling to cope with the sharp decline in military pro-curement in the aftermath of the Boer War.[146] It was thus hoped that two capital ship contracts per year plus orders from overseas would be sufficient to keep solvent the four principal warship building firms, i.e., Vickers, Armstrong-Whitworth, the Fairfield Shipbuilding Company, and John Brown & Co. Ltd.[147] In late 1905, the Admiralty deliberately invited the three last named firms to build the three *Invincible* class battles cruisers authorized to be laid down that year, rather than following the normal practice of putting the contracts out for tender. Although this controversial procedure was not repeated, it should be noted that not until the exceptional ten capital ship program of 1909 did the Admiralty award a big ship contract to a firm outside this quartet.

The Admiralty was not motivated by altruism. There were good rea-sons not to ruin the private shipbuilders. First, they generally could turn out warships faster and cheaper than the dockyards. Second, the Admiralty wanted to combat the spreading unionization among dockyard workers and the reluctance by politicians to discharging unwanted men during periods of inactivity.[148] It was hoped that competition from the pri-vate sector would help curb militancy and help keep costs down.[149] Third, in the event of war the Royal Dockyards were expected to be fully occu-pied with repairing damaged ships, and that consequently building would be suspended.[150] During a period of hostilities, therefore, the navy would have to rely upon private yards for new ships to maintain the flow of up-to-date warships into the fleet. (There is no evidence to suggest the Admiralty envisaged the suspension of large warship construction during a major war.) Lastly, the Board recognized that to keep the Dockyard workmen fully employed "would result in the destruction, if not the total extinction, of an advantage which this country possesses over her neighbours, viz., the power to produce war vessels in large numbers, in a short time, and at moderate cost."[151] As the head of the Admiralty's contracts department explained to his counterpart in the War Office, the navy felt it was "of special importance" to award a large proportion of contracts to private firms "in order to keep open those sources of supply against times of need."[152] The Admiralty had other reasons to maintain the level of shipbuilding capacity in the country against the possibility of a future "arms race." More compelling was the fact that although the state dockyards had the ability to build the hulls of large armored vessels, by 1905 they had become totally dependent upon the private sector for expertise in the design and production of technologically sophisticated components such as big-gun mountings, armor-plate, and turbine engines.[153] Together these three items accounted for well over 50 percent of the cost of a capital ship.

Several internal memoranda confirm that the Admiralty's resistance to deep cuts in the naval construction budget after 1905 was substantially motivated by concern at the damaging impact upon the armaments industry. In July 1906, in a document written at the height of the first major Treasury onslaught against the navy estimates, the Board noted that if, as threatened, no armored vessels were laid down, then:

> shipbuilding yards, armor plate factories, and arsenals [will be] thrown out of gear by a cessation of work and the discharge of skilled mechanics . . . [A] day will come when our naval supremacy will again be challenged, and when, by consequence, the ability to rapidly build warships in considerable numbers will be a national asset of incalculable importance. To starve the construction vote in the present will, should expansion ever again become necessary, not merely inevitably enhance the cost of any future program, but will greatly impair the national power of rapid naval recuperation in the vital matter of our output of new warships.[154]

The same argument was prominent in the sea lords' memorandum to the first lord of 3 December 1907, protesting against Cabinet instructions to delete the sole dreadnought from the 1908–9 program.

> Although it is quite true that our preponderance in battleships at the present moment might justify the omission of the solitary battleship proposed, yet with the full knowledge and absolute certainty (now afforded by the German program just issued) of having to commence a large battleship program in 1909/10, it would be most unbusinesslike, and indeed disas-

trous to close down the armor plate industry of this country by the entire cessation of battleship building. It would be similarly disastrous to abruptly stop the manufacture of heavy gun mountings.[155]

By 1905, the Royal Navy had become completely dependent upon the private sector to supply the mountings and turrets for the 12-inch guns that had become the standard main armament for all its capital ships.[156] Messrs. Vickers Ltd. and Armstrong-Whitworth & Co. were the only two firms in England with the facilities to build these enormously complex machines with the necessary expertise and precision. The design of the mountings was originally the property of the Armstrong Company. Since the late 1890s, moreover, these two private firms had been colluding. They had pooled their technical knowledge, agreed to share the research and development burden, and had cut their manufacturing costs by standardizing their product. The response by the Admiralty had been to approach other firms and provide them with copies of the Armstrong plans. In 1903, the Admiralty had been obliged to award Vickers and Armstrong an effective oligopoly in the supply of big-gun mountings in return for the companies' agreement to drop legal proceedings against the Controller's Department for back-payment of royalties and infringement of their patents.[157] As a result, Messrs. Beardmore and John Brown Ltd. had been forced to close their brand-new gun mounting plants for want of contracts.

Although the granting of this concession certainly narrowed the field of supply for big-gun mountings, for a period the Royal Navy benefited from the arrangement. The speed at which a manufacturer could supply such specialized naval equipment was closely correlated to its stock of manufacturing plant and pool of experienced machinists. Neither factors could be improvised. The scale of the plant required to construct big-gun mountings may be gauged from the fact that it required no fewer than five hundred machines to build just one unit.[158] Many were custom-made for the job.[159] As a consequence, their supply was highly inelastic. The Admiralty could not purchase gun mountings on demand. Battleship turrets had to be ordered at least six months—large orders required nine months—before the ships for which they were required were laid down. For obvious reasons, the Admiralty wanted their suppliers to keep a large margin of surplus capacity in anticipation of the need to accelerate naval construction. But for private firms this made no economic sense. Experience had taught them that the Royal Navy's demand for capital ships (and thus big-gun mountings) was unpredictable. In addition, the costs of retaining extra skilled workmen and underemploying factories equipped with up-to-date machine tools were prohibitive, especially at a time when the cost of capital depreciation was high owing to the rapid pace of technological progress.[160] There were, moreover, few alternate uses for such specialized machinery. Not even the British government was prepared to incur the costs of retaining the desired level of spare industrial capacity at a royal ordnance factory. It was too expensive.

Private companies, however, were in a position to cover some of their plant overheads by selling their products overseas. What is more, the Admiralty actively encouraged them to do so.[161] During the first decade of the twentieth century, Vickers earned between 20 and 30 percent of their incomes generated by their gun mountings factories from exports. This freedom to exploit overseas markets coupled to an oligopoly in their home market, gave Vickers and Messrs. Armstrong the confidence to maintain larger plant than they required to supply the Royal Navy, and thus allowed them to exploit significant economies of scale in production.[162] As a result, they were in a position to make big-gun mountings substantially faster than any other potential supplier. Or to put it another way, two large companies could deliver big-gun mountings quicker than the combined efforts of three or four smaller firms. During the Fisher administration, speed of manufacture was all-important. As the director of Naval Ordnance explained in July 1907 to a parliamentary select committee inquiring into why the Admiralty refused to employ the state-owned Royal Gun Factory:

> The fact is that Woolwich [Arsenal] could, no doubt, manufacture 12–inch hydraulic gun machinery to the designs of private firms if time were not a factor . . . [but] it is to be observed that without considerably increasing both the plant and staff of the Arsenal, it is not possible for Woolwich to manufacture hydraulic gun machinery in time to meet the present requirements—it being pointed out that battleships and cruisers are now required to be completed in two years.[163]

The facilities of the Woolwich gun factory were not required even after the surge in demand for big-gun mountings after the introduction of all-big-gun ships. Whereas predreadnought battleships carried four 12-inch guns in two turrets, dreadnoughts would require ten of these big-guns mounted in five turrets. Again, "rapidity of manufacture of heavy gun mountings," the controller (Capt. Henry Jackson) explained to the military superintendent of the arsenal in July 1907, "is of the greatest importance under present conditions of naval shipbuilding, and it is possible to meet requirements only by plant, facilities, and organization of the very best. The resources of the private Trade have been latterly greatly increased to meet the new requirements, and are now ample, and are much in advance of those at Woolwich."[164]

By 1909, however, the advantages of relying upon an oligopoly to supply critical components were less clear. It is possible that the navy had became overly reliant upon Vickers and Armstrong. At a meeting between the sea lords and senior government ministers in February 1909, it emerged that for the previous three years the Admiralty had been subsidizing both firms. In return for retaining their production capacity for gun mountings at a level higher that their expectations for orders warranted, the companies had been paid inflated prices for the few gun mountings they had completed.[165] The minutes of this meeting also show that the traditionally aggressive posture adopted by the Admiralty towards their suppliers was being tempered by recognition that the navy was in a position of absolute dependence. Those officials present initially proposed solving this problem by modernizing and extending the plant at Woolwich. But the Admiralty at once rejected this idea on the grounds of time and cost. Furthermore, the chancellor of the Exchequer had to be disabused of his notion that, if enough pressure was applied, private firms could always meet the navy's requirements. It was explained to him that the manufacturing capacity simply did not exist; and anyway the Admiralty no longer had the necessary leverage to employ such tactics. Previously, in 1888, during the 1890s, and again in 1902, the Admiralty had easily bullied or coaxed either Vickers or Armstrong to extend their gun making capacity by threatening to give contracts to another firm.[166] During the 1909 "Navy Scare," however, the then first lord of the Admiralty explained "we could not go to these firms now and say, 'we will give you nothing unless in return for these orders, which may not be very valuable, you will undertake to spend so many hundred thousand pounds.'" The Admiralty estimated that a new firm entering the industry would require at least two years experience to even match the existing output of either Vickers or Armstrong, plus the promise of a full order book for several years. Moral suasion, thus advised the first lord, was now the only pressure that could be feasibly applied, but even then "for the last two or three years they have not made such a profit out of us as to put us on a very good footing with them."[167]

Another important reason why the Fisher administration chose not to rely exclusively upon the Royal Dockyards to build armored ships was that by 1905 the navy had become dependent upon the private armaments giants for the development of new weapon systems. The costs of developing updated or improved versions of existing equipment during a period of rapid technological progress were invariably high and frequently unpredictable. For the Royal Dockyards to have tried to keep abreast of improvements to every piece of naval equipment aboard a battleship would have been financially impossible. In the words of Sir William White, the former director of Naval Construction, "the progress of invention and discovery [in naval armaments] is *increasing,* rapid changes occur unceasingly, the outlay is enormous, the task is never-ending."[168] At the turn of the century, firms such as Vickers were providing their scientists with sums amounting "on average to 6–12 per cent of annual net profits."[169] Development also required a sustained effort. Teams of skilled designers, draftsmen, and workmen took years to train and assemble; and the plant required to build warship components could not be improvised overnight. Any firm that wished to compete in the design of big-gun mountings, for instance, required a team of over one hundred experienced first-class (and highly paid) draftsmen for the design team alone.[170]

At the turn of the twentieth century the Royal Navy was badly placed to carry out research and development projects that required specialized expertise or sustained effort.[171] The navy's shortage of technical staff was so acute that sometimes it could not properly maintain and service sophisticated equipment it already had, led alone find the personnel to develop improved models. The Royal Ordnance was in no better position. When, for instance, in 1907 the chief superintendent of the ordnance factory suggested that Woolwich should be allowed to participate in "design work for heavy mountings," the director of Naval Ordnance reminded the Board that:

> No Woolwich design of even the smallest naval gun mounting has ever yet been accepted, although the designs sent in are usually close copies of existing mountings; and the only large gun mountings ever designed by the Royal Carriage Department, viz., the 9.2–inch mountings of HM Ships "*Powerful*" and "*Terrible,*" have been regarded as absolute failures ever since they were installed. Large sums of money have been and are being spent in endeavors to improve them, but they will never be satisfactory owing to the initially bad design.[172]

At the same time the ability of the navy to encourage civilian inventive talent was constrained by the reluctance to allocate public money on developing promising yet still unperfected inventions. This best documented example of this situation is the squabble between the Argo Company and the Admiralty in the development of the Pollen gunnery fire control computer.[173] Rather than continue to subsidize this small and financially shaky company, the Ordnance Department repeatedly urged the inventor sell-out his patents to one of the armaments giants. He refused. Although perhaps insensitive and high-handed, the Admiralty's behavior toward Pollen was understandable. Because research and development programmed were expensive and required sustained development effort, only large firms like Vickers Ltd. or Armstrong-Whitworth were in a position to assume the risks and costs normally associated with the sponsorship of inventions.[174] The Royal Navy would then step forward and buy the finished product.

In return for private companies continuing research and development, and maintaining construction capacity, the navy was obliged to direct a steady flow of orders for naval equipment to ensure the firms remained sufficiently profitable. In other words the relationship between the Admiralty and the private shipbuilding firms had evolved into one of mutual dependence. The navy had entered what historian William McNeill has termed the age of "command technology."[175] In order to obtain up-to-date naval equipment the Admiralty was compelled to underwrite the research and development efforts of private firms by promising lucrative contracts for the perfected weapon system. Only rarely did companies experience difficulties in justifying the costs of research and development to their customer. Under special circumstances, the Admiralty could reward firms with the promise of an oligopoly in the distribution of contracts, such as in the case of big-gun mountings. But costs of developing improved big gun mountings were so large they could be amortized only by directing towards those firms a steady flow of orders for large armored warships. These contracts were so lucrative they effectively determined which companies in Britain flourished and which foundered. During the period 1905–14, a dozen or so yards teetered on the verge of bankruptcy, maintaining their cash flow only by taking orders for merchant ships at cut prices and depleting reserves.[176] Some, like Thames Iron Works in 1912, went under.

This brief sketch of the interconnections between the Admiralty shipbuilding policy and the armaments firms will have demonstrated to the reader that Fisher's defense of battleship construction was not necessarily symptomatic of his anxiety to acquire the "dreadnoughts" themselves. His efforts in this direction can be also attributed to recognition of the need to preserve the warship-building industry. Obviously this could never be stated explicitly to Cabinet. The idea that an essential plank of British naval policy was to guarantee large contracts to the "armaments ring" was not likely to appeal to Liberal ministers on either economic or ideological grounds.[177] This is not to say that Fisher did not want any dreadnoughts. For his purposes they were better than pre-dreadnoughts and as he often used to remark, "half a loaf is better than no bread." Even so, in view of his stated preference for battle cruisers (which he continued to believe would one day be adopted as the standard armored warship for the Royal Navy), and his acknowledgment that the fleet was already amply provided with capital ships, suggest that his efforts to resist cuts in the construction budget probably stemmed more from industrial than military considerations.[178] After all, battle cruisers also required armor, big-guns and turbine engines.

There is other evidence for thinking that industrial considerations were at least as important as strategic ones. When in August 1908 the Cabinet offered to buy for the Royal Navy (at discount!) three Brazilian dreadnought battleships then under construction in England to prevent them being possibly sold to Germany, the Admiralty declined.[179] "We should prefer," the Board replied, "to give the shipbuilding trade, which is very depressed, the benefit of the work and the wages arising from fresh construction."[180] Fisher had yet another reason to refuse the offer. In the autumn of 1908, the DNC was working on the design of "Sans Pareil"—a new battle cruiser armed with eight new model 13.5-inch guns. There is overwhelming evidence that Fisher hoped this vessel would be adopted as the model for all six (later eight) capital units projected for the 1909–10 program.[181] But that came later.

Submarine Design and Production

While there were manifest advantages in exploiting private firms, the Admiralty recognized the drawbacks to the Royal Navy relying upon them too heavily. Fundamentally, private companies did not exist for the benefit of the state. Their ultimate goal was profit.[182] Consequently, while the Admiralty directed contracts towards selected firms in order to preserve productive capacity, at the same time they had to be careful to keep the field of supply wide enough to prevent collusion in pricing. In addition to exploiting the "invisible hand" of competition, the Admiralty also used the Royal Dockyards to monitor the costs of labor and material within the industry. Civil servants employed by the contracts department kept prices under review to ensure that the navy was not being exploited.[183] Profiteering was most difficult to detect in the submarine industry. This was because submarine construction was a highly specialized business about which few people properly understood. Furthermore, the Admiralty Board of 1902 had inadvertently made the task harder by granting Vickers a seven-year monopoly on submarine contracts in return for assuming all the costs of development and on the understanding sufficient capacity would be retained to meet all the navy's requirements. In 1905, due mainly to growing concern in Whitehall that Vickers were making "super-normal" profits on submarine contracts, the navy delayed the introduction of an improved type of submarine.[184]

The last major advance made by the navy in the field of submarine design was the **B** type approved at the end of 1903. Except for minor improvements in the arrangements of the batteries the **C** class was basically the same craft. In 1903, submarine design had been still very much constrained—rather than led—by the limits of engineering and technological knowledge.[185] Although the Admiralty acknowledged the superiority of the 300 ton vessels of the **B** class over earlier models, it was felt that "for seagoing purposes they will be of little use."[186] What the navy really wanted, declared the controller in January 1904, was a long-range vessel capable of operating on the high seas in any weather. "The sea limitations" of a submarine, he recognized, "will always be governed by the size of the boat." With this objective in mind, Captain Bacon was instructed "to rough out the design of a boat of 1000 tons displacement."[187] Nothing came of this exercise. And not until 1905 was the possibility of building an "oversea" boat again seriously considered when the Admiralty secured an appropriation under the 1905–6 estimates for one improved submarine.

On 23 June 1905, Capt. Henry Jackson, who had recently succeeded Admiral May as controller of the navy, assembled a select group of officers at the Admiralty to consider two alternative submarine designs.[188] Both sets of plans differed greatly from existing British boats. As French naval designers had discovered some eight years earlier, with existing engineering knowledge there was an effective limit to the size of a mono-hulled submarine. The easiest way of overcoming this technological barrier was to place the "ballast tanks" outside the pressure hull thereby leaving more room inside the hull for additional fuel or larger engines. Both prototypes laid before the submarine committee of 1905 incorporated this feature. This indicates that the Admiralty's principal goal was to develop larger submarines. The French, of course, had adopted the Laubeuf double-hull system. The British solution was somewhat different. The "C2" design had its ballast tanks on top, the "D" was given side or "saddle" tanks. The task of the committee was to chose which model to adopt as the prototype for future development. Eventually the "D" plans were chosen largely on account of its better anticipated underwater performance. It was "also agreed at the meeting that heavy-oil [diesel] engines should be adopted as soon as a suitable engine working with it is available."[189] The advantages were manifest: "a diesel engine which is about twice the weight and one and a half times the volume of a petrol engine for the same power" consumes "about half the weight and less than half the volume of fuel than an oil engine." In other words, for a given quantity of fuel a submarine propelled by diesels could proceed twice as far than it could if driven by a petrol engine. Diesel fuel, moreover, cost less than half the price of gasoline.[190] There is no evidence that the "D" type was selected in expectation of future operational requirements in the North Sea. If anything, the Submarine Committee appeared more concerned at keeping pace with the French.[191] In 1905, most if not all the Royal Navy's torpedo craft were still being designed primarily for action in the Channel.[192]

The contract for the new experimental submarine was not let in 1905–6. The Board of Admiralty was most annoyed to learn that Vickers was demanding £84,000 to build the new vessel. The price was £30,000—or 60 percent—more than the cost of a **C** class vessel. Jackson shared the Board's outrage.[193] At the meeting of the Submarine Committee he and Captain Bacon had "pointed out that the extra expense was a serious consideration in the case of vessels which must be built in numbers."[194] On 8 August Fisher set the limit "for the moment" at £60,000 per boat.[195] The Admiralty "preferred to have twelve single screw rather than eight or nine twin screw" submarines.[196] Other reasons for delay were also given. For instance, the committee was concerned that a suitable diesel engine had not yet been "made and *tried.*" After the meeting Bacon reminded Jackson that in his experience "makers are so apt to take a rosy view of the difficulties attending producing an engine" that "nothing short of the exact engine at work should be taken for granted."[197] In time Bacon's caution was proved justified. To some officers, however, this was no excuse for not constructing an experimental craft with an improved hull-form propelled by gasoline engines.

Capt. Edgar Lees, the new inspecting captain of submarines, was especially unhappy to be told that the type "D" project had been suspended. The news prompted him to write several forceful letters to Jackson urging him to reconsider, insisting that the technical objections to ordering the vessel immediately had been grossly exaggerated.[198] In a letter signaling him to "lay off," Bacon explained to Lees that the Admiralty had an ulterior motive for not placing the contract.[199] The 1902 Vickers's monopoly agreement included a clause which provided for both parties to share ownership of any subsequent patents taken out by either party connected with submarine boats. Vickers, however, had retained the right to set the final price on the finished product. Ever since the firm had habitually demanded what the Admiralty considered exorbitant prices for making the most trivial improvements to their submarines. The tender for the "D" type had been the last straw; subsequently the Admiralty became determined to renegotiate its agreement with Vickers and establish a closer check over prices and costs before letting further contracts. The navy could best be accomplish this goal by negotiating the right to build a few submarines in a Royal Dockyard under license from

Vickers.[200] "I started the designs of the C2 and D types," Bacon revealed, so as "in no way to infringe the Holland patents."[201] By thus intimating to Vickers that the navy was capable of designing and building its own submarines, the Admiralty hoped to bring about a moderation in prices.[202] The decision to order just seven of the twelve submarines authorized for 1905 was possibly another attempt to apply pressure.

In his reply to Captain Lees, Bacon explained that the Admiralty did not want to break totally with Vickers or incur the inconvenience of having to build all the navy's submarines in Royal Dockyards. "We cannot do better than cooperate with Messrs Vickers in building the number we want. They have experience which it would take three years for any other firm or the Dockyards to acquire."[203] Besides, he added, "for the Admiralty to have suddenly repudiated the validity of the patents would have been a very unfair proceeding."[204] The Admiralty only wanted Vickers to moderate their prices. Negotiations with the company, however, proceeded much slower than expected. Vickers was not so easily intimidated. In November, with still no compromise in sight, Lees lost patience and again wrote to the controller with his "views as to the real necessity of proceeding with the D design if we are not to be left hopelessly behind the French."[205] Bacon, however, continued to insist that the Admiralty should wait until a new agreement had been signed with Vickers.[206] It took another six months pressure before Vickers finally caved in. On 17 May 1906, Vickers licensed the Royal Navy to construct submarines in Royal Dockyards. Three months later the "D" type craft was ordered from Vickers at a contract price of £69,000.[207] Ironically, Bacon never realized the true magnitude of Vickers's profit margin. The company still made enormous profit—perhaps as much as 70 percent.[208] The net result of these shenanigans was that the experimental submarine H.M.S. *D1* did not begin her trials until late 1908. During the interim the Admiralty had little choice but to continue ordering the superseded C class.

The Home Fleet Saga

In May 1906, the Board of Admiralty decided that the only way to head off demands for more cuts in the next (1907–8) construction program would be to reduce the number of ships in full commission.[209] Decommissioning eleven armored ships was calculated to yield £250,000.[210] Added to further savings in naval works, Fisher calculated that enough money could be freed to meet the chancellor's demands for an overall reduction in expenditure without having to sacrifice the third armored warship projected under the 1906–7 program. "By no other means can we reduce the Navy Estimates as promised," Fisher insisted.[211] Lord Tweedmouth, however, was not at all happy with the trade-off. He realized that paying off battleships was a particularly "visible" economy, and one which was bound to attract accusations that Britain's naval supremacy was being jeopardized. It was with considerable mis-givings, therefore, that in June he reported to Cabinet that in order to achieve the government's set spending targets the Admiralty was plan-ning to retire seven battleships (three from the Channel Fleet and two each from the Atlantic and Mediterranean Squadrons) and four armored cruisers from active service and place them in nucleus crew reserve.[212]

For political reasons the first lord delayed warning the commanders in chief that the number of ships in their squadrons was about to be reduced.[213] In July, the government had came under fierce attack in the press and Parliament for departing from the Cawdor program by cutting an armored ship from the naval construction budget, and Tweedmouth had no wish to further inflame his critics. Thus it was not until the end of August 1906 that the news was released. To his dismay, Tweedmouth was immediately subjected to a most uncomfortable barrage of objec-tions from angry fleet commanders.[214] In an effort to calm his nerves, the first sea lord assured him:

> The present naval force at sea is greater in power than at the time of the Dogger Bank incident, when it was possible for France and Russia to have thrown in their lot against us, and we considered our naval strength *then* was amply sufficient. Now Russia is annihilated, France our friend, and Germany our only possible foe, many times weaker than ourselves; so how can we support or justify keeping up our strength at sea at a higher pitch than that?[215]

Before the Admiralty was able to publish the scheme of redistribution an officer on the staff of the commander in chief, Mediterranean, leaked the gist of the proposals to a hostile newspaperman.[216] "I am afraid we are likely to be in a great hucker about naval affairs," Tweedmouth subse-quently reported to the prime minister on 15 October, "the placing of six battleships and four armored cruisers in the nucleus crew reserve at home has now come out and there is a great outcry arising about it."[217] In an effort to quell the agitation, ten days later Fisher announced to the press that the Admiralty was planning to use the crewmen thus freed to improve the war readiness of the nucleus crew reserve by organizing the best ships into distinct squadrons. The ten armored warships scheduled to be withdrawn from active service in April 1907 would form the corps d'elite of a new "Home Fleet." In order that these ships could be mobi-lized even quicker than hitherto was possible, they would be manned by 60 percent of their war complements. Hitherto, two-fifths had been the normal.[218] In addition, the highly regarded Rear Adm. Sir Francis Bridgeman was to be made solely responsible for their fighting efficiency.[219] Fisher's attempt to dampen criticism had little effect. If anything, it served only to confuse matters by creating the impression that a second "fleet" was being established in home waters quite distinct from the Channel Fleet.[220]

Hostility to the new fleet organization was fueled by negative coverage given to the proposals in the press. Tory activists in Fleet Street, who had become restless at what they perceived as a lack of vigor displayed by their Party's leaders in attacking cuts in the House, deliberately amplified objections raised by Fisher's personal enemies.[221] The controversy over the "Home Fleet" was to have much more serious implications. From the moment he became first sea lord, Sir John Fisher had been subjected to constant abuse from various serving and retired naval officers, back-bench politicians and uninformed naval interest groups who disagreed with his policies and methods. But his opponents had been unable to mount effective opposition because they were themselves divided over which of Fisher's reforms were bad for the service. Although press criticism of the Admiralty briefly subsided in December 1906, the decision to create the Home Fleet had served as a rallying point for Fisher's enemies. The disparate groups subsequently coalesced into what became known as "the syndicate of discontent."[222] Their one common objective was to remove Sir John Fisher from power.

Compared to the activities of Col. Sir George Clarke, the press campaign waged against the formation of the Home Fleet was only a minor irritant. Readers will recall that throughout 1906, the secretary of the CID had been sniping at the Admiralty and giving support to the Cabinet campaign for drastic reductions in naval construction. To his indignation, Clarke first learned of "the proposed battleship reduction" from the *Standard*.[223] The prime minister, evidently, had not troubled to inform the CID of the decision he had endorsed some four months previously.[224] "I think that if reductions are to be made of this kind," he protested to Lord Esher on 15 October from his desk in the CID, "they ought to be considered here."[225] Clarke, it should be noted for future reference, was one of the very few men to notice that although the Admiralty was proposing net reductions in the "battleship force," at the same time they planned "to increase our torpedo boat and submarine preponderance."[226] He disapproved. The former army officer had never been impressed with submarines. Nor had he been receptive to the concept of the torpedo armed flotilla.[227] He persisted in equating naval power with battleships.[228]

Over the next four weeks Clarke synthesized the various arguments circulating against the formation of the Home Fleet and presented them

on paper to Campbell-Bannerman.[229] "I can conceive a case being made
out at the present time for reducing the number of ships in commission
with a view to economies," he reported to the prime minister on 15
November, "on the other hand, there are strong political reasons for
not reducing the Channel fleet."[230] What he most objected to was the proposal to reduce the number of fully commissioned battleships kept
in home waters down to fourteen—which was two fewer than the
strength of the High Sea Fleet across the North Sea. (Fisher had ignored
warnings this would be an easy opening for his critics to exploit.)[231]
The possession of a numerically stronger Channel Fleet, he argued,
always gave the British government a "moral and *political* advantage."[232]
Furthermore, "numerous writers in this country have been endeavouring
for some time to create a German scare, and one of the alarming
brochures of this nature received the imprimatur of Lord Roberts. It
is clear that this propaganda has produced in this country a certain
feeling of uneasiness and of suspicion of which it is necessary to take
account."[233] Clarke believed that in the public mind a numerically
stronger fleet "served the important purpose of interposing between our
shores and the imagined invasion, a force always superior to that of
Germany."[234]

There is sadly no direct evidence to indicate how much weight
Clarke's opinions carried with the prime minister, though he certainly
boasted his influence was great.[235] By contrast Fisher's reaction to the
paper was unequivocal. Colonel Clarke, he assured King Edward, had
mistaken the function of the new Home Fleet and had overstated the tactical weakness of the Channel Fleet.[236] The remaining fourteen battleships were by themselves qualitatively superior to the entire German
High Sea Fleet.[237] Although to naval experts this claim was tenable, laymen, who measured naval strength by counting numbers of battleships,
were not convinced.[238] Clarke was right: there was no way a British government could afford to be seen reducing the number of fully commissioned battleships in home waters below the strength of a rival navy. The
public did not understand such qualitative arguments. For that matter
neither did most government officials. Sir Charles Hardinge, for
instance, the permanent undersecretary at the Foreign Office, thought
that "the weakness of the Channel Fleet in comparison with the German
Fleet under Prince Henry is a positive scandal."[239] In November, he tried
to drum up support within the government for an independent inquiry
into the distribution of the fleet.[240]

The first sea lord very quickly became impatient at having to answer
every new point raised by his critics.[241] But he consistently refused to
divulge the function of the Home Fleet: this, he insisted, "is the

inscrutable secret of the Admiralty, and will remain so."[242] His refusal to explain clearly his strategic policy lost him a considerable number of friends. "In a country like ours, governed by *discussion,*" Lord Esher wrote to the Admiral, "a great man is never hanged. He hangs himself. Therefore pray be Machiavellian, and play upon the delicate instruments of public opinion with your fingers and not with your feet—however tempting the latter may be."[243] Thanks to Sir George Clarke's agitation, opposition to the Home Fleet within official circles refused to subside. By the beginning of 1907, Fisher had become sufficiently unnerved to consider modifying his stance.[244] In February, Clarke confided to Esher that the Channel Fleet would "probably be returned to sixteen if what I know is true."[245] Clarke expected the Atlantic squadron would be recalled from Gibraltar and amalgamated into the Channel Fleet.[246]

To everyone's surprise Fisher did not do this. Instead, reported an incredulous Louis Battenberg, "it is the intention of J[ohn] F[isher] to form the Sheerness/Chatham division of the Home Fleet of our eight best battleships." With good reason he asked: "where is the sense of this"?[247] The decision to attach the most powerful ships in the navy, including *Dreadnought* and the three *Invincible* class all-big-gun cruisers to what had been originally conceived as a reserve fleet was manifestly illogical.[248] Subsequent charges that the Home Fleet now was "neither a reserve nor a striking force" were fully justified.[249] Some years later Battenberg suggested to one correspondent that Fisher took this errant step because he had become so antagonized by attacks on his administration from Lord Charles Beresford, who had been selected to inherit command of the Channel Fleet, that he "was determined that Beresford would not have so big and honourable a command."[250] This charge may have had some basis, but the thought does not appear to have occurred to Battenberg until several years later. It is more likely that Fisher, in trying to side-step criticism, inadvertently tripped himself into making an even greater publicity blunder. On 5 March 1907, the first sea lord was summoned to explain the changes in fleet distribution to the Cabinet. Again Fisher refused to go into details, insisting that "to explain the matter clearly involves making public what must be kept most secret—our fighting plans."[251] Instead he impressed upon the assembly "the enormous advantage of the nucleus crew system."[252] Ministers were each given a memorandum which drove home the point: to keep the entire fleet fully manned would cost an additional four million.[253] This was language that the Cabinet understood. Approval for the creation of the new Home Fleet was subsequently granted.[254] Meanwhile, Sir George Clarke was left spluttering that "the entire organization (naval) in home waters is thoroughly bad."[255]

The Silent Fanfare

From the beginning it was Fisher's intention to organize the Home Fleet into a "real fighting fleet of the first quality and *peculiarly* adapted for the first onslaught of war."[256] The word in italics should be noted. When he first wrote to Tweedmouth with his idea for "a fresh 'Home Fleet,'" he indicated there were a number of subtle aspects to the scheme.[257] "You will see when I explain the details (too intricate for a letter)," he hinted, "how everything fits into our purpose."[258] Alas he never set down on paper what exactly he intended. As a result historians have assumed the squadron of battleships based at Chatham formed the core of the Home Fleet—taking little notice of the first sea lord's claim that things were not what they seemed.[259] "It is surely obvious to all," he hinted in another memorandum prepared for Cabinet, "that the whole of the vessels in reserve are not of equal fighting importance, and also it is manifest that some vessels, such, for instance, as torpedo craft and submarines, are wanted sooner than others."[260]

Under the order of council which created the Home Fleet:

> the entire flotilla of torpedo craft . . . and all submarines in full commission which are not allocated for local defense of Home Ports, together with all scouts, torpedo-gunboats, destroyers and their respective parent vessels, repair ships and mine laying vessels now in commission with nucleus or special service crews, under the command of the Admiral (D) and respective Captain (D)s will be affiliated to the Home Fleet, and be placed under the supreme command of the Commander-in-Chief, Home Fleet.[261]

Fisher, however, for some reason decided not to publicize this fact.[262] As a result, while the eyes of the politicians and public were fixed on the reshuffling of several old battleships, the redistribution of more than one hundred flotilla craft passed unnoticed.[263] One of those who did notice it was Capt. (later Adm.) Douglas Brownrigg. In November 1906, he wrote to Balfour's secretary drawing his attention to the unobtrusive movements of flotillas from the south to the east coast. Additional destroyers were brought home from overseas. "It is natural that no flourish of trumpets should be required over *this*," he cryptically noted.[264] The concentration of flotilla craft in home waters would have been even more noticeable if the Admiralty had gone ahead with plans to reallocate submarine flotillas to Dover, Harwich, Hull and Dundee. But "in view of the contiguity of existing facilities" at Portsmouth, and doubtless the cost of setting up new bases, it was decided that in peace time only a reinforced flotilla at Harwich would be permanently maintained on the east coast.[265] What Fisher hinted at but never explained was that the torpedo flotillas were the core of the Home Fleet; and flotilla defense was the strategy *"peculiarly* adapted" for the defense of the narrow seas.

In a confidential memorandum written to mollify angry fleet commanders who had been stripped of their destroyer flotillas, the Admiralty clearly explained that:

> it has to be observed that new strategic conditions necessitate the employment of the largest practicable number to be obtained of these vessels for North Sea service, and for this reason a number of torpedo-boat destroyers have been brought home from China, the Mediterranean and Gibraltar to strengthen the home force, leaving only a small proportion of torpedo craft abroad. [Also] the political circumstances were quite different when originally twenty-four destroyers were attached to the Channel Fleet.[266]

To take their place, the Admiralty encouraged those self-governing Dominions interested in forming their own navies to build large flotilla craft capable of supporting Royal Navy armored squadrons operating in distant waters.[267]

Fisher's boast that the torpedo craft of the Home Fleet were intended to be "the advanced guard and first striking force of the whole fleet," in other words the core of the Home fleet, is corroborated by evidence of changes in the distribution of personnel manning ships in home waters.[268] Subsequent to the decommissioning of the eleven armored vessels in 1906–7, the crews of all torpedo craft in nucleus crew reserve were strengthened from 40 to 80 percent of their war complements. Between October 1906 and April 1907, personnel allocated to flotilla craft jumped 20 percent from 10,315 to 12,486.[269] Colonel Repington, military correspondent for the *Times,* grasped what was intended. Commenting on the plans to establish submarine and destroyer bases on the east coast, he explained to his editor, "this *apparently* defensive organization will not prevent Sir J[ohn] F[isher] from using the whole of the boats offensively when he pleases, and that knowledge of the existence of this mobile defense on the east coast would be a far greater deterrent to me if I were a German officer than the existing distribution."[270]

The ability to rely upon "flotilla defense" to prevent invasion also gave the Admiralty far greater flexibility in deployment of squadrons of armored warships. Whereas "the constitution of the Home Fleet, and its effective administration and efficiency, entirely rests on its retention in home waters," the Admiralty explained in June 1907, that "the Channel and Atlantic Fleets are on another and entirely different basis. They are commissioned definitely for two years' service, and could be sent tomorrow on distant and prolonged service, involving indefinite absence from home, should political considerations render it necessary, without its causing any administrative inconvenience."[271] Flotilla defense was, therefore, the hinge of Fisher's naval policy. Together with an incomparable network of coaling stations and overseas bases, the Admiralty now had the ability to send squadrons of armored vessels to reinforce the outer marches of the Empire without exposing the British Isles to the risk of invasion.[272]

CHAPTER 6

Illusions and Realities: Naval Strategic Planning, 1905–1909

There is another theory with regard to the submarine. We are going to
have a new British tradition, and a new British doctrine, that the main
fleet is to remain in harbour because the fleet is in danger at sea! . . .
Nelson would turn in his grave . . .

Adm. Lord Charles Beresford, May 1914.

Before 1914, few Englishmen would have disagreed that the maintenance of naval supremacy was the foundation of British commercial
prosperity and imperial security. Public confidence in the Royal Navy
was concomitantly absolute and latent determination to uphold naval
strength whatever the cost was a political factor that no British government could disregard.[1] This troubled certain Liberal ministers, who saw
that current high levels of defense expenditure precluded spending on
social reform. Despite the Cabinet's best efforts, in 1908 the Royal Navy
still swallowed about 25 percent of annual state revenue. To some, the
Admiralty's ability to withstand government pressure for cuts in the navy
estimates was deeply frustrating. "In the present humour of the country
about warships, there is no economy to be looked for in that quarter,"
complained John Morley (secretary of state for India) in 1908, "the more
we spend in novelties of every sort upon the water, the more popular will
be the spending ministers with the public."[2]

Compared with men like Balfour, Arnold-Forster, Lansdowne and
Selborne, Liberal ministers were ignorant of how sea power actually
worked. They assumed that naval combat was an affair of close block-
ades and battleships. Whenever naval officers tried to explain the necessity of maintaining a balanced force, invariably the politicians asked
them to simplify their demands by expressing their requirements in numbers of battleships. Yet, for a combination of financial and political rea-

sons, the Admiralty did little to disabuse their new masters of these out-dated notions. During the Fisher administration, for instance, the two-power standard was recognized as an effective bulwark against drastic cuts in the navy estimates. Though it must also be acknowledged that even if circumstances had been different, an attempt by the sea lords publicly to declare that the utility of battleships had declined would have been a difficult and dangerous undertaking. The truth was by no means self-evident even to "naval experts" with a fuller understanding of naval war-fare. Furthermore, the Liberal Cabinet's simplistic understanding of naval affairs was not entirely the product of lack of interest in or study of the subject. Politicians of all colors were generally predisposed to thinking about the Royal Navy more as an instrument of deterrence and diplomat-ic influence than as a fighting force. From this viewpoint, prestige count-ed for more than operational effectiveness. Battleships, they had been told for many years, were the ultimate symbols of naval power. Changing such deep-rooted attitudes could not be accomplished overnight.

Historians are no less guilty of misunderstanding the nature of British sea power. To be fair, however, it must be said that this is large-ly attributable to the fundamental errors of leading scholars in the field. By misrepresenting events, historians of Edwardian naval policy have compromised the efforts of their political and diplomatic history colleagues. British naval policy and state financial policy were more complicated and interrelated than has been generally realized. Most his-torians have accepted without question the proposition that up to August 1914, Britain's naval leaders envisaged fighting the next war against Germany; that their strategy for victory involved nothing more sophisti-cated than offensive operations against the enemy coast; and that naval operations would climax in a decisive clash of battle fleets somewhere in the southern half of the North Sea.[3] Marder, for instance, while rec-ognizing that Fisher in fact "had no great use" for close blockade, insisted that his strategy for war against Germany involved a "modified" system of observation blockade by light craft inside the Heligoland Bight and intended to keep the supporting main fleet a respectable distance away from "the nearest German destroyer base."[4] He also believed that an integral part of Jacky's plan involved "the capture of one or more German islands, to be established as an oversea base for the [observa-tional] blockading flotillas."[5] Marder also insisted that Fisher saw deci-sive battle as the ultimate end of naval strategy. Other writers have read much more into Fisher's expressions of interest in amphibious warfare. A few have gone so far as to suggest that aggressive "brown water" com-bined operations were at the heart of his strategic vision: that he envis-aged "the massing of overwhelming naval strength on the very doorstep of the enemy, beating in all his naval and coastal defences, and opening the enemy's seaboard to the possibility of a British military descent."[6] But it is not easy to reconcile Fisher's supposed advocacy of such reckless amphibious schemes with his more frequent prophecies on the power of the torpedo armed flotilla.[7] Those who propound such theories, moreover, tend to ignore his explicit predictions about the impact submarines would have upon the conduct of war.[8]

The one fact even the best historians accept is that Fisher was an unimaginatively conventional strategist. Paul Kennedy has suggested that although the admiral possessed a genius for recognizing the potential of new weapon systems even before they had been perfected, paradoxically:

> [Jacky] appears to have had little *consistent* appreciation of the many practical ways in which this newer weaponry would undermine the effectiveness of his beloved Royal Navy: for example, that neither the German *nor* the British fleets dare cruise in the North Sea when those waters were infested by submarines; that a close blockade was a thing of the past; that amphibious landings [on the German coast] would be immensely difficult, if not impossible to carry out in the face of the enemy.[9]

Critics and admirers alike have generally agreed Fisher expended most of his energy dealing with questions of matériel policy and so "had little or no time—or inclination—to consider the fundamentals of naval strategy and particularly the extent to which the new technology was revolutionising the conduct of naval warfare."[10] As a corollary to this, historians have generally assumed that Fisher introduced all-big-gun armored vessels merely to improve the fighting efficiency of the battle fleet.[11] His strategic myopia has been partially excused by suggestions that most of his contemporaries appeared to share this same weakness. Historians have thus concluded that the entire British naval leadership possessed a "crudely Mahanian vision of the workings of sea power."[12] Or put another way: "the Admiralty fixed its mind on the prospect of a single great battle that would decide the command of the sea" and would not even consider other ways of applying naval force.[13] In light of the evidence already reviewed these criticisms of Fisher seem unjustified.[14] While the majority of naval officers serving before 1914 may have possessed a broadly Mahanian outlook, historians should not be automatically assume that the opinions expressed by fleet officers ever reflected "that imponderable and unknown quantity—the mind of the British Admiralty."[15] As Capt. Charles Ottley explained to War Minister Richard Haldane on 11 December 1909, "not one naval officer out of fifty has any knowledge of what the British fleet will do in war, or how it will do it."[16]

Recent scholarship has presented a more rational basis for Fisher's strategic thinking on a war against Germany. Avner Offer conclusively disproved Arthur Marder's assertion that "British naval thinking in the prewar decade did not anticipate the extraordinary degree to which blockade would throttle the German war economy in 1914–18."[17] He showed that during Fisher's administration, the trade division of the Naval Intelligence Department made a detailed (albeit simplistic) study of Germany's vulnerability to systematic economic blockade.[18] Not only did the Board of Admiralty consider this scheme, he argued, but sometime between 1905 and 1908 it "became a central element in British war preparation."[19] The evidence seems irrefutable. Yet despite having argued so forcibly that the Admiralty pursued a more sophisticated understanding of naval grand strategy than previously suspected, there are indications that the author found it difficult to let go of the idea that the navy's operational policy remained essentially Mahanian.[20] He offered no explanations for how precisely the Admiralty intended to enforce the commercial blockade, or what measures were thought to be necessary to contain the High Sea Fleet inside the North Sea while the Royal Navy was throttling the German economy.

Discovering the Admiralty's operational intentions is complicated by the paucity of formal expositions of "strategic policy" dating from this period.[21] Few such documents were ever written. It must be remembered that at the beginning of the twentieth century the majority of Britain's naval leaders worked in offices along the dark corridor leading from the staircase outside the Admiralty board room. Most discussion on naval strategy was informal and conducted orally. Naval leaders did not consider the creation of detailed written war plans to be necessary, and made no attempt to compile such documents before 1912. Fisher encouraged this informality. Aware that there was considerable opposition to his radical theory of naval war, even within Whitehall, he deliberately avoiding expressing his strategic thoughts in official writing for fear such documents might be used against him. Most other clues to the Admiralty's preparations for war have been lost with the destruction of nearly all the files of administrative correspondence generated within the departments of intelligence, ordnance, mobilization, and personnel.[22] Fragments have survived only by chance. The only set of papers from this period which appear to offer historians any coherent picture of the Admiralty's thoughts on North Sea strategy are the verbal and written statements given by naval officers to the Committee of Imperial Defense.[23]

⟹◆⟸

Between 1906 and 1910, the Liberal Cabinet conducted three major investigations into aspects of national defense that compelled the

Admiralty to give the CID an explanation of their strategic policy. No sooner had the Conservative ministry left office, indeed, than various interest groups began pressing the incoming government to exhume the old strategical problems recently laid to rest by Arthur Balfour. The most vocal and certainly most persistent of these was the National Service League which since the end of the Boer War had been campaigning for the introduction of some form of military conscription for all male adults in Britain.[24] The appointment of Field Marshal Lord Roberts, one of the country's most respected soldiers, to head this organization in early 1906 provided the National Service League with a clearer sense of direction. Roberts demanded the formation of a large home defense army to serve as an insurance against the possibility of a sudden invasion. So strongly did he feel on this subject, indeed, that several months earlier he had resigned as special representative to the CID after Balfour had dismissed such a precaution as unnecessary.[25] As soon as the Conservatives were out of office, Roberts and his band started agitating for this decision to be reviewed in light of recent changes in diplomatic conditions. Mr. Balfour, they pointed out, had examined the possibility of a French rather than German invasion. The Admiralty had persuaded him that a "bolt from the blue" was impossible largely because the French lacked sufficient commercial shipping to gather in secret the transport to carry an invasion army.[26] Since then, Roberts and his followers claimed, Germany had become a more likely and much more formidable threat to British interests. The campaign for an inquiry into the possibility of a German invasion also received quiet encouragement from the newly constituted Army General Staff.

Throughout 1906 and 1907, Sir John Fisher fought hard against the establishment of a new invasion inquiry.[27] From his perspective the navy had nothing to gain and everything to lose. In 1904, the prime minister had placed the entire responsibility for protecting the country against invasion and raids in the hands of the Admiralty.[28] And along with these responsibilities the navy had received priority in the allocation of limited defense resources. Fisher was convinced that the generals were interested only in exploiting every opportunity that occurred during such an investigation to demand a larger slice of the defense budget.[29] And any War Office success would inevitably jeopardize future naval estimates. In his opinion, securing adequate funding for the navy was much more important than achieving harmony in national strategic policy. Following the appointment in 1907 of Gen. William Nicholson as chief of the General Staff,[30] the first sea lord's suspicions of the army's motives bordered on paranoia.[31] After being humiliated at the 1903 invasion inquiry, he reminded the DNI, Nicholson had defiantly proclaimed "his day would yet come to conquer."[32] The general had always refused to admit the pri-

macy of the Royal Navy in imperial defense; he was, moreover, a notoriously abrasive personality who antagonized almost everyone with
whom he came into contact.[33] Cooperation with such a man was quite
impossible.

Of course Fisher could not express his opposition to the establishment of a government inquiry in such bold terms. Instead he blustered
that another invasion inquiry so soon after the last would suggest to the
public that the government lacked confidence in the Board.[34] This was a
weak argument and he knew it.[35] It also earned him admonitions from
some of his staunchest friends. "Your functions are not only to believe
that you possess a navy strong enough to defeat the Germans at all
points," warned Lord Esher, "but to justify the belief that is in you, wherever and whenever required! Tiresome perhaps but part of your day's
work."[36] Fisher, however, was unrepentant. The generals, he replied to
Esher, "will trot out reams of foolscap and miles of railway sidings at
Hamburg and Bremen, and millions of German soldiers who can get in
and out of a train in 5 seconds," then go on to explain how quickly the
German army could disembark on the east coast of Britain.[37] But they
would never say, the first sea lord protested, how the invasion army
would pass across the North Sea without being intercepted by the Royal
Navy. Ultimately, in September 1907, Campbell-Bannerman appointed
Chancellor Asquith to chair a subcommittee of the CID to investigate this
possibility.

Fisher had other reasons for not wanting to face such an inquiry at
this time. He was especially concerned that any investigation would
force him to discuss the navy's operational plans for the North Sea. This,
he explained to Lord Tweedmouth, had to be avoided at all costs.[38]
Security had little do with it. Fisher was more afraid that an open discussion of current strategic policy would expose the widening schisms
within the service caused by growing opposition to his administration
among fleet officers. According to Capt. Charles Ottley, there were at
this time at least "half a dozen schools of thought within the navy" each
with their own strategic theories; and all the others regarded Fisher's
policy as "retrograde."[39] Such rifts were not new. In the early 1890s, for
instance, there had been a fierce debate within the navy over whether
fleet commanders should use a newly developed signaling system to control the movements of all ships in their squadron, or allow individual
captains to use their own initiative in bringing the enemy to action.[40] In
1907, however, Fisher's determination to engineer his revolution in
strategic policy, and the sometimes "ruthless, relentless and remorse-
less" methods he used to force through reform, had exacerbated these
natural schisms within the service to extremes. As a result, Fisher found

that support for his reforms was at times insecure even within the Board of Admiralty. But so long as he could rely upon the unanimous support of his closest followers, often referred to as the "fishpond," he was generally able to implement his policy. As we shall see, however, Fisher increasingly discovered that his supporters were themselves divided over the wisdom of his more radical proposals. At these times Jacky was vulnerable to counterattack.

On no subject was the Royal Navy more divided than over the question of North Sea strategy. Opposition was already growing to the adoption of flotilla defense among senior fleet officers. Up to this time, the Admiralty had managed to conceal from outsiders the strength of opposition to official policy from within the service, by a combination of appeals for loyalty and threats of courts-martial for dissenters who betrayed secrets. Members of the syndicate of discontent, however, were only too keen to broadcast this fact as justification for an open ended investigation of Fisher's administration.[41] And giving evidence before a CID inquiry, of course, would allow them to criticize Fisher's board without danger of disciplinary action. Chief among these antagonists was Adm. Lord Charles Beresford, the fleet commander in chief, who had long aspired to the office of first sea lord. So keen was he to eject Fisher from Whitehall that he seemed deaf to warnings that his actions threatened to undermine public confidence in the service, or that such displays of disharmony prejudiced the Admiralty's dealings with the government. Politicians disliked inconsistent or conflicting advice on defense matters. Since their embarrassing performances in front of Balfour's CID, the soldiers had learned to suppress ruthlessly all internal dissent over military policy. These underlying political considerations must always be kept in mind when analyzing the Admiralty's presentation to the 1907 invasion inquiry.[42]

The testimony given to the CID by Fisher, Tweedmouth and the director of Naval Intelligence between December 1907 and May 1908, has given scholars the impression that the Board of Admiralty during this period was steering a conventional strategic course. In the words of one naval historian, during committee meetings "the air was thick with historical arguments drawn from earlier wars."[43] The naval representatives to the CID, it is argued, built their entire defense upon the argument that history taught no hostile power had ever attempted to invade the British Isles without first seeking to win command of the sea in order to secure their army's lines of communication.[44] It thus followed that so long as the British fleet remained supreme invasion would remain a chimera.[45] Without doubt, the Admiralty's case was a masterly exposition of the principles of naval warfare in the age of sail. But it clearly offered little relevance to the conduct of naval war against Germany in the twentieth century. It also conveyed the impression that the Royal Navy's approach to strategy before 1914 was amateurish and outdated. Nothing, for instance, was said about the value of submarines and mines as a deterrent to offensive naval operations inside the North Sea.

What critics have failed to realize, however, is that both sets of service chiefs who attended the 1907 invasion inquiry were much more interested in maneuvering for political position than debating real strategic problems.[46] At the 1913 invasion inquiry, the then first lord of Admiralty—Winston Churchill—frankly explained that:

> five years ago the position of the Admiralty was that the Army estimates ought to be greatly cut down—that was Lord Fisher's position—in order to economise and spend money on the Navy, and that, if that were done, there was absolutely no need of any regular army at all, or of only a small one. That was the sort of position that was taken up. The Admiralty arguments were all pitched in that tone from beginning to end, and lots of statements were made which required considerable modification. Truths were pushed to the point where they ceased really to carry a truthful meaning. The War Office, on the other hand, took the opposite line. . . .[47]

In other words, the arguments employed by both sets of service chiefs were inspired more by financial and political considerations than strategic principles. Indeed, at the time, several ministers recognized documents purporting to be statements of Admiralty policy to be in fact examples of "Sir John's semi-confidential manifestos, printed for the advantage of the press." Fisher made these "secret" documents available to anyone with a platform who was willing to amplify his navalist propaganda.[48] Examples can be found in the private papers of many prominent journalists and politicians.

The explanation for why the Admiralty misrepresented their true strategic opinions at the CID, and why Fisher chose to employ the "historical" case rather than explain "flotilla defense," is found in the private correspondence of the naval representatives involved in the invasion inquiry. From the very beginning, Fisher declared he was far too busy fighting battles over the estimates to spend time himself preparing the Admiralty's brief to the CID.[49] He thus delegated "the whole thing" into the hands of the director of Naval Intelligence.[50] Although obliged to attend the meetings, Fisher made no attempt to hide his disdain for the proceedings and used the occasions to catch up on his correspondence.[51] "I am here wasting my time," he wrote to one friend during one particularly slow afternoon at Number 2, Whitehall Gardens, "considering an invasion of England by Germany under the inconceivable conditions of the 'bolt from the blue' school."[52]

The invasion inquiry came at a most inconvenient time for the Admiralty. After having serving more than three years as DNI, in September 1907 the experienced Capt. Charles Ottley retired from the service. He subsequently became secretary of the CID in succession to Sir George Clarke. While the appointment of a sailor to this post was certainly of benefit to the navy generally, Fisher suffered as a result of the transfer. Ottley had been perhaps his most stalwart lieutenant inside the Admiralty. More than any other officer's his strategic views mirrored those of his chief. Nevertheless Ottley had to go. The Board had already granted him one extension to his term of office in Whitehall, a second was impossible. Also, having never commanded a line of battle ship for a minimum of six years he was not eligible for promotion to flag rank on the active list and was thus facing mandatory retirement.

The officer nominated to become Ottley's successor was something of an unknown quantity to the first sea lord. Capt. Edmund Slade had a reputation within the service as an intellectual and a keen student of history. He was also something of a loner. Prior to his appointment as DNI he had served as the president of the War College.[53] When the two had first met Fisher had thought Slade "clever."[54] But this initially favorable impression quickly evaporated after it became apparent that he was an officer who firmly believed that historical "principles" of maritime strategy transcended advances in technology and were thus applicable to the strategic environment of the early twentieth century.[55] Slade, for instance, firmly believed in amphibious warfare and in the practicability of close blockade.[56] As one historian has noted, his strategic thought had a decidedly eighteenth-century flavor.[57] Slade was also politically rather naive.[58] Being a straight-forward character, he regarded all inter-service rivalry as "childish" and political maneuverings (even by politicians) as "dishonest."[59] He once seriously suggested that the Admiralty ought to endorse the army's campaign for increased estimates: he thought Fisher's refusal to do so a symptom of his small-mindedness![60] He never seemed to understand that the upholding of Britain's naval supremacy depended first and foremost upon the negotiation of adequate funding. Slade could never quite grasp why Fisher would not find time to work out strategic problems with him in detail, preferring instead to spend his time entertaining politicians. He never saw the connection—although at times he came close. "I think it is as much or even more the estimates than invasion which is waying [*sic*] on his mind," he speculated in a letter to the historian Julian Corbett dated 1 December 1907.[61] But twelve months later he was still complaining that Fisher's "whole energies are now given up to intriguing with the politicians and not to working out war problems."[62] Whereas Ottley had worked closely with the first sea lord in the preparation of the navy estimates and had been a member of the

Admiralty estimates committee, his successor was rarely invited to participate in discussions concerning financial questions.[63] It is fair to say that Slade's intellectual horizon was strictly limited to that of a naval theorist.[64]

As early as August 1907, Sir John Fisher had commenced shooting his own broadsides at the invasion lobby. At the end of that month he circulated a document entitled "Invasions and Raids," containing a miscellaneous collection of documents prefaced with a memorandum of his own composition.[65]

> We have now a permanent flotilla of our latest type of submarine, with their attendant vessels, stationed at Harwich . . . similarly there are permanently on the same coast the active service destroyers of the Eastern group . . . is it conceivable that with these never absent, always ready, irresistible weapons of attack, able to commit unutterable havoc amongst helpless thousands crowding the transports, the masses of transports necessary to effect the operation of an invasion, or even the lesser number obligatory for a raid, would dare to emerge from the German ports until these vessels have been swept away? But who is to sweep them away? We have 123 destroyers and forty submarines. The Germans have 48 destroyers and one submarine![66]

Days later Fisher came close to revealing flotilla defense. "If we are not safe from invasion," he wrote angrily to the Prince of Wales, "then make us so. Spend money on submarines, destroyers, etc., but don't waste money on an armed mob."[67] [A conscript army.]

Slade, with his strong belief in the lessons of history, disliked Fisher's revolutionary strategic theory of "flotilla defense." Throughout his term of office as DNI he consistently deprecated the value of submarines.[68] Though by this time it was Slade, not Fisher, who was out of step with majority opinion within the Admiralty. In November 1907, the officers serving on the naval estimates committee unanimously agreed that in future conflicts "the use of submarines on enemy coasts" was "inevitable" and recommended that money should be set aside for building a flotilla of suitable craft.[69] In 1908, Captain Ottley observed that "it *is* today *absolutely* certain that a single British torpedo boat or submarine manned by a dozen men can send two or three Atlantic liners (each holding perhaps 3000 or 4000 troops) to the bottom by merely pressing a button."[70]

When Fisher first asked Slade in the autumn of 1907 how he proposed to handle the invasion inquiry, the DNI suggested that instead of risking controversy by outlining the flotilla concept, the Admiralty should instead emphasize there was no historical precedent for any power attempting to launch an invasion before attaining command of the sea.

He wanted—in his own words—to avoid "figures and details" and "keep the thing on broad principles."[71] Fisher certainly realized that this approach offered advantages, aware as he was that the invasion lobby was intending to call Adm. Lord Charles Beresford, the fleet commander in chief, "to give evidence against the Admiralty."[72] Beresford, as we shall see below, was utterly opposed to flotilla defense. Not discussing current operational policy, however, removed the justification for calling Beresford to testify. This is probably why Fisher subsequently authorized Slade to employ his historical arguments. Last minute doubts were allayed after the DNI recruited his personal friend Julian Corbett, the naval historian, whose opinions Fisher respected.[73] Unbeknown to Fisher, however, Slade was also keen to see the Admiralty mend some fences with the War Office. "The more I think of this invasion business," the DNI privately told Corbett after the latter agreed to serve as his assistant, "the more I am pleased it should have come up, as we now ought to have a good chance of shewing that the Army and Navy are not two separate forces, but only divisions of one force."[74] Corbett agreed.[75] Publicly admitting the army had a role to play in home defense, both felt, would help "bringing the two services together a little more."[76] While steps in this direction were certainly desirable, in the prevailing financial climate, they were neither attainable nor wise.

On the morning of 9 December, Fisher and Lord Tweedmouth were finally allowed to see the position paper drafted by Slade and Corbett. Both immediately lodged strong protests at the proposed concessions to the War Office it contained. Fisher doubtless recalled that at the last invasion inquiry the soldiers had made a great deal out of the Admiralty's admission that however unlikely raids were still possible.[77] The first lord was apparently even more "bloodthirsty" than Sir John Fisher.[78] "Since you left I have seen Lord Tweedmouth," Slade reported to Corbett later that day. "He wanted to cut out all references to the Army and I had a great fight with him over that. He wants [merely] to say that our Navy must be sufficiently strong to cope with any consideration."[79] Considering that at that moment the Admiralty was battling with the Cabinet and War Office over the 1908–9 estimates, it is slightly surprising that the DNI managed to dissuade his superiors from insisting upon these changes.[80] Thanks to Slade, nevertheless, during the opening days of the invasion inquiry the Admiralty exercised noticeable "self-effacement" and "self-restraint" while the invasion lobby presented its case.[81] As the concurrent naval estimates crisis intensified, however, the DNI came under more pressure from his superiors to assume a more aggressive posture towards the War Office. On 20 December, Slade reported to Corbett that his masters were again "very anxious to go back to the contention that the Navy can guarantee that nothing comes across but I don't want to put it in such a bold way. It will only get the military backs up all round—we want them to see they are required [so] as long as they do not take too great a view of their relative importance."[82] Against their better judgement Fisher and Tweedmouth again withdrew their objections.[83]

As the inquiry progressed, Sir John Fisher became steadily more uneasy with Slade's presentation. "He thinks we have got ourselves into a hornets nest," the DNI informed Corbett on 24 December.[84] "It is only because he will not be honest with himself and looks at the whole thing from a partisan point of view rather than from a broad stand point."[85] From the first sea lord's perspective, however, Slade's historical arguments were abstractions. The DNI failed to emphasize the value of wireless telegraphy and the development of the torpedo armed flotilla, or explain that because of these inventions overseas invasion was now a much more difficult operation than it had been in the age of sail— arguments that had impressed the CID back in 1903. At times Fisher's annoyance at Slade's timidity boiled over. On several occasions he elbowed his advocate aside and launched himself at the soldiers. On 4 April 1908, Slade recorded in his diary that "Sir J. said a great deal about submarines—never becoming obsolete—no enemy's ships reaching our coasts etc.—very wild statements."[86] Afterwards Slade managed to persuade Fisher to have the entire text of his views on "flotilla warfare" expunged.[87] The minutes of that meeting show the secretariat subsequently deleted the offending paragraphs.[88] Although on this occasion Fisher acquiesced, at subsequent meetings he again publicly contradicted the DNI by stressing the importance of submarines.[89]

By sticking to his historical arguments and employing narrow definitions of sea power Slade may have managed to score a series of debating points at the CID.[90] But in his final report Asquith failed to reendorse the absolute primacy of the navy in national defense.[91] "There is," as Lord Esher explained to the king:

> a novel condition attached by the committee, which has come prominently forward in consequence of the evidence laid before them by Lord Roberts, and it is in order to make sure an expedition fitted out secretly in German ports, could not effect a landing by *evading* the *fleet*, an Army must be kept *in this country*, at all times, of such strength, that any hostile Force, in order to have a chance of success, must come 70,000 strong.

This condition, Esher felt, "very materially strengthens the hands of the Secretary of State for War against those who have been anxious to reduce the Army."[92] This of course did not please Fisher, or do much for

Slade's career prospects. Anything that strengthened the army's hand weakened the navy's claim upon limited defense resources. An officer who proved successful as DNI could have expected to remain in the post for at least three years: Slade's term lasted just one year and four months. At the end of 1908 he was "kicked upstairs" with the rank of rear admiral and shipped off to the East Indies because, as Capt. Herbert King-Hall explained to his brother, George, a rear admiral, "the Admiralty wished to get rid of him as DNI."[93]

Naval War Planning against Germany

The Admiralty did not begin making formal preparations for war against Germany before the so-called Moroccan crisis during the summer of 1905.[94] It began in early 1905 with an attempt by France to extend her influence in North Africa. Germany took exception to French action in Morocco and a quarrel ensued. The British, who cared little for Morocco, at first paid little attention. As the Germans became more aggressive in pressing their point of view, however, the British moved steadily closer towards declaring open support for France.[95] The increasingly Euro-centric shift in the orientation of British foreign policy created a major problem for the Board of Admiralty. Hitherto, the Royal Navy had been organized and equipped as a force for imperial defense. It had been expected that the next war would be fought on the world's oceans protecting British merchant shipping from marauding squadrons of French or Russian armored cruisers, not supporting military operations on the European continent.[96] An oceangoing fleet designed to achieve control of the trade routes could not be easily adapted to fight coastal operations. There was another consideration. How, during a period of financial limitation, could the Royal Navy afford to build warships suitable for offensive operations in the North Sea and still maintain a fleet capable of meeting its imperial commitments?

The foundation of the Admiralty's first plan for war against Germany was built upon the Royal Navy's ability to interdict all oceanic trade passing through the North Sea and the English Channel. In June 1905, Charles Ottley, then DNI, noted that "the British Isles, lying like a breakwater six hundred miles long, athwart the path of German trade with the west" gave the Royal Navy a stranglehold over German trade; an effective "blockade of the German ports would today *sever* an artery, essential, it seems to me, to the financial existence of Germany."[97] In April 1906, Fisher referred to the commercial blockade as being "our great anti-German weapon."[98] Two years later, Ottley reminded the first lord that "throughout the whole time I was DNI the Admiralty claimed that the geographical position of this country and her preponderant seapower combined to give us a certain and simple means of strangling Germany at sea."[99] The idea that the destruction of German oceanic trade would be sufficient to compel Germany to sue for peace was acknowledged by one officer serving in the NID in 1907, "to represent the view of a considerable section of those well qualified to judge."[100] Papers in the Admiralty archives confirm that between 1906 and 1909 the trade division of the NID made a detailed appraisal of the impact a blockade would have upon the German economy.[101] The secret instructions given to the British naval delegation (led by the ubiquitous Charles Ottley) attending the 1907 Hague Peace Conference, further indicate that the Admiralty was intent on waging economic warfare against Germany.[102]

While the Admiralty planners agreed that a commercial blockade would form the main thrust of the navy's war effort, this consensus did not extend to operational policy inside the North Sea. Setting up cordons to interdict German oceanic trade would consume only a fraction of the navy's resources and provided no role for the armored squadrons. There seemed little glory to be won in performing such operations. More optimistic officers hoped that sooner or later the High Sea Fleet would put to sea in an attempt to break up the lines of blockade, thus offering the British battle fleet an opportunity to win a second Trafalgar, but Fisher was not so sure the Germans would be so foolish. Indeed, he expressed reservations at the wisdom of the British fleet actively seeking battle. The first sea lord did not object to the idea of bringing the enemy to action under favorable circumstances. He simply believed that deploying armored warships in the North Sea was always going to involve a high degree of risk. He consistently maintained that to avoid a surprise torpedo attack, "our armored units are not wanted there at the first outbreak of war."[103] Fisher was even more secretive about what he planned to do in the second phase of the war—once the fleet was fully mobilized. It is possible that he had not yet finally made up his own mind.

A number of senior officers thought that such a policy of "wait and see" would be the wisest course. Admiral of the Fleet Sir Arthur Wilson, the man designated to command the war fleet in any major conflict, believed that "the action to be taken would depend so entirely on extremely complicated and uncertain political conditions that it would be extremely difficult to frame any plan of operations beforehand."[104] This was also Ottley's view. He thought that "to lay down a hard and fast plan of sea operations against an enemy the disposition of whose forces cannot be accurately foreseen, and without information as to the political circumstances under which hostilities might be expected, is futile."[105] Another secret report written by Ottley in January 1907, indicates he was sympathetic to Fisher's idea of employing only flotilla craft in the North Sea.

[E]ven today, in her numerous flotilla of fast craft (scouts, destroyers and torpedo-boats) this country already possesses the nucleus of a mosquito fleet, which, while it admittedly does not possess the wide radius of action of our present unarmoured cruisers, will at all events be able to press home its investigations off enemy's ports fronting upon the *Narrow Seas* and *German Ocean*, [North Sea] with a well grounded confidence that, if chased, it may show a clean pair of heels to an enemy in superior force.[106]

Whether or not political opinion would have allowed Fisher to rely upon "steady pressure" exerted by the commercial blockade and flotilla defense to deny the North Sea to the enemy's large ships is another question.

After the war scare in January 1906, the Board of Admiralty had good reasons to believe that in a war against Germany, Britain would probably be allied to France, and that a commercial blockade "might not be sufficiently aggressive to suit French ideas," or, for that matter, the ideas of British politicians. Naval leaders recognized there was a strong possibility that the government of the day might ask the British armed forces to make a more active contribution to the joint war effort.[107] This prospect placed Fisher in a dilemma. As we have seen, he had been utterly convinced that operating fleets of large ships in the narrow seas in the face of a torpedo armed flotilla was too dangerous. Distant commercial blockade, he also believed, was the only way the Royal Navy could hurt Germany without losing too many ships. The need to preserve Britain's capability to provide imperial security was always in the back of his mind. Yet at the same time the first sea lord realized that unless the navy met the demand for an offensive policy against Germany, the government would probably turn to the army. Of course war with Germany might never come. But that was not the point. The real danger, from Fisher's perspective, was that in anticipation of possible conflict the politicians might reallocate defense resources in favor of the War Office. The refusal of successive prime ministers to rule out the possibility of sending most of the British army to the continent to fight alongside the French can only have spurred the Admiralty into devising alternate plans.[108] These did not have to be genuine or withstand close scrutiny. All that was required was something on paper to show politicians to justify the existing levels of naval expenditure—and of course demonstrate that the navy would be capable of meeting the government's demands should a more active policy in support of France be wanted.

In the winter of 1906, Fisher appointed a small committee under Capt. George Ballard to examine the feasibility of various amphibious schemes that had been submitted to him.[109] During the first Moroccan crisis, for instance, Admiral Wilson had proposed landing British military forces in Denmark and Schleswig-Holstein with the object of distracting German soldiers away from the French frontier.[110] Another of his ideas was to capture the island of Heligoland to facilitate a close blockade of the North Sea coast. Another plan, put forward by Slade in December 1905, while serving at the War College, advocated the use of "a mobile army of say 10,000 or 15,000 men embarked in the fastest transports we can get."[111] According to a letter written by Ottley several years later, the Ballard committee reported that any combined operations against the German coast or the Island of Heligoland were "utterly impracticable."[112] This negative appraisal, however, did not stop Fisher from allowing others to consider similar schemes.[113] Some officers, notably Slade, believed that such operations were practicable. But they were exceptions. Other officers serving in Whitehall regarded these plans as "councils of desperation" that were "entertained solely because no others are feasible."[114] Before proceeding, readers are asked to remember to keep in mind the distinction between feasibility studies and actual plans for war.

During the first half of 1907, some dozen officers drawn from the NID and the War College were instructed to explore the strategic options open to the Royal Navy in case "the destruction or enforced idleness of shipping under the German flag is not in itself considered sufficient to bring Germany to terms."[115] This group was quite separate from the Ballard Committee.[116] The Whitehall Committee, as it was referred to, wrote a number of papers some of which were bound together in June 1907 under the title of "War Plans." This document outlined schemes for the capture of various North Sea islands to facilitate a close blockade and the bombardment of German naval bases.[117] Although outwardly very impressive (one copy ran to almost eight hundred pages of print) the schemes were manifestly impracticable, and have since, therefore, been held up as the prime example of inadequate strategic planning by the Admiralty before 1914.[118] Actually these were not real war plans but strategic studies.[119] In the preface to the proof copy is a disclaimer which reads—"the opinions and plans herein (to which others will be added from time to time) are not in any way to be considered as those definitely adopted, but are valuable and instructive of the variety of considerations governing the formulation of war schemes."[120]

The real function of the 1907 war plans was twofold. Firstly they served to show government ministers that the navy could offer an offensive strategy against Germany. Secondly, they rebutted claims by Adm. Lord Charles Beresford and other members of the syndicate of discontent that the Admiralty had no ideas on how to fight a war against Germany.[121] There is a substantial amount of evidence to indicate that the 1907 war plans were intended to serve as no more than a smoke screen. One copy has attached to the front a highly suggestive memorandum written by Fisher which states in the first paragraph that "the

780 pages herewith of print and manuscript are sufficient evidence of the close thought and study given to war planning during the last four years."[122] Portions of the document were circulated widely to influential Cabinet ministers including avowed pacifists![123] Several years after the war plans had served their purpose, moreover, Fisher confided to several of his friends that they had been produced solely for the consumption of his critics.[124] Sir Arthur Wilson, he recalled some years later, "not being a Machiavelli, wouldn't tell the Cabinet anything. I, on the contrary, told them so much that they thought me perfect. I gave them 600 pages of print of war plans!"[125] The exclamation mark was Fisher's.

In 1908, Fisher authorized a third investigation into the practicability of waging amphibious warfare against Germany. The plan, to capture the islands controlling the entrance to the Baltic Sea, was the brainchild of DNI Edmund Slade, who, it will be recalled, was a consistent advocate of combined operations.[126] He believed that a mobile amphibious force "would paralyse all German initiative and would tie up a large portion of their forces to the sea coast."[127] On 1 February, Slade was authorized to develop his plan in conjunction with officers at the Naval War College. On this occasion, the DNI went so far as to hold talks with his opposite number in the War Office, and over next few months much interdepartmental correspondence was accumulated.[128] The contents of these papers did not, however, signify the determination of the Admiralty to adopt the strategy and should not thus be so interpreted.[129] From the outset everyone involved (except Slade) was skeptical of the Baltic project.[130] On 20 May 1908, the DNI moaned in his diary that the first sea lord could never find time to discuss the plan. He also noted "I don't think he likes my ideas at all."[131] Later that summer Capt. Osmond de Brock (deputy director of Naval Intelligence) confessed to a staff officer in the War Office that he and his colleagues regarded the Naval War College's Baltic plan as "a mass of verbiage."[132] Nor was the president of the War College, Rear Adm. Lewis Bayly, under any illusions. He recognized that Fisher only wanted the plan on paper to serve his political purposes. "These war plans," Bayly dryly noted in his memoirs, "were duly put into a drawer by him."[133] Some years afterwards, Captain Ottley made an oblique reference to the project in a letter to Lord Esher to illustrate the state of war planning in the Admiralty during the period 1907–9. "Preposterous notions were at the time abroad regarding the functions of the Naval War College! People solemnly suggested that the educational establishment was to prepare war plans! As though the secrets of the first sea lord were to be discussed in lecture room debates of a score of perfectly irresponsible half pay commanders and captains!"[134]

If the Admiralty had been truly committed to a strategy of combined operations in the North Sea, then Slade's grandiose "Baltic project" would almost certainly have been revealed to the CID subcommittee convened on 3 December 1908.[135] In his memoirs Fisher described this gathering as a plenary meeting to discuss British strategy in the event of war with Germany. On this occasion the General Staff explained their continental strategy to the government for the first time. This seemed to be the moment for the Admiralty to respond with its plan of amphibious attack. But they did not. Just before the meeting, the first sea lord ordered Slade not to say one word about his Baltic plan.[136] Instead the Admiralty submitted to the CID a detailed plan for an economic blockade of Germany which was immediately approved.[137] When at a subsequent meeting of the CID the War Office tried to embarrass the Admiralty by leaking the gist of Slade's plan, Fisher immediately distanced himself from the whole scheme. He categorically replied that the Admiralty had concluded "it would *not* be essential to British naval success that an effort should be made to regain access to the Baltic."[138] He followed this up with memorandum composed by the new DNI, Rear Adm. Alexander Bethell, which more or less repudiated the entire Baltic plan.[139] Only after Slade had left Whitehall did it finally dawn on him that his plans had always been "purely academic."[140]

The Submarine Question

By the end of 1908, Fisher was certainly convinced of the practicability of using the flotilla defense strategy in the North Sea. At the end of that year the big (600 ton) submarine HMS *D1* finally commenced her builders' trials. This craft promised to be capable "*of maintaining itself at sea, unaided, for long periods.*" To draw attention to the implications of this fact, at the end of 1908 Fisher drafted perhaps one of his most prescient documents on naval warfare. Entitled "The Submarine Question," it served notice that a "revolution" had occurred in the method of conducting of naval war "with *any* power, particularly with any European power, on account of the narrow waters of the North Sea and Baltic, English Channel and Mediterranean, being denied to large ships of war until the submarine is cleared out."[141] Although Fisher had made this prophecy before, on this occasion he was more assertive. Not only had the Royal Navy successfully tested its prototype "oversea" submarine, but more ominously Germany also was now beginning to spend considerable sums on a submarine development program.

It is inevitable when the Germans fully realize the capability of this type of submarine—they probably do not do so yet, on account of having small experience with them at sea (they have but 3 to our 60)—the North Sea and all its ports will be rendered uninhabitable by our big ships—until we have cleaned out their submarines.[142]

"The first practical necessity that arises from a consideration of the above facts," Fisher concluded, was that "this country must produce more than the six a year which our present vote provides."[143] In addition, the navy must resume its efforts to combat the submarine. Both these suggestions were swiftly acted upon. In the spring of 1909 the Admiralty secretly established an "anti-submarine" committee.[144] Later that summer Fisher "told the first lord we must have one million next year for submarines"—more than double the existing submarine construction budget.[145] At the same time, the committee engaged in estimating the navy's personnel requirement for the next five years, under Vice Adm. Francis Bridgeman, was warned that a large expansion in the submarine fleet was impending. Sadly the original figures given to the manning committee have not survived. Although in an interim report, Bridgeman noted that according to his calculations, based upon the figures given him, the Admiralty was planning to build over this five year period almost one hundred additional submarines.[146]

In April 1909, Fisher circulated a second draft of "The Submarine Question" to selected officers within the Admiralty.[147] Alas only the comments from Rear Adm. John Jellicoe, then serving as controller of the navy, have survived. Jellicoe's reply was: "I entirely agree in the conclusions that we must spend more money on submarines and that we must devise something in the shape of a submarine destroyer." But, he went on to suggest, Germany could not possibly build enough submarines to saturate the North Sea for another eight or ten years.[148] Even then:

> it seems to be going rather too far to say that the German submarine development must render the North Sea and all its ports uninhabitable by big ships and that this fact inevitably points to big ship battles being fought in more open waters. My reasoning is as follows:—In the early stages of a war with Germany it will no doubt be the case, when the German submarines become very numerous. At this stage it would seem that the command of the narrow waters will be fought for by small craft and submarines, the big ships kept in safety. But a time will come when the submarines will have been so reduced in numbers by this fighting that present conditions will be reproduced, the big ships will get into the North Sea and the decisive action may well be fought in those waters . . . therefore the time must come when our own Battle Fleet will be forced into the North Sea to endeavor to bring the German fleet to action.[149]

"I don't agree" Fisher scrawled in the margin alongside this last sentence.[150] Unfortunately further discussion of "The Submarine Question" was suspended for six months. The file did not reach the desk of the first lord of the Admiralty until the end of September 1909.[151] During the interim Fisher was fully occupied in fending off criticisms of his administration and strategic policy before a Cabinet select committee chaired by prime minister H. H. Asquith.

Charlie B

On 24 March 1909, Adm. Lord Charles Beresford hauled down his flag as commander in chief, Channel Fleet. Ordinarily he could have expected to remain in this post for another year. But the Board of Admiralty could no longer tolerate his constant sniping at official policy and gross insubordination. Beresford not surprisingly was most indignant at having been effectively sacked. The order to "come ashore" represented an ignominious end to his distinguished albeit checkered career, and also the death of his life-long ambition to become first sea lord. Within a week Beresford took his revenge. On 2 April, he wrote to the prime minister accusing the Board of Admiralty of failing to ensure the construction of sufficient small craft, strategic incompetence in the distribution of the fleet, and not providing the fleet with properly formulated strategic plans for war. He also intimated to Asquith that if his government failed to take appropriate action the letter would be published.[152] At first, Sir John Fisher thought he had little reason to be concerned. Although "Charlie B" had a large following in the country and many influential society friends,[153] the first sea lord believed that it was not in the government's interest to investigate the charges. The Cabinet was largely responsible for any shortage of modern warships, and the prime minister himself had endorsed the decision to sack Beresford after having been convinced of his incompetence.[154] Also, it was widely known that there was personal animosity between the two admirals. Most of London society, indeed, knew that the first sea lord and the commander in chief had for several months not been on speaking terms.[155] Beresford's accusations, therefore, could easily have been dismissed as the ravings of an embittered and jealous man.

It thus came as a considerable shock when Fisher learned, ten days later, that Asquith had resolved to chair a subcommittee of the CID to investigate Beresford's complaints.[156] More ominously the prime minister had deliberately excluded from his committee those regular members of the CID known to think highly of the first sea lord, men such as Lords Esher, Crewe and Morley. Considering that Asquith could have safely ignored Beresford's complaints, his decision to hold an inquiry was probably motivated more by political considerations than a desire to investigate the rift within the navy. At that particular moment the prime minister was furious with the Admiralty for having repeatedly defied Cabinet instructions to request money for just four dreadnoughts under the 1909–10 program.[157] Asquith, it will be recalled, believed that the Cabinet should always have the dominant voice in fixing the size of the construction budget and as chancellor of the Exchequer had fought to curtail the Admiralty's influence.[158] In early 1909, however, Fisher, supported by the new first lord, Reginald McKenna, had refused to withdraw the Admiralty's request for the construction of six capital ships that year plus six more the following year on the grounds that naval-industrial intelligence indicated an expansion in German warship-building capacity. Ultimately, the British government had been compelled to fund no fewer than eight units in 1909–10, despite receiving money from Australia and New Zealand to pay for two additional battle cruisers.[159] More seriously for Asquith, McKenna and Fisher's intransigence had produced in the public mind a major "navy scare," and their blunt refusal to compromise had in March nearly split the Cabinet.[160] In addition, the bill for the additional capital ships had threatened to upset the Cabinet's electoral promise to introduce a system of old age pensions. In order to finance the unexpected increase in naval expenditure and retain their program of social reform, the Cabinet had consequently forced into taking a political gamble by endorsing David Lloyd George's "radical" budget. Asquith thus had ample reason in May 1909 to seek a change of leadership at Whitehall and to try exerting tighter control over the Admiralty. Yet he was also aware that public opinion would not allow him to dismiss Fisher or McKenna without cause. He first needed a lever.

The ensuing investigation, which amounted to the Liberal Cabinet's most determined effort to learn the details of naval policy before 1914, failed to uncover any evidence of mismanagement at Whitehall. Though not through want of effort. The committee's search disrupted the administration of the Admiralty for half a year. "The enquiry has quite upset the Admiralty," Fisher wrote to Admiral May on 9 May, "everyone [is] employed getting up evidence to give against their superiors."[161] In the aftermath Captain Ottley observed that "it is scarcely too much to say that for the six months during which the Beresford Enquiry was proceeding the entire thinking machinery of the Admiralty was concentrated on that question, and every other matter was necessarily shelved."[162] The upset was compounded by the suspension of two senior captains in the NID caught passing confidential papers to Beresford. By the end of 1909, the already understaffed Admiralty was faced with a large backlog of work and as a result could not give proper attention to a number of important files.[163] These included Fisher's "The Submarine Question," and reports of a major flaw in the design of all existing armor piercing shell. Indeed the thoroughness with which Asquith and his committee searched the Admiralty records lends color to the suspicion that they were less interested in listening to Beresford's quite specific complaints than in finding out more about the true workings of the naval administration.

Most historians have interpreted the extraordinary feud between Fisher and "Charlie B" as little more than a personality clash.[164] Others have attributed their bickering to Beresford's public criticism of a number of Fisher's reforms, "more particularly with the fleet redistribution scheme" of 1906.[165] These simplistic explanations, however, do not adequately explain either the origins of the dispute or why their "personal" quarrel embroiled and so divided most of the navy's officer corps. It is hardly sufficient to attribute the intensity of the feud to Beresford's naturally "bellicose Irish temperament," or to suggest that he was egged on by members of the syndicate of discontent.[166] One of those best in a position to judge was Reginald Bacon. After serving as assistant to the first sea lord in 1905, then as a captain in Beresford's fleet for two years, Bacon returned to Whitehall in 1908 as director of Naval Ordnance. In his biography of Lord Fisher, Bacon suggested that Beresford started the feud after Fisher was promoted to the rank of admiral of the fleet, thus allowing him to remain as head of the navy beyond the normal retirement age of sixty-five.[167] Beresford, he claimed, who was only five years younger and very ambitious, subsequently realized that he had to depose Fisher if he was ever to succeed him. "In fairness to Lord Charles," he nevertheless conceded, "it must be stated that both he and those around him considered he would make a better first sea lord than Fisher." Why Bacon did not say exactly; but he implied that there were fundamental disagreements between the two admirals over important questions of naval policy.[168] Evidence in the Admiralty archives confirms this impression.

Beresford's naval career was most unusual and merits close examination. Lord Charles Beresford, the younger son of an Irish peer, had always been immensely popular within the service. Yet while he may have commanded the loyalty of his subordinates, he had always possessed an undeniable talent for antagonizing his superiors which provides an important context for looking at the Fisher-Beresford dispute. The records show that during his career as an admiral, the Board of Admiralty formally censured him on no fewer than five occasions; once in 1895, twice in 1902, once in 1903 and once in 1904.[169] Fisher did not bother.[170] Lord Walter Kerr, the former senior naval lord, found Beresford to be "childish and unreasonable" as well as hopelessly "insubordinate."[171] He too found him unresponsive to reason. "Beresford is a curious man," Kerr remarked to Lord Selborne after one such quarrel, "it is a marked 'trait' in his composition that when he is completely pulverised by arguments and facts, he always starts again as if nothing has happened. I have observed this odd feature in him for a long time past . . . ."[172] Fisher, Kerr, and even their predecessor, Sir Frederick Richards, all tried to force Beresford into retirement. But he always survived, thanks mainly to his numerous social and political connections. Whenever the naval establishment tried to place the querulous admiral on the beach he always managed to get himself elected to Parliament.[173] From this platform he would then proceed to harangue the Board with impunity! In 1874, 1885, 1897 and again in 1902, Beresford was returned to Westminster. The last three occasions were by-elections. In 1886, he even secured the nomination of the new Conservative government for one of the junior ministerial posts at the Admiralty which normally went to a civilian; on accepting he rejected a bizarre offer to become chief commissioner of the London Metropolitan Police Force.[174] Two years later Beresford dramatically resigned from the Admiralty and returned to Parliament—to attack his former colleagues! A naval officer "serving" in the House of Commons was allowed to remain on the active list and be promoted according to the normal rules of seniority. He could not, therefore, be forced by the Admiralty into retirement. During his naval career which lasted from 1878 till 1909, Beresford served just eight years and two hundred and fifty days at sea and no less than fourteen years in Parliament.[175] On his retirement from the service in 1909, moreover, Beresford was elected member for Portsmouth, a seat he held until his elevation to the peerage in 1916.

Relations between Fisher and Beresford were outwardly cordial when the latter took command of the Channel Squadron in April 1907. If "Charlie B" was truly smoldering over Fisher's promotion to admiral of the fleet he had succeeded in keeping his envy under control for more than eighteen months. Although during the preceding winter there had been some antagonism between them, this was nothing more than a symptom of their tumultuous relationship.[176] Similarly, although Fisher certainly flirted with the idea, he did not try to cancel Beresford's appointment to command the Channel Fleet.[177] In fact, it had been Jacky who had first recommended that Beresford succeed the eminent Sir Arthur Wilson as commander in chief, despite gnawing doubts over his judgement and knowing him "to be ambitious, self-advertising and gassy in his talk."[178]

As Bacon implied, the root of the Fisher-Beresford dispute seems to have been a serious disagreement over British naval strategy. Shortly after Beresford hoisted his flag as commander in chief, he informed the first lord (and shortly afterwards most of London) that he thought the existing distribution of the fleet to be "a fraud and a danger to the Empire."[179] He also petitioned the Admiralty to clarify the navy's plan for war against Germany. By return he was notified that he had already been given a set of war orders outlining the navy's strategic objectives. Beresford was further reminded that as the commander in chief he was responsible for the operational control of the fleet and thus he himself should propose his own plan of campaign and submit it to the Admiralty for approval. It is important here to understand that the written war orders handed to the admiral provided only a vague summary of the Admiralty's views. For reasons of secrecy the details were communicated verbally. No formal records of the meetings remain.[180] Fortunately, Beresford's official correspondence and his testimony to the CID in 1909, yield several clues about what he was told during his briefing at the Admiralty.[181] From these sources it would appear that Fisher told him that, because of the danger from the numerous German torpedo craft, in the event of war the Admiralty intended to deploy only the Home Fleet (including the flotilla) in the North Sea. Beresford's main (Channel) battle fleet would stay in reserve.

The commander in chief held very different ideas. Fundamentally, he was much more confident in the ability of a battle fleet to ward off torpedo attack and thus could not see the necessity of flotilla defense. On 13 May 1907, Beresford forwarded his "plan of campaign" to Whitehall. Not surprisingly, it prescribed a strictly orthodox naval offensive, involving an observational force of destroyers positioned off the German ports, backed by cruisers, with the battle fleet ready to intercept any large hostile force that dared to attack the inshore squadron.[182] Submarine operations were limited to defending the Straits of Dover.[183] The plan clearly embodied Beresford's own ideas on the strategic objectives to be pursued rather than those given him by the first sea lord. Along with his plan of campaign, the commander in chief also sent the Admiralty his critique of the 1907 "War Plans."[184] In this paper Beresford denounced the entire idea of a distant commercial blockade as "radically unsound."[185] Specifically, he objected to the Royal Navy attempting nothing more ambitious than "the destruction of German merchant shipping."[186] According to this plan, he complained, no cruisers would be deployed "to prevent the German battle fleet or other German fleets from going through the Kiel canal round the Skaw to the west, entering into a large space, totally unwatched, with a chance of getting to the rear of the British battle fleet."[187] (Assuming, of course, that the battle fleet would be in the southern half of the North Sea.) Even if this strategy was adopted, he observed, "the cordon must fail in the object for which it is created" because, "it is too far from the German bases." Beresford estimated that even with "double" the number of cruisers presently at his disposal, the fleet "could not make a complete cordon in the North Sea."[188] As Captain Ballard pointed out: "It is evident that he [Beresford] entirely fails to grasp the main ideas. These cruisers are not watching cruisers in any sense of the word as regards watching for the exit of the enemy's fleet, but placed solely to intercept trade . . . Our object is to force them to proceed a distance of more than 300 miles from their own sheltered base to defend their trade and then fall on them when outside, or cut off their retreat."[189]

In June 1907 Fisher responded to Beresford's patently "absurd" plan of campaign by asking Lord Tweedmouth to endorse a new set of war orders to the commander in chief specially composed "with the object of disabusing him of the idea that now possesses him that his is the sole responsibility for the conduct of a naval war."[190] Several weeks later, the Admiralty asked Beresford to submit a new plan of campaign based upon these amended war orders. They defined his duties as: first, to watch all enemy forces in the vicinity of the United Kingdom; second, interdict enemy sea borne trade; and last, prevent invasion. They contained not a word about a close observational blockade.[191] Fisher was exasperated after Beresford wrote back complaining that he did not have adequate forces at his disposal to achieve these objectives and thus could not draw up a plan. On 5 July, the first lord summoned both admirals to his rooms in an effort to negotiate a rapprochement between them.[192] The attempt at mediation failed largely because the commander in chief either could not or would not articulate his complaints.[193] Fisher subsequently lost all patience with the argumentative fleet commander and began demanding his dismissal on the grounds of insubordination.[194] Initially Tweedmouth refused. By the end of 1907, however, he too was looking to rid himself of the tiresome Charlie B.

In May 1908, Reginald McKenna took over as first lord of the Admiralty. Soon thereafter, Fisher persuaded him that Beresford's insubordination had become intolerable and that the admiral should strike his flag and come ashore. For more than a year, the first sea lord complained, the commander in chief had still not submitted his plan of campaign—ostensibly because he was too busy. Meanwhile he abused the Admiralty in public with impunity. Fisher suggested to McKenna that if he wished to allow Beresford to save face, he could plausibly say that the commander in chief's resignation was compelled by the need to merge the Home and the Channel Fleets for strategic reasons.[195] The following month, Fisher's personal assistant, Cmdr. Thomas Crease, asked the prominent naval correspondent Arnold White to quiet raging speculation in the press about the feud. "The end is in sight, so do use your influence to keep the subject in the background for the next two weeks."[196] Although McKenna was persuaded, to Fisher's dismay, however, Asquith refused to sanction Beresford's dismissal at this time.[197] The new prime minister was probably wary of stirring up a major political storm so early into his ministry. Besides, the likelihood of conflict with Germany was remote. And Fisher made no secret of his intent in the event of a conflict to recall Sir Arthur Wilson as fleet commander anyway.[198] Beresford, incidentally, was formally notified of this fact in late 1908.[199]

Once the Admiralty realized they were "stuck" with Beresford they sent him another set of revised instructions.[200] The war orders issued in July 1908 must have been much more to his liking. They prescribed an observational blockade off the main German ports and across the entrance to the Baltic. Indeed, they were so much in accord with Beresford's personal views, and so contradicted the previous orders issued to him, that there must be doubts that they truly represented the Admiralty's strategic views. It is more than likely they were specially written to keep him quiet. It is known that some months earlier Fisher had allowed representatives of the NID to meet with the commander in chief to—"fog out"—a new war plan. Slade, who was equally contemptuous of Beresford, recorded in his diary that it had been agreed to "discuss a plan with him [Beresford] and let him perhaps imagine it was this plan that was going to be adopted."[201] There are other indications that the Admiralty was no longer playing straight with the fleet commander. In November 1908, the first sea lord made a point of reminding McKenna to be evasive when answering queries from Beresford on strategic matters.

> [T]he War Orders were intended to convey to him "the general intentions of the Admiralty" and it was added in the same paragraph "that considerable departures from them maybe necessary to suit the exigencies of the moment." And consequently and manifestly the detailed statement he requires as to the exact places from which the battle fleet, cruiser squadrons and destroyers will proceed to act cannot be given![202]

Perhaps the strongest evidence that the 1908 War Orders were "fake" is that Beresford himself believed so. One of his loudest complaints he made to the prime minister in 1909 was that the Admiralty had never taken him fully into their confidence over strategic matters.[203] And it is highly suggestive that after Beresford was finally dismissed as commander in chief in March 1909, these orders were immediately withdrawn.

At the opening of the Beresford Enquiry in May 1909, the plaintiff intimated to the prime minister that two years earlier the Admiralty had told him that in event of war with Germany a distant blockade strategy would be employed.[204] Beresford lectured Asquith that the distant blockade strategy—this "pedagogue plan" as he called it—was "a defensive policy that we cannot afford to adopt."[205] It would "be like playing football when you have got the football always at your goal."[206] Instead, he advised, "we have got to have an attacking policy . . . [w]e have got to watch the enemy's coast with watching cruisers; they have only two egresses, and when they come out the Admiral should know they have come out."[207] Incidentally, during cross-examination, Beresford surprised his audience by admitting that he "did get things which called themselves plans, but which [he] did not regard worthy of name."[208] Yet, he refused to concede that his original letter of complaint to the prime minister had been misleading, his admission notwithstanding.

The former commander in chief went on to berate the Fisher administration for having scrapped over one hundred small cruisers without building replacements. Ever since, he complained, the Royal Navy had been chronically short of vessels suitable for blockade duties off enemy ports.[209] In reply, the first lord explained to the assembly that the development of fast armored cruisers had rendered all these old cruisers obsolete. Besides, he added, replacements had been built. The Admiralty believed that submarines had taken over this function of the small cruiser.[210] Several weeks later McKenna was to let slip in the House of Commons that the Admiralty thought submarines could be used "for blockading the enemy's ports."[211] Testifying before the Beresford Enquiry, however, McKenna could have been more explicit. He did not say, for example, that the Admiralty believed an observational blockade of the North Sea German coast to be impossible, chiefly because the navy could not maintain its battle fleet in a position to support the inshore squadrons without prohibitive risk of torpedo attack.

Very little was said during the committee meetings about the ability of torpedo craft to make attack on the battle fleet. Admittedly this subject did not properly fall within the terms of reference of the enquiry, but understanding the positions of Fisher and Beresford on this subject is essential to understanding their differences of opinion on strategic matters. During cross-examination Beresford publicly confessed that he "attached no importance to submarines."[212] His reasoning was not easy to follow:

A propos [sic] of what I said with regard to shortage [of cruisers], if the submariners are to take their place, I want to point out that all submarine warfare is entirely theoretical. I will not say they will not "put down" ships, but they will not revolutionise [naval] warfare unless the Admirals are afraid of them. It is like mining the Channel and the Straits. We must go to sea and fight anything we have got to grapple with. Now the submarine is always in a fog. The one thing that beats a seaman on the top of the water is a fog. So it is entirely theoretical.[213]

On being asked by the first lord to explain what he meant by the statement that "navigating a submarine is like navigating a ship in fog," Beresford became incoherent.[214] All he would say was "fancy trusting to submarines! You have covered all our coasts with submarines—with 30 or 40 submarines—and [consequently] we have not got the small cruisers and catchers [destroyers] upon which we shall depend in war." Turning to Asquith he advised—don't "let the country trust to them [submarines] to defend it in war."[215]

Documents submitted by Beresford to the CID in support of his arguments confirm that he had at least heard of "flotilla defense." In one memorandum he dismissed the idea that "our defense is to consist chiefly of submarines and torpedo craft in home waters" as "entirely theoretical and speculative."[216] During his cross-examination McKenna asked him point blank if he was aware that "the modern C and D classes of submarines are designed for offensive work."[217] "Yes," Beresford replied, "I know the idea is that every German ship will be put down [sunk] the day after war is declared. I have heard a lot of funny little things like that."(!)[218] Later he admitted that he had never seen a submarine at sea![219] His only experience was a single nearly fatal dive in a London dock aboard a primitive experimental submarine-boat some twenty years earlier.[220] This was an extraordinary confession, considering that for the past two years Beresford had been in command of the navy's premier battle fleet. It must also cast serious doubts on the validity of his assessment on the military value of submarines.

Despite Beresford's clear prejudice against submarines, there is no denying he was a most able commander of surface ships. As commander in chief, he had contributed towards the development of long range gunnery in the navy. He stood as one of the chief sponsors for the Pollen fire-control system. He also had carried out a number of difficult experiments with his battle fleet to test the possibility of a battle squadron concentrating their fire against a single target.[221] Undoubtedly his experiences as a fleet commander encouraged him to believe that the torpedo threat was overrated and consequently that North Sea strategy should still be based upon the use of a predominant battle fleet. Many officers believed that a battle squadron properly trained in tactics of fire and maneuver could easily ward off torpedo-boat attacks: at least in conditions of good light and weather. Beresford was not completely blind to the dangers associated with operating armored squadrons close to the German coast. His experiences in maneuvers had taught him that if German torpedo boats could one night put to sea undetected his "the battle fleet w[ould] not be safe within two hundred miles of the German coast."[222]

Back in October 1907 Beresford had conducted a series of exercises to test his arrangements for the blockade of Heligoland Bight. These maneuvers had convinced him that the Royal Navy did not possess enough small craft to maintain an effective watch of German ports at night.[223] Rather than keep his battleships well away from the German coast as Fisher suggested, however, Beresford chose to interpret the results as justification for his demand that the Royal Navy must build more destroyers and small cruisers. Exercises conducted the following year by elements of Vice Adm. Sir Francis Bridgeman's Home Fleet reconfirmed the conclusions of the Irish Sea maneuvers held three years earlier, that to maintain an effective observation "the blockers should be to the blockaded as three is to one."[224] To implement Beresford's plan, therefore, the Royal Navy would have required a force of about three hundred small craft. The cost of building and especially maintaining such a force in peace (both in terms of money and men) was, of course, prohibitive. One can thus sympathize with Fisher's inability to comprehend why Cabinet ministers courted Beresford. The "chief plank" of his alternate policy, the first sea lord often used to protest, "is the immediate additional expenditure of millions in small cruisers and destroyers."[225]

In August 1909, one of the assistant secretaries at the CID surreptitiously handed Arthur Balfour copies of the voluminous minutes taken during the Beresford Enquiry. Burdened with parliamentary work the Conservative leader passed these on to his secretary, Jack Sandars, to précis for him. Shortly afterwards Sandars wrote to Lord Esher with his impressions. "I thought Charlie B's evidence extraordinarily ineffective," he began:

> he did not know his case in detail—he was pushed from one point to another: had he been before a court of law the ordinary cross examiner would have broken him in one afternoon. Reading the evidence one never knew what he was driving at, such as preparations for war, organization for war. I think Charlie, with every possible indulgence given him, failed and failed badly. He could have been made to fail [even] worse. Now I am not sure whether Asquith and Haldane were wise in fooling him into the belief that he was doing well before the committee; that they did fool him is plain from the conversation which he held with outsiders like myself.
>
> I think McKenna's presentation of Jackie's case was admirable. It seemed to me to be well balanced in argument, and particularly moderate in form; and Charlie B made no resistance to it that was worth a moment's consideration.[226]

Sandars found "the most interesting thing in the whole proceedings" was the evidence given by Admiral of the Fleet Sir Arthur Wilson.[227] At the final gathering of the committee, Beresford had tried to coax his notoriously reticent predecessor to agree with him that the navy was "dangerously short" of destroyers and small cruisers. He had refused. When pestered to explain why not, Wilson snapped back at Beresford "my point is that, as I do not want to work over on the German coast, I do not want so many."[228] Sandars (correctly) interpreted this to mean that Wilson "does not believe in Charlie's strategy—he does not believe in going over to the German coast and watching there day and night."[229] To Sandars, who was a layman in naval matters, the idea that some British naval officers had no intention of operating off the enemy coast was something of a revelation—although not, it seems, to Balfour.[230]

To Fisher's disgust, but not his surprise, many criticisms of Lord Charles Beresford originally contained in the committee's draft report were deleted from the published version.[231] If the committee had wanted, he wrote, they could have "smashed Beresford in their report and proved him out of his own mouth a blatant liar and imbecile in his ignorance of the naval situation."[232] After only the third meeting of the committee, Fisher was complaining to Sir William May, the new commander in chief, that so far "Beresford has been flattened out on every single point—but I don't think the evidence matters one way or the other one bit."[233] The "bias shown by Asquith" throughout the inquiry convinced Fisher and McKenna that the prime minister was looking for an excuse to force them both out of office.[234]

After the publication of the final report, it was well known in political circles that Asquith had gone out of his way to protect Beresford's reputation. The first sea lord was not the only naval officer who felt that during the proceedings Beresford had "shewed much ignorance" of the parameters of modern naval warfare.[235] In August Lord Esher wrote to Jack Sandars confirming that the original version of the report had been quite different from the one finally published. Esher blamed the "middle class ministers" for allowing themselves to be "open to social influence" from Beresford's aristocratic friends.[236] Yet it is also quite possible that Asquith, like Arthur Balfour, realized the dispute between Fisher and Beresford was more complex than it appeared.[237] Each represented a different school of thought within the navy. Condemning one man or the other therefore would have amounted to taking sides in a highly technical debate over the conduct of war at sea.[238] This story will be continued in the next chapter.

Flotilla Defense: a Postscript

In mid-1910 Reginald McKenna, still the first lord of the Admiralty, tried to obtain Cabinet approval for all fully commissioned battleships in the Royal Navy to gather off Portugal for combined maneuvers. He sent two letters to senior Cabinet colleagues both of which merit quotation at length. The first went to the foreign secretary, Sir Edward Grey:

> A paper has gone to the Foreign Office in which you will see that we pro-pose to send the First and Second divisions of the Home Fleet, the Atlantic Fleet, and the Mediterranean Fleet to Aroso Bay [off Spain] for joint exer-cises next month. It may excite alarm that we shall be denuding the North Sea of battleships, but it must be remembered that our fleet could be recalled by W/T within two days, and that our destroyers and submarine flotillas, *which are the true defense against invasion* will be stationed on the East Coast.[239] [my italics]

The second was addressed to the prime minister:

> I need hardly assure you that there is not the slightest danger. Our destroyers and submarine flotillas will be so disposed as to constitute a complete defense for our coasts, and the battleships can at any moment be brought back by W/T orders . . . it would in fact be an advantage to acclimatize the public to the idea of not keeping our new battleships per-manently tied to the Home Ports.[240]

Both letters clearly allude to flotilla defense being the foundation of Admiralty policy against invasion. But perhaps the real significance of these letters is that they were written by the political head of the Admiralty in the fall of 1910—some nine months after Sir John Fisher had retired as first sea lord.

PART III

CHAPTER 7

Aberrations:
The Grand Fleet of Battle,
1910–1912

> In the old days the battleship was the conception of a ship which nothing else on these waters could sink. But now the battleship is no longer the ultimate power on the sea: it may be sunk by the smallest vessel afloat. Therefore it has lost its primary function; or one of its primary functions, namely the ability in itself to defend oversea expeditions against anything on water. Now to make up for that inability she must have attendant torpedo craft which will keep the other torpedo craft at a respectful distance . . .
>
> *Rear Adm. Reginald Bacon, March 1913.*

Sir John Fisher was deeply offended by the implied censure inserted by the prime minister into the published findings of the Beresford Enquiry. He also felt betrayed by the failure of many of his political allies of either party to protest at the unfairness of the final report.[1] "Jack is evidently very sore and he has every reason to be so," observed the King's private secretary Lord Knollys.[2] More seriously, Asquith's verdict had undermined the first sea lord's personal authority within the service and damaged public confidence in the Board of Admiralty. As a consequence, by the autumn of 1909 it had become clear to a number of observers that Fisher's continued presence at Whitehall was no longer in the best interests of the service.[3] Although Fisher had been considering retirement for several months, "what is keeping him back is fear that his policy would be upset," explained the second sea lord, Vice Adm. Sir Francis Bridgeman.[4] In October, however, after having reflected upon his position while vacationing on the Continent, Fisher finally made up his mind to go. On 20 October, Asquith agreed to elevate Fisher to the peerage in the king's birthday honors on the understanding that he would quit the Board at the first opportunity, probably the following April after the passage of the navy estimates through Parliament.[5]

The task of finding a replacement for Sir John Fisher posed a major dilemma for Reginald McKenna, the first lord. If he followed the rules of convention he was bound to choose one of the twelve full admirals on the active service list. The problem was that none of them possessed anything like Fisher's knowledge of technical matters or his skills as an adminis- trator. At least four were "yellow" admirals—officers of mediocre ability who had risen to the top of the flag list by virtue of their seniority but who had never been trusted with command of a fleet or a seat on the Board of Admiralty.[6] The field of talent was further narrowed by McKenna's reso- lution that whoever succeeded Fisher must agree not to reverse the reforms introduced over the preceding five years. This ruled out the five admirals known to belong to the so-called syndicate of discontent: Charles Beresford, Reginald Custance, Lewis Beaumont and Arthur Moore.[7] The other, Assheton Curzon-Howe, was dying of cancer. Of the remaining alternatives, the former second sea lord Charles Drury was too closely identified with Jacky's regime,[8] while Sir William May had only recently been appointed to the post of commander in chief, Home Fleets.[9] Although on paper the latter certainly appeared to be the strongest can- didate, for McKenna to have appointed May as first sea lord would have provoked a storm of dissent within the service while satisfying no one.

William May was regarded by his peers as arrogant, vain, opulent, and generally incompetent. Indeed many naval officers regarded him as "wholly unfit for the great command of the Home Fleet."[10] In August 1909, Jack Sandars was reliably informed that he retained the post only because the Board of Admiralty shrank from taking action so soon after the recent controversies. "They say 'we must let the service settle down: we cannot afford to have another Charlie B case.'"[11] "It is incredible that May should have risen so high," Lord Esher remarked to Sandars, "if he is as bad as some of his professional colleagues seem to think."[12] How justified was the criticism of May is difficult to establish; but what can be said is that over the preceding decade he had served in three admin- istrative posts at the Admiralty and on each occasion had failed to shine. Fisher, who liked May personally, often described him as "wood painted to look like iron." And it is suggestive that in 1905, Fisher had been instrumental in May's early departure from the office of controller.[13] If, in 1909, Fisher had been prepared to consider him as his successor then it was only because all the alternatives seemed worse.[14] But ultimately May's aspirations were destroyed by Bridgeman's warning to McKenna that he would sooner resign than serve under this officer for whom he had "a contempt."[15] That effectively settled the matter. And so, when Fisher's retirement was formally announced, therefore, the first lord had no obvious successor in hand.[16]

Political turmoil at the end of 1909, however, forced McKenna to quickly make up his mind. In November, the Conservative peers in the House of Lords rejected Lloyd George's "Peoples Budget," prompting the Liberal Cabinet to dissolve Parliament and appeal to the country for a mandate. The general election was scheduled for the third week of January 1910. Fisher greeted the news with horror.[17] He feared that if, as expected, the Liberals were returned to power, Asquith would have a golden opportunity to remove the stalwart Reginald McKenna from his new ministry. He could then, without controversy, offer the portfolio of first lord of the Admiralty to someone more sympathetic to demands from the radical wing of the party for reductions in naval expenditure.[18] If, on the other hand, the Conservatives won the election, Fisher was afraid that the Admiralty would be captured by the syndicate of discontent. He had been tipped off by friends inside the party that Walter Long had been nominated for the office of first lord and Adm. Arthur Moore designated to become his first sea lord.[19] The solution, Fisher concluded, was to announce his retirement before the election in order to allow his successor to be established in Whitehall by 25 January "so as to avoid any difficulties in the event of any change in the First Lord of the Admiralty."[20] He calculated that no government would risk the controversy of sacking a brand new first sea lord. It only remained to select the candidate.

More out of desperation than inspiration, Fisher and McKenna turned to the eminent and reclusive Admiral of the Fleet Sir Arthur Wilson *VC*.[21] At the beginning of 1910, Wilson was universally regarded as the best fleet commander of his generation, and although he had been retired from active service for almost three years it was widely expected that in the event of war he would be offered command of the fleet. Within the service his skills in seamanship and naval tactics were legendary. More recently Wilson had acquired a following within government circles. Having remained aloof from service politics since his retirement in 1907, he had not been tarnished by the Fisher-Beresford dispute, and was, as a consequence, regarded as something of a paragon. Largely because of Wilson's reputation as a nonpartisan yet competent officer, in April 1909 Asquith had appointed him special advisor to the Committee of Imperial Defence for the Beresford Enquiry. That summer his "clear and straight forward manner" had impressed the senior cabinet ministers present.[22] One of the committee members, Lord Morley, noted that while Fisher and Beresford each had their good qualities, "Sir A. Wilson strikes me, and I think the others of us, as much the best-balanced sort of man, to say nothing of his having proved himself as a first rate commander."[23] Despite all Wilson's qualities, he was a surprising successor to Sir John Fisher nonetheless.[24] Recalling an officer to active service after three years in retirement was most irregular.[25] And it was mainly for this reason that Wilson was initially unwilling to return to active duty. Only after King Edward VII was recruited to appeal to the admiral's keen "sense of duty" was Wilson finally persuaded "how necessary it is in the interests of the service that you should become First Sea Lord in succession to Sir John Fisher."[26] Fisher was delighted by the confirmation. "I don't think any intrigues can now displace Wilson after his being thus appointed before the General Election," he gloated to his friend Lord Knollys, "it has been a knock-down blow to the Beresford party and totally unexpected by them."[27]

Whatever McKenna or anyone else might have said in public, it is highly unlikely that Wilson was resurrected primarily to heal the rifts within the Royal Navy.[28] For one thing, "Old 'Ard 'Art," as he known by the lower deck, was a notoriously abrasive personality with the reputation of being something of a "martinet."[29] Throughout his career he had tended to bully his subordinates and habitually ignored their opinions or advice. Officers at Whitehall who had previously served with him dreaded his arrival. "I dare say that *under the circumstances* Wilson is the best solution," sighed Francis Bridgeman, "but I know from experience with him that there is no joy to be found in serving either with him or under him! Deadly dull and uncompromising, as you know. He will never consult anyone and is impatient in argument, even to being impossible."[30] The second sea lord's concern at Wilson's inflexibility of mind was shared. The normally imperturbable King Edward VII was reported to have declared after an interview with the admiral that he found him "one of the most obstinate men I ever came across!!"[31] Meanwhile, in the fleet, officers joked among themselves that with Wilson at the helm the other lords commissioners of the Admiralty could be expected to occupy only a very "humble" position.[32] Even Fisher was initially doubtful of his suitability for the post of first sea lord. "I wasn't sweet on it at first as Wilson is such a stonewall," he confessed to McKenna after his candidacy was first suggested, "however you made a good point which converted me in saying that for two years a stone wall was desirable."[33]

What Fisher meant was that Wilson was chosen to occupy the seat of first sea lord only until a more suitable candidate emerged.[34] In March 1912, moreover, Wilson would reach his seventieth birthday and thus be compelled by regulations to retire from the service. The conspirators felt that for such a short period he could be trusted to steer Admiralty policy along the course charted by his predecessor.[35] Under Wilson's regency, meanwhile, McKenna would prune the line of rightful succession by making liberal use of another regulation which empowered the first lord to place on the retired list any admiral who had been unemployed for more than two years.[36] To this end, one of Jacky's last acts was to fill all flag appointments "as far in advance as possible" with officers he considered to be his allies.[37] If all went according to plan, then in March 1912 Fisher's true heir would be installed as first sea lord; or possibly he himself would be restored to power. As a final precaution, McKenna promised Fisher that in the unlikely event of war breaking out within the next two years he would be immediately recalled as first sea lord.[38]

The only flaw in this truly Machiavellian (some might say characteristically "Fishy") scheme was that the chosen puppet did not prove to be as malleable as Fisher and McKenna had first hoped. In addition, the first lord soon found that Wilson's abrasive personality was far worse than he had realised and very quickly produced discord within the Admiralty.[39] On 4 January 1910 McKenna confided to his friends that already he was beginning to have second thoughts. Sir Francis Bridgeman had been affronted at being publicly told by Wilson that he was "only his second," and generally treated "as if he were a second lieutenant on board a ship."[40] During their first week of working together, apparently, the second sea lord threatened resignation on no less than three occasions.[41] McKenna's concerns were echoed by Capt. Ernest Troubridge, the naval secretary, who on 7 January noted pithily in his diary that "Wilson is autocratic."[42] This was nothing new. Wilson inability to delegate had been almost legendary within the service. As controller of the navy between 1897 and 1901, his methodical work habits and tendency to centralize had created administrative chaos within his department.[43] But few officers knew, and certainly none remembered, that in March 1901 Lord Selborne, then first lord, has dismissed Wilson for his uncompromising and dogmatic attitude.[44] "I never did a better days work in my life than when I removed him from the Admiralty where he was an utter failure and a mischievous failure too," Selborne later recalled.[45] In 1910, Fisher acknowledged that his successor had not mellowed with age and that his overbearing manner might create problems. "McKenna is a splendid fighter! He won't go under unless Wilson wrecks him—I must work there like hell!" he half joked with Esher.[46]

Wilson's Strategy

When Fisher handed over to Wilson he had known that his successor's views on the conduct of war did not mirror his own. In 1908, Fisher had admitted to Lord Tweedmouth that he and Wilson were at "variance" over several details of the navy's plan for war against Germany.[47] At the strategic level, Wilson was skeptical of the effectiveness of an economic blockade.[48] He thought that the only sure way of bringing Germany to terms was for the Royal Navy's battleships to engage and decisively beat the High Sea Fleet. Surprisingly, though, their views on tactical and operational policy were broadly similar. Wilson shared Fisher's concern at the dangers posed by torpedo craft to large ships cruising the narrow seas and agreed that in the event of war with Germany the battle fleet must ordinarily be kept out of the North Sea. He accepted that "the rendezvous would be in the Orkneys, and there the fleet would lie, ready for battle, only cruisers and destroyers in the North Sea."[49] There was only one point of divergence. Whereas Fisher would have preferred the main fleet always to remain in northern waters, seeking battle only under exceptionally favorable tactical conditions near to the British coast, Wilson was prepared to risk sending the fleet southward on periodic "sweeps" in the hope of catching enemy warships at sea.[50] The plan was not unreasonable and several of Fisher disciples, including Jellicoe, approved. Otherwise Wilson and Fisher were in total agreement over the operational deployment of the fleet in a war against Germany. Or so it seemed to Fisher when he finally relinquished the reigns of power on 25 January 1910.

On the afternoon of 23 August 1911, at a special meeting of political and military leaders convened by the secretary of state for war to discuss British action in case the "Agadir crisis" escalated into war with Germany,[51] Wilson demonstrated that he held a fundamentally different view of North Sea strategy from his predecessor.[52] The background to the crisis will be examined properly in the next chapter. Responding to a request from Prime Minister Asquith to explain the navy's intentions in the event of war with Germany, the first sea lord proceeded to outline an extraordinary war plan involving the close blockade of "the whole German North Sea coast," backed by units of the main fleet in close support.[53] While Reginald McKenna listened in horror, Wilson explained that the Royal Navy "had no wish to prevent the German Fleet from coming out [but] unfortunately, if we left them free to do so, their destroyers and submarines could get out also, and *their* exit it was essential to prevent."[54] Anticipating likely objections, the first sea lord went on to explain that the navy lacked sufficient destroyers to employ a flotilla strategy or an observational blockade, and consequently the only way of keeping an effective watch over German ports was to impose a close blockade. To alleviate some of the obvious logistical difficulties in operating destroyers so far from the British coast, Wilson proposed immediately to dispatch the Royal Marines supported by up to a division of regular troops to seize the German island of Heligoland for use as an advanced refueling base by the inshore squadron. He closed his presentation by observing that he "did not anticipate any difficulty" with such an operation.[55]

Wilson's presentation left his audience of senior political and military leaders incredulous. It was not so much the patent absurdity of the plan that shocked the politicians so much as Wilson's insistence on the need for absolute secrecy.[56] (The often remarked impracticability of his scheme has become much more glaring with hindsight.) The prime minister could hardly believe his ears when the first sea lord declared that his plan of operations "was not even known to the fleet."[57] Yet it was true. According to Vice Adm. Prince Louis of Battenberg, who then commanded the third and forth divisions of the Home Fleet, and who shortly afterwards joined the Board of Admiralty as second sea lord, no one, not even the "First Lord [McKenna] nor War Minister [Haldane] (both present) [had] heard a word of this scheme, which Wilson had worked out in minute detail."[58] Even Charles Ottley, the former DNI and now secretary to the CID, was dumbstruck. He too he had never heard about this "lunatic" plan before.[59] This being so, it is more than likely the scheme had not even been appraised by the Admiralty's own Naval Intelligence Department;[60] Ottley still had many friends inside the Admiralty including the current DNI, Rear Adm. Alexander Bethell, with whom he regularly discussed strategical questions.

Six weeks after the meeting Ottley wrote to Winston Churchill, the home secretary, who had also been present at the meeting:[61]

When I was DNI (in 1906)—a special committee of officers of which Captain Ballard was one, of which Captain [Maurice] Hankey was secretary, sat, by Sir John Fisher's orders to investigate the plan of campaign for a war with Germany. We then came to the conclusion that—much as we should have liked to take Heligoland—the scheme was utterly impractical. It could not be done. . . . Now, I don't say we were right or wrong. But I will wager any money that the committee's work was never considered by Sir A. K. Wilson when he decided, off his own bat, in a contrary sense.[62]

Without exception, historians who have read the minutes of this meeting have subsequently condemned Sir Arthur Wilson as dangerously poor strategist who was blind to the impact of technological change upon the conduct of war at sea. How was it possible, they cry, that one of the most respected admirals in the Royal Navy could have proposed, in 1911, in the age of mines and submarines, a return to the close blockade strategy? Yet none have ever seriously attempted to answer this question. It was simpler, they found, to tar all other naval planners of this period with the same brush.[63] But what these historians have failed to realize is that, after being appraised of their nature, the majority of senior naval officers in the fleet roundly condemned Wilson's anachronistic strategic plans. Naval opinion was so strongly against any idea of a close block-ade of Germany, indeed, that it is highly doubtful that Wilson's blockade strategy or his Heligoland scheme would have been executed in the event of war. Internal Admiralty documents show that when Arthur Wilson announced his plan to the CID in August 1911, the appropriate war orders had not yet been drawn up.[64] When, several weeks later, they were finally issued to the fleet, Francis Bridgeman—who in February 1911 had been appointed commander in chief—immediately protested the plan therein was unworkable.[65] His second in command, Vice Adm. Sir George Callaghan, was equally opposed to any suggestion of operat-ing the fleet off the German coast or trying to capture an advanced base, as was Vice Adm. Battenberg.[66] The admirals could see the logic behind Wilson's plan; the navy lacked sufficient destroyers to maintain a force in such an exposed position without an advanced base. But they doubt-ed the practicability of capturing the Island of Heligoland for the pur-pose.[67] In early September, Bridgeman and Callaghan refused point-blank to endorse the draft War Orders prepared for the Commodore (T) designated to command the inshore squadron. Before the dispute over the proposed close blockade strategy could be resolved, however, Wilson and McKenna were expelled from the Admiralty. Sir Francis Bridgeman became first sea lord and Winston S. Churchill the new first lord. According to Bridgeman, "Churchill laughed at the idea, and in conse-quence the scheme went by the board."[68]

This still leaves one question: if the opinions expressed by Wilson on 23 August 1911 were genuine, how could Fisher possibly have been per-suaded that their opinions on naval strategic policy in a war against Germany were broadly similar—as he undeniably claimed and seemed genuinely to believe? The explanation is simple. When Fisher resigned as first sea lord, he had every right to believe that his successor was utter-ly opposed to all close blockade strategies. Between 1906 and 1909, Sir Arthur Wilson explicitly and consistently stated that he believed a close blockade of the German coast to be impracticable. In 1907, he declared his opinion that even if such a strategy were effective it would not lead to any decisive results.[69] "The actual capture of their vessels at sea will do them much more harm than merely rendering them inactive in their ports," he argued on one paper, "and if eventually they come to the con-clusion that the risk is too great to venture out, we shall have arrived at the same result as if we blockaded them in, with *much less risk and loss to ourselves.*"[70] In 1909, Wilson reaffirmed his convictions when testifying before the Beresford enquiry. "I came to the conclusion," he explained to the prime minister, "that you could not keep a really close watch off the German ports, and that therefore you must adopt the policy of giving the enemy every possible opportunity of getting to sea in the hope you will catch him when he is at sea."[71] Towards the end of his cross-examination, moreover, Wilson openly castigated Beresford for proposing to deploy British destroyers right up to the German coast.[72] When Asquith had asked him to clarify his views on the best strategic disposition of the fleet against Germany he had replied that:

> after a great deal of consideration I decided that you could not keep a really effective watch off the German ports, because of the risk. If you send a small force of destroyers there, they are liable to be overwhelmed by the larger force of German destroyers. If, on the other hand, you send a large force of destroyers, you will get such an awful confusion . . . besides that, there is the impossibility of keeping a large force over there.[73]

At no time did Wilson give the slightest hint of being interested in close blockade strategies or plans to capture advanced bases on the German coast. Furthermore, when pressed by Beresford to give an estimate of how many destroyers the Royal Navy would need if it ever he wanted to impose an effective close blockade of the German ports, Wilson reply had been as uncompromising as it was emphatic. "As I do not want to work on the German coast," he had retorted, "I do not want so many."[74]

Unlikely as it may seem for a man so renowned for his inflexibility, it would seem that between 1909 and 1911 Wilson completely changed his mind about the desirability of close blockade. It is impossible to say what exactly triggered this dramatic reversal. Unless his private papers and diary are recovered we shall never fully understand his motives.[75] Yet it does seem that the growing submarine menace had been a major consideration. According to Capt. Roger Keyes (inspecting captain of submarines, 1910–15) the "enterprising exploits" of HMS *D1* during the summer maneuvers of 1910, "opened the eyes of the First Sea Lord, Admiral Sir Arthur Wilson, to the offensive possibilities of submarines, which he had hitherto regarded as defensive vessels."[76] Operating 600 miles from Portsmouth, *D1* had successfully "torpedoed" two hostile armored cruisers before returning to base. Although a decade earlier Wilson had stood out against the Royal Navy developing the submarine, it will be recalled, at the same time he had accepted that in time the submarine would evolve into a formidable threat to British naval supremacy. To most people these two opinions were contradictory: but not to Sir Arthur Wilson. As illogical as it may sound today, it was precisely *because* "his eyes had been opened" to the offensive possibilities of submarines that in 1911 he began advocating a close blockade of Germany!

A close examination of the minutes taken on 23 August 1911 shows that this was the explanation Wilson provided to the CID for why close blockade was "essential."[77] He clearly stated his opinion that: "the safety of our fleet depended upon preventing the German destroyers from getting out."[78] He further explained that: "if destroyers knew the position of a fleet accurately they were almost certain to meet with success at night. If a destroyer got within 3,000 yards of a battleship at night it could sink it."[79] Finally, he insisted that "all the experience of recent manoeuvres showed that close blockade was necessary" because "[a]ny other policy [such as an observation blockade or flotilla defense] would require a greatly increased number of destroyers."[80] Put another way, Wilson believed that the Royal Navy lacked the destroyers to cast a "flotilla net" fine enough to be sure of catching German flotillas seeking to ambush the British battle fleet on one of its periodic "sweeps" of the southern half of the North Sea. Warships on observation duties, moreover, were not in a position to prevent hostile submarines from putting to sea or getting into positions to shoot torpedoes at the British fleet. The only place the Royal Navy could be certain of intercepting German torpedo craft, therefore, was in the shallow waters off their own ports. This then was the reasoning behind Wilson's close blockade strategy; his object was to safeguard the British battle fleet from submarines while it was cruising in the North Sea looking for an opportunity to fulfill the Royal Navy's primary strategic objective, the destruction of the enemy's main fleet.

When in 1913 Sir Arthur Wilson again appeared before the CID to discuss North Sea strategy, he reaffirmed his conviction that he thought it imperative for the Royal Navy to maintain a close blockade of German ports in order to prevent their submarines escaping to the open seas. "I see no way of stopping this," he said, "except catching them in shoal water at the mouths of their own rivers."[81]

> I think that the advent of the submarine is the reason which makes the close blockade absolutely necessary, and the Admiralty must put its wits together to see how they will keep that close blockade or else the submarines will get out. The principal danger [to the British battle fleet] is the submarine which will get out.[82]

To summarize: while on the one hand Sir Arthur Wilson correctly appreciated the danger to the British fleet from torpedo craft and realized that it was not practicable for the British battle fleet constantly to patrol the North Sea ready to intercept the High Sea Fleet, on the other he refused to accept that battleships were redundant in narrow seas and remained determined to employ the battle fleet in the North Sea. Although Wilson far better understood the submarine's potential than the majority of senior naval officers, he simply would not accept the view that submarines made close blockade impossible. He believed that by blockading the enemy's ports, hostile submarines could be prevented from getting to sea—thus neutralizing the torpedo danger in the North Sea. To most people this reasoning was illogical—but not to Wilson.

A clue to understanding how Wilson developed his paradoxical reasoning lies in the report he submitted to the Admiralty in March 1904 on the series of exercises he arranged off Portsmouth between the early Holland submarine boats and the Channel Fleet.[83] While observing the maneuvers, Wilson developed very definite ideas on the capabilities and weaknesses of submarines. He noted, for instance, that the underwater craft had experienced difficulties in attacking smaller targets such as torpedo boats and steam pinnaces, and appeared to be handicapped when operating in shallow water.[84] In the process, he turned a deaf ear to claims that the submarines had been ignoring the flotilla craft in order to save their torpedoes for more valuable targets. After the Irish Sea maneuvers of August 1904, Wilson again ignored the contrary opinions expressed by the majority of his subordinates and reported to the Admiralty that his efforts to protect his fleet against submarine attack with small craft had been "on the whole successful."[85] Thereafter Wilson never wavered in his belief that submarines could be deterred from putting to sea by the threat of being rammed in shallow water by small surface craft which he believed were immune to torpedo attack.[86]

When six years later Wilson was placed in charge at the Admiralty, he was still blind to the true capabilities of the submarine. One of his first acts as first sea lord was to forbid the removal of cumbersome picket boats (fifty-foot-long steam pinnaces) which cluttered the decks of battleships, on the grounds that they would be required "for defence against submarines."[87] He simply would not listen to warnings from two successive inspecting captains of submarines, Sydney Hall and Roger Keyes, that however vigilant the patrolling destroyers and pinnaces, "there should be no difficulty in getting a number of submarines to sea past an inshore blockading squadron of light craft."[88] After trials between a submarine flotilla and the First Destroyer Flotilla led by Commodore (T) Robert Arbuthnot conducted during the summer of 1911, Keyes reemphasized his conviction that if the navy deployed destroyers inshore "off the coast of an enemy possessing submarines, it would court certain disaster. Any of the older craft [submarines] using the oldest type of torpedo we possess could not have failed to successfully torpedo such an easy prey."[89] Wilson remained unmoved.

Another step Sir Arthur took shortly after joining the Admiralty was to expand Fisher's secret anti-submarine committee.[90] In March 1910, the new body was placed on a firmer footing under the command of Rear Adms. Cecil Burney and Reginald Tupper. They were given the authority (and a considerable budget) to investigate all conceivable methods of detecting and attacking submarines. To make trials as realistic as possible they were allowed to use several old submarines as targets. One vessel, HMS *A1,* was fitted with a mechanical device which enabled it to run without a crew.[91] It could dive, maneuver, and then surface automatically. Unfortunately in February 1911 a mechanical breakage resulted in the motors failing to disengage after surfacing, and before the pursuing motor boats could catch her, the *A1* disappeared. Attempts to locate the vessel were unsuccessful. Other experiments involved the use of aircraft to find and bomb submarines. And in 1912 an intriguing attempt was made "to obtain an indication of the presence of a submerged submarine by an electric or magnetic apparatus."[92] "The idea of using ultrasonic waves for signalling and locating purposes," recalled one scientist involved with the development of ASDIC (Sonar) during the First World War, dated from the time of the *Titanic* disaster in 1912.[93] Sadly, the details of these experiments have not survived.

While Sir Arthur Wilson clearly recognized the danger to the Royal Navy posed by the development of "oversea" submarines and was alarmed at the size of the German budget for these craft, after becoming first sea lord he shelved plans drawn up by his predecessor to increase Britain's own submarine construction budget. Between 1910 and 1912, spending on new craft actually fell.[94] Instead of ordering eight (**D** class) submariners under the 1910 estimates, as his predecessor had intended, Wilson deleted two and decreed that for the remainder of his administration the navy would build no more than six craft a year.[95] He provided no explanation. There was certainly no pressing financial reason for the decision. The shortsightedness of the decision prompted Fisher shortly afterwards to confide in Rear Admiral Jellicoe his fear that Wilson did not seem to realize "the immense alteration in both tactics and strategy which the development of the submarine *now* causes," which was a curious remark for a man who had satisfied himself that his successor understood the conditions of modern naval warfare.[96]

In February 1910, Wilson arbitrarily directed that the thirty-eight destroyers and torpedo boats which had been detailed to cooperate with the seagoing submarine sections for operations in the North Sea were reassigned to destroyer flotillas.[97] Vice Adm. George Neville (commanding the nucleus crew divisions of the Home Fleet) privately explained to the distraught inspecting captain of submarines: "Sir A. K. W. won't hear of destroyers working with submarines, he says the latter should be attended on by their own parent vessels, the torpedo-boat destroyers being wanted for other work."[98] The first sea lord insisted that British submarines must be restricted to local defense duties. In wartime, the flotillas were to be broken up and reorganized into what can best be described as "fire brigades" comprised of "three boats plus a parent ship or tender," distributed "at various strategic points on the [east] coast ready at short notice to go anywhere they may be required."[99] In "their Lordships opinion," Admiral May noted acidly, submarine "patrol in the sense of a continuous watch at sea will *only* be required in the Pentland Firth [between Scotland and the Orkneys] and at the approaches to the Thames and in the Straits of Dover."[100] Even then, they were to be posted no more than ten to twelve miles offshore; a distance of twenty-eight miles was considered to be too far.[101] Most flag officers thought the change in deployment was a mistake and frequent representations were made to the Admiralty for the decision to be reversed.[102]

Wilson's efforts to diminish the role of the submarine in British naval strategy provoked strong criticism from the admirals afloat. Although there were flag officers serving in the Home Fleet in 1910 who believed that submarines were a waste of money, such as Rear Adm. Doveton Sturdee, they were exceptions to the rule.[103] The fleet commander in chief, by contrast, Adm. Sir William May, fully appreciated the utility of the submarine. In mid-1910, he decreed that "admirals and captains should be more conversant with submarines and their methods, and that more exercises should take place in conjunction with the fleet."[104] To this end he circulated a memorandum to all officers commanding warships in his fleet outlining the capabilities and tactics of submarines.[105] Admiral May further demonstrated his appreciation of the submarine by informing the Admiralty of his wish to deploy them in large numbers to support any surface squadrons operating near the German coast.[106] Papers written by the Mobilization Department confirm that in November 1910, two of the navy's seven submarine flotillas were redesignated "offensive" sections "for use oversea under the orders of C-in-C, Home Fleets."[107] Wilson's thoughts on this matter are not recorded.

Complexity and Confusion: On the Problems of Using a Battle Fleet in the North Sea

By 1910, most British admirals had been convinced that "the German Fleet is recognised as practically our only likely opponent (and a formidable one too) for some time to come."[108] A large (and increasing) proportion of the fleet was based, trained and exercised in home waters. From the commander in chief downwards, every British naval officer eagerly prepared for the second Trafalgar. Yet while there was a broad consensus among senior officers as to their ultimate objective, at the same time many realized that before they could forge the sword that would give them victory over the sixteen battleships of the High Sea Fleet, they first had to find solutions to several problems with operating a large battleship fleet in the usually misty waters of the North Sea. Put another way, although admirals unanimously believed that their goal was the destruction of the High Sea Fleet in battle, there was serious disagreement over how exactly this should be accomplished. Some officers favored a small highly capable fleet—the precision of the rapier—others wanted to employ the largest number of battleships possible—the brute force of the cutlass. For at least twenty years, fleet tactics had been a controversial subject in the Royal Navy.[109] About the only aspect upon which admirals could agree was that the navy would engage its adversary with a "battle fleet" consisting of no more than two or three squadrons of battleships deployed in a single line, each squadron comprising between four and eight units. Beyond that there was little consensus.

The largest obstacle to a large battle fleet was the problem of command and control. While the firepower, range and speed of warships had advanced tremendously since the age of sail, the ability of ships to communicate with one another was relatively underdeveloped. The Royal Navy still relied upon visual flag or lamp signals to control its ships at sea. In 1909, Rear Adm. Edward Bradford, who for many years had served as flag captain to the eminent Sir Arthur Wilson, declared that no fleet commander could reasonably hope to control a line of more than twenty battleships.[110] Many officers thought even this number would be unwieldy, however. The respected tactician Adm. Hedworth Lambton, for instance, believed that it was impracticable to control a line of battle longer than ten units.[111] Any more than that number and the admiral commanding in the lead ship would not be able to see—and thus control—the rearmost ship in his line; or more accurately, the rear ship would not be able to see the flagship's signals.

Rapid advances in gunnery technique further confused the debate. After the navy adopted long-range firing, the leading gunnery experts of the day insisted that all such tactical discussion was academic. They contended that it was simply impractical for a long line of warships to shoot effectively at an enemy fleet. Live firing experiments conducted in 1908 had shown that even at ranges as short as 8,000 yards, ships towards the end of a line simply could not see their targets through the smoke emanating from the funnels and guns of the battleships ahead of them. Furthermore, the Japanese navy had experienced exactly the same problem in fleet actions against Russian squadrons in 1904 and 1905.[112]

Gunnery experts therefore recommended that a line of battle consist of no more than six to eight units. But few senior officers listened to them; gunnery tactics was also a controversial subject within the navy about which there was equally little consensus.[113] Other "experts" could always be found refute any argument. Some gunnery officers, for instance, argued that the visibility problem for ships at the end of a line would be eliminated after the perfection of Adm. Percy Scott's "director" gunlaying system, then under development. The Scott director was, more or less, a master gunsight positioned atop the ship's control tower high above interference from sea spray and smoke. It helped, but it was not finally adopted by the Royal Navy until 1913.[114]

There was an alternative solution to the problem of commanding a large force. The commander in chief could split the fleet into divisions of four battleships each and allow them in battle to maneuver independently of one another. These tactics had first been tested back in the 1890s by Sir George Tryon. But after his death in 1893, as a result of his flagship being rammed and sunk by another battleship during an exercise, they were quickly abandoned.[115] Interest in divisional tactics revived after British officers learned that Admiral Togo had employed them at the Battle of Tsushima in May 1905.[116] For the next six years the Royal Navy spasmodically attempted to perfect divisional tactics but with little energy. Again and again it was found that existing communications equipment was simply not up to the task. Amidst the confusion of battle, visual signals were often missed and wireless messages went astray. In addition, because of the lack of an agreed tactical doctrine within the Royal Navy, the commander in chief could not rely upon his subordinates to anticipate his movements correctly. Admiral Togo had experienced the same problem at Tsushima.[117] The perils of allowing subordinates to act independently had been demonstrated to British fleet commanders by (acting) Comm. Hugh Evan-Thomas during the 1909 maneuvers. Flushed with a couple of minor victories, he had proceeded forward at top speed with his division straight into the path of the enemy main fleet and had been promptly annihilated.[118] At least a fleet formed in single line could not be defeated in detail.

Another reason for the lack of consensus on tactics was the mixture of dreadnought and predreadnought type battleships in the Home Fleet. Not until the end of 1911 did the Royal Navy possess enough all-big-gun ships to form its first homogenous "dreadnought" squadron, and it would take another two years before sufficient all-big-gun ships had been completed to equip the entire Home Fleet. In the meantime, fleet commanders were compelled to form harlequin squadrons. When deployed together in line of battle, the older types handicapped the more modern ships. In addition, whereas predreadnoughts, armed with powerful batteries of medium caliber quick-firing guns, fought best at shorter ranges, the all-big-gun ships had been purposely designed to fire deliberate salvoes only at relatively longer ranges. Whether the commander in chief chose to engage the enemy at long or short range, therefore, at least half his line would be compelled to fight at a disadvantage.

Not all the flag officers holding appointments in the Home Fleet in 1910 had yet been won over to the advantages of fast, all-big-gun armored ships. "It is said, and obviously with reason," revealed Rear Admiral Sturdee to one correspondent:

> that she [*Dreadnought*] can choose her range, and that at 10,000 yards she can inflict such damage on her opponents, in the opening stage of a fight that the opponent will not care about it and the matter will be settled there and then: i.e. the opponent will be demoralised. . . . Those who favour a smaller and consequently cheaper type [of battleship] argue, again with considerable truth, that taking the whole year round there are, in the North Sea, on average, twenty-five days out of every thirty on which you cannot see 10,000 yards, and that about 6,000 yards is the distance at which fire will be opened, and such being the case one of the great advantages of the *Dreadnought* disappears at once.[119]

Sturdee subscribed to the latter view; though he was prepared to admit that "the last word has not been said in 12-inch gun laying, and there is every reason to hope that the rate of hitting with this gun will be improved presently."[120] But there were no guarantees. Before then, the navy had to develop and perfect new fire-control gear, and overcome reluctance to pay for all units of the battle fleet to be fitted with up-to-date instruments.[121] In the meantime, even Sir William May found himself bound to confess that he anticipated the weather would probably restrict battle ranges in the North Sea to no more than 6,000 yards.[122] The supposition that battle would most likely take place at shorter ranges was greatly strengthened by intelligence assessments that the High Sea Fleet was determined to fight at ranges considerably less than 8,000 meters, and probably less than 5,000 meters where they could employ their quick-fire secondary batteries.[123] By 1910, British naval intelligence had established that the Germans had recently given up practicing long-range gunnery in favor of seeking battle at close range. This, as it happened, suited the Royal Navy. Development problems with the highly sophisticated helm-free Pollen fire-control system, not to mention escalating costs, encouraged the Admiralty to abandon its five year effort to develop a mechanized system of gunnery fire-control.[124] The decision in 1909–10 to prepare for fleet action at ranges of 6,000 to 8,000 yards had implications which extended far beyond battle tactics and gunnery policy.[125]

Another major problem in operating a battle fleet in the North Sea was the danger from torpedoes. Between 1909 and 1911, more and more officers came to accept that the steadily increasing range and power of the torpedo posed an undeniable threat to battleships cruising narrow seas. The Admiralty picked a bad time to abandon the "quest for reach" in gunnery. In December 1908, a 21-inch "heater" torpedo (mark 1) had run 7,500 yards at thirty knots. By late 1909, these new weapons were beginning to reach the fleet and the commander in chief was anxious for deliveries to be accelerated.[126] In June 1910, the DNI, Rear Adm. Alexander Bethell, confidentially noted that "the range and speed of the Whitehead torpedo has enormously increased in the last few years, and there is every probability of its being still further developed. *It is likely therefore that a range exceeding that of the gun will be obtained, and that fleet actions may have to be fought within torpedo range—that has already been nearly arrived at.*"[127] [my italics] Bethell, whose previous job had been director of torpedoes in the Ordnance Department, was one of the few officers in the service who knew that the navy was already developing an improved model designed to run 12,000 yards at full speed: a distance well beyond the then effective range of naval gunfire.[128] The officer now responsible for development of torpedoes was Rear Adm. Reginald Bacon. In March 1910, shortly after quitting the post of director of Naval Ordnance for a job in the private sector, Bacon informed an audience of senior officers that:

> the introduction of the torpedo has brought about a very considerable limitation in the powers of the battleship. Not only is the battleship itself open to attack by small craft which it cannot engage on equal terms, but it is powerless to protect any form of vessel against the attacks of such craft. Whereas forty years ago the battleship was practically supreme, it can now only be looked upon as supreme against vessels of more or less corresponding class. . . . [T]hese days, the battleship has developed merely into a vessel for fighting other battleships, and it shuns, as far as possible, encounters with most other classes of vessels. It is this defencelessness against the torpedo which has changed, to a certain extent, the tactical and strategical uses of battleships.[129]

The development of the long range torpedo had significant implications for North Sea strategy and a host of related issues such as warship construction policy, battle tactics, gunnery policy and—as will be shown—submarine design. Among the questions that most worried officers was: how could the Royal Navy deploy a line of battle in the North Sea if the big-gun became outranged by the torpedo? Under Sir Arthur Wilson, the Board of Admiralty expressed no official concern at the problem. This, of course, did not mean that the other sea lords did not have their own ideas. Bridgeman, Jellicoe, and Rear Adm. Charles Madden (respectively the second, third and fourth sea lords) all gave this question careful consideration.[130]

Before 1910, nearly every senior British admiral believed that except for a couple of small cruisers for signaling duties, the battleships alone would participate in fleet actions. Cruisers and destroyers, they felt, had no role to play in fleet actions. Some flag officers, notably Rear Adm. Lewis Bayly, wanted destroyers banned from ever attacking battleships.[131] Fleet commanders had no notion of a "Grand Fleet"; that is, an integrated fighting fleet comprising squadrons of battleships, and cruisers, and divisions of destroyers—the cumbersome formation the Royal Navy was to employ during the First World War. The concept of "grand fleet of battle," as it was known, did not begin to evolve until the period 1910–14. Not even Fisher, during his time in the Mediterranean, considered such tactics.[132] Although the Japanese under Admiral Togo had added destroyers to their main fleet in August 1904, midway through the Russo-Japanese War, another six years were to pass before any British fleet commander seriously considered following suit.[133] Serious discussion among Royal Navy flag officers on the concept of a "grand fleet of battle" did not emerge until 1910, and it was no coincidence that this occurred shortly after the new long-range torpedoes entered service.[134]

In the spring of 1910, Adm. Sir William May informed the Admiralty that he and his flag officers had been contemplating what ramifications the new torpedoes would have for fleet tactics, ever since the Intelligence Division had informed them that "the Germans propose to use two of their flotillas (twenty-two in number) with the High Sea Fleet."[135] May went on to report his conviction that hostile destroyers "would very likely succeed" getting within effective torpedo range of his battleships during the confusion of battle. A line of battleships, he imagined, would offer a marvelous target for torpedoes. May thought that the best method of protecting the battle line from this threat would be either to employ divisional tactics or to attach scout cruisers and destroyers to the Home Fleet and employ them to ward off hostile torpedo craft.[136] Of the two options May preferred the latter. In 1910, it must be stressed again, this was a novel and controversial idea. The overwhelming majority of May's flag officers, indeed, were opposed to the idea of seeing squadrons "hampered by having destroyers in company." When faced with an enemy torpedo attack, squadron commanders wanted to have the sea room to maneuver their battleships immediately out of harm's way without danger of ramming friendly destroyers. Only Vice Adm. Louis Battenberg (commanding the Atlantic battle squadron) was prepared to "advocate their use."[137] And even he was only a recent convert.[138] Nevertheless, all conceded that something had to be done to better protect the battle fleet from torpedo craft.

A better solution, in the opinion of May's flag officers, was to provide battleships with more guns. They complained that the new dreadnoughts lacked an auxiliary battery of quick-firing guns capable of warding off a hostile torpedo attack in the middle of a fleet action. Besides their 12-inch main armament, the new type of capital ship was armed with nothing larger than 4-inch guns mounted in the open on the upper deck. At ranges beyond 5000 yards these weapons would be of little use against larger destroyers, and in fleet action their crews would probably find their positions untenable owing to shell-splinters from the enemy's big-guns. "It might be most unpleasant," noted one officer, if during a fleet action the enemy "forced you to take your 12-in. guns off your opponent in order to fire at destroyers."[139] There was another objection to deck mounted anti-torpedo-boat guns. Practical experiments indicated that in fleet actions gun crews in the open might be concussed by the blast from their own big turret guns.[140] The solution, argued the flag officers, was to incorporate into future dreadnought designs a well shielded battery of 6-inch guns with which to fend off hostile torpedo craft. Six-inch guns could not only shoot farther, but practical trials had shown that a single 6-inch shell would effectively wreck a modern destroyer.[141] Thus, believed the flag officers, a battle fleet armed with a battery of quick-firing 6-inch guns, and without attendant destroyers to hamper them, would have the firepower to sink any threatening destroyers and the maneuverability to avoid their torpedoes.[142] Faced with virtual unanimity among his subordinate commanders, Admiral May reversed his opinion and endorsed the call to reintroduce the 6-inch gun in future battleship designs.[143]

The request from the Home Fleet was not well received by officers serving in Whitehall. For one thing, implementing the idea required further increases in the size and cost of future capital ships which the first lord was reluctant to endorse.[144] For another, neither Bridgeman, Jellicoe, nor Bethell thought that fitting larger anti-torpedo-boat guns would be either an appropriate or effective response to enemy flotilla craft carrying long-range torpedoes.[145] All three preferred instead the idea of attaching destroyers to the fleet to perform this task. Bridgeman thought that any additional weight added to capital ships could be better allocated to improving underwater protection. Jellicoe agreed—but for different reasons. After considering the complex gunnery problems associated with the proposed "fire and manoeuvre" tactics, he came to the conclusion that, in fleet action an admiral might find himself in the uncomfortable position of having to choose between maintaining effective gunfire on the enemy line of battle with his main armament, or maneuvering to engage hostile torpedo craft with his quick-firers and to avoid torpedoes in the water.[146] With existing fire control equipment a British admiral could not do both.[147] "We object most strongly," agreed Reginald Bacon:

> to the fire of the big guns being interfered with by the use of smaller guns at the same time with all the smoke and mess that are engendered by them. The attention of the Observing Officers is distracted; their sight is to a greater extent obliterated, and even the theoretical result of the small guns is not worth the candle . . . The ordinary six-inch gun in a battleship is, as regards torpedo-boat attack, of just as much use as a stick is to an old gentleman who is being snow-balled: it keeps his enemy at a respectful distance but still within the vulnerable range of the torpedo. In these days the locomotive torpedo can be fired at ranges at which it is absolutely impossible even to hope or think of hitting the Destroyer which fires the torpedoes at you. You may try to do it, but it is quite useless. Very well, then; the six-inch gun does keep the Destroyer at a longer range than would be the case if the six-inch gun were not there, but that's all.[148]

Bacon thought that "the better place for the 6-in. gun is in the auxiliary vessel that should form an integral part of the battleship unit."[149] But not until late 1912 did the Royal Navy start to built such vessels: which became known as light cruisers.

It is significant that only after Admirals Bridgeman and Jellicoe left Whitehall to take command of the Home Fleet and Atlantic Fleet respectively, did the Board of Admiralty at the last minute add a battery of 6-inch guns to the battleships laid down under the 1911–12 program.[150] Why this was done is still not clear. It is possible that the desire to improve the battleships' anti-torpedo-boat defenses may not have been the only motive for their addition. A number of senior naval officers actually wanted to fight the enemy at the shorter ranges (6,000 yards) where 6-inch projectiles could hurt battleships. A constant "hail" of shot from the "secondary battery" of quick-firing guns, many officers still believed, would prove more destructive and demoralizing to the enemy than occasional hits from the slower firing main 12-inch or 13.5-inch gun battery.[151] It is also significant that Bacon and Jellicoe's successors insisted that 25 percent of the 6-inch projectiles carried by the battleships of the 1911–12 program must be armor piercing "for use against armoured vessels."[152] Although to the eye there was little difference between an *Iron Duke* class "dreadnought" fitted with 6-inch guns and the original *all-big-gun* HMS *Dreadnought*, if the 6-inch guns were intended to serve as a "secondary battery" then conceptually the two were totally different types of battleships.[153] Fisher certainly feared this might be the case.[154] It is, however, difficult to say with any certainty why the 6-inch guns were added because the Admiralty dockets on the subject have been destroyed, as have the private papers of Sir Arthur Wilson. Similarly, little is known about the views of Vice Adm. Sir George Egerton (who replaced Bridgeman) or even more importantly Rear Adm. Charles Briggs (who succeeded Jellicoe as controller at the end of 1910). Opinion among officers serving in the fleet was as usual confused.[155]

The only other officer to read all the submissions on "the employment of destroyers in fleet action" by the various admirals commanding squadrons in the Home Fleet, was Herbert Richmond, Admiral May's flag captain. Richmond was widely acknowledged as one of the most gifted—and intellectually arrogant—officers of his generation. In one characteristically scathing letter to his chief dated May 1910, Richmond observed "a certain lack of consistency in some reports, which while saying that the attack has every prospect of success in thick weather and good prospects if delivered late enough in fine weather, yet also say that destroyers should not accompany a fleet: and thus recommend denying ourselves a weapon which is admitted to be a most valuable one."[156] Richmond found it incredible that not one admiral in the Home Fleet had been prepared to endorse an "offensive" plan calling for British destroyers to be thrown against the enemy's line of battle during a fleet action.[157] Only one, Milne, had been prepared even to consider the idea: but he had concluded that even in thick weather "although they might do a certain amount of damage, the majority would be sunk."[158]

Richmond was not the only senior captain in the fleet to criticize his superiors' lack of imagination on this point. Capt. Walter Cowan, a former destroyer officer, was also "strongly of the opinion that a battle fleet at sea and likely to fight should always have its attendant flotilla." He believed that "nothing would stop them inflicting such damage as would justify any losses they themselves might suffer, either in clear or thick weather." Recalling in 1911 recent various informal discussions on the subject, Cowan noted that:

some flag officers and captains who have only served in armoured ships will perhaps disagree with this, and have said whilst discussing the manoeuvres of last December [1910] that destroyers acting as I have described would be annihilated by gunfire before ever getting within striking distance; but I cannot think it, as no system of [fire] control in the Navy

is quick enough to cope with vessels closing each other [head on] at perhaps nearly fifty knots' speed.[159]

Cowan's views were warmly endorsed by Admiral Bridgeman who saw to
it that his paper was circulated round Whitehall.[160]

While their observations may have carried force, those officers
calling for the Royal Navy to use destroyers to attack the enemy fleet in
conjunction with its battle fleet overlooked the immense difficulties in
command and control of such a "grand fleet of battle." With the relatively primitive communication equipment available to the navy in 1910,
admirals were already experiencing difficulties in controlling a line of sixteen battleships.[161] Most admirals shuddered at the thought of having to
control an additional thirty or forty smaller craft in battle.[162] Even those
officers who favored attaching destroyers to the battle fleet for defensive
purposes, such as Jellicoe, did not like the idea of trying to use them
offensively as torpedo boats.[163] All squadron commanders doubted the
ability of battleship gun crews, in the heat of battle and amidst all the
smoke, to identify an approaching destroyer as friend or foe.[164] The easiest solution, it was agreed, would be to ban friendly destroyers from
approaching within 10,000 yards of the battle fleet and shoot on sight any
vessel that tried to steam closer. Berkeley Milne, Admiral May's second
in command, suggested that at night this distance should be increased to
fifteen miles.[165] This was adopted.[166]

Sir William May's personal views on the command and control problem were ambiguous. The "recent experience I have had now in thirty-
four tactical exercises," he informed the Admiralty in early 1910, "tends
to prove that it would be almost impossible to get a signal through, on
account of the smoke from the funnels and the guns."[167] But, without suggesting how, he went on to assert that the command and control difficulties would eventually be overcome. Besides, he added, the "question
as to whether a fleet operating in home waters should be accompanied
during the daytime by a flotilla of destroyers is practically solved for us
by the fact that at least one foreign nation is known to carry out tactical
exercises with destroyers taking part."[168] The Royal Navy was compelled,
he thus concluded, to attach "at least" six cruisers and twenty-four modern destroyers to the battle fleet.

This seemingly modest demand was not so easily granted, however.
In 1910, the Royal Navy had only eighty-six destroyers built or building
that "may be counted on as capable of working on [or up to] the German
coast in any weather, from a distant base."[169] And allocating this number
of destroyers to cruise with the Home Fleet would leave the British flotillas on observation duties in the southern half of the North Sea outnum-

bered and incapable of maintaining an effective watch. Notwithstanding the shortage, however, Sir Arthur Wilson directed that two flotillas of destroyers be attached to Admiral May's fleet.[170] Readers will see that Wilson's decision to endorse the tactics of "grand fleet of battle" and his subsequent proposal for a strategy of close blockade because of the shortage of modern destroyers, were related. The former, to a very large extent, determined the latter.

The Fleet Submarine Project

As we have seen, while most flag officers serving in the Home Fleet in 1910 recognized the potential of the new long-range torpedoes, for a variety of reasons they did not much like the idea of using destroyers to attack the enemy battle line.[171] More interest was shown in the possibility of shooting long-range torpedoes from the submerged torpedo tubes fitted to most battleships.[172] There was of course another type of small craft that could carry torpedoes to within firing range of an enemy battle fleet: namely the submarine torpedo boat. Submarines, of course, would not only be invisible to the enemy but also immune to their gunfire. In addition, the very fact that they operated underwater meant that they would not obstruct the battle fleet in action. It is not too much to say that from the moment naval officers appreciated the tactical capabilities of the submarine, they immediately began to investigate the possibilities of adding them to the "grand fleet of battle."[173]

The biggest drawback to the idea was the lack of sufficient progress in the development of the internal combustion engine. Existing submarines were all far too slow to keep pace with battle squadrons searching for the enemy in the blue water—though this had not stopped Vice Adm. Sir Francis Bridgeman in 1907 from trying to cruise submarines in company with his battleships during fleet maneuvers. During the first ten years of the twentieth century it was simply not possible to build submarines of battleship speed because suitably powerful engines did not yet exist.[174] But there was every reason to hope that the situation would improve before another decade passed. It is interesting to note that those officers who favored attaching flotillas of destroyers to the Home Fleet, i.e., Battenberg, Bridgeman, Jellicoe, and Bethell, were also among the first to envisage submarines being deployed in an auxiliary "torpedo" squadron to the main battleship fleet.[175] Discussion on the real practicability with "fleet submarines" was encouraged in late 1909, by information gathered by the Intelligence Department that several European navies were working in this direction. The NID had long suspected that submersibles already in service with the French navy were significantly faster and more seaworthy than British submarines; but they could never prove it. "The closest security is still maintained about everything connected with French submarines," as one intelligence officer noted—"like other nations [they] imagine they are the only other navy that have them."[176]

Then in late 1909, the Scottish shipbuilding firm of Messrs. Scott of Greenock notified the Admiralty that it had purchased a licence from the Italian firm of FIAT-Laurenti to build their patented high surface speed submersibles. On 4 November, the senior directors of Scott were granted an interview in London with the controller of the navy and the director of naval construction.[177] Rear Adm. John Jellicoe and Sir Philip Watts were sufficiently impressed by the Scott's presentation to consider purchasing their submarine. There were, however, potential legal complications. Eight months previously the Admiralty had agreed with Messrs. Vickers to renew their so-called "monopoly" agreement in return for the manufacturers waiving all royalties on submarines built in the Royal Dockyards.[178] Although the navy's lawyers claimed the agreement could be circumvented by using a loophole in the contract, any attempt by the Admiralty to do so was certain to be resisted by Vickers with accusations of sharp practice.[179] The controller's department was not as yet so persuaded that acquiring the Italian submarine design was worth antagonizing the navy's principal supplier. But that opinion would soon change. In the meantime the papers were forwarded to the inspecting captain of submarines, Sydney Hall, for his thoughts on the subject.

Before the Admiralty administration managed to deliver the file to Hall, however, a FIAT submersible en route to Stockholm for delivery to the Swedish navy "happened" to stop over at Plymouth and Royal Navy officers were allowed on board to inspect her. Although the 250-ton *Hvalen* was not a particularly modern design nor fitted with the latest engines (Scott was offering the Admiralty a much larger vessel fitted with new high power two-stroke diesels), she could nevertheless steam fourteen knots on the surface—or two knots faster than the equivalent British **C** class boat. To the officers of the Naval Intelligence Department the voyage of the *Hvalen* from Italy to England was at last proof positive that foreign submersibles were better craft than the Royal Navy submarines. Several days later this impression was reinforced when the department learned that the French boat had recently steamed the 1,200 miles from Rochfort to Oran inside five days; a performance "not approached by any British submarine," noted the assistant DNI Capt. Thomas Jackson in an accusing tone.[180] "There is no doubt," he declared, "that the Italian type presents a submersible torpedo boat capable in most circumstances, of rendering valuable service."[181]

Captain Hall was skeptical. Until 1909, he had always managed to bamboozle fleet submarine enthusiasts with technical data to show that building such vessels was not practicable. But faced with *Hvalen* moored in Plymouth Sound, and an offer to build an improved submersible already on the table, Hall was thrown on to the defensive. After personally inspecting the vessel, his first response was to barrage the officers of the NID with facts and figures. Hall insisted that their analysis based upon the comparisons between the "paper" performance of the Italian and British submarines was flawed. The *Hvalen,* he began, had been especially designed for surface navigation.[182] Her impressive surface speed was due entirely to the hull form favored by Italian designers which offered less resistance to water at higher surface speeds. "As I have so often pointed out," he added,

> a gain in speed of a knot or two on the surface or submerged sinks into insignificance compared with the many qualities that do not appear in contract trials. *Where such a gain is obtained at the expense of the other qualities,* as in the case of the FIAT submarine, where undoubtedly submerged qualities suffer for exaggerated surface performance, I do not consider that they are at all desirable and I see no reason to justify the claim of these FIAT submarines to superiority over other designs of equal displacement.[183]

Hall also disputed the assertion that submersibles were better sea-boats, and to demonstrate the fact he sent a **B** class (1903 vintage) submarine on a continuous run of 1,420 miles.[184] He also pointed out that the proven underwater performance of the British **C** class was markedly superior to even the paper figures claimed for the Italian craft; our "endurance at five knots is about twenty hours, a result the *Hvalen* cannot approach."[185]

Hall's arguments in favor of the Royal Navy continuing to develop "a sound reliable vessel with no one quality exaggerated at the expense of any other" fell on deaf ears at Whitehall, however, and a bitter argument ensued over the direction of British submarine policy. "It seems to me," observed Rear Adm. Alexander Bethell, the director of Naval Intelligence, that

> sea-worthiness and surface speed are *all important* in submarines. The first consideration is that they should be able with certainty and rapidity to reach their scene of action, and this must be done on the surface. A great radius of action when submerged, is not essential . . . nor is it desirable that any seaworthiness or surface speed should be sacrificed to obtain this.[186]

"I submit," Hall retorted, "that the principle of adding to surface speed at the expense of submerged qualities is unsound."[187] The capability to fight when action developed, rather than obtaining speed to get into action, should be the governing consideration in submarine design, Hall insisted. "The amount of endurance the DNI advocates, is, in my opinion, dangerously small, and no officer of experience in submarine attacks would be found to support it."[188] A submarine with the *Hvalen's* battery power, he protested, would have barely sufficient endurance to approach her target within torpedo range let alone escape over the horizon afterwards. Without electrical power she would be forced to the surface and "if she is harassed by any enemy she will be captured," he advised. Providing submarines with inadequate underwater endurance, Hall concluded, was analogous to "sending a ship into action short of coal."[189]

In February 1910, the inspecting captain of submarines was forced to respond to a petition from the NID for the Admiralty to abrogate the Vickers agreement and award a contract to Scott. In addition to reiterating the weaknesses of the Italian design, Hall drew up a long list of reasons why the Admiralty should not break with Vickers.[190] Most importantly, he pointed out, the navy had forged a close working relationship with the design team at Barrow-in-Furness. Vickers also possessed a unique capacity to design and build new models of submarine within a very short period. Hall was not opposed to seeing Vickers lose its monopoly when the contract lapsed, but he did not want to see the company upset before then through Whitehall high-handedness.[191] He had his reasons. Shortly before the agitation for "fleet submarines" began, Hall had petitioned the Admiralty for money to build an 800-ton experimental submarine of his own design.[192] In addition, Hall was anxious to equip the new vessel with beam firing torpedo tubes.[193] The results of recent experiments with "beam discharges for torpedoes from submarines," he explained to Jellicoe, "are so far reaching and important [that] I do not think at this stage that any [submarine] design without them is worth consideration."[194] Hall knew that the quickest way of acquiring the craft would be through cooperation with Vickers in modifying the design of the existing **D** type submarine,[195] hence his anxiety not to see the waters muddied by ill-judged talk of building fleet submarines and breaking the Vickers monopoly.

In March 1910, Jellicoe promised Hall that one possibly two of the 600-ton **D** type "patrol" submarines projected under the 1910–11 construction program would be modified to incorporate beam torpedo tubes as he had requested.[196] The enlarged (and more expensive) 800-ton version, known originally as "D-mod x," was later designated the type **E** submarine and was to form the backbone of the British submarine service during World War One. Three months later the controller resolved to go even further. At a meeting of the Admiralty Submarine Design Committee held in June 1910, Jellicoe announced that, subject to Board approval, no fewer than six of the seven vessels to be ordered that financial year would be built to "D-mod x" design.[197] Hall must have been delighted. But there was more: Jellicoe went on to reveal that the seventh submarine to be ordered that year would be a fleet submarine—or a "diving destroyer" as he preferred to call it.[198] Unbeknownst to the inspecting captain of submarines, the controller had ordered the Constructors Department to sketch a design for an experimental craft capable of attaining a surface speed of twenty knots and displacing 1,000 tons. To an extent, Hall was mollified by an assurance that this leviathan would be ordered from Vickers. The projected craft was essentially a still larger version of the original **D** type submarine and hence classified as the "D-mod y" design. In addition, Jellicoe had deferred to Hall's tactical expertise by stipulating the vessel must also have beam torpedo tubes, a requirement that complicated the design.[199] Even so, Hall was sufficiently upset at being so blatantly ignored that he seriously considered quitting the navy for private industry. Several weeks later, he secretly entered negotiations with Alfred Yarrow to spearhead Yarrow Shipbuilding's efforts to break into the submarine construction business.[200] In the meantime Jellicoe went on to explain to the Submarine Committee that he had felt compelled to order a "diving destroyer" because the Naval Intelligence Department had informed him that the French navy had laid down a class of high speed submersibles. "It is understood," he had been told, "they will be fully sea-going ships capable of keeping the sea with the fleet."[201] The department had further uncovered that the French craft would be propelled by two enormous diesel engines, each weighing over fifty tons and rated at 2,400 horsepower, to be built by the Franco-Belgian firm of Carrels. These two-stroke diesels, moreover, would generate more than three times the power of the Vickers four-stroke engine intended for the **E** class. Jellicoe was so disquieted by the huge disparity between the rated output of the French and British diesels that he asked the director of Naval Construction to approach Carrels to see if they would be willing to sell engines to the Royal Navy in the event that Vickers were found unable to supply such powerful units.[202] He also directed further enquiries to be made in Germany.[203]

Jellicoe's hopes for the fast submarine project were soon deflated. On 27 June, Edward Froude, the superintendent of the Admiralty Research Establishment, advised the controller that experiments conducted with models of the "D-mod y" hull-form in the testing tank at Haslar had yielded unexpectedly discouraging results. Based on the preliminary figures, Froude predicted that when propelled by 4,800 horsepower. engines the projected submarine might just attain a surface speed of twenty knots, but only if the hull was lengthened to two hundred and thirty feet. This meant the "D-mod y" had to be substantially redesigned.[204] But in August, Froude reported that further experiments with new lengthened models had demonstrated that the consequent improvement in speed was "practically nil."[205] Furthermore, the longer vessel was found to be dangerously unstable with a marked "tendency to dive" at higher speeds: "a little roughness of water, or a slight accidental excess of trim by the bow would probably turn the scale in favour of diving."[206] How exactly the Submarine Design Committee reacted to this news is uncertain because the Admiralty copies of the reports and remarks thereon have not survived. Jellicoe must have been disappointed: but not Hall. He was quite content with a more moderate speed. "I cannot see what is the virtue of twenty knots as opposed to sixteen or seventeen knots for a submarine," he thought.[207]

In any case, before the final sketch designs of "D-mod y" were sent to Vickers at the end of October 1910 they were amended. The proposed craft was now fitted with smaller engines and given an enhanced underwater endurance. The reworked design, in fact, was remarkably similar to the **L** type submarine ordered by the Admiralty in 1916. It was probably Hall who was responsible for the changes because he subsequently became much more enthusiastic about the "D-mod y" project.[208] Just days before the Board of Admiralty was due to award the contracts for the submarines of the 1910–11 program, Hall was prodded by Admiral Fisher, his old mentor, to submit a last minute plea for his own "D mod x" (**E** type) design to be set aside in favor of the amended Admiralty "D-mod y" plans. "I do not think the 800 ton design is large enough to give sufficient comfort for the vessel to fully realise the sea keeping qualities she otherwise possesses," he now thought, "but the 1000 ton design with four beam tubes should do so." In a remarkable turn around, Hall advised that "I think she would be better value."[209]

Ironically, however, Hall's new appeal was ignored. On 2 February 1911, the Admiralty placed contracts for six **E** type submarines, plus another two on behalf of the Australian government, at a price of £105,415 per boat. The tender for "D-mod y" was rejected by the Admiralty ostensibly because the price Vickers was asking—almost £200,000—was considered too much.[210] In fact, the decision not to order the experimental craft that year had been taken several months earlier.[211] In December, someone at the Admiralty had instructed the DNC to put the plans for "D-mod y" in a drawer for reconsideration in six months.[212] That someone was almost certainly Rear Adm. Charles Briggs who at the end of 1910 had succeeded Jellicoe as controller upon his appointment to command the Atlantic Fleet.[213] The colorless Briggs had a reputation for being a timid and ponderous administrator.[214] No one had informed Hall of the decision to suspend the project because in December 1910 he had been fired as inspecting captain of submarines.

The decision to sack Hall probably had much to do with the Admiralty's discovery of his flirtation with Yarrow.[215] Sir Arthur Wilson, who had long regarded Hall as "too damned pertinacious," was reportedly furious at what he regarded as an attempt by an officer to sell naval secrets to private industry for personal gain.[216] The measure of the first sea lord's displeasure is illustrated by Hall's subsequent fate. He was effectively banished from England: his next command was a dilapidated third-class cruiser detached from the Mediterranean Fleet for police duties off Crete. He was accompanied into exile by a commander and four lieutenants who had all recently served in submarines.[217] It says something of Hall's character that his ship, HMS *Diana,* soon acquired "a reputation for being a pirate and for avoiding rather than conforming to the customs of the service."[218] The new inspecting captain of submarines, Roger Keyes, was an officer of a very different kidney. Dashing, flamboyant, and well-connected socially, he was more at home on the polo field than in "the trade." More importantly he was neither a qualified torpedo officer nor a submariner. He was, in his own words, "a mere *Salt Horse.*"[219] Until then it had been the custom of the outgoing inspecting captain to choose his own successor. Hall, for instance, had nominated Capt. Frank Brandt as his heir. In his memoirs, Keyes claimed that Wilson appointed him to the post especially to break the "closed shop" and "to bring the submarine service into close touch and co-operation with the fleet."[220]

Had the post of inspecting captain of submarines not still carried with it the responsibility for the development of matériel, Wilson's decision to appoint a nonspecialist officer would have been an inspiration. When Keyes first accepted his new commission, he had been conscious there still existed an "awful stigma of being attached to the creation of Bacon and Fisher."[221] A significant number of captains and commanders serving in the fleet remained prejudiced against submarines and submariners generally, largely because they were so closely identified with "the streaky one" and "radical jack." By the end of his appointment, the "potentiality" of the submarine had become much better understood by these middle-ranking officers, and the submarine service had become "very much recognised as part of the sea-going fleet."[222] When Keyes proclaimed in 1911 that the new **D** class "oversea" vessels "would be able to remain self supporting in an enemy coast for some days," previously skeptical officers sat up and took notice.[223] With justification, therefore, Keyes believed that his personal popularity and well-known independence from Fisher's influence had contributed to the new willingness within the fleet to take submarines seriously.

On balance, however, Keyes' term as inspecting captain (commodore from May 1912) of submarines was not a success. Subsequent events were to show that he had neither the qualifications nor the temperament for a job that required him to coordinate the actions of designers, engineers and manufacturers, and which also required a sound grasp of technical detail. Even his best friends agreed that he did not have an outstanding intellect.[224] "To me," Keyes himself confessed, "machinery and materiel detail were a closed book."[225] To help compensate for his deficiencies, the new inspecting captain gathered around him a small committee of advisors. Inexperienced young officers, his predecessor chided, who were "not in a position to judge the ultimate effect of their recommendations and just the people likely to be influenced by the advertising quacks of rival types of submarines."[226] More seriously, during discussions in the Submarine Design Committee, Keyes habitually deferred to the DNC's department. As we shall see, the inability or unwillingness of the head of the submarine service to stand up to the constructors was to have a profound impact upon the efficiency and capability of the British submarine arm before 1914.

Most significantly, as soon as Hall vacated his desk in Whitehall agitation for the fleet submarine revived. Keyes, who seems to have been predisposed to favor the idea, was immediately informed by Sir Philip Watts that the first priority of the design committee was to reconsider the fleet submarine project. The DNC informed Keyes that the Vickers design "did not lend itself to further development."[227] Armed with the latest reports from the Haslar testing tank facilities, he went on to explain that the only way of achieving a higher surface speed was by adopting a more streamlined hull form to reduce resistance to water, and increasing the surface buoyancy thereby counteracting the tendency to dive involuntarily in choppy seas.[228] These two requirements, Watts advised, could only be met by adopting a double hull design. If "the circular section of pressure resisting hull would be given up as in the Italian boats, and a torpedo boat shape adopted," he explained further, "the hull form is made more favourable for surface propulsion."[229]

In May 1911, Keyes asked Haslar to test more submarine models incorporating radically different hull forms.[230] The new hulls, apparently, were taken from stolen copies of plans for Italian and French double hull submersibles "which got into Sir Philip Watt's hands in an illicit way!"[231] The consequences of the decision to adopt the Italian hull form were important, and Keyes recalled the discussions when drafting his memoirs. "The definitely limited speed of the **E** type," he recorded, "made it desirable to build submersible rather than submarine vessels, for work with the fleet."[232] More specifically, "I was advised by the technical experts that an extension of the E design [the 'D mod y'] could not be driven at a higher speed than about fifteen knots without considerable risk of diving while running on the surface, but the French and Italian designs could be driven safely at considerably higher speeds."[233]

At a subsequent meeting of the Submarine Design Committee attended by Briggs, Keyes and Watts, and their principal assistants, Cmdr. Percy Addison and Constructor Harris Williams, it was unanimously agreed that the most important feature of the next class of submarines would be a high surface speed.[234] Although the minutes of the meeting have not survived, Keyes recorded most of what was said in a letter he wrote to his predecessor, Sir Philip Watts, Keyes informed Hall, insisted "the saddle tank monstrosity" (alias the "D-mod y") could not possibly fulfil the navy's requirement for a fast submarine and thus was immediately "wiped out" from consideration.[235] The DNC and his assistant had then gone on to extol the virtues of Italian submersibles. But when asked to design one they had "funked," according to Keyes. "They said it was very doubtful whether they could build them satisfactorily in England without any experience, owing to the very confined spaces between the inner and outer plating."[236] Matters had not been helped by the refusal of the submarine design team at Vickers Ltd. to assist. As a consequence, Keyes reported, the assembly resolved that the only remaining option was to acquire an Italian designed vessel "for the sake of experiment and comparison," from either Scott's of Greenock or direct from the FIAT company.[237] Hall replied that having seen the *Hvalen,* he considered the purchase would yield "doubtful advantage."[238]

The decision in the summer of 1911 to buy an Italian designed submersible from Scott's set the Admiralty firmly on a collision course with Messrs. Vickers Ltd. Relations between the two were already in a poor state. Earlier in the year the company had discovered the Admiralty's negotiations with foreign firms to supply the Royal Navy with high powered diesels and promptly threatened legal action claiming that their long-standing "monopoly" agreement extended to all fixtures and fittings in the boats. The firm's submarine business was highly profitable and worth fighting for.[239] According to Vickers's internal papers, the firm's mark-up on diesel engines yielded more than a third of overall profits on submarine construction.[240] Faced with an Admiralty counterclaim that the company was "failing to meet the Navy's requirements," the directors of Vickers had responded by offering to develop a suitably powerful diesel engine of their own. But the Admiralty had not been impressed. Vickers produced only heavy four-stroke diesel cylinders whereas the navy required for its fleet submarines the more powerful and theoreti-cally more advanced two-stroke lightweight version of the engine. There was little chance that the British firm could develop a new type of engine cylinder within two years. Vickers, nevertheless, began development work on the new cylinder.

The Vickers engineers were from the start doubtful of success. They advised their managers that the French, Italian, and even German diesel manufacturers had all greatly underestimated the difficulties in perfect-ing the two-stroke diesel engine. And as subsequent events would show, they were correct. Not only was the science of metallurgy not yet suffi-ciently advanced, but a host of technical problems with experimental engines had not been correctly identified. Torsional vibration, for instance, was still not properly understood. As a consequence, when the foreign designed engines under development in 1911 were tested two years later, they literally disintegrated on their mountings.[241] Although the Vickers personnel had not understood torsional vibration either, they had recognized a problem existed and had accidentally found a partial remedy. Building deliberately heavy engines and mounting them on sub-stantial foundations enabled Vickers to supply the Royal Navy with what was certainly the most reliable albeit crude diesel built for submarine propulsion developed before the First World War.[242] But all this did not become apparent until much later. Meanwhile, in 1911, rather than lis-ten to warnings from Vickers that two-stroke engines could not be made reliable without considerably more development, the Admiralty chose to believe that British engineers were backward compared with their Continental rivals.[243] Parenthetically it is interesting to note that in 1914 the German navy dropped the Krupp-made two-stroke submarine diesel in favor of the more reliable four-cycle MAN diesel.[244]

The reaction of the Submarine Design Committee to the Vickers legal challenge was at once to petition the Board of Admiralty to cancel the monopoly agreement. Keyes pleaded that the special agreement clearly had "outlived its uses, and is in fact a hindrance to development if, as has been stated, it debars us from ordering engines from other firms."[245] In support, Watts composed an inflammatory report which claimed, but failed to prove, that for the past few years the firm had been consistently "overcharging" the navy by as much as 25 percent.[246] In so doing, the DNC was aware that a month earlier the sea lords had been most unhappy at having to pay £106,768 for each of the new E class sub-marines when they had only been paying some £80,000 for each D class vessel.[247] Watts's report, in other words, was probably written to under-mine the last remaining goodwill towards Messrs. Vickers. It worked. On 31 March 1911, the Admiralty had served notice on Vickers of its intention to cancel the monopoly agreement, though a clause in the contract meant that links could not be finally severed for another two years.[248] Whether, at this stage, the Admiralty had truly decided to part with Vickers or was merely posturing in order to secure a better standard of service and lower prices (as the Fisher administration had done back in 1906) is not clear.[249] By September, however, after Vickers had refused to develop a double-hull submarine for the navy without financial guarantees, the Admiralty's demeanor towards the company noticeably hardened. Egged on by an adamant Roger Keyes, the Board resolved "to adhere to the cancellation of the agreement" using the excuse that "the firm has not met the Admiralty's requirements" by failing to deliver the new **D** class submarines on time.[250] The Vickers directors responded by again threatening legal action, but ultimately withdrew their claim after "the First Lord saw Sir Trevor Dawson [of Vickers], and told him very plainly that relations with his firm would become strained if the firm endeavoured to stop other firms from building for us."[251] In short, Vickers made much more money from capital ship contracts.

In the summer of 1911, the Submarine Design Committee had no intention of obeying the spirit of the now defunct Vickers agreement by waiting two years before procuring a FIAT submersible. Readers will recall that in 1909 the Admiralty legal department claimed it had identified a loophole in the Vickers contract. According to the "sea-lawyers," the terms did "not preclude us [the navy] from obtaining submarine vessels by competition provided they are not to a specification prepared by the Admiralty i.e. the design and requirements must be left entirely to the tenders."[252] This meant that the submersible could be purchased provided members of the Submarine Design Committee did not collaborate in the design of the craft.[253] To do so would clearly violate the letter of the agreement.[254] The drawback to "buying off the shelf" was that standard equipment used in British submarines covered by joint Vickers-Admiralty patents, such as beam firing torpedo tubes, could not be fitted to the craft. But as the officers of the Submarine Committee were mainly interested in the Italian hull form this was not seen as a major problem.

By coincidence, Keyes had previously served as British naval attaché in Rome. Through his contacts in Italy he was thus able to arrange for FIAT to send the Admiralty a supposedly unsolicited invitation for Royal Navy officers to visit their yards and inspect their submarines.[255] In September 1911, a team of submariners led by Cmdr. Percy Addison was sent to inspect the FIAT works at La Spezia.[256] Their report was full of lavish praise. Doubts over the reliability of the diesel engines raised by Engineer Cmdr. Hugh Garwood were brushed aside: a fact which tends to strengthen the argument that the principal object was to acquire the hull form.[257] Acquiring the streamlined Italian hull design had become still more urgent after the Admiralty had learned in August that Carrels had derated their high-power diesels by thirty percent.[258] So, on 6 September, Keyes reported to the first sea lord that he urgently recommended "the purchase of one of these craft through Messrs Scott" for the purpose of experimentation and to "keep pace with foreign powers—to evolve a type of fast sea-going submersible."[259] The Board approved. On 23 January 1912, the Admiralty signed a contract with Scott's for one submersible which later was commissioned as HMS *S1*.[260]

Finally, in February 1912, Keyes was instructed by the first lord of the Admiralty to form a committee "to put forward definite recommendations as to future design."[261] For this task Keyes selected only his personal advisors, making no effort to consult other experts in the field such as Captains Hall, Bacon or Brandt. After only a week, Keyes unhesitatingly recommended that all future submarines should be built with a double hull to facilitate improved surface performance.[262] The report stated that in future the navy would require two types of craft. First, "a high buoyancy ship-shaped vessel of sufficient speed to accompany a battle-fleet, and . . . capable of keeping the sea for extended operations. The speed required to carry out the role of 'fleet' submarine should be at least the speed of the fleet—at present about twenty knots"[263] and second, a smaller model of about 350 tons for coastal defense duties "to replace the submarines which have become non-effective." Both designs, Keyes admitted, were "very frankly copied" from FIAT plans.[264] But the most significant result was that the Royal Navy was henceforth committed to a long-term fleet submarine development program.

Epilogue

Over the next two-and-a-half years, Keyes would discover he had made a number of miscalculations. When in 1911 the Submarine Committee resolved to cancel the Vickers monopoly, they had forgotten that the DNC's department did not yet have its own submarine design team. At most only two or three naval constructors knew anything about submarines. Also, the Royal Navy was totally dependent upon Vickers draftsmen to produce working sets of blueprints for any new design. Until the monopoly contract finally lapsed, moreover, the Admiralty was barred from collaborating with engineers at other firms. It was to Vickers, therefore, that Keyes was forced to turn in June 1912 to design the *Nautilus*—the Royal Navy's first full-sized fleet submarine—whose hull form had been copied from the FIAT plans.[265] It is highly probable that Keyes illegally tried to evade this restriction by secretly sending specifications of the Admiralty's ideal submarine to foreign designers.[266] Later in 1912 he was caught passing such information to French designers.[267] Fortunately for the Admiralty the directors at Vickers did not find out.

The adoption of the fleet submarine development program had other repercussions. Most importantly, Keyes was alarmed to find that deliveries from Vickers slowed after the monopoly finally lapsed. He had anticipated that increased competition would have the opposite effect. There were several reasons why it did not: first, after March 1913 the company was no longer bound to give priority to submarine building for the Royal Navy and was now free to sell its latest designs for export.[268] In 1913, for instance, Vickers won competitions to supply submarines (Admiralty **E** type!) for the navies of both Turkey and Greece. Second, Vickers found their output disrupted by the new firms in the industry poaching their skilled workmen and experienced draftsmen. This problem became so serious that in 1913 the directors responded by offering all members of their submarine design team an unheard-of five year personal contract.[269] The Admiralty, incidentally, also suffered from the effects of head-hunting. At the end of 1912, Constructor Harris Williams, the navy's top submarine designer, was lured to Armstrong and Engineer Cmdr. Hugh Garwood was recruited by Vickers. Third, Keyes had not fully appreciated just how reliant upon Vickers the entire British submarine industry would be for a variety of key components. This was brought home to him in 1913 after the "superior" Italian and German diesel engines he had purchased proved to be totally unreliable. As we have seen, the Vickers diesels may have been crudely and heavily built, but their reliability and performance was better than anything else available before the war.[270] Much to Keyes' embarrassment, in 1913 the Submarine Committee was forced back to designing their new improved (**F** type) coastal submarine around the Vickers diesel.[271] The rate at which the Royal Navy could add submarines to the fleet once again became governed by the output from the Vickers diesel engine plant.[272]

Another consequence of the decision to cancel the Vickers monopoly was that the performance capabilities of Royal Navy patrol submarines did not improve for three years. The reason for this was more complex. Essentially, so long as the Vickers monopoly agreement remained in force the company was entitled to claim joint ownership over any new patents taken out by the Admiralty relating to submarines. This included all new equipment developed by the navy or improved features incorporated into the design of submarines built in the Royal Dockyards.[273] As one Admiralty lawyer noted: "There would thus be some risk that designs or inventions really made by the Admiralty either with or without the assistance of Messrs: Vickers might be patented by the contractors, and royalties afterwards claimed against the Admiralty or their contractors."[274] And as Sir Philip Watts had observed several years previously, "the first result of [a contractor] being requested by the Admiralty to submit a design . . . would probably be that they would take out patents for all possible arrangements they could think of."[275] Naturally, the Admiralty did not want Vickers to be able to claim ownership of any more patents than was necessary. So it was probably for this reason that the Royal Navy stuck with the basic type **E** design for over four years, at a time when the submarine was evolving rapidly on the Continent, and why the Admiralty ignored repeated requests from the submarine service for improvements in design.

The most important consequence resulting from the fleet submarine development program was the cost of persuading other firms to enter the submarine industry in competition with Vickers. Originally, the Admiralty expected Messrs. Scott to jump at the chance of building a submersible for the Royal Navy. When approached, however, Scotts refused to make the necessary investment in plant and labor unless they were guaranteed contracts for six such boats over the next three years.[276] The Admiralty had no alternative but to agree to this demand. In July 1912, the Admiralty encouraged Armstrong Ltd. to enter the industry "as a rival to Scott's."[277] This firm subsequently purchased a license from the French company of Schneiders after they were guaranteed contracts for four boats within two years. In 1913, six other British shipbuilders were enticed to build submarines for the navy. They too had to be promised a minimum number of contracts and given a relatively simple design to build in order they might gain experience. At the end of that year, therefore, the Admiralty awarded contracts for seven new 350-ton submarines which the submarine service really did not want.[278]

The net result of the decision to obtain the Italian hull form was that between 1912 and 1914 the navy ordered a total of twenty-six submarines of eight different designs of which more than half were known to be either "obsolete" or "unsuitable" for operational purposes.[279] Over the same period the production of submarines designed for operational purposes slowed to a trickle. "It is tragic," lamented the former inspecting captain of submarines, Captain Hall, in a letter addressed to Fisher dated April 1914, that over the previous four years "our vote for submarines should be frittered away on freaks and coastals."[280] During this period Keyes added just ten **E** class "patrol" submarines to the eight ordered by Hall under the 1910–11 program. As a consequence, when war with Germany commenced in August 1914, the Royal Navy found itself chronically short of modern patrol submarines and unable to implement the strategy of flotilla defense in the North Sea.

CHAPTER 8

The Churchill Administration, 1911–1913

The [naval] estimates for the forthcoming year should show some reduction from the abnormal level at which they now stand.
Winston Churchill (first lord of the Admiralty), 10 November 1911

Readers will recall that when Mr. Asquith became prime minister in April 1908, one of his first acts had been to dismiss Lord Tweedmouth as first lord of the admiralty for failing to keep a tight reign on expenditure. Before his elevation to the premiership, it will also be recalled, Asquith had served two years as chancellor of the Exchequer. During that period his inability to control naval spending had more than once threatened to embarrass the government's fiscal policy. Although Asquith had suspected that the Admiralty was manufacturing arguments to support their case for more funds than the Treasury considered necessary, lacking any expertise in naval affairs he had been unable to prove his suspicions. But an energetic "economist" minded minister planted inside the Admiralty, he had hoped, might have more success.[1] Asquith's first choice for this mission was the young Winston Churchill— but he unexpectedly refused the portfolio of first lord and it had been taken instead by Reginald McKenna. Since the beginning of the Liberal administration in 1905, the little-known McKenna had earned himself the reputation for being an excellent administrator. His first post in the government had been that of chief secretary to the Treasury, a position that bought him into close contact with Asquith who was quickly impressed by his first-rate mathematical brain and sound grasp of finance.[2] In early 1907, accordingly, McKenna had been promoted to the Cabinet as president of the Board of Education and charged with the task of salvaging the government's education policy after the House of Lords rejected its nonconformist inspired reform bill.[3]

When Asquith moved McKenna to the Admiralty in April 1908, he had believed his disciple to be a confirmed "economist." The prime min-

235

ister soon learned his mistake. Instead of dismissing the obstinate Sir John Fisher from the Board—as many had expected he would do—McKenna had developed an unexpected rapport with the first sea lord.[4] The two quickly became friends and together became a formidable administrative team, committed to upholding Britain's naval supremacy.[5] Their greatest achievement was to force the Cabinet in early 1909 to swallow the eight capital ship construction program that resulted in a 10 percent increase in the navy estimates. That summer McKenna had risked his political career by vigorously defending the first sea lord's administrative record before the Beresford Enquiry. Fisher often boasted proudly that his friend had "pretty near wrecked himself for the Navy's good."[6] Despite winning the case against Beresford, though, the first sea lord's reputation had been too badly damaged and in January 1910 he retired. Even after Fisher left the Board of Admiralty, Reginald McKenna continued to champion the navy's cause much more effectively than the prime minister had thought likely or possible. His skills as an advocate (he had practiced at the bar before entering the House of Commons) had enabled him to resist attempts by the Cabinet to impose cuts on naval expenditure after panic of 1909 subsided.[7] David Lloyd George, the chancellor of the Exchequer, more than once remarked with rueful admiration that "McKenna could make the best departmental 'defence speech' [*sic*] of any man in the House of Commons."[8] Though it does seem that McKenna's effectiveness owed much to the fact that for many months after his official retirement, Fisher continued to prepare the first lord's brief.[9] McKenna, it seems, not being a naval professional, lacked either the initiative or confidence to implement reform without the approval of Arthur Wilson.[10] Herein lay the seeds of his eventual downfall.

Towards the end of 1910, Reginald McKenna began to loose his grip on the Admiralty bureaucracy and his sense of administrative direction. In part this was due to recurrent bouts of poor health.[11] In January 1911, serious illness resulting in a major operation kept him out of action for six weeks and it was many months before he was fully recovered.[12] But most of the blame for the growing confusion in naval policy rested upon the shoulders of the first sea lord. Sir Arthur Wilson had not only failed to provide the first lord with adequate guidance or support, but, as has been mentioned, his "autocratic tendencies" generated serious disharmony inside and outside Whitehall. During Wilson's term as first sea lord the Admiralty earned the reputation among the other departments of being "difficult" to deal with and slow to reply to official correspondence.[13] This certainly was not McKenna's fault. He was renowned for being able to state his case "lucidly and logically," and it was well known that he dealt with "all his official papers the moment they arrived."[14] Both

Asquith and Lloyd George spoke often of his "characteristic efficiency."[15] Yet despite his reputation as a gifted administrator, McKenna proved incapable of dispelling the growing impression within the Cabinet that his Board of Admiralty seemed to have no definite policy before it—except to defy all attempts by the Treasury to deflate the levels of naval expenditure.[16] McKenna's stock with his colleagues had never been high. He had always depended heavily upon the prime minister's patronage. By the spring of 1911, however, his popularity had fallen so low that a number of Cabinet ministers believed the time had come to replace him as first lord of the Admiralty.

Prominent among the first lord's detractors was the recently ennobled Viscount Haldane. Since the Liberals took power in December 1905, Haldane, as secretary of state for war, had been performing a miracle of reorganization at Pall Mall by transforming the army into an efficient fighting force. In addition to setting up the General Staff and restructuring the regular battalions, he had successfully reformed the militia and volunteer reserves into the so-called Territorial Army.[17] Undoubtedly his most notable achievement was the creation of a much needed rapid reaction force. Haldane conceived the British Expeditionary Force (or BEF) in January 1906 as a "highly-organised and well-equipped striking force which can be transported, with the least possible delay, to any part of the world where it is required."[18] Contrary to the assertions of many historians, the size and composition of the BEF were not determined by Continental strategic considerations;[19] rather its character was dictated by a "rigid financial ceiling" placed on the army estimates, the constraints imposed by a voluntary system of military recruiting, and the number of battalions required for imperial garrison duties.[20] In the words of Haldane's biographer, "any speculation about the strategic role or the military capability of the force was merely an attempt to rationalise a body, earmarked for war, whose size was determined by the restrictions of peacetime criteria."[21] That being said, however, the War Office did make preparations for the BEF to operate on the Continent in the event of a German invasion of France, but realised that it was too small to play a major role in the defense of France.[22]

Haldane had no pretensions to be a military strategist. He saw his role as a reformer of the administrative machine and was content to leave the details of military policy to his new general staff.[23] That being said, however, he was deeply concerned at the aggressiveness of Germany foreign policy. Like many other officials serving in the government at this time, he seems to have been driven by the belief that Britain could not afford to allow Germany to establish a political or military hegemony in Europe.[24] In short, Haldane was committed to the idea of direct British intervention in the event of war between France and Germany.[25] Reasoning that the Royal Navy could do little to stop the German army from reaching Paris, Haldane believed that the only politically viable option open to the British government in the event of war with Germany was to send the expeditionary force to the Continent. Haldane thus encouraged the chief of the General Staff, Gen. Sir William Nicholson, to prepare the aforementioned contingency plans for the dispatch of the expeditionary force to the continent—though he does not seem to have realized before mid-1911 these plans were incomplete. He also allowed his staff officers to continue secret talks with their French counterparts to hammer out logistical details. He further authorized preparations to draw reinforcements from the self-governing Dominions. The war minister convinced himself that the urgency of the situation overrode all departmental or broader imperial defense considerations—though not, apparently, financial ones.[26]

Haldane knew full well he had no chance of persuading the Treasury to provide the army with the additional funds necessary to develop and expand the expeditionary force. Trying to argue the point, he also realized, was futile because the majority of his Cabinet colleagues were not interested in military affairs. So instead he fixed his attention on tapping some of the navy's budget. While Haldane claimed he did not question the Admiralty's claim for primacy in the allocation of defense resources, he undoubtedly wanted to see more spent on the Army. He recognized that against Germany, the Royal Navy could do no more than impose an economic blockade and further suspected that the strength of the fleet was larger than necessary for that purpose.[27] Meanwhile, in Whitehall, the Board of Admiralty were well aware that "the whole War Office is permeated and saturated with the idea of our being in collusion with the Continental armies on their own ground."[28] They were also conscious that the generals were conspiring "to undermine the vital [maritime] principles on which the Defence of the Empire is at present based."[29] Since the beginning of 1910, it had been an open secret that Haldane had been quietly pressing his claim to succeed McKenna as first lord.[30] And it was also was well known that the war minister favored the creation of a unified ministry of defense and saw himself as the ideal candidate for the job.[31] The navalists and imperial defense lobby hoped that for so long as McKenna remained at the Admiralty, and while public support for the Royal Navy remained strong, the army's bid for a greater share of the defense budget would fail.

By 1911, the secretary of state for war was no longer the only member of the Cabinet keen to see stronger leadership at Whitehall. For some months there had been growing dissatisfaction within the Liberal

Party at McKenna's inability to offset the costs of increased dreadnought construction with economies in other areas of naval expenditure, or to say when the Navy Estimates would finally enter the long-promised "era of reduction."[32] In February that year, during the preparations for the upcoming budget, a group of ministers led by David Lloyd George (chancellor of the Exchequer) and Winston Churchill (home secretary) voiced their concerns at naval expenditure breaking the £44 million barrier: a figure that had been considered "the utmost" the 1909 "Peoples Budget" could be "expected to sustain."[33] In addition, having to provide for higher-than-expected naval spending, the chancellor also had to cope with the unexpectedly high costs associated with the implementation of the government's new welfare programs. Thus far, the chancellor had been able to meet demands upon the Treasury without recourse to higher taxation because a boom in economic activity had produced greater-than-expected revenues. But Lloyd George believed that this bounty would not last for long. And he saw that further raising taxation to cover prospective fiscal deficits was politically impossible. Hence he insisted in the spring of 1911 that both social and, especially, naval expenditure must be brought under control at once. Lloyd George, with Churchill's help, was able to persuade the Cabinet that a fiscal crisis was looming. As a result, the Cabinet overruled the first lord's objections to the formation of a special Cabinet subcommittee to scrutinize the navy estimates. Although Lloyd George and Churchill were subsequently authorized by the prime minister to audit the Admiralty's accounts, as one senior civil servant recalled in his memoirs, "the emissaries had been [deliberately] so snowed under by the mass of figures presented to them that they had been quite unable to arrive at the true facts."[34] McKenna's refusal to cooperate with them succeeded in protecting the naval budget from significant cuts in 1911, but only at the price of further antagonizing the powerful "economist" wing of the Liberal Party.[35]

In a letter to one of his journalist friends dated 15 April 1911, Fisher complained that politicians from across the spectrum were lining up "to get McKenna 'knocked out.'"[36] The following month he wrote to McKenna's wife with the latest gossip and intelligence:

> Esher writes a whole lot about the military conspiracy to raise the Army Estimates, and the Generals on the Committee of Imperial Defence all being banded to depreciate the Navy, but he adds quite conclusively, "*the country will never stand it,*" but "Lord Viscount Napoleon B." [Haldane] is so extremely artful . . . that one does not know what mischief might not be done, when you consider how glad both L[loyd] G[eorge] and Winston [Churchill] might be to give your dear Reggie a fall![37]

The Agadir Crisis

McKenna fell in October 1911. The pretext for his dismissal was the Admiralty's poor showing that summer during the so-called Agadir crisis. Actually the navy's leadership had not performed that badly during the crisis. After the war scare subsided, no one could point to one false step. Nevertheless there was an impression that the navy had been caught unprepared, and that was used by McKenna's enemies to collapse confidence in his administration. At the height of the crisis, for instance, on 27 July, Winston Churchill phoned the Admiralty to recommend the dispatch of Royal Marines to guard the armament depots in the east end of London from German fifth columnists. His call was taken by Rear Adm. Charles Madden, the fourth sea lord.[38] After the confused (or bemused) naval officer refused to take the proferred advice, the latter rang off and on his own authority arranged for some armed policemen to do the job: minutes after they arrived a company of guardsmen, sent by Haldane, appeared on the scene. "By the next day," Churchill proclaimed in his memoirs, "the cordite reserves of the navy were safe"![39] But what he omitted was that the admiral had in fact been quite right; responsibility for the security of the depots had belonged to the War Office. Whether or not the armament depots had been truly in danger was not the point, however. Madden's response was used to fuel the rumors of laxity at the Admiralty. This impression was reinforced the following week by McKenna's decision to allow the majority of Whitehall officials to go ahead with their planned summer vacations. While the admirals went on holiday, representatives from the General Staff were sent across to Paris to finalize the details of their Continental plan.

On 15 August, Capt. Maurice Hankey (the naval representative attached to the secretariat of the CID) tipped off McKenna that the War Office was plotting to exploit the situation. He reported that the generals wanted to force the Cabinet into making an instant decision as to whether or not to dispatch the expeditionary force to France in the event of war with Germany. "It is of course notorious," Hankey informed the first lord, "that the D.M.O., General Wilson, who has bought this question to the front, has a perfect obsession for military operations on the continent."

> He holds the view, not only that military action is indispensable in order to preserve the balance of power in Europe, but that we require a conscript army for the purpose. If he can get a decision at this juncture in favour of military action he will endeavor to commit us up to the hilt; and in a few months time he will prove that with our existing forces we could not have rendered France proper assistance, and will seek to show that without conscription we cannot fulfil our obligations.[40]

Hankey went on to suggest that if the prime minister agreed to refer the matter to the CID the Admiralty could frustrate the War Office's efforts by refusing "to say how long it will be before the transport of troops will be feasible." Alternatively, he recommended, the Admiralty "can stick to the line they took in 1908 that the policy of sending an expedition is altogether a wrong one."[41] Five days later, McKenna received another letter (this time from Fisher) echoing the warning of a War Office plot to introduce "compulsory service and an increase of the Army estimates and military influence."[42] The former first sea lord advised his friend "*to trust in Hankey implicitly.*"[43]

The promised gathering at the CID was convened much earlier than the Admiralty had expected. Wilson and Bethell (DNI) were hurriedly recalled from vacation to attend the meeting scheduled for 23 August 1911. Indeed the DNI arrived late and missed the morning session. Haldane, who was responsible for the invitations, deliberately excluded from his list anyone he thought might be opposed to his military policy. Among this group were several supposedly "permanent members" of the CID including Lords Morley, Crewe, and Fisher. The most notable—and inexcusable—absentee was Viscount Esher.[44] Once the meeting began, Gen. Sir Henry Wilson subjected his audience to a barrage of facts, figures, and charts, showing the War Office's reasoning for sending the entire expeditionary force to the Continent. It was a thoroughly "professional" presentation.[45] He successfully concealed from the politicians the full details of Anglo-French cooperation, the recent changes in the French command and war policy, and most importantly the resource implications for adopting such a strategy. By juggling the number of divisions available to each power at the beginning of a war, and by assuming that Germany would not infringe upon Belgian territory north of the River Meuse, General Wilson claimed that the immediate dispatch of the entire BEF to the town of Mauberge would provide the French with a numerical superiority at the key point in their line.[46] Of course the idea that just six British divisions could provide a decisive contribution to the defense of France was far-fetched.[47] Yet despite harboring grave reservations as to the military value of the six divisions,[48] Haldane endorsed the argument and laid great stress on the necessity to land the expeditionary force on the Continent as quickly as possible.[49] The logic appealed to the civilians present.

In reply, McKenna took Hankey's advice and "pleaded ignorance of the whole scheme" to transport a military expeditionary force across the Channel.[50] This proved to be a bad mistake and one that McKenna regretted for the rest of his life.[51] After the meeting, Haldane skillfully exploited the Admiralty's reply and the refusal to provide transports for the BEF to dramatize the endemic lack of cooperation between the two service departments over strategic planning.[52] These allegations, not surprisingly, served to fuel the now widespread rumors that Whitehall was in administrative chaos. A particularly inept performance by Sir Arthur Wilson at the CID meeting further reinforced the impression that the Admiralty had been unprepared for war during the Agadir crisis.[53] On 25 August, in a move calculated to maintain pressure on Whitehall, Haldane forwarded to the Admiralty details of the army's revised transport requirements and demanded an immediate reply. When after three weeks nothing had been heard (because the director of Naval Transports was away on vacation),[54] Haldane "intimated to the Prime Minister that he would not continue to be responsible for the War Office unless a Board of Admiralty was called into being which would work in full harmony with the War Office plans, and would begin the organisation of a proper Naval War Staff."[55] The following week the war minister put himself forward as the only man in the party suitably "equipped with the knowledge and experience that were essential for fashioning a highly complicated organisation" for the navy.[56]

At the beginning of October, the Lord Haldane finally persuaded the prime minister that the first lord had lost control of the Admiralty and that administrative reform was overdue. "McKenna has done fairly well as defender of Admiralty policy in Parliament," Asquith confided to Lord Esher, "but he has been entirely dominated by (a) Jackie (b) by Wilson, and that he would never be inclined or able to reorganise the internal naval policy of the department."[57] The prime minister might have had other reasons for wanting a change of leadership at the Admiralty. More than one commentator has noted that since the autumn he had again been leaning towards the radical "economist" wing of his party, and was now prepared to endorse Treasury-endorsed cuts on the navy.[58] Even Sir Edward Grey, normally the navy's staunchest ally, was unwilling to oppose calls for naval retrenchment.[59] He had his own problems to worry about.[60] Clearly, therefore, Asquith had more than one motive to see McKenna "promoted elsewhere."[61] But outright dismissal was impossible; McKenna had intimated to Asquith that if forced out of the Cabinet he would reveal to Parliament the true extent of Britain's secret diplomatic and military commitments to France.[62] The prime minister recognized that finding him a suitable billet within the government was not going to be easy.[63] Who would make way and who would take his place? Asquith was both wary of Haldane's ambition and afraid to inflict more damage on the navy's already tarnished reputation by sending the War Office minister directly across to the Admiralty.[64]

The solution to this dilemma came with a request from Winston Churchill at the end of September to be transferred from the Home Office to the Admiralty.[65] His candidacy was strongly backed by Lloyd George.[66] While Haldane may have been primarily responsible for undermining McKenna's defenses, it was Lloyd George and Churchill who successfully exploited the weakness. Churchill was keen to find a more exciting and less tedious post within the government. "I'm sick of the Home Office," he is reported as having told the king in late August 1911, "These women (suffragettes) will be the death of me"![67] After a short deliberation, the prime minister finally resolved that Churchill and McKenna should exchange offices. On 10 October Asquith wrote to the incumbent first lord offering him promotion to the Home Office.[68] At the same time the impression put about was that Churchill was in fact being demoted "for his indiscreet conduct as Home Secretary."[69] Rumors circulated London society that the brash young minister was lucky not to be banished to the Irish Office.[70] McKenna, however, was not deceived by Asquith's invitation and immediately declined, only to be ordered, three days later, to accept or leave the government.[71] McKenna, it should be noted, never forgave Churchill for his part in what he justifiably regarded as a conspiracy to remove him from the job he loved. This animosity soon developed into hatred.[72]

A Heaven Sent Strategist!

Winston S. Churchill took office as first lord of the Admiralty on 25 October 1911, with the reputation of being an uncompromising "economist." Back in 1909, despite being the most junior member in the Cabinet, Churchill had led the radical wing of the party that had stood against proposed increases in naval spending on the grounds that they were unnecessary and would interfere with concurrent plans to further extend the welfare system. He was deeply committed to the party's social reform program for both moral and pragmatic reasons.[73] He professed, for instance, to be in favor of land reform and the imposition of a national minimum wage for agricultural laborers.[74] After being promoted home secretary in 1910, Churchill had continued to agitate for a substantial cut in naval expenditure.[75] The following year he had served on the Cabinet subcommittee appointed to review the navy estimates, and had been mainly responsible for the demand for the Admiralty to revise the costly plan to reestablish a fleet in the Pacific.[76] Despite what he later claimed in his memoirs, when Churchill arrived at Whitehall he was still bent on imposing large cuts in the naval budget.[77] While he may have experienced a "metamorphosis" in his "attitude" towards Germany and the "alleged German threat,"[78] he still nevertheless believed that significant cuts in naval expenditure were both desirable and practicable. In a major political speech delivered to the Guildhall Banquet on 9 November 1911, for instance, Churchill assured his audience that "the [naval] estimates for the forthcoming year should show some reduction from the abnormal level at which they now stand . . . the high-water mark, at any rate, has been reached."[79]

Churchill took office determined to appoint a new first sea lord as soon as possible. Sir Arthur Wilson's display on 23 August had shocked him. "No man of real power," he had afterwards told Asquith, "c[oul]d have answered so foolishly."[80] After interviewing most of the senior officers on the flag list, the new first lord chose Vice Adm. Prince Louis of Battenberg to become his "principal councillor."[81] Churchill felt that he and the admiral were "in cordial agreement" on "nearly every important question of naval policy."[82] He was thus not at all pleased when Asquith blocked Battenberg's appointment out of fear of public disapproval at the appointment of a "German" born officer as head of the Royal Navy.[83] In addition, the prime minister was still anxious to subdue rumors of the Admiralty's poor performance during the recent crisis. He thus insisted that Wilson must remain in office until his compulsory retirement for age the following March.[84] Churchill, however, was not so easily put off.[85] Within a fortnight he found his excuse: on 5 November 1911 Churchill complained to Asquith that the first sea lord was stubbornly blocking plans to introduce a naval staff system, a reform which Haldane had convinced the prime minister was vital.[86] By the end of the month, therefore, the prime minister gave his grudging consent to replacing Wilson with the supposedly malleable Sir Francis Bridgeman. Prince Louis of Battenberg was appointed second sea lord after Vice Adm. George Egerton was summarily ordered to vacate the post with "less warning than a footman gets."[87]

Shortly after Bridgeman arrived for duty at the Admiralty he reported to his old mentor, Lord Fisher, that "Churchill is strongly on the economy drive" and was "full of new schemes of strategy which are almost too bold to be believed!"[88] What the first sea lord had not yet realized, however, was that the inspiration for Churchill's radical strategic theories was none other than Admiral of the Fleet Lord Fisher! Winston and Jacky were old friends. They had first met in April 1907 while visiting mutual friends in Biarritz. Looking back on that occasion in the 1920s, Churchill recalled: "we talked all day long and far into the nights. He told me wonderful stories of the Navy and of his plans—all about dreadnoughts, all about submarines." Churchill confessed to being captivated by the admiral. "When I returned to my duties at the Colonial Office I could have passed an examination on the policy of the then Board of Admiralty," he wrote.[89] For the next eighteen months the two were close friends and dined together regularly.[90] Although during the passage of the 1909 navy estimates the two had ceased communicating—Fisher accused Churchill of betraying the navy by opposing his demands for an eight dreadnought construction program—the spat had been short-lived and within twelve months they were again on speaking terms. Thus "[a]s soon as I knew for certain that I was to go to the Admiralty I sent for Fisher: he was [then] abroad in sunshine," Churchill recalled in his memories.[91]

On sitting down at his new desk the new first lord immediately wrote to Jacky at his hotel in Italy begging an audience.[92] Three days later the pair were closeted for a long weekend at Reigate Priory in Surrey.[93] Churchill later claimed that by the end of their meeting he had "almost made up his mind" to place Fisher again as head of the naval service.[94] Political expediency, however, compelled him to rely upon "Radical Jack" in no more than an unofficial capacity. Except for one more secret rendezvous at Plymouth Dockyard (18–20 November), Fisher deliberately remained in Italy to dampen speculation about the existence of links between them.[95] Even so, Churchill continued to send him numerous confidential Admiralty documents carried by diplomatic courier to the British consulate in Naples.[96] During the winter of 1911–12, Fisher and Churchill corresponded on an almost daily basis. Fisher relished the opportunity to exercise influence without responsibility. This extraordinary clandestine relationship operated until Churchill "shocked" Fisher the following spring by giving appointments to three senior admirals who he considered incompetent.[97] The admiral was informed by the equally disapproving Rear Adm. Ernest Troubridge that the first lord had "truckled" to court influence; the new King George V—himself a former naval officer—had pressured Churchill into employing the three admirals, all of whom were personal friends.[98]

During the winter of 1911, Fisher managed to persuade his disciple that he could achieve his goal of finding significant savings in naval expenditure without endangering British naval supremacy by embracing the battle cruiser concept and the strategy of "flotilla defence."[99] Rough notes taken by Churchill at Reigate Priory in October show that he was given a very frank explanation of Fisher's radical vision of naval war. The Admiral revealed when he had been first sea lord he had visualized the entire southern half of the North Sea being saturated with submarines, into the Heligoland Bight and the Skaggerak, and that he had planned to send a force of submarines into the Baltic to help the Russian navy protect St. Petersburg from bombardment by the German High Sea Fleet.[100] Several days after the interview Fisher wrote a triumphant letter to a close friend claiming that he had put the question of expanding the submarine service to Winston and had "converted him."[101] Churchill was also persuaded to reinstigate flotilla defense in the North Sea—or at least a version of that strategy. Within six months he arranged for the command and control of all flotilla craft stationed on the east coast of Britain to be returned to the control of a single flag officer reporting to the Admiralty rather than the commander in chief. The new scheme, it will be noted, bore a marked similarity to the original "Home Fleet" organization the former first sea lord had proposed back in 1906.[102]

Fisher also persuaded Churchill to cancel the battleships projected under the 1912/13 program and instead "plunge" for a new model battle cruiser. In November 1911, the admiral forwarded his pupil sketch plans of a warship armed with eight 15-inch guns, fitted with oil fired boilers capable of propelling the ship at thirty knots and which relied upon extensive internal subdivision rather than heavy armor for protection.[103] He promised Churchill that not only would these ships be qualitatively superior to anything then afloat but they would force all other navies to reconsider their own ship designs: which, as a result, would compel them to recast their building programs. Fisher calculated that if the Admiralty concealed the change until the last possible moment, Britain could afford to relax her own capital ship program for at least one year. The "whole secret" of successful naval administration, Fisher preached, "is 'plunging'—it stupefies foreign Admiralties."[104]

> put off to the very last hour the ship (big or little) *that you mean to build* (or perhaps not build her at all!). You see all your rival's plans fully developed, their vessels started beyond recall, and then in each individual answer to each such rival vessel you *PLUNGE* with a design 50 per cent. better! knowing that your rapid shipbuilding and command of money will enable you to have your vessel fit to fight as soon if not sooner than the rival vessel.[105]

Initially Churchill took steps in the directions indicated. He began by asking his senior Whitehall advisors to reconsider the 1912 construction program. Previously, McKenna had planned to ask Parliament for money to lay down four battleships, five light cruisers, twenty destroyers and six submarines. Altogether the Admiralty planned to incur new liabilities totaling £11.3 million, of which £8.4 million would be taken by the four capital ships. On 10 November Churchill informed Battenberg (who had not yet been officially appointed to the Board) that instead of ordering the battleships he "contemplated" laying down four improved battle cruisers.[106] He also anticipated "a multiplication of torpedo craft" to be financed by savings resulting from the paying off and disposal of old ships.[107] "You will see that the more we can reduce expense of the upkeep of our obsolescent tail," Churchill explained, "the more we shall have for the development of new teeth and claws."[108] The combination of a ruthless scrapping policy and the anticipated deceleration in the pace of dreadnought construction over the next three years, he hoped, would allow the Admiralty "easily to be able to satisfy the economists at the same time as we strengthen the fleet."[109]

Battenberg was initially doubtful. He advised that many of the economies that appeared feasible on paper would in practice be difficult to achieve. He was also concerned by appearances. The sea lords, he warned, would be most reluctant to be seen "cutting down" so soon after Wilson's departure. But later he suggested that "the withdrawal of six fully manned battleships from the Mediterranean to home waters offers great possibilities."[110] This, Battenberg calculated, would release a modest half-million pounds. It was again Fisher who came up with an alternative way of funding an increased flotilla program. "I think in view of the immense *increase of gun power* in your new ships," he wrote to Churchill on 20 November, that instead of ordering four armoured vessels under the 1912 program, "you might only have 3 & take the money for the 4th for submarines—*chiefly*—& a few more destroyers."[111] Even by Fisher's standards this was a bold scheme. Possibly too bold—it required the new first lord to sacrifice the Liberal Party's last remaining "fig leaf" of naval respectability and for the sea lords to display considerable political nerve.[112] The deletion of even one ship from the declared building program was bound to expose the Admiralty to accusations they were endangering naval supremacy. Nevertheless Churchill resolved to take the "plunge" after assuring himself that he had found a way to protect the Liberal Party's modesty. His solution was to renege on the agreement reached with the Dominions in 1909 to establish a battle cruiser squadron in the Pacific. In December Churchill explained to the Board:

> In order to maintain 60 per cent preponderance over Germany in capital ships in home waters four should be laid down this financial year. But this is on the assumption that the *Indomitable* should be sent to China in January [1912], and that the *New Zealand* should follow when completed. If the *Indomitable* be retained in home waters it is clear that the numerical requirements will be satisfied by a construction of three capital ships in the 12–13 programme . . . I therefore propose as an alternative to the programme submitted that we should build three new capital ships and retain the *Indomitable,* thus saving £2,100,000.[113]

This money would pay for ten additional submarines (making sixteen in all) and ten more torpedo boat destroyers (making thirty in all).[114] Although aware that Grand Admiral Tirpitz was lobbying for an amendment to the German navy law to which the Royal Navy might have to react, at this stage Churchill was more concerned with finding money within his existing budget to pay for more flotilla craft. "IF the Germans increase their navy law by laying down an extra [battle] cruiser," he conjectured, "we could immediately reply by adding two battle cruisers to our programme."[115]

At the end of 1911 Churchill rapidly retraced his steps when he found that none of his official advisors at the Admiralty were prepared to support such radical changes to the construction program.[116] "The new first lord is a young man in a hurry and what is more he is—in his opinion—a heaven born strategist both military and naval," reported one junior staff officer to a friend on distant service; "whether all his schemes are quite sound I shouldn't like to say. . . ."[117] The three senior members of the Board—Briggs, Battenberg and especially Bridgeman, were equally opposed to giving up battleships in favor of the battle cruiser concept.[118] Indeed, the first sea lord wanted "to get rid of the battle cruiser type" altogether.[119] He championed the development of the heavily armored (and considerably more expensive) fast battleship type which later became known as the *Queen Elizabeth* class.[120] On learning that Churchill had backed down Fisher became irate. In bold handwriting he rebuked his pupil for listening to his "effete experts," condemning the fast-battleship design as a "damned hybrid."[121] Fisher became even more angry when he learned that the Board had refused to reallocate other monies to pay for additional submarines. "I deeply regret your halting steps," Fisher wrote Churchill on 30 December. "You say 'but I got no encouragement to spend the additional £400,000'—still less was there in those past years to spend a million."[122] To outsiders, however, Fisher was careful to defend Churchill's hesitation. "Every step he contemplates is good," he assured the naval publicist Gerald Fiennes in February 1912. Unfortunately the first lord "can't go quite as far as I urge him, as his instruments [a reference to the sea lords] are inadequate. They shiver on the brink and won't take the great plunge. He can't well plunge alone."[123]

The sea lord's emphatic rejection of the substitution policy and the battle cruiser concept quickly dampened Churchill's enthusiasm for Fisher's radical strategic ideas. While he did not entirely repudiate his naval mentor's theories, he subsequently adopted a more orthodox approach to naval strategy. But there was a price. Appeasing his official advisors antagonized Fisher and more importantly left him with little room for fiscal maneuver. To achieve his primary objective of cutting the navy estimates, Churchill was thrown back onto his original idea of "tackling the number of old ships to be kept in commission."[124] He was fortunate that a closer inspection of the Navy List revealed that the Wilson administration had built up a substantial hoard of "miser's junk" in the reserve fleet. A policy of ruthless scrapping, Churchill calculated, would produce considerable savings in the maintenance budget which when added to the sums already found by the second sea lord (principally resulting from the paying off the six battleships stationed at Malta) would yield almost two million.[125] On 20 January 1912, the first lord indicated he planned to surrender about 1.4 million to the Exchequer in 1912–, with further more modest reductions in the navy estimates in the two subsequent financial years.[126] Obstacles raised by Rear Adm. Alexander Bethell, the long-serving director of Naval Intelligence, were swept aside by transferring him out of Whitehall to the East Indies station.[127]

The net result of Churchill's proposals would have been to transform the character of the Royal Navy's fighting fleets. The main battle fleet would have been reduced to just sixteen fully manned dreadnoughts in home waters, plus a harlequin squadron of six battleships at Gibraltar.[128] (A total of twenty-two battleships.) Within two years the last of the pre-dreadnoughts would have been finally displaced, and most of the oldest vessels scrapped. Both Bridgeman and Battenberg supported the creation of a homogenous all big-gun line of battle. The tactical advantages (already explained) were obvious. In addition, Churchill intended that the 4,500-odd trained men released from the Mediterranean battleships would be reallocated to the 50-odd flotilla craft then under construction.[129] These additional men would allow the navy to man the new vessels without having to pay off older craft. The net result would be two more flotillas in full commission which could be attached either to the admiral of patrols or the grand fleet of battle.

The Novelle: New German Naval Law

In January 1912, Churchill took lateral steps to reduce the level of naval construction. With the blessing of Sir Edward Grey, the foreign secretary, he quietly approached the German government with the offer of a "naval holiday." His idea was for both powers to suspend battleship construction for one year. The initial negotiations were conducted through an international financier of Anglo-German ancestry by the name of Sir Ernest Cassel.[130] He was chosen because of his personal links with ministers in both countries.[131] Churchill's disarmament initiative quickly yielded an unexpected dividend. On 31 January 1912, Cassel returned to London with an outline of the plan to expand the German navy.[132] Two weeks later the Admiralty was supplied with an advanced copy of the "Novelle" (new fleet law) due to be published the following month. Although British naval intelligence had anticipated some further increase in the High Sea Fleet, the Admiralty was left stunned by the proposed "extraordinary increase in the striking force" of the German navy. This, the first lord explained to the Cabinet, was the result of the proposal to raise the establishment from 66,700 in 1912, to 101,500 men by 1920.[133]

> From the general indications which they had previously received they were inclined to think that the new construction would be its most serious feature. But on examining the text they found that while the new construction was limited to three, or it maybe two, capital ships in six years, the increase of personnel and the increases in the vessels of all classes maintained in full commission constituted a new development of the very highest importance . . . It would enable the German Government to have available at all seasons of the year twenty-five, or perhaps twenty-nine, fully commissioned battleships; whereas at the present time the British Government have in full commission in home waters only twenty-two, even counting the Atlantic Fleet. Compared to this predominant fact, any alteration of the *tempo* of the proposed additional new construction appeared comparatively a small thing.[134]

This news wrecked Churchill's plan to cut his navy estimates. The most that he could now hope to achieve was containment of the rate of increase in naval expenditure. It was evident that instead of cutting the number battleships in full commission from twenty-eight to twenty-two, as he had hoped to do, "on the contrary some increase is necessary."[135] "Ag[ain]st 25 battleships we c[oul]d not keep less than forty available within twenty-four hours," was his first estimate.[136] The preparations to trim the reserve fleet were also shelved. As a result, old warships which had been destined for the scrap heap in 1911 were still afloat three years later.[137]

Churchill recognized that if the Germans went ahead with their plans, the Royal Navy would have no alternative but to strip the Mediterranean and Atlantic squadrons of their battleships to increase Britain's strength in the North Sea. On 1 February 1912, he formally asked the newly appointed chief of the War Staff, Rear Adm. Ernest Troubridge, "*with this important need in view* [to] examine the Mediterranean position; and report what reasons there are which would justify or prevent the battleships there being brought to home waters."[138] In their place, Churchill revealed, "I contemplate of course flotillas."[139] In other words, the first lord hoped to safeguard British interests in the Mediterranean by relying upon Fisher's system of flotilla defense. Jacky was delighted. "Let the French take care of the Mediterranean," he advised, "and a hot time they'll have of it with submarines poking about in that lake! We are well out of it."[140] Bridgeman too believed that a sizeable force of torpedo craft would provide a formidable obstacle to any hostile power trying to exercise control of the Mediterranean Sea.[141] Troubridge, however, demurred.[142] In his opinion, "flotillas of torpedo craft left in the eastern basin of the Mediterranean on the withdrawal of our battle fleet would soon fall easy prey to a Mediterranean enemy" with a battle fleet.[143] "At best," he thought, they might delay the enemy from seizing the Royal Navy's principal bases; but they certainly would not be able to protect commerce passing between Gibraltar and Suez. A battle fleet, he insisted, was the only universally accepted "symbol and measure of British power." And the Royal Navy could not credibly claim to protect British interests in the Mediterranean without one.[144]

It was probably because of this conflicting advice that the first lord asked the Cabinet on 14 February if he could "defer" explaining how exactly the Admiralty planned to respond to the new German naval law.[145] The following day Churchill curtly informed Troubridge that his appraisal of the Mediterranean situation missed the point. The navy's first priority was to preserve British dominance in the North Sea and this could only be achieved by bringing home the battle squadron from Malta, because whatever response the Admiralty finally adopted would require more personnel in home waters.[146] "It is not so much the ships but the men who are wanted."[147] After further deliberation, Churchill ruled out the option of relying upon flotilla defense to provide strategic deterrence in the North Sea and instead adopted an orthodox strategy that gave the battle fleet this primary role. His advisors persuaded him that the only credible response to the expansion of the High Sea Fleet was to increase the strength of the Home Fleet. An "overwhelming" numerical superiority, the sea lords considered, would overawe and deter the Germans. Eventually the Admiralty settled upon a fleet of thirty-three battleships in full commission plus eight more in immediate reserve. Meanwhile, the decision on how best to defend the Mediterranean was deferred.

Besides being unimaginative, the decision to create a "deterrence" force of thirty-three battleships for the North Sea seriously undermined the ability of the Royal Navy to project British sea power in more distant regions. It also represented a major departure from previous policy. During Fisher's administration the Admiralty had been satisfied with maintaining sufficient ships in full commission to assure Britain a "reasonable" margin of superiority over Germany; the Royal Navy's superior strength lay in the better quality of its ships and crews, plus the possession of a much larger flotilla supported by the fleet reserve. After Churchill took the helm, however, the Admiralty proposed to give the navy the *luxury* of an "overwhelming" 50 percent superiority in the number of fully commissioned modern capital ships kept in the North Sea. Finding the hulls was no problem. In 1912, the Royal Navy still possessed a large stock of serviceable predreadnought battleships in reserve. Before the end of 1912, moreover, ten new dreadnoughts were due to enter service. The problem was in finding the men to form the required additional crews. "We have not got and cannot get the 33 ships," Churchill explained to the Cabinet, because "the rate at which our margins can be increased depends entirely upon the number of trained officers and men available."[148] For reasons explained earlier, British warships were designed to be manned by a high proportion of skilled personnel. As it took six years to train a recruit, a shortage of personnel could not be met by simply increasing recruitment.[149] In the short run the only way to provide the 3,500 trained seamen required to man the battleships was to reallocate them from cruisers and flotilla craft, and by diluting the proportion of skilled personnel manning older battleships. Although these measures constituted major reversals in policy, particularly the decision to reduce the number of flotilla craft in commission, this is exactly what the Admiralty did.[150]

Subsequent practical exercises conducted by the fleet show clearly that the Board had given little thought to the tactical implications of their decision to increase the strength of the Home Fleet from twenty-two to thirty-three battleships and possibly forty-one. As we have seen in the last chapter, in an attempt to compensate for the tactical shortcomings of a traditional battleship fleet, the Royal Navy had adopted the concept of "grand fleet of battle." In addition to his capital units, the commander in chief was already expected to control some two dozen light cruisers, at least forty destroyers, and, ultimately, flotillas of fleet-submarines. Admirals were already experiencing problems in controlling a more modest "grand fleet" comprised of twenty-two battleships and fifty-odd auxiliaries. In May 1912, Battenberg confessed to the first lord that "I think I may truthfully say that at this moment *no-one* has any clear idea how the Commander-in-Chief, wherever he maybe in the line, is to effectively command such a fleet" of battleships.[151] The maneuvers of 1912 and 1913 served only to accentuate the debate over this problem, which will be considered further in the next chapter.

The Mediterranean Fiasco

Churchill announced the redistribution of the fleet in his introduction of the navy estimates to the House of Commons on 18 March, 1912.[152] The plan was to shuffle the Atlantic Fleet from Gibraltar to Portland and slide the Mediterranean battle squadron over to Gibraltar where it could act "eastward or westward," with a solitary squadron of four old armored cruisers to be retained at Malta.[153] In the same speech, the first lord formally revised the battleship standard. Henceforth, instead of being guided by the two-power standard, he explained, the Admiralty would maintain a 60 percent superiority in dreadnought capital ships over the German fleet. The new rule was to hold valid only so long as the Royal Navy's late predreadnought battleships, of which the Germans had nothing equivalent, could be counted as effective. Thereafter, Churchill stated, from about 1917, the percentage would be increased.[154] What he could not say was how much this would cost the British taxpayer; so much depended on the actions of Germany. Unable to reveal the government's knowledge of the Novelle, Churchill deliberately made no direct reference to the expansion of the High Sea Fleet.[155] Instead he issued a veiled warning to the kaiser that the Admiralty would respond to any increase in the hitherto published German building tempo by laying two keels to one. With the other hand, he again held out the offer of a "naval holiday."[156]

Like the Earl of Tweedmouth, Churchill soon discovered that it was not such an easy matter for the Admiralty to redistribute old battleships without provoking heavy criticism. Churchill's announcement was interpreted as a decision by the Royal Navy to "withdraw" from the Mediterranean, which raised a storm of protest from interested diplomatic, political and military parties.[157] Such a shift in policy, these argued, had far reaching non-naval implications that deserved consideration alongside those of the Admiralty.[158] The army's General Staff, for instance, complained that without British command of the Mediterranean the garrisons at Malta and in Egypt would have to be increased by as many as three divisions.[159] No less serious criticism came from the imperial federation lobby led by Lord Esher, which envisaged the British empire evolving into a global superpower. He objected strongly to the Admiralty narrowing their "strategic outlook" to focus exclusively on the German threat.[160] Such a step, he protested, would be tantamount to surrendering the principle of British global naval supremacy.[161] Esher consoled himself with the conviction that the British public would not tolerate the abandonment of naval supremacy, and began lobbying his contacts in the press.[162] "These people who want to concentrate every ship in the North Sea are mad," he exclaimed to the editor of *The Westminster Gazette*.

Remember that it must be followed by demands for large expenditure on the east coast, and then the kaleidoscope changes *politically* and our relations with Foreign Powers change, and all the money is wasted. Whereas the history of Europe as well as of Great Britain shows that the

Mediterranean is *permanently* the centre of naval strategic gravity in
Europe because it is and always has been the main artery of seaborne
trade.[163]

It is interesting to note that Esher did not object to the withdrawal of the
battleships. His close association with Fisher had persuaded him that
battle fleets were obsolete. "I should be far happier," Esher informed
Arthur Balfour, "if I could see the standard of [our] strength measured
by (1) personnel; (2) submarines; (3) destroyers; (4) large armoured
[battle] cruisers; (5) armoured cruisers; (6) battleships—in that
order."[164] Esher's complaint, rather, was the inadequacy of the naval
force Churchill proposed to leave behind to defend British interests in
the Mediterranean. He also suspected that the first lord was also preparing to reduce the strength of the other station fleets. With justification.
Not only had Churchill recommended such a policy of systematic
retrenchment back in 1911,[165] but more ominously, Esher discovered,
the Admiralty was already trying to extricate itself from promises made
at the 1909 and 1911 imperial defense conferences to reestablish a
modern fleet in the Pacific in conjunction with the self-governing
Dominions.[166] "If the Board of Admiralty could have their way," Esher
warned one correspondent, "the whole of the Dominion fleets (when they
come into being) will be in the North Sea. It is madness. Talk to Admiral
Troubridge and see what he says about the 'fighting value' of such a force
concentrated in one theatre of war."[167] Esher rightly feared that the
Admiralty's "unimaginative" new policy of "force concentration," as he
termed it, would have significant repercussions for the defense of British
imperial interests elsewhere around the globe.[168]

Yet, the Whitehall strategists retorted, if North Sea supremacy was
the navy's first priority, and the battleship was the decisive instrument
of naval warfare, then what other alternatives were open to the
Admiralty? As Churchill made clear to the unhappy Lord Haldane on 6
May, "of course if the Cabinet & the House of Commons like to build
another fleet of dreadnoughts for the Mediter[ranea]n the attitude of the
Adm'y will be that of a cat to a nice fresh dish of cream." But "it w[oul]d
cost you 3 or 4 millions a year extra to make head against Austria & Italy
in the Mediter[ranea]n & still keep a 60% preponderance in the North
Sea" and therefore "I do not look upon this as practical politics."[169]
Churchill went on to suggest, oblivious to the irony of the idea, considering his treatment of Australia and New Zealand over his dismantling of
the Imperial Pacific Fleet, that only the self-governing Dominions could
afford to pay for an additional battle squadron for the Mediterranean.[170]
There was a chance, he believed, that the Canadian government could be

induced to pay for two or three dreadnoughts.[171] This possibility he saw could not be relied upon—but there were no other options.

The first lord did not need to belabor the point. The situation was pretty well understood. In a private letter to the British ambassador in Paris, Sir Arthur Nicholson (permanent undersecretary to the Foreign Office) reflected that:

> There seem to me only two courses to take if the naval people insist upon evacuating the Mediterranean, and this is, first, either to add a very considerable sum to our naval budget so as to enable us to organise a fleet specially for the Mediterranean, but as this would mean a large addition to the £45,000,000 already voted for the Naval Budget, I imagine the Government would hardly be disposed to put forward such a proposal. The other alternative is to come to an understanding with France on the subject which would, I do not deny, be very much in the character of a naval alliance. I think certain members of the Cabinet see this very clearly and would be disposed to agree to it, but I do not know if they would be able to carry all their colleagues with them. In fact I doubt such would be the case.[172]

Privately Nicholson believed that a formal "understanding" with France "offers the cheapest, simplest and safest solution."[173] He favored the signing of a formal alliance.[174]

At the end of April 1912, Asquith agreed to accompany Churchill aboard the Admiralty yacht on what was described to the press as "an inspection of the Mediterranean station."[175] In reality, they were headed for Malta to hear objections against the naval "evacuation" raised by the consul-general of Egypt, Field Marshal Lord Kitchener, who was an acknowledged expert on Eastern affairs.[176] The party also planned to stop over in Naples to discuss the matter with Lord Fisher.[177] Also on the agenda for discussion (drawn up by Hankey in conjunction with Esher) were "the scale of defences and the garrison required at Malta," and "the effect of the new naval dispositions on India and the dominions and the colonies east of the Mediterranean."[178] Originally, a considerable number of senior government advisors from various departments were supposed to have attended the Malta conference. But pressure from the many Cabinet members who had been left out, including Lords Morley and Haldane, obliged Asquith to withdraw most of the invitations. In the end, the prime minister and first lord were accompanied only by Battenberg (second sea lord), Rear Adm. David Beatty (naval secretary), and Gen. Sir John French (chief of the Imperial General Staff).[179] Curiously, neither Bridgeman nor Troubridge—supposedly the two naval officers with official responsibility for strategic matters—were included. The first sea lord was reported to be furious at having been cut.[180] Just before the party set off in mid-May, Bridgeman impressed upon Churchill to "please think and talk about submarines and destroyers together with their bases in the Mediterranean. I am convinced of their necessity and let them be doled out with no meagre hand!"[181]

On 31 May, Lord Kitchener presented a formidable case against the plan to withdraw the Mediterranean battle fleet. All present at Malta were deeply impressed by his speech.[182] The field marshal's argument was based upon the paramount importance of upholding British prestige in the Near East.[183] This, he insisted, could only be accomplished by the continued presence of a battle squadron at Malta. Small craft, however numerous, could never counterbalance the diplomatic weight of powerful-looking battleships. Kitchener's assessment of the diplomatic situation was loudly echoed by the Foreign Office. In addition to holding Turkey in check, the diplomats advised, a strong British naval presence in the Mediterranean was the best deterrent against Italy and possibly also Spain gravitating towards the Triple Alliance.[184] Realizing that the Admiralty's policy was about to be overturned, Churchill assured the assembly that the Admiralty was "anxious" naval dispositions "should command general agreement."[185] On the spur of the moment he offered to station two *Invincible* class battle cruisers in the Mediterranean, albeit based on Gibraltar, and upgrade the four armored cruisers to be retained at Malta. Such a force, he claimed, could outfight any smaller force and outrun anything stronger.[186]

On the morning of 1 June, the first lord cabled the essence of the "Malta Compromise" to Sir Francis Bridgeman, who was most indignant at not having being first consulted. On his return, Churchill was greeted by a letter from the first sea lord insisting that if modern battle cruisers were sent to the Mediterranean "we must have something to replace them at home." But after reflecting on the personnel dimension, Bridgeman expressed himself "bound to confess that if the policy of bringing the [six] battleships home *can* be satisfied with these two battle cruisers—we shall have got out of a serious difficulty very cheaply."[187] As Churchill had put it in his telegram, "we gain 4 battleship crews on balance."[188] In a further memorandum on the subject dated 9 June, Bridgeman confessed that "the question of prestige (about which Lord Kitchener makes a strong point) has a great deal in it."[189] For this reason he agreed to the dispatch of the battle cruisers to Gibraltar, but only "on the understanding that their places must be filled in the Home Fleets by two others of new construction."[190] Nevertheless, Bridgeman continued to insist, "in addition to these two battle-cruisers, it is undoubtedly important that the destroyer and submarine force should be increased."[191] Rough figures at the end of his paper suggest that he envisaged more than doubling the flotilla stationed at Malta, and dispatching additional craft to Alexandria.[192] The first lord gave his qualified approval.[193]

Churchill had left Malta under the impression that the Admiralty's critics had been placated. On arriving back home he soon found this was not so. Kitchener, it transpired, had been left with the impression that the Admiralty could be persuaded to station more battle cruisers at Malta.[194] "I think if you insist they will find three of these," he advised Sir Edward Grey, the foreign secretary.[195] The prime minister, he added, was already half persuaded. Meanwhile Sir Arthur Nicholson, the permanent undersecretary at the Foreign Office, informed Grey that he was equally unimpressed with "the Malta Compromise" and warned him that he would voice his concerns if asked, even if it meant contradicting his minister.[196] Churchill encountered yet more opposition from within Cabinet. Egged on by Reginald McKenna, who was relishing his successors discomfort, the rump of ministers insisted upon the provision of a full battle squadron for the Mediterranean. On 24 June, the ex-first lord provocatively suggested that if the six battleships of the Mediterranean fleet were too old they could be replaced by the eight newer *King Edward* class earmarked for the nucleus crew reserve.[197] Churchill could not persuade his colleagues that if the Royal Navy tried to deploy predreadnought battleships against the modern dreadnoughts now being built by Italy and Austria "they would only be a cheap and certain spoil."[198] Nor would they accept his contention that because of the shortage of trained personnel "we cannot afford to keep 6 battleships in the Mediterranean in full commission."[199]

After two weeks of bickering with his colleagues, Churchill finally accepted that he was not going to persuade the Cabinet to accept the Malta compromise. Yet he could hardly ignore the advice from the sea lords that keeping more than two capital units at Malta was simply impossible because of the personnel shortage. Churchill, accordingly, had no alternative but to overrule the War Staff's objections to flotilla defense. On 15 June, the first lord cautiously suggested in Cabinet that "arrangements" could "be made which will enable us, without undue expense, to provide for the protection of our special interests in the Mediterranean."[200] But, he hastened to add, "it must be plainly recognised that we must adopt the *rôle* in this minor theatre appropriate to the weaker naval power, and while in the North Sea we rely upon the gun as our first weapon, we must in the Mediterranean fall back mainly on the torpedo."[201] By transforming Malta into "a nest of submarines and torpedo craft" and stationing an additional flotilla of oversea submarines at Alexandria, claimed the first lord, Britain's naval bases could be "safeguarded from capture" at the beginning of a war.[202] Later, after command of the North Sea had been secured, the Admiralty could dispatch a powerful surface fleet to relieve the port defense flotillas. Readers should take note that to his political colleagues Churchill hesitated to suggest flotilla craft would be able to contest the command of the sea in the Mediterranean.[203] He claimed only that they could prevent the main naval bases in that sea from being captured by amphibious assault. But the first lord said enough for McKenna to understand, and privately approve, of what was actually envisaged.[204] The rest of the Cabinet, though, found the idea more difficult to swallow.

Churchill's proposals for flotilla defense in the Mediterranean were vigorously supported by Lord Fisher. On 21 June the Admiral, who had recently returned from Italy to chair a royal commission on the supply of oil fuel for the navy, made plans "to interview Sir E. Grey, Lord Haldane, Lloyd George, M'Kenna [sic], Sir Arthur Nicholson, and Sir Robert Chalmers [of the Treasury]."[205] Fisher's first call was to the Foreign Office. "The object of his visit," Nicholson reported to the absent Grey, "was to tell us confidentially that since he was C-in-C in the Mediterranean he foresaw that we should have to rely upon our submarines and torpedo craft for the defence of our interests in the Mediterranean." Also, "we could defend Alexandria and the entrance to the Suez Canal with submarines and torpedo craft—and Malta could hold out for three months easily"![206] "Of course," Nicholson haughtily added, "he apparently has not taken into consideration other than strictly naval questions," by which he probably meant the matter of diplomatic prestige. Grey's reply has not survived.[207]

On 4 July 1912, Asquith convened a general council of officials and interested parties to discuss the Mediterranean situation at the offices of the CID.[208] Among those present were Sir Arthur Wilson and Lord Fisher. After a heated discussion lasting from eleven in the morning until six at night,[209] the "Malta Compromise" was finally rejected on the grounds that two battle cruisers could not provide sufficient protection to British commercial interests and trade passing through the Mediterranean. The Admiralty was instructed to put forward alternative proposals.[210] While much of what Churchill said at the meeting and the conclusions reached have been analyzed in minute detail, very little attention has been given to the remarks made by Lord Fisher. While Jacky certainly endorsed the recall of the Mediterranean battle squadron, he was not, as has been suggested, motivated by a desire to strengthen the main fleet in home waters.[211] Although the minutes only summarized what was said at the meeting (the CID did not employ a proper stenographer), the substance of Fisher's thoughts have been recorded with remarkable clarity.[212] When asked by Asquith for his opinion Radical Jack told the assembly:

> He had absolute confidence in the power of the submarine and did not believe that any heavy ship was safe from them in narrow waters. Therefore if we had an adequate flotilla of submarines and destroyers, at Malta, Gibraltar and Alexandria, no battleship could move in the Mediterranean. He did not believe that any trade could pass through the Mediterranean in time of war.[213]

Whereupon Reginald McKenna chipped in with an observation "that if this estimate of the power of the submarine was correct then surely the North Sea was equally unsuitable for battleships." Replying to his friend's prompt, Fisher went on to explain that he believed in wartime "our battle fleet would not be in the North Sea. It would be off the north coast of Scotland, or outside the Straits of Dover. If the German Fleet came out it would be attacked by submarines and destroyers [only], if it came out far enough would it have to fight our battle fleet."[214] These remarks provoked Churchill to reply: "that the Board of Admiralty did not exactly accept Fisher's views on submarines. They did not think they could deny open water in the Mediterranean to battleships, but they did agree that the Mediterranean might become a very precarious route."[215]

Churchill's dismissal of Fisher's opinion sparked a major row between the first lord and McKenna, his predecessor, during which much was said about naval strategic thinking during the Fisher—McKenna regime. Though the argument was not recorded in the minutes, the incident was remembered by several witnesses.[216] Fisher reported to his son that throughout the day "McKenna and Winston were tearing each other's eyes out."[217] According to Maj. Adrian Grant-Duff, assistant secretary to the CID and the officer responsible for taking the minutes, "Winston was very flushed after lunch and lashed out more than once at McKenna."[218] Although details are vague, it seems that the two argued over the practicability of adopting flotilla defense for the North Sea—McKenna for, and Churchill against.[219] The former contended that the latter's policy of "overwhelming" superiority in the decisive theater was ill-conceived and endangered Britain's maritime position elsewhere around the globe. On this point McKenna received support from Loulou Harcourt, the colonial secretary, and Lord Esher. But no one else, it seems, was prepared to consider flotilla defense strategy. Indeed, this rather technical debate was probably over the heads of most of those present. The minutes indicate that after tempers were calmed, the conversation returned to the discussion on the number of battleships that ought to be retained in the Mediterranean. Grant-Duff noted that immediately after the meeting Asquith remarked: "Fisher has a 'kink' in his brain" about submarines.[220]

The significance of the debate at the CID, for the purpose of this study, is that it shows Churchill was not yet sufficiently confident in Fisher's theory of naval warfare to throw overboard all the conventional "strategic principles" of naval warfare. More simply, he was not prepared to suggest that flotilla defense should become the basis of British naval strategic policy for the Mediterranean—let alone the North Sea. Having probed Cabinet opinion over the previous fortnight, the first lord seems to have concluded that the government was not yet ready to accept any departure from the battleship standard as the ultimate measure of maritime supremacy. Furthermore, whatever his personal convictions might have been, Churchill knew that his authority within the Admiralty was not yet sufficiently strong to insist upon such a change. Although Sir Francis Bridgeman was certainly ready to endorse the strategy of flotilla defense (it is significant that he remained silent at the CID) Admirals Battenberg and Troubridge (also present) most certainly were not.[221] Three days after the meeting, moreover, Prince Louis sent Churchill a memorandum disparaging the "quite novel principles of the art of war at sea put forward" recently at the CID.[222] "It was assumed," he sneered, "that the German main fleet would never face the peril from the torpedo near our shores" and that "fleet action would only become a feature in the later development of the war" in the North Sea.[223] "To count on the German High Sea Fleet not daring to come out" would be "absolutely fatal," he insisted. Battenberg found it equally "unthinkable" to imagine "that its splendid units should rust away in cowardly inactivity under the protection of the coast batteries, whilst its torpedo craft and light cruisers are engaged in fierce fighting close by and the wealth of the nation in its merchant ships becomes the easy prey of British cruisers"(!).[224] Other commentators noticed that Battenberg resented Fisher's influence over Churchill.[225]

Actually, the meeting of the CID on 4 July settled nothing, nor had it been expected to. The final vote always remained with the Cabinet. On 16 July, accordingly, ministers voted for a resolution calling for the Admiralty to keep "a battle fleet" in the Mediterranean equal to the next strongest naval power in the region, though excluding France. It was an essentially conventional arrangement.[226] The only concession extracted by Churchill was an agreement that the navy would not be compelled to dispatch more than four first-class heavy units until after sufficient dreadnoughts had been built to meet North Sea requirements.[227] But having to station even four battle cruisers at Malta posed a considerable manpower problem. The Board of Admiralty agreed to these terms only after Churchill revealed the Canadian prime minister had promised him during an informal conversation at the recent Spithead review, that the Dominion would pay for the construction of three additional dreadnoughts for the Royal Navy.[228] Notwithstanding the confusion over the exact composition of the Mediterranean Squadron, on 17 July the Admiralty notified the French naval attaché of their new one-power Mediterranean standard. This communication, which had sometimes been interpreted as signifying the start of formal "naval conversations" between Britain and France, was intended by the Admiralty as no more than an act of courtesy to a friendly power intended to avoid any misunderstanding.[229] Whether this gesture in fact had diplomatic implications is more open to question.

In October 1912, Sir Francis Bridgeman assessed the recent events with his friend Jack Sandars. Privately, the first sea lord thought that Churchill had made a complete "mess" of the Mediterranean arrangements.[230] Besides repeatedly failing to consult his senior advisor (i.e., Bridgeman) the first lord, he had allowed the Admiralty to be pushed by the government from pillar to post over the distribution of its ships and, perhaps more importantly, its limited manpower. In addition, as we shall see in the next chapter, Churchill had not fully appreciated the financial costs attached to his supreme North Sea battle fleet policy.

War Plans 1912—The North Sea Problem

The aforementioned review of North Sea strategy undertaken by the Admiralty during the first half of 1912, exposed substantial disagreement within the leadership of the Royal Navy. Outside the Admiralty, the most important character in this story was the new commander in chief, Home Fleet. Upon Sir Francis Bridgeman's promotion to the office of first sea lord in December 1911, Vice Adm. Sir George Callaghan, the second in command, had been appointed to this post. Callaghan, whose career until then had been unremarkable, had been elevated to command the fleet because Churchill had feared controversy at appointing any of the better known flag officers, such as Berkeley Milne.[231] Originally Callaghan's appointment was only temporary. But after proving himself more than competent at the job, he was invited to stay until the end of 1914. Callaghan was a naturally cautious officer who not only questioned the prevailing dogma on the importance of "offensive" warfare, but also possessed a realistic understanding of difficulties a battle fleet would face when operating in the North Sea. By consistently objecting to the more aggressive war plans put forward by various Whitehall strategists, this obscure officer served as perhaps the most important influence upon British naval strategic planning during the entire Churchill administration.

In a letter dated 9 January 1912, Callaghan informed the Admiralty that he found his war orders to be incomprehensible. The documents he was referring to, of course, were those that had been drafted the previous August by Sir Arthur Wilson and which prescribed a close blockade of the German North Sea coast.[232] Not only were they confused in detail and riddled with inconsistencies, Callaghan complained, but certain aspects of the plan they prescribed were astonishing. "The employment of a portion of the *Main Fleet* in operations against land defences, as recommended in these notes," for instance, "appears to me to be open to grave objection."[233] He also requested that "the whole question of the Heligoland Bight blockade, which depends so largely on the policy with regard to Heligoland [island], may be reviewed."[234] Callaghan, like his predecessor, Bridgeman, thought personally that the plan was madness. But he saw that unless an advanced base for the flotilla was acquired, then a close blockade was impossible because still "our present margin of superiority in destroyers seems insufficient to establish a watch on the mouths of the [German] rivers in the manner suggested." In April 1912, Adm. George Callaghan was at last notified formally that the plan calling for "the blockade by the British fleet of the whole German coast on the North Sea is to be discontinued."[235] Most curiously, however, the Admiralty's reply was not accompanied with fresh instructions.[236] The initial delay in replying to Callaghan's letter was due to Churchill's insistence that the newly constituted War Staff must draw up considered "war plans." This took time.[237] Not until 8 March 1912, did Troubridge report that new plans and war orders would "very shortly be ready for issue."[238]

The 1912 war plans represented the first attempt by the Admiralty to set down on paper the Royal Navy's real plan of campaign in the event of war. Germany was assumed to be the enemy and the North Sea the theater of operations. In these plans, Churchill wanted to see the strategic objectives identified, the operational policy for achieving these objectives prescribed, and initial deployments of every ship in the fleet agreed. The experiment proved a failure; partly because there was serious disagreement within the War Staff on the plan to adopt, and partly because the planning committee was constituted on the wrong principles. The war plans committee did not include any representatives from the staff of the commander in chief, and because the first sea lord was not a member it also lacked executive authority. While Troubridge, the chairman, had many friends within the service, he was never admired for his intellect. Also, not having held a sea-going command for at least four years, and never having commanded so much as a cruiser squadron, his opinions commanded little respect from senior admirals afloat.

The strategy outlined in the 1912 war plans is usually described by historians as an intermediate blockade.[239] The general idea was for the battle fleet to cruise the relatively safe waters off the coast of Scotland. Meanwhile large numbers of scouts would be stretched along the line from the southwest tip of Norway to the Dutch coast, to search for hostile ships at sea. When contact had been made and the enemy's position reported, the Grand Fleet was supposed to proceed to intercept and sink the enemy fleet. Even at the time the weaknesses of this plan were regarded as transparent.[240] Other officers protested that Troubridge had ignored all the evidence of recent maneuvers. Practical exercises conducted by Admiral Bridgeman and the Home Fleets during 1911, it was pointed out, had conclusively shown that the navy's entire "force of 48 modern destroyers, supported by 8 light cruisers, were unable to watch effectively a patrol line of 60 miles in length."[241] Germany's North Sea coast was 150 miles long; while Troubridge's proposed blockade line was closer to three hundred miles in length. Furthermore, with the number of modern flotilla craft then available there was a high degree of probability that a raiding force might slip past the observation line undetected (especially in misty weather); more seriously the patrolling British light cruisers would be vulnerable to counterattack by enemy submarines or battle cruisers. Effective support by heavier warships could not be provided to the observation line while the Grand Fleet remained concentrated in the north. Yet detaching a battle squadron for this purpose was seen as even more dangerous as it risked defeat in detail.

Towards the end of March 1912, the first lord mentioned in a letter to his wife that "the war plans put forward by the staff have several stupid features about them wh[ich] have caused me some worry. I am gradually purging them of foolishness." He further remarked: "it is extraordinary how little some of these officers have really thought upon war on the largest scale."[242] In his memoirs Churchill recalled:

> In 1912 the War Staff, under the guidance of the then first sea lord, Sir Francis Bridgeman, proposed as an experiment, a plan for an immense cordon of submarines and destroyers, supported by the battle fleet, from the coast of Norway to a point on the east coast of England. To a military eye this system appeared unsound. I quoted repeatedly Napoleon's scathing comment in 1809: "these long thin cordons of troops are good enough to stop smuggling, but after fourteen years of war one does not expect to see such follies."[243]

If, as it appears, Troubridge not Bridgeman drew up the plan, then Churchill's public indictment of the latter in his memoirs is unfair. But otherwise the matter is of little real significance.

Thanks to Churchill, and Callaghan, this intermediate blockade strategy was never formally adopted.[244] On 25 May, in what Bridgeman described as a "truly Winstonian telegram," the first lord suddenly instructed his advisors to suspend the new war orders until the practicality of the cordon system had been tested in maneuvers.[245] Troubridge was outraged. How, he protested to Bridgeman, could the collective opinion of the "Sea Lords and the superior officers of the War Staff" be "set aside" by a civilian "whose knowledge of fleets and their tactical limitations and possibilities is theoretical and not founded upon even the smallest experience that may be expected of even a Lieutenant"?[246] For a civilian first lord of the Admiralty to overrule professional naval officers on an operational question was almost unprecedented. Nonetheless Churchill was unabashed.[247] He justified his actions by claiming that "outside the Admiralty it [the plan] was generally condemned by naval opinion."[248] By "naval opinion" he seems to have meant Adm. George Callaghan. After several long talks with him on the subject, the first lord had been convinced that the admiral held very "sensible" views on naval strategy.[249] Bridgeman too respected his judgement.

During the summer maneuvers of 1912, Troubridge's cordon system "was completely exposed and broken down," as was his reputation.[250] Churchill, by contrast, was vindicated. Practical exercises had demonstrated beyond reasonable doubt that the Royal Navy had too few cruisers and destroyers to sustain an effective observation line across the North Sea. For the task of rewriting the war plans Churchill resolved to employ more competent officers.[251] "The War Staff has begun bravely," he wrote to the prime minister shortly after the maneuvers, "but it requires more brain and more organising power at the top."[252] Accordingly he arranged to have Troubridge relieved of his post at the end of the year.[253] In his place, he selected the volatile and irascible Vice Adm. Henry Jackson (then serving as president of the Naval War College). At about this time, the first lord also began plotting to rid himself of Sir Francis Bridgeman who was becoming increasingly resentful at being circumvented during strategic discussions. Churchill decided that he could not allow the first sea lord to resign in a blaze of publicity, as he was threatening to do, and thus resolved to strike first. At the end of November, Bridgeman was blackmailed into resigning on the grounds of ill-health.[254] Prince Louis of Battenberg was subsequently promoted to first sea lord, and his seat on the Board taken by Sir John Jellicoe.[255]

It took the War Staff the rest of 1912 to rethink the war plans. In the interim, Callaghan asked for and received temporary war orders which gave him "absolute control of all Battle Cruisers, Cruisers, Light Cruisers, and Destroyer movements in the North Sea" and allowed him "to prepare his own plan of operations."[256] This, of course, had been the practice that existed before the formation of the War Staff. After Callaghan was given the freedom to adopt the operational policy he thought best, he proved most reluctant to surrender control back to the Admiralty. Surviving correspondence between the Admiralty and the commander in chief shows that there were frequent squabbles between them over the operational deployment of the fleet and the demarcation of responsibilities between them. Callaghan insisted on maintaining what might be termed the traditional prerogatives of the commander in chief. He contended that the officer responsible for executing operational policy must be allowed the dominant voice in the formulation of war plans. Callaghan, in addition, had little respect for the opinions of Whitehall planners, and battled constantly to have various aspects of the war plans revised. As late as August 1913, he was still complaining about the lack of "a solid basis of understanding between the War Staff and the service afloat" over North Sea strategy.[257] Much to Churchill's chagrin, some officers at the Admiralty were sympathetic to Callaghan's interpretation of his privileges. Prominent among them was one George Ballard, director of the War Staff's Operations Division.[258]

Captain George A. Ballard was one of the most powerful "naval intellectuals" of his generation. In 1911, Sir Charles Ottley rated him as "100% the ablest officer of his rank and standing now in the service."[259] Maurice Hankey shared this opinion.[260] Other admirers included Fisher, Beresford, Callaghan, Esher and Battenberg.[261] Ballard's career was unusual in that he served many years at Whitehall while still only a relatively junior officer. After four years as an assistant to the director of Naval Intelligence (under Battenberg and then Ottley), Ballard was promoted captain and appointed as naval representative to the Owen commission charged with the task of inspecting the state of coastal defenses at defended ports throughout the empire. On his return to England at the end of 1906, Fisher selected Ballard to chair a secret committee set up to investigate the practicability of amphibious operations against the German coast. Between 1907 and 1910, Ballard was given successive commands in the reserve fleet so that he might remain available to the Admiralty for consultation when needed. During Sir Arthur Wilson's administration, he was briefly shunted aside to command a battleship in Callaghan's Second Battle Squadron. But he was not forgotten. In 1911, McKenna had him penciled in to succeed Rear Adm. Alexander Bethell as director of Naval Intelligence.[262]

After the change of leadership at the Admiralty in October 1911, Fisher pressed Churchill hard to endorse Ballard's selection as the next head of the intelligence department.[263] Although the new first lord accepted the recommendation to recall this officer to Whitehall, he wanted a more senior officer for the top job in the reconstituted NID (the War Staff). So instead, Ballard was appointed director of the Operations Division (DOD). Being able to write coherently and expressively, Ballard easily outshone Rear Adm. Troubridge—who Churchill had hand-picked to head the War Staff.[264] Troubridge, incidentally, was also a golfing friend of the prime minister.[265] But according to Major Grant-Duff of the imperial defense secretariat (who dealt with both men on a regular basis), "Ballard," who "has more brains in his little finger than Troubridge has in his great woolly head, [found] himself ignored and practically a cipher."[266] It seems that Churchill himself was as much responsible for this state of affairs as the apparently jealous Ernest Troubridge. In October 1912, Grant-Duff heard that Churchill "is said to refuse to speak to Ballard because he won't compromise his opinions."[267] This rumor seems to have had foundation. Dockets in the Admiralty archives testify to the DOD's frequent criticisms of the first lord's strategic ideas. More conclusively, the first lord confessed his dislike of Ballard in a private letter addressed to Battenberg discussing future changes in personnel in the War Staff. "I cannot feel that he sees deeply into the great problems with which he deals," Churchill observed in September 1913.[268] Although Ballard was due to be made rear admiral within twelve months (in these days promotion to flag rank for senior captains was automatic) the first lord proposed to transfer him out of Whitehall by giving him command of a battleship until his promotion. As Churchill did not regard Ballard as suitable flag officer material, he thus seemed destined to be remain on the beach until compulsory retirement two years later.[269] Fortunately for Ballard subsequent events did not run to plan. His friends at the Admiralty persuaded the first lord to keep him on as DOD for another seven months. Then, instead of being passed over for a flag appointment, he was given an accelerated promotion! Despite not yet having reached the rank of rear admiral, in May 1914 Ballard was appointed admiral of patrols with responsibility for the defense of the entire east coast of Britain from invasions and raids.[270] For reasons that will become clear below, in 1914 this was perhaps one of the most important posts in the navy.

Returning to Admiralty war planning in 1912. At the end of November draft copies of the new plans were forwarded to the commander in chief for his approval.[271] "You will observe that the general idea of these plans is to exercise economic pressure upon Germany by cutting off German shipping from Oceanic trade," Callaghan was informed.[272]

> It is believed that the prolongation of a distant blockade will inflict injury upon German interests, credit and prestige sufficient to cause serious eco-

nomic consequences to Germany. Provided that the entrances to the North Sea from the westward and the northward are closed to all shipping under the German flag, a close commercial blockade is unnecessary. . . . To relieve such a situation, Germany would be tempted to send into the North Sea a force sufficient not only to break up the lines of lighter vessels actually employed upon the blockade but to offer a general action. Such an action or actions would take place far from the German coast and close to our own.[273]

As Callaghan had previously requested, all instructions to maintain a fixed line of observation across the North Sea had been deleted; a decision which left "the British coasts themselves [as] the only true and certain line of observation."[274] Based on the Firth of Forth, the commander in chief was still expected to "sweep and patrol" the southern half of the North Sea with his fleet, but details of how frequently or how far south were not specified except that his cruiser squadrons were "not to pass east of [the] 4th Meridian" (roughly halfway across the North Sea).[275] Given the latitude he wanted, Callaghan approved.[276]

The idea of a strictly defensive commercial blockade did not sit well with everyone in the Admiralty. Just before he vacated the post of naval secretary in January 1913 before taking up command of the First (Battle) Cruiser Squadron, Rear Adm. David Beatty sent a memorandum to Churchill protesting at the vagueness of Callaghan's war orders and the lack of what might be termed "offensive spirit." He thought it ridiculous that "no indication is given the Commander-in-Chief of how Their Lordships expect him to so dispose of the forces under his command: beyond the frustration of the enemy's landing of an invasion force !!! or the breaking up of the lines of distant blockade."[277] Beatty was also disturbed at the lack of arrangements for coordinating movements of the main fleet with the coast patrol flotillas.[278] These complaints appear to have reignited doubts in Churchill's own mind. There can be little doubt that the first lord was uncomfortable at the idea of ignoring the "historical" traditions of the service by ordering the navy to assume a posture of "purely passive defence."[279] Just before he was dismissed from the Board, Sir Francis Bridgeman had noted that the first lord was "not in agreement" with the revised 1912 war plans.[280]

Churchill was worried that with the bulk of the fleet stationed in the north, the Royal Navy could do little to prevent German warships from interfering with the transport of the British Expeditionary Force across the Channel. He was especially and justifiably concerned at the apparent vulnerability of the east coast of Britain to enemy raids. There was no question that the Grand Fleet of battle was more than capable of annihilating any German force it encountered. But at the same time it was becoming clear to him (and others) that the fleet was too far north to react against German strikes further south. Without any warning that the enemy was at sea, the Grand Fleet was powerless to stop small amphibious landings or bombardments of towns between the Forth and the Thames. Even trying to intercept the enemy ships returning to their base would require a considerable amount of luck. The new chief of the War Staff, Vice Adm. Henry Jackson, admitted as much when he noted we must "trust to our flotillas and shore batteries to inflict much damage to them during the raid."[281] The only consolation, he added, was that such eccentric attacks would probably not achieve any significant military results. Churchill, as the politician who would be held responsible for failing to prevent such an insult, did not find this to be much consolation.

Despite the navy's growing confidence in the power of the torpedo armed flotilla, the idea that the local patrol flotillas and coastal batteries could drive off a raiding force before it could do any serious damage was open to doubt. Although by 1913 the Royal Navy possessed over two hundred surface torpedo craft and almost seventy submarines, nothing like this number were available for coastal "flotilla" defense duties. A large number of modern destroyers and light cruisers had been sucked into the Grand Fleet to meet the insatiable demands from the commander in chief for more escorts. The remainder had been organized into an independent scouting force for the main fleet, known as Force T. After deducting the vessels allocated to the Dover Straits patrol and the oversea submarine flotillas, the admiral of patrols (Rear Adm. John de Robeck—later Captain Ballard), who was charged with the responsibility for the east coast, was left with only sixty-eight obsolescent destroyers and forty submarines with which to defend six hundred miles of coastline.[282] For the next couple of years, moreover, all new destroyers would be replacing worn-out craft. There would not, therefore, be any net addition to the flotilla. Projected deliveries of new submarines were even worse. As was explained in the previous chapter, after Keyes committed the navy to a fleet submarine development program the building of new patrol submarines had almost ceased.

At the beginning of January 1913, Churchill ordered a complete review of the war plans in light of the vulnerability of the east coast to attack. He saw that even if a German raid would not achieve any significant military result, the political cost to the government of the day might be ruinous. Better protection, he insisted, would have to be provided. The War Staff were undoubtedly spurred into taking this question seriously after the prime minister announced on 13 January that once again the CID would examine the possibility of serious invasion at length.[283] The enquiry was established at the request of the new secretary of state for war, Jack Seely, after he somehow learned that the Admiralty was no longer so sure that the navy could prevent German raids on the east coast of Britain.[284] In the meantime Churchill drafted a scheme of his own to discourage German raids. "Whatever maybe said in favour of distant blockade as the guiding policy of a long war," he postulated in a letter to his new first sea lord (Battenberg) on 17 February, "and I agree with what is said, such a policy can only be effectively maintained on a basis of moral superiority." Although the Royal Navy possessed a battle fleet capable of annihilating the High Sea Fleet, it was incapable of deterring individual German squadrons from roaming the southern half of the North Sea. "Until our enemy has felt and learned to fear our teeth," Churchill reasoned, a distant blockade strategy was thus "impracticable." He therefore called for the Royal Navy to adopt "an offensive at the outset and a recurrence to it from time to time throughout the war."[285] "We must conduct so ourselves that the sea is full of nameless terrors" for the German fleet. This could most easily be accomplished, he argued, by imposing a close blockade of German ports during the first week of the war and periodically thereafter. Churchill believed that for one week the Royal Navy could achieve a temporary "flotilla superiority" in the Heligoland Bight, because "the whole flotilla fleet can be used together for the duration of a week, and not merely one relief of a third at a time."[286]

When the first lord's letter was passed on to the War Staff for comment, every officer who saw it ridiculed the ideas. The key flaw in Churchill's reasoning, Jackson pointed out, was his assumption that all the navy's flotilla craft were suitable for operations off the German coast. Most destroyers then in service did not carry sufficient coal for sustained operations.[287] And if only the newer oil fueled craft were sent over (which could be refueled at sea) they would find themselves outnumbered by at least two to one. Finally, "on the principle that it is unwise to underrate your enemy, may we not credit the German flotillas as being as efficient as our own, especially when they are acting in their own waters" he asked.[288] Ballard developed this point further. He pointed out that a temporary close blockade with destroyers could only be maintained in the face of superior numbers by accepting a potentially crippling rate of attrition.[289] Captain Herbert Richmond, his assistant, was even more forthright in his condemnation. Punctuating his assessment with stinging historical examples (Churchill professed to be a historian) Richmond tore into the "fantastic measures" put forward by the first lord and predicted that his scheme would "result in appalling disaster."[290] Fisher was equally "unhappy" with Churchill's scheme, but for another reason. He feared that admissions that the navy could not protect the country from raids would inevitably be exploited by the War Office. "It means ruin to the Navy and a Flemish Army," Fisher warned. "Build more submarines—that's the remedy—not more lobsters [soldiers]."[291]

Churchill's determination to find an alternative to the distant blockade strategy may be gauged from his willingness to reconsider Admiral Wilson's plan to capture an advanced base off the German coast. In early 1913, the first lord instructed Rear Adm. Lewis Bayly "to investigate and report on the question of seizing a base on the Dutch, German, Danish or Scandinavian coasts for operations of flotillas on the outbreak of war with Germany."[292] He did so, it must be stressed, in defiance of majority opinion at the Admiralty.[293] Only Beatty, his former assistant, and Hankey, the secretary to the CID, favored such operations.[294] It was no surprise therefore that Bayly's favorable report, which postulated that a force of 12,000 troops should be able to capture a base close to the Heligoland Bight, was condemned by the Staff. "These projects," Ballard commented in July 1913, "are in the nature of a gamble. Gambles in war are justified, but here that does not appear to be the case."[295] Jackson's remarks were equally scathing. As were Callaghan's. "It is understood," the latter noted, "this policy of close blockade was seriously considered a few years ago and abandoned as being impracticable. As it appears to be still more impractical now, it is useless to reconsider it."[296] But Churchill refused to abandon the idea.[297] As late as June 1914 he remained deaf to warnings that such expeditions were "not worth the cost in ships and men."[298]

The War Staff's solution to problem was to lay a huge minefield off Heligoland Bight. This scheme had first been put forward by Capt. George Ballard the previous September.[299] He had argued that not only would the threat of mines inhibit the enemy from making hostile movements into the North Sea, but if the German battle fleet ever did put to sea it would have to be accompanied by slow minesweepers which would hinder its mobility, and thus give the Grand Fleet more chance to intercept.[300] In addition, he had cryptically noted, "the mines would probably provide a useful auxiliary to our commercial blockade." The giant minefield idea was certainly more practicable than Churchill's close blockade, but it did not appeal to Troubridge who immediately shelved the idea. Ballard, however, was not easily discouraged. Shortly after Vice Adm. Henry Jackson succeeded Troubridge as chief of the War Staff, in February 1913, the DOD resubmitted his plan.[301]

The revised paper is a remarkable document. In it, Ballard stressed the value of mines as a deterrent to neutral vessels trying to run the blockade into German ports. The switch in emphasis was deliberate. Ballard knew that the CID was currently discussing the practicability of the navy's blockade strategy. Several Cabinet ministers, led by David

Lloyd George, were pressing Asquith to endorse a more comprehensive wartime blockade of Germany by imposing rationing upon all imports into contiguous neutral countries.[302] Even the War Office was in favor.[303] After developing this theme in his paper, Ballard went on to explain that because of the impossibility of stationing an inshore squadron off the German coast, nothing could prevent neutral merchant ships from flouting the British commercial blockade by sailing from neutral Dutch territorial waters to German ports. As a consequence, he reasoned, "the actual effect of our naval pressure upon Germany in war is likely therefore to be greatly minimised by neutral action." There was only one way of "overcoming this unsatisfactory state of affairs," he advised, "and that is by resorting to the use of mines." Ballard estimated that a minefield extending from the coast of Belgium to Denmark, would "produce a paralysing moral effect on trade in the east part of the North Sea including the approaches to Dutch and Belgian ports."[304] He displayed no qualms in suggesting that "if a [neutral] steamer or two on the way from Rotterdam to Hamburg were blown up off the Texel, the traffic to German ports would almost certainly cease at once."[305] Ballard justified this ruthlessness by pointing out that:

At the last Hague Conference, Great Britain on behalf of neutral interests proposed as a general principle that no mine-laying should be permitted on the high seas, but this proposal was voted down by other states. The actual convention (No. VIII) which deals with mine-laying, and which was signed by 37 out of 44 States taking part, imposes no restriction whatever as to the localities wherein moored mines may be laid. . . . By adopting a policy of mine-laying, it is true that Great Britain would be acting in opposition to the above-mentioned principle as enunciated by the British representatives at the Hague. But only for a very sufficient reason. Finding that it is the palpable intention of other powers—as evidenced by their votes—to use mines at their own discretion, the British Government cannot be expected to deny itself the undoubted strategical advantage which a judicious use of mines affords. The other States . . . having chosen to ignore British warnings at the Hague, must abide by the consequences [and] will only have themselves to thank.[306]

Jackson was enthusiastic. With his backing, in April 1913 Ballard's mining strategy was provisionally approved by the Board of Admiralty. The only other officers who were aware of this decision were Callaghan and the senior members of the War Staff. Subsequently, the Board directed that a more powerful type of mine be developed, stocks increased, and 14,500 copies of the "notice to mariners" printed for distribution to captains of merchant ships on the outbreak of war.[307] Claims that "Churchill alone was interested in the scheme—until he got the figure for the cost of 50,000 mines" or that "when war came, Britain had no mining policy and consequently very few mines" are not supported by the documents.[308] The policy was in place and the mines were on order.

━━▷•◆•◁━━

It is impossible to say with any authority what Britain's naval policy would have been in the event of war with Germany between 1910 and 1913. Certainly the documents called the 1912 war plans cannot be regarded as a definitive statement of Admiralty strategic policy. Opinions varied: so much depended upon the beliefs of individual officers serving at the Admiralty at any particular moment and the balance of opinion within Whitehall. For instance Churchill insisted in his memoirs that

> The policy of distant blockade was not adopted from choice, but necessity. It implied no repudiation on the part of the Admiralty of their fundamental principle of aggressive naval strategy, but only a temporary abandonment of it in the face of unsolved practical difficulties; and it was intended that every effort should be made, both before and after a declaration of war, to overcome those difficulties.[309]

Most officers involved in the preparation of the navy's 1912 war plans acknowledged the distant blockade strategy was not ideal. But they could see no other way of keeping the battle fleet safe from attrition and ready to inflict the decisive blow on the enemy fleet. In other words the Grand Fleet had to stay out of "the torpedo-infested waters" and remain in northern waters.[310] Naval planners accepted that the price of keeping the battle fleet safe was an acceptance that the Royal Navy had abdicated control of the North Sea which left the east coast exposed to the possibility of attack. In the opinion of first lord the degree of risk was unacceptably high. In mid-1913, Churchill became so fearful for the defense of the east coast that he admitted to the CID that the navy could not guarantee the protection of key ports and towns from raids and suggested, accordingly, that the army strengthen their coast defense batteries and always retain a mobile field army in the country.[311] Before the consequences of this admission became apparent, however, war intervened.

Historians must also recognize that throughout Churchill's administration Britain's naval leaders were divided over a range of important strategic issues. The frequent arguments between the commander in chief and the Whitehall strategists have already been alluded to, and will be examined more closely in the next chapter. Perhaps more serious, however, were the divisions that existed amongst the flag officers holding appointments in the Home Fleets. There was a serious "conflict in style" over battle tactics. Some officers favored relying upon big-guns to overwhelm the enemy fleet: others on a combination of gun and torpedo attacks. There was no real consensus on battle ranges, the importance of maneuvering to repel torpedo attacks, or the role of destroyers, or whether the fleet should risk battle in misty weather. More fundamentally there were still major doubts as to whether a Grand Fleet formation comprising of thirty-three battleships plus up to one hundred smaller craft could be effectively controlled in battle. Many officers felt that the task was too great for one man and advocated giving individual squadron commanders freedom of action in battle. Others predicted that such "radical" tactics would create confusion and result in disaster. Because there was no agreed doctrine within the Royal Navy a commander in chief could not depend upon his subordinate commanders correctly anticipating his wishes. In short, British naval opinion was totally fragmented.

CHAPTER 9

The Revolution, 1913–1914

> The reader must now prepare himself for what looks like a reversal of
> policy; but which indeed had been the real policy throughout. No sooner
> had I won from the Cabinet the authority to order the four super-
> dreadnoughts of the year 1914 than I immediately resumed my plans for
> converting two of these ships into a much larger number of smaller ves-
> sels. I proposed to treat these dreadnoughts not as Capital Ships but as
> units of power . . .
>
> *Winston S. Churchill, first draft of "The World Crisis" manuscript*

In March 1912, Winston Churchill promised the House of Commons
that henceforth the Royal Navy would maintain a battle fleet of dreadnought
capital ships at least 60 percent more numerous than the established
strength of the High Sea Fleet. In addition, for every extra battleship
Germany added to her published building program Great Britain would
respond by laying down two.[1] The German rejection of the Churchill "naval
holiday" initiative and the publication of the Tirpitz *novelle* two weeks later,
accordingly committed the Board of Admiralty to increase their 1913–14
capital ship program from three to five ships. In October, however,
Churchill shocked his senior naval advisors by suddenly declaring that "he
should not fulfil his pledge."[2] Instead, he proposed to order just four battleships and ask Parliament to give the navy an additional £1,000,000 for
submarines.[3] This amounted in effect to a repudiation of "two keels to one."
Bridgeman and Battenberg, his senior advisors, greeted this "startling
change of policy" with incredulity. Earlier that summer, the first lord had
publicly ridiculed before the Committee of Imperial Defence all suggestions
that the Royal Navy could rely upon submarines in place of capital ships.[4]
Both sea lords thought that such a turn about would be "difficult to defend"
before Parliament and the navy. Winston was reported to have replied:
"leave it to me. I will manage the H[ouse] of Commons."[5] This was no flip-
pant remark. Minutes written by the first lord a fortnight later on the draft
report of the naval estimates committee show that he was still "inclined" to
favor the substitution.[6] To comprehend Churchill's attempt to reverse his
own policy, we must return to the beginning of 1912.

There can be little doubt that tightening financial constraints had induced Churchill to change tack. After the Cabinet first received intelligence on the German *novelle* in January 1912, the first lord had assured the chancellor of the Exchequer that, even after taking into consideration the need to respond to expansion of the High Sea Fleet, over the next five years the Admiralty would require only a "modest" increase in funds. By the summer of 1912 it had become clear that this forecast had been wildly optimistic. The original figures had not taken into account the decision, for instance, to upgrade the four battleships to be ordered under the 1912–13 program into oil-fired "super dreadnoughts." Ships of the *Queen Elizabeth* class *each* cost £600,000 more to build than the coal burning *Iron Duke* class battleships.[7] The switch in fuel also committed the navy to increasing its strategic reserve of oil. Accordingly, expenditure on oil fuel was projected to rise by at least £500,000 a year for the next four years.[8] There were further causes for financial worry. Inflation within the economy was exerting upward pressure on the naval budget. Prices for "shipbuilding material [were] up more than 5%, and gun machinery between 10% and 12%."[9] This added another half a million to the cost of the capital ship program. There was also a sharp rise in the price of coal. On top of all this, at the beginning of the year the Board had resolved that the enlisted men had a legitimate grievance over pay, which had not risen over the preceding five years (in spite of increases in the cost of living).[10] The sea lords insisted that pay and pensions must rise that year.[11] Churchill's unwillingness or inability to adopt flotilla defense as the basis of British naval policy in the Mediterranean meant that there were no economies to offset these higher costs.

Churchill was slow to recognize the magnitude of his department's financial difficulties but even slower to recognize his own consequent vulnerability. During a Cabinet review of naval policy conducted on 16 July, he revealed that his department now anticipated that over the next five years naval expenditure would have to rise from £44 to more than £49 million.[12] The news was not well received.[13] But it must have been something of a surprise to the first lord (considering that the German increase was not his fault) when during his presentation David Lloyd George passed him a private note across the table remonstrating that: "Bankruptcy stares me in the face"![14] The Treasury could not afford such an increase without raising taxation. Outwardly Churchill had remained unimpressed.[15] He had continued to insist that the Cabinet was committed to providing enough capital ships to uphold the 60 percent margin in the North Sea and the one power standard in the Mediterranean, and that these policies determined the level of naval expenditure. "Your only chance is to get [an extra] £5,000,000 next year," he retorted to the chancellor of the Exchequer, "and put the blame on me."[16]

What the first lord evidently did not dare go on to admit was that his £49 million figures were based upon the assumption that the Royal Navy would be receiving substantial financial assistance from the self-governing Dominions. On the strength of the Canadian prime minister's promise to finance the construction of three battleships, Churchill had deleted their cost (nine million) from the Admiralty's revised calculations.[17] In so doing, he had deliberately turned a blind eye to signals that Borden's task would not be an easy one.[18] Yet clinging to this possibility must surely have been easier than telling the chancellor of the Exchequer and the rest of the Cabinet that to carry out all the government's naval policy would mean that by 1915 annual naval spending might rise to the staggering sum of £53 million.[19] (Which would inevitably happen if the British treasury alone had to pay for the implementation of the Mediterranean arrangement, the 60 percent North Sea standard, and the policy of "two-keels to one.") This would have been equivalent to an increase of 25 percent in the navy estimates within a three-year period. Privately, even Churchill accepted that a rise of this magnitude "would place an undue strain on the taxpayer" and would probably have to be met by borrowing.[20]

Parenthetically, it is interesting to note that the leaders of the opposition Conservative Party also suspected that Churchill's naval policy might prove ruinously expensive to uphold.[21] Although they publicly approved and voted for Churchill's policy in 1912, the Unionist leaders avoided committing themselves to upholding either the 60 percent or "two keels to one" standards should they assume power. Lord Lansdowne, for instance (who had served as foreign secretary in the Balfour administration), was especially keen "to avoid tying ourselves to a programme of construction the extent of which will be determined by the rate at which other Powers may think proper to build."[22]

Churchill would also have been aware that any Cabinet investigation of naval policy would reveal that the upward pressure on the navy estimates had been exacerbated by decisions he had taken earlier in the year (such as initiating the super-dreadnought program) and to which the Admiralty was now committed. To a large extent, therefore, the situation was of his own making and that fact made him politically vulnerable. Churchill's moves, earlier in the year, to clothe himself as the champion of naval supremacy compounded his difficulties. During his first six months in office, Churchill had delivered numerous speeches pledging himself unequivocally to uphold Britain's naval position.[23] This, he had announced to Parliament, would be accomplished by maintaining a 60 percent dreadnought standard—augmented by the policy of two keels to one—instead of the old two-power standard. It is clear that when he did so he had not fully appreciated the costs such a change in policy entailed. Churchill's position in July 1912 may be summed up as thus: unless he could abandon either his 60 percent standard or the policy of two keels to one to which he had committed the government in the spring of 1912, then without Canadian assistance the Admiralty could not implement the Cabinet's Mediterranean policy unless taxes were raised to politically unacceptable levels. At the same time, Churchill could not admit this situation without attracting charges of mismanagement. Yet, neither could he ignore the warning he had received from Lloyd George. The chancellor's note had impressed upon the first lord the necessity to trim the navy estimates before resubmitting them to the Cabinet after the summer vacation.[24] Hence his suggestion in October to repudiate the policy of two keels to one and instead ask for just an additional £1 million for submarines.

The initial response by the sea lords to the "substitution policy," as it was called inside the Admiralty, made it clear to Churchill that he was proposing a politically dangerous course. Before the policy could be proclaimed, the Board of Admiralty had first to persuade the service that recent improvements in the capabilities of the submarine had reduced the need for such a large battle fleet. Then the first lord had to convince the Cabinet that a dilution of the "dreadnought standard" would not leave the government vulnerable to criticism that it was endangering British naval supremacy. Actually, Churchill had ample justification for making such a case. The performance of the **D** class submarines which had participated in the maneuvers that summer had been outstanding. There is no doubt that Churchill—for once—paid careful attention to a memorandum written in September 1912, by Capt. George Ballard drawing attention to their recent successes. Speculating on the implications for North Sea strategy, the DOD had argued that any attempt by the Royal Navy to operate a squadron of large armored warships or to maintain a line of observation across the North Sea in the face of modern submarines was clearly impracticable. "An effective watch [in the North Sea] is virtually impossible," he concluded, "unless by a very large force of submarines able to keep the sea for at least ten days in any weather."[25] Ballard had closed his report with a request for the Board to endorse "an immediate change in the war orders for our **D** class submarines" and redeploy them "to occupy positions as an advanced force on the German coast."[26] He further pointed out that the Royal Navy needed many more submarines.

When Churchill first proposed his substitution policy he must have been confident that he could count on the first sea lord's support.

Although taken aback at Churchill's audacity, Bridgeman admitted to his old friend Jack Sandars that he did indeed find the scheme attractive.[27] Sandars subsequently reported to Arthur Balfour that "Bridgeman is in favour of laying out this million on submarines," having been greatly impressed by their performance in the recent maneuvers. "I understand the idea is to employ submarines on the work of blockade of the enemy's ports in spite of Mahan's theory of naval warfare."[28] This assertion is corroborated by a private letter from the chief of the War Staff to the admiral of patrols. On 20 September 1912, Troubridge informed de Robeck that the Admiralty was considering a proposal to remove a number of submarines from his command and redeploy them for offensive work in the North Sea.[29] There is another indication of a significant change in stance by the Admiralty at this time. At about this time Fisher again began to crow that Churchill's "whole soul is saturated with the submarine."[30] Delighted, the admiral promised to use his influence with the Conservative Party to minimize the political backlash in Parliament against the sudden change of stance.[31]

The Board of Admiralty was further encouraged to reconsider the substitution policy later in November by warnings that Austria was planning yet another increase in her dreadnought program.[32] The Naval Intelligence Department had learned that the head of the Austrian navy recently had asked his political masters to finance the construction of a second division of dreadnought battleships.[33] Churchill was dismayed by the news.[34] He saw that if the Austrians went ahead and built four more dreadnoughts, then in order to meet the Cabinet's one-power Mediterranean standard, the Royal Navy would have no alternative but to follow suit. And if, as was appearing increasingly likely, Borden failed to deliver the three Canadian dreadnoughts, then within the next three years the British treasury would have to finance the building of no fewer than seven extra capital ships for the Mediterranean Fleet, pushing the navy estimates up to a fantastic level. "It is no use being vexed with me and reproaching me," Churchill pleaded to Lloyd George on 18 November, "I can no more control these facts than you can. We shall have to take further measures. What measures I cannot now say; but an *equal* provision in some form or another will be necessary."[35]

The meaning of this last remark is clarified by an Admiralty memorandum written by Captain Ballard entitled: "Considerations as to the Best Composition of the Mediterranean Fleet in 1915." Dated 20 November (thus written only two days after Churchill's letter to Lloyd George) this document reviews the possibility of matching a numerically stronger Austrian battle fleet with a smaller British armored squadron but supported by a large flotilla of destroyers and submarines.[36] Ballard concluded that because the mouth to the Adriatic was only forty miles wide, a flotilla force guarding the straits could be relied upon to weaken any Austrian squadron that tried to break into the Mediterranean. "To what extent it would actually suffer must, of course, remain a matter of conjecture," he noted, "but even if only two first class units were put out of action the gain would be appreciable and a similar danger would await the Austrians on every occasion of return to their bases and every subsequent venture into Mediterranean waters. In time they would almost certainly suffer serious reduction."[37] A force of twenty destroyers and twenty submarines plus depot ships, he calculated, would cost less to build than two modern dreadnoughts. In addition, the flotillas would absorb fewer personnel (an important consideration) and would also be cheaper to maintain. Although the War Staff was generally in favor of Churchill's idea, Ballard warned that large armored vessels were more mobile than submarines and thus better suited for imperial defense purposes. And so, he cautioned, "the substitution of submarines for battleships should be kept within strict limits until the development of submarines has proceeded much further than it has as yet."[38]

Two weeks after the sketch navy estimates had been submitted for Treasury approval, the Board of Admiralty were still toying with the idea of financing an expansion of the flotilla by dropping a battleship from the 1913–14 building program.[39] In a memorandum dated 8 December, Churchill explained to the sea lords that it was neither desirable nor necessary to "complicate" negotiations with the Treasury by talk of "substituting for a battleship or battleships increased programmes of smaller vessels." The Admiralty's first priority was to secure money from the Treasury, or to use his words, "alternatives for the application of money available can be considered after the main number has been established and agreed."[40] Then, "it will always be possible at any time before the construction of the last two battleships in the programme is actually commenced to decide on a change of policy and to substitute for them greatly increased programmes of submarines and destroyers or small cruisers."[41] The first lord further pointed out that "it is most undesirable to raise such a question now while the Canadians and the Federated Malay States are committing themselves to the construction of great ships. The adumbration of such a new idea would only darken council [sic] and greatly embarrass those who are working on our behalf."[42]

Churchill knew full well that he could not implement the substitution policy on his own authority or successfully "force his views on the Board"—though some of his critics believed he could.[43] To execute what amounted to a fundamental shift in British naval policy required the unanimous and unequivocal support of the Board of Admiralty. Considering the confusion within Whitehall over naval strategy generally during the winter of 1912–13, the willingness of all the sea lords to endorse such a step must have been doubtful. Churchill nevertheless tried. Jellicoe, who had only just been appointed to the Board, asked for time to consider such a radical proposal.[44] And the other sea lords showed signs of hesitation. Everyone realized that once the decision had been taken, there was no turning back. The Board would only be able to maintain public confidence by insisting that technology had fundamentally changed the conditions of naval warfare and by arguing that battleships were no longer "the final arbiters of naval power." This, of course, would have delivered a shattering blow to the axiom that battleships were the very symbols of Britain's naval supremacy. A naval administration which allowed the number of battleships in commission to fall slightly below the declared numerical standard could still justifiably claim to be upholding that standard if sufficient additional ships had been ordered or were under construction. A Board that did not build up to the standard and at the same time consciously deleted a ship from the building program could not.

Early in 1913, Churchill suddenly dropped his substitution policy. He did so for three reasons. First, the Austrian parliament had postponed their decision on whether or not to finance a second dreadnought squadron.[45] Second, the Federated States of Malaya paid for the addition of a fifth super-dreadnought to the 1912–13 construction program thus fulfilling the declared policy of "two keels to one." Although officially the Admiralty was not supposed to include either this vessel or the recently completed battle cruiser *New Zealand* in their calculations of British naval strength, they certainly did so when the first lord found it to be convenient.[46] And third, higher than expected yields from existing taxation had enabled the chancellor to swallow his objections to the inflated 1913–14 navy estimates and meet the cost of the Admiralty's four capital ship program without recourse to higher taxes. In return, Churchill had pledged himself to support Lloyd George's controversial Land Reform Bill.[47]

A Summer of Discontent

On 10 June 1913, Churchill asked the third sea lord, Rear Adm. Archibald Moore, to provide him with "details of maximum submarine output."[48] Two days later the first lord was informed that any rapid expansion of the submarine fleet would be handicapped by the shortage of firms in the country engaged in their construction. Moore explained that presently only Vickers, Armstrong, and the small Clydeside firm of Messrs. Scott were set up to build submarines. The only way to expand building capacity in the industry sufficiently to meet the navy's future material requirements, he advised, while at the same time ensuring sufficient competition within the industry to keep a check on prices, was to encourage new firms to tender for submarine contracts.[49] If other firms could be persuaded to enter the industry then within a year the building capacity in the country might be doubled to approximately thirty new hulls per year.[50] The limiting factor at this point, apparently, was the supply of diesel engines from Vickers Ltd.[51] Assuming that steps were taken to bring new firms into the industry, Moore estimated, the Admiralty could order twenty-five new submarines of the new **F** class designed by Commodore Roger Keyes and his committee, plus two improved *Nautilus* type experimental fleet submarines.[52] This would represent a capital investment of approximately £4.25 million, payable over a period of about two years. But, Moore added, for the navy to embark upon a large submarine building program next year it would be "necessary at once to give the new firms definite promises for orders" so as to give them time enough to retool.[53]

The following day (13 June) the first lord instructed Moore "to make plans for spending the maximum sums outlined." Over the next three weeks the first and second sea lords added their endorsements.[54] The Board of Admiralty also resolved that the enlarged submarine program must be kept secret until construction was under way. It was agreed that to minimize the chance of a leak not even the Treasury would be told.[55] Churchill declared that the magnitude of the change in policy justified such extraordinary secrecy. On 8 July, accordingly, Moore opened secret negotiations with eight private shipbuilders with the object of enticing them to switch from the construction of destroyers to building submarines.[56] In return, the firms were probably guaranteed contracts for half a dozen vessels spread over a period of years.[57] Meanwhile, Churchill asked the Operations Division of the War Staff to consider the proposals "in light of the War Plans." Two weeks later Captain Ballard replied that he and his staff thoroughly approved of an expansion of the submarine program and agreed "that every encouragement should be given to private building firms to lay down a submarine construction plant."[58] They advised that the additional vessels could be paid for by reducing the number of destroyers ordered in future programs.[59] Thus far, the degree of unanimity within the Admiralty was remarkable. But it was not to last.

By mid-July 1913, naval opinions began to diverge. While everyone at the Admiralty generally agreed that building more submarines was desirable, when it came to placing contracts they began to squabble over the exact role and function of the new craft. In addition, questions began to be asked about the suitability of the designs being considered. This, of course, was the responsibility of the inspecting captain of submarines. It will be recalled that since the end of 1910, this post had been held by Capt. Roger Keyes who championed the development of fleet-keeping submarines. In February 1912, Keyes had been appointed chairman of an Admiralty committee set up to consider the Royal Navy's future materiel requirement. The submarine design committee had reported that "the Royal Navy henceforth needed two types of submarine; a vessel of small displacement" for coastal patrol duties and an "oversea" type. In considering the design of the latter, "it was considered that this type should be capable of accompanying a modern fleet to sea and should possess the highest possible speed for strategic reasons."[60] Although diesel engines of sufficient power had not yet been designed to drive a vessel at twenty knots on the surface, as an interim measure Keyes had recommended the construction of a large experimental craft named the *Nautilus* which displaced 1,500 tons and was expected to attain 18 knots on the surface. In addition to this experimental fleet submarine, Keyes had also designed the "Admiralty coastal"—later designated the **F** class. This small craft displaced less than 350 tons and was expected to possess only a limited radius of action. These were the only "official" designs available to the Admiralty in 1913.

The War Staff's preliminary appraisal of the revised flotilla program written early in July 1913, concluded that the additional submarines could most usefully be employed to patrol the approaches of enemy harbors thus "reviving the strategy of close blockade."[61] Ballard (DOD) imagined the ideal patrol submarine would possess good habitability to enable it to remain on station for over a week and superior underwater performance to operate effectively in hostile waters. A high surface speed, he considered, "though desirable," was not "an essential feature."[62] In a further paper on the subject dated 20 July 1913, Ballard, supported by Jackson, his chief, issued a direct appeal for priority to be given to the building of patrol types.[63] The staff Operations Division estimated that an effective blockade of the North Sea German coast could not be attempted with less than thirty-six vessels. Presently the Royal Navy possessed less than twenty such craft built or building—and that figure included the prototype **D** class vessels. Ballard was worried that neither the "fleet" *Nautilus* design nor the "coastal" **F** class appeared to be suitable for blockade duties. This concern was shared by Sir John Jellicoe.[64] While the second sea lord was enthusiastic for the *Nautilus*, he considered the **F** type submarine would be too small for offensive operations off the German coast.[65] Both Jellicoe and the War Staff officers thought that instead the navy should continue building more of the proven **E** type (800 ton) craft.

Keyes' subsequent attempt to defend his construction policy only served to confuse matters. On 15 August, he replied that his **F** design should be perfectly "capable of operating on the enemy's coast."[66] But in the same paper he went on to admit that they would be "on the small side for this work in severe weather and have not the offensive value of the **E** class."[67] His ambivalence created, not surprisingly, a great deal of confusion at the Admiralty over whether or not the **F** class was really suitable for blockade duties. Nevertheless Keyes landed one telling blow—one which was calculated to be noticed by the first lord. At a price of only £55,000 per boat, **F** class submarines cost less than half that of the **E** type vessels.[68] To replace the twenty-five **F** class submarines projected in the third sea lord's proposed "maximum" submarine program with the larger **E** type vessels would push up the price from £4 to £6 million, an unacceptable increase. Any increase in the navy estimates, of course, was politically out of the question. But the War Staff's opposition to seeing money "diverted from the building of battleships and other ocean going vessels towards increasing the submarine program" kept this door shut.[69] Yet even if all the funds presently earmarked for destroyers were switched to the submarine program, as Churchill considered doing, there still would not be enough money to build twenty-five patrol submarines. Clearly the number of vessels in the submarine program had to be cut: the question was whether to build fewer patrol types or delete the experimental fleet submarines?

Churchill hesitated to choose. He recognized that the navy required as soon as possible a large number of patrol submarines for its immediate operational requirements. A submarine blockade, he realized, also offered the best chance of creating a consensus within Whitehall on North Sea strategy for the first time in many years. According to the most conservative estimates, "to maintain a continuous blockade of the German rivers" the navy would require forty-eight patrol submarines. Still more craft would be needed for the Mediterranean.[70] Such a force, Churchill accepted, "could be created largely at the expense of the destroyers."[71] Yet giving top priority to the construction of "improved **E** boats" meant slowing or even suspending the fleet submarine development program—something he was loath to do because in this type he saw a path towards his long-term goal of overall cuts in naval expenditure.[72] As we shall see, Churchill believed that if the Royal Navy could develop a submarine "with sufficient speed to overhaul a battle fleet so as to be able to anticipate it at any point, or get ahead of it in order to dive and attack," then these vessels could serve as "a decisive weapon of battle [and] as such must count in partial substitution of battleship strength."[73] In a memorandum on the subject dated 20 July 1913, he speculated that a "battle group" comprised of "3 or 4 ocean submarines of 24 knots speed [supported by] 2 light cruisers of 30–31 knots" fitted to carry sea planes, "should be considered equal as a decisive fighting unit to a first class battleship or battle cruiser."[74] Such a squadron, moreover, would be cheaper to build and maintain than a battleship. The realization of this "fleet submarine" vision, however, required substantial and immediate investment. But in 1913 the Royal Navy simply could not afford to continue the fleet submarine development program, and at the same time produce sufficient numbers of patrol submarines to meet its operational requirements. At the end of August, Churchill decided to await developments.

⇒◆⇐

It is against this background that the Admiralty strategists continued to discuss North Sea strategy. As we have seen, after the 1912 maneuvers there was a growing conviction within Whitehall that the best chance of resolving the "North Sea problem" rested with the Royal Navy making greater use of submarines in one role or another.[75] Throughout the first half of 1913 the Admiralty remained divided on the exact strategy to adopt in the event of war with Germany. Angry correspondence between the first lord and the War Staff during the early weeks of 1913 demonstrate that the strategy of distant blockade prescribed in the war plans had not yet been definitely set. Churchill was still gravely concerned over the vulnerability of the east coast to enemy raids. So much so, indeed, that at the beginning of 1913 the first lord indicated to several other members of the CID invasion committee that he was now prepared to consider the need for some form of compulsory military training for all male adults.[76] Though this could have been just a ploy to slide the inflated navy estimates through Cabinet. At the end of February 1913 the Admiralty agreed to leave the North Sea question in abeyance until after the "dispositions of our fleet and defence against raids" had been tested.[77] The naval strategists hoped the maneuvers scheduled for the end of July would settle the argument once and for all. Practical exercises would either confirm "the results obtained by the red fleet last summer, or show that the apparently successful raid on the east coast was illusory."[78]

For the 1913 maneuvers, Adm. Sir George Callaghan (commander in chief) retained control of the main British (blue) fleet and Rear Adm. John de Robeck (admiral of patrols) the blue patrol flotillas. Command of the opposition (red) fleet was given to the second sea lord, Vice Adm. Sir John Jellicoe. After ten days red claimed a decisive victory. De Robeck's patrol flotillas entirely failed to detect the location of Jellicoe's fleet or prevent the red invasion force from landing 3,500 marines at Immingham harbour. Though it should be noted that just before the landings a questionable umpiring decision ruled the entire blue submarine flotilla guarding the Humber estuary out of action.[79] This led several officers to believe that the result had been fixed for "political reasons."[80] Nevertheless, in his official report Callaghan conceded defeat. He advised that a fleet stationed in the North of Scotland could not properly defend the east coast of Britain. The best solution, he agreed with Churchill, was to ask the army to strengthen their coast defense batteries.[81] If the Admiralty continued to insist on assuming full responsibility for the defense of the British Isles against invasion and raids, warned the commander in chief, "the battle fleet must cruise further south than would otherwise be the case, and, in consequence, will be more exposed to the attack of torpedo craft."[82] Such a deployment, he prophesied, would result in heavy—possibly disastrous—losses. Callaghan's certitude is unquestionable. In a follow-up report on this subject he reemphasized that "unless steps can be taken to prevent systematic mining in the North Sea, the Grand Fleet should not come south to play any part in preventing invasion."[83] Mines, torpedoes and "the submarine" rendered these waters too dangerous for battleships.[84]

The failure of the blue fleet to locate and bring the red fleet to action during the maneuvers arguably had an even greater impact upon Britain's naval planners. After two weeks at sea, Callaghan's large scouting force did not catch even a glimpse of Jellicoe's fleet; and de Robeck's coastal patrol flotillas were no more successful at vectoring the blue fleet towards its objective. The Whitehall strategists were so dismayed at these failures in their war plan that their first reaction was to consider an updated version of the discredited Troubridge scheme to scatter observation squadrons across the North Sea. The commander in chief did not agree. Callaghan expressed his opposition to the deployment of independent warships for observation duties so forcibly indeed, that he was accused by Churchill of carrying "arrangements for the safety of the cruisers almost to the point of neglecting the safety of the country."[85] But Callaghan refused to be intimidated. "As I have stated," he retorted, "it is necessary to abandon the plan of stationing cruiser observation squadrons across the North Sea."[86] He insisted that all available modern light cruisers were needed as scouts for the battle fleet.[87]

Callaghan was equally scathing of an alternate plan suggested by the War Staff which called for the flotillas and light cruiser squadrons periodically to sweep "intermediate areas" between the British and German coasts. He condemned this idea as "a compromise which is unsound in principle and dangerous in practice. Unsound because it would only be an off chance that they would be met, and dangerous because they might encounter a superior force too far from effective support."[88] Callaghan spelled out his reasoning as follows:

> The advent of submarines and the introduction of ships which combine high speed and great gun-power have introduced factors which necessitate the concentration of [our] cruisers and flotillas in the same area as the battle fleet. If our torpedo craft are widely separated from the heavy ships, not only will they be absent when required, but are liable to be destroyed in detail. It is not the enemy's torpedo craft that they may expect to meet but his cruisers and even battle cruisers which can steam as fast as they can in ordinary weather.[89]

After Jellicoe expressed concurrence with Callaghan that the proposed strategy of sending flotillas or cruiser squadrons "vaguely into the North Sea in anticipation of meeting hostile ships" would be "of little use," the idea was dropped.[90] Churchill's board resolved, though with some misgivings, to keep the battle fleet in northern waters and retain the distant blockade strategy. In view of Callaghan's intransigence on the point little else was immediately possible.

Instead of tampering with the deployment of the Grand Fleet, the Admiralty instructed the War Staff to devise a "different organisation" for the east coast patrol flotillas—one "more suitable to their restricted and local spheres of action." Henceforward, Battenberg directed, they would be regarded "no longer 'patrol flotillas' but 'défenses mobile' (to use the French term), or simply coast defence flotillas."[91] A change in leadership was also felt to be necessary. Early in 1914, Rear Admiral de Robeck was dismissed as admiral of patrols and replaced in this key post by the man who had drafted the new defense scheme, Capt. George Ballard.[92] Although the entire system was not in place before the outbreak of war in August 1914, draft documents show that the War Staff contemplated giving a major role to the embryonic Royal Naval Air Service. In addition to his old destroyers and submarines, the admiral of patrols was to be given fifty new airplanes fitted with wireless telegraphy (W/T) capable of searching at distances up to one hundred miles from their bases.[93] Recent trials had demonstrated that an airplane could "be relied on to carry 5 hours fuel, pilot and W/T operator with outfit."[94] Another advantage of using aircraft for reconnaissance was that they were less handicapped than surface ships by the patches of low lying fog than often prevailed in the North Sea.[95] With an eye on the future, over the next two years the Admiralty anticipated spending almost £1 million on setting up the ground infrastructure (such as aerodromes) needed to support naval air power.[96] Far from buttressing "the Admiralty's fear of a successful raid," therefore, the development of aviation was seen by naval strategists as a major part of the solution to the navy's difficulties in protecting the east coast from attack.[97]

Callaghan's failure to intercept and engage the enemy fleet during the 1913 maneuvers not only fueled concerns over the adoption of the distant blockade strategy, but also revived doubts over the practicability of the Grand Fleet tactical system. A growing number of "thinking" officers were concerned that if the concentrated might of the Royal Navy ever stumbled to within striking range of the High Sea Fleet, the commander in chief would be unable to control such a cumbersome armada with the existing visual signaling equipment. Prominent among the decentralizers was Rear Adm. David Beatty, who recently had taken command of the Battle Cruiser Squadron.[98] But he was by no means the only flag officer in the Home Fleets thinking along these lines at this time.[99] During the 1913 maneuvers Callaghan and Jellicoe had both "kept their destroyers with their battleships in order to make use of them in fleet actions." Each, it should be noted, commanded a much smaller force than the "Grand Fleet of battle" the Royal Navy proposed to deploy in a war against Germany. Jellicoe, for instance, was given just fourteen battleships, two battle cruisers, ten cruisers and forty destroyers.[100] Yet when at sea with even this relatively modest armada, he found that contact "between the flotillas and the Commander-in-Chief is very quickly lost." Jellicoe reported that experience had taught him that an admiral could "neither signal his orders by wireless to the flotilla, nor can the flotilla give him information obtained." Without adequate means of communication the admiral's power "to organise and control his flotilla is [therefore] very much reduced."[101] Echoing Jellicoe's remarks, Callaghan admitted he had found using destroyers at night to be virtually impossible because "no-one knew where to send them." He blamed their lack of success upon "the fact that it is only recently a systematic start has been made to train them to work with a battle fleet," concluding, "it is evident that they require much more practice."[102]

Sir George Callaghan's attempts to improve the Grand Fleet system by incorporating more and more warships into the formation predictably exacerbated the strain on existing methods of command and control. Since his appointment as commander in chief at the end of 1911, the size of the Grand Fleet of battle had grown into forty-one battleships and tactics had become more complex. "A line formed of these 41 ships at the new close order intervals of 2½ cables would measure exactly ten nautical miles or 20,000 yeards."[103] The roles of destroyers, for instance, were no longer limited to scouting and warding off attacks on the battle squadrons by enemy torpedo craft. Under Callaghan they were regarded as an integral component of the Grand Fleet's strike capability.[104] Callaghan may have been encouraged to place more reliance upon the torpedo in particular by serious doubts over the standard of the fleet's gunnery.[105] In any case, in early October 1913 the commander in chief reminded officers serving in Whitehall that since "the introduction of the long range torpedo, opinion, however decided it may have been previously, is now more favourably disposed towards using our destroyers offensively against the enemy's capital ships."[106] And he was not the only officer keen to see destroyers being fitted to carry more torpedoes, even if this meant sacrificing gun-power.[107]

Callaghan's report left the Admiralty in no doubts as to his tactical intentions. "It is evident," he lectured, "that gun attack by itself cannot have the same effect as combined gun and torpedo attack, and it is undoubtedly true that, in combination with the gunfire of a fleet, torpedo attacks by large numbers of destroyers is a danger which a battle fleet, already heavily engaged, would find it almost impossible to resist."[108] What he did not explain, however, was how he proposed to coordinate such an attack. While the War Staff acknowledged that there was "no doubt much to be said in favour of their [destroyers] use as a battle support to a fleet," they cautioned "this might be carried too far." The staff officers reminded the commander in chief that destroyers could also profitably be employed acting independently at night. "We ourselves know that the proximity of destroyers is a source of perpetual apprehension to battle fleets" during the hours of darkness.[109] The role of destroyers, they agreed, deserved careful consideration.

Two months later, in December 1913, Callaghan again demonstrated his faith in the torpedo by asking the Admiralty to authorize destroyers attached to his fleet to carry one spare torpedo for each torpedo tube. At that time, destroyers did not carry any reloads. Again Callaghan took the opportunity to advise the Admiralty "that, in the past few years, the torpedo has improved to an unprecedented extent in power, range, speed, and accuracy." Destroyers "could reach positions for favourable torpedo fire with little risk to themselves" and thus ought to carry more than one salvo of long-range torpedoes.[110] At the Admiralty, only the junior sea lord disagreed with the commander in chief's assessment on the efficacy of long-range torpedoes. More serious objections were voiced at "the C. in C.'s proposals to load up the decks of TDB's with spare torpedoes to the detriment of the vessels proper role as torpedo boat destroyers." Stowing an estimated three and a half tons of equipment on the upper deck of a destroyer, it was feared, would compromise their stability as gun platforms. "I would rather see the sea-going [fleet] submarine developed," noted the third sea lord. Battenberg agreed that "loading up a destroyer with torpedoes of great weight is undesirable."[111] For this reason, Callaghan's request was refused.

One of the few facts upon which Britain's naval leadership was unanimously agreed after the maneuvers was the stunning success of the big "oversea" submarines. By the end of the first week Callaghan was judged to have lost no less than 40 percent of his capital ships to submarine attack. In his report he acknowledged that submarines posed "a far greater menace than the fleet had given them credit for."[112] He was so much shaken by the experience that he subsequently determined that the battle fleet should never under any circumstances put to sea without a strong escort of destroyers and cruisers. Jellicoe was equally impressed. "So far as the North Sea and Great Britain and Germany are concerned," he reported, "these vessels [submarines] can remain in positions off any hostile port for a week or more, and they go far to deny the use of German ports to German ships and similarly British ports to British ships, except at great risk to the surface vessel. They can undoubtedly carry out a blockade of an enemy's coast in the old sense of the word."[113]

Attempts by a few senior officers to belittle the achievements of the submarines were resisted by the officers serving at the Admiralty. For instance, at the end of the maneuvers Churchill invited Adm. Reginald Custance (now retired) to comment on reports submitted by the umpires and fleet commanders.[114] Custance, readers will recall, had been one of Fisher's most implacable opponents. As second in command to Lord Charles Beresford between 1906 and 1908, he had encouraged the view that the strategy of close blockade against Germany was still practicable. He continued to believe this as late as 1915. Custance, moreover, was notorious for his view that submarines were "untried" and that the torpedo was an "overrated" weapon.[115] Even so, Churchill valued his opinions. So highly did he rate him, indeed, that in September 1913 the first lord considered appointing Custance chief of the War Staff in place of the disappointing Henry Jackson.[116] Battenberg was horrified when told of the idea. "It is no use going back to the Russo-Japanese war to illustrate the failings of the torpedo craft," protested the first sea lord, "both the weapon and its carrier have made immense strides since then, and their effect cannot be brushed aside so lightly. On the submarine he is of course quite wrong."[117] The point was taken. Churchill conceded that "Sir Reginald Custance in my opinion underrates the submarine altogether," and began looking elsewhere for a successor to Henry Jackson.[118]

Views expressed by men like Battenberg, Jackson, Jellicoe, Moore and Callaghan represented the opinion of the Royal Navy's leadership. Their thoughts are recorded in private correspondence with each other and in the dockets that circulated Whitehall. What naval officers serving in the fleet thought about submarines and torpedo warfare at this time is much more difficult to discern. Because the Admiralty rarely surveyed the opinion of fleet officers on any question, there is very little written evidence with which to form any definitive conclusions. In addition, fleet officers were far more likely to discuss their theories in conversation rather than communicate them in writing. Sufficient evidence has survived, however, to contradict widespread assertions of myopia among British naval officers with regard to the submarine. It is quite wrong to assert, as most historians have done, that "[d]own to 1914 the Fleet, generally speaking, regarded submarines as merely local defence vessels whose officers and men dressed like North Sea fisherman, were almost a service apart."[119]

In 1913, one of the most articulate and respected officers in the fleet was the recently promoted Rear Adm. Mark Kerr. Related to the former senior naval lord and a close personal friend of the current first sea lord, Kerr was also highly regarded by Fisher.[120] In June 1913, Kerr was asked to head the new British naval mission to Greece. In recommending him to his opposite number in Athens, Churchill described Kerr as "one of the most gifted and brilliant officers in our service, of whom we fully expect in the future that he will rise at an early age to the most important commands."[121] Arriving in Athens at the end of the summer, Kerr's first job was to formulate an affordable construction program. Accordingly, in September, he advised the minister of marine that Greek interests in the Aegean could best be protected by a large force of destroyers, submarines, and aircraft, supported by a squadron of specially designed fast heavy cruisers and a small aircraft carrier (!). Forwarding his recommendations, Kerr explained that:

> Experience has shown that capital ships, viz., *Dreadnoughts* and *Dreadnought* cruisers, in narrow waters, cannot live long against a modern flotilla well handled. Air-craft can cover such an area by sea, sending the information by wireless to the flotilla, that in ordinary weather it is impossible that the capital ships can escape the attack of the flotilla either by day or night. It is apparent, therefore, that capital ships are only of value in the open sea out of the radius of action of the flotilla, and it follows, therefore, that Greece, having no colonies, can protect herself and attack (in the best and most economical method) her enemy by means of flotilla warfare.[122]

The scheme was not well received. Kerr was "startled" to learn that Greek officers had no confidence in flotilla craft against dreadnoughts. "They say that they have been brought up to believe only in the big ship, and that, although some of them have been almost persuaded that the day of the big ship in narrow waters is over, yet the moral effect of not having the name *dreadnought* behind them will be so bad that they will go into action with such a feeling of depression as to risk defeat."[123] "In the British Navy," Kerr assured the minister in reply, "we have come to believe in the destroyer and submarine far more than in the large ship; it therefore never occurred to me that the effect could be so opposite [sic] among the officers of the Royal Hellenic Navy."[124] Kerr went on to warn that a dreadnought would add an unnecessary and costly burden to the construction budget. But if this "depression of *morale*" could be "done away with" by the purchase of a battleship, he conceded, "it may be well worth Your Excellency's consideration to expend this money as an investment against the great expense of a war."[125] The Greek navy subsequently placed an order with a German firm for one dreadnought battleship. Parenthetically, it is interesting to note that both Ballard and Churchill at the Admiralty in London fully endorsed Kerr's advice for Greece to establish a fleet of flotilla craft, though they were less happy about the proposed fast heavy cruisers which they regarded as potentially dangerous to British interests.[126]

Just how far Kerr's views reflected the opinion of senior British naval officers outside Whitehall is difficult to say. Yet it is worth noting that a letter written by Sydney Hall (the former inspecting captain of submarines) to Fisher in April 1914, claimed that among those senior captains attending the War College with him "there does *not* seem to be any lack of appreciation of the potentiality of the submarine."[127] This seems equally true of the flag officers. In May 1914, the Admiralty asked all squadron commanders in the Home Fleets to submit topics for discussion at the forthcoming joint conference to be held at the end of July.[128] Their replies indicate, with just one exception, that every admiral in the fleet (including Beatty, Pakenham, Warrender, Madden and Burney) took it for granted that flotilla craft would pose a "formidable" danger to squadrons operating in the North Sea, and especially when returning to base for coal. Vice Adm. Charles Briggs, for instance, felt that unless provided with a large escort his (Fourth) battle squadron would be "at the mercy of any small craft which may sight it."[129] If historians must make generalizations, it would be more accurate to say that most senior officers seemed to recognize the submarine menace—but few properly understood the implications. Which was understandable. More importantly, no one seemed able to suggest any practicable counter measures except to screen the movement of big ships with ever greater numbers of destroyers.[130]

The Fleet Submarine

Since the middle of 1912, Admiral Lord Fisher had been engaged as chairman of the royal commission set up to investigate the supply of fuel oil for the Royal Navy.[131] He had been charged "to find the oil: to show how it can be stored cheaply: how it can be purchased regularly and cheaply in peace; and with absolute certainty in war."[132] Like the experienced chairman he was, Jacky at once packed the committee with friends known to hold similar views. Among them were Captain Hall (the former head of the submarine service), and Vice Adm. Sir John Jellicoe (the current second sea lord). Driven by Fisher's unmatched energy and enthusiasm, the commission had virtually finished its work by the beginning of 1913—though for political reasons Churchill would not allow it to disband until the beginning of the following year.[133] In the interim, Fisher used his position of authority first to acquire information on the Admiralty's submarine policy and then as a platform to wage a campaign for an increase in the submarine budget. To this end he encouraged Hall to publish in the newly established journal for officers, *The Naval Review*, a series of articles on "the influence of the submarine upon naval policy."[134] The articles were of course published anonymously.[135] Although it is impossible to say precisely what impact they had upon service opinion, they did serve to initiate discussions on the subject within the fleet. At the end of March 1913, Fisher began circulating to selected commentators drafts of a paper outlining his own views on the importance of submarines in future naval wars.[136] His main argument was simple: it was essential that the Royal Navy at least double submarine construction because it was "the only type of vessel capable of maintaining any form of blockade" on the enemy coast.[137] He also asked his readers to consider the possibility of submarines attacking and sinking merchant ships.[138]

In May 1913, Fisher began to recast his paper after hearing rumors that in an effort to accelerate the fleet submarine development program the Admiralty was contemplating the adoption of steam power plants in place of diesels.[139] Quite independently from Keyes and his committee, the new director of naval construction, Tennyson d'Eyncourt, had taken an interest in the fleet submarine concept.[140] With the encouragement of Churchill and the third sea lord, the DNC believed he could build a vessel capable of steaming at 24 knots on the surface. Designed to be propelled by steam turbines, 338 feet long and displacing 2,260 tons, d'Eyncourt's craft was more than twice the size of any other submarine then afloat.[141] This design was the prototype of **K** class submarines that would be ordered in 1915.[142] Fisher was quickly persuaded by Captain Hall that the technical difficulties of using steam would be insurmountable.[143] Hall also took the opportunity to complain more generally that his successor's single-minded pursuit of his fleet submarine program had resulted in disaster for the submarine service. In June, Fisher confided in Jellicoe:

I am extremely anxious about the Admiralty development of the submarine. The more I hear, the more d—d fools they seem to be! I've written a memorandum on the subject, but if I sent it to Winston, it would mean open war with the Admiralty, so I withhold it. The most fatal error imaginable would be to put steam engines in a submarine.[144]

In October, Jacky proved unable to contain himself when he learned that the Admiralty, with the approval of Keyes, were about to place a contract with Messrs. Scott of Greenock for a smaller experimental steam powered submarine to be christened *Swordfish*. Fisher swiftly despatched the first lord a note telling him "whatever you do don't go for steam in a submarine! Simply fatal!"[145] Clearly annoyed at being lectured in such peremptory tones, Churchill reposted: "if the submarine is to be a substitute for battleship strength or battleship preponderance, not merely a substitute for destroyers, it must possess strategic speed which will enable it effectively to overhaul or circumvent a battle fleet." Only fleet-keeping submarines, he believed, could be regarded as instruments of strategic deterrence. "If this speed can be attained at the present time or in the immediate future by any other path except by those of size and steam I should be delighted to learn it."[146] The first lord closed his letter with a request to see a copy of "The Oil Engine and the Submarine." Apparently Fisher had not allowed him to see one of the six early draft copies.[147] But not until November was the first lord sent a copy.[148]

What has always most impressed historians about this famous paper was Fisher's prediction that submarines would sink unarmed merchant ships without warning, an assertion that at the time was regarded as fantastic, but was made to seem all the more prophetic by the amount of scorn with which it was greeted. Neither Battenberg, Keyes nor Churchill believed "this would ever be done by a civilised power."[149] This, however, was not the central message of the paper.[150] "The Oil Engine and the Submarine" was in fact written as an attack on the fleet submarine program.[151] On the first page Fisher condemned the dissipation of the inadequate submarine budget on experimental vessels. He went on to point out that the practicality of working fast submarines alongside capital ships had not yet been proved and that if they had to be fitted with steam engines then it was not desirable to build such craft. Whereas the value of patrol submarines had already been proved in exercises and a coherent doctrine for their use had been agreed by the War Staff and the Admiralty. In short, the experimental fleet submarine program was creating an acute shortage of modern patrol submarines needed for immediate operational requirements. Fisher insisted that more submarines suitable for blockading the German coast had to be built at once because they *were "the only type of vessel capable of maintaining any form of blockade."*[152] Building adequate numbers of patrol submarines would mean halting the development of the fleet submarine which, he knew, Churchill was reluctant to do.

Wary of probing at what was clearly a sensitive area, Fisher tried hard to avoid hurting Churchill by attacking his encouragement of the fleet submarine. Instead, he directed his criticism at the men who had advised him that steam propulsion was practical:

> the development of the submarine has been entirely based and dependent upon the development of the internal combustion engine, and on that development the future great advance of the submarine must patiently wait. . . . Although an increase in surface qualities and advantage could have been given them by the substitution of steam turbines for the natural internal combustion engine, these have never even been considered in the past and quite rightly so—because thereby all the important advantages as a submarines would have been impaired[153]

Fisher's paper contained other, not very convincing gestures, to avoid confrontation over the concept of the fleet submarine itself.[154] His attempts to attack "steam" and not the idea of the fleet submarine (and thus Churchill) can be seen in the following passage:

> it is open to grave doubts whether a steam submarine proceeding at say, twenty knots could shut down and dive within a period of three minutes. Rapidity in diving from surface work being an essential quality to save the vessel being caught and easily destroyed on the surface, it need hardly be pointed out how grave this disadvantage would be. . . . *These difficulties to some extent dispose for the present of the very natural desire for submarines to accompany battle fleets.*[155]

Historians have always thought that the Board of Admiralty never studied "The Oil Engine and the Submarine."[156] This is not correct. There is clear evidence that it was discussed fully and provoked "no small commotion" when it was presented at an Admiralty conference held on 9 December 1913 to discuss submarine construction policy.[157] Those present included Churchill, Jellicoe, Moore, Jackson, d'Eyncourt and Keyes. At the assembly it was agreed that "the policy to be worked for is the revival of the blockade of German ports."[158] Initially, the Board thought that the F class submarine would be "suitable for a blockade" of the German coast.[159] Until Keyes (belatedly) admitted "this was not the case." In the process he torpedoed Churchill's last hope that the navy could afford to build adequate numbers of patrol submarines and maintain the pace of development for the fleet submarine project.[160] Keyes, however, refused to allow the Admiralty to order more **E** class submarines. He insisted that because the type did not possess a double-hull it was now regarded by his experts as obsolete.[161] Instead, he proposed that a brand new type should be designed incorporating "the best features" of the **E** and **F** types. Accordingly, the following day, instructions were sent to the naval constructors department to produce a sketch design immediately. The result was a double-hulled Admiralty "improved E type" submarine.[162] But because Moore had already placed contracts for seven **F** class vessels, there was only enough money left in the budget for just two "improved" **E** class patrol submarines that year. The contracts could not be canceled without breaking faith with the companies that Moore had enticed into the submarine construction business.[163]

The meeting then moved on to discuss whether or not to order a 24 knot, "K" type fleet submarine. Given the affirmation that priority was to be given to the production of patrol submarines, it does seem curious to find recorded in the minutes of this meeting that "no serious objection was raised by anyone present to the laying down of one experimental vessel except that the money might be better spent."[164] Four **E** class patrol submarines could be built for the price of one "K" boat. Although Keyes expressed reservations at proceeding "too fast" with the pace of development, his warnings were discounted. Churchill, Moore, and Battenberg were all enthusiastic to acquire fleet submarines as soon as possible. It was resolved that the question of ordering the new fleet submarine "should be further considered towards the end of 1914, with a view to including the type in the 1914/15 programme."[165]

The ambivalence of the resolutions passed at the meeting reflected exactly the state of Churchill's own mind. From a strategical point of view he knew that unless he were to "put-off for another year at least the means for re-establishing any effective blockade of the German ports," he must give priority to the production of patrol submarines. But he still hankered after the fleet submarine.[166] On Christmas day Churchill finally made up his mind.

> Since the submarine blockade of the German ports is one of the tactical objects we have in view, we must build a suitable class of vessel for that purpose. Since the proposed new programmes, both ordinary and extraordinary were put forward by the Third Sea Lord on [document number] S0367, grave doubts have been thrown upon the value of the Admiralty coastal [**F**] design for oversea work. . . . The type on which we must now concentrate is a vessel big enough to maintain itself effectively on the German coasts and yet small enough to dive in German coastal waters. I assume the double-hulled **E** is the best design we have at present for this

purpose. [Therefore we must] recast the ordinary programme of 1914/15 so as to provide for the maximum number of double-hulled **E**'s and eliminate the new *Swordfish* [steam fleet submarine] and as many of the seven [**F**] admiralty coastals as possible.[167]

On the other hand, he continued:

We are now at work upon a design which, if it receives board approval, will supply us with ocean submarines of the required speed and sea-going qualities, and if these are to be constructed they must be a substitute for the battleship preponderance and paid for out of the money that would otherwise have gone into battleships. We have another six months at least before a decision is required.[168]

Churchill concluded his memorandum by ordering Moore to work out the costs of the "extraordinary substitution programme as verbally discussed at our last meeting."[169] The meaning of this last instruction is clarified by a minute the first lord wrote three weeks later on an apparently "secret" docket relating to the 1914/15 construction program that strangely is not listed in the Admiralty's official registers of correspondence.[170] On 14 January, Churchill asked the third sea lord to calculate how many submarines could be built for the price of one *Revenge* class battleship.[171] On 22 January he further enquired from Moore: "what will be the latest dates at which the fourteen [**E** type] submarines substituted for the forth or Plymouth battleship [*Resistance*] would have to be begun in order that the whole batch might be ready by June 1917, i.e., the date when this ship is required"? At the bottom of the page the first lord directed that: "Extreme secrecy must be observed in handling this paper."[172]

The 1914 Estimates Crisis

Back at the beginning of 1913, readers will recall, Churchill had approached, then shied away from, the idea of substituting submarines for battleships. He had recognized that proposing such a radical shift in British naval policy would be highly controversial both within and outside the service. In addition, he had not been assured of support from all the sea lords. And furthermore, the fiscal situation did not appear to justify such a desperate political gamble. At the last minute, higher-than-expected tax revenues had enabled Lloyd George to accept higher navy estimates which in turn had allowed Churchill to continue building dreadnoughts in sufficient numbers to maintain the 60 percent standard. For these reasons the battleship substitution policy had been shelved. By the end of 1913, however, the financial outlook for the Admiralty had again clouded.[173] When on 5 December, Churchill notified the Cabinet that naval expenditure for next year would have to rise by another £3 million to over £50 million, his sketch estimates were thrown out.[174] A chorus of more than one hundred Liberal back bench MP's added their voices in protest at the magnitude of the sum requested.[175] Churchill also came under fierce attack from the Liberal press.[176] Even Asquith regarded the sum as excessive. "If one can't be a little economical when all foreign countries are peaceful I don't know when we can," he remarked to the chancellor.[177] Surprisingly, however, Lloyd George was not among the malcontents[178] Earlier in the year, he had struck a bargain with Churchill: in return for supporting his controversial land reform bill, he had promised the first lord more money for the navy.[179]

On 8 December, the Cabinet suggested that instead of laying down four capital ships in 1914–15, the navy should build just two. Churchill replied that was impossible. The construction of four battleships "only just maintains the 60 per cent standard."[180] It was therefore the minimum number that could be built. He did not need to add that he had mortgaged his political reputation to the implementation of a four ship capital program. On 17 December, Sir Francis Hopwood, a senior civil servant at the Admiralty, explained the recent events to the king's private secretary:

> The Cabinet has become thoroughly scared by the Radicals who are for a smaller navy, and is putting pressure upon Churchill to reduce the *programme*. This he cannot do for the simple reason that he was fool enough to tell the world what his programme was going to be for about half a dozen years ahead. It is said that practically all the Cabinet is for a reduction. What they mean by it I cannot imagine for the numbers are deeply committed. Not only did they not dissent when Churchill made his speech about building 4.5.4.4.4.4. battleships each year but they made themselves party to the despatch laid on the table of the Canadian Parliament in which the coming programme is set forth.[181]

What Hopwood could not understand was why the Cabinet appeared so keen to pick a fight with the Admiralty on such a weak pretext. "Is it possible they are riding for a fall or do they merely want to shed Winston," he speculated.[182] In the opinion of Lord Riddle, the second possibility was closer to the truth. His contacts told him that the junior members of the Cabinet, "[Herbert] Samuel, [John] Simon, and [Walter] Runciman, are doing their utmost to force [Churchill] out of the Cabinet." There was a strong feeling within the Cabinet, even among his admirers, that Winston had "lost touch with liberalism" and since joining the Admiralty had become "a man of one idea."[183] Some ministers feared that such a large increase in naval spending might provoke the defection of the Labour members of the coalition and several Liberal backbenchers.[184]

After another week, the outcry against Churchill in Cabinet had become so deafening that even Lloyd George was taken aback at its volume. As the row over the navy estimates intensified, moreover, the Chancellor became increasingly uncomfortable in Cabinet at having to stand back and watch the "beagles"—as the prime minister dubbed his junior ministers—demand the government make economies in armaments. The sight was doubly irritating to Lloyd George because he had long regarded himself as champion of this particular cause and also the leader of the "junior radicals" who comprised the "social progressive" wing of the party. By 16 December he could stand it no longer. That afternoon, during a cabinet meeting, the Chancellor signaled his intention to renege on his pledge with Churchill and switch sides by openly imploring the first lord to reconsider his estimates.[185] The latter, enraged, refused. At that point, according to Charles Hobhouse, the postmaster general, Winston "protested his inability to carry on and went off characteristically banging the dispatch box and the door as he went out as loud as he could . . ."[186]

Worse news was to follow. On 19 December Churchill telegraphed Borden to inquire whether a cut in the British capital ship program would affect the willingness of the Canadian parliament to finance the three dreadnoughts promised for the Mediterranean Fleet. Borden was emphatic: if that occurred "it would be quite impossible for us to persevere in proposals which were based upon considerations of an urgency which were vigorously proclaimed."[187] Anticipating Borden's reply, however, Churchill had already taken the precaution of assuring the prime minister that if necessary he could shore-up Britain's naval position in the Mediterranean without having to demand additional sums from Lloyd George. "Borden will act," he explained. "If he succeeds, the Cabinet policy in the Medit[erranea]n can be carried out. If he fails—then 6 months from now I can develop an argument ab[ou]t submarines in that sea wh[ich] will obviate a further constr[uctio]n of battleships for this 2dary [secondary] theatre. Either way we can get through."[188] Churchill now turned to meet his critics within the Cabinet.

In January 1914, Churchill's task was made a good deal harder after he was forced to raise his demand to no less than £53 million, in order to pay for the delivery of ships that had been delayed by earlier labor unrest in the shipyards.[189] Lloyd George, taken aback at this sum, promptly replied that the naval budget could no longer be financed without raising fresh taxes. For a number of reasons this was something he was loath to do. As part of the Liberal's strategy for reelection in 1916, Lloyd George had been preparing to overhaul the system of local government finances.[190] The essence of the plan was to subsidize town hall expenditure with "exchequer grants" from central government funds; in other words income tax would be raised to pay for cuts in property taxes. Unfortunately, it was administratively impossible to introduce the proposed reforms a year early, thereby allowing a single increase in taxation to pay for both his land reform and a larger navy budget—a strategy which had succeeded in 1909. For obvious political reasons the Liberals did not want to raise taxes in consecutive years.

All this time Reginald McKenna had been keeping a close watch on proceedings, quietly waiting for his chance to revenge himself on Churchill. The astute McKenna was the first to suspect that the chancellor would be the first to back down and that Churchill would win his battle over the size of the capital-ship program. On 16 January 1914, he discussed recent events with his friend Lord Riddle. The latter recorded in this diary that night, that according to McKenna, "Winston has shown his fangs and they are pretty big fangs. He has cornered the PM who is committed up to the hilt to all Winston has done. He has it all down chapter and verse. McKenna fears that L[loyd] G[eorge] will have to change his attitude as he also is committed."[191] By 23 January, sure enough, the chancellor was visibly wavering.[192] Ultimately, on the 28th, to the dismay of his radical friends, Lloyd George announced in Cabinet that he was now prepared to allow the 1914–15 navy estimates to reach £53 million.[193] Churchill had promised in return that naval expenditure would fall back to "under £50 millions" in 1915–16.[194] Lloyd George went on to explain that he could balance the books by raising new taxation in 1914–15 and using it to pay for the increase in the navy. The following year (1915–16) these new revenues would be reallocated to fund his scheme of exchequer grants to local authorities.[195] The plan depended, of course, upon the materialization of the promised reduction in the 1915 navy estimates.[196] Hitherto, no historian has ever seriously considered how Churchill could have ever have kept his "pledge" without sacrificing the battleship standard.[197] The answer, of course, is that he was prepared to do so. He planned to adopt a new naval standard which included submarines. The details were kept secret from the Cabinet and were known only to members of the Board of Admiralty, Asquith and Lloyd George.[198]

Drafting his memoirs after the First World War, Churchill recalled the drama surrounding the negotiations over the 1914–15 estimates and explained his motives. In the first draft of his manuscript, Churchill wrote that he proposed to treat the four dreadnoughts "not as capital ships but as units of power which could, if desirable, be expressed in any other form."[199] He explained that "the finance of the transformation was most complicated." Battleship took three years to build "whereas the kind of craft we were contemplating could be completed in from fifteen to eighteen months." This meant "the contractors would therefore be able to earn the whole of the money value of the battleship in half the time." Accordingly it was agreed that the Admiralty would order the small craft "at such dates as would space out the payments due to the contractors so that a similar amount fell in each year."[200] Alternatively (and this in fact seems to have been what was really intended), the Admiralty could cancel the battleship(s) projected under the 1914–15 estimates and delay placing the contracts for the replacement submarines until the end of 1915, thereby affording "substantial relief" to the naval construction budget for 1915–16 (the election year).[201] Churchill believed that so long as the additional submarines were complete by June 1917, he could simultaneously maintain Britain's naval supremacy and provide the chancellor with the a reduction in naval expenditure in the election year. However, Churchill expunged all references to the substitution policy in the published version of his memoirs. Why he did so is still not clear.

——— ≫•◆•≪ ———

In June 1914, Vice Adm. Sir John Jellicoe left the Board of Admiralty for a six month "rest-cure" before taking up the post of commander in chief, Home Fleets, in December.[202] He was replaced as second sea lord by another court favorite, Vice Adm. Sir Frederick Tower Hamilton.[203] Before the latter was formally offered the appointment, Churchill personally acquainted him with the proposed substitution program. Hamilton was given the clear impression that the plans to substitute submarines for battleships would definitely be carried out at the end of the year.[204] Afterwards, he assured the first lord "there is nothing in them to which I feel myself to be antagonistic and much of which I heartily agree."[205] Once he had accepted the job, Jellicoe and Moore sent Hamilton a set of notes intended to familiarize him with the details of the plan.[206] These reveal that in addition to substituting fourteen submarines for the *Resistance,* Churchill also wanted to cancel a second capital ship, the *Agincourt* (a special battle cruiser version of the *Queen Elizabeth* class), and in its place build six torpedo craft of a radically new type referred to as "Polyphemus."[207] Suffice to explain that "Polyphemus" was an armored semi-submersible torpedo-boat designed to launch six or eight long-range torpedoes at an enemy line of battle.[208]

More significantly, the Hamilton papers show that the professional members of the Board of Admiralty entirely accepted the principles underlying Churchill's policy. Summarizing the information given to him, Hamilton noted that:

The time has come when the proportion of torpedo craft (especially submarines) to battleships should be increased—It is understood that it is proposed to commence this process this year by substituting for some of the approved programme certain extra torpedo craft. The alternatives to be discussed are understood to be as follows:

(a) To drop one battleship and substitute 6 of the proposed "Polyphemus" class.
(b) To drop a second battleship and substitute about 16 submarines of the latest pattern.
(c) To drop all the programme of destroyers in the programme except 2 or 3 large ones designated for leaders of divisions of flotillas, and substitute submarines.[209]

The sea lords all realized that Churchill's motives were predominantly financial. Jellicoe emphasized to his successor that "he wishes to save money by the change, and this substitution programme is designed to do this i.e. the cost of the substitutes is *less* than the cost of the battleships."[210] Moore estimated "the effect of the proposed changes is a saving on materiel varying in amounts up to £900,000."[211] Nevertheless, the admirals agreed that the change would be justifiable on naval and well as financial grounds. Contemporary documents support Churchill's later claim that "the First Sea Lord, like myself, was convinced that the change proposed would add to our naval power. We should get better value for money out of the small craft."[212] Indeed he does not appear to have been exaggerating when he wrote "it was with very great pleasure and even excitement that we [the Board] now addressed ourselves to the agreeable task of planning this enormous addition to the torpedo vessels of the fleet."[213]

The sea lords disagreed only about the pace at which the battleship standard should be abandoned. Moore was particularly concerned at the public reaction to such a dramatic change in policy. Even Churchill expressed uneasiness that "the change of view will not be easy to explain to the public or to the service without to some extent reflecting on the Admiralty policy of former years."[214] He recognized that "the public understood dreadnoughts and the House of Commons was deeply versed in the controversy about the standard of supremacy in dreadnoughts."[215] Jellicoe, on the other hand, predicted that the strongest resistance would come from the Cabinet. He reflected that in his experience "it is perfectly easy to devise a new standard and almost impossible to get a government to adopt it." Previous attempts by the Royal Navy to move away from the battleship standard in 1906 and 1912 had been opposed by the same Liberal government. Hamilton, Jellicoe's successor, expressed fewer reservations. He felt sure "it should certainly not be past the wit of man to conceive a new standard of comparison which, although it may lack the simplicity of the present arithmetical standard, will be really more valuable and not beyond the comprehension of the public."[216]

In May 1914, Churchill reported to Fisher that "Battenberg was in favour of substituting submarines for a battleship," but that Jellicoe was against the idea.[217] This report, however, was misleading. Jellicoe was not opposed to the building of more submarines; rather, he wanted to see first if they could be built in Canada in place of a Canadian-funded dreadnought. Jellico thought there was a far greater chance of extracting a Canadian contribution to imperial defense by asking them to build submarines for the Royal Navy in their own yards instead of paying for battleships to be constructed in Britain. Jellicoe "never thought the Admiralty advice to Canada sound."[218] In fact Churchill, without revealing any secrets, had already taken steps in this direction. In March 1914 he had quietly encouraged Borden to amend the Canadian offer. "It maybe more convenient for you," Churchill had suggested, to offer the Royal Navy "two capital ships and convert the third into cruisers or other craft" to be built in Canada: "if so, the Admiralty would certainly approve such a decision."[219] In July arrangements were made for Jellicoe to visit Canada to discuss a new formula for the Canadian naval contribution.[220]

More revealing was the Admiralty's reaction to the publication in the *Times* of a letter by Adm. Sir Percy Scott, in which he claimed that battleships were obsolete in the age of submarines.[221] Previously, historians have used Scott's letter as evidence to support the argument that prior to the outbreak of war, the Admiralty had been filled with conservative, unimaginative officers (unlike the maverick Scott) who had not given proper consideration to the potential of submarines.[222] The true story is quite different. The Admiralty were quietly furious with Scott for having given rival powers any hint of current thinking in Britain on this subject. They had hoped that the suddenness and unexpectedness of the sudden change in policy would "paralyse" Britain's naval rivals. As Churchill put it: "[I] intended to let the Germans lay down and be thoroughly committed to their whole dreadnought programme for the year, so that we should be given the advantage of the change at any rate for a year before them."[223] "Percy Scott has banged the door on Borden I fear!" complained Fisher in a letter to Churchill dated 7 June; "it is a great pity that this submarine scare has prematured [*sic*] before a bit more Austrian and Italian dreadnoughts were laid down."[224] Several days later, however, Fisher appeared slightly less annoyed when he reported to Julian Corbett:

> a conversation three days ago with Winston Churchill as to Percy Scott's effusion. He angry, but I told him providence has come along and helped

England as usual. The effect of Percy Scott's diatribe has been to besmirch unjustly the submarine . . . so the Triple alliance will lavish their money on vessels that will be securely blockaded by our submarines, as the Mediterranean and the North Sea will be securely locked up.[225]

On 12 July, Churchill sent the sea lords a memorandum for discussion at the next meeting of the Board of Admiralty to be convened the following Wednesday. "I am convinced the time has come for action," he wrote in a covering letter sent to Battenberg, "the steps are serious but I do not feel any anxiety about taking them. They will add greatly to the power of the fleet and bring great credit to all associated with them."[226] The enclosed paper set out in detail the amended 1914–15 construction program. Gone was the *Resistance* and gone was the *Agincourt* : in their places were twenty submarines. On 29 July, the Admiralty placed contracts with Armstrong and Coventry Ordnance to supply big-gun mountings for just two capital ships.[227] This evidence is conclusive. Big-gun mounting had to be ordered at least nine months before the ship that was intended to receive them was laid down.

There was no time for the revolution in British naval policy to become apparent to all. On 4 August 1914, Britain declared war on Germany.

Appendix 1

Naval Expenditure, 1889–1914

Years	Naval Estimates (Net Naval Spending)	Gross Naval Expenditure[1]	%Age of Add'l	Spending on Shipbuilding, Repairs, and Maintenance Votes 8+9[2]	%Age of Gross	Spending on Naval Works Vote 10+ NDA[3]	%Age of Gross	Spending on Personnel Votes 1,2, 7,13,14[4]	%Age of Gross
1889–1890	13,643,968	15,588,502	14	6,460,001	41	437,316	3	6,374,311	41
1890–1891	13,910,732	18,061,816	30	6,676,628	37	411,563	2	6,640,375	37
1891–1892	14,278,049	18,150,638	27	6,746,216	37	385,762	2	6,912,539	38
1892–1893	14,325,948	17,402,741	21	6,635,612	38	413,739	2	7,116,460	41
1893–1894	14,306,546	16,327,641	14	6,357,457	39	397,149	2	7,343,120	45
1894–1895	17,642,424	18,595,685	5	9,113,968	49	654,675	4	7,588,186	41
1895–1896	19,637,238	21,264,377	8	10,934,554	51	1,176,501	6	7,934,887	37
1896–1897	22,271,901	23,886,177	7	13,215,564	55	1,177,890	5	8,234,668	34
1897–1898	20,848,863	22,547,844	8	11,239,225	50	1,337,863	6	8,594,869	38
1898–1899	23,880,875	26,145,598	9	13,462,803	51	1,958,581	7	9,355,440	36
1899–1900	25,731,220	28,478,842	11	15,043,853	53	2,265,471	8	9,771,314	34
1900–1901	29,998,529	33,302,260	11	18,411,543	55	3,021,126	9	10,147,182	30
1901–1902	30,981,315	34,994,553	13	19,114,676	55	3,627,696	10	10,511,508	30
1902–1903	31,003,977	35,525,731	15	18,573,040	52	3,988,937	11	10,971,611	31
1903–1904	35,709,577	40,503,873	13	22,360,630	55	4,230,042	10	11,683,599	29
1904–1905	36,859,681	41,696,313	13	22,575,297	54	4,353,334	10	12,275,095	29
1905–1906	33,151,841	38,175,045	15	19,059,433	50	4,127,064	11	12,012,387	31
1906–1907	31,472,087	35,693,850	13	17,658,932	49	3,133,789	9	12,047,839	34
1907–1908	31,251,156	33,950,169	9	16,368,536	48	2,377,186	7	12,247,174	36
1908–1909	32,181,309	34,775,752	8	16,974,653	49	1,899,237	5	12,043,061	37
1909–1910	35,734,015	37,385,460	5	19,784,032	53	1,388,643	4	13,055,683	35
1910–1911	40,419,336	43,903,499	9	24,064,361	55	1,716,113	4	13,414,318	31
1911–1912	42,414,257	46,793,789	10	25,242,570	54	1,917,669	4	13,903,589	30
1912–1913	44,933,169	48,742,182	8	27,419,414	56	1,699,545	3	14,390,697	30
1913–1914	48,732,621	52,920,960	9	29,792,872	56	2,241,338	4	15,235,171	29

Source: Jon Sumida, *In Defence of Naval Supremacy* (London, 1989): appendix, tables 3, 6, 7, 13

[1] Includes navy estimates, appropriations in aid, and naval loans; see Sumida, table 3.
[2] Includes vote 8 (shipbuilding, repairs, and maintenance), and vote 9 (naval armaments).
[3] Includes navy estimates, vote 10 (works); appropriations in aid; Naval Works Act see Sumida, table 7.
[4] Includes vote 1 (pay), vote 2 (victuals), vote 7 (naval reserve), vote 13 (half-pay), and vote 14 (pensions) see Sumida tables 12 and 13.

Appendix 2

British Naval Construction by Type*

Year	A Gross Naval Expenditure	B Spent on New Battle-ships	C Spent on New Armored Cruisers	D Spent on New Smaller Cruisers	E Spent on Surface Flotilla	F Spent on New S/M	G Total Spent New Warships (Columns B, C, D, E, F)	H New Const'n as % of Gross Naval Spending	I S/M as % of New Const'n	J Surface Flotilla % of New Const'n	K Minor Cruisers as % of New Const'n	L Armored Cruisers as % of New Const'n	M Battle-ships as % of New Const'n
1895	21,264,377	3,372,239	828,047	1,264,793	732,911	—	6,197,990	29	0	12	20	13	54
1896	23,886,177	2,678,315	1,846,607	1,573,365	1,506,015	—	7,604,302	32	0	20	21	24	35
1897	22,547,844	2,166,066	1,416,127	1,058,070	581,187	—	5,221,450	23	0	11	20	27	41
1898	26,145,598	3,406,912	1,954,761	859,747	605,692	—	6,827,112	26	0	9	13	29	50
1899	28,478,842	3,926,203	2,486,473	300,106	824,830	—	7,537,612	26	0	11	4	33	52
1900	33,302,260	4,105,749	3,802,752	105,380	990,073	—	9,003,954	27	0	11	1	42	46
1901	34,994,553	3,892,866	4,484,122	261,016	341,938	162	8,980,104	26	0	4	3	50	43
1902	35,525,731	3,216,036	4,076,702	255,812	971,771	220,453	8,740,774	25	3	11	3	47	37
1903	40,503,873	4,373,831	4,671,896	1,204,171	888,756	238,851	11,377,505	28	2	8	11	41	38
1904	41,696,313	4,547,657	4,018,013	1,642,284	1,075,111	310,584	11,593,649	28	3	9	14	35	39
1905	38,175,045	4,103,692	4,247,609	446,470	534,193	650,352	9,982,316	26	7	5	4	43	41
1906	35,693,850	3,351,935	4,494,448	237	780,400	430,487	9,057,507	25	5	9	0	50	37
1907	33,950,169	3,723,412	2,692,610	180,524	1,013,886	349,126	7,959,558	23	4	13	2	34	47
1908	34,775,752	4,298,530	1,231,813	376,359	1,149,632	533,652	7,589,986	22	7	15	5	16	57
1909	37,385,460	4,578,805	1,074,752	1,549,929	2,070,475	522,272	9,796,233	26	5	21	16	11	47
1910	43,903,499	5,884,374	2,556,455	1,792,481	2,560,484	321,852	13,115,646	30	2	20	14	19	45
1911	46,793,789	6,056,072	2,436,216	1,228,878	1,782,396	486,919	11,990,481	26	4	15	10	20	51
1912	48,742,182	7,203,164	1,662,513	1,407,087	2,077,536	748,913	13,099,213	27	6	16	11	13	55
1913	52,920,960	8,134,959	936,325	1,929,141	2,046,615	767,307	13,814,347	26	6	15	14	7	59

Source: Sumida, table 8. Figures taken from Naval Appropriations Accounts

*Regarding nomenclature of warships, HMS *Swift* (1905) was classified as a "destroyer." The next generation of "super swift's" HMS *Arethusa* (1912) was classified as a light cruiser. The term "light cruiser" was introduced only in 1912.

Appendix 3
Royal Navy Personnel
Crews in Commission and Reserve Each Quarter

Year	A Numbers Borne Active Service RN Personnel	B Allocated to Ships in Comm'n or in	C Col. B as % Col. A	D Manning RN Ships in Comm'n	E Manning RN Ships in Reserve	F Manning All Ships at Home	G Manning All Ships Overseas
1897/1	88,792	57,542	65	54,980	2,562	27,606	29,303
1897/2	94,467	60,431	64	57,767	2,664	26,217	30,130
1897/3	94,467	62,411	66	60,923	1,488	28,998	29,228
1897/4	94,467	63,413	67	60,219	3,194	28,238	30,703
1898/1	94,467	64,070	68	60,814	3,256	27,079	30,962
1898/2	99,999	65,008	65	61,533	3,475	27,488	31,779
1898/3	99,999	66,934	67	63,724	3,210	27,144	33,455
1898/4	99,999	66,750	67	63,394	3,356	29,161	33,597
1899/1	99,999	67,628	68	63,826	3,802	28,972	34,176
1899/2	105,924	69,591	66	66,011	3,580	29,687	34,397
1899/3	105,924	71,160	67	67,774	3,386	29,764	33,941
1899/4	105,924	69,176	65	65,567	3,609	29,224	35,121
1900/1	105,924	70,130	66	67,058	3,072	28,592	35,451
1900/2	110,978	72,552	65	69,650	2,902	31,610	35,352
1900/3	110,978	73,133	66	70,364	2,769	32,903	36,383
1900/4	110,978	75,676	68	72,683	2,993	33,652	38,482
1901/1	110,978	76,421	69	73,714	2,707	32,755	39,245
1901/2	113,589	78,724	69	76,066	2,658	32,971	39,992
1901/3	113,589	78,897	69	76,762	2,135	34,273	39,641
1901/4	113,589	78,112	69	76,008	2,104	33,913	39,879
1902/1	113,589	79,041	70	77,474	1,567	35,218	40,764
1902/2	118,884	79,604	67	77,843	1,761	36,033	40,294
1902/3	118,884	80,245	67	78,707	1,538	36,322	41,973
1902/4	118,884	80,041	67	78,319	1,722	36,277	41,417
1903/1	118,884	80,282	68	78,574	1,708	37,086	41,328
1903/2	124,413	81,229	65	79,056	2,173	37,447	40,980
1903/3	124,413	80,603	65	79,600	1,003	37,621	39,909
1903/4	124,413	81,439	65	80,024	1,415	38,013	39,160
1904/1	124,413	83,940	67	82,209	1,731	39,487	40,806
1904/2	128,270	85,929	67	84,534	1,395	40,813	40,948
1904/3	128,270	86,737	68	84,797	1,940	41,550	41,802
1904/4	128,270	86,431	67	84,074	2,357	42,915	40,838
1905/1	128,270	85,326	67	78,278	7,048	34,760	44,693
1905/2	130,078	83,855	64	75,074	8,781	39,742	41,908
1905/3	130,078	85,891	66	76,390	9,501	40,620	40,581
1905/4	130,078	88,789	68	76,282	12,507	42,001	42,459
1906/1	130,078	88,380	68	77,221	11,159	43,013	40,966
1906/2	127,366	90,922	71	79,029	11,893	45,017	40,055
1906/3	127,366	87,238	68	74,846	12,392	46,348	38,364
1906/4	127,366	88,001	69	74,633	13,368	47,477	38,881
1907/1	127,366	87,600	69	73,245	14,355	49,154	37,109

Crews in Commission and Reserve Each Quarter*

Year	A Numbers Borne Active Service Personnel	B Allocated to Warships in Comm'n or in Reserve	C Col. B as % of Col. A	D Manning Ships at Home	E Manning Ships Overseas
1907/2	127,028	92,532	73	55,670	34,079
1907/3	127,028	93,262	73	58,816	33,695
1907/4	127,028	93,436	74	58,660	33,552
1908/1	127,028	92,451	73	56,823	33,647
1908/2	127,534	93,165	73	57,325	33,349
1908/3	127,534	92,351	72	57,601	33,070
1908/4	127,534	91,787	72	57,162	32,915
1909/1	127,534	92,174	72	57,354	32,876
1909/2	126,935	93,983	74	56,015	33,484
1909/3	126,935	93,751	74	56,224	33,738
1909/4	126,935	92,873	73	56,240	34,923
1910/1	126,935	93,206	73	56,522	34,935
1910/2	128,871	93,750	73	56,775	34,320
1910/3	128,871	93,593	73	57,813	33,975
1910/4	128,871	94,989	74	58,312	33,294
1911/1	128,871	94,645	73	58,384	33,790
1911/2	131,871	94,174	71	57,970	33,720
1911/3	131,871	94,469	72	58,412	34,074
1911/4	131,871	94,693	72	58,747	33,787
1912/1	131,871	96,124	73	59,361	33,791
1912/2	133,698	94,732	71	57,957	34,102

*After the 1907 Home Fleet reforms, for statistical purposes the distinction between warships in commission and warships in reserve was abolished.

Appendix 4

Royal Navy Personnel

Distribution by Ship Type

Year	A Men in Ships	B Men Forming Crews for Ships in Comm'n	C Men Forming Crews for Ships in Reserve	D Crews for Battle- ships in Comm'n	E Crews for BB in Reserve	F Crews for all BB as % of Col.A	G Crews for Cruisers in Comm'n	H Crews for CC in Reserve	I Crews for all CC as % of Col.A	J Crews for Flotilla in Comm'n	K Crews for FF in Reserve	L Crews for all FF as % of Col.A
1897/1	57,542	54,980	2,562	16,428	768	30	22,191	1,475	41	6,154	319	11
1897/2	60,431	57,767	2,664	16,107	818	28	23,959	1,452	42	6,137	394	11
1897/3	62,411	60,923	1,488	19,236	662	32	24,587	613	40	5,985	213	10
1897/4	63,413	60,219	3,194	19,759	738	32	24,427	2,059	42	6,564	397	11
1898/1	64,070	60,814	3,256	19,260	861	31	24,617	1,928	41	6,367	467	11
1898/2	65,008	61,533	3,475	19,538	920	31	24,892	2,052	41	6,350	503	11
1898/3	66,934	63,724	3,210	21,069	925	33	25,738	1,740	41	6,080	545	10
1898/4	66,750	63,394	3,356	21,084	904	33	25,257	1,854	41	6,166	598	10
1899/1	67,628	63,826	3,802	20,576	909	32	24,872	2,332	40	6,534	561	10
1899/2	69,591	66,011	3,580	21,523	882	32	26,934	2,183	42	6,689	515	10
1899/3	71,160	67,774	3,386	21,473	905	31	28,580	1,965	43	6,840	516	10
1899/4	69,176	65,567	3,609	20,907	945	32	26,821	2,115	42	6,851	549	11
1900/1	70,130	67,058	3,072	21,823	886	32	27,432	1,691	42	6,897	495	11
1900/2	72,552	69,650	2,902	23,707	809	34	27,526	1,668	40	7,383	425	11
1900/3	73,133	70,364	2,769	23,453	805	33	27,854	1,576	40	7,806	388	11
1900/4	75,676	72,683	2,993	25,105	694	34	27,545	1,956	39	8,138	343	11
1901/1	76,421	73,714	2,707	25,398	670	34	28,526	1,671	40	8,138	366	11
1901/2	78,724	76,066	2,658	24,908	869	33	30,435	1,476	41	7,993	313	11
1901/3	78,897	76,762	2,135	25,949	637	34	30,175	1,175	40	7,874	323	10
1901/4	78,112	76,008	2,104	26,130	567	34	29,302	1,173	39	7,566	364	10
1902/1	79,041	77,474	1,567	26,100	191	33	30,666	1,037	40	7,734	339	10
1902/2	79,604	77,843	1,761	27,078	294	34	29,847	1,157	39	7,710	310	10
1902/3	80,245	78,707	1,538	27,161	220	34	30,788	954	40	7,553	364	10
1902/4	80,041	78,319	1,722	27,116	296	34	30,448	1,063	39	7,499	363	10
1903/1	80,282	78,574	1,708	26,953	212	34	30,975	1,103	40	7,138	39	,9
1903/2	81,229	79,056	2,173	27,521	221	34	30,467	1,456	39	7,388	496	10
1903/3	80,603	79,600	1,003	26,662	151	33	32,192	615	41	7,287	237	9
1903/4	81,439	80,024	1,415	26,528	377	33	33,143	815	42	6,925	223	9
1904/1	83,940	82,209	1,731	26,330	383	32	35,515	1,026	44	7,042	322	9
1904/2	85,919	84,534	1,385	26,808	223	31	37,054	819	44	7,240	343	9
1904/3	86,737	84,797	1,940	26,653	503	31	37,423	950	44	7,378	487	9
1904/4	86,431	84,074	2,357	27,801	421	33	35,023	1,465	42	7,593	471	9
1905/1	85,320	78,278	7,042	26,618	2,011	34	32,351	3,468	42	7,069	1,563	10
1905/2	83,855	75,074	8,781	24,631	2,246	32	31,348	5,015	43	6,832	1,520	10
1905/3	86,283	76,390	9,893	26,141	2,600	33	31,014	5,010	42	6,968	2,283	11
1905/4	88,789	76,282	12,507	24,173	3,111	31	32,793	6,067	44	7,125	3,329	12
1906/1	88,380	77,221	11,159	,24,128	3,111	31	34,358	5,498	45	7,825	2,550	12
1906/2	90,922	79,029	11,893	,24,865	3,102	31	35,904	6,051	46	7,531	2,740	,11
1906/3	87,238	74,846	12,392	,23,490	2,618	30	32,987	7,163	46	7,640	2,611	,12
1906/4	88,001	74,633	13,368	,24,443	3,149	31	32,468	7,408	45	7,504	2,811	,12
1907/1	87,600	73,245	14,355	,25,247	3,319	33	30,641	8,117	44	7,536	2,919	12

Distribution by Ship Type: Post Home Fleet Reform

Year	A Active Service Naval Personnel Allocated to Ships in Comm'n or Reserve	B Forming Crews for Battle- ships	C B as % of A	D Forming Crews for Cruisers	E D as % of A	F Forming Crews for Flotilla	G F as % of A
1907/2	92,532	28,624	31	41,267	45	12,486	13
1907/3	93,262	28,095	30	42,800	46	12,058	13
1907/4	93,436	28,485	30	42,428	45	12,187	13
1908/1	92,451	28,485	31	41,732	45	12,148	13
1908/2	93,165	28,483	31	42,476	46	12,119	13
1908/3	92,351	27,692	30	42,379	46	12,197	13
1908/4	91,787	27,315	30	42,014	46	12,345	13
1909/1	92,174	27,239	30	42,638	46	12,126	13
1909/2	93,983	27,819	30	42,936	46	12,518	13
1909/3	93,751	26,938	29	43,815	47	12,417	13
1909/4	92,873	26,776	29	43,389	47	12,593	14
1910/1	93,206	26,892	29	43,029	46	12,570	13
1910/2	93,750	27,024	29	43,526	46	12,719	14
1910/3	93,593	27,818	30	42,736	46	12,618	13
1910/4	94,989	27,740	29	43,107	45	12,575	13
1911/1	94,645	26,957	28	43,544	46	13,703	14
1911/2	94,174	26,795	28	43,665	46	13,887	15
1911/3	94,469	26,806	28	44,000	47	13,742	15
1911/4	94,693	26,868	28	44,118	47	13,696	14
1912/1	96,124	26,973	28	44,537	46	13,872	14
1912/2	94,732	25,921	27	43,625	46	14,916	16

Appendix 5

Royal Navy Personnel

*Summary of Recruitment, 1896 1914**

Year	Authorized Number of Personnel (Vote A)	Numbers of Personnel Borne at End of the Fiscal Year	Increase or (Decrease) over Previous Year	Natural Wastage	Total Recruitment over the Year
1896/97	93,750	94,467	—	—	—
1897/98	100,050	99,999	5,532	—	—
1898/99	106,390	105,924	5,925	5,959	11,884
1899/00	110,640	110,978	5,054	7,644	12,698
1900/01	114,890	113,589	2,611	8,485	11,096
1901/02	118,625	118,884	5,295	8,971	14,266
1902/03	122,500	124,413	5,529	7,496	13,025
1903/04	127,100	128,270	3,857	7,588	11,445
1904/05	131,100	130,078	1,808	7,252	9,060
1905/06	129,000	127,366	(-2,712)	10,724	8,012
1906/07	129,000	127,028	(-338)	8,664	8,326
1907/08	128,000	127,534	506	9,072	9,578
1908/09	128,000	126,935	(-599)	9,105	8,506
1909/10	128,000	128,871	1,936	9,167	11,103
1910/11	131,000	131,871	3,000	10,110	13,110
1911/12	134,000	133,698	1,827	11,305	13,132
1912/13	136,000	139,408	5,710	12,258	17,968
1913/14	146,000	145,574	6,166	10,507	16,673

Source: Admiralty, "RN & RM Recruiting Report for the Year Ending 31st March, 1914,"
and"RN & RM Recruiting Report for the Year Ending 31st March, 1906,"
both P822K, [N.L.M.D.]

*The Admiralty could change its mind over how many men had been recruited or discharged in a specific year as many as five years later. As a result the numbers borne were always subject to revision.

Appendix 6
Royal Navy Personnel
Distribution by Station

	A	B	C	D	E	F	G	H	I
Year	Numbers Bourne	Crews for Ships at Home in Comm'n	Crews for Ships at Home in Reserve	Col. B as % of Col. A	Crews for Ships Overseas	Col. E as % of Col. A	East of Suez	Med'n Fleet	Atlantic Fleet
1897/1	88,792	25,044	2,562	28	29,303	33	10,987	11,307	—
1897/2	94,507	23,553	2,664	25	30,130	32	10,931	12,129	—
1897/3	94,507	27,510	1,488	29	29,228	31	10,896	11,588	—
1897/4	94,507	25,044	3,194	26	30,703	32	11,363	11,957	—
1898/1	94,507	23,823	3,256	25	30,962	33	12,322	11,482	—
1898/2	99,999	24,013	3,475	24	31,779	32	12,335	12,242	—
1898/3	99,999	23,934	3,210	24	33,455	33	13,817	12,397	—
1898/4	99,999	25,805	3,356	26	33,597	34	13,837	12,349	—
1899/1	99,999	25,170	3,802	25	34,176	34	13,877	13,153	—
1899/2	105,924	26,107	3,580	25	34,397	32	13,770	13,211	—
1899/3	105,924	26,378	3,386	25	33,941	32	13,892	12,735	—
1899/4	105,924	25,615	3,609	24	35,121	33	14,123	13,673	—
1900/1	105,924	25,520	3,072	24	35,451	33	14,133	14,147	—
1900/2	110,978	28,708	2,902	26	35,352	32	14,176	14,246	—
1900/3	110,978	30,134	2,769	27	36,383	33	14,255	14,942	—
1900/4	110,978	30,659	2,993	28	38,482	35	16,851	14,195	—
1901/1	110,978	30,048	2,707	27	39,245	35	17,819	14,407	—
1901/2	113,589	30,313	2,658	27	39,992	35	18,515	14,358	—
1901/3	113,589	32,138	2,135	28	39,641	35	17,513	15,056	—
1901/4	113,589	31,809	2,104	28	39,879	35	17,632	15,444	—
1902/1	113,589	33,651	1,567	30	40,764	36	17,813	16,283	—
1902/2	118,884	34,272	1,761	29	40,294	34	16,950	16,726	—
1902/3	118,884	34,784	1,538	29	41,973	35	16,534	18,905	—
1902/4	118,884	34,555	1,722	29	41,417	35	15,693	18,963	—
1903/1	118,884	35,378	1,708	30	41,328	35	15,663	18,841	—
1903/2	124,413	35,274	2,173	28	40,980	33	15,379	18,977	—
1903/3	124,413	36,618	1,003	29	39,909	32	15,436	18,067	—
1903/4	124,413	36,598	1,415	29	39,160	31	15,489	17,265	—
1904/1	124,413	37,756	1,731	30	40,806	33	16,359	18,001	—
1904/2	128,270	39,418	1,395	31	40,948	32	16,443	18,059	—
1904/3	128,270	39,610	1,940	31	41,802	33	16,240	19,128	—
1904/4	128,270	40,558	2,357	32	40,838	32	16,375	18,029	—
1905/1	128,270	27,712	7,048	22	44,693	35	13,966	17,075	10,294
1905/2	130,139	30,961	8,781	24	41,908	32	13,903	12,817	10,811
1905/3	130,139	31,119	9,501	24	40,803	31	12,103	12,455	11,531
1905/4	130,139	29,494	12,507	23	42,793	33	10,591	13,385	13,351
1906/1	130,139	31,854	11,159	24	41,325	32	10,644	12,662	12,413
1906/2	127,469	33,124	11,893	26	40,263	32	10,097	12,937	12,041
1906/3	127,469	33,956	12,392	27	38,390	30	10,386	11,565	11,929
1906/4	127,469	34,109	13,368	27	39,036	31	10,409	12,307	12,016
1907/1	127,469	34,799	14,355	27	37,264	29	10,242	12,171	10,822
1907/2	127,147	55,670		44	34,267	27	10,474	10,389	9,665
1907/3	127,147	58,816		46	33,897	27	10,581	10,449	8,922
1907/4	127,147	58,660		46	33,754	27	10,581	10,449	8,779
1908/1	127,147	56,823		45	33,849	27	10,476	10,429	8,779
1908/2	127,534	57,325		45	33,551	26	10,476	10,189	8,615
1908/3	127,534	57,601		45	33,304	26	10,376	10,183	8,661
1908/4	127,534	57,162		45	33,149	26	10,230	10,183	8,652
1909/1	127,534	57,354		45	33,068	26	10,230	10,151	8,648
1909/2	126,935	56,015		44	33,676	27	10,311	10,137	9,219
1909/3	126,935	56,224		44	33,944	27	10,530	10,135	9,233
1909/4	126,935	56,240		44	35,129	28	10,530	10,873	9,221
1910/1	126,935	56,522		45	35,155	28	10,530	10,872	9,234
1910/2	128,871	56,775		44	34,554	27	10,650	10,133	9,228
1910/3	128,871	57,813		45	34,224	27	10,576	10,058	9,042
1910/4	128,871	58,312		45	33,543	26	9,895	10,058	9,042
1911/1	128,871	58,384		45	34,038	26	10,384	10,069	9,034
1911/2	131,920	57,970		44	33,968	26	10,301	10,078	9,038
1911/3	131,920	58,412		44	34,322	26	10,229	10,081	9,414
1911/4	131,920	58,747		45	34,035	26	10,229	10,081	9,127
1912/1	131,920	59,361		45	34,040	26	10,313	9,360	9,038
1912/2	135,000	57,957		43	34,351	25	10,518	10,126	9,101

Notes

Introduction

1. Arthur J. Marder, *A History of British Naval Policy in the Pre-Dreadnought Era, 1880–1905* (London, 1940; reprint, Hamdon, CT: Archon Press, 1964; hereafter cited as *Anatomy*); Arthur J. Marder, *From the Dreadnought to Scapa Flow: The Road to War,* first of 5 vols. (Oxford, 1961–1970; hereafter cited as *FDSF*). See also commentaries in Arthur J. Marder, *Fear God and Dread Nought: The Correspondence of Admiral of the Fleet Lord Fisher of Kilverstone,* 3 vols. (London, 1952–1959; hereafter cited as *FGDN*).

2. George Monger, *The End of Isolation: British Foreign Policy, 1900–1907* (London, 1963); Zara Steiner, *Britain and the Origins of the First World War* (London, 1977); Samuel Williamson, *The Politics of Grand Strategy; Britain and France Prepare for War, 1904–1914* (pbk. ed., 1990; first pub. Cambridge, Mass., 1969); Paul Kennedy, *The Rise of the Anglo-German Antagonism, 1860–1914* (London, 1980).

3. Paul Kennedy, *The Rise and Fall of British Naval Mastery* (London, 1976); Paul Kennedy, *The Rise and Fall of the Great Powers* (London, 1980); Paul Kennedy, "Strategy versus Finance in Twentieth Century Great Britain," *International History Review,* 3 (1981): 45–52; Aaron Friedberg, *The Weary Titan: Britain and the Experience of Relative Decline* (New Jersey, 1988); Paul J. Cain and Anthony G. Hopkins, *British Imperialism: Innovation and Expansion, 1688–1914* (New York, 1993), 450–52.

4. Kennedy, "Strategy versus Finance in Twentieth Century Great Britain," 46.

5. Kennedy, *British Naval Mastery,* 245.

6. Jon T. Sumida, *In Defence of Naval Supremacy: Finance, Technology and Naval Policy, 1889–1914* (London, 1989).

7. See Appendix, table 1.

8. Captain Alfred Mahan, "The Hague Conference of 1907, and the question of immunity for belligerent merchant shipping," *National Review* July 1907, 49. I am indebted to Professor Jon Sumida for rediscovering this quote for me.

9. Friedberg, *Weary Titan,* 168–74; Marder, *FDSF,* I, 5–6, 11–12, 25–26, 105–10; Kennedy, *British Naval Mastery,* 254–72.

10. Marder, *Anatomy,* 456–14.

11. Arthur Marder first coined this phrase in 1952. See *FGDN,* I, 147. He used it again in 1962 in *FDSF,* I, 6.

12. Marder, *FDSF,* I, 367.

13. Nicholas Lambert, "Economy or Empire; the Quest for Collective Security in the Pacific, 1909–1914," in Keith Neilson and Greg Kennedy eds., *Far Flung Lines: Essays in Honour of Donald Mackenzie Shurman* (London, 1996), 55–83.

14. Further details of Fisher's radical tactical theory can be found in Lambert, "Economy or Empire."

15. Jon Sumida, "Sir John Fisher and the Dreadnought: The Sources of Naval Mythology," *The Journal of Military History,* 59 (October 1995): 619–38; and Nicholas Lambert, "Admiral Sir John Fisher and the Concept of Flotilla Defence, 1904–1910," *The Journal of Military History,* 59 (October 1995): 639–60.

16. Keith Neilson, *Britain and the Last Tsar: British Policy and Russia, 1894–1917* (Oxford, 1996).

17. Jon Sumida and David Rosenberg, "Machines, Men, Manufacturing, Management and Money: The Study of Navies as Complex Organisations and the Transformation of Twentieth Century Naval History," in John Hattendorf ed., *Doing Naval History: Essays Towards Improvement* (Newport, 1995), 25–39.

18. Sumida, *In Defence,* chapters 2–4.

19. Charles H. Fairbanks, "The Origins of the Dreadnought Revolution: A Historiographical Essay," *International History Review,* 13/2 (May 1991): 246–72.

Chapter One: The Price of Naval Supremacy

1. *Parliamentary Debates,* vol. 333 (1889) Hamilton, 7 Mar 1889.

2. Paul Kennedy, *British Naval Mastery,* 1–11, 183–84, 201–7, 209–11, 227–28.

3. Marder, *Anatomy,* 88, 106.

4. Sumida, *In Defence,* 6.

5. Sir Thomas Brassey, *The British Navy: Its Strength, Resources, and Administration* (London, 1882) five parts in 5 volumes, III, 7.

6. Ruddock Mackay, *Fisher of Kilverstone* (Oxford, 1973), 179–82.

7. Donald Schurman, *The Education of a Navy: The Development of British Naval Strategic Thought, 1867–1914* (London, 1965), 3.

8. *Parliamentary Debates,* vol. 333 (1889) Hamilton, 7 Mar 1889.

9. Ibid.

10. Edward Woodward, *Great Britain and the German Navy* (Oxford, 1935), 455–73; Marder, *Anatomy,* 105–7.

11. *Parliamentary Debates,* vol. 333 (1889) Hamilton, 1171–85, cited in Sumida, *In Defence,* 15.

12. Ibid.

13. Minute (15 Oct 1898) by Richards in "Mediterranean: Protection of Trade Route," ADM 1/7376B [Admiralty Papers, Public Record Office, Kew].

14. Ibid.

15. Commander Stephen King-Hall, "The Evolution of the Cruiser," 1928, ADM 1/8724/93.

16. For acknowledgment that 6 inches of Harvey armor could resist 6-inch

AP projectiles see: Minute (22 Jan 97) by White (DNC), "Type of Battleship to be Contemplated in 1897–98," ADM 116/878.

17. Marder, *Anatomy*, 283.

18. Goschen to Hicks-Beech, 23 Jul 97, PCC/83, Hicks-Beech Mss [Gloucester Record Office]; permission to lay down a fifth and sixth *Cressy* was not requested until May 1898: see minute (2 May 1898) by Richards to Goschen, "Provisional Programme for New Construction, 1898–99," ADM 116/878. But according to the appropriations accounts they were paid for under the 1897 estimates: Sumida, *In Defence*, table 17.

19. Marder, *Anatomy*, 282–85.

20. Minute (11 Jan 98) by Richards, "Type of Battleship to be Contemplated in 1897–98," ADM 116/878.

21. Admiral Hopkins (C-in-C Mediterranean) to Admiralty, 27 Feb 1898, in "Mediterranean: Protection of Trade Routes," ADM 1/7376B. See also minutes thereon (19 Mar 98) by Richards and (4 Apr 98) by Goschen.

22. Goschen, "Navy Estimates and Shipbuilding programme, 1898–99," 17 Feb 98, CAB 37/46/20.

23. Marder, *Anatomy*, 285; Sumida, *In Defence*, 19.

24. Minute (7 Oct 98) by Wilson, "Design for New Cruisers—Supplemental Programme, 1898–99" (copy) in f.74, ADM 1/8724/93; Minute (6 Apr 1898) by Moore, on memorandum by Wilson entitled, "Tactics of New Armoured Cruisers as Affecting their Design," ADM 1/7377.

25. Marder, *Anatomy*, 286–287.

26. Sumida, *In Defence*, appendix, tables 16 & 17.

27. Minute (4 Feb 1898) by Richards (print) "Shipbuilding Programme 1898–99," printed 11 Jun 1898, p. 39, ADM 116/878.

28. Minute (27 Jan 1898) by Goschen, ibid; see also Marder, *Anatomy*, 287.

29. Goschen to Hicks-Beech, 26 Nov 97, PCC/83, Hicks-Beech Mss; Minute (7 Oct 98) by Wilson, "Design for New Cruisers—Supplemental Programme, 1898–99" (copy) in f.68, ADM 1/8724/93.

30. Goschen, "Russian Naval Construction," 6 Jun 1898, CAB 37/47/39; Goschen to Hicks-Beech, 6 Jun 98, PCC/83, Hicks-Beech Mss.

31. Marder, *Anatomy*, 308; Neilson, *The Last Tsar*, 117.

32. Goschen, "Navy Estimates and Shipbuilding Policy, 1898–99," 17 Feb 98, CAB37/46/20.

33. Goschen to Hicks-Beech, 21 Jul 98 (second letter) PCC/83, Hicks-Beech Mss.

34. Peter Gatrell, *Government, Industry, and Rearmament in Russia, 1900–1914* (Cambridge, 1994), 20–24.

35. Goschen, "Russian Naval Construction," 6 Jun 1898, CAB 37/47/39.

36. Goschen to Hicks-Beech, 20 Jul 98, PCC/83, Hicks-Beech Mss.

37. Goschen to Hicks-Beech, 21 Jul 98 (first letter) PCC/83, ibid.

38. Goschen to Hicks-Beech, 21 Jul 98 (second letter) PCC/83, ibid.

39. Minutes (7 Oct 98) Wilson (17 Oct 98) Bedford (19 Oct 98) Moore, and (22 Oct) Richards, all "Design for New Cruisers—Supplemental Programme, 1898–99" (copy) in f.74, ADM 1/8724/93; Minute 27 Jan 1898) by Goschen

(print) "Shipbuilding Programme 1898–99," printed 11 Jun 1898, p. 33, ADM 116/878.

40. Keith McBride, "The First County Class Cruisers of the Royal Navy," *Warship* 46 (April 1988): 19–27. I am indebted to Jon Sumida for bring these articles to my attention.

41. Goschen to Hicks-Beech, 1 & 24 Dec 98, PCC/83, Hicks-Beech Mss.

42. Goschen, "Navy Estimates, 1899–1900," 31 Jan 99, p. 8, CAB 37/49/7.

43. Goschen to Hicks-Beech, 4 Feb 99, PCC/83, Hicks-Beech Mss.

44. Theodore Ropp, *The Development of a Modern Navy: French Naval Policy, 1871–1904* (N.I.P.: Annapolis, 1987), 162–65.

45. The idea was set out in: François Fournier, *La Flotte Necessaire, ses advantages stratégiques, tactiques, et économiques* (Paris, 1896); see also documents cited in Nicholas Lambert, "The Influence of the Submarine upon Naval Strategic Thought, 1896–1914," D.Phil. diss. (Oxford, 1992). Fournier's clearest explanations of his theory are in the Procès Verbal and papers considered by the Conséil Superiérure de la Marine [catalogued in BB8 2424, French Naval Archives, Vincennes]; see especially, Fournier to Ministre, "Program naval à adopter dans l'ordre d'urgence," 10 May 05, and "Note sur l'importance du role des flottilles sousmarines dans la guerre navale et sur les consequéces de ce role," 8 May 05, dossier 3, BB8 2424(6).

46. Ropp, *Development of a Modern Navy,* 165–78; Henri Le Masson, *Histoire du Torpilleur* (Paris, 1967), chapters 1–4.

47. Walser, "France's Battlefleet," 64–68.

48. Ropp, *Development of a Modern Navy,* 288, 296–98.

49. Edouard Lockroy, *La Défense Navale* (Paris, 1900); idem, *La Marine de guerre; six mois de rue royale* (Paris, 1897).

50. For an account of French submarine policy see chapters on the French navy in Lambert, "The Influence of the Submarine upon Naval Strategic Thought," chapters 2 & 3.

51. Vice Admiral de la Saille (prefect 5ème arr., Toulon) to EMG2 (second section, naval staff), 15 Dec 1898, enclosing copy of report submitted by Lt. Mottez to Commandant Défence Mobiles, Toulon, 9 Dec 1898, GG2 76/3. [Service Historique de la Marine—Vincennes].

52. Vice Admiral de la Saille au Minister. 15 Dec 1898, ibid.

53. Brassey's, *Naval Annual,* 1899, 37; for a confused analysis see: Marder, *Anatomy,* 357–62.

54. Mottez to his wife, 9 Jan 1899, in Mottez Papers (I am indebted to Capitaine de Vasseau Claude Huan for providing me with a copy of this document.)

55. Journal Officiel, Chambre des Députés, débats parlementaires, seance du 17 Mar 1899, M. le Ministre de la Marine, 938–39.

56. Admiral Hopkins (c. in c., Mediterranean) to Admiralty, 5 Apr 1898, 8, and minutes thereon by Custance (DNI) and Richards (SNL) in "Mediterranean: Protection of Trade Routes," ADM 1/7376B

57. Selborne, "Navy Estimates, 1901–1902," 17 Jan 01, 5–6, CAB 37/56/8.

58. Selborne, "The Navy Estimates and the Chancellor of the Exchequer's Memorandum on the Growth of Expenditure," 16 Nov 01, CAB 37/59/118.

59. Sumida, *In Defence,* 12–13.

60. Ibid.

61. Mallet, *British Budgets,* 474.

62. Salisbury to Hicks-Beech, 2 Jan 1896, f.111, PCC/69, Hicks-Beech Mss.

63. Hicks-Beech to Salisbury, 12 Oct 98, PCC/34, ibid.

64. Mallet, *British Budgets,* Appendix.

65. Hicks-Beech to Salisbury, 21 Jan 99, PCC/34, Hicks-Beech Mss.

66. Ibid.

67. Salisbury to Hicks-Beech, 24 Jan 1899, f.166, PCC/69, ibid.

68. A. N. Porter, "Lord Salisbury, Foreign Policy and Domestic Finance, 1860–1900," in Lord Blake and Hugh Cecil, eds., *Salisbury: The Man and his Policies* (Macmillan: London, 1987), 148–84.

69. Hicks-Beech to Salisbury, 30 Jan 1899, 3M/E, Salisbury Mss, cited in Friedberg, *Weary Titan,* 105.

70. Hicks-Beech to Salisbury, 30 Jan 99, PCC/34, Hicks-Beech Mss.

71. Salisbury to Hicks-Beech, 24 Jan 1899, f.166, PCC/69, ibid.

72. Mallett, *British Budgets,* 497, table 16, col. 11.

73. Sumida, *In Defence,* table 15.

74. Goschen to Hicks-Beech, 26 Jan 1900, PCC/83, Hicks-Beech Mss.

75. Hicks-Beech to Salisbury, 24 Jan 1900, PCC/34, ibid.

76. All figures taken from Sumida, *In Defence,* 20–23.

77. Hicks-Beech to Salisbury, 21 Oct 00, PCC/34, Hicks-Beech Mss; see also minute (22 Oct 00) by Kerr on warship construction program, f.11–23, Selborne Mss 158 [Bodleian Library, Oxford].

78. Salisbury to Hicks-Beech, 29 Oct 00, f.185, PCC/69, Hicks-Beech Mss.

79. Hicks-Beech to Selborne, 23 & 28 Nov 00, f.181–184, Selborne Mss 26.

80. Minutes (22 Oct 00) and (27 Oct 00) by Kerr on "Shipbuilding Programme," 19 Oct 1900, f.11–23, Selborne Mss 158.

81. Goschen to Hicks-Beech, 4 Feb 99, PCC/83, Hicks-Beech Mss.

82. Minute (27 Dec 00) by Kerr to Selborne, "Shipbuilding Programme," f.11–23, Selborne Mss 158.

83. Selborne acknowledged Kerr's persuasiveness on this issue in: Selborne to Kerr, 12 Sep 01, f.145, Selborne Mss 27.

84. Selborne to Hicks-Beech, 29 Dec 00, PCC/83, Hicks-Beech Mss.

85. Hicks-Beech to Selborne, 2 Jan 01, f.186, Selborne Mss 26.

86. Selborne, "Navy Estimates, 1901–1902," 17 Jan 01, CAB 37/56/8.

87. Ibid., p. 8.

88. Kerr to Selborne, 14 Feb 01, f.30, Selborne Mss 27.

89. Capt. [later Adm. Sir] George King-Hall, diary, reporting conversation with Kerr at Malta, 16 Mar 01, King-Hall Mss. At the time, King-Hall was chief of staff to the commander in chief, Mediterranean, Sir John Fisher.

90. Unfunded debt rose during fiscal year 1901–02 from £16 million to £78 million, for which see Mallet, *British Budgets,* 494, table 15, column 3.

91. Hick Beach, "Financial Difficulties: Appeal for Economy in Estimates," Oct 01, CAB 37/58/109.

92. Cited in Sumida, *In Defence*, 23.

93. Kerr to Selborne, 5 Oct 01, f.188, Selborne Mss 27.

94. Selborne, "The Navy Estimates and the Chancellor of the Exchequer's Memorandum on the Growth of Expenditure," 16 Nov 01, 7, CAB 37/59/118.

95. Selborne to Salisbury, 31 Oct 01, cited in Boyce, 128–29.

96. Salisbury to Hicks-Beech, 14 Sep 01, f.191, PCC/69, Hicks-Beech Mss.

97. Selborne to Kerr, 12 Sep 01, f.145, Selborne 27; Minute (24 Sep 01) by Kerr, f.24, Selborne Mss 158.

98. Kerr to Selborne, 11 Mar 02 (f.34) and 6 Apr 02 (f.42), both Selborne Mss 31.

99. Kerr to Selborne, 28 Apr 02, f.68, ibid.

100. Selborne to Balfour, 12 Jul 02, Sanders Mss 736 [Bodleian Library, Oxford].

101. Balfour to Hicks-Beech, 11 Jul 02, PCC/88; Hick Beach to Balfour, PCC/12, Hicks-Beech Mss.

102. Selborne to Curzon, 17 Jul 02, box 2 part 2, Curzon Mss (cited in Monger, 76).

103. Sumida, *In Defence*, 24–26.

104. Aaron Friedberg, *The Weary Titan*, 101–34.

105. Richard Rempel, *Unionists Divided: Arthur Balfour, Joseph Chamberlain and the Unionist Free Traders* (Newton Abbot, 1972); Alan Sykes, *Tariff Reform in British Politics, 1903–1913* (London, 1979).

106. Balfour to Arnold Forster, 16 Dec 02, f.23, Add Mss 50289, and 28 Oct 03, f.36, Add Mss 49706 [Additional Manuscripts Series, British Library, London].

107. Selborne to the Admiralty Permanent Secretary, 16 Feb 03, in "Distribution of Business, 1904" (31 Dec 04), ADM 1/7737, cited in Sumida, *In Defence*, 26.

108. Nicholas d'Ombrain, *War Machinery and High Policy* (Oxford, 1973), 1–6, 27–29.

109. For the only coherent explanation of this relationship, see Sumida, *In Defence*, chapters 2 & 3.

110. Friedberg, *Weary Titan*, 167–68, 172–80, 207.

Chapter Two: Complexity and Duplicity

1. Sir Thomas Brassey, *The British Navy*, iii, 3–8.

2. Cited in Arthur Marder, *Anatomy*, 351; see also Alex Rowland, *Underwater Warfare in the Age of Sail* (Indiana U.P.: Bloomington, 1978), 112, notes 14–15.

3. Michael W. Dash, "British Submarines Policy, 1853–1918," Unpublished Ph.D. diss. (London University, 1990), 36–46, 61–80.

4. Ibid.

5. Memorandum (21 Jan 01) by A.K. Wilson, on docket "New Docket — Submarine-boats," ADM 1/7515.

6. Report by Capt. William Arthur RN, naval attaché report No. 90, 2 Aug

1881, FO 115/673, cited by Dash, "Submarine Policy," 73, nt. 171; I am also indebted to Dr. Douglas Furgol of the naval museum, Washington Navy Yard, for information that British naval officers also examined *Intelligent Whale.*

7. Minute (6 Mar 1899) by White, on Jackson to Admiralty (report No. 14) , 22 Jan 1899, in "Trials of French submarine boat Gustave-Zédé and other submarines," (FO 26 Jan 1899) ADM 1/7422A. N.B. reference to five reports dated 1885–1887.

8. Various reports in docket "French Navy and Coast Defences," (FO 26 Feb 00) ADM 1/7471.

9. Capt. Henry Jackson, "Report on French Coast Defences, Torpedo-boats and submarine boat Le Goubet," 2 Apr 98, ADM 1/7471; Admiralty, "Submarine boats," NID 577, May 1900, pp. 46–49, HMS *Dolphin* Submarine Museum.

10. Minute (20 Apr 98) by Beaumont, on Jackson's Report, ADM 1/7471; for White's reputation see Fisher to Selborne, 5 Jan 01, *FGDN*, I, 178; Frederick Manning, *The Life of Sir William White* (London, 1923).

11. Minute (5 May 98) by White, on Jackson's Report, ADM 1/7471.

12. Minute (22 Jan 1899)) by Monson, on Jackson to Admiralty (report No.14), 22 Jan 1899, in "Trials of French submarine boat Gustave-Zédé and other submarines " (FO 26 Jan 1899) ADM /7422A.

13. Minutes (15 Mar 1899) by Egerton and (16 Mar 1899) by Captain Jeffreys, on report No.14, ibid.

14. Ibid.

15. Minute (25 May 00) by Goschen, on "Submarine boats Considered by the USA House Committee" (ADM 18 May 00) ADM 1/7462; minute (16 Mar 1899) by Wilson, on Jackson to Admiralty (report No. 14), 22 Jan 1899, in "Trials of French submarine boat Gustave-Zédé and other submarines," (FO 26 Jan 1899) ADM 1/7422A.

16. "Reliable Information Concerning the French Submarine boat Gustave-Zédé," May 1899, ibid.

17. Minute (2 May 99) by Custance, on "Reliable Information Concerning the French Submarine boat Gustave-Zédé," ibid.

18. Ibid.

19. Journal Officiel, Chambre des Députés, débats parlementaires, seance du 17 Mar 1899, 938–39, m. le ministre de la marine, 938–39.

20. Minutes (2 May 1899) by Custance and (15 May 1899) by White (FO 26 Jan 1899) ADM 1/7422A.

21. Report by Captain Charles Ottley, on "U.S. Submarine-boat Holland," 18 Dec 1899 (FO 3 Jan 00) ADM 1/7471.

22. Attaché Report by Douglas Gamble, 22 Jan 00, "France—submarine boats—latest trials and experiments," ADM 1/7482.

23. Minute (20 Feb 00) by Kerr, in docket "Report No.51: Probable adoption of Government Proposals respecting shipbuilding programme," 22 Jan 00, ADM 1/7482.

24. Minute (5 Feb 00) by Sturdee (a/DNO), on "Submarines" (FO 16 Jan 00) ADM 1/7471; Custance, "Proposal to Print a Report on Submarine Boats," 21 Apr 00, ADM 1/7461B; Admiralty Print, "Submarine-boats" (NID report 577) May 1900, HMS *Dolphin* Submarine Museum.

25. "Blockade Mines—Use of, for defence against submarine boats" (G2778/00), extract from report by captain of HMS *Vulcan*, 5 Feb 00, and extract from submission from c. in c., Mediterranean, 26 Feb 00, both in "Principle Questions Dealt with by the Director of Naval Ordnance," 1900 (Hereafter cited as PQ), pp. 105–8, ADM256/39.

26. Minute (14 Apr 00) by Capt. Charles Robinson (Vernon), p.105, PQ 1900, ibid.

27. Minute (14 Apr 00) by Jeffreys, p.106, ibid.

28. ibid; see also minute (25 Apr 00) by Jeffreys on "Submarine boats—Methods of resisting attack by towing torpedoes," p. 110, ibid.

29. Minutes (24 Apr 00) by Kerr (23 Apr 00) by Custance, and (18 Apr 00) by Wilson, ibid.

30. Minute (30 Apr 00) by Kerr, ibid.

31. Minute (4 May 00) by Kerr, p. 112, ibid.

32. Admiralty to C. in C.'s Devonport and Portsmouth, 17 May 00, ibid.

33. Minute (18 May 00) by Sturdee (a/D.N.O.) on "Submarine-boats considered by USA House Committee" (ADM 18 May 00) ADM 1/7462.

34. Beresford to Fisher, 21 Jun 00, f.104, enclosed in Beresford to Balfour, 21 June 00, f.96, Add Mss 49713.

35. Minute (22 May 00) by Walter Kerr (ADM 18 May 00) ADM 1/7462.

36. Minutes (3 May 00) by Wilson (4 May 00) by Kerr, and (6 May 00) by Goschen, on "Submarine boats—method of resisting attack by towed torpedoes," 111, P.Q.1900, ADM 256/39.

37. Minute (3 Aug 00) by Wilson, "Submarine boats considered by the USA House Committee," (ADM 18 May 00) ADM 1/7462.

38. Minute (3 Aug 00) by Wilson (ADM 18 May 00) ADM 1/7462.

39. Minute (May 00) by Goschen, ibid.

40. See Rice to Goschen, 17 Sep 00; Rice to Rothschilds, 13 Jul 00; and Rothschilds to Goschen, 23 Jul 00, enclosed in docket "Holland Type Submarines" (ADM 15 Jan 01) ADM 1/7515.

41. Ibid.

42. Minute (19 Sep 00) by White (DNC), "Submarine boats," ADM 1/7515.

43. Notes on interview between Rice, Wilson and White, 16 Oct 00 (Approval of arrangement with Vickers, 18 Oct 00), ibid.

44. Minute (17 Sep 00) by Wilson, "Submarine boats," ADM 1/7515.

45. First draft of letter from Wilson to the Treasury, 23 Oct 00, ibid.

46. Minute (24 Oct 00) by Goschen, ibid.

47. Minute (26 Oct 00) by Kerr, and final draft of Admiralty to Treasury, 6 Nov 00, ibid.

48. Minute (30 Jan 01) by Kerr on "Holland submarine boats," ADM 1/7515.

49. Salisbury to Selborne, 27 Oct 00, in D. G. Boyce, *The Crisis of British Power: The Imperial and Naval Papers of the Second Earl of Selborne, 1895–1910* (Historians Press: London, 1990), 103.

50. *Parliamentary Debates,* 4th Series, 86, 333, 17 Jul 00, Goschen speaking.

51. Ibid.

52. Lt. F. D. Arnold-Forster diary, entry 13 Jan 01, F. D. Arnold-Forster Mss, HMS *Dolphin* Submarine Museum.

53. Selborne to Hicks-Beech, 29 Dec 00, in Boyce, *Selborne,* 106.

54. Selborne, "Naval Estimates 1901–1902," 11, 17 Jan 01, CAB 37/56/8.

55. Minute (15 Jan 01) by Selborne, on docket "Holland Type Submarine," (ADM 15 Jan 01) ADM 1/7515.

56. Capt. Lewis Bayly, "United States, [attaché] report No.9," 3 (ADM 22 Dec 00) ADM 1/7465C.

57. Various minutes on "Submarine boats designed by Captain Hovgaard of the Danish Navy," (Admiralty 25 Jan 01) ADM 1/7516; N.B. Arnold-Forster to Selborne, 10 Jan 01, f.4, Add Mss 50294.

58. Ibid.

59. Minute (15 Jan 01) Selborne, "Holland Type Submarine," ADM 1/7515.

60. Minute (28 Jan 01) by Admiral Douglas, ibid.

61. Minute (19 Feb 01) by McGriggor, ibid.

62. Marder, *Anatomy,* 359.

63. Ibid; most recently expressed by Dan Van der Vat, *Stealth at Sea: The History of the Submarine* (London, 1994), 33–34.

64. Minute (21 Jan 01) by Wilson, on "New docket—Submarine Boats," ADM 1/7515.

65. Minute (30 Jan 01) by Kerr, ibid.

66. Nicholas Lambert, "Admiral of the Fleet Sir Arthur Wilson VC," in Malcolm Murfett ed., *The First Sea Lords: From Fisher to Mountbatten* (Praegers: Westport, 1995); and Selborne to Wilson, 19 Mar 01, Selborne Mss 28; Selborne to Balfour, 20 May 15, f.251, Add Mss 49707.

67. Undated note from Atkinson to McKecknie (both executives at Vickers) enclosing extract for the *Glasgow Herald* f.8, Vickers Mss 632; also telegram, 25 Feb 01, f.18, Vickers Mss 1003 [Cambridge University Library].

68. For Arnold-Forster's character: see Rhodri Williams, *Defending the Empire* (Yale: New Haven, 1992), 41–45, 68; For his habit of pressing his views see: Kerr to Selborne, 4 Nov 03, f.3, Selborne Mss 34.

69. Minute (19 Mar 01) by Arnold-Forster, ADM 1/7515.

70. Arnold-Forster to Selborne, 3 Jun 02, f.179, Add Mss 50280; also Arnold-Forster to May, 1 Jul 02, f.132, Add Mss 50281.

71. "Value of Submarines in War," enclosed in Arnold-Forster to Selborne, 8 Aug 01, f.13, Add Mss 50294.

72. Selborne, "The Navy Estimates and the Chancellor of the Exchequer's Memorandum on the Growth of Expenditure," 16 Nov 01, p. 15, CAB 37/59/118. (Three submarines—A2, A3 and A4—were laid down under the 1902/03 program.)

73. Ibid., p. 15.

74. Ibid., p. 18.

75. Selborne to Arnold-Forster, 3 Oct 01, f.58, Selborne Mss 28.

76. Adm. Sir Reginald Bacon, *From 1900 Onwards* (Hutchinson: London, 1940), 50–65.

77. Lt. F. D. Arnold-Forster (nephew of parliamentary secretary to the

Admiralty) diary entry and letter to his father both dated 6 Apr 02, F. D. Arnold-Forster Mss, HMS *Dolphin.*

78. Selborne, "Navy Estimates 1901/02," 17 Jan 01, p. 11, CAB 37/56/8.

79. Bacon, *From 1900 Onwards,* 61.

80. Minute (18 Jan 02) by Selborne, on the importance of weather in gauging the true efficiency of submarines, "France—Submarine boats—Latest trials and experiments," CAP G119/1900, ADM 1/7482.

81. Bacon to May (controller), 13 May 01, in "Admiralty 18 May 00," ADM 1/7462.

82. Minute (n/d) by H. G. Deadman, on Bacon to White (DNC), 30 Jul 01, f.6, Ships Covers 185 [also known as ADM 138 series: Brass Foundry, National Maritime Museum].

83. See Bacon memorandum, 26 Aug 05, cut 4, Ships Covers 290.

84. Schedule of commencement and launch of submarines, f.19, Ships Covers 185.

85. The contrast between the seagoing qualities of Holland and A1 is set out in Bacon, "Submarine A1, report of ICS on passage from Barrow to Portsmouth," 3 Aug 03, A730/03, ADM1/7644.

86. Admiralty to C. in C.'s Devonport and Portsmouth, 17 May 00, p. 112, P.Q.1900, ADM 256/39.

87. ART 1901, Appendix C, 171–73.

88. Handwritten book entitled "Captain Bacon's Notebook," 57, HMS *Dolphin* Submarine Museum.

89. Ibid., 57–59.

90. Ibid., 57.

91. Ibid.

92. Ibid., 187–89.; see also Bacon, "Report on the Running of Submarine boats," 31 May 03, ADM 1/7795.

93. ART 1903, 82; and HMS *Vernon* to C. in C. Portsmouth, 15 Sep 03, f.26, Ships Covers 185.

94. Ibid; references to anti-submarine trials in, minute (5 Jan 01) by Admiral May, ADM 1/7717.

95. Minutes (30 Jun 04) by May and (1 Jul 04) by Kerr, on "Remarks by C. in C. Portsmouth" (John Fisher), enclosed in docket: "H.M.S. Thames: Report on the Manoeuvres recently carried out between submarine boats and one division of the Portsmouth Destroyer flotilla," by Captain Bacon and Captain Charlton, ADM 1/7719. Further details can be found in the 1901 to 1904 volumes of "Annual Report of the Torpedo School" (cited as ART) (Ministry of Defence Admiralty Library).

96. Capt. George Egerton to C. in C. Portsmouth, 15 Sep 03, in reference to "H.M.S. Starfish" anti-submarine trials, f.26, Ships Covers 185.

97. Experiments were revived briefly in June 1907, by the third Captain (S) SS Hall, ADM 189/99.

98. Bacon, "Report on running of submarine-boats," 31 May 03, ADM 1/7795.

99. Ibid.

100. Ibid., 1–34.

101. Ibid., 12–16.

102. Marder, *Anatomy*, 365–67.

103. Ibid., 365.

104. Custance, "Memorandum on Sea Power and the Principles Involved in it," July 1902, Selborne Mss 134.

105. Minute (16 Apr 02) by Selborne on paper by Custance, "Australian Naval Question," Selborne Mss 133.

106. Bacon, "Report on Running of Submarine Boats," 31 May 03, p. 13, ADM 1/7795.

107. Selborne, "Navy Estimates 1903/04," 17 Oct 02, p. 11, CAB 37/63/142.

108. In October 1902, Selborne projected 40 destroyers, 40 torpedo-boats and 40 submarines, CAB 37/63/142. A year earlier he had envisaged building 49 destroyers, 45 Torpedo-boats and 20 submarines, CAB 37/59/118.

109. Minute (20 Jan 03) by May, "Controller, 20 Jan 03," ADM 1/24200.

110. Marder, *Anatomy*, 365, citing minute by Battenberg on docket in Admiralty archives since lost.

111. Admiralty Correspondence Digests, cut 55, ADM 12/1377 (1902) and ADM 12/1389 (1903).

112. Arnold-Forster to May, 1 Jul 02, f.132, Add Mss 50281.

113. Minutes, "France—submarine boats—latest trials and experiments," (11 Jan 02) CAP G119/1900, ADM 1/7482.

114. Rough notes attached to a letter from Selborne to Kerr, 12 Sep 01, suggest that the Board agreed the Royal Navy should build a fleet of thirty-five submarines to match the French, f.150, Selborne Mss 27.

115. Fisher to Selborne, 25 Jul 02, Selborne Mss 198.

116. "Report of a Conference between the Admiralty and War Office Representatives to Consider the Strategic Conditions Governing the Coast Defence of the United Kingdom in War as Effected by Naval Conditions," printed November 1903, 3/1/9A, CAB 38/1/4.

117. Admiralty, "Admiralty Instructions on Defence Matters," 10 Feb 03, Paragraph 17, 3/1/2A, CAB 38/2/3. Re-affirmed in May 1904, for which see copy, f.12, Add Mss 50308.

118. Marder, *Anatomy*, 378.

119. D'Ombrain, *War Machinery*, 1–30.

120. War Office, "Provision of Land Forces for the Defence of the United Kingdom," 14 Feb 03, p. 2, para. 7, 3/1/3A, CAB 38/2/5; and Admiralty, "Naval Remarks on the Military Paper, 'Provision of Land Forces for the Defence of the United Kingdom,' of the 14th February, 1903," 4 Mar 03, 3/1/8A, CAB 38/2/11. The Home Ports were the three principal naval bases at Portsmouth, Devonport, and Chatham.

121. Admiralty, "Naval Remarks on the Military Paper, 'Provision of Land Forces for the Defence of the United Kingdom,' of the 14th February, 1903," 4 Mar 03, p. 1, 3/1/8A, CAB 38/2/11.

122. Ibid., p. 2; and Admiralty, "Our position as regards Invasion on the supposition that our battle fleet in Home Waters has sustained a reverse and is

unable to leave Port in face of a Hostile Fleet in superior strength," 31 Mar 03, 3/1/11A, CAB 38/2/19.

123. Admiralty, "Remarks on M.I.D. Paper 13A," 14 Jul 03, p. 2, 3/1/16A, CAB 38/3/60.

124. Ibid.

125. "Naval Remarks on the Military Paper, 'Provision of Land Forces for the Defence of the United Kingdom,' of the 14th February, 1903," by Battenberg, 4 Mar 03, p. 1, 3/1/8A, CAB 38/2/11.

126. War Office, "Provision of Land Forces for the Defence of the United Kingdom," 14 Feb 03, p. 3, 3/1/3A, CAB 38/2/5.

127. Ibid; for strength of overseas garrisons see Selborne (Admiralty), "The Defence of Naval and Commercial Harbours," 17 Dec 04, CAB 37/73/165.

128. Draft letter Selborne to Arnold-Forster, 14 Nov 03, f.7, Selborne Mss 34. Reference to "Instructions of Defence Matters."

129. War Office, "Remarks on the Memorandum Prepared by the Naval Intelligence Department, dated March 31 1903, on 'The Possibilities of Invasion During the Temporary Loss of Command of the Sea in Home Waters,'" 27 Apr 03, 3/1/13A, CAB 38/2/24.

130. "Notes on Submarine Mines" enclosed in Clarke to Balfour, 24 Nov 04, f.215, Add Mss 49700.

131. Admiralty Docket, "Thames and Medway Defences," 29 Feb 1896, ADM 1/7642; also Paul Cowie, *Mines, Minelayers and Minelaying* (London, 1949), 24–26.

132. Draft letter Selborne to Arnold-Forster, 12 Nov 03, f.7, Selborne Mss 34.

133. Ibid.

134. Sir George Clarke to Balfour, 25 Nov 04, f.220, Add Mss 49700.

135. Brodrick to Admiralty, 15 Jan 03, on "Proposed removal of Submarine mining School from Chatham to Sheerness" (WO 15 Jan 03), ADM 1/7717.

136. Ibid.

137. Minute (6 Feb 03) by Captain Egerton, ibid.

138. Minute (16 Feb 03) by Capt. Henry Jackson, ibid.

139. Ibid.

140. Minute (26 Feb 03) Captain Battenberg, ibid.

141. Battenberg, "Naval Remarks on the military paper, 'provision of land forces for the defence of the United Kingdom,' of 14th February 1903," 4 Mar 03, p. 2, 3/1/8A, CAB 38/2/11.

142. Selborne, "Garrisons of Coaling Stations," 17 Jun 01, CAB 37/57/60; Lansdowne, "Proposed Transfer of Coaling Stations to the Admiralty," 20 Jan 1898, CAB 37/46/8; Lansdowne, "Proposal to Employ Marines to Garrison Coaling Stations," 11 Dec 1896, CAB 37/43/54; Brodrick to Selborne, 11 Jan 01 and 11 Mar 01, f.138, Selborne Mss 26.

143. Minute (Feb 01) by Custance, "Proposed Transfer to Admiralty of Certain Coaling Stations," f.11, ADM 1/7516.

144. Kerr to Selborne, 15 Nov 00, f.2; 28 Jan 01, f.24–30; 11 Mar 01, f.41, all Selborne Mss 27.

145. Minute (26 Feb 03) by Battenberg (WO 2 May 03), ADM 1/7717.

146. Minute (4 Mar 03) by Selborne, ibid.

147. Committee formed 11 May 03, report 7 Jan 04 (WO 2 May 03), ADM 1/7717.

148. Bacon, "Report on running of submarine boats," 31 May 03, p. 18, ADM1/7725; May to Selborne 19 Mar 03, f.2, Selborne Mss 36.

149. Admiralty, "Memorandum on Possibility of Invasion During Temporary Loss of Command of the Sea in Home Waters," 31 Mar 03. p2, 3/1/11A, CAB 38/2/19.

150. Custance to Selborne, 31 Sep 04, and Lambton to Selborne, 28 Jan 04, Selborne Mss 23.

151. Haldane, "Memorandum of Events between 1906–15," Apr 1916, f.29, Haldane Mss 5919.

152. Williams, *Defending the Empire*, 41.

153. Richard Rempel, *Unionists Divided: Arthur Balfour, Joseph Chamberlain and the Unionist Free Traders* (Newton Abbot, 1972).

154. Cited in Marder, *Anatomy*, 121.

155. Balfour to Esher, 30 Jul 04, Add Mss 41718; See also Williams, *Defending the Empire*, 41–43.

156. Arnold-Forster, "Needs for Organisation for War," Add Mss 50289; for the offer of the post see diairy, f.3, Add Mss 50335; for understanding of the Esher Committee's role see diary, f.9, Add Mss 50335.

157. Arnold-Forster's diary for 1903 gives a blow by blow account of his attempts to reform the War Office, f.4–133, Add Mss 50335.

158. Arnold-Forster, "Army Reform Notes," 15 Jan 1897, f.15, Add Mss 49722.

159. Arnold-Forster diary, 1 Nov 03, f.70, Add Mss 50335.

160. Arnold-Forster's diary, 30 Oct 03, f.68, Add Mss 50335.

161. Kerr to Selborne, 3 Nov 03, f.3, Selborne Mss 34.

162. Minute (4 Mar 03) by Selborne (War Office 15 Jan 03), ADM 1/7717.

163. Arnold-Forster diary, 1 Nov 03, f.70, Add Mss 50335.

164. Arnold-Forster to Selborne 2 Nov 03, f.1, Selborne Mss 34.

165. Ibid; examples of confusion in command and control given in Arnold-Forster's "Organisation for War," 20 Oct 02, f.155, Selborne Mss 118.

166. Marder, *Anatomy*, 365.

167. Ibid.

168. Kerr to Selborne 4 Nov 03, f.3, Selborne Mss 34.

169. Kerr admitted having discussed the relative merits of submarines and mines with Arnold-Forster some days before, ibid; also Arnold-Forster diary, 30 Oct 03, f.68, Add Mss 50335.

170. Selborne to Arnold-Forster, 14 Nov 03, f.9, Add Mss 50308. More "forceful" drafts can be found in f.7–12, Selborne Mss Box 34.

171. Kerr to Selborne, 4 Nov 03, Selborne Mss 34.

172. Marder, *Anatomy*, 370–71.

173. See: Tweedmouth, "Memorandum" [Navy Estimates 1907/8], 26 Jun 06, CAB 37/83/60.

174. Balfour, "Draft Report on Possibility of Serious Invasion," November 1903, 3/1/18A, CAB 38/3/71.

175. Ibid., p. 7.

176. Ibid., p. 8.

177. Ibid., pp. 8, 14–15.

178. Ibid; note the similarity of arguments employed in: Admiralty, "Remarks on M.I.D. Paper 13a," 14 Jul 03, 3/1/16A, CAB 38/3/60.

179. Selborne to Balfour, 16 Nov 03, f.148, Add Mss 49707.

180. Battenberg, "Strategic Position of British Naval Bases in Western Atlantic and West Indies," 24 Nov 03, 5/1/5C, CAB 38/3/74.

181. Minutes of 24 Meeting of CID, 25 Nov 03, CAB 38/3/75.

182. [War Office], "Memorandum on the Defence of Bermuda" [December 1903], 5/1/6C, CAB 38/3/78.

183. Ibid.

184. [Admiralty] Battenberg, "Garrison of Bermuda," 19 Mar 04, 5/1/9C, CAB 38/4/9.

185. Balfour to Fisher, 3 Jan 04, f.71, Add Mss 49710.

186. Lord Esher, "National Strategy," 27 Mar 04, Add Mss 49718.

187. Fisher to Balfour, 5 Jan 04, enclosing letter from Admiral May dated 3 Jan 04, f.75, Add Mss 49710.

188. Balfour to Selborne, 7 Jan 04, f.1, Selborne Mss 39.

189. Minute (14 Dec 03) by Battenberg, on docket "Submarine Defences—Substitution of Submarines for existing Mine-fields at certain places," ADM 1/7717.

190. Captain Bacon, "Report on the suitability of R.E. submarine mining stations at Portsmouth, Devonport, & Sheerness as depots for s.m. boats," 13 Dec 03, enclosed in "Submarine Defences," ibid.

191. Minute (16 Dec 03) by Kerr addressed to Admirals Drury and Durnford, on docket "Submarine Defences," ibid.

192. Memoranda (29 Dec 03) by Vice Adm. Charles Drury and (24 Dec 03) by Rear Adm. John Durnford (Admiralty 15 Jan 03), ADM 1/7717.

193. Memo (24 Dec 03) by Durnford, ibid.

194. Memo (29 Dec 03) by Drury, ibid.

195. Memo (24 Dec 03) by Durnford, ibid.

196. Memo (5 Jan 04) by May (controller), ibid.

197. Memo (6 Jan 04) by Kerr, ibid.

198. Ibid.

199. Minute (7 Jan 04) by Selborne on memorandum by Kerr dated 6 Jan 04, ibid.

200. Correspondence between Balfour and Selborne, Jan 1904, Add Mss 49707.

201. Arnold-Forster, "No 1. Memorandum," 4 Dec 03, f.5–6, Add Mss 50300 and f.230, Selborne Mss 120.

202. Arnold-Forster, "No.3. Memorandum," 8 Dec 03, p. 6, Selborne Mss 120; Williams, *Defending the Empire,* 46–47.

203. Ibid., p. 6.

204. The capital cost of transferring the responsibility for the coaling stations was calculated in 1901 to be £1,286,000. It would also add £769,740 per annum to the naval estimates, for which see Admiralty, "Considerations Affecting the Proposal to Transfer the Responsibility of Defence of Coaling Stations to the Admiralty," Jun 01, f.17, Selborne Mss 160.

205. Arnold-Forster to Lyttleton (CIGS), 19 May 04, f.4, Add Mss 50308; also Arnold-Forster to Selborne, 31 Jan 02, enclosing memo on coaling stations, f.102, Add Mss 50280.

206. Arnold-Forster, "Summary of Years Work at War Office," 31 Jan 05, Selborne Mss 120; Arnold-Forster to Lyttleton, 19 May 04, f.4, Add Mss 50308.

207. Arnold-Forster to Selborne, Dec 02, f.23–33, Add Mss 50284.

208. Arnold-Forster diary, 21 Nov 03, f.97, Add Mss 50335. Arnold-Forster frequently complained in his diary about the slow rate at which his reforms were introduced, and recorded his growing impatience with their obstruction by soldiers.

209. Kerr to Selborne, 6 Jan 04, Selborne Mss 41.

210. Minutes of Board meeting forwarded by Selborne to Secretary of the Admiralty, 13 Jan 04, ADM 1/7717.

211. Bacon, "Submarine-boats and Bases," 4 Feb 04, CAP B127/1904, ADM 1/7739.

212. Draft minutes of Board meeting held on 13 Jan 04, ADM 1/7717.

213. Minute (7 Jan 04) by Selborne on memorandum by Kerr dated 6 Jan 04, attached to Board minutes, ibid.

214. Minute (4 Jun 04) by Cmdr. George Ballard, on docket "Functions of Submarine Mines in War," dated 27 Feb 04, ADM 1/7717.

215. Draft minutes of Board meeting held on 13 Jan 04, ADM 1/7717.

216. Lyttleton to Arnold-Forster, 29 Jul 04, f.12, Add Mss 50308; Minute (6 Jun 04) by Cmdr. George Ballard, on docket "Functions of Submarine Mines in War," dated 27 February, 1904, ADM 1/7717.

217. Minutes (4 Jun 04) by Cmdr. George Ballard (a/DNI) and (6 Jun 04) by Kerr, ibid.

218. Minute (21 Aug 04) by Selborne on docket "Submarine Mine Defences in its Naval Aspects" (ex-WO 22 Apr 05) ADM 1/8879.

219. John McDermott, "The British Army's Turn to Europe," in Paul Kennedy ed., The War Plans of the Great Powers (Allen & Unwin: London, 1979; reprint 1985), 105; d'Ombrain, War Machinery, 6.

220. Letter (M.0314) from Army Council to Admiralty, Feb 1904, ADM 1/7717.

221. Arnold-Forster to Lyttleton (C.I.G.S.), 19 May 04, f.4, Add Mss 50308; Lyttleton to Arnold-Forster, 29 Jul 04, f.12, ibid; Arnold-Forster to Lyttleton, 16 Aug 04 and Arnold-Forster to Lyttleton, 3 Oct 04, ff.16, Add Mss 50300.

222. War Office, "The Strength of the Regular Army and Auxiliary Forces, having regard to peace and war requirements," 1 May 04, 3/1/22A, CAB38/4/40; see also d'Ombrain, War Machinery, 54.

223. Williams, Defending the Empire, 47–50.

224. Balfour to Esher, 30 Jul 04, f.120, Add Mss 49718.

225. Arnold-Forster was one of the first to be aware of Fisher's appointment; for which see Arnold-Forster diary, 16 May 04, f.43, Add Mss 50337.

226. Arnold-Forster diary, 8 Jul 04, f.20, Add Mss 50339.

Chapter Three: Radical Jack Fisher

1. The three major biographies are: Reginald Bacon, *The Life of Lord Fisher of Kilverstone* (Hodder & Stoughton: London, 1929); Richard Hough, *First Sea Lord: An Authorised Biography of Admiral Lord Fisher* (London, 1969); Ruddock Mackay, *Fisher of Kilverstone* (Clarendon: Oxford, 1973). The minor biographies are: Ester Meynell, *A Woman Talking* (London, 1940) and Richard Ollard, *Fisher and Cunningham: A Study of Personalities of the Churchill Era* (Constable Press: London, 1991); the caprice (and most successful attempt to capture the character of the man) is Jan Morris, *Fisher's Face* (Viking Press: London, 1995).

2. See letter from Geoffrey Penn to the editor, *Naval Review,* Jan. 1996; biographic note on Barry Gough in the list of contributors, *The First Sea Lords: From Fisher to Mounbatten,* ed. Malcolm Murfett (Praeger: Westport, 1995).

3. Bacon, *Lord Fisher,* I, 227–28.

4. Ibid., citing remarks of G. L. Garvin, the long-time editor of the *Observer* newspaper..

5. Marder, *FGDN,* I, 9.

6. Jan Morris, *Fisher's Face,* 10.

7. Fisher to Arnold Forster, 16 Jan 01, cited in Mackay, *Kilverstone,* 247.

8. Fisher to Mrs. Reginald Neeld (his daughter), 23 Mar 1899, *FGDN,* I, 139.

9. Fisher to Earl Spencer, 28 Mar 02, *FGDN,* I, 238; Lord Hankey, *The Supreme Command,* 1914–1918 (2 vols.; George Allen and Unwin: London, 1961) I, 14–15.

10. Fisher, *Kilverstone,* 224–25.

11. Fisher to Selborne, 25 Jul 01, Selborne Mss 198; Fisher to Thursfield, 27 Apr 00, *FGDN,* I, 155; and Bacon, *Lord Fisher,* I, 128.

12. Mackay, *Kilverstone,* 224–26, 230, 233–36; Marder, *FDSF,* I, 12; idem, *Anatomy,* 395.

13. Hankey, *Supreme Command,* I, 19; also cited in Mackay, *Kilverstone,* 225

14. Fisher to Selborne, 19 Dec 00, FP56, Fisher Papers 1/2; more generally: Sumida, *In Defence,* 41–44.

15. Fisher, Feb 1900, p. 105, P.Q.1900, ADM 256/36; p. 24, ART 1900, Admiralty Library.

16. Beresford to Balfour, 21 Jun 00, f.104, Add Mss 49718; For evidence Beresford took submarines seriously, see Beresford to Domville, 7 Dec 03, "War Plans: Mediterranean and Channel Fleets," ADM 116/3111.

17. Fisher to Selborne, 19 Jul 02 and 25 Jul 02, Selborne Mss 198; Fisher to Admiralty, 16 Jul 01, on "Serious Disadvantage to the Public Service Caused by British Consul being on Leave of Absence during French Naval Manoeuvres off Ajaccio," ADM 1/7505.

18. See, for example, Fisher, "Notes for Successor," 14 May 02, in "Mediterranean," ADM 1/7597; and Morris, *Fisher's Face*, 109–11.

19. Fisher to Selborne, 25 Jul 02, Selborne Mss 26.

20. Fisher, "Mediterranean Fleet Lectures," 75, FP4702, Fisher Papers 8/1.

21. Fisher, "Purging the Navy of Obsolete Vessels" in Kemp, *F.P.1*, 35.

22. Fisher, "Notes for Successor," paragraph 24, 14 May 02, in "Mediterranean," ADM 1/7597; Fisher to Wilson, 12 Feb 02, *FGDN*, I, 227.

23. Fisher, "Notes on the important necessity of possessing Powerful Fast Armoured Cruisers and their Qualifications," Feb 02, FP4198, Fisher Papers 5/9; and Fisher, "Notes for Successor," Apr 02, FP4196, Fisher Papers 5/8.

24. Selborne to Chamberlain, 30 Sep 03, cited in Boyce, *Selborne*, 156.

25. Minute (20 Jan 01) by Custance, on Fisher to Admiralty, 25 Dec 00, enclosing "Further Report on the number of Destroyers Required on the Mediterranean Station," Admiralty 24 Dec 1900, ADM 1/7465C.

26. Fisher to Wilson, 12 Feb 02, *FGDN*, I, 227.

27. Fisher to Selborne, 25 Jul 01, Selborne Mss 198; Fisher, Synopsis of first portion of French naval maneuvers in the Mediterranean, 25 Jul 01, N807, ADM 1/7507; Admiralty, "France—Naval Manoeuvres 1900," NID Report 595, p. 7, Noel Mss Box 6A [National Maritime Museum].

28. Remarks by Captain Egerton, "*Majestic,*" 13 January 1900, in "Report on Trials of Gyroscopes Carried Out in Channel Squadron and Remarks by Vernon," 36–39, ART 1900, Admiralty Library.

29. Fisher to Selborne, 29 Jul 01, f.21, Selborne Mss 21; Rawson (c. in c., Channel Squadron, 1901) to Admiralty, 15 Jan 01, in "Mediterranean Fleet Exercises," ADM 1/7450B.

30. Selborne, "Naval Estimates, 1901–1902," 17 Jan 01, p. 8., CAB 37/56/8.

31. Fisher to Selborne, 6 Oct 01, Selborne Mss 198; see also Jon Sumida, "The Quest for Reach: The Development of Long-range Gunnery in the Royal Navy, 1901–1912," in Stephen D. Chiabotti, ed., *Tooling for War: Military Transformation in the Industrial Age* (Imprint Publications: Chicago, 1996), 49–97.

32. Admiral Beaumont to Selborne, 5 May 02, f.41, Selborne Mss 17. Beaumont, a former DNI, was later C. in C. Australia Squadron.

33. Wilson, Report on Torpedo running in Channel Fleet, p. 49–50, ART 1903, Admiralty Library.

34. Fisher to Selborne, 19 Jul 02, *FGDN*, I, 253.

35. Mackay, *Kilverstone*, 226–30; for evidence that quick-firing guns were preferred over big guns at this time see Sumida, *In Defence*, 41–42.

36. Sumida, "The Quest for Reach," 3.

37. Fisher, "Mediterranean Fleet Lectures, 1899–1902," 89, FP4702, Fisher Papers 8/1; Extracts from Report on use of destroyers by Captains Louis Battenberg, Charles Briggs, Charles Madden, 42–47, ibid.

38. Fisher to Admiralty, 16 Jan 00, enclosed in "Mediterranean Fleet Exercises," N848/00, ADM 1/7450B.

39. Fisher to Selborne, 1 Dec 00, 19 Dec 00, 5 Jan 01, and Fisher to Thursfield, 27 Apr 00, 29 Jan 01, *FGDN*, I, 155–186.

40. For Kerr's views on the role of destroyers see Minute (27 Dec 00) by Kerr on "Shipbuilding Programme," 8 (f.16–23), Selborne Mss 158.

41. Kerr to Selborne, 25 Aug 01, f.129, Selborne Mss 27.

42. Ibid; Minutes (24 Jul 01) by Kerr and (23 Jul 01) by Custance, on "Third Series of Operations," ADM 1/7450B; Minute (5 Mar 01) by Custance, on Fisher to Admiralty, 25 Dec 00, "Mediterranean Stations," ADM 1/7465C; and Marder, *Anatomy,* 399.

43. Minute (2 Aug 01) by Custance, on "Mediterranean Fleet Exercises" (between NID 638 & 639), ADM 231/35.

44. Kerr to Selborne, 26 Feb 02, f.26, Selborne Mss 31.

45. Matthew Allen, "Rear Admiral Reginald Custance: Director of Naval Intelligence, 1899–1902," *The Mariner's Mirror,* 78 (February 1992): 61–75.

46. Fisher, "Invasion and Raids," ADM 116/942.

47. May to Fisher, 3 Jan 04, f.76, Add Mss 49710; Instructions to form Torpedo Design Committee in Admiralty to Fisher, 6 Feb 02, p. 229, P.Q.1904, ADM 256/40.

48. Statement by Captain Sir Robert Arbuthnot dated 6 Jan 04, cited in Bacon, *Lord Fisher,* I, 249–50.

49. Admiralty, "Application of Heat to compressed air for torpedoes; consideration of commercial offer" (13 Mar 03), ADM 1/7657; and Admiralty, "First Report of Torpedo Design Committee," Feb 04, appendix G. Superheaters, 132, ART 1904, Admiralty Library.

50. Selborne to Fisher, 14 May 04, enclosing "Memorandum" paragraph 7, cited in Kemp, *F.P.1,* xxi.

51. Beresford to Selborne, 31 Sep 04, f.16, Selborne Mss 18.

52. Selborne, "Naval Estimates 1901–1902," 17 Jan 01, 8, CAB 37/56/8.

53. Minute (2 Dec 03) by May, "Experiments with Torpedo-proof Hulls," (DNO, 1 Aug 03) ADM 1/7687; May to Selborne, 4 Sep 03, Selborne Mss 36; p. 37, ART 1903, Admiralty Library.

54. May to Selborne, 4 Sep 03, Selborne Mss 36.

55. Mackay, *Kilverstone,* 253–55.

56. "Complements & Training of crews for submarine boats," 8 May 03, ADM 1/7644; "Crews for submarine-boats," 29 May 03, ADM 1/7666.

57. Fisher to Balfour, 6 Dec 02, f.2, Add Mss 49710; also Fisher, Mediterranean Lectures, p. 73, FP4702, Fisher Papers 8/1.

58. Minute (30 Jan 01) by Kerr, "New Docket Submarine-boats," ADM 1/7515.

59. Bacon, *From 1900 Onwards,* 54.

60. Marder, *Anatomy,* 345.

61. Lord Fisher, *Memoirs and Records* (New York, 1919), II, 86–90. Speech to Royal Academy banquet, 14 May 1903.

62. Roger Keyes, *Memoirs of Roger Keyes* (London, 1940), I, 28.

63. Fisher to Sandars, 5 Dec 03, f.57, Add Mss 49710; Fisher, "Invasion and Submarines," ibid.; Fisher, "Notes on AJB's Invasion Paper," f.56, Add Mss 49710.

64. Lt. F. D. Arnold-Forster diary, 12 Sep 03, HMS *Dolphin* Submarine Museum; also Fisher to Sanders, 5 Dec 03, ibid.

65. Leaflet printed from Admiralty House Portsmouth, "A Visit to Portsmouth and Osborne on 12 September 1903," Esher Mss 17/3.

66. Fisher to W.T. Stead, 10 Dec 03, Stead Mss 1/27 [Churchill College, Cambridge].

67. Mackay, *Kilverstone,* 297.

68. Bacon, "Running of Submarines 31 June to 30 December 1903," 16 Jan 04, enclosed in Portsmouth submission 258/45, 25 Jan 04, ADM 1/7725.

69. Comments by Reginald Bacon on "Lecture on the Submarine by Mr Alan Burgoyne" (1904), *Journal of the Royal United Services Institute* 48: 1288–1305.

70. Ibid.

71. Bacon, "Report on Submarines," 31 May 03, p. 28, ADM 1/7795; Bacon, "Report on Suitability of R.E. Submarine Mining Stations," 13 Dec 03, in "Submarine Defences: Substitution of Submarine for existing Mine-fields at certain places," ADM 1/7717.

72. Bacon to Admiralty, 7 Nov 03 (S30250/03), "Type of Submarine boat for 1904," Ships Covers 185A; Bacon to May, 19 Dec 03, on "Staff for Submarine-boat Design," ADM 1/7745.

73. Minute (29 Jan 04) by May, on Fisher to Admiralty, 25 Jan 04, enclosing "Tactical and Other Exercises of Submarine boats 1 June to 31 December 1903," ADM 1/7725.

74. Bacon, *Lord Fisher,* I, 218.

75. Fisher, "Invasions and Submarines," Dec 1903, ADM 116/942.

76. Bacon, "Report on Running of Submarine," 31 May 03, p. 2, ADM 1/7795.

77. Ibid., pp. 13–14.

78. Fisher to Balfour, 5 Jan 04, f.75, Add Mss 49710.

79. Fisher to White, 12 Mar 04, *FGDN,* I, 305.

80. Fisher to May, 20 Apr 04, and Fisher to Esher, 23 Apr 04, *FGDN,* I, 308.

81. See reference to Admiralty letter M01441/03 of 13 January 1904, in Wilson to Admiralty, 23 Feb 04, paragraph 28, D53, ADM 1/7725; but see also Adm. Sir Edward Bradford, *The Life of Admiral of the Fleet Sir Arthur Knyvett Wilson* (London, 1923), 190.

82. Minute (29 Dec 03) by Drury, on the substitution of mines for submariners, ADM 1/7717.

83. Admiralty, "Great Britain; Torpedo Craft Manoeuvres 1904," N.I.D. report 754, p. 5, ADM 231/43.

84. Bradford, *Wilson,* 190; Admiralty, "Technical History 40," (1919), Admiralty Library.

85. Wilson to Selborne, 24 Feb 04, f.1, Selborne Mss 21.

86. Evaluations of maneuvers (22 Mar 04) by Admiral Wilson, p. 44, and (24 Mar 03) by Captain Bacon, p. 46, in "Report of Manoeuvres between Home Fleet and Submarines 8–18th March, 1904," ADM 1/7795.

87. Minute (22 Mar 04) by Wilson, p. 44, ibid; Wilson to Noel, 22 May 04, Noel Mss 5.

88. Report on "Loss of Submarine A1," A555, ADM 1/7718, and Report of "Court of Enquiry on loss of A1," A690/04, ADM 1/7719.

89. Fisher to Selborne, 31 Mar 04, Selborne Mss 24; Bradford, *Wilson*, 193.

90. Fisher to Esher, 20 Apr 04, Esher Mss 10/41.

91. Fisher to Knollys, ? Mar 04, Royal Archives, W56/113.

92. Report by Bacon on manoeuvres, 24 Mar 04, p. 46, ADM 1/7795.

93. Report by Umpire in Chief, Captain Robert Arbuthnot, pp. 50.53, ibid.

94. Marginal comments, Fisher, "Submarines: Second Postscript" April 1904, f.139, Add Mss 49710; Fisher to Sandars, f.100, Sandars Mss 748.

95. Bacon & Charlton, "H.M.S. Thames—Report of Manoeuvres recently carried out between submarine-boats & one division of the Portsmouth Destroyer Flotilla," 6 Jun 04, A1065/04, ADM 1/7719.

96. Ibid.

97. Minute (17 Jun 04) by Fisher, on docket cover, ibid.

98. Minute (1 Jul 04) by Kerr, ibid.

99. Minute (30 Jun 04) by May, ibid.

100. Wilson to Admiralty, 23 Aug 04, A1065/04, ADM 1/7719.

101. Minute (8 Sep 04) by Jackson (D.N.O.) on Wilson to Admiralty, 28 Aug 04, ADM 1/7719.

102. Esher to M. V. Brett, 14 Mar 04, Maurice Brett, *Journals and Letters of Reginald Viscount Esher*, 4 vols. (London, 1934) ii, 50.

103. Bacon, "Second Annual Report of The Submarine Flotilla," 1904, Appendix, Irish Sea Manoeuvres; "General Orders for Submarine-boats," ADM 1/7725.

104. Ibid.

105. Extracts from Chief Umpires report (Rear Admiral Hugh Grenfell) in "Torpedo Craft Manoeuvres," N.I.D. report 754, pp. 70–71, ADM 231/43.

106. N.I.D. report 754. "GB Torpedo Craft Manoeuvres 1904." Report by Admiral Charles Robinson p. 77, ADM 231/43

107. M. S. Partridge, "The Royal Navy and the End of the Close Blockade: 1885–1905," *Mariner's Mirror,* 75 (May 1989): 119–30.

108. Fisher, "Invasion and Submarines," appendix B, Dec 03, ADM 116/942.

109. Bacon, *The Life of Lord Fisher,* I, 217–18.

110. Fisher to Sandars, 22 Oct 03, and Fisher to Cecil Fisher, 22 Oct 03, *FGDN,* I, 288–89; Balfour to Selborne, 22 Oct 1903, f.35, Selborne Mss 34.

111. Fisher, "A Brief Précis of the Principal Considerations that must Influence our Future Naval and Military Policy," n/d [Sept. 1903] f.3, Add Mss 49710. The Admiralty stationery suggests that this was written before Oct 1903.

112. Mackay, *Kilverstone,* 291

113. See also Fisher to Sandars, 23 Jan 04, f.108, Add Mss 49710.

114. Fisher to Esher, 19 Nov 03, cited in Brett, *Esher,* ii, 54.

115. Fisher, "A Brief Précis of the Principal Considerations that Must Influence our Future Naval and Military Policy," n/d [August 1903], f.6, Add Mss 49710.

116. Fisher, "An Addenda" [Nov 1903], f.49, Add Mss 49710.

117. Fisher, "A Brief Précis of the Principal Considerations . . ." [Aug 03], f.6, Add Mss 49710.

118. Ibid.

119. Mackay, *Kilverstone*, 285–91.

120. Fisher to Cecil Fisher, 14 Sep 03, cited in Mackay, *Kilverstone*, 286.

121. Fisher, "Invasions and Submarines," appendix a, ADM 116/942.

122. Arnold-Forster, "Suggested War Office Reforms—for the personal information of Sir John Fisher and his colleagues only," 7 Dec 03, f.51, Add Mss 50305; Arnold-Forster to Selborne, 31 Jan 02, f.86, Add Mss 50280.

123. Arnold-Forster diary, entries 5, 6 Dec 03, f.116, Add Mss 50335; Fisher to Esher, 7 Dec 03, *FGDN*, I, 292.

124. Balfour, "The Possibility of Serious Invasion," 11 Nov 03, 3/1/18A, CAB38/3/71.

125. Fisher to Balfour, notes on "Serious Invasion" Nov 03, f.55, Add Mss 49710.

126. Fisher, "Invasion and Submarines," appendix A, Dec 1903, ADM 116/942.

127. Mackay, *Kilverstone*, 302.

128. Balfour to Fisher, 3 Jan 04, f.71, Add Mss 49710.

129. Fisher to Esher, 7 Dec 03, *FGDN*, I, 292.

130. Fisher to Sandars, 29 Dec 03, f.59, Add Mss 49710.

131. Arnold-Forster, "Number 1 Memorandum," 4 Dec 03, p. 6, Selborne Mss 120; Arnold-Forster's diary shows that between 4 and 6 December 1903 he was staying with Fisher at Portsmouth, f.115, Add Mss 50335; Fisher to Esher, 7 Dec 03, *FGDN*, I, 292.

132. Fisher to Arnold-White, 12 Mar 04, *FGDN*, I, 305.

133. Fisher to Balfour, 5 Jan 04, f.75, Add Mss 49710.

134. Fisher to Bridgeman, Jan 04, FP112, Fisher Papers 1/3.

135. Marder, *FGDN*, I, 282; the only hint that Fisher was lead candidate is in Selborne to Balfour, 6 May 03, f.27, Selborne Mss 34.

136. Noel to Selborne, 14 Jul 04, Noel Mss 5; King-Hall, diary, reporting views of Admirals Seymour (24 Aug 03) Beaumont (15 Oct 03) Noel (9 Dec 03), King-Hall Mss.

137. For Kerr's hostility to Fisher see Rear Adm. [later Adm. Sir] George King-Hall, diary, 2 Oct 02, 9 Dec 03, King-Hall Mss; Kerr to Selborne, 17 Dec 01, cited in Boyce, *Selborne,* 136–39; Kerr to Selborne, 13 Aug 01, f.113, Selborne Mss 27.

138. Fisher to Cecil Fisher, 14 Nov 02, *FGDN*, I, 266.

139. Sir Charles Walker, notes on "Recollections of Jackie Fisher," cited in *FGDN*, I, 243.

140. King-Hall, diary, 2 Oct 02, King-Hall Mss.

141. Battenberg to Fisher, 18 May 04, f.112, Selborne Mss 198.

142. Sumida, *In Defence,* appendix, table 17.

143. Appendix 1; the figure would have been above 12 million had Fisher not canceled 13 destroyers.

144. Mackay, *Kilverstone*, 305–8.

145. Fisher to Balfour, 5 Jan 04, f.75, Add Mss 49710.

146. Statement by Capt. Robert Arbuthnot, 6 Jan 04, cited in Bacon, *Lord Fisher,* 249.

147. Fisher, "The Fighting Characteristics of Vessels of War," 7, enclosed in "Admiralty House—Portsmouth," printed May 1904, ADM 116/942; also cited in Kemp, *F.P.1*, 41; and Sumida, *In Defence*, 52.

148. Ibid.

149. For instance, see memorandum (16 Jun 02) by Reginald Custance (DNI) on "New French Programme," f.68, Selborne Mss 158; Custance, "Memorandum on Sea Power and the Principles Involved in it," 1902, f.196, Selborne Mss 134.

150. Kemp, *F.P.1*, 40.

151. Sumida, *In Defence*, 53.

152. Ibid., 51–61; for later attempts see: Nicholas Lambert, "Concept of Flotilla Defence," 643–45.

153. Selborne to Balfour, 23 Aug 05, f.88, Add Mss 49707.

Chapter Four: Necessary Reforms

1. Mackay, *Kilverstone*, 313.

2. Fisher to Esher, 28 Jul 04, *FGDN*, I, 320; Note salutation in Selborne to Fisher, 21 Oct 04, cited in Kemp, *F.P.1*, 5. N.B.: There are at least three different versions of "Naval Necessities, volume 1." Wherever possible citations will be from the version edited by Peter Kemp and published by the Naval Records Society. But many of the most instructive prints are bound only in Fisher's and Selborne's private copies kept by the Naval Historical Branch and the Admiralty Library.

3. Fisher to Esher, 28 Jul 04, *FGDN*, I, 320.

4. Fisher to Esher, 21 Aug 04, *FGDN*, I, 324.

5. Sanders to Balfour, 14 Sep 04, f.120, Add Mss 49762 ,cited in Williams, *Defending the Empire*, 64; Beaumont to Noel, 26 Jun 04, Noel Mss 5, cited in Mackay, *Kilverstone*, 308; Fisher to Selborne, 2 Aug 04, *FGDN*, I, 321.

6. Fisher to Selborne, 19 Oct 04, *FGDN*, I, 330.

7. Sumida, *In Defence*, 52–54; some arguments Fisher employed may have been borrowed from papers written by his assistants, for which see Oscar Parkes, *British Battleships* (London, 1957), 468–72.

8. Kemp, *F.P.1*, 2.

9. Fisher, "Organisation for War," 14 May 04, cited in Kemp, *F.P.1*, 17.

10. Admiralty, "Report on the Redistribution of the Fleet in Home and Foreign Waters," Nov 04, ADM 1/7736.

11. Lt. Robert Wigglesworth (gunnery instructor, Whale Island) to Arnold White, 18 Nov 04, White Mss, box 3. Extracts from these documents are cited by Lt. Peter MacNamara (gunnery instructor, Whale Island) in "Concentration of Fire, its Effect and its Further: from experience gained during trials carried out by the different modern battle fleets and cruiser squadrons in the past and present. The uses of Director Firing for this purpose and the value of different ships using different coloured shell bursts," April 1909, in file on "Fleet fire and Concentration," special documents cabinet, HMS *Excellent* Mss. [Whale Island, Portsmouth].

12. Selborne, "Memorandum" [Distribution of the fleet], 6 Dec 04, CAB 37/73/159.

13. Ibid.

14. Ibid.

15. Ibid.

16. *Navy List,* October 1904. A "fleet" consisted of at least twelve ships of the line. "Squadrons" were formed of four or more ships.

17. *Navy List,* July 1904.

18. Selborne, "Memorandum," 6 Dec 04, CAB 37/73/159.

19. Ibid.

20. Battenberg to Selborne, 6 Apr 04, f.15, Selborne Mss 44.

21. Minute (2 Apr 02) by Selborne, f.156, Selborne Mss 158.

22. Selborne, "Memorandum," 6 Dec 04, CAB 37/73/159.

23. Admiralty, "Report on the Redistribution of the Fleet in Home and Foreign Waters," forth progress report, 1 Dec 04, ADM 1/7736; also cited in "Naval Necessities, volume 2," 495, Admiralty Library.

24. Selborne, "Memorandum," 6 Dec 04, CAB 37/73/159.

25. Fisher, "Fleet Reorganisation," Jan 05, p. 458, "Naval Necessities, volume 2," Admiralty Library.

26. Minutes (27 Jan 1898) by Richards and (4 Feb 1898) by Goschen, on crews for armored cruisers, in "Shipbuilding Programme, 1898–99," printed 11 June 1898, ADM 116/878.

27. Custance to Selborne, 31 Aug 04, f. 47, Selborne Mss 23.

28. Bacon, *The Life of Lord Fisher,* I, 287.

29. Selborne, "Memorandum," 6 Dec 04, CAB 37/73/159.

30. Selborne to Admiralty, 4 Apr 02, f.156, Selborne 158. Note marginalia by Selborne dated 21 Oct 04; also Arnold-Forster diary, November 1904, f.89, Add Mss 50341.

31. Ibid; also Kerr to Selborne, 29 Apr 02, f.62, and Kerr to Selborne, 15 Oct 02, f.167, both Selborne Mss 31.

32. Minute (21 Oct 04) by Selborne on copy of memorandum by Selborne dated 4 Apr 02, f.156, Selborne Mss 158.

33. Fisher, "The Strategical Distribution of Our Fleets," 25 Feb 02, FP 90, Fisher Papers 1/2; also cited in Mackay, *Kilverstone,* 260–63.

34. Fisher to Selborne, 4 Dec 04, enclosing "Rough notes for First Lord," f.59, Selborne Mss 42.

35. Kemp, *F.P.1,* 29.

36. Kerr to Selborne, 11 Dec 04, f.299, Selborne Mss 41.

37. Marder, *Anatomy,* 496; Williams, *Defending the Empire,* 64, note 34.

38. Marder, *FDSF,* I, 41–42.

39. Marder, *FDSF,* I, 41; see also Kennedy, *British Naval Mastery,* 257–58; Philip Towle, "The Effect of the Russo-Japanese War on British Naval Policy," *Mariner's Mirror* 60 (1974): 383–94.

40. Marder, *FDSF,* I, 41–42; idem, *Anatomy,* 489.

41. Kennedy, *Anglo-German Antagonism, 1860–1914,* 417–20; Monger, *The End of Isolation* (London, 1963).

42. Kennedy, *Anglo-German Antagonism;* Monger, *End of Isolation;* Zara Steiner, *The Foreign Office and Foreign Policy, 1898–1914* (Cambridge, 1969); idem, *Britain and the Origins of the First World War* (Macmillan: London, 1977).

43. See generally: Neilson, *The Last Tsar*, introduction; Keith Wilson, *The Policy of Entente: Essays on the Determinants of British Foreign Policy, 1904–1914* (Cambridge, 1985); idem, "The Question of anti-Germanism at the British Foreign Office before the First World War," *Canadian Journal of History* 18 (1983): 23–42.

44. Neilson, *The Last Tsar*, xii-xv, 118–43, 238–64.

45. See, for instance, Nicholas Lambert, "Economy or Empire"; idem, "The Opportunities of Technology; British and French Strategy in the Pacific, 1905–09," in Nicholas Rodger ed., *The Perimeters of Naval Power* (Macmillan, 1996).

46. Jonathan Steinberg, *Yesterday's Deterrent: Tirpitz and the Birth of the German Battle Fleet* (London: Macmillan, 1965), chapter 5.

47. Minute (21 Nov 04) by Selborne, on First and Second Progress Report, of the committee appointed to consider the "Redistribution of the Fleet in Home and Foreign Waters," ADM 1/7736.

48. Mackay, *Kilverstone*, 316.

49. Neilson, *The Last Tsar*, 238–64; Balfour to Lansdowne, 31 Dec 04, f.34, Add Mss 49729.

50. Fisher to Selborne, 28 Nov 04, f.33, Selborne Mss 42.

51. Ruddock Mackay, "The Admiralty, the German Navy, and the Redistribution of the British Fleet, 1904–05," *Mariner's Mirror* 56 (August 1970): 341–46.

52. Mackay, *Kilverstone*, 313–18.

53. Mackay, "Redistribution of the British Fleet," 344.

54. Marder, *Anatomy*, 496; for exact words, Selborne, "Memorandum," 6 Dec 04, CAB 37/73/159.

55. Minute (29 Jan 02) by Battenberg on Fisher's "The Strategical Distribution of our Fleets," Feb 02, FP86 & FP90, Fisher Papers 1/2; also cited in Mackay, *Kilverstone*, 260–65.

56. Aaron Friedberg, *Weary Titan*, chapter 4, especially 207.

57. Ibid., 192, note 201.

58. Ibid., 137.

59. Ibid., 194.

60. Kerr to Selborne, 11 Oct 04, f.282, Selborne Mss 41.

61. Battenberg to Selborne, 16 Oct 04, f.41, Selborne Mss 44.

62. Battenberg to Selborne, 20 Oct 04, f.44, Selborne Mss 44.

63. Memorandum (7 Nov 04) by Battenberg (initialed by John Fisher 7 Nov), FP139, Fisher Papers 1/4.

64. Battenberg to Selborne, 16 Oct 04, f.41, Selborne Mss 44.

65. Ibid.

66. Kerr to Selborne, 14 Oct 04, f.284, Selborne Mss 41.

67. Kerr to Selborne, 11 Oct 04, and 14 Oct 04, f.282–284, Selborne Mss 41.

68. Kerr to Selborne, 14 Oct 04, f.284, Selborne Mss 41; see also minute (n/d) by Kerr cited in Marder, *Anatomy*, 496.

69. Fisher, "Mediterranean Fleet, 1899–1902," p. 85, FP4702, Fisher Papers 1/8.

70. Fisher, *Kilverstone,* 262–63.

71. Quoted in Sumida, *In Defence,* 52–53.

72. Ibid., 51–61.

73. Fisher, "The Fighting Characteristics of Vessels of War," May 04, cited in Kemp, *F.P.1,* 26–27.

74. Fisher to Selborne, 2 Aug 04, and Selborne to Fisher 4 Aug 04, cited in Boyce, *Selborne,* 180–81.

75. Selborne to Fisher, 4 Aug 04, ibid., 181.

76. Undated minute by Selborne omitted by Kemp in his version of "Naval Necessities" cited by Sumida, *In Defence,* 52.

77. Sumida, ibid.

78. Ibid., 58–61.

79. Ibid.; The most important document is: "Meeting held at the Admiralty Saturday, 2nd December 1905," part 3, "Fusion design of battleships and armoured cruisers," in report of "Naval Estimates Committee 1906/07," printed 10 Jan 06, prints box, Crease Mss [Admiralty Library]; see also Lambert, "Concept of Flotilla Defence."

80. Battenberg to Selborne, 6 Apr 04, f.15, and Battenberg to Selborne, 4 Aug 04, f.39, both in Selborne Mss 44; see also minute (8 Aug 04) by Battenberg cited in Marder, *Anatomy,* 495–96; Battenberg to Fisher, 7 Apr 02, enclosed in "Notes for Successor," Mediterranean, 14 May 1902, ADM 1/7597.

81. Battenberg to Fisher, 10 May 04, MB1/T93, Battenberg Mss [Southampton University Library]; see also Battenberg to Selborne, 14 Jul 04, f.35, Selborne Mss 44.

82. First Progress Report, 10 Nov 04, p. 3, of the committee on "Redistribution of the Fleet in home and Foreign Waters," ADM 1/7736.

83. Battenberg to Selborne, 6 Apr 04, f.15, Selborne Mss 44.

84. Lambert, "Economy or Empire."

85. For evidence of Battenberg's viewpoint see: Battenberg to Selborne, 6 Apr 04, f.15, Selborne Mss 44.

86. Robert S. Wood, "Domestic Factors, Regime Characteristics, and Naval Forces," and Volker Berghahn, "Navies and Domestic Factors," in Hattendorf, ed., *Doing Naval History,* 67.

87. Sumida, *In Defence,* 18–28.

88. Mackay, *Kilverstone,* 306–7; and Chamberlain to Selborne, 10 May 04, f.137, Selborne Mss 39.

89. Quoted in Sumida, *In Defence,* 26–27; Selborne to Fisher, 14 May 04, quoted in Kemp, *F.P.1,* xvii.

90. Fisher to Esher, 17 Jun 04 and 28 Jul 04, *FGDN,* I, 319–20; Fisher to Selborne, 2 Aug 04, p. 322.

91. Marder, *FDSF,* I, 23–24; idem, *Anatomy,* 484.

92. Mackay, "Redistribution of the British Fleet," 341.

93. Friedberg, *Weary Titan,* 193.

94. Kemp, *F.P.1,* 25.

95. Selborne to Fisher, 17 Oct 04, f.3, Selborne Mss 42.

96. Ibid; also Chamberlain to Selborne, 3 Sep 04, f.155, Selborne Mss 39; also Mackay, *Kilverstone,* 307–8 (especially Beaumont to Noel, 26 Jun 04).

97. Selborne to Chamberlain, 11 Nov 04, f.157, Selborne Mss 39.

98. Memorandum enclosed in Selborne to Fisher, 14 May 04, cited in Kemp, *F.P.1*, xviii.

99. Selborne to Kerr, 16 Dec 01, cited in Boyce, *Selborne*, 136; Fisher to Selborne, 23 Sep 02, f.46, Selborne Mss 32.

100. Selborne, Memorandum, 6 Dec 04, CAB 37/73/159.

101. Fisher, "Navy and Dockyards," revised proof 14 Nov 05, p. 14, Cawdor Mss, Naval Library.

102. For a typical complaint on the shortage of trained men, see Beresford to Admiralty, 16 Mar 01, enclosed in Fisher to Admiralty, 29 Mar 01, "Observations of Rear Admiral The Lord Charles Beresford on Inspection of H.M.S. Hood," N327/01, ADM 1/7504.

103. Fisher to Selborne, 24 Dec 02, f.72, Selborne Mss 32.

104. Selborne to Knollys, 16 Nov 04, R.A. W56/147, enclosing memorandum addressed to King Edward, p. 1, Royal Archives, W56/148.

105. Sumida, *In Defence*, appendix, table 22. In 1889, vote A stood at 65,400; and Selborne, "Memorandum," 6 Dec 04.

106. Fisher, "The Personnel," Mar 07, p. 1, FP4824, Fisher Papers 8/23.

107. Fisher, "Navy and Dockyards," p. 15, Cawdor Mss, Admiralty Library.

108. "Effect on Personnel of Withdrawal From Sea of Ships of Small Fighting Value," Fisher, Jul 07, FP4942, Fisher Papers 8/26.

109. "Why we must continue to weed out," Fisher, 1905, Kemp, *F.P.2*, 9–13; Report of meeting held at the Admiralty on 8 Oct 05, p. 2, in "Committee on Navy Estimates," Manning the Fleet in War, 5 October 1905, ADM 1/7813.

110. Fisher to Tweedmouth, 24 Apr 06, *FGDN*, I, 79.

111. Fisher, "Non-Effective Charges in Relation to Long Service System," Jan 05, in Kemp, *F.P.2*, 47–51; for exact figures of the growth in costs see: Sumida, *In Defence*, appendix, tables 12 & 13.

112. Minutes (n/d) by Selborne, and (13 Jun 01) by Kerr, "Manning of the War Fleet in 1905/06" (Admiralty 6 Jun 01), ADM 1/7522.

113. Kerr to Selborne, 22 Dec 02, f.174, Selborne Mss 31; Fisher to Selborne, 23 Sep 02, f.46, Selborne Mss 32.

114. Fisher, "Non-Effective Charges in Relation to Long Service System," Jan 05, in Kemp, *F.P.2*, 47.

115. Minute (March 1902) by Selborne, f.136, Add Mss 50281.

116. Minute (28 Apr 37) by DCNS in "Distribution of the Fleet," ADM 1/9181. In 1935 the proportion was just 20 percent.

117. Appendix, table 5; Battenberg, "Manning Summary," [1911] MB1/T14/68, Battenberg Mss. The number of recruits entered during 1901–2 alone was 14,266.

118. Jon Sumida, "British Naval Administration and Policy in the Age of Fisher," *The Journal of Military History* 54 (January 1990): 1–26; for a brief survey on the importance of a balanced career structure see Lambert, "Economy or Empire"; Mackay, *Kilverstone*, 312; Admiralty, "Proposal to Reduce the Commission of Ships to Two Years," Admiralty 19 May 03, ADM 1/7658; Kemp, *F.P.1*, 19–20; Fisher,

"Navy and Dockyards," unrevised draft, 14 Nov 05, p. 5, 13–15, prints, Cawdor Mss, Admiralty Library.

119. Fisher, "Non-Effective Charges in Relation to Long Service System," Jan 05, in Kemp, *F.P.2,* 48.

120. Sumida, "Naval Administration on the Age of Fisher," 10–11; Admiralty, "Manning the Fleet Committee: remarks on Mr. McKenna's memorandum," printed March 1907, FP4826, Fisher Papers 8/23. (I am indebted to Jon Sumida for bringing this document to my attention.)

121. Fisher, "Navy and Dockyards," p. 15, 35.

122. Appendix, table 3.

123. Ibid.

124. Ibid.

125. Appendix, table 4a.

126. Appendix, table 3.

127. Ibid.

128. Kemp, *F.P.1,* 99, and Table K, 129.

129. *Navy List,* October 1904 and 1905; see also memorandum (4 Apr 02) by Selborne, f.156, Selborne Mss 158.

130. Kemp, *F.P.1,* 36–38.

131. Fisher, "Mediterranean Fleet, 1899–1902," p. 85, FP4702, Fisher Papers 1/8.

132. Marginal comment by Fisher on "First and Second Progress Report," paragraph 4, 10 Nov 04, by the committee for "Redistribution of the Fleet in Home and Foreign Waters," Admiralty 6 Dec 1904, ADM 1/7736.

133. Kemp, *F.P.1,* 99, and Table K, 129.

134. First and Second progress Report, p. 7, 10 Nov 04, of the committee on "Redistribution of the Fleet in Home and Foreign Waters," ADM 1/7736. To patrol the Far East, the committee recommended: 3 (rather than 6) armored cruisers; 2 (6) first-class cruisers; 9 (8) second-class cruisers; 7 (10) third-class cruisers. (Fisher's recommendations in brackets.)

135. Battenberg to Selborne, 20 Oct 04, f.44, Selborne Mss 44.

136. Minute (7 Nov 04) by Battenberg, MB1/T93, Battenberg Mss; Battenberg, Redistribution of the Fleet, Nov 04, FP139, Fisher Papers 1/4.

137. Kemp, *F.P.1,* 12, 41, 105–7, 128–34; and Fisher to Tweedmouth, 5 Oct 06, *FGDN,* I, 96.

138. Kemp, *F.P.1,* 13, 67; also *Navy List,* October 1905, 270b. N.B.: In all, there were 25 cruisers in reserve; also Table O showing the effect on the nucleus crew system of the retention of the five battleships in China in full commission, in "Naval Necessities, volume 1," Admiralty Library.

139. Ibid., 40–43.

140. Fisher, "The Subsidiary Services of War," Jun 05, cited in Kemp, *F.P.2,* 6.

141. Selborne to Battenberg, 23 Nov 04, f.64, Selborne Mss 44.

142. Balfour, "The Possibility of Serious Invasion: Home Defence," pp. 14–18, 3/1/18A, CAB 38/3/71.

143. Selborne to Balfour, 16 Nov 03, f.148, Add Mss 49707.

144. Selborne, Memorandum, 1904, f.158, Selborne Mss 158.

145. Fisher, "Naval Necessities, volume 1," p. 133, Admiralty Library.

146. Marginal comment by Selborne, ibid.

147. Fisher, "Defence of Naval Arsenals," cited in Kemp, *F.P.1,* 69.

148. Ibid., p.68.

149. Battenberg to Selborne, 19 Dec 04, f.75, Selborne Mss 44; Battenberg to Selborne, 28 Dec 04, f.41, Selborne Mss 39.

150. Fisher, "The Defence of Naval Ports," Nov 1904, f.156–160, Add Mss 49710; and Fisher, "Defence of Naval Arsenals," *F.P.1,* p.68–72.

151. Arnold-Forster to C.G.S., 3 Oct 04, f.16, and related correspondence f.4–19, Add Mss 50308.

152. Memo (17 Aug 04) by Battenberg and minute (21 Aug 04) by Selborne, "Submarine Mines in its Naval Aspect" (ex-WO 22 Apr 05), ADM 1/8879.

153. "Submarine Mines: Questions addressed to the Admiralty with regard to the Naval aspects of employment of submarine mines in British ports," 24 Oct 04, 4/1/40B, CAB 38/6/103.

154. Ibid.; and 58th meeting of CID, CAB 38/6/110.

155. Arnold-Forster diary, 22 Nov 04, f.108, Add Mss 50341.

156. Ibid.

157. Ibid.

158. Memorandum by the Chancellor of the Exchequer, 13 Nov 04, 4/1/42B, CAB 38/6/106.

159. Arnold-Forster diary, 22 Nov 04, f.108, Add Mss 50341.

160. Arnold-Forster diary, 23 Nov 04, Add Mss 50341; and 1 Mar 05, f.1, Add Mss 50344.

161. Arnold-Forster to Lyttleton, 22 Nov 04, f.175, Add Mss 50318.

162. War Office, "Submarine Mine Defences," 24 Nov 04, 4/1/43B, CAB38/6/111.

163. Admiralty, 25 Nov 04, 4/1/44B, CAB38/6/113.

164. Arnold-Forster diary, 25 Nov 04, f.125, Add Mss 50341.

165. Letters from Clarke to Balfour, 24 to 30 Nov 04, f.213–55, Add Mss 49700; see also George Clarke, *Military Fortifications* (London, 1894).

166. Minutes of 59th meeting of CID, 25 Nov 04, CAB 38/6/112.

167. Arnold-Forster to Balfour, 30 Nov 04, f.246, Selborne Mss 39.

168. Minutes of 60th meeting of CID, 2 Dec 04, CAB 38/6/117; Selborne to Balfour, 18 Feb 05, f.76, Add Mss 49708.

169. Selborne to Balfour, 16 Jan 05, f.70, Add Mss 49708.

170. Arnold-Forster diary, 22 Nov 04, f.108, Add Mss 50341.

171. Minutes of 60th meeting of CID, 2 Dec 04, CAB 38/6/117.

172. Conclusions of 64th meeting of CID, 1 Mar 05, CAB 38/8/19.

173. Arnold-Forster diary, 23 Nov 04, f.111, Add Mss 50341.

174. Selborne to Balfour, 16 Jan 05, f.70, Add Mss 49708.

175. For complaints of War Office procrastination see Selborne to Balfour 7, 18 Feb 05, f.73–76, Add Mss 49708; and undated War Office Memorandum, f.258, Add Mss 50318. The total value of the property and land transferred to the Navy amounted to £908,216. See also ADM 1/7860.

176. D'Ombrain, *War Machinery,* 59–63.

177. Arnold-Forster diary, 1 Mar 05, f.1–3, Add Mss 50345; Clarke to Balfour, 23 Mar 05 and 26 Apr 05, f.103, Add Mss 49701.

178. Arnold-Forster diary, 1 Mar 05, f.1–3, Add Mss 50345; Minutes of the 64th meeting of CID, CAB 38/8/19.

179. Williams, *Defending the Empire*, 49–55.

180. Ibid.

181. D'Ombrain, *War Machinery*, 61–68.

182. Fisher to Balfour, 24 Jan 05, enclosing "Submarines Used Offensively" f.165–77, Add Mss 49710.

183. Ibid.

184. Ibid.

185. Ibid.

186. Selborne to Balfour, 23 Aug 05, f.88, Add Mss 49708.

187. Cawdor (Fisher?), "Submarine Boats," March 1905, CAB 37/75/57.

188. Balfour, Arnold-Forster, Selborne, Lansdowne, Chamberlain, Cawdor.

189. Admiralty, "Submarine Boats," Mar 05, CAB 37/75/57.

190. Ibid., pp. 4–5.

191. Fisher to Arnold-White, 12 Mar 04, *FGDN*, I, 305; Fisher to Balfour, 5 Jan 04, f.75, Add Mss 49710.

192. Fisher to Cromer, 22 Apr 05, *FGDN*, II, 54.

193. Bacon to C-in-C Portsmouth, 15 Dec 04. Distance from Portsmouth to Dover is 115 miles. Completed in 11 hours; weather force 4 to 7, A1007/04, ADM 1/7719.

194. Bacon, "Confidential Report enclosed in Portsmouth Submission No.258/5, of 25 January 1904," ADM 1/7795.

195. According to Captain SS Hall in a minute written in 1910, the furthest distance traveled by a B type submarine, unassisted and uninterrupted was 1,420 miles, ADM 1/8220.

196. Perhaps the best illustration of Fisher's attitude when he was recalled to the Admiralty in November 1914, his first priority was to order forty-six submarines within three days of taking office and twenty more a week later. See Memo (11 Nov 14) by Director of Contracts on CPD1458/14, Contracts Dept., Branch 8, Keyes Mss 4/11.

197. "The Effect of Submarine Boats," November 1903; Fisher to Esher, 20 Apr 04, enclosing memorandum entitled "Submarines," 10/41, Esher Mss.

198. Fisher to Selborne, 29 Dec 04, f.84, Selborne Mss 42.

199. Admiralty, "Organisation of Torpedo Craft in Home Waters," 21 Feb 04, D342/04, ADM 1/7725.

200. Ibid.

201. Minute (8 Mar 05) by Ottley, in "Revision of arrangements for the constitution and concentration of Torpedo Craft Flotillas in War," D342/04, ADM 1/7725.

202. Appendix 1.

203. Ibid.

204. Naval Estimates Committee 1906/07, 10 Jan 06, prints, Crease Mss.

205. "Memorandum on the first meeting of committee on Naval Estimates 1906–07," 20 Jul 05, f.37–43, Add Mss 49711.

206. Ibid., table: appendix 2, "sketch estimates for 1906–07."

207. Ibid; and Fisher, "The Strategic Aspects of our Building Programme," p. 14, in "Report of Navy Estimates Committee 1905/06," 16 Nov 05, prints, Cawdor Mss, Admiralty Library.

208. Ships Covers 214, "Torpedo-boats 1–12." Jane's *Fighting Ships* (1906–7), 82. See also Crease Mss, 3/23, "Shortage of Torpedo boats," 10 Mar 09.

209. Edgar March, *British Destroyers* (London, 1966), 82.

210. Memo on CN25464/4 (22 Dec 04) by Dunston and Watts, Ships Covers 214 (Torpedo Boats 1–12). A coastal destroyer cost £41,000, a River class destroyer about £75,000.

211. Ibid., these carried oil sufficient for 8 hours at full speed or 1000 miles at economical speed.

212. I am indebted to Mr. Edward Cadwallader (late of the Royal Canadian Navy) for bringing these trials to my attention and providing me with a file of papers to overcome my skepticism. Among these is a note from the *Naval and Military Record*, of 16 Aug 1906, and an extract from the London *Times* dated 8 Aug 1906.

213. Hall to Keyes, 7 Oct 11, Keyes Mss 4/22 [Keyes Papers, British Library, London].

214. Fisher, "Financial Effects of Fleet Redistribution," f.201, Add Mss 49698.

215. Fisher, "The Personnel," Mar 07, p. 2, FP4824, Fisher Papers 8/23; see also Fisher, "Navy and Dockyards," Nov 05, p. 1, Cawdor Mss, Admiralty Library.

216. *FGDN*, II, 23.

217. Julian Corbett, *Some Principles of Maritime Strategy* (London, 1911) , 91–106, 114–15.

218. Lambert, "Concept of Flotilla Defence."

Chapter Five: Defending British Naval Supremacy

1. Williams, *Defending the Empire*, 79.

2. Enclosure of letter from Clarke to Haldane, 6 Feb 05, f.147–157, Haldane Mss 5906 [National Library of Scotland, Edinburgh].

3. Williams, *Defending the Empire*, 77–87.

4. Bernard Mallett, *British Budgets*, 148–254.

5. Michael Bentley, *The Climax of Liberal Politics: British Liberalism in Theory and Practice* (London, 1987), 114–16.

6. Note by Haldane for his autobiography, Aug 1926, f.15, Haldane Mss 5923.

7. Williams, *Defending the Empire*, 78.

8. Clarke to Haldane, 6 Feb 05, f.145, Haldane Mss 5906.

9. For the progressives see Peter Clarke, *Lancashire and the New Liberalism* (London, 1971) and "The Progressive Movement in England," *Transactions of the Royal Historical Society*, 5th series, 24 (1974): 159–81; Michael Feeden, *The New Liberalism: An Ideology of Social Reform* (London,

1978). For the radicals see H. Weinroth, "Left Wing opposition to naval armaments in Britain before 1914," *Journal of Contemporary History* 6 (1971): 93–120; Gerald Jordan, "Pensions not Dreadnoughts," in *Edwardian Radicalism*, ed. A. J. A. Morris (Routledge: London, 1974), 162–69.

10. Fisher to Cawdor, 23 Jan 06, *FGDN*, II, 67.

11. Haldane to Asquith, 28 Dec 05, f.194, Asquith Mss 10 [Bodleian Library].

12. Asquith to Tweedmouth, 10 Jul 06, Tweedmouth Mss A65 [Admiralty Library].

13. Williams, *Defending the Empire*, 96–99.

14. Sumida, *In Defence*, 21–25.

15. Asquith to Tweedmouth, 23 May 06, Tweedmouth Mss, A62.

16. Ibid., 24 May 06.

17. Admiralty, "Memorandum of a meeting of the Sea Lords at the Admiralty on Saturday, 26 May 1906, to consider future shipbuilding arrangements &c.," "Naval Necessities, vol. 4," Admiralty Library.

18. Tweedmouth [Navy Estimates 1907/8], 26 Jun 06, CAB 37/83/60.

19. For evidence that Asquith was handed a proof copy of Fisher's "Navy and Dockyards," dated 14 Nov 05, see covering note from Masterton-Smith (first lord's private secretary) to Tweedmouth, n/d, attached to copy of this paper in Cawdor Mss, Admiralty Library.

20. Tweedmouth, [Navy Estimates 1907/8], 26 Jun 06, p. 3, CAB 37/83/60.

21. Ibid., p. 2, & table B.

22. Asquith, "Naval Expenditure," 9 Jul 06, CAB 37/83/62.

23. Ibid.

24. Ibid.

25. The Admiralty case was set out in "The Balance of Naval Power, 1906," printed Apr 06, ADM 1/7876; for the clearest definition of the standard see: Admiralty, "Relative Strength of the British Navy," Jan 1905, "Naval Necessities," vol. 2, Admiralty Library.

26. Asquith, "Naval Expenditure," 9 Jul 06, CAB 37/83/62.

27. Ibid.

28. Ibid.; see also Tweedmouth to Campbell-Bannerman, 21 Nov 06, f.134, Add Mss 41231.

29. Asquith, "Naval Expenditure," 9 Jul 06, CAB 37/83/62.

30. Asquith to Tweedmouth, 10 Jul 06, Tweedmouth Mss, A65.

31. "Notes of a Conversation between Mr. Haldane, Mr. McKenna and Colonel Repington [military correspondent for the *Times*] at Mr. Haldane's Houses," 8 May 08, Esher Mss, 16/12.

32. Haldane to Campbell Bannerman, 10 Jul 07, f.175, Add Mss 41218; for Haldane's concerns for his own estimates see: Haldane to his mother, 14 Mar 06, f.115, Haldane Mss 5975.

33. Asquith, "Naval Expenditure," 9 Jul 06, CAB37/83/62.

34. Jellicoe to Fisher, 15 Jul 06, and "Remarks by the Board of Admiralty on the Attached memorandum," n/d, both ADM 116/3095; see also Tweedmouth, "Memorandum relative to meeting, under presidency of the

Prime Minister, on Thursday, July 12, at 10 Downing Street," 17 Jul 06, CAB 37/83/65.

35. Tweedmouth to Asquith, 10 Jul 06, Tweedmouth Mss A66; Capt. Charles Ottley, "The Admiralty and the Reduced Naval Building Programme," 28 Jul 06, Royal Archives, W57/75; it is possible that Fisher hoped all the 1907 ships would be laid down as battle cruisers, for which see Fisher to Noble [director of Messrs. Armstrong], 14 Apr 06, *FGDN*, I, 74.

36. Admiralty, "Admiralty Policy," Oct 1906, Crease Mss 2/22.

37. Asquith to Tweedmouth, 10 Jul 06, Tweedmouth Mss, A65 and A66 (two letters).

38. Tweedmouth, "Memorandum relative to meeting, under presidency of the Prime Minister, on Thursday, July 12, at 10 Downing Street," 17 Jul 06, CAB 37/83/65.

39. Sir George Clarke, "Memorandum," Jun 06, and "Remarks by the Board of Admiralty on the attached memorandum:—(Notes on comparative Naval Strength), July 1906, both ADM 116/3095; and Clarke to Ponsonby, 30 Jul 06, f.200, Add Mss 41213.

40. Bacon, *Fisher*, II, 95–97.

41. Knollys to Esher, 3, 8 Sep 06, Esher Mss 10/49.

42. Fisher, "Statement Regarding Admiralty Responsibility for the Strength of the Navy," July 1906, p. 1., and Clarke to Fisher, 18 Jul 06, ADM 116/3095; Bacon, *From 1900 Onwards*, 101–2.

43. Fisher to Tweedmouth, 9 Jul 06, *FGDN*, II, 83.

44. Ibid.

45. Esher to Fisher, 4 Feb 07, Brett, *Esher*, II, 219.

46. Fisher to Esher, 15 Oct 07, Brett, *Esher*, II, 251.

47. Minute (6 Oct 05) by Commander G. A. Ballard (ADM 1/7859) cited in d'Ombrain, "The Military Departments and the Committee of Imperial Defence," 49.

48. Clarke, "Notes on Comparative Naval Strength," June 1906, ADM 116/3095.

49. Admiralty, "Remarks by the Board of Admiralty on the attached memorandum:—(Notes on comparative naval strength," n/d [May or June 1907], attached to Clarke memorandum, ibid.

50. Admiralty, "HM Ships *Dreadnought* and *Invincible*," in Kemp, *F.P.2*, 260–81.

51. Jon Sumida, "The Quest for Reach," 56–70.

52. Admiralty, "The Building Programme of the British Navy," printed Feb 1906, FP4715, Fisher Papers 8/8.

53. Minute (17 Nov 06) by D.N.O. on Beresford to Tweedmouth, 16 Nov 06, in "Experimental Battle Practice carried out by H.M.S. *Britannia*," G17211/6, PQ 1907, ADM 256/43.

54. Sturdee to Sandars, 3 Mar 09, enclosing untitled memorandum, f.97, Sandars Mss 758; Balfour to Esher, 16 Apr 09, Esher Mss 16/13.

55. Ottley to King Edward VII, 8 Nov 08, Royal Archives, W59/67.

56. Balfour to Esher, 16 Apr 09, Esher Mss 16/13.

57. See Marder, *FDSF*, I, 57.

58. Marder (*FDSF*, i 57) argued that Fisher "knew" in the Spring of 1904 the United States Navy intended to order the all big gun battleships *Michigan* and *South Carolina*. It is difficult to see how. Originally these ships were designed to carry a conventional mixed battery. Not until late *1906* did the board on construction amend the armament from four to ten 12-inch guns, for which see "Proceedings of the Board on Construction," meetings of 21 Nov 05, 29 Jun and 27 Jul 06, Entry 179 (box 2 of 3), R.G. 80 [National Archives Record Administration, Washington, DC].

59. Clarke, "The Effectiveness of Naval Fire," Sep 07, copy enclosed in Tweedmouth to Fisher, 25 Apr 08, FP4982, Fisher Papers 8/45.

60. Esher to Brett, 3 Sep 06, *Esher* ii, 179.

61. Clarke to Asquith, 17 Jul 06, f.196, Add Mss 41213.

62. Marder, *FDSF*, I, 56.

63. "Barfleur," "The Growth of the Capital Ship," *Blackwood's Magazine* 179 (May 1906): 577–96; idem, "The Growth of the Cruiser," *Blackwood's Magazine* 180 (January 1907): 21–35.

64. Cited in Marder, *FDSF*, I, 56.

65. Campbell-Bannerman to Asquith, 4 Jan 07, f.220, Asquith Mss 10.

66. Ibid.

67. Asquith to Grey, enclosing memorandum on sale of two battleships, n/d [January 1907], f.253, Asquith 19; Fisher to Campbell-Bannerman, 4 Jan 07, f.281, Add Mss 41210.

68. Sumida, "The Historian as a Contemporary Analyst: Sir Julian Corbett and Sir John Fisher," in *Mahan Is Not Enough: The Proceedings of a Conference on the Works of Sir Julian Corbett and Admiral Sir Herbert Richmond*, ed. James Goldrick and John Hattendorf (Newport, 1993), 129.

69. Fisher to Corbett, 4 Jan 07, Corbett Mss box 13; for evidence of Corbett's receipt of this document see the copy in envelope containing various prints returned to Fisher's secretary by Corbett (on shelf in cellar) Admiralty Library; there is also a later version of this print among the documents handed to Admiral Richmond by Corbett's widow, Richmond Mss, 9/1 [National Maritime Museum].

70. Corbett and Ottley, "Recent Admiralty Administration," printed Jan 07, run of 20, Crease Mss box 3.

71. Corbett, "Recent Attacks on the Admiralty," *The Nineteenth Century* 61 (February 1907): 198–210 (the final version of "Recent Attacks on the Admiralty"); Fisher to Corbett, 15 Jan 07, *FGDN*, II, 113.

72. Corbett, "The Capture of Private Property at Sea," *The Nineteenth Century* 61 (Jun 1907): 918–32; idem, The Strategical Value of Speed in Battleships," *Journal of the Royal United Services Institution* 51 (Jul 1907): 824–39; in November 1907, a third article on the possibility of invasion was refused by the editor of *The Nineteenth Century*. Corbett never again wrote articles on current affairs.

73. Asquith to McKenna, Jul 08, cited in Stephen McKenna, *Reginald McKenna, 1863–1943* (London, 1948), 65.

74. Asquith to Campbell-Bannerman, 30 Dec 06, Add Mss 41210.

75. Campbell-Bannerman to Asquith, 4 Jan 07, f.220, Asquith 10.

76. Ibid.

77. Tweedmouth to Campbell-Bannerman, 21 Nov 06, f.135, Add Mss 41231.

78. Ibid.

79. G. H. Murray, "Naval and Military Expenditure," 20 Nov 07, CAB 37/90/98.

80. H. Weinroth, "Left Wing Opposition to Naval Armaments in Britain before 1914," *Journal of Contemporary History* 6 (1971): 97.

81. G. H. Murray, "Naval and Military Expenditure," 20 Nov 07, CAB 37/90/98.

82. Tweedmouth to Asquith, 21 Nov 07, in "Navy Estimates 1908–09" volume, Tweedmouth Mss.

83. Asquith to Tweedmouth, 21 Nov 07, ibid.

84. Weinroth, "Left Wing Opposition to Naval Armaments in Britain before 1914," 106; Jordan, "Pensions not Dreadnoughts," 162–69; Bentley, *Climax of Liberal Politics,* 114–15.

85. Tweedmouth, "Navy Estimates, 1908/09," 18 Dec 07, CAB 37/90/112.

86. Note from "10, Downing Street," 26 Nov 07, Navy Estimates 1908/9 Volume, Tweedmouth Mss.

87. Ibid.

88. Slade to Corbett, 1 Dec 07, Corbett Mss 6 [National Maritime Museum].

89. Vincent Badderly (secretary) to Jackson (controller) 29 Nov 07, outlining Fisher's suggestions, "Navy Estimates 1907/08" volume, Tweedmouth Mss.

90. Admiralty, "Memorandum by the Sea Lords for the Information of the First Lord," 3 Dec 07, "Navy Estimates 1907/08" volume, Tweedmouth Mss; copy in May Mss, box 9 [National Maritime Museum collection]; see also Mackay, *Kilverstone,* 387–92.

91. Slade to Corbett, 3 Jan 08, Corbett Mss 6.

92. Ibid.

93. Nash (PM's secretary) to Ponsonby (king's secretary), 1 Jan 08, cited in John Wilson, *CB—A life of Sir Henry Campbell-Bannerman* (London, 1973), 539.

94. Esher Journals, 8 Dec 07, and 7 Feb 08, Brett, *Esher,* II, 268, 281.

95. Esher Journals, 4 Jan 08 and 4 Feb 08, Brett, *Esher,* II, 272, 280.

96. Esher Journals, 7 Feb 07, Brett, *Esher,* II, 280–84. For a description of Haldane's tactics see "Notes of a Conversation between Mr. Haldane, Mr. McKenna and Colonel Repington at Mr. Haldane's Houses," 8 May 08, p. 7, Esher Mss 16/12.

97. Slade Diary, 7 Feb 08, reel 2, Slade Mss [microfilm copies, Queens University, Kingston, ON, Canada]; Esher Journals, 7 Feb 08, Brett, *Esher,* 283–84; further evidence of the duplicitous negotiations between Fisher and the Cabinet at this time can be found in A. J. A. Morris, *Radicalism Against War, 1906–1914: The Advocacy of Peace and Retrenchment* (London, 1972), 126–28.

98. Sir Philip Magnus, *King Edward the Seventh* (London, 1964), 375–76.

99. Asquith to King Edward VII, 6 Apr 08, cited in McKenna, *Reginald McKenna,* 23, 46–47; For further evidence of Tweedmouth's senility see: Asquith

to Venetia Stanley, 31 Oct 14, Brock and Brock, *H. H. Asquith: Letters to Venetia Stanley,* 300.

100. Fisher to Esher, 2 Feb 08, Esher Mss 10/42.

101. Mackay, *Kilverstone,* 179–83.

102. Alfred Gollin, *The Observer and J. L. Garvin, 1908–1914* (Oxford, 1960), 28–56.

103. Ibid., 46–47.

104. Ibid.

105. Tweedmouth to Campbell-Bannerman, 11 Feb 08, f.175, Add Mss 41231.

106. Tweedmouth to Campbell-Bannerman, 12 Feb 08, f.244, Asquith 19.

107. Churchill to Asquith, 14 Mar 08, f.10, Asquith Mss 11; Asquith to King Edward VII, 6 Apr 08, cited in McKenna, *Reginald McKenna,* 23, 46–47; Jon Sumida, "Churchill and British Sea Power: The Politician and Statesman as an Advocate and Antagonist of Royal Navy Expansion, 1908–1929," in Alister Parker, ed., *Sir Winston Churchill, Europe the Empire, and the United States* (London, 1995), 7–8.

108. Reginald Mckenna was one of the five ministers in February 1908 who renounced Campbell-Bannerman's settlement with the Admiralty and demanded cuts in naval spending, for which see Esher journals, Brett, *Esher,* II, 281.

109. Tweedmouth to Asquith, 11 Apr 08, f.87, Asquith Mss 11.

110. Fisher to Tweedmouth, 13 Mar 08, enclosing "Memorandum Respecting Large Armoured Cruiser to be Laid Down in 1908/09," Crease Mss, 3/22.

111. Ibid.; see also Watts (DNC) to May (3SL), 27 Nov 07 enclosing legend for "Cruiser E," ADM 1/24200.

112. Mackay, *Kilverstone,* 358, 371–72, 382–91, 409.

113. Fisher to Tweedmouth, 26 Sep 06, *FGDN,* II, 93; see also a delightfully ambiguous minute by Fisher (10 Nov 06) in "Admiralty file 30 Apr 1906," ADM 1/7876.

114. Fisher to King Edward, 4 Oct 07, *FGDN,* II, 141.

115. Marder, *FDSF,* I, 23–25, 126–29, 137.

116. Hand written insert on page four by Captain Charles Ottley on "Recent Admiralty Administration" (originally a draft article by Julian Corbett), printed Jan 1907, Crease Mss 3/6.

117. Admiralty, "First meeting of Committee on Naval Estimates 1906/7," 20 Jul 05, f.37, Add Mss 49711.

118. Fisher, "The Strategic Aspects of our Building Programme," Richmond Mss, 9/1.

119. Appendix 1.

120. Admiralty, "A Statement of Admiralty Policy," Command 2791, *Parliamentary Papers* (Commons), 1906, Vol. 70:6.

121. Sumida, *In Defence,* 70, note 172.

122. Williams, *Defending the Empire,* 79.

123. Ibid., Marder, *FDSF,* I, 126.

124. Ibid; Fisher, "Navy and Dockyards: a Statement of Admiralty Policy," revised proof, 14 Nov 05, prints box, Cawdor Mss, Admiralty Library.

125. Fisher, *Records,* 109.

126. Ibid., 108–9.

127. Sumida, *In Defence,* 61, 98–100.

128. J. D. Scott, *Vickers: A History* (London, 1962), 35–39, 46–52.

129. William Ashworth, "Economic Aspects of Late Victorian Naval Administration," *Economic History Review* 22 (1969): 492.

130. Clive Trebilcock, *Vickers Brothers,* 23, 52–57; idem, "Spin-Off in British Economic History: Armaments and Industry, 1760–1914," *Economic History Review* 22 (1969): 480.

131. Minute (6 Dec 1898) by Wilson to Richards, on armoured cruisers, "programme for 1899–00," ADM 116/878.

132. John Brown (Clydebank), Fairfield, Vickers, Armstrong, Palmers, Scotts, Beardmore, Cammell Laird, Thames Iron Works, Swan Hunter, Harland and Wolff, London & Glasgow, Laird & Co, Hawthorn Leslie, and Greenock Foundry Co.

133. Asquith to Campbell-Bannerman, 30 Dec 06, Add Mss 41210; Unsigned memorandum (but probably by Haldane) on battleships completed, 18 Nov 07, Haldane Mss 6108A.

134. Meeting held at the Admiralty on Friday, 6 Jan 1905, to discuss "Scheme of Shipbuilding and Repairs," in "Naval Necessities," vol. 2, 521–26, Admiralty Library.

135. Mackay, *Kilverstone,* 171, 193–95, 207, 254–55, 344–48; Fisher to Knollys, 3 Mar 05, *FGDN,* II, 53.

136. Fisher, "The Strategic Aspects of Our Building Programme," in Report of the Navy Estimates Committee, 16 Nov 05, p. 14, Crease Mss.

137. Admiralty, "Shipbuilding—Remarks on Votes for Further Programmes of New Shipbuilding in Successive years, and on the enormous advantages arising from rapid building," May 1905, "Naval Necessities," vol. 2, 117–19, Admiralty Library.

138. Ibid.

139. Admiralty, "The Advantages of Rapid Shipbuilding," appendix D in "Report of Naval Estimates Committee, 1906/07," printed 10 Jan 06, prints, Crease Mss; Bacon, *The Life of Lord Fisher,* I, 261.

140. Admiralty, "The Advantages of Rapid Shipbuilding," 10 Jan 06, Crease Mss, prints box.

141. Admiralty, "Shipbuilding in Royal Dockyards in Relation to Employment of Workmen," meeting held 26 May 05,"Naval Necessities," vol. 2, 112–16, Admiralty Library.

142. Admiralty, "Shipbuilding and Repairs," 6 Jan 06,"Naval Necessities," vol. 2, 525, Admiralty Library. The price of repairs and refits was 40 percent higher when done by private yards.

143. Admiralty, "Naval Establishments Enquiry Committee," volume 1, preliminary report, 20 Jul 05, pp.5–11, Naval Historical Branch. Copy also in ADM 1/7735.

144. J. M. Haas, *A Management Odyssey: The Royal Dockyards, 1714–1914* (University of America Press, 1994), 176.

145. Admiralty, "Naval Establishments Enquiry Committee," volume 1, preliminary report, 20 Jul 05, p. 114, Naval Historical Branch; also Fisher to Tweedmouth, 26 Sep 06, *FGDN,* II, 92.

146. Trebilcock, *Vickers Brothers,* 74–82.

147. In 1905/06, John Brown, Fairfield and Messrs. Cammell-Laird combined their gun making efforts to form the Coventry Ordnance Works.

148. Fisher to Tweedmouth, 26 Sep 06, *FGDN,* II, 92–93.

149. Remarks by Fisher and Selborne, in Kemp, *F.P.1,* 23; for the consistency of Fisher's views on this point since the 1880s see Mackay, *Kilverstone,* 187–93, 199–200.

150. Admiralty, "Scheme of Shipbuilding and Repairs," 6 Jan 05, and "Shipbuilding in Royal Dockyards in Relation to Employment of Workmen," 26 May 05, in "Naval Necessities," vol. 2, 112–14, 521–26, Admiralty Library.

151. Admiralty, "Scheme of Shipbuilding and Repairs," meeting 6 Jan 05,"Naval Necessities," vol. 2, 521–26, Admiralty Library.

152. Minute (20 Jul 07) by Director of Contracts, on "Report of Conference in Regard to Making Additional Articles at Woolwich Arsenal," (G11099/07) p. 107, PQ 1907, ADM 256/43.

153. Captain John Jellicoe, "Paper prepared by the Director of Naval Ordnance and Torpedoes for the information of his successor," 7 Jul 07, pp. 12–14, Admiralty Library.

154. Admiralty, "Remarks by the Board of Admiralty on the attached memorandum:—(Note on comparative naval strength), July 1906, ADM 116/3095.

155. "Memorandum by the Sea Lords for the information of the First Lord," 1908/09 Naval Estimates volume, Tweedmouth Mss.

156. For an outline history see Peter Hodges, *The Big Gun: Battleship Main Armament 1860–1945* (Naval Institute Press: Annapolis, 1981).

157. Memorandum by DNO, "Supply of Naval Guns—Proposed Arrangements with Armstrong and Vickers" (G15963/04), 18 Nov 04, pp. 662–79, P.Q.1906, ADM 256/41; Trebilcock, *Vickers Brothers,* 61–63; Admiralty, "Royalties on Gunmountings," ADM 116/528.

158. William McNeill, *The Pursuit of Power* (Chicago, 1982), 265–74, 290; Trebilcock, *Vickers Brothers,* 7–10.

159. Ibid.; see also Bacon, *From 1900 Onwards,* 183–93.

160. Minutes (12 May 06) by DNO and (6 Jul 06) by DNC, in "12-inch Double Turrets—Capabilities of Messrs. Vickers and Messrs. Armstrong for Annual Output," Apr 1906, pp. 723–25, P.Q.1906, ADM 256/41; McNeill, *Pursuit of Power,* 270–72; Trebilcock, "Armaments and Industry," 480.

161. Fisher, "Navy and Dockyards: a Statement of Admiralty Policy," p. 65, revised proof, 14 Nov 05, prints box, Cawdor Mss, Admiralty Library; Fisher to Churchill, 6 Dec 13, *FGDN,* II, 496.

162. McLaren (MD of Vickers) to McKenna, 21 Apr 09, ADM 1/8046, cited in Haas, *A Management Odyssey,* 176.

163. Minute (17 Jul 07) by DNO on "Report of Conference in Regard to making Additional Articles in Woolwich Arsenal," (G11099/07) p. 106, P.Q.1907, ADM 256/43.

164. Minute (25 Jul 07) by Controller, ibid.; Parliament, "Report on Production Possibilities of the Shops and Machinery of Royal Arsenal," 1907, SUP 6/657 [Ministry of Supply Papers, Public Record Office, Kew].

165. Testimony of Reginald McKenna, "Navy Estimates: minutes of a conference held in the Prime Minister's room, House of Commons, on Tuesday, February 23, 1909," f.130–137, Asquith Mss 21.

166. Trebilcock, *Vickers Brothers,* 1–25, 54–55.

167. Testimony of Reginald McKenna, "Navy Estimates: minutes of a conference held in the Prime Minister's room, House of Commons, on Tuesday, February 23, 1909," f.130–137, Asquith Mss 21.

168. Extract from F. L. Manning, *The Life of Sir William White* (London, 1923), 484.

169. Trebilcock, "Armaments and Industry," 481.

170. Interview with Mr. Travers at Elswick by J. T. Scott, 29 Sep 60, Vickers Mss 674; see also remarks by Mr. Lloyd George, "Navy Estimates: minutes of a conference held in the Prime Minister's room, House of Commons, on Tuesday, February 23, 1909," f.124, Asquith Mss 21.

171. Sumida, "Naval Administration and Policy in the Age of Fisher," 1–26.

172. Minute (17 Jul 07) by DNO on "Report of Conference in Regards to Making of additional Articles in Woolwich Arsenal," p. 107, P.Q.1907, ADM 256/43.

173. Sumida, *In Defence,* chapters 2–7; idem, "British Naval Administration," 6–7.

174. For the case of Adm. Sir Percy Scott, see Peter Padfield, *Aim Straight* (Hodder & Stoughton: London, 1966), 262–68.

175. McNeill, *Pursuit of Power,* 279–89.

176. Hugh Peebles, *Warship Building on the Clyde: Naval Orders and the Prosperity of the Clyde Shipbuilding Industry, 1889–1939* (John Donald: Edinburgh, 1987), 69–73.

177. Undated memo in Asquith's handwriting, f.167, Asquith 21.

178. See report of conversation between Fisher and Sandars in Sandars to Balfour, 2 Apr 07, f.34, Add Mss 49765.

179. McLaren to McKenna, 27 Jul 08, f.4, and Grey to Asquith, 17 Aug 08, MCKN 3/3 McKenna Mss [Reginald McKenna Papers, Churchill College, Cambridge].

180. McKenna to Grey, 16 Aug 08, f.170, FO 800/87.

181. Lambert, "Admiral Sir John Fisher," 643–45.

182. Gary Weir, *Building American Submarines, 1914–40* (Washington, DC, 1991), 1–4, 11–13.

183. McNeill, *Pursuit of Power,* 278, 289.

184. Lord Graham to Tweedmouth, 26 Oct 07, B447, Tweedmouth Mss.

185. Bacon to May, 7 Nov 03, enclosing memorandum on S30250/03 "Type of Submarine Boat for 1904," Ships Covers 185.

186. Minute (29 Jan 04) by William May, on Fisher to Admiralty, 25 Jan 04, in "Tactical and Other Exercises of Submarine Boats 1 June to 31 December 1903," A1052/04, ADM 1/7719.

187. Ibid.

188. "Meeting of Submarine-boat Design Committee," 23 Jun 05, Ships Covers 290.

189. Ibid.

190. Minute (4 Jul 05) by A. J. Durston, f.1, Ships Covers 212.

191. "Meeting of Submarine Design Committee," 24 Jun 05, Ships Covers 290; Lees (ICS) to Jackson (controller), 16 Nov 05, on CN20123/05, f.10 & 12, Ships Covers 212.

192. Note radius of action for Torpedo boats 1–12 on Docket CN25462/4, 22 Dec 04, Ships Cover 214. In 1908 Beresford claimed that no more than 34 of the 120 destroyers in the fleet were suitable for North Sea operations: Beresford to Balfour, 7 Mar 08, f.179, Add Mss 49713.

193. Head of N Branch to Fisher, 23 Jun 05, f.10 Ships Covers 212.

194. Submarine Committee to First Sea Lord, 23 Jun 05, f.10, Ships Covers 212.

195. Minute (10 Aug 05) by Fisher, f.10, Ships Covers 212.

196. Hall to Keyes, 7 Oct 11, Keyes Mss 4/22.

197. Minute (4 Jul 05) by Bacon, f.1, Ships Covers 212.

198. Some of these are found in Lees to Controller, 16 Nov 05, f.10–12, Ships Covers 212.

199. Bacon memorandum, 28 Aug 05, cut 4, Ships Covers 290.

200. Fisher to Balfour, 12 Sep 05, f.112, Add Mss 49711.

201. Bacon to Lees, 26 Aug 05, Ships Covers 290.

202. Ibid.

203. Ibid.

204. Ibid.

205. Lees to Jackson, 16 Nov 05, Ships Covers 212.

206. Minute (17 Nov 05) by Bacon, ibid.

207. DNC to Controller, 7 Aug 06, "New Construction 1906," f.159, ADM 116/1012.

208. Trebilcock, *The Vickers Brothers*, 105–8; Dash, "British Submarine Policy," (Ph.D. diss., University of London, 1990), 109–11.

209. Tweedmouth to Asquith, 10 Jul 06, A66, Tweedmouth Mss.

210. Fisher to Tweedmouth, 11 Oct 06, *FGDN*, II, 98.

211. Fisher to Tweedmouth, 4 Oct 06, *FGDN*, II, 93–95.

212. Tweedmouth, "Navy Estimates," 26 Jun 06, CAB 37/83/60.

213. Admiralty, "Admiralty Policy—Replies to Criticisms," pp. 38–41, reprint of letter dated 18 Aug 06, Crease Mss, 2/22.

214. Fisher to Tweedmouth, 11 Oct 06, *FGDN*, II, 98–99.

215. Fisher to Tweedmouth, 4 Oct 06, *FGDN*, II, 95.

216. Fisher to Tweedmouth, 5 Oct 06, *FGDN*, II, 96.

217. Tweedmouth to Campbell-Bannerman, 15 Oct 06, f.127, Add Mss 41231; N.B. during the summer of 1906 one of the seven battleships, HMS *Montagu*, was wrecked off Lundy Island.

218. Fisher to Tweedmouth, 11 Oct 06, *FGDN*, II, 98.

219. Fisher to Tweedmouth, 11 Oct 06, Tweedmouth Mss A104; Admiralty, Letter to the Press dated 23 Oct 06, in "Distribution of the Fleets, 23 Oct 06," ADM 1/7880.

220. Historians have also been confused: Williams, *Defending the Empire*, 122–23.

221. Ibid.

222. Admiralty, "Recent Admiralty Administration" (January 1907), Crease Mss 3\6.

223. Clarke to Esher, 25 Sep 06, enclosing clipping from the *Times,* Esher 10/39.

224. "Memorandum of meeting, under presidency of the Prime Minister . . . ," 17 Jul 06, CAB 37/63/85; also Tweedmouth to Campbell-Bannerman, 15 Oct 06, f.127, Add Mss 41231.

225. Clarke to Esher, 15 Oct 06, Esher Mss 10/39.

226. Ibid.

227. Marginal comment by George Clarke, on Balfour's "Draft report on the possibility of serious invasion," 27 Jun 04, f.43, Add Mss 49700; Clarke to Balfour, 16, 23 Dec 05, f.193–200, Add Mss 49702.

228. Admiralty, "Invasions and Raids," August 1907, p. 29, part 21(d), Richmond Mss 9/1; Clarke to Esher, 16 Nov 06, Esher Mss 10/40.

229. Clarke to Campbell-Bannerman, 15 Nov 06, enclosing "Notes on the redistribution of our Naval Forces," f.236, Add Mss 41213; Clarke to Esher, 16 Nov 06, Esher Mss 10/40.

230. Clarke to Campbell-Bannerman, 15 Nov 06, f.236, Add Mss 41213.

231. Mark Kerr, *Prince Louis of Battenberg—Admiral of the Fleet* (London, 1934), 219.

232. Clarke to Campbell-Bannerman, 15 Nov 06, enclosing "Note on re-distribution," f.236, Add Mss 41213.

233. Ibid.

234. Ibid.

235. Clarke to Ponsonby, 15 Feb 07, f.267, Add Mss 41213.

236. Fisher to King Edward, 22 Oct 06, *FGDN,* II, 103.

237. Fisher to unknown recipient, 24 Jan 07, *FGDN,* II, 116.

238. Table showing comparative value of "The Fleets of the Great Powers." Channel fleet consisted of six *King Edwards;* four *Majestics;* two *Swiftsures;* and two *Canopi:* Jane's *Fighting Ships* (1906–7), 386.

239. Hardinge to Knollys, 9 Jul 07, Knollys Mss, File 1907, Royal Archives; also Fisher to King Edward, 3 Nov 06, *FGDN,* II, 105.

240. Hardinge to Colonial Office, ? Nov 06, file 41147S [Colonial Office papers, Public Record Office, Kew], CO 537/342.

241. Esher to Fisher, 21 Oct 06, Brett, *Esher,* II, 199.

242. Admiralty, "Navy Reform—A summary" (January 1907), p. 7, f.98, Sandars Mss 755.

243. Esher to Fisher, 21 Oct 06, in Brett, *Esher,* II, 199.

244. Esher to Fisher, 4 Feb 07, Brett, *Esher,* II, 219–20; and Knollys to Esher, 4 Feb 07, "Your letter to Jacky has terrified him. He came to me about it this morning, and I sent him to the Prince of Wales who, I believe, has more or less converted him on the question of the distribution of ships."

245. Clarke to Esher, 1 Feb 07, Esher Mss 10/40.

246. Clarke to Campbell-Bannerman, 27 Feb 07, Add Mss 41213.

247. Battenberg to Thursfield, 23 Jan 07, cited in Mackay, *Kilverstone,* 362.

248. Admiralty, "The Home Fleet—December 1906," printed 2/07, Crease Mss, 2/27(i); The three *Invincible* were to have been attached to the Channel Fleet, "Admiralty Policy," October 1906, p. 32, Crease 2/22,

249. Beresford Enquiry, p. 40, CAB 16/9A.

250. Fisher to Lambert, 21 Jan 07, and Fisher to Tweedmouth, 18 Feb 07, *FGDN*, II, 115, 118; Battenberg to King-Hall, 24 Feb 09, cited in Mackay, *Kilverstone*, 363.

251. Fisher, "The Personnel," printed February 1907, copy sent to Lord Knollys for King Edward, Royal Archives, W58/62.

252. Marginal comment by Fisher on copy of "The Personnel," ibid.

253. Fisher to unknown recipient, 24 Jan 07, *FGDN*, II, 116.

254. Fisher to Corbett, 9 Mar 07, *FGDN*, II, 120.

255. Clarke to Ponsonby, 3 May 07, f.289, Add Mss 41213.

256. Fisher to Tweedmouth, 27 Oct 06, Crease, 2/21.

257. Fisher to Tweedmouth, 11 Oct 06, *FGDN*, I, 99.

258. Ibid.

259. Admiralty, " The Home Fleet," Dec 06, Crease Mss 2/27.

260. Ibid. also Fisher, "The Personnel," 25–3/07, FP4824, Fisher Papers 8/23.

261. Admiralty, "The Home Fleet—Part ii (for office use only)," Feb 07, p. 9, Crease Mss, 2/22(ii).

262. Ibid.

263. *FGDN*, II, 33–34; Mackay, *Kilverstone*, 357–58.

264. Browrigg to Sandars, 30 Nov 06, f.165, Sandars Mss 752.

265. Report by Captain Bacon, 19 Nov 06, ADM 1/7880.

266. Admiralty, "The Distribution of the Fleet," Jan 07, Crease Mss 3/2.

267. Speech by Lord Tweedmouth to the 1907 Colonial Conference, Apr 07, p. 130, CAB18/11A.

268. Admiralty, "The Distribution of the Fleet," Jan 07, Crease Mss 3/2.

269. Appendix 4.

270. "Notes of a Conversation between Mr. Haldane, Mr. McKenna and Colonel Repington at Mr. Haldane's Houses," 8 May 08, Esher Mss 16/12.

271. Fisher, "War Arrangements," 25 Jun 07, Crease Mss, 3/16.

272. Lambert, "The Opportunities of Technology," 41–59.

Chapter Six: Illusions and Realities

1. Fisher to J. A. Spender (editor of the *Westminster Gazette*) 22 Apr 10 and 8 Aug 10, f.82, 92, Add Mss 46390.

2. Morley to Clarke, 7 Aug 08, f.49, Morley Mss 573/42a,b [India Office Library].

3. Woodward, *Great Britain and the German Navy* (Oxford, 1935).

4. Marder, *FDSF*, I, 369.

5. Ibid., 372, 383–88.

6. Kemp, *F.P.2*, 316–17; Paul Hayes, "Britain, Germany, and the Admiralty's Plans for Attacking German Territory, 1906–1916" in Robert O'Neill, ed., *Strategy and International Politics: Essays in Honour of Sir Michael Howard* (Oxford, 1992), 97.

7. Neil Summerton, "The Development of British Military Planning for a War against Germany, 1904–1914" (Ph.D. diss., University of London, 1970), 23–51.

8. Mackay, *Kilverstone*, 369–71.

9. Paul Kennedy, "Fisher and Tirpitz Compared," in *Strategy and Diplomacy, 1870–1945*, 122.

10. Ibid., 114; Marder, *FDSF*, I, 401–4; Friedberg, *Weary Titan*, 193.

11. Marder, *Anatomy*, 489–91; idem, *FDSF*, I, 25, 36–45, 87.

12. Paul Kennedy, "The Relevance of the Pre-war British and American Maritime Strategies to the First World War and its Aftermath, 1898–1920," in John Hattendorf and Robert Jordan, ed., *Maritime Strategy and the Balance of Power* (Macmillan: London, 1989), 171.

13. Ranft, "Protection of Seaborne Trade," 15, cited in Avner Offer, *The First World War: An Agrarian Interpretation* (Oxford: Oxford University Press, 1989), 234.

14. Sumida, "Sir Julian Corbett and Admiral Sir John Fisher," 138–39; idem, "Sir John Fisher and the Dreadnought: The Sources of Naval Mythology," 6.

15. Draft of letter sent by Arthur Pollen to the editor of the *Morning Post*, 18 Mar 10, Pollen Papers PLLN3/6; I am indebted to Professor Sumida for bringing this document to my attention.

16. Ottley to Haldane, 11 Dec 09, f.209, Haldane Mss 5908.

17. Marder, *FDSF*, I, 383.

18. Offer, *The First World War*, 230–32, 236–43.

19. Ibid., 227, 242–43.

20. Ibid., 234.

21. Ibid., 227.

22. Sadly, two cases of correspondence on "war arrangements" dating from this period have been destroyed: ADM 12/1442, cut 50 (Mobilisation), reference to secret cases 0085 and 0086.

23. For an excellent essay on the evidentiary problems with writing the naval history of this period see Sumida, "The Sources of Naval Mythology," 619–38.

24. Williams, *Defending the Empire*, 143–47.

25. Ibid., 138–47.

26. Tweedmouth to Campbell-Bannerman, 7 Aug 07, f.161, Add Mss 41213.

27. Tweedmouth to Campbell-Bannerman, 22 Feb 07, f.152, and Fisher to Campbell-Bannerman, 17 Aug 07, f.163, both Add Mss 41231.

28. Fisher to Campbell-Bannerman, 17 Aug 07, f.163, Add Mss 41231; Haldane to Esher, 23 Aug 07, Brett, *Esher*, II, 246.

29. Mackay, *Kilverstone*, 381.

30. Fisher to Esher, 16 Sep 07, cited in Mackay, *Kilverstone*, 383.

31. D'Ombrain, *War Machinery*, 63.

32. Fisher to Ottley 18 Sep 07, cited in Mackay, *Kilverstone*, 383.

33. Haldane to Rosebery, 19 Dec 05, f.282, Haldane Mss 5906; Knollys to Haldane, 29 Oct 06, f.110, Haldane Mss 5907; Slade to Corbett, 15 Feb 08, Corbett Mss 6; Fisher to Sandars, 25 Jan 04, f.108, Add Mss 49710.

34. Fisher to Campbell-Bannerman, 17 Aug 07, f.163, Add Mss 41231; Haldane to Esher, 23 Aug 07, Brett, *Esher*, II, 246.

35. Fisher to Esher, 8 Sep 07, Brett, *Esher*, II, 248.

36. Esher to Fisher, 1 Oct 07, Brett, *Esher*, II, 249.

37. Fisher to Esher, 7 Oct 07, *FGDN*, II, 143.

38. Fisher to Esher, 18 Sep 07, *FGDN*, II, 135.

39. Ottley to Haldane, 11 Dec 09, f.209, Haldane Mss 5908.

40. Andrew Gordon, *The Rules of the Game* (John Murray: London, 1996). My thanks to Dr. Gordon for this information.

41. Fisher to Balfour, 29 Nov 07, f.21, Add Mss 49712; Sumida, "Sir Julian Corbett and Admiral Sir John Fisher," 125–40.

42. Campbell-Bannerman to Tweedmouth, 27 Aug 07, f.164, Add Mss 41231.

43. Marder, *FDSF*, 348.

44. Ibid.

45. see Julian Corbett, *Some Principles of Maritime Strategy* (London, 1911; reprint, Brassey's, 1988), 209–27.

46. D'Ombrain, "The Military Departments and the Committee of Imperial Defence," 220–25.

47. Testimony of Winston Churchill to CID inquiry on "Attack on the British Isles from Overseas," 3 Dec 13, Q.2558, p. 311, CAB 16/28A.

48. Repington, "Notes of a Conversation between Mr. Haldane, Mr. McKenna, and Colonel Repington at Mr. Haldane's Houses," 8 May 08, p. 5, Esher Mss 16/12; see also Jon Sumida, "The Sources of Naval Mythology."

49. Esher to Fisher, 1 Oct 07, Brett, *Esher*, II, 249.

50. Slade to Corbett, 28 Nov 07, cited in Donald Schurman, *Julian S. Corbett, 1854–1922* (London, 1981), 83.

51. Morley to Clarke, 4 Dec 07, f.9, Morley Mss, 573/42a, b.

52. Fisher to Spender, 22 Apr 08, f.82, Add Mss 46390. Note "Whitehall Gardens" notepaper.

53. Slade to Corbett, 16 Dec 05 and 26 Dec 05, Richmond Mss, RIC9.

54. D'Ombrain, *War Machinery*, 91.

55. Slade to Corbett, 11 & 18 Nov 07, Corbett Mss 6; Slade to Corbett, 16 Dec 05, Richmond Mss 9.

56. Slade to Corbett, 16 Dec 05 and 26 Dec 05, Richmond Mss 9.

57. Mackay, *Kilverstone*, 396.

58. Slade diary entry 20 May 08 and 7 Feb 08, Slade Mss.

59. Slade diary, Feb 08, Slade Mss.

60. D'Ombrain "The Military Departments and the Committee of Imperial Defence," 249–50, citing Slade diary, 23 Jul 08.

61. Slade to Corbett, 1 Dec 07, Corbett Mss 6.

62. Slade diary 13 Nov 08, Slade Mss.

63. Slade to Corbett, 3 Jan 08, Corbett Mss 6, N.B. phrase "i hear there is great trouble over money matters. . . ."

64. Slade diary, 1 Feb 08 & 22 Feb 08, reel 2, Slade Mss.

65. Memorandum by First Sea Lord, "Invasions and Raids," 22 Aug 07, p. 3, Richmond Mss 9/1.

66. Ibid.

67. Fisher to Prince of Wales, 16 Oct 07, *FGDN*, II, 147.

68. Slade, "Invasions and Raids," 16 Aug 07, Richmond Mss 9/1.

69. Admiralty, "Naval Estimates Committee—1908/09" (November 1907), p. 50, Crease Mss 3/19; See Sumida, *In Defence*, for the committees repeated refusal to accept Fisher's favored capital ship design.

70. Ottley to Fisher, 24 Nov 08, FP338a, Fisher Papers 1/7.

71. Slade diary, 15 Feb 08, Slade Mss.

72. Fisher to Corbett, 4 Dec 07, *FGDN*, II, 152; see also Corbett to Fisher, 4 Dec 07, Corbett Mss box 13.

73. Slade to Corbett, 25 Nov 07, Corbett Mss 6.

74. Slade to Corbett, 1 Dec 07, ibid.

75. For the strength of his feeling on this point see Corbett, *Principles of Maritime Strategy*, 10–11.

76. Schurman, *Corbett*, 88–89, 94; Mackay, *Kilverstone*, 392–93.

77. D'Ombrain, "The Military Departments and the Committee of Imperial Defence," 43–44.

78. Slade to Corbett, 6 Dec 07, Corbett Mss 6.

79. Slade to Corbett, 9 Dec 07, Corbett Mss 6.

80. Ibid.

81. Fisher to Esher, 12 Dec 07, *FGDN*, II, 153.

82. Slade to Corbett, 20 Dec 07, Corbett Mss 6.

83. Schurman, *Corbett*, 93–95.

84. Slade to Corbett, 24 Dec 07, Corbett Mss 6.

85. Slade to Corbett, 11 Jan 08, Corbett Mss 6.

86. Slade diary, 4 Apr 08, Slade Mss.

87. Ibid.

88. Conversation between Haldane and Fisher on "flotilla warfare," Meeting on Invasion Enquiry, 2 Apr 08, p. 239, CAB 16/3A.

89. Slade diary, 8 Apr 08; Fisher to McKenna, 20 Apr 08, f.1a, MCKN 3/4, McKenna Mss.

90. Schurman, *Corbett*, 96–98; Mackay, *Kilverstone*, 396–97.

91. Final Report of Invasion Enquiry, CAB16/3B.

92. Esher to King Edward, 2 Nov 08, Royal Archives, W41/79.

93. Vice Adm. George King-Hall diary, entry 21 Nov 08, reporting conversation between Sir Francis Bridgeman and his brother Capt. Herbert King-Hall.

94. The key Admiralty docket on this subject, "British Intervention in the Event of an Attack on France by Germany," which was seen by Professor Marder during the 1930s, had since disappeared from the archives (Marder, *Anatomy*, 502). Unfortunately Marder cites only part of the second half of the crucial memorandum written by the DNI on 26 Jun 05, and focuses upon the "promiscuous" discourse by Ottley on whether the Admiralty should take the risk of losing a few ships and deploy elements of the fleet still more aggressively.

95. Kennedy, *Anglo-German Antagonism*, 275–88.

96. Brian Ranft, "The Protection of British Seaborne Trade and the Development

of Systematic Planning for War, 1860–1906," in *Technical Change and British Naval Policy*, ed. Ranft (London, 1977), 1–22.

97. Ottley to Corbett, 1 Jun 05, Richmond Mss, RIC9.

98. Fisher to Fortescue, 14 Apr 06, *FGDN*, II, 72.

99. Ottley to McKenna, 5 Dec 08, MCKN 3/7, McKenna Mss.

100. Introductory Remarks to 1907 War Plans, cited in Kemp, *F.P.2*, 363.

101. Trade Division papers, ADM 137/2749, and files 137/2864 to 2872 cited by Offer, *First World War*, 230–32.

102. Ottley to Sir William May (second sea lord), 15 Sep 07, Tweedmouth Mss, A163.

103. Fisher, "Remarks on the War Plans by Admiral Wilson" [Apr 1907], ADM 116/1043B; Fisher to Grey, 23 Jan 08, *FGDN*, II, 157; Fisher to Tweedmouth, 23 Jan 08, *FGDN*, II, 158.

104. Wilson, "Remarks on the War Plans," n/d [1907], FP4231, Fisher Papers 5/13. N.B. This is the original hand-written copy by Wilson. The passage cited is heavily underlined by Fisher.

105. Minute (8 Mar 06) by Ottley memorandum by Beresford, 5 Feb 06, ADM 116/900B.

106. Ottley, "The Strategic Aspects of our Building Programme, 1907," 7 Jan 07, p. 34, RIC 5, Richmond Mss.

107. D'Ombrain, *War Machinery*, chapter 3.

108. Fisher to Esher, 15 Mar 09, *FGDN*, II, 233.

109. Lord Hankey, *The Supreme Command*, I, 39–40.

110. Marder, *Anatomy*, 504–5.

111. Slade to Corbett, 16 Dec 05 and 26 Dec 05, Richmond Mss 9.

112. Ottley to Churchill, 2 Nov 11, CAB17/8.

113. Admiralty, "Planned attack on Borkum," Apr 07, f.591, and "Plan to Seize Heligoland," f.608, volume 3, ADM 116/1043B2; Conversation with Admiral Lowry in George King-Hall diary, 14 Jun 09.

114. Minute by unknown NID officer on "Plan to Seize Heligoland," [1907] f.608–609, ADM 116/1043B2.

115. Introductory Remarks to 1907 War Plans, cited in Kemp, *F.P.2*, 364.

116. Testimony of Reginald McKenna, to the Beresford Enquiry, May 09, pp. 245–46, especially Q.2189, CAB16/9A; this evidence contradicts the interpretation of the Ballard report given in Offer, *The First World War*, 235, citing Lord Hankey, *Supreme Command*, I, 39–40; see also Ottley to Churchill, 2 Nov 11, CAB17/8.

117. Kemp, *F.P.2*, 316–18; see also Admiralty, "War Plans," ADM 116/1043B1.

118. Kemp, *F.P.2*, 316–18; Hayes, "Britain, Germany and the Admiralty's plans for attacking Germany, 1906–1916," pp. 96–116; The case of supporting documents to the "War Plans" (0073 now known as ADM 116/1043B) was created in November 1936 from miscellaneous papers in the Admiralty record office. All of the documents, including several supporting documents in typescript are unsigned. Although some historians have attempted to assign authorship of some of the documents to certain officers the "evidence" submitted to support their arguments is speculative to say the least!

119. Ballard to Fisher, 3 May 09 enclosing "Remarks on the framing of certain plans for war with Germany now at the Admiralty," in "War Plans" (Ady 3 August 1933) ADM 1/8997.

120. ADM 116/1043B2, volume 3, f.331; N.B. The War Plans were printed at the Foreign Office by Harrison's rather than the Admiralty printers.

121. See also a cryptic reference in Fisher to Tweedmouth, 13 Oct 06, Tweedmouth Mss, A105.

122. Admiralty, "War Plans and the Distribution of the Fleet," n/d, War Plans 1907/8, ADM 116/1043B1 (the other surviving copy of this preface exists in the Fisher papers).

123. Foreign Secretary Edward Grey was sent a copy; see Fisher to Grey, 23 Jan 08, *FGDN*, II, 155; An incomplete set also exists in the private papers of Lewes "Loulou" Harcourt (first commissioner of works) Harcourt Mss dep. 510 [Bodleian Library].

124. D'Ombrain, "The Military Departments and the Committee of Imperial Defence," 157–58.

125. Fisher to Leyland, 7 Nov 11, *FGDN*, I, 412.

126. Slade diary, 17 Jan 08, Slade Mss; Mackay, *Kilverstone*, 386.

127. Slade diary, 1 Feb 08, Slade Mss.

128. D'Ombrain, "The Military Departments and the Committe of Imperial Defence," 248.

129. Summerton, "The Development of British Military Planning," 130 et seq.; N.B. this thesis is widely cited as being authoritative on this subject, a judgment with which I do not agree.

130. Mackay, *Kilverstone*, 396, 405; Slade diary, 22 Feb 08, Slade Mss.

131. Slade diary, 20 May 08, Slade Mss.

132. Captain Osmond de Brock to Colonel Gleichen, 19 Oct 08, cited in Mackay, *Kilverstone*, 405–7.

133. Lewis Bayly, *Pull Together: The Memoirs of Admiral Sir Lewis Bayly* (London, 1939), 131.

134. Ottley to Esher, 8 Oct 11, Esher Mss, 4/3.

135. Invasion Enquiry, 1907/8, CAB 16/5a.

136. Slade diary, 28 Nov 08, Slade Mss.

137. Minutes of first and second meetings, CID, "Military Needs of the Empire," 3, 17 Dec 08, CAB16/14. N.B. Appendix 5, "The economic effect of war upon German trade," Admiralty, 12 Dec 08.

138. Third meeting of CID subcommittee, 23 Mar 09, CAB 16/4.

139. Admiralty, CID paper E8, 4 Feb 09, appendix X, pp. 45–48, "Military Needs of the Empire," CAB 16/4.

140. Slade to Asquith, 8 May 09, Beresford Enquiry, f.195, CAB 16/9B.

141. Fisher, "The Submarine Question," n/d [November 1908], FP4238, Fisher Papers 5/13.

142. Ibid., part 3.

143. Ibid.; Hall to Keyes, 15 Dec 12, Keyes Mss 4/22.

144. Hall to Keyes, 15 Dec 12, Keyes Mss 4/22; see Reginald Tupper,

Reminiscences (London, 1932), 110; Admiralty, "The Official History of the War," Technical History 40, Admiralty Library.

145. Fisher to Hall, 24 Sep 09, FP412, Fisher Papers 1/8; Jellicoe to McKenna, 11 Nov 09, f.6, MCKN 3/22, McKenna Mss.

146. Bridgeman, "Interim report of the committee on manning requirements," 18 Jun 09, p. 2, ADM 1/8048.

147. Navy War Council, minutes, ADM 116/3090

148. Jellicoe to Fisher, 18 Apr 09, FP413, Fisher Papers 1/8.

149. Ibid.

150. Ibid.; see also Hall to Fisher, 3 Aug 09, enclosed with Fisher to McKenna, 24 Sep 09, FP413, Fisher Papers 1/8.

151. Fisher to McKenna, 24 Sep 09, FP413, Fisher Papers 1/8.

152. Fisher to McKenna, 8 Apr 09, *FGDN*, II, 242.

153. Jan Morris, *Fisher's Face*, 161–62.

154. Fisher to Lambert, 5 Apr 09, *FGDN*, II, 240.

155. Morley to Clarke, 29 May 08, f.37, Morley Mss, 573/42a&b.

156. Fisher to McKenna, 8 Apr 09, and 14 Apr 09, Fisher to Ponsonby, 24 Apr 09, *FGDN*, II, 242–47; Esher to Balfour, 15 Apr 09, Brett, *Esher*, II, 383.

157. Esher Journals, 14 May 09, Esher Mss 2/11.

158. Asquith, "Naval Expenditure," 9 Jul 06, CAB 37/83/62.

159. Nicholas Lambert, "Concept of Flotilla Defence," 644–45; idem, "Economy or Empire."

160. Haldane to his mother, 24 Feb 09, f.72, Haldane Mss, 5981.

161. Fisher to May, 9 May 09, May Mss [N.B.: private collection].

162. Ottley to Haldane, 11 Dec 09, f.209, Haldane Mss 5908.

163. Sumida, "Naval Administration and Policy in the Age of Fisher," 1–26.

164. Mackay, *Kilverstone*, 365–66, 370–74, 412–15; Geoffrey Bennett, *Charlie B: A Biography of Admiral Lord Charles Beresford of Metemmeh and Curraghmore* (London, 1968).

165. Marder, *FDSF*, I, 90.

166. Marder, *FDSF*, I, 90–91.

167. Bacon, *The Life of Lord Fisher*, II, 30.

168. Ibid., 31–50.

169. Flag officers records: Charles William de la Pour Beresford, Admiral, f.39, ADM 196/86.

170. See untitled memorandum by Fisher for the Board of Admiralty on behavior of Admiral Beresford, printed June 1907, box 3, Crease Mss.

171. Kerr to Selborne, 16 Apr 04, f.102, Selborne 41; Kerr to Selborne, 5 May 02 (f.72), 16 May 02 (f.80), 1 Jul 02 (f.102) all Selborne Mss 31.

172. Kerr to Selborne, 1 Jul 02, f.102, Selborne 31; see also McKenna's exchanges with Asquith in CID p. 182 (Q.1767), p. 193 (Q.1863), CAB16/9A.

173. Beresford served as MP for: Waterford, 1874–80; East Marylebone, 1885–89; York, 1897–1900; Woolwich, 1902–3; and Portsmouth, 1910–16.

174. Gordon, *Rules of the Game*, 333. I am indebted to Dr. Gordon for this reference.

175. Beresford Enquiry, p. 67 (Q.721), CAB 16/9A.

176. File of correspondence relating to relations between Adm. Lord Charles Beresford and the Board of Admiralty, 1906–9, ADM 116/3108.

177. Fisher to Tweedmouth, 18 Feb 07 (2 letters), Tweedmouth Mss, A121 and A122.

178. Tweedmouth to Fisher, 8 Jun 07, Tweedmouth Mss, A135; Fisher to Tweedmouth, 27 Jul 06, enclosing undated memorandum by Ottley (DNI), *FGDN*, II, 84–85; Fisher to Tweedmouth, 31 Dec 06, Tweedmouth Mss, A109; Fisher to Tweedmouth, 10 Feb 07, A122, Tweedmouth Mss.

179. Beresford to Admiralty, 8 May 07, f.18, ADM 116/1037.

180. Fisher to McKenna, 26 May 08, f.10, MCKN3/4, McKenna Mss; Beresford Enquiry, p. 60 (Q.636–637), p. 68 (Q.733), p. 72 (Q.761), CAB16/9B.

181. Beresford Enquiry, pp. 51–64 (Q.582–664), ibid.

182. Fisher to McKenna, 26 May 08, *FGDN*, II, 177–79.

183. Beresford, "Plan of Campaign—Channel Fleet," 9 May 07, pp. 3–16, ADM 116/1043B/2.

184. Beresford, "Remarks on War Plan 1," 8 May 07, ADM 116/1037; Fisher to McKenna, 26 May 08, *FGDN*, II, 177; Kemp, *F.P.2*, 372.

185. Beresford Enquiry, remarks by Admiral Beresford, 29 Apr 09, p. 62 (Q.659–664), CAB16/9B.

186. Beresford to Admiralty, 8 May 07, enclosing general remarks on Plan A in "Correspondence Relating to War Orders & Position of C-in-C Channel Fleet etc.," ADM 116/1037.

187. Ibid.

188. Ibid.

189. Ballard to Fisher, 3 May 09, in "War Plans," Ady 3 Aug 1933, ADM 1/8997.

190. Fisher, "War Arrangements," 25 Jun 07, 3/16, Crease Mss; Slade to Corbett, 6 Dec 07, Corbett Mss 6.

191. Draft War Orders sent to Commander-in-Chief, 14 Jun 07, B250, Tweedmouth Mss; Fisher to McKenna, 26 May 08, *FGDN*, II, 177–79.

192. Tweedmouth to Fisher, 8 Jun 07, *FGDN*, I, 125; Transcript of meeting between Tweedmouth, Fisher and Beresford, 5 Jul 07, f.234–253, Add Mss 49711.

193. Ibid., f.254, Remarks, Fisher, 5 Jul 07.

194. Remarks by Fisher on Beresford to Fisher, 16 Jul 07, *FGDN*, I, 127; Minute by Fisher, on Beresford to Admiralty, 16 Jul 07, ADM 116/1037.

195. Fisher to McKenna, 25 May 08, f.11, MCKN 3/4, McKenna Mss; Minute (Jun 08) by McKenna in file of correspondence relating to relations between Adm. Lord Charles Beresford and the Board of Admiralty, 1906–9, ADM 116/3108.

196. Crease to White, 22 Jul 08, White Mss 76 [National Maritime Museum].

197. Fisher to Esher, 31 Jan 08, *FGDN*, II, 161; Fisher to McKenna, 16 Apr 08, *FGDN*, II, 173.

198. Fisher, "War Arrangements," 25 Jun 07, 3/16, Crease Mss.

199. Esher, Journals 9 Nov 08, f.188, Esher Mss, 2/11; McKenna to Asquith,

n/d [Nov 1908], f.8, Asquith Mss 21; Fisher to King Edward, 31 Jan 09, f.6, W59/69, Royal Archives; Fisher to McKenna, 25 Jun 09, f.25, MCKN 3/4, McKenna Mss.

200. "War Orders—Channel Fleet," 1 Jul 08, ADM 116/1043B2.

201. Fisher to Grey, 23 Jan 08, *FGDN*, II, 155; Slade diary, 8 Jan 08, Slade Mss.

202. Fisher to McKenna, 10 Nov 08, ADM 116/1037.

203. Fisher to Ottley, 29 Aug 09, *FGDN*, II, 263.

204. Beresford Enquiry, pp. 51–64 (Q.582–664), testimony of Admiral Beresford, CAB 16/9B.

205. Ibid., p. 62 (Q.659), Beresford speaking.

206. Ibid., p. 52 (Q.582).

207. Ibid., p. 10 (Q.112), pp. 51–53 (Q.582–584).

208. Ibid., p. 60 (Q.636), Asquith speaking.

209. Ibid., pp. 51–52 (Q.580–582).

210. Beresford Enquiry, final report, pp. 240–44 (Q.2128), CAB 16/9A; see also Ottley, "The Strategic Aspects of our Building Programme, 1907," 7 Jan 07, RIC 5, Richmond Mss.

211. *Parliamentary Debates,* fifth series, vol. 8. Mr Lee, 3 Aug 09, p. 1800.

212. Beresford Enquiry, p. 187 (Q.1814), CAB 16/9B.

213. Ibid., p. 51 (Q.582).

214. Ibid., p. 188 (Q.1818–1821); for a slightly more coherent explanation see remarks by Admiral Beresford on paper by Sir John Biles, "On the Protection of Battleships against Submarine Attack," in *Transactions of the Institute of Naval Architects,* 57 (1914): 268–70.

215. Beresford Enquiry, pp. 188–89 (Q.1820–1822), CAB 16/9B.

216. Proof of CID document No.7, "Small cruisers and torpedo craft—statement by Lord Charles Beresford," dated 29 Apr 09. p. 1, Royal Archives X40–42,

217. Admiralty reply to "Cruisers and Torpedo Craft," paper 24, 12 May 09, CAB16/9a.

218. Beresford Enquiry, p. 189 (Q.1822), CAB 16/9B.

219. Ibid. p. 187. Q1816. See also Beresford proposed distribution of submarines in "Plan of campaign—Channel Fleet," 9 May 07, p. 16, ADM 116/1043 part 2.

220. Bacon, *From 1900 Onwards,* 54.

221. Experiments involving concentration of fire by battleships: Beresford to Hamilton (inspector of target practice), 1 Dec 07, Hope to Hamilton, 2 Dec 07, Craig to Hamilton, 12 Dec 07, all Hamilton Mss, box 118A; Lt. Peter Macnamara, "Concentration of Fire, its Effects and its Future," April 1909, in "Fleet Fire," special documents cabinet, HMS *Excellent* Mss; also Sumida, "The Quest for Reach," 61.

222. Beresford to Admiralty, 9 Dec 07, ADM 116/1037 (copy in f.35 CAB 16/9B).

223. Ibid.; Beresford, "Second Plan of Action for British Fleet," 1 Jun 08, ibid., generally, "Tactical Exs—Channel Fleet, 5C.S., Scouts and Destroyers," D675/07, ADM 1/7926.

224. Ibid.; Minute (31 Oct 08), by Vice Adm. Francis Bridgeman (c. in c.,

Home Fleet) on report by Commodore T (Lewis Bayly), "Destroyers Watching mouths of Rivers," (H.F.2560/030), 4 Aug 08, ADM 116/1037.

225. Fisher to Tweedmouth, 16 Jun 08, B248, Tweedmouth Mss.

226. Sandars to Esher, 15 Aug 09, Esher Mss 5/31.

227. Ibid.

228. Beresford Enquiry, p. 314 (Q.2598) CAB 16/9B.

229. Sandars to Esher, 15 Aug 09, Esher Mss 5/31.

230. Balfour to Fisher, 15 Oct 10, F.P.499, Fisher Papers 1/10.

231. Knollys to Fisher, 19 Sep 09, *FGDN*, II, 267; Fisher to Esher, 20 Oct 11, *FGDN*, II, 396.

232. Fisher to Knollys, 24 Sep 09, Royal Archives, Add C/7 (Navy).

233. Fisher to May, 9 May 09, May Mss [N.B.: private collection].

234. Esher Journals, 14 May 09, Esher Mss 2/12.

235. George King-Hall diary, entry 25 Sep 09, reporting conversation with Adm. Charles Drury; Crease (assistant to Fisher), "Notes for First Sea Lord on letters from C-in-C Grand Fleet," 16 Apr 15, ADM 1/28268; Troubridge diary, 28 Feb 10, Troubridge Mss (Imperial War Museum collection).

236. Esher, Journals, 14 May 09, Esher Mss 2/12.

237. Balfour to Esher, 16 Apr 09, Esher Mss 16/13.

238. Esher to Sandars, 18 Aug 09, f.115, Sandars Mss 759.

239. McKenna to Grey, 12 Dec 10, f.226, FO 800/87 [Grey Papers, Foreign Office Papers, Public Record Office, Kew].

240. McKenna to Asquith, 17 Dec 10, MCKN 3/17, McKenna Mss.

Chapter Seven: Aberrations

1. Sandars to Esher, 25 Aug 09 and 8 Sep 09, Esher Mss 5/31.

2. Knollys to Esher, 2 Sep 09, Esher Mss 10/51.

3. Sandars to Esher, 8, 16 Sep 09, both Esher Mss 5/31; Marder, *FDSF*, I, 204–7; Stephen Roskill, *Hankey Man of Secrets* (Collins: London, 1970), 98.

4. Sandars, "Notes on interview with F.B. 12 May 09," f.216–220, Sandars Mss 758; Crease to Troubridge, 4 Jul 09, C3, Troubridge Mss [National Maritime Museum collection].

5. Fisher to McKenna, 12 Oct 09 and Asquith to Fisher, 26 Oct 09, *FGDN*, II, 272–73; *FDSF*, I, 204–205; McKenna to Knollys, 20 Oct 09, Royal Archives, W59/89.

6. Arthur Fanshawe, Wilmot Fawkes, William Acland and Charles Atkinson fell into this category; *Navy List,* January 1910. (Correct to November 1909.)

7. Ibid.

8. Lady Wester Wemyss, *The Life and Letters of Admiral of the Fleet Lord Wester Wemyss* (London, 1935), 87.

9. The *Navy List* for April 1909 shows May hoisted his flag on 24 March 1909.

10. Sandars to Esher, 25 Aug 09, Esher Mss 5/31.

11. Ibid. Sandars's source for this information was almost certainly his close friend Sir Francis Bridgeman.

12. Esher to Sandars, 26 Aug 09, Brett, *Esher*, II, 402.

13. Fisher to Churchill, 5 Mar 12, *FGDN*, II, 439; Fisher to Churchill, 14 May 12, f.124, Chart 13/43.

14. Nicholas Lambert, "Admiral of the Fleet Sir Arthur Knyvett Wilson," in *The First Sea Lords: From Fisher to Mountbatten,* ed. Malcolm Murfett (Praeger: Westport, CT, 1995), 35–53.

15. Fisher to McKenna, 12 Oct 09, *FGDN*, II, 272.

16. Lambert, "Wilson."

17. Ibid.; also Fisher to Yexley, 13 Jan 10, *FGDN*, II, 290.

18. Marder, *FGDN*, II, 285. ft.1.

19. Ibid.; Esher to Brett, 13 Sep 09, Brett, *Esher*, II, 409.

20. Fisher to King Edward VII, 27 Nov 09, Royal Archives, W59/93; see also very similar texts in Fisher to McKenna, 17 Nov 09, *FGDN*, II, 285; Fisher to Esher, 5 Aug 10, *FGDN*, II, 333–34.

21. Fisher to McKenna, 8 Nov 09, *FGDN*, II, 217.

22. Esher to Sandars, 18 Aug 09, f.115, Sandars Mss 759.

23. Morley to Clarke, 20 Aug 09, f.113, Morley Mss, Eur.D.573.47/49.

24. See Fisher's stunned reaction to the news of Wilson's appointment to the CID in Fisher to McKenna, 14, 19 Apr 09, *FGDN*, II, 244–46.

25. Lambert, "Wilson," 35–38.

26. McKenna to Wilson, 19 Nov 09, and Wilson to McKenna, 20 Nov 09, both f.43a, McKenna Mss, 3/9; Fisher to Knollys, 3 Nov 09, *FGDN*, II, 276.

27. Fisher to Knollys, 1 Dec 09, Royal Archives, W59/93a.

28. Roskill, *Hankey Man of Secrets,* 98; Beresford to Balfour, 12 Dec 09, *FDSF,* I, 212.

29. Oscar Parkes, *British Battleships,* 543.

30. Bridgeman to Fisher, 21 Nov 09, *FGDN*, II, 282.

31. Knollys to Esher, 30 Dec 09, cited in Marder, *FDSF,* I, 213.

32. Battenberg to Hamilton, 5 Dec 10, Hamilton Mss 118A [National Maritime Museum].

33. Fisher to McKenna, 8 Nov 09, MCKN3/4, McKenna Mss.

34. Fisher to Pamela McKenna, ? Dec 10, *FGDN*, II, 344; Fisher to McKenna, 23 Feb 11, *FGDN*, II, 356.

35. Fisher to White, 13 Nov 09, *FGDN*, II, 277.

36. Lambert, "Wilson."

37. Troubridge diary, 7 Jan and 1 Feb 10, Troubridge Mss (IWM).

38. Fisher to White, 12 Jan 10, *FGDN*, II, 297; Fisher to Esher, 20 Oct 11, *FGDN*, II, 395.

39. Lambert, "Wilson"; see also: Maj. Adrian Grant-Duff, diary, 21–25 Jul 11, Grant-Duff Mss, DC/MISC/77 [Imperial War Museum]; and for an example of Wilson's reluctance to delegate, Wilson to Sir Arthur Nicholson (Foreign Office), 8 Jun 11, f.155a, FO 371/1140/19617.

40. Esher to MV Brett, 4 Jan 10, *Esher,* II, 433; Bridgeman seems to have been a habitual victim of bullies. During the 1890s while serving as executive officer to the infamous Captain "Pompo" Henage, Bridgeman reportedly locked himself in his cabin and refused to come out until given a transfer; see Andrew Gordon, *Rules of the Game,* 175.

41. Troubridge diary, 7 Jan 10, Troubridge Mss (IWM); Conversation between Esher and McKenna, *FDSF*, I, 213; Lambert, "Wilson," 39.

42. Troubridge Diary, 7 Jan 10, Troubridge Mss (IWM); see similar observations in: Pollen to Slade, 24 Jan 10, and Graham Greene (secretary to the Admiralty) to Slade, 16 May 11, both in reel 1, Slade Mss.

43. Selborne, "Memorandum," March 1901, f.158/p. 146, Selborne Mss 158.

44. See chapter 2.

45. Selborne to Balfour, 20 May 15, f.251, Add Mss 49707; Selborne to Wilson, 19 Mar 01, Selborne Mss 28.

46. Fisher to Esher, 3 Jan 10, Esher Mss 10/43.

47. Fisher to Grey, 23 Jan 08, and Fisher to Tweedmouth, 23 Jan 08, in Marder, *FGDN*, II, 155–57.

48. Offer, *The First World War*, 285, 296–98; testimony of Admiral Wilson to the CID, 24 Jun 09, pp. 305–15, CAB 16/9A.

49. Esher Journals, 21 Aug 08, Esher Mss 2/11.

50. Fisher to Grey, and Fisher to Tweedmouth, both 23 Jan 08, *FGDN*, II, 155–58; testimony of Sir Arthur Wilson, 24 Jun 09, p. 308, Q.2540, CAB 16/9A.

51. For the background to the crisis see Steiner, *Origins of the First World War*, 66–78, 197–203.

52. Nicholas d'Ombrain, "The Imperial General Staff and the Military Policy of a 'Continental Strategy' during the 1911 International Crisis," *Military Affairs* (February 1970): 88–93.

53. Minutes of 114th meeting of CID, 23 Aug 11, p. 11, Sir Arthur Wilson speaking, CAB 2/2.

54. Ibid. [my emphasis]

55. Ibid.

56. Asquith to Haldane, 31 Aug 11, f.140, Haldane Mss 5909; Haldane, "Memorandum of Events between 1906 and 1915" [Apr 1916], f.390, Haldane Mss 6109 (II).

57. Minutes of 114th meeting of CID, A. K. Wilson, p. 14, CAB2/2; Asquith to Crewe, ? Aug 11, cited in Roy Jenkins, *Asquith* (London, 1964) 164.

58. Hand-written statement by Battenberg, 24 Jun 16, Battenberg Mss, MB1/T39/378; see also views of Francis Bridgeman (c. in c., Home Fleet) , Bridgeman to Sandars, 12 Jan 15, f.12, Sandars Mss, 768.

59. Ottley to Churchill (first lord of the Admiralty), 2 Nov 11, CAB 17/8.

60. Graham Green to Slade, 16 May 11, and Capt. Osmond de Brock to Slade, 28 Dec 11, both reel 1, Slade Mss; see also "Minutes of Navy War Council," p. 4, which shows that between April 1910 and November 1911 not a single meeting of the council was convened, ADM 116/3090.

61. Ottley to Churchill, 2 Nov 11, CAB 17/8; for the results of this meeting see also chapter 8.

62. Ibid.; Ottley also cited the findings of the 1905 joint service committee on amphibious operations chaired by General Plummer which concluded that "the operation of [opposed] landing in the face of a determined enemy was out of the question."

63. Hayes, "The Admiralty's Plans for Attacking German Territory," 95–116, especially 99, 103–4, 111–12; Mackay, *Kilverstone*, 431; *FDSF*, I, 245.

64. "Heligoland Bight Blockade Squadron—Preliminary War Orders for Commodore T," issued by W. H. May, January 1911 and approved by Admiralty on paper M071/11, 1 Mar 11, ADM 116/3096.

65. Lambert, *Wilson;* see also: Bridgeman to Sandars, 12 Jan 15, f.12, Sandars Mss 768.

66. Callaghan to Admiralty, 9 Jan 12, handwritten addenda "War Plans—pages 1–24, Remarks by C-in-C Home Fleet," (VII) section on War Stations, ADM 116/3096.

67. Vice Admiral commanding 1st and 2nd Divisions (Callaghan) to Admiralty, 31 Aug 11, "Blockade of North Sea Coast of German Empire," ADM 1/8132.

68. Bridgeman to Sandars, 12 Jan 15, f.12, Sandars Mss 768.

69. Wilson, "Remarks on War Plans," April 1907, FP4231, Fisher Papers 5/13.

70. Ibid., p. 6.

71. Evidence of Sir Arthur Wilson, 24 Jun 09, p. 308, Q.2540, CAB 16/9B.

72. Answers to: Q.2602, p. 314l; Q.2539, p. 307; Q.2541, p. 308, and p. 315, ibid.; see also Beresford, "Plan of Campaign—Channel Fleet," 9 May 07, pp. 3–16, ADM 116/1043B.

73. Evidence of Sir Arthur Wilson, 24 Jun 09, Q.2539, p. 307 and Q.2541, p. 308; Q.2554, p. 309, all CAB 16/9A.

74. Wilson, Q.2596–2599, Q.2602, Q.2604, p. 314, ibid.

75. Bradford, *Wilson,* viii.

76. Keyes, *Memoirs,* 23.

77. Minutes of the 114th meeting of the CID, A. K. Wilson, p. 14, CAB2/2.

78. Ibid.

79. Ibid.

80. Ibid.

81. Churchill citing a report by Wilson, Q.2741, p. 324, CAB 16/28A.

82. Testimony by Wilson (3 Dec 13) Q.2661, p. 311, ibid.

83. See chapter 3.

84. Wilson to Admiralty, 22 Mar 04, "Reports of Manoeuvres between Home Fleet and Submarines," ADM 1/7725.

85. Extract from report by vice admiral commanding blue fleet, August 1904, NID 754, appendix 2, p. 72, ADM 231/43.

86. Wilson to Bradford, 14 Feb 15, cited in Bradford, *Wilson,* 193, 242.

87. Minute (16 Apr 10) by Wilson, G0230/10, f.38, Ships Covers 338.

88. Keyes to Battenberg (then commanding 3rd and 4th divisions, Home Fleet), 3 Jul 11, Keyes Mss, 4/13.

89. Keyes to Rear Adm. Lewes Bayly (commanding blue fleet), 1 Jul 11, Keyes Mss 4/13.

90. Hall to Keyes, 15 Dec 12, Keyes Mss 4/22. Reference to formation of subcommittee on 4 Apr 09.

91. Minute (29 Dec 10) by Wilson, on "Proposals of Fitting to Submarine to Make Vessel Dive," ADM 1/8132; Plans for modifications to A1, f.71, Ships Covers 290A.

92. "Submarine Committee: General Summary," 21 Sep 12, f.39, Ships Covers 290B.

93. Report by Dr. R. W. Boyle, dated 31 Dec 18, p. 17, ADM 116/1430, cited in Mackay, *Kilverstone*, 508.

94. Appendix 1.

95. "Estimate of the Manning Requirements of the Navy up to 1914," printed Nov 1910, but dated July, MB1/T7/40B, Battenberg Mss.

96. Fisher to Jellicoe, 10 Jan 11, f.6, Add Mss 49006.

97. Neville to SS Hall. 16 Feb 10, X1677/10, ADM 1/8120.

98. Neville (3, 4 BS) to Keyes, 23 Jan 11, Keyes Mss 4/13.

99. Battenberg (3 BS) to Keyes, 12 Apr 11, Keyes Mss 4/13

100. May to Battenberg, 1 May 11, Keyes Mss 4/13.

101. "Enclosure No.14 to Local War Orders," 26 Dec 11, and Battenberg to Keyes, 2 Sep 11, both in Keyes Mss 4/13.

102. Neville to Hall, 16 Feb 10, "Destroyer Flotillas Reorganisation," X1677/10, ADM 1/8120; Keyes to May, 11 Feb 11, and Bridgeman to Keyes, 1 May 11, both Keyes Mss 4/13; Minutes (19 Dec 11) by VA Hamilton on "Captain (D) Conference," in "Flotilla Scouts, Cruisers and Depot Ships," ADM 1/8273.

103. Sturdee to Sandars, Mar 1909, f.97, Sandars Mss 758; see also remarks by Vice Admiral Sturdee on "The Submarine Menace" dated 1913, umpire's report for 1913 Manoeuvres, part 5, ADM 116/3381.

104. May to Admiralty, 3 May 10; May to Neville, 19 Jan 11; Keyes to May, 11 Feb 11; and May to Battenberg, 1 May 11, all Keyes Mss 4/13; Keyes, "Submarines, Memorandum On," X1596, ADM 1/8119.

105. Keyes, "Memorandum by Captain (S) to Commanding Officers of all Ships," X1596/10, ADM 1/8119.

106. "Preliminary War Orders for Commodore (T)," by Admiral May, 11 Feb 11, p. 8., and "Revision of War orders for Submarines," Minute (23 Mar 11) Wilson to DNM, both in ADM 116/3096; Minute (24 Nov 10) by D.N.M. (Capt. Herbert King-Hall) on "Organisation of Submarine Flotillas," reference to "offensive sections," X1763/10, ADM 1/8121; "Submarine Committee Report No 14." Minute by May to Admiralty, 15 Aug 10, ADM 1/8128.

107. Minute (24 Nov 10) by King-Hall (DNM) on chart showing option for war stations for submarines enclosed in Hall to Neville, 11 Nov 10, X1763/10, ADM 1/8121; Minute (23 Mar 11) Wilson to King-Hall (DNM), on "Revision of War Orders for Submarines," ADM 116/3096.

108. Battenberg (c. in c., Atlantic Fleet) to McKenna, 20 Apr 09, MB1/T6/37, Battenberg Mss.

109. For a survey of "conflict in style" in fleet tactics from 1890–1916, see Andrew Gordon, *Rules of the Game.*

110. E. E. Bradford to MacNamara, n/d [1909], in folder on "Fleet fire and Concentration," June 1909, special documents cabinet, HMS *Excellent* Mss.

111. Lambton to Fisher, 11 Nov 03, enclosure f.94, Fisher Papers 1/3.

112. Lt. Peter Macnamara, "Concentration of Fire, its Effect and its Further: from experience gained during trials carried out by the different modern battle fleets and cruiser squadrons in the past and present. The uses of Director Firing for this purpose and the value of different ships using different coloured shell bursts," April 1909, in file on "Fleet fire and Concentration," HMS *Excellent*. In 1910, Macnamara was serving on the staff

of the gunnery school, HMS *Excellent;* he had been the senior gunnery officer to participate in the 1907 *Hero* gunnery experiments. This file also contains correspondence with many of the leading gunnery officers of the day, most of whom agreed with his analysis; for further details on this subject see Gunnery Branch, "Fleet Fire and Concentration of Fire Experiments," G.0132/10, 1910, p. 1040 (bound in miscellaneous papers on gunnery subjects), Ja.010, Admiralty Library.

113. Sumida, *In Defence,* 163–66, 171–76, 196–206, 249–56.

114. Adms. Percy Scott and Richard Pierce, "Final Report of the Committee on Director Firing," 5 Nov 12, MB1/T22/161, Battenberg Mss; see also Sumida, "Quest for Reach," 70–81.

115. Gordon, *Rules of the Game,* chapters 10, 11.

116. Julian Corbett, *Maritime Operations in the Russo-Japanese War, 1904–1905,* 2 vols. (Admiralty, 1913; reprint, N.I.P.: Annapolis, 1994) I, 310–19, 474–91, II, 232–35, 240–48.

117. Ibid., II, 258.

118. Gordon, *Rules of the Game,* 372 [my thanks to Andrew Gordon for this reference].

119. Sturdee to Sandars, 9 Mar 09, f.97, Sandars Mss 758.

120. Ibid.; for further evidence of poor prevailing weather in the North Sea see Hugh-Onslow's memo on fire control cited by Sumida, "Quest for Reach," 70.

121. Sumida, *In Defence,* 196–220.

122. May to Admiralty, 16 Apr 10, enclosing report on "the possible effects of Gunnery Technique on the new developments in fleet tactics," paper 2, "The Value of Plotting"; Minute (15 Jun 10) by Bethell, on May to Admiralty, 17 May 10, in "Employment of Destroyers in Fleet Action," X1751, ADM 1/8120; for evidence of widespread hostility to all-big-gun ships within the service see Balfour to Esher, 16 Apr 09, postscript, Esher Mss 16/13.

123. Jon Sumida, "The Quest for Reach," 70–72; idem, *In Defence,* 252–54, 285, note 369.

124. Ibid.

125. Minutes (24 May 10) by Moore (DNO) (18 May 10) by Peirse (ITP), on Admiral May, "Gunnery: effects on (a) plotting for range (b) rate of change of bearing and range (c) possibility of concentration of fire etc. of new developments in Fleet Tactics," 25 Apr 10, ADM 1/8051.

126. By November 1910, 49 torpedoes had been delivered and another 794 were on order, p. 8, ART 1910, Admiralty Library; Minute (16 Apr 09) by DNO, on G.5891/09, f.178, ADM 256/124.

127. Minute (15 Jun 10) by Bethell (DNI) on May to Admiralty, 17 May 10, in "Employment of Destroyers in Fleet Actions," ADM 1/8120.

128. Minutes (17 Dec 08) by Capt. Bernard Currey (A.T.D.) and Rear Adm. Reginald Bacon (DNO) on memo "As to allowance of 21-inch torpedoes in ships," f.34 (G18176/8) in Ships Covers 224 (*Australia* and *New Zealand*).

129. Bacon, "The Battleship of the Future," 16 Mar 10, in *Transactions of the Institute of Naval Architects* 52 (1910): 1–21.

130. For evidence of Madden's views see Madden to Fisher (plus enclosure), 9 Nov 13, FP 741, Fisher Papers 1/14.

131. Memo (4 Nov 08) by L. Bayly on "Duties of Destroyers in War"; also Bridgeman to Bayly, 18 Aug and 31 Oct 08, all in "Tactical Exs," X950/08, ADM 1/7988.

132. But see Fisher to Lady Fisher, 29 Sep 00, *FGDN*, I, 161–62.

133. Corbett, *Russo-Japanese War*, I, 316, Admiralty Library.

134. May to Admiralty, 12 Jun 10, enclosing paper by Sturdee, "Tactical importance of submerged tube torpedo fire," 13 May 10, f.42, Ships Covers 338 (*King George V* class battleships); Ottley to Esher, 8 Oct 11, Esher Mss 4/3.

135. May to Admiralty, 17 May 10, "Employment of Destroyers in Fleet Actions," X1751/10, ADM 1/8120.

136. Ibid.

137. Enclosures by Admirals Sturdee (27 Apr 10), Colville (1 May 10), Battenberg (2 May 10), Milne (2 May 10), ibid.

138. For contradictory view see Battenberg to Fisher, 3 Aug 09, FP 404, Fisher Papers 1/8.

139. Kerr to Watts (DNC), 27 Jun 09, cited in Parkes, *British Battleships*, 545.

140. Minute (10 Jun 14) by Tudor (DNO) on G.15927/14, f.325, *IQDNO*, vol. 3, 1914, Admiralty Library.

141. Admiralty, "Anti-torpedo boat armament on capital ships," (G02343/14) ADM 1/8367/27.

142. Synthesis of arguments expressed in the following documents. Letters addressed to Admiral May from Admirals Sturdee (27 Apr 10), Colville (1 May 10), Battenberg (2 May 10), Milne (2 May 10), in "Employment of Destroyers in Fleet Actions," X1751/10, ADM 1/8120; May, "Notes on Tactical Exercises—Home Fleet, 1909–1911, printed Sep 1911, 411–30, EB 012, Admiralty Library.

143. May to Admiralty, 17 May 10, "Employment of Destroyers in Fleet Actions," X1751/10, ADM 1/8120; see also May, "Notes on Tactical Exercises," p. 415, EB 012, Admiralty Library.

144. Parkes, *British Battleships*, 538, citing Reginald McKenna.

145. Bridgeman, "Fitting 12-pounder gun," 25 Nov 12, f.49, Ships Covers 294 (Queen Elizabeth class battleships); there is a copy in Admiralty, "Anti-torpedo boat armament on capital ships" (G02343/14) ADM 1/8367/27; Bridgeman to Bayly, 18 Aug and 31 Oct 08, in "Tactical Exs," X962/08, ADM 1/7988; Minute (4 Jul 10) by Jellicoe, "Destroyers in Fleet Actions," X1751/10, ADM 1/8120.

146. Minute (10 Jun 14) by Jellicoe, Admiralty, "Anti-torpedo boat armament on capital ships" (G02343/14) ADM 1/8367/27; see also Jellicoe to Fisher, 29 Nov 14, FP890a, Fisher Papers 1/17.

147. This is made very clear in Jellicoe's "First Draft of War Orders, 2nd Division Home Fleet 1912," c. Jan 12 to Apr 12, f.3, Add Mss 49,012; see also Sumida, *In Defence*, 206, 238, 305–6.

148. Bacon, remarks on paper by Alan Burgoyne MP, "Recent Developments in Battleship Type," 12 Mar 13, in *Transactions of the Institute of Naval Architects* 55 (1913, part 1): 1–19; further evidence on Bacon's tactical theory can be found in Lambert, "The Fleet Unit Concept," 55–83.

149. Bacon, remarks on paper by Alan Burgoyne, "Recent Developments in Battleship Type," 12 Mar 13, in *Transactions of the Institute of Naval Architects* 55 (1913, part 1): 16.

150. The *Iron Duke* class; for evidence of the lateness of the decision see Parkes, *British Battleships*, 47 and see also Briggs to Wilson, 31 Jul 11, on "Design of Armoured Cruiser for 1911–12 Programme," f.34, and "Report of Conference under Presidency of the DNO to consider crews for 6-inch anti-torpedo boat armament," 1 Apr 12, f.37, both in Ships Covers 279 (*Tiger*).

151. Capt. Mark Kerr (Battenberg's flag captain) to Watts (DNC), 27 Jun 09, cited in Parkes, *British Battleships*, 545–46; Sturdee to Sandars, 9 Mar 09, f.97, Sandars Mss 758.

152. Minutes (8 Aug 11) by Moore (DNO) and (10 Aug 11) by Briggs (3SL), on "6-inch Shell," G.0517, f.11–14, *IQDNO*, vol. 1, 1912, Admiralty Library.

153. Madden to Fisher, 9 Nov 13, enclosing articles from the *Times*, FP741, Fisher Papers 1/14.

154. Fisher to McKenna, 22 Nov 11, MCKN 6/3; see also Parkes, *British Battleships*, 538, 547; Churchill to Fisher, 2 Nov 11, FP537, Fisher Papers 1/10; Sumida, *In Defence*, 258–60.

155. Précis of opinions expressed by officers in the Home Fleet, in "Armament for Defence Against Torpedo Craft," G.0243/14, f.365–372, *IQDNO*, vol. 3, 1914, Admiralty Library.

156. Minute (6 May 10) by Richmond on, "Employment of T.B.D.s [torpedo boat destroyers] in varying weathers against a battle fleet," May Mss 9/1 (NMM).

157. Minute (6 May 10) by Capt. Herbert Richmond, "Employment of T.B.D.s in varying weathers against a battle fleet," May Mss 9/1 (NMM).

158. Milne to May, 2 May 10, X1751/10, ADM 1/8120.

159. Cowan to Bridgeman, 9 Oct 11, "On use of destroyers in wartime," p. 3, BTY2/3/2 [Beatty Mss].

160. Note on front cover of docket, endorsements (26 Feb 12) by Battenberg (2d sl) and (28 Feb 12) by Churchill (1st lord), ibid.

161. Bacon, "The Battleship of the Future,"17—see note 1 above; see also Gordon, *Rules of the Game*, 354–70.

162. Ibid.; see especially report by Vice Adm. Sir John Jellicoe on, "Naval Manoeuvres, 1913," 6 Aug 1913, p. 4–6, ADM 116/3381.

163. Jellicoe, "First Draft of War Orders, 2nd Division Home Fleet 1912," section on "destroyer attack on enemy's line," f.15, Add Mss 49012.

164. Minute (9 Jun 10) by King-Hall (D.N.M.) on May to Admiralty, 17 May 10, and also Colville to May, 1 May 10, ADM 1/8120.

165. Submissions by Rear Adm. Bradford (1 May 10) and Vice Adm. Berkeley Milne (2 May 10), ibid.

166. May, "Notes on Tactical Exercises," p. 425, EB 012, Admiralty Library.

167. May to Admiralty, 17 May 10, "Employment of Destroyers in Fleet Actions," X1751/10, ADM 1/8120.

168. May, "Notes on Tactical Exercises," p. 411, EB 012, Admiralty Library.

169. Minutes (4 Feb 10) by Rear Adm. Alexander Bethell (DNI) and Capt. Herbert King-Hall (DNM) on "Pacific Fleet—provision and disposition of," ADM 116/1270.

170. Lambert, "Economy or Empire," 67–71.

171. May, "Notes on Tactical Exercises," p. 424, EB 012, Admiralty Library.

172. May to Admiralty, 12 Jun 10, forwarding paper by Rear Admiral Sturdee on "The Tactical Importance of Submerged tube Torpedo Fire," dated 13 May 10, in f.42, Ships Covers 260 (*King George V*).

173. Leverson (DOD) to Jackson (COS), 12 May 14, folder on "investigation 11," Keyes Mss 4/14.

174. Keyes to Admiralty via V.A. commanding 3rd & 4th Divisions, Home Fleet, 3 Jun 11, Keyes Mss 4/13.

175. Ibid.; minute (15 Jun 10) by Bethell, on May (c. in c.) to Admiralty, 17 May 10, on "Employment of Destroyers in Fleet Actions," X1751/10, ADM 1/8120; further evidence of Jellicoe and Battenberg's enthusiasm for fleet submarines is cited below.

176. Notes by Lt. Col. N. A. Paris RMA, dated 1910, contained in volume "Reports on Foreign Navies" (extracts from NID reports), HMS *Dolphin* Submarine Museum.

177. Minute (22 Nov 09) Watts to Jellicoe, on "Submarine boat design submitted by Messrs Scott of Greenock," (CN01029/09) f.40, Ships Covers 290A.

178. Admiralty to Vickers, 25 Mar 09 and reply dated 27 Mar 09, f.131, Ships Covers, 290.

179. Memorandum by contracts department on CN.0580/10, [Jan 1910], f.39, Ships Covers 290A.

180. Minute (23 Dec 09) by Capt, Thomas Jackson for DNI on "Report on the Swedish Submarine hvalen and Discussion of its Merits in Comparison with British and French Types of Submarine," Keyes Mss 4/1.

181. Ibid.

182. SS Hall to Admiralty, 15 Nov 09, ibid.; Hall to Jellicoe (controller), 2 Dec 09, Ships Covers 290A.

183. Hall to Admiralty, 19 Nov 09, Keyes Mss, 4/1.

184. "Memorandum by Captain (S) to commanding officers of all ships," X1596/10, ADM 1/8119. Contrast with *Hvalen* report by A/DNI Capt. T. Jackson, 23 Dec 09, Keyes Mss 4/1.

185. *Hvalen* report, Hall to Admiralty, 19 Nov 09, ibid.

186. Minute (23 Dec 09) by Capt. T. Jackson (A/DNI), ibid.

187. SS Hall to Admiralty, 2 Feb 10, ibid.

188. *Hvalen* report, "Further remarks by ICS," 2 Feb 10, ibid.

189. Ibid.

190. "Memorandum" dated 20 Feb 14, Thorneycroft Mss file X123.

191. Hall to Fisher, 15 Jun 10, FP 489, Fisher Papers 1/9.

192. Hall to Jellicoe, 12 Nov 09 (on CN0936/09) f.1, Ships Covers 291.

193. Hall(ICS) to Jellicoe (3S.L.), 12 Nov 09; Hall (ICS) to Captain Hornsby (HMS *Vernon*), 11 Aug 09, f.1, ibid.

194. Hall to Jellicoe, 2 Dec 09, f.40, Ships Covers 290A.

195. It was also essential to keep secret the Admiralty's decision to adopt broadside tubes for which see Minute by H.G. Watts, 27 Dec 09, ibid.

196. Notes on submarine construction, shows that an appropriation was

made: £537,552 was voted for submarine construction for 1910/11, but only £321,852 was actually spent, ADM 1/8380/150.

197. Minutes of meeting held on 2 Jun 10, f.2, Ships Covers 291.

198. Keyes to Hall, 19 Oct 12, Keyes Mss 4/22.

199. Constructor Harris Williams (a/DNC) to Keyes, 22 Nov 11, Keyes Mss, 4/1; Cmdr. A. Percy Addison to Keyes, ? Dec 17, Keyes Mss, 4/11.

200. Fisher to Hall, 21 Jun 10, *FGDN*, II, 328–29. Further correspondence on this subject is found in the Fisher Papers. See especially, Hall to Fisher, 15 Jun 10, FP 489, Fisher Papers 1/9.

201. "New Submarine-boat Designs 1910–11," enclosed with Williams to DNC, 25 Oct 10, f.7b, Ships Covers 291.

202. Watts, Memorandum handed to the DNC for the Controller, 2 Jun 10, f.2, Ships Covers 291.

203. Watts suggested approaches to MAN (Nurnberg) GMB, and Busch-Sulzer, ibid.

204. Report on submarine design (TE) of 27 Jun 10 and design (TG) of 14 Jul 10, f.178, ADM 226/16.

205. Report on model TE, 19 Aug 10. f.174–182, ibid.

206. Report on model TG, 1 Mar 11, p. 3, f.219, ibid.

207. Hall to Keyes, n/d [c. 1911], Keyes Mss 4/22.

208. Fisher to Gardiner, 19 Jan 11, *FGDN*, II, 352.

209. Hall to Keyes (n/d), enclosing Hall to Briggs, 7 Feb 11, Keyes Mss 4/1; Fisher to Hankey, 3 Nov 11, cited in Mackay, *Kilverstone,* 432.

210. Vickers to Admiralty, 2 Feb 11, f.13, Ships Covers 291.

211. Admiralty to Vickers, 2 Feb 11, f.13, and note by H. G. Williams, 7 Feb 11, f.7a, both in Ships Covers 291; also reports on submarine design (TD) of 23 Jun 10, report dated 1 Apr 12, f.358, ADM 226/16.

212. Ibid.

213. The *Navy List* for January 1911 shows Jellicoe hoisting his flag as c. in c., Atlantic Fleet, on 20 Dec 1910.

214. Fisher to McKenna, 20 Nov 09, *FGDN*, II, 281; Fisher to Jellicoe, 9 May 11, *FGDN*, II, 369.

215. Wilson to McKenna, 8 Feb 11, f.28, MCKN 3/22.

216. Fisher to Churchill, 30 Dec 11, cited in Randolph Churchill, *Winston S. Churchill—Young Statesman* (London, 1967), companion vol. 2, 1364; see also notes on Hall and Yarrow (n/d), FP 497, Fisher Papers 1/10.

217. *Navy List,* January 1911, officers of HMS *Diana.*

218. Keyes to Hall, Dec 1913, Keyes Mss 4/22.

219. Roger Keyes, *The Naval Memoirs of Sir Roger Keyes* (London, 1934), 23.

220. Ibid.

221. Keyes to Hall, 7 Dec 13, Keyes Mss 4/22.

222. Hall to Fisher, 26 Apr 14, FP803, Fisher Papers 1/15; Keyes to Hall, Dec 1913, Keyes Mss 4/22.

223. "Memorandum," enclosed with Keyes to Admiralty, 3 Jun 11, Keyes Mss 4/13; Further examples of Keyes' views can be found in: Keyes to Bayly (c.o. blue fleet) 1 Jul 11, and 3 Jul 11, Keyes Mss 4/14; Keyes to de Robeck, 10 Aug 13, f.420–425, ADM 137/1926.

224. Beatty to Jellicoe, 7 May 16, BTY13/22/12, Beatty Mss [National Maritime Museum].

225. Keyes, *Memoirs*, 27.

226. Keyes, *Memoirs*, 25; Hall to Fisher, 17 Feb 14, FP 783, Fisher Papers 1/13.

227. Keyes, draft manuscript for *Memoirs*, p. 8 (deleted in published version), Keyes Mss 18/1.

228. Memorandum by the DNC Watts, 31 Aug 11, f.1, Ships Covers 289A. For evidence that Keyes fully understood this question see deleted text in the draft of his memoirs, pp. 8, 17, Keyes Mss 18/1.

229. Memorandum by H. G. Watts, 31 Aug 11, f.1, p. 2, Ships Covers 289A; for earlier speculation on the possibilities with Italian hulls see minute (27 Dec 09) by H. G. Watts, f.40, Ships Covers 290A.

230. Report on hull TG and TK, dated 17 Jul 11, f.247, and report on hull form TS, dated 18 Dec 12, paragraph 18, reference to receipt of instructions received on 2 May 11 and 12 May 11 for hull forms TJ and TK, f.428a, all in ADM 226/16; Watts to Briggs, 1:0:11, on "Programme 1911–1912" (CN02218/11), f.31, Ships Covers 291.

231. Keyes to Hall, 19 Oct 12, Keyes Mss 4/22; also report on submarine design (TS), dated 18 Oct 12: paragraphs 18–19 refer to submarine design (TJ) 2 May 11, and (TK) 12 May 11, f.428a, ADM 226/16.

232. Keyes, draft manuscript for *Memoirs*, p. 8 (deleted in published version), Keyes Mss 18/1. N.B.: Keyes generally referred to all saddle tank designs (including "D-mod y") as "E types."

233. Ibid., see also Williams to Keyes, 22 Nov 11, Keyes Mss 4/4.

234. Draft letter Keyes to Hall, 19 Oct 12 [11], Keyes Mss 4/22.

235. Ibid.

236. Ibid.

237. Ibid.; also Controller to First Sea Lord (Wilson), 30 Aug 11 (on CN02430/11) f.38, Ships Covers 291.

238. Hall to Keyes, 7 Oct 11, Keyes Mss 4/22.

239. Trebilcock, *The Vickers Brothers*, 105–8.

240. Table showing costs and prices, dated 7 Sep 12, document 590/12, Nautilus file, Vickers Mss 1110.

241. For the Admiralty's recognition of the reliability problems with foreign diesels see Keyes, "Development of British Submarines," May 1914, pp. 4–5, ADM 137/2067; extracts from N.I.D. "Reports on Foreign Navies," Germany, p. 26 (n/d, 1913), p. 38 (12 Nov 13), France, p. 135, volume held at HMS *Dolphin* Submarine Museum.

242. Hall to Briggs, 7 Feb 11, Keyes Mss, 4/1; Keyes, "Report as to Immediate Future Construction of Submarine Boats," appendix on engine design, CN0420/12, enclosed in Hall to Briggs, 9 Mar 12, Ships Covers 306 (Nautilus class submarine). For technical explanations see Norman Friedman, *U.S. Submarines Through 1945* (N.I.P.: Annapolis, 1995), appendix a, "submarine propulsion," 255–58; Lambert, "The Influence of the Submarine Upon Naval Strategic Thought."

243. See unfavorable report on Italian and German engines by Eng. Cmdr. Hugh Garwood, "Report on Visit to Fiat San Georgio Works at La Spezia," CN43282/11, 6 Sep 11, Keyes Mss, 4/2; for typical opinion on the virtues of foreign designs see Williams (a/DNC) to Keyes, 22 Nov 11, Keyes Mss, 4/4.

244. Eckhart Roessler, *The U-boat* (Arms & Armour Press: London, 1981); for an account of the French navy's disastrous experience see Lambert, "The Influence of the Submarine Upon Naval Strategy," chapter 3.

245. Keyes to Admiralty 20 Jul 11 (CN02408/11) and reply from Vickers, 25 Jul 11, Keyes Mss 4/17; Admiralty, untitled memorandum on using clause C, 28 Jul 11, Keyes Mss 4/18.

246. Watts, memorandum dated 8 Mar 11, f.19, Ships Covers 291.

247. Vickers costed the building of an E type submarine at £79,039, table showing costs and prices, 7 Sep 12, Vickers Mss 1110.

248. For a similar story of the relations between the Admiralty and Arthur Pollen's Argo Company, see Sumida, *In Defence,* from 220.

249. Keyes to Admiralty 20 Jul 11 (CN02408/11) and attached papers notably Vickers to Admiralty, 25 Jul 11, all in Keyes Mss 4/17; notes on Vickers letter to Admiralty, 12 Dec 11, f.50, Ships Covers 291; and especially Minute (13 Sep 11) by Briggs on "Further remarks on CN.02408/11, f.85, Ships Covers 290A.

250. Endorsements by (14 Sep 11) by Wilson, and (18 Oct 11) by McKenna, ibid.; see also remarks of Capt. Murray Sueter cited in J. D. Scott, *Vickers: A History* (Weinfield & Nicholson: London, 1962), 67.

251. Minute (7 Jul 12) by Sir Francis Hopwood, on "Construction of Future Submarine boats—Procedure," CN0492/12, f.34, Ships Covers 290B.

252. See copy of memorandum by Admiralty legal department dated 19 Mar 09, in the possession of Roger Keyes, Keyes 4/5; unsigned memorandum on CN0580/10 [1910], f.39, Ships Covers 290A.

253. Minute (16 May 12) by A. W. Smallwood of the legal department, f.34, Ships Covers 290B.

254. Minute (14 Jun 12) by Admiralty solicitor Mr. B. A. Cohen, ibid.

255. Briggs to Wilson, 1 Sep 11, f.38, Ships Covers 291.

256. Cmdr. Percy Addison, "Report on Visit to FIAT San Georgeo Works at Spezia," 6 Sep 11, Keyes Mss 4/2.

257. Hugh S. Garwood, "Report on Engines" (n/d) (CN43282/11), ibid.

258. Minute (1 Sep 11) by Watts on "Programme 1911–12," f.31, Ships Covers 291.

259. Minute (6 Sep 11) by Keyes, on "FIAT Submarines—Report by Commander Addison," ibid.

260. Contract dated 23 Jan 12, f.5, Ships Covers 289a.

261. Keyes, *Memoirs,* 27–32; and First Draft of Memoirs, p. 13, Keyes Mss 18/1.

262. Keyes to 3rd sea lord, 9 Mar 12, enclosing "Report as to Immediate future Construction of Submarine Boats" (CN0420/12) f.1, Ships Covers 306 (Nautilus class submarine).

263. Keyes, "Memorandum for Successor," 6 Apr 14, section 27, ADM 137/2067.

264. Keyes to Hall, n/d [June 1914], Keyes Mss 4/22.

265. "New Design of Submarine by Messrs Vickers," 3 Jun 12, f.4, Ships Covers 306 (Nautilus).

266. See memoranda by Admiralty legal department cited above.

267. Minutes of meeting between Lt. Martin Nasmith RN and Armstrongs, copy of "Statement of Requirement for a Submarine boat" handed to Charles Ottley (CN02069/12) Keyes Mss 4/1; Watts to Keyes, 16 Sep 12. and 21 Sep 12, Keyes 4/23. Note: these letters were sent to Keyes' home address.

268. Keyes to Admiralty, 7 Jan 14 (CP01202) Keyes Mss 4/1; Keyes to Admiralty, 22 Nov 11, Keyes 4/4.

269. J. E. Morpurgo, *Barnes Wallis—A Biography* (London: Penguin, 1973), 76. Barnes Wallis, the inventor of the legendary "Dambusting—bouncing bomb" in 1943, was employed before the First World War as a submarine designer for Vickers and Messrs. White of Cowes.

270. Keyes to Briggs, 9 Mar 12, "Report as to Immediate Future Construction," f.1, Ships Covers 306 (Nautilus).

271. Keyes to Dawson (MD of Vickers), 20 Aug 13, Vickers Mss, 741.

272. For boosted output at the plant see Mr. Wardropper (works superintendent) to McKechnie, 20 Nov 12, in Nautilus file, Vickers Mss 1110.

273. Hall to Fisher, 17 Feb 14, FP 783, Fisher Papers 1/14; Minute (18 Jul 10) by DNC Watts, on "Invention of Gun Mounting on submarine," ADM 1/8127; also Hall to Keyes, 15 Dec 12, Keyes Mss 4/22.; Briggs to Wilson, 30 Aug 11, on CN02430/11, f.38, Ships Covers 291.

274. Memorandum by legal branch on CN.0580/10, f.39, Ships Covers 290A.

275. Handwritten minute (27 Dec 09) by Watts on rough paper, ibid. The minute refers to asking Scotts to design a beam torpedo tube.

276. Minutes of meeting held in third sea lord's rooms, 29 Jan 13, f.12, Ships Covers 289A; Keyes, Memorandum for Successor, 6 Apr 14, section 20, ADM 137/2067; for terms offered to Messrs. Armstrong see minute (18 Jun 14) by Moore, Ships Covers 330; further details on the Armstrong built W class submarines can be found in Ships Covers 307.

277. Minutes (14 Sep 12) by Moore (3d s.l.) and Churchill (1st l.), and (23 Nov 12) by Moore, on CN02069/12, Keyes Mss 4/1.

278. Minute (14 Sep 12) by Keyes on memo CN02069/12, and Keyes to Moore, 28 Nov 12, and Keyes to DNC, 3 Nov 12, all ibid.

279. Ibid.

280. Hall to Fisher, 26 Apr 14, FP 803, Fisher Papers 1/13.

Chapter Eight: The Churchill Administration

1. Stephen McKenna, *Reginald McKenna*, 46–47, see especially Asquith to McKenna, Jul 1908, cited on 65; for evidence that McKenna had previously campaigned for cuts in the navy estimates see Fisher to King Edward VII, 11 Apr 08, *FGDN*, II, 172.

2. Riddle diary, 26 Sep 13, f.32, Add Mss 62973.

3. Stephan McKenna, *Reginald McKenna*, 2–13, 23, 46–47.

4. Sir Charles Walker, *Thirty-Six Years at the Admiralty* (Lincoln Williams Ltd.: London, 1933), 57, 66. (Walker was a career civil servant who served for two years as Fisher's private secretary and ultimately rose to become deputy secretary of the Admiralty); Fisher to Leyland, 1 Jan 11, *FGDN*, II, 356.

5. Fisher to Esher, 5 May 08, *FGDN*, II, 175.

6. Fisher to Cecil Fisher, 24 Oct 11, *FGDN*, II, 396; the only reliable account of the events surrounding the dismissal of McKenna and the strategic discussions during the Agadir crisis is found in d'Ombrain, *War Machinery*.

7. Steiner, *Origins of the First World War*, 139–44.

8. Riddle diary, reporting conversations with Lloyd George, 18 Apr 13, f.116, Add Mss 62972, and 26 Sep 13, f.32, Add Mss 62973.

9. Fisher to Esher, 5 Aug 10, Esher Mss, 10/43.

10. Ibid. (See also Fisher, *Memories*, 200.)

11. McKenna, *Reginald McKenna*, 118–19.

12. Fisher to May, 10 May 11, May Mss [N.B.: private collection].

13. The diary of Maj. Adrian Grant-Duff (secretary to the CID) contains frequent references to the unpopularity of the Admiralty at this time: diary entries 16–21 Jan 11, 24 Mar 11, 21 Jul 11, Grant-Duff MSS, DC/MISC/77.

14. Riddle diary, 26 Sep 13, f.32, Add Mss 62973, and 26 Apr 13, f.127–128, Add Mss 62972.

15. Asquith to Venetia Stanley, 7 Mar 15, cited in Brock and Brock, *H. H. Asquith: Letters to Venetia Stanley*, 464; see also biographical note on McKenna, 635.

16. Marder, *FDSF*, I, 215–221.

17. Williams, *Defending the Empire*, chapters 8 and 10.

18. Haldane, A Preliminary memorandum on the Present Situation, 1 Jan 06, f.44, Haldane Mss 5918, cited in Williams, *Defending the Empire*, 101.

19. Most recently, David Hermann, *The Arming of Europe and the Making of the First World War* (Princeton, 1996), 55–56.

20. Williams, *Defending the Empire*, 101–2.

21. Edward Spiers, *Haldane: An Army Reformer* (Edinburgh UP, 1980), 53–56, 192–95; idem, *The Army and Society, 1815–1914* (London, 1980), 268–84; Samuel Williamson, *The Politics of Grand Strategy* (Harvard, 1969),165–92.

22. Spiers, *Haldane: An Army Reformer*, 53–56, 192–95.

23. D'Ombrain, *War Machinery*, 80–89, 97–99; J. McDermott, "The Revolution in British Military Thinking from the Boer War to the [First] Moroccan Crisis," in *The War Plans of the Great Powers 1880–1914*, ed. Paul Kennedy (London, 1979), 99–117.

24. Kennedy, *Anglo-German Antagonism, 1860–1914*, 423–29; David French, *British Strategy and War Aims, 1914–16* (London, 1986),1–13.

25. D'Ombrain, *War Machinery*, 97; Williamson, *Grand Strategy*, 170.

26. Haldane, "Memorandum of Events between 1906 and 1915" [Apr 1916], f.15, Haldane Mss 5923.

27. Diary entry, 9 Nov 10, Grant-Duff MSS, DC/MISC/77.

28. Fisher to Spender, 27 Feb 11, *FGDN*, II, 359.

29. Ottley to Bethell, 16 Jan 11, ADM 1/8896 and CAB17/107; Fisher to May, 21 May 11, May Mss [N.B.: private collection].

30. D'Ombrain, *War Machinery*, 97–107; idem, "The Military Departments and the Committee of Imperial Defence," 287–99.

31. Fisher to McKenna, 19 Jun 11, *FGDN*, II, 376.

32. McKenna, "Navy Estimates," 16 Feb 11, CAB37/105/12.

33. Cabinet notes, Asquith to the King, 1 Mar 11, f.14, Asquith 6; Asquith to McKenna, 15 Oct 11, McKenna Mss, 4/1; Churchill to Lloyd-George, 12 Jul 12, Randolph Churchill, *Young Statesman*, 4 vols. including 3 companion vols. (Heinemann: London, 1967–69), companion vol. 3, p. 1613 (hereafter cited in format *YS*, c3, 1613).

34. Walker, *Thirty-six Years*, 67.

35. Diary entry, 7 Feb 11, Grant-Duff MSS, DC/MISC/77.

36. Fisher to White, 15 Apr 11, *FGDN*, 11, 366–67.

37. Fisher to Mrs McKenna, 4 May 1911, *FGDN*, II, 368.

38. Madden to McKenna, 28 Jul 11, MCKN 4/4, McKenna Mss.

39. Winston Churchill, *World Crisis*, I, 47–48.

40. Hankey to McKenna, 15 Aug 11, cited in Roskill, *Hankey: Man of Secrets*, 101–2.

41. Ibid., 102.

42. Fisher to McKenna, 20 Aug 11, *FGDN*, II, 380.

43. Ibid.; for very similar advice see Fisher to McKenna, 18 May 11, *FGDN*, II, 371.

44. Nicholas d'Ombrain, "The Imperial General Staff and the Military Policy of a Continental Strategy during the 1911 International Crisis," *Military Affairs* (Oct 1970): 88–93; idem, *War Machinery*, 100–105, 253–59.

45. Williamson, *Grand Strategy*, 165–69, 182–92.

46. Wilson, minutes of 114th meeting of the CID, p. 5, 23 Aug 11, CAB2/2.

47. Steiner, *The First World War*, 126.

48. Spiers, *Haldane*, 192.

49. Haldane, minutes of 114th meeting of the CID, p. 10, 23 Aug 11, CAB2/2.

50. Diary entry, 25 Aug 11, Grant-Duff MSS, DC/MISC/77.

51. D'Ombrain, "Continental Strategy," 88–93; for McKenna's regret see McKenna, *Reginald McKenna*, 330.

52. Secret memorandum on Transports for the BEF enclosed in Nicholson to Haldane, 25 Sep 11, f.212–219, Haldane Mss 6129[1].

53. For contrasting reports on the proceedings see: Hankey to Fisher, 24 Aug 11, FP530A, Fisher Papers 1/10; Churchill to Asquith, 13 Sep 11, Churchill to Lloyd George, 14 Sep 11, Lloyd George to Churchill, 15 Sep 11, all in Churchill, *Young Statesman*, I, 531–35; Haldane to Grey, 11 Sep 11, f.138, Grey Mss, FO 800/102; Asquith to Haldane, 31 Aug 11, f.140, Haldane Mss 5909.

54. Asquith to McKenna, 18 Sep 11, McKenna Mss 4/1; McKenna to Asquith, 19 Sep 11, f.43, and Haldane to Asquith, 25 Sep 11, f.48, both Asquith Mss, 13,

55. Churchill, *World Crisis*, 56; d'Ombrain, "The Military Departments and the Committee of Imperial Defence," 288–95.

56. Richard Haldane, Autobiography.

57. Esher Journals, 4 Oct & 24 Nov 11, Esher Mss 12/1.

58. Esher to Spender, 8 Aug 11, f.22, Add Mss 46392; Riddle diary, reporting conversation with Charles Masterman, 18 Dec 13, f.100, Add Mss 62973.

59. Neilson, *The Last Tsar*, 28.

60. Steiner, *Origins of the First World War*, 91, 139–43.

61. Fisher to Cecil Fisher, 24 October 1911, *FGDN*, II, 396.

62. D'Ombrain, "The Military Departments and the Committee of Imperial Defence," 292–94; French, *British Strategy and War Aims*, 3.

63. D'Ombrain, *War Machinery*, 259.

64. Asquith to Crewe, 7 Oct 11, Asquith Mss 46; Violet Bonham-Carter, *Winston Churchill as I Knew Him* (London: Eyre & Spottiswoode and Collins, 1965), 235.

65. Lady Randolph Churchill (his mother) to Churchill, 1 Oct 11, *YS*, c2, 1294.

66. Riddle diary, reporting conversations with Lloyd George and Churchill, 11 Nov 11, f.103, Add Mss 62968, and 6 Jan 14, f.7, Add Mss 62974, and with Charles Masterman, 18 Dec 13, f.100 Add Mss 62973.

67. Battenberg, "Statement made to me by Sir Francis Hopwood, additional Civil Lord at the Admiralty," 24 Jun 16, MB1/T24/378, Battenberg Mss. For Churchill's equivocal attitude towards women's suffrage see John Grigg, *Lloyd George: From Peace to War, 1912–16* (Berkeley, CA: University of California Press, 1985), 72.

68. Asquith to McKenna, 10 Oct 11, MCKN 4/1, McKenna Mss.

69. Montagu to McKenna, 15 Nov 11, MCKN 4/1, McKenna Mss, cited in d'Ombrain, "The Military Departments and the Committee of Imperial Defence," 291; Sandars to Balfour, 14 Dec 11, f.3, Add Mss 49768.

70. Riddle diary, 11 Nov 11, f.102, Add Mss 62968.

71. McKenna to Asquith, 17 Oct 11, Asquith to McKenna, 18 Oct 11 and McKenna to Asquith 19 Oct 11, all MCKN 4/1, McKenna Mss.

72. Gilbert, *Organiser of Victory*, 53, 131–35.

73. Sumida, "Churchill and British Seapower"; Randolph Churchill, *Young Statesman*, 30–32; George Bernstein, *Liberalism and Liberal Politics in Edwardian England* (Boston: Allen & Unwin, 1986), 96–104, 114–15, 125–28; Michael Bentley, *The Climax of Liberal Politics* (London, 1987), 112.

74. Riddle diary, reporting conversations with Churchill, June—August 1911, f.86–97, Add Mss 62968.

75. Churchill, "Naval Expenditure," 15 Jul 10, CAB37/103/32; Churchill, "Secret" [Navy Expenditure], 3 Feb 11, CAB37/105/7; Churchill, "The Mediterranean Fleet," 15 Mar 11, CAB37/105/27.

76. Nicholas Lambert, "Economy or Empire," 55–84; Churchill to Crewe, 14 Feb 11, f.3, Churchill to Lloyd George, 14 Feb 11, f.4, Lloyd George Mss, C/3/15 [House of Lords Records Office].

77. Churchill, *World Crisis*, 76.

78. Williamson, *Grand Strategy*, 185.

79. "The Guildhall Banquet—Mr. Churchill on Naval Expenditure," reported in the *Times*, 10 Nov 11, p. 10, col. 2.

80. Churchill to Asquith, 13 Sep 11, *Young Statesman*, 531; Churchill, *World*

Crisis, 56, 78–82; see also Churchill to Lloyd George, 5 and 14 Sep 11, Lloyd George Mss, C/3/15/9 and C/3/15/12.

81. Churchill, *World Crisis,* 89.

82. Churchill to Asquith, 5 Nov 11, f.58, Asquith 13.

83. Esher diary, 4 Oct 11, Esher Mss 12/1.

84. Esher Journals, 4 Oct 11, Esher Mss 1/12; Asquith to Crewe, 7 Oct 11, Asquith Mss 46.

85. Churchill to Asquith, 16 Nov 11, Churchill, *YS,* c3, 1336.

86. Churchill to Asquith, 5 Nov 11, f.58, Asquith 13; see also Ottley to Churchill, 3 Nov 11, CAB1/31; Carter, *Winston Churchill as I Knew Him,* 235.

87. Admiral George King-Hall, diary 28 Dec 12, King-Hall Mss.

88. Bridgeman to Fisher, 4 Dec 11, FP547, Fisher Papers 1/11.

89. Sumida, "Churchill and British Seapower"; Churchill, *World Crisis,* 71.

90. For an insightful analysis of their relationship see Morris, *Fisher's Face,* 180–88.

91. Ibid., 75; Churchill to Fisher, 25 Oct 11, *YS,* c2, 1298.

92. Fisher to Esher, 29 Oct 11, cited in Fisher, *Memories,* 205.

93. Churchill, notes on conversations with Lord Fisher, 28, 29, 30 Oct 1911, *YS,* c2, 1300; Fisher to Spender, 31 Oct 11, *FGDN,* II, 409.

94. Churchill, *World Crisis,* 76–77; Churchill to Asquith, 5 Nov 11, f.58, Asquith Mss 13.

95. Percy Scott to White, 29 Nov 11, Arnold White Mss, 172; Riddle diary, 9 Dec 11, f.133, Add Mss 62968.

96. Fisher to Churchill, 5 Mar 12, f.75, and Churchill to Fisher, 12 Apr 12, f.24, Chart 8/177; Fisher to Esher, 2 Apr 12, *FGDN,* II, 442.

97. Fisher to Troubridge, 19 Apr 12 and 27 Apr 12, F1, Troubridge Mss (NMM); Fisher to Churchill, 22 Apr 12, FP 570, Fisher Mss 11/1; Churchill's reply: *YS,* c3, 1545–1548; Fisher's reply: 2 May 12, f.110, Chart 13/14; for evidence that initially Fisher had no idea of why the appointments were made see Fisher to Mrs McKenna, 20 Apr 12, *FGDN,* II, 446.

98. Fisher to Troubridge, 19 and 27 Apr 12, both F1, Troubridge Mss (NMM); Fisher to Esher, 29 Apr 12, and Fisher to Cecil Fisher, 6 and 9 May 12, *FGDN,* II, 457–60

99. Fisher to Churchill, 6 Nov 11, f.16, Chart 13/2.

100. Fisher to Churchill, n/d, note by John Fisher on employment of submarines in northern waters. The references to the anticipated visit of the head of the Russian navy to England—Admiral Grigorovich—and that the letter was addressed from Naples indicate this letter was written in Dec 1911, f.5–8, Chart 13/43. Note, the requests for 15-inch guns in the new ships and more submarines indicates the letter was written about or before January 1912, Chart 13/14; Fisher to Knollys, 29 Jan 09, enclosures "German War Vessels in Danish Waters and Secret Orders to the IX German Army Corps," and Fisher to McKenna, 26 Jan 09, Royal Archives, W59/72.

101. Fisher to Hankey, 4 Nov 11, cited in Mackay, *Kilverstone,* 434; Fisher to Churchill, 22 Nov 11, f.41, Chart 13/2.

102. Churchill to Fisher, 10 Jan 12, *YS,* c3, 1495.

103. Fisher to Churchill, 22 Nov 11 and 3 Dec 11, Churchill, c2, 1341, 1349; Churchill to Battenberg, 10 Nov 11, MB1/T9/46, Battenberg Mss.

104. Fisher to Churchill, 30 Dec 11, and Fisher to Churchill, 6 Dec 11, *YS*, c2, 1351, 1365.

105. Fisher to Churchill, 13 Feb 12, *FGDN*, II, 431.

106. Churchill to Battenberg, 10 Nov 11, MB1/T9/46, Battenberg Mss.

107. Churchill to Battenberg, 18 Nov 11, MB1/T9/46, ibid.

108. Ibid.; similar language is found in Churchill to Fisher, 3 Dec 11, *YS*, c2, 1350.

109. Ibid.

110. Battenberg to Churchill, 20 Nov 11, cited in Kerr, *Prince Louis of Battenberg*, 233.

111. Fisher to Churchill, 20 Nov 11, *YS*, c.2, 1338.

112. Sumida, "Churchill and British Seapower"; Churchill to Fisher, 12 Apr 12, FP568, Fisher Papers 1/11.

113. Churchill, "Naval Programme 1912/13," n/d [Dec 1911], f.69, CAB1/32.

114. Ibid.

115. Ibid.

116. Fisher to Churchill, 30 Dec 11, f.77, Chart 13/2.

117. Osmond de Brock to Slade, 28 Dec 11, reel 1, Slade.

118. Nicholas Lambert, "Fisher and the Concept of Flotilla Defence," 644–45; Bridgeman to Churchill, 21 May 12, f.50, Chart 13/9.

119. Minute (27 Oct 12) by Churchill, p. 117, FLM, Admiralty Library.

120. Churchill, *World Crisis*, 132–33, see also "first draft," f.13, Chart 8/59.

121. Fisher to Churchill, 6 Dec 11, Churchill, c2, 1351. The two experts were Sir Philip Watts (DNC) and Rear Adm. Charles Briggs (controller).

122. Fisher to Churchill, 30 Dec 11, f.77, Chart 13/2; for more detailed survey of Churchill's capital ship policy see: Sumida, *In Defence*, 258–65.

123. Fisher to Fiennes, 8 Feb 12, *FGDN*, II, 430; Fisher to Esher, 2 Apr 12, Esher Mss 10/43.

124. Churchill to Battenberg, 18 Nov 11, MB1/T9/46, Battenberg Mss.

125. Battenberg to Churchill, 7 Dec 11, MB1/T9/49, ibid.; Fisher to Churchill, 16 Jan 12, f.18, Chart 13/14; see also Hall to Keyes, 31 Jan 12, Keyes Mss 4/22. In January 1912, the First Battle Squadron was to comprise entirely of dreadnoughts, the Second of 2 dreadnoughts, 2 *Lord Nelson*, and 4 *King Edward* class; see also Churchill to War Staff, enclosing memorandum marked "Secret," 15 Feb 12, paragraph 2, ADM 116/3099.

126. Churchill to Lloyd George, 12 Jul 12 [not sent], *YS*, c3, 1609.

127. Minute (1 Nov 11) by Bethell, on Churchill proposal to reduce the Mediterranean Fleet, f.12a, Chart 21/20.

128. Battenberg to Churchill, 7 Dec 11, MB1/T9/49, Battenberg Mss; Minute (8 Jan 12) by Battenberg, MB1/T15/71, ibid. This document shows that the Admiralty intended to form a Third Division of the Home Fleet comprised of eight *King Edward*s, but manned with 60 percent nucleus crews. This would leave 16 fully manned dreadnoughts in the First and Second Squadrons, plus six other battleships in full commission at Gibraltar—a total of 22.

129. Churchill to Battenberg, 26 Dec 11, MB1/T10/58, Battenberg Mss. The six Mediterranean battleships were scheduled to be reduced in July 1912 and their crews turned over; see Admiralty, "Confidential Nucleus Crews Turn Over Lists—Chronological Relief List (for six months from 1 Mar 12)," 29 Feb 12, MB1/T89; Fisher to Churchill, 22 Nov 11, f.41, Chart 13/2.

130. Marder, *FDSF,* I, 275–87.

131. Churchill to Cassel, 7 and 26 Jan 12, f.34, MB1/X4, Cassel Mss [Southampton University Library].

132. Churchill to Grey, 31 Jan 12, enclosing note on "observations," *YS,* c3, 1504.

133. Churchill, "Amendment to the Laws of June 14, 1900, and June 5, 1906, Concerning the German Fleet," 14 Feb 12, CAB 37/109/21; the figure for the establishment of the Navy in 1912 is taken from *Brassey's Naval Annual,* 1913.

134. Churchill, "Admiralty Memorandum on New German Naval Law," 9 Mar 12, CAB 37/110/43.

135. Churchill to War Staff, 15 Feb 12, ADM 116/3099; Admiralty, "Confidential Nucleus Crew Turn Over Lists," 29 Feb 12, MB1/T89, Battenberg Mss.

136. Churchill to Grey, 31 Jan 1912, *YS,* c3, 1504.

137. Churchill to Masterton-Smith, 23 May 14, f.106, CAB 1/33; Churchill, "Manning Requirements for the Navy," 26 Jun 12, CAB 37/111/82; Churchill, "The Naval Situation III," 25 Jun 12, CAB 37/111/80.

138. Churchill to Troubridge, 1 Feb 12, ADM 116/3099; Churchill to Grey, 31 Jan 12, Churchill *YS,* c.2, 1504.

139. Ibid.

140. Fisher to Churchill, 5 Mar 12, *FGDN,* II, 437.

141. Bridgeman to Churchill, 21 May 12, f.50, Chart 13/9.

142. Esher to Spender, 5 Jun 12, f.80, Add Mss 46392.

143. Troubridge to Churchill, 7 Feb 12, ADM 116/3099.

144. Ibid.

145. Churchill, 14 Feb 12, CAB 37/109/21.

146. Churchill to War Staff, 15 Feb 12, f.20, ADM 116/3099.

147. Churchill, "Naval Situation in the Mediterranean," Churchill, 15 Jun 12, p. 1, CAB 37/111/76.

148. Churchill to War Staff, 15 Feb 12, f.20, ADM 116/3099.

149. Churchill, "The Naval Situation," 22 Jun 12, p. 2, CAB 37/111/78.

150. Capt. John Dumaresq to Tupper, 28 Dec 13, Tupper Mss [Portsmouth Naval Museum].

151. Battenberg to Churchill, 10 Jul 12, f.1, CAB 1/33.

152. *Parliamentary Debates,* 5th series, vol. 35 (1912), 1556, 1563–68, Churchill, 18 Mar 12.

153. Marder, *FDSF,* I, 287–88; Admiralty, Report of interview with the French minister of marine, Adm. Boue de Lapreyere, 21 Jan 12, ADM 116/3109.

154. *Parliamentary Debates,* 5th series, vol. 35 (1912), 1556, 1563–68, Churchill, 18 Mar 12.

155. Churchill, *World Crisis,* 101.

156. *Parliamentary Debates,* 5th series, vol. 35 (1912), 1556, 1563–68, Churchill, 18 Mar 12.

157. Foreign Office, "Effect of a British Evacuation of the Mediterranean on Question of Foreign Policy," 8 May 12, ADM 116/3099.

158. Halpern, *Mediterranean,* 21–23.

159. War Office, "Effect of Loss of Sea power in the Mediterranean upon British Military Strategy," 9 May 1912, Asquith Mss 107.

160. For Esher's views see Brett, *Esher,* vol. 3, especially Esher to Balfour, 1 Jul 12, III, 95–98.

161. Esher to his son (M. V. Brett), Brett, *Esher,* III, 99–100.

162. Esher to Fisher, 20 Apr 12, Brett, *Esher,* III, 88.

163. Esher to Spender, 5 Jun 12, f.80, Spender Mss, f.80, Add Mss 46392.

164. Esher to Balfour, 23 Jul 12, Brett, *Esher,* III, 103.

165. Churchill, "Secret" [Navy Expenditure], 3 Feb 11, CAB 37/105/7; Churchill, "The Mediterranean Fleet," 15 Mar 11, CAB 37/105/27.

166. Nicholas Lambert, "Economy or Empire," 55–84.

167. Esher to Spender, 5 Jun 12, f.80, Spender Mss, f.80, Add Mss 46392; Nicholas Lambert, "Economy or Empire," 55–84.

168. Esher to Balfour, 1 Jul 12, Brett, *Esher,* III, 96.

169. Churchill to Haldane, 6 May 12, Haldane Mss cited in *YS,* c3, 1549.

170. Churchill to Asquith, 14 Apr 12, Chart 13/5; for the hostile reaction from Australia see Lambert, "Economy or Empire," 74–75.

171. Ibid.

172. Sir Arthur Nicholson (permanent undersecretary to the Foreign Office) to Sir Francis Bertie, 6 May 12, cited in G.P. Gooch & H. Temperley, *British Documents on the Origins of the War* (London, 1926–38), volume x (part 2), 584.

173. Nicholson to Grey, 6 May 12, f.94, Grey Mss, FO 800/94; see also Keith Neilson, *The Last Tsar,* 326.

174. Williamson, *Grand Strategy,* 269–72.

175. Churchill to Hankey, 25 Apr 12, and reply Hankey to Troubridge, 27 Apr 12, ADM 116/3099.

176. Hankey to Grey, 30 Apr 12, *British Documents,* 580–81.

177. Churchill to Fisher, 15 May 12, Churchill, *YS,* c3, 1553.

178. Enclosure 2, ibid.

179. Asquith to Churchill, 10 May 12, Churchill, *YS,* c3, 1552.

180. Esher journals, 6 Jun 12, Esher Mss 2/12.

181. Bridgeman to Churchill, 21 May 12, f.50, Chart 13/9.

182. Brian Ranft, ed., *The Beatty Papers* (2 vols.; Naval Records Society: London, 1990–1994), vol. 2, 16–19. Beatty to Admiralty, December 1918.

183. Draft telegram, Churchill to Bridgeman, 1 Jun 12, f.237, CAB 1/33.

184. Halpern, *Mediterranean,* 19–30.

185. Draft telegram, Churchill to Bridgeman, 1 Jun 12, f.237, CAB 1/33.

186. Ibid.

187. Bridgeman to Churchill, 1 Jun 12, f.189, CAB 1/33.

188. Draft telegram, Churchill to Bridgeman, 1 Jun 12, f.237, CAB 1/33.

189. Bridgeman, "Mediterranean," 9 Jun 12, f.53–57 ADM 116/3099.

190. Ibid.

191. Ibid.

192. Ibid.

193. Minute (25 Jun 13) by Churchill, p. 242, FLM, Admiralty Library.

194. Kitchener to Grey, 2 Jun 12, cited in *British Documents,* x, part 2, 594.

195. Ibid., enclosure.

196. Nicholson to Grey, 30 Jun 12, f.115, Grey Mss, FO 800/94.

197. McKenna, [The Mediterranean Situation], 24 Jun 12, CAB 37/111/79.

198. Churchill, "Naval Situation in the Mediterranean," Churchill, 15 Jun 12, p. 1, CAB 37/111/76.

199. Ibid., p. 2.

200. Churchill, "Naval Situation in the Mediterranean," 15 Jun 12, CAB 37/111/76.

201. Ibid.

202. Ibid.

203. Churchill, Cabinet paper marked "Not Circulated," 6 Jul 12, p. 2, CAB 37/111/89.

204. McKenna, [The Mediterranean Situation], 24 Jun 12, CAB 37/111/79.

205. Fisher to ?, 21 Jun 12, cited in Bacon, *Lord Fisher,* II, 154.

206. Nicholson to Grey, 21 Jun 12, f.112, Grey Mss, FO 800/94.

207. Ibid.

208. Minutes of 117 meeting of CID, 4 Jul 12, CAB2/2.

209. Fisher to Cecil Fisher, 5 Jul 12, *FGDN,* II, 470; Esher, Journals, 5 Jul 12, Esher Mss.

210. Halpern, *Mediterranean,* chap. 2.

211. Ibid., 35.

212. Fisher to Cecil Fisher, 6 May 12, *FGDN,* II, 460. Just before the meeting Fisher sent Churchill a memorandum suggesting that British flotilla craft operating from Malta should try to stop all merchant traffic in the region; see Fisher, "Battleships and Trade in the Mediterranean," n/d [June 1912], f.196, CAB 1/33; for edited copy see: Fisher to Stamfordham, 25 Jun 12, enclosure, *FGDN,* II, 469.

213. Minutes of 117th meeting of CID 4 Jul 12, CAB 2/3.

214. Ibid.

215. Ibid.

216. Fisher to Cecil Fisher, 5 Jul 12, *FGDN,* II, 470; Esher to Balfour, 23 Jul 12, Brett, *Esher,* III, 103.

217. Fisher to Cecil Fisher, 5 Jul 12, *FGDN,* II, 470.

218. Diary entry, 4 Jul 12, Grant-Duff Mss, DC/MISC/77.

219. See memorandum by Battenberg, 7 Jul 12, MB1/T20/103B, Battenberg Mss.

220. Diary entry, 4 Jul 12, Grant-Duff Mss, DC/MISC/77.

221. Minutes of 117th meeting of CID 4 Jul 12, CAB 2/3.

222. Memorandum by Battenberg, 7 Jul 12, MB1/T20/103B, Battenberg Mss.

223. Ibid.

224. Ibid.

225. Beatty to his Wife, 24 May 12, cited in Ranft, *Beatty Papers,* I, 46.

226. Halpern, *Mediterranean,* 39–40.

227. Asquith to the King, 16 Jul 12, f.156–157, Asquith Mss 6, N.B. secret enclosure.

228. Lambert, "Economy or Empire," 73–74; Borden and Churchill met at the Spithead review on 9th July 1912.

229. Williamson, *Grand Strategy,* 286–91.

230. Sandars to Balfour, 10 Oct 12, f.27, Add Mss 49768.

231. Pencil note by Churchill on paper outlining list of appointments, f.68, Chart 13/1.

232. Admiralty to C-in-C, 23 Aug 11, f.8, ADM 137/1936.

233. Ibid.

234. Callaghan to Admiralty, 9 Jan 12, enclosing "War Plans pages 1 to 24— Remarks by the C. in C. H.F.," hand-written secret enclosure entitled VII, War Stations, p. 10, "Watch on German Rivers," ADM 116/3096.

235. Admiralty to Callaghan, 9 Apr 12 (M001/12), ADM 116/3096.

236. War Plans issued on M0025, 18 Jan 13, ibid.

237. D'Ombrain, "The Military Departments and the Committee of Imperial Defence," 295–99.

238. Troubridge to Bridgeman, 8 Mar 12, ADM 116/3096.

239. Drafts of War Staff, "Memorandum Approved for issue to Flag officers," 15 Apr 12. (marked not issued), ADM 116/3096.

240. Admiralty, "Memorandum Approved for issue to flag officers," dated 15 Apr 12, but never issued, ADM 116/3096; Battenberg to Churchill, 10 Jul 12; Chart 13/13, Churchill to Bridgeman, 27 Sep 12, f.1, CAB 1/32; Churchill, "Notes on the Manoeuvres prepared for the PM by the First Lord, 17 Oct 13, ADM 116/3381.

241. Minute (11 Mar 13) by Jackson, on "Remarks on War Plans and on the First Lord's Notes on the Subject," f.199, ADM 116/3412.

242. Churchill to Clementine Churchill, 25 Mar 12, *YS,* c3, 1529.

243. First draft of *World Crisis,* f.4, Chart 8/60.

244. Some historians have mistakenly argued that this intermediate blockade strategy was adopted; see Marder, *FDSF,* i. 372; Richard Hough, *The Great War at Sea* (Oxford, 1983).

245. Telegram (24 May 12) from Churchill to Admiralty, f.1, ADM 116/1169; Bridgeman to Troubridge, 25 May 12, B6, Troubridge Mss (NMM).

246. Memorandum by Troubridge for the First Sea Lord, 26–30 May 1912, in Troubridge's handwriting, f.1, ADM 116/1169.

247. Diary entry 25 Apr 12, Grant-Duff Mss, DC/MISC/77.

248. Churchill, *World Crisis,* 153.

249. Churchill to Clementine Churchill, 24 Mar 12, ibid.

250. Churchill, first draft of *World Crisis,* f.4, Chart 8/60; Churchill to Bridgeman, 27 Sep 12, Chart 13/13; Churchill, "Notes on the Manoeuvres prepared for the PM by the First Lord, 17 Oct 13, ADM 116/3381.

251. Churchill to Battenberg, 18 Sep 12, f.212, Chart 13/22B.

252. Churchill to Asquith, 15 Aug 12, *YS,* c3, 1633.

253. Ibid.; Battenberg to Churchill, n/d [reference to Bridgeman's illness dates this paper to Aug or Sep 1912], discussing possible replacements, CAB 1/34; See also Churchill to Battenberg, 18 Sep 12, f.212, Chart 13/22B; Churchill to Troubridge, 14 Nov 12, C2, Troubridge Mss (NMM).

254. Lambert, "Admiral Sir Francis Bridgeman," 69–70; see also note by "Bal" (Lord Lindsay of Balcarres) to Sandars, 5 Dec 12, f.22, Sandars Mss 765.

255. Ibid.

256. Ballard, memorandum, Sept. 1912, ADM 116/866B; Ballard, "Remarks by D.O.D.," n/d [March 1913], on Churchill to Battenberg, 17 Feb 13, f.204, ADM 116/3412.

257. Callaghan to Admiralty, 28 Aug 13, in "Naval Manoeuvres, 1913—North Sea Strategy," ADM 116/3130.

258. Ballard, "Observation force in the North Sea: Remarks on War Orders for, in connection with lessons of 1912 manoeuvres," 16 Sep 12, ADM 116/866B; Bridgeman to Troubridge, 6 Dec 12, B6, Troubridge Mss (NMM).

259. Ottley to Esher, 8 Oct 11, Esher Mss 4/3.

260. Hankey to Esher, 5 Oct 11, Esher Mss 4/3.

261. Confidential reports on G. A. Ballard by Beresford and Callaghan, f.29, ADM 196/90.

262. Grant-Duff diary, n/d (after entry of 25 Aug11), Grant-Duff Mss, DC/MISC/77.

263. Fisher to Churchill, 26 Oct, 11, 4 Nov 11, *YS,* c3, 1300, 1321.

264. For Churchill's responsibility in Troubridge's selection see: Churchill to Battenberg, 19 Nov 11, MB1/T9/43, Battenberg Mss.

265. Asquith to Troubridge, 1 Sep 10, A1, Troubridge Mss (NMM).

266. Diary entry 25 Apr 12, Grant-Duff Mss, DC/MISC/77.

267. Diary entry 11 Oct 12, ibid.

268. Churchill to Battenberg, 18 Sep 13, f.212, Chart 13/22B.

269. Ibid., 2–3.

270. Despite being still only a captain, Ballard was appointed admiral of patrols in succession to Rear Adm. John de Robeck: *Navy List,* June 1914.

271. Ibid.

272. Admiralty to C. in C., 16 Dec 12, enclosing draft War Orders on M0020, f.47, ADM 116/3412.

273. Admiralty, War Orders, "Part 1—General Instructions," f.10, ADM 116/3412.

274. Churchill to Asquith, "Notes on the Manoeuvres Prepared for the PM by the First Lord," 17 Oct 12, ADM 116/3381.

275. Admiralty, "War Plans & War Orders," part 1, November 1912, 25 Nov 12, ADM 116/3412. The draft War Orders in force from April to November cannot be located; they may never have existed.

276. Ballard, "Remarks by D.O.D.," n/d [March 1913], f.204, ADM 116/3412.

277. Beatty, notes, n/d [1913], f.188, ADM 116/3412. N.B., Beatty was succeeded as naval secretary on 8 Jan 13.

278. Ibid.

279. Churchill to Battenberg, 17 Feb 13, f.190, ADM 116/3412; and testimony of Churchill to the CID invasion enquiry, 3 Dec 13, p. 310 (Q.2655), CAB 16/28A.

280. Bridgeman to Troubridge, 26 Nov 12 and 6 Dec 12, B6, Troubridge Mss (NMM).

281. Jackson, "Remarks on War Plans and on the First Lord's Notes on the Subject," 11 Mar 13, f.194, ADM 116/3412.

282. Ibid.

283. Marder, *FDSF*, I, 354–57.

284. Seely to Asquith, 3 Jan 13, f.13–15, Mottistone Mss 13 [Papers of Jack Seely, Nuffield College, Oxford].

285. Jackson, "Remarks on War Plans and on the First Lord's Notes on the Subject," 11 Mar 13, f.194, ADM 116/3412.

286. Ibid.

287. Ibid.

288. Ibid.

289. Ballard, "Remarks by D.O.D.," Ballard, n/d [March 1913], f.201, ibid.; Ballard, "Memorandum on Seizure of Advanced Base," n/d, f.296, ADM 116/866B.

290. Richmond, "Remarks on First Lord's Paper," unsigned [but Richmond's handwriting], n/d [March 1913], f.205, ADM 116/3412; the three staff assessments are quoted at length in Marder, *FDSF*, I, 372–400.

291. Fisher to Churchill, 24 Apr 13, f.12, Chart 13/21.

292. Mackay, *Kilverstone*, 456; Admiralty to Bayly, 31 Jan 13, ADM 137/452.

293. Minute (26 Mar 13) by Jackson to Battenberg, on "Points raised by C. in C. Home Fleet," MB1/T23/184, Battenberg Mss; Jackson to Battenberg, 5 Apr 13, MB1/T23/199, ibid.

294. Beatty to Churchill [7 Apr 12], Ranft, *Beatty Papers*, I, 44–45; Beatty to Churchill [7 Apr 12], cited in Ranft, *Beatty Papers*, I, 44–45; There is a remarkable similarity of the language in this document and that in Churchill's letter to Battenberg of 17 Feb 13; see also Hankey to Churchill, 9 Sep 13, f.51, CAB 1/32.

295. Ballard to Jackson, 10 Jul 13, ADM 137/452.

296. Callaghan to Admiralty, 3 Oct 13, enclosing paper on "Employment of Destroyers," MB1/T26/240, Battenberg Mss.

297. Testimony by Churchill to Invasion Enquiry 1913, 3 Dec 13, Q.2655, p. 310, CAB 16/28A.

298. Minutes (27 Jul 14) by Jackson on "Plan L" (a) and (b) f.15, ADM 137/0968; Churchill to Battenberg, 11 Jun 14, ADM 116/3096.

299. Ballard, "Observation Force in the North Sea," 16 Sep 12, p. 3, f.290, ADM 116/866B.

300. Ibid.

301. Minutes (6 Feb 13) by Ballard and (11 Feb 13) by Jackson, on "Proposals for the use of Mines in anti-German War," f.493, ADM 116/3412.

302. Minutes of 120th CID, 6 Dec 12, CAB 2/3.

303. Minute (n/d) by General David French (CIGS) on paper by Henry Wilson (DMI) addresses to Seely, 20 Jan 13, f.29, Mottistone Mss 2.

304. Ballard, Memorandum, f.493, ADM 116/3412.

305. Ballard, "Observation Force in the North Sea," 16 Sep 12, p. 3, f.290, ADM 116/866B.

306. Ballard, "Secret Proposals Regarding the Use of Mines in Support of an Offensive Strategic Plan," 6 Feb 13, f.542, ADM 116/3412. For Board approval see Admiralty to Callaghan, 23 Apr 13 (Letter M0033/13) f.504, 542, ibid.; see also Jackson to Battenberg, 5 Apr 13, Battenberg Mss MB1/T23/199.

307. Minute (21 Nov 13) by chief hydrographer, referring to instructions dated 22 September, f.500, ibid.

308. Marder, *FDSF*, I, 328–29.

309. Churchill, *World Crisis*, 152.

310. Testimony by Churchill to Invasion Enquiry 1913, 3 Dec 13, p. 313 (Q.2672) CAB 16/28A.

311. Ibid., pp. 310–311 (Q.2655).

Chapter Nine: The Revolution

1. *Parliamentary Debates*, 5th series, vol. 35 (1912), 1556, 1563–68, Churchill, 18 Mar 12.

2. Sandars to Balfour, 16 Oct 12, *YS*, c3, 1655.

3. Ibid.

4. Minutes of 117th meeting of CID, 4 Jul 12, CAB 2/2.

5. Sandars to Balfour, 16 Oct 12, *YS*, c3, 1655.

6. Churchill to Moore, 27 Oct 12, pp. 114–16, FLM, Admiralty Library.

7. Sumida, *In Defence*, table 16.

8. Churchill to Lloyd George, 12 Jul 12, CAB 37/111/92.

9. Churchill to Lloyd George, 29 Oct 12, *YS*, c3, 1658.

10. Churchill to Lloyd George, 3 Nov 12, *YS*, c3, 1659.

11. Churchill, "Proposed Scale of Pay—Royal Navy," 1 Oct 12, 35 pages, Mottistone Mss [N.B. this paper is not listed in the CAB 37 series of Cabinet Papers]; idem, "Navy Pay (November 1911)," printed 7 Nov 12, P.902K, Admiralty Library.

12. Churchill to Lloyd George, 12 Jul 12, CAB37/111/92; also Asquith to the King, 16 Jul 12, f.156, Asquith Mss 6.

13. Fisher to Esher, 2 Aug 12, *FGDN*, I, 475.

14. Cabinet notes, 16 Jul 12, Lloyd George Mss, cited in *YS*, c3, 1619.

15. Minute (16 Jul 12) by Churchill on Lloyd George's Cabinet note, ibid.

16. Ibid.

17. Initially Churchill had planned to inform the Cabinet of the full costs but later changed his mind after securing Borden's offer. See: Churchill to Lloyd George, 12 Jul 12, CAB 37/111/92 [Marked "not sent"].

18. Borden to Churchill, 3 Oct 12, c3, 1650; Asquith to Harcourt, 15 Sep 12, f.188, Harcourt Mss, dep. 421.

19. Churchill to Lloyd George, 12 Jul 12, CAB37/111/92 ["not sent"].

20. Ibid.

21. Williams, *Defending the Empire*, 208–12.

22. Lansdowne to Selborne, 4 Sep 12, f.117, Selborne Mss 79, cited by Williams, 209–10, ibid.

23. For instance: Speech given at Guildhall Banquet, reported in the *Times*, 10 Nov 11, p. 10, col. 2; Williams, *Defending the Empire*, 206–8.

24. Churchill to Lloyd George, 29 Oct and 3 Nov 12, *YS*, c3, 1658–60.

25. Ballard, "Observation force in the North Sea: Remarks on war orders for, in connection with lessons of 1912 manoeuvres," 16 Sep 12, ADM 116/866B. For evidence this paper was noticed by Churchill and the Sea Lord's see Churchill to Bridgeman, 27 Sep 12, Chart 13/13.

26. Ibid.

27. Sandars to Balfour, 16 Oct 12, f.29, Add Mss 49768. Note: the most important part of this letter was deleted by Randolph Churchill (*YS*, c3, 1655).

28. Ibid.

29. Troubridge to de Robeck, 20 Sep 12, De Robeck Mss, 3/31 [Churchill College, Cambridge].

30. Fisher to Churchill, 8 Nov 12, f.107, Chart 8/177.

31. Ibid.; Fisher to Bonar Law, 27 Jul 12, Bonar Law Mss, 26/5/42 [House of Lords Record Office].

32. Milan Vego, *Austro-Hungarian Naval Policy, 1904–1914* (Frank Cass: London, 1996), 136; Lawrence Sondhaus, *The Naval Policy of Austria-Hungary, 1867–1918: Navalism, Industrial Development, and the Politics of Dualism* (West Lafayette, Ind.: Purdue U.P., 1994), makes no mention of the proposed increase.

33. Sir F. Cartwright (British ambassador in Vienna) to Foreign Office, 19 Sep 12, f.274, and telegram (16 Oct 12), Cartwright to Foreign Office, f.304, 43537, FO 371/1298; Churchill to Lloyd George, 18 Nov 12, *YS*, c3 1671; Halpern, *Mediterranean*, 172–74.

34. Churchill to Lloyd George, 18 Nov 12, *YS*, c3, 1671.

35. Ibid.

36. Ballard, "Considerations as to the best composition of the Mediterranean fleet in 1915," 20 Nov 12, f.77, ADM 116/3099.

37. Ibid.

38. Ibid.

39. Admiralty, "Reports of the Finance Committee of the Admiralty on the Sketch Navy Estimates 1913–14, Prepared in October-December 1912," 19 Dec 12, ADM 1/8275; Lord Riddle, diary, 27 Apr 13, f.140, Add Mss 62972.

40. The original docket containing the minutes cited in the volumes of First Lord's Minutes at the Admiralty Library (see note 2 above) is not in the Public Record Office.

41. Churchill, "New programme 1913/14," 8 Dec 12, *YS*, c3, 1695–97.

42. Ibid.

43. For more evidence of complaints against Churchill's forcefulness see Sumida, *In Defence*, 254–55.

44. Extracts from Jellicoe's autobiographical notes (Add Mss 49038, pp. 239–50) cited in Temple Patterson, *The Jellicoe Papers* (N.R.S.: London, 1966), vol. 1, 27.

45. Vego, *Austro-Hungarian Naval Policy,* 147–54.

46. Churchill, "The Strength of the Navy, 1914/15," printed 1 Jan 14, f.112, CAB 1/32.

47. Lord Riddle, diary, 31 Oct 13, f.59/60, Add Mss 62973; Brinkley Gilbert, *Lloyd George: Organiser of Victory* (London, 1992), 55–66.

48. Minute (10 Jun 13) by Churchill, "Submarine Construction, 1914/15: Précis of Papers," Keyes Mss 4/5.

49. Average costs of warships in 1913: Battleship *Queen Elizabeth* (including outfits) £2,760,337; "M" class destroyer (average) £125,000; E class submarine (*E17 & E18*), £105,560.

50. Minute (12 Jun 13) by Moore, "Submarine Construction 1914–15: précis of papers," Keyes Mss 4/5.

51. Keyes to Dawson, 20 Aug 13, Vickers Mss 741; See also J. R.Wardropper (works superintendent at the Vickers diesel engine plant) to J. Meckechie (director), 20, 25 Nov 12, Vickers Mss 1110; Fisher to Asquith, Mar 1916, *FGDN,* III, 326.

52. Minute (12 Jun 13) by Moore, Keyes Mss 4/5.

53. Minutes (12, 18 Jun 13) by Moore, ibid.

54. Minutes (24 Jun 13 & 26 Jun 13) by Battenberg, and (3 Jul 13) by Jellicoe, ibid.

55. Minutes (2 Jul 13) by Churchill and Lambert (financial secretary), ibid.

56. Minute (8 Jul 13) by Moore, ibid. Firms approached were: Yarrow, White, Hawthorn Leslie, Swan Hunter, Denny, Thorneycroft, Fairfield and Beardmore. For evidence of receipt of this approach see Admiralty to Thorneycroft, 16 Jul 13, Thorneycroft Mss X175.

57. Minutes of meeting held 29 Jan 13 shows these were the terms offered to Armstrongs, Whitworth Ltd., and Messrs. Scott, f.12, Ships Covers 404B.

58. Ballard, "General Policy of Submarine Development," 14 Jul 13, X3341/12, ADM 1/8331.

59. For evidence that shipbuilders that specialized in building destroyers were aware of the Admiralty's intentions see Nicholas Lambert, "British Naval Policy 1913/14: Financial Limitation and Strategic Revolution," *The Journal of Modern History* 67:3 (September 1995): 605; Messrs Thorneycroft internal letters, 13, 17 Mar 13, file X175, and Thorneycroft to Admiralty, 5 Feb 13, file X123, all in Thorneycroft Mss; Churchill to Chief of War Staff, 11 Mar 13, p. 205, FLM, Admiralty Library; Churchill, "New programme 1913/14," 8 Dec 12, *YS,* c3, 1695–97.

60. Keyes, "Commodore S Minute on Submarines," 15 Aug 13, DEY 31, d'Eyncourt Mss [National Maritime Museum].

61. Ballard, "General Policy of Submarine Development," 14 Jul 13, X3341/12, ADM 1/8331.

62. Ibid.

63. Jackson, "War Staff Minute on Submarines" n/d. [July 1913] DEY 31, d'Eyncourt Mss.

64. Minute (3 Jul 13) by Jellicoe, "Submarine Construction 1914–15," Keyes Mss 4/10.

65. Ibid.

66. Keyes, "Commodore S Minute on Submarines," 15 Aug 13, DEY 31, d'Eyncourt Mss.

67. Ibid., p. 2.

68. Ibid.; see also a restatement of the arguments, in Keyes to Battenberg, 18 Aug 13, Keyes Mss 4/11.

69. Ballard, "General Policy of Submarine Development," 14 Jul 13, X3341/12, ADM 1/8331; Jackson, "War Staff Minute on Submarines," July or August 1913, DEY 31, d'Eyncourt Mss.

70. Churchill, "First Lord's Minute on Submarines," 20 Jul 13, DEY 31, d'Eyncourt Mss.

71. Ibid.

72. Churchill to 1st and 3rd Sea Lords, 15 Aug 13, 1911–13, p. 256, FLM, Admiralty Library.

73. Churchill, "First Lord's Minute on Submarines," 20 Jul 13, DEY 31, d'Eyncourt Mss.

74. Ibid.

75. Docket, "Naval Manoeuvres 1913" subtitled "North Sea Problem—War Plans," 29 Jan 13, ADM 116/1214.

76. Lord Riddle, diary, 21 Mar and 5 May 13, f.62, 153, Add Mss 62972.

77. Docket, "Naval Manoeuvres 1913" subtitled "North Sea Problem—War Plans," 29 Jan 13, ADM 116/1214; for reference to the primary object of the maneuvers see minutes (8 Sep 13) by Ballard and Jackson on criticisms of the manoeuvres by Admiral Custance, ADM 116/1169.

78. Minute (12 Feb 13) by Jackson on "Naval Manoeuvres 1913," ADM 116/1214.

79. Adm. Sir William May, "Naval Manoeuvres 1913: Report of Umpire in Chief," p. 6, MB1/T26/231; Minute (20 Aug 13) by de Robeck on Keyes to de Robeck, 10 Aug 13, f.425, ADM 137/1926; Jellicoe to May, 1 Aug 13, p. 4, ADM 116/1214; Keyes to Admiralty, 1 Nov 14, p. 7, ADM 137/1926; Hall to Fisher, n/d [Aug 1913] FP648, Fisher Papers 1/12.

80. Hall to Fisher, ibid.

81. For critique by the War Staff see "Remarks on Comments by the Commander-in-Chief on the 1913 Manoeuvres," 29 Sep 13, ADM 116/1214; also a highly critical letter from Churchill to Callaghan dated 29 Jul 13, Chart 13/5.

82. Callaghan, "Naval Manoeuvres, 1913: North Sea Strategy," p. 11, ADM 116/3130. Copies also found in f.48, ADM 137/1936 and ADM 116/1214.

83. Report of Committee under Sir George Callaghan on the function of the Grand Fleet, October 1914, Richmond Mss, RIC 2/2.

84. Ibid.

85. Callaghan to Admiralty (No.1472/H.F.7.S.) 2 Oct 13, citing Admiralty letter to c. in c. M0036/13, of 22 Jul 13, Battenberg Mss, MB1/T26/240.

86. Callaghan to Admiralty, 2 Oct 13, ibid.

87. Callaghan, "Review of War Plans after Manoeuvres," 2 Oct 13, ibid.

88. Callaghan, "Employment of Destroyers in War," paragraph 4, enclosure, ibid.

89. Ibid.

90. Jellicoe, "Naval Manoeuvres, 1913," 6 Aug 13, ADM 116/3381.

91. Battenberg, Memorandum on coastal defence, n/d, MB1/T37/377, and War Staff, "Districts, Areas and Groups on the east coast of Scotland and England," 6 Jun 13, MB1/T25/227, Battenberg Mss.

92. Robeck's dismissal was forecast in testimony by Churchill to 1913 Invasion Enquiry, 3 Dec 13, pp. 319–320 (Q.2726) CAB16/28A.

93. Minute (n/d) by Battenberg, on War Staff memorandum "Organisation of Patrol Flotillas and Coastal Watching (3 Apr 14), MB1/T32/302, Battenberg Mss; War Staff, "Draft report on Coast Defence," 15 Dec 13, MB1/T33/317; Minute (n/d) by Battenberg on previous report in MB1/T37/377; Minute (12 Nov 13) by Churchill, on transferring control of RNAS to Admiral of Patrols, FLM, 4th series, p. 5; Minute (18 Jun 14) by Capt. Arthur Leverson (DOD), MB1/T36/354, Battenberg Mss.

94. Burney to Callaghan, 23 Jul 14, enclosing "B8 How far aircraft are likely to replace the advanced cruiser line in the near future. How far they are likely to replace the Patrol flotillas," f.86, ADM 137/1939.

95. Minute (26 Feb 13) by Churchill, on Admiralty, "Aerial Warfare," 26 Jul 13, ADM 1/8331.

96. The total sum to be spend on the RN Air Service in 1914 and 1915 was to be £978,473. In addition, 1,452 naval personnel were to be allocated to the RNAS, for which see Jellicoe, "Aerial Warfare," 16 May 13, Admiralty "Aerial Warfare," ADM 1/8331.

97. This mistaken view was expressed by Samuel Williamson, *The Politics of Grand Strategy*, 308, note 22.

98. Gordon, *The Rules of the Game*, 25–28, 55.

99. Burney to Callaghan, 23 Jul 14, enclosing "B5: decentralisation of command, i.e.— to what extent Junior Flag officers should act on their own initiative and responsibility without signals and orders from the Commander-in-Chief," f.83, Adm137/1939; CQI (alias Capt. E. W. Hardinge), "Naval Tactics, Studies in the Theory of" (in four parts), *Naval Review* (1913): 12, 82, 208, (1914), part 4: 123.

100. Jellicoe, testimony to 1913 Invasion Enquiry, p. 315 (Q.2687), CAB 16/28A.

101. Jellicoe, "Naval Manoeuvres, 1913," 6 Aug 13, ADM 116/3381.

102. Callaghan, "Naval Manoeuvres, 1913," 28 Aug 13, p. 19, ADM 116/3130.

103. Battenberg to Churchill, 10 Jun 12, f.1, CAB 1/33.

104. Minute (22 Apr 13) by Battenberg, on "Fitting of Mines in Torpedo Boat Destroyers—reports and minutes on G.01358/12," f.318, *IQDNO*, vol. 3, 1914, Admiralty Library.

105. Sumida, *In Defence*, 250–51, 255–56.

106. Callaghan, "Employment of Destroyers in War," Callaghan, 3 Oct 13, Battenberg Mss, MB1/T26/240; see also Burney to Callaghan, 23 Jul 14, enclosing "B4: The use to which light cruisers and torpedo craft are to be applied in a fleet action, and the defence against the same," f.82, ADM 137/1939.

107. Remarks by Richmond on C. in C. HF's letter on North Sea Strategy, p. 7, ADM 116/1169.

108. Callaghan, "Employment of Destroyers in War," Callaghan, 3 Oct 13, MB1/T26/240, Battenberg Mss.

109. War Staff, "Remarks on Comments by the Commander-in-Chief on the 1913 Manoeuvres," 29 Sep 13, ADM 116/1214.

110. Callaghan to Admiralty, 11 Dec 12, G.01313/13, f.314, *IQDNO*, vol. 3, 1914, Admiralty Library.

111. Minutes (21 Jan 14) by Lambert, (24 Jan 14) by Moore, and (26 Jan 14) by Battenberg, on "Outfit of Torpedoes for Torpedo boat destroyers of First Fleets," f.311–313, ibid.

112. War Staff, "Remarks on Comments by the Commander-in-Chief on the 1913 Manoeuvres," 29 Sep 13, ADM 116/1214; Callaghan to de Robeck, 6 Aug 13, pp. 414–19, ADM 137/1926.

113. Jellicoe, "Naval Manoeuvres, 1913," 6 Aug 13, p. 5, ADM 116/3381.

114. Custance to Churchill, 28 Sep 13, enclosing annotated copy of Callaghan's "Naval Manoeuvres, 1913: North Sea Strategy"; Churchill to Battenberg, 30 Aug 13, MB1/T26/238, Battenberg Mss; Custance to Churchill, 10 Aug 14, f.43, Chart 13/43.

115. Custance to Churchill, 10 Aug 14, f.43, Chart 13/43; Custance to Churchill, 30 Aug 13, and Churchill to Asquith, 30 Aug 13, ADM 116/3381.

116. Churchill to Battenberg, 18 Sep 13, f.212, Chart 13/22b; typed memorandum by War Staff on Admiral Custance's critique, 8 Sep 13, notes marked "received 8/9/23," ADM 116/1169; Bridgeman to Troubridge, 6 Sep 13, B6, Troubridge Mss (NMM).

117. Battenberg to Churchill, 24 Oct 13, f.109, CAB 1/33.

118. Minute (n/d) by Churchill, on Custance to Churchill, 30 Aug 13, ADM 116/3381.

119. Marder, *FDSF*, I, 330.

120. Fisher to Churchill, 26 Oct 11, 2 & 4 Nov 11, *YS*, c2, 1299–1321; in 1920, Kerr wrote Battenberg's biography.

121. Churchill to Greek Minister of Marine, 2 Jun 13, *YS*, c3, 1751.

122. Kerr, "Greek Naval Construction Policy," print, n/d [Sept. 13], ADM 116/3486.

123. Kerr to Greek Minister of Marine, 4 Oct 13, print, ADM 116/3486.

124. Ibid., p. 4.

125. Ibid.

126. Ballard, "Remarks on Proper Shipbuilding Policy for Greece," 7 Jan 13; Minutes (2 Jan 13) by Churchill and (7 Jan 13) by Troubridge, in "Greece, Shipbuilding and Islands," ADM 116/3098.

127. Hall to Fisher, 26 Apr 14, FP803, Fisher Papers 1/15; see also Hall to Fisher, 14 Jun 14, FP809, ibid.

128. Warrender to Callaghan, 8 Jul 14, f.35, ADM 137/1939; see also other submissions ff.40–90.

129. Briggs to Callaghan, 22 Jun 14, f.41, ADM 137/1939.

130. Minute (16 May 14) by Keyes on, submarine committee to Admiralty, 5 May 14, f.460–464, ADM 137/1926; Capt. John Dumaresq to Rear Adm. Reginald Tupper, 28 Dec 13, Tupper Mss. See reference to views of Vice Adm. Doveton Sturdee in Hall to Fisher, 26 Apr 14, FP803, Fisher Papers 1/15.

131. Mackay, *Kilverstone*, 439.

132. Churchill to Fisher, 11 Jun 12, cited in Churchill, *World Crisis*, 137–38; also in Marder, *FDSF*, I, 270; Churchill to Fisher, 26 May 12 and Hopwood to Churchill, 1 Jun 12, *YS*, c3, 1928.

133. Fisher to Churchill, 24 Apr 13, *YS*, c3, 1939.

134. Anonymous [Hall], "The Influence of the Submarine upon Naval Policy," *Naval Review* (1913): 256–61, 396–402, (1914): 47–52.

135. For evidence of Hall's authorship see: "Author List for The Naval Review, 1913–1930," in, *Mahan is Not Enough*, ed. Goldrick and Hattendorf, 342–46.

136. Various drafts sent from Fisher to Balfour, f.87 et seq., Add Mss 49712; Sydenham to Fisher, 24 Jun 13, and 28 Jun 13, FP704 & 705, Fisher Papers 1/13.

137. Fisher to Churchill, 31 Mar 13, *YS*, c3, 1937.

138. Fisher to Balfour, 15 May 13, f.95; memo entitled "Submarines and Commerce," 28 May 13, f.105, both Add Mss 49712.

139. Engineer Lt. C. J. Hawkes (DNC's department) to Fisher, n/d [May 1913], FP698; Fisher to Hopwood, 16 Jun 13, FP690, Fisher Papers 1/13.

140. Moore to Keyes, 12 May 13, Keyes Mss 4/23.

141. Tennyson d'Enycourt, "Proposed Submarine" [c. May 1913], DEY 31, d'Eyncourt Mss.

142. Admiralty, Memorandum prepared by the DNC's department on "The Development of the Submarine," p. 9, printed 31 Dec 18, ADM 1/8547/340.

143. Hall to Fisher, 4 Jul 13, FP708, and 19 Aug 13, FP717, both Fisher Papers 1/13.

144. Fisher to Jellicoe, 1 Jun 13, *FGDN*, II, 489, ft.1.

145. Fisher to Churchill, ? Oct 13, *YS*, c3, 1955.

146. Hall to Fisher, 19 Aug 13, FP717, and Churchill to Fisher, 30 Aug 13, FP720, Fisher Papers 1/13.

147. Between May and November 1913 this paper was printed in runs of 6, 2, 25, 6.

148. Churchill to Fisher, 12 Nov 13, *YS*, c3, 1795.

149. Churchill to Fisher, 1 Jan 14, FP763, Fisher Papers 1/14; See also Mackay, *Kilverstone*, 453.

150. Marder, *FDSF*, I, 363; Mackay, *Kilverstone*, 441–51.

151. Fisher, "The Oil Engine and the Submarine," Run of 6, printed 11/13, FP4293, Fisher Papers 5/13.

152. Ibid.

153. Ibid., p. 2.

154. Ibid., p. 9.

155. Ibid.

156. Marder, *FDSF*, I, 363–64.

157. Hall to Fisher, 11 Dec 13, Fisher Papers 1/14, FP758. (This letter is dated Thursday, 11 December 1913, and refers to a meeting having taken place the previous Tuesday—9 December); see also reference in Churchill to Sea Lords, 25 Dec 13, f.261, Chart 13/22B, f.261; and Keyes, "Record of Conference held in First Lord's room, 9 December 1913," Keyes Mss 4/10.

158. Ibid.

159. Keyes, "Record of Conference held in First Lord's room on 9 December 1913," paragraph 2, Keyes Mss 4/10; this was also Jellicoe's impression for which see: Jellicoe to Board of Admiralty (addressed to First Lord), 19 Dec 13, MB1/T49/25, Battenberg Mss.

160. Ibid.

161. Keyes to Trevor Dawson (managing director of Vickers Ltd.), 20 Aug 13, Vickers Mss 741; Keyes, Memorandum addressed to First Lord, January 1914, Keyes Mss 4/11.

162. The Improved **E** was later designated as **G** class for which see: Ships Covers 330, G class submarines, f.1, d'Enycourt to Mr. Johns, 10 Dec 13; Moore to Keyes, 30 Dec 13, Keyes Mss 4/4.

163. Jellicoe to Board of Admiralty (addressed to First Lord), 19 Dec 13, p. 1, MB1/T49/25; in fact, faith was broken at the end of December: Churchill to Sea Lords, 25 Dec 13, f.261, Chart 13/22B; Jellicoe, Memorandum to 1st Lord, 1st and 3rd Sea Lords, 19 Dec 13, T49/25, Battenberg Mss; Admiralty, "Request for Tenders," 28 Oct 13—due 10 Dec 13—Thorneycroft Mss X123.

164. Keyes, "Record of Conference. . . ." Keyes Mss 4/10.

165. Ibid., paragraph 7.

166. Jellicoe to Board of Admiralty (addressed to first lord), 19 Dec 13, p. 1, MB1/T49/25; for reply see Churchill to Jellicoe, 16 Jan 14, f.23, Chart 13/29.

167. Churchill to First, Second and Third Sea Lords, 25 Dec 13. f.261, Chart 13/22B.

168. Ibid.

169. Ibid.

170. For reference to the "secret file" see Churchill to Masterton-Smith, 2 Jan 14, f.6, Chart 13/29.

171. Churchill to Moore, 14 Jan 14, vol 2, p. 9. FLM, Admiralty Library.

172. Churchill to Moore, 22 Jan 14, p. 16, ibid.

173. Churchill to Battenberg, 26 Dec 13, MB1/T28/261, Battenberg Mss.

174. Churchill, "Naval Estimates 1914/15," 5 Dec 13, CAB 37/117/86.

175. The hard-line economists were Herbert Samuel (postmaster general), John Simon (attorney general), Charles Hobhouse (duchy of Lancaster), Walter Runciman (Agriculture and Fisheries), and Joseph Pearce (Education). They were supported by McKenna (home secretary) McKinnon Wood, Lord Beauchamp, and Lewis Harcourt (colonial secretary), for which see Simon to Asquith, 29 Jan 14, f.29, Simon Mss 50 [Bodleian Library]; Churchill, *Young Statesman,* 659, 668.

176. Lord Riddle, diary, 18 Dec 13, f.98, Add Mss 62973, & 16 Jan 14, f.31, Add Mss 62974.

177. Asquith to Lloyd George, 17 Nov 13, cited in Churchill, *Young Statesman,* 655–66.

178. Cabinet notes between Churchill and Lloyd George, 16 Dec 13, and Hopwood to Stamfordham, 11 Jan 14, both cited in Churchill, *Young Statesman,* 661, 668; McKenna to Riddle, cited in Lord Riddle, diary, 31 Dec 13, f.91–93, Add Mss 49673.

179. Lord Riddle, diary, 31 Oct 13, f.59/60, Add Mss 62973; Brinkley Gilbert, *Lloyd George: Organiser of Victory* (London, 1992), 55–66; see also Ian Packer, "The Liberal Land Campaign and the Land Issue, c.1906–1919" (Ph.D. diss., Oxford, 1995); Bridgeman to Sandars, 2 and 11 Jan 14, f.13, Sandars Mss 766.

180. Churchill, "Naval Estimates: Notes on Various Suggestions for Reduction," 13 Dec 13, CAB 37/117/93.

181. Hopwood to Stamfordham, 17 Dec 13, cited in Randolph Churchill, *Young Statesman*, 661–62.

182. Ibid.

183. Lord Riddle, diary, 18 Dec 13, f.98–100, Add Mss 62973.

184. Simon to Asquith, 29 Jan 14, f.30, Simon Mss 50.

185. Cabinet notes passed between Churchill and Lloyd George, *YS*, c3, 1833.

186. E. David, ed., *Inside Asquith's Cabinet: From the Diaries of Edward Hobhouse* (London, 1977), 20 Dec 13, 154, cited in Gilbert, *Lloyd George*, 70–74.

187. Churchill to Borden, 19 Dec 12, and Borden to Churchill, 31 Dec 13, MG26H, OC659, volume 126, 67914 (Microfilm reel C4349), Borden Mss [Canadian National Archives]; for an informed assessment of the implications see Hopwood to Stamfordham, 5 Jan 14, Churchill, *Young Statesman*, 667.

188. Churchill to Asquith, 18 Dec 13, *YS*, c3, 1834; for the eventual adoption of this policy see Churchill to Asquith, 4 Jul 14, p. 7, fifth series, FLM, Admiralty Library.

189. Churchill to Lloyd George, 19 Jan 14, f.160, Asquith Mss 25.

190. Bruce Murray, "Battered and Shattered: Lloyd-George and the 1914 Budget Fiasco," *Albion* 23/3 (Fall 1991): 483–507; F. W. Wiemann, "Lloyd George and the Struggle for the Navy Estimates of 1914," *Lloyd George: Twelve Essays*, ed. A. J. P. Taylor (Atheneum: New York, 1971), 71–91.

191. Lord Riddle, diary, 16 Jan 14, f.16, Add Mss 62974.

192. Lord Riddle, diary, 23rd to 25th January, f.31–34, ibid.; Churchill to Asquith, 23 Jan 14, *YS*, c3, 1852; correspondence between Churchill to Lloyd George, 26 Jan 14 (2 letters), 27 Jan 14 (2 letters), *YS*, c3, 1853–56; J. B. to Chancellor of Exchequer, 26 Jan 14, C24/3/23, Lloyd-George Mss.

193. Churchill to Lloyd George, 19 Jan 14, f.160, Asquith Mss 25; Asquith to the King, 29 Jan 14, f.93, Asquith Mss 7.

194. Churchill to Asquith, 2 Feb 14, *YS*, c3, 1860.

195. Wiemann, "The Navy Estimates of 1914," 486–87; Asquith to the King, 29 Jan 14, Cabinet notes, Asquith Mss 6.

196. Churchill, first draft of "World Crisis," f.27, Chart 8/61.

197. Murray, "Battered and Shattered," note 2; Avner Offer, *Property and Politics, 1870–1914* (Cambridge, 1973), 396–400; Packer, "The Liberal Land Campaign" (Ph.D. diss., Oxford, 1995), 244.

198. Churchill, first draft of "World Crisis," f.27–30, Chart 8/61.

199. Ibid.

200. Ibid.

201. Minutes (22 Jan 14 and 1 Jun 14) both by Churchill to Moore, vol 2, p. 16, 62, FLM, Admiralty Library.

202. Churchill to Borden, 6:3:14, MG26H, OC 659, vol. 126, 68013. (microfilm reel C4349) Borden Mss; the *Navy List* shows that Vice Adm. Sir George Warrender's two-year term as admiral commanding the First Battle Squadron was due to end 16 Dec 14.

203. Bridgeman to Sandars, 8 Mar 16, f.62, Sandars Mss 759.

204. Hamilton to Churchill, n/d. [June 1914], Hamilton Mss 125.

205. Ibid.

206. Minutes (n/d) by Jellicoe and Moore, on undated handwritten memorandum by Hamilton (returned within Moore to Hamilton 17 Jul 14), box 124, Hamilton Mss (hereafter cited as Hamilton Memorandum).

207. Churchill to Controller, 11 Jun 14, vol.2, p. 67, FLM, Admiralty Library; Churchill to Sea Lord's, 1 Jun 14, MB1/T34/322, Battenberg Mss.

208. Vice Adm. Doveton Sturdee (chief of naval staff), "What is the Raison d'être of a Polyphemus at the present time?" and "What is the Strategic and Tactical Value of a Polyphemus?" both dated 24 Jul 14, MB1/T37/361 & /362, both Battenberg Mss; see also Ships Covers 333A (Polyphemus type) 1914; Diary entry 18 Nov 13, DEY31, d'Enycourt Mss.

209. Ibid.

210. Minute (n/d) by Jellicoe, Hamilton Memorandum, Hamilton Mss 124.

211. Minute (n/d) by Moore, ibid.

212. Churchill, first draft "World Crisis," f.28, Chart 8/61.

213. Ibid.

214. Churchill to Sea Lords, 1 Jun 14, MB1/T34/322, Battenberg Mss.

215. Churchill, first draft "World Crisis," f.28, Chart 8/61.

216. Hamilton, Hamilton Memorandum, Hamilton Mss 124.

217. Fisher to Jellicoe, 25 May 14, FGDN ii, 506.

218. Minute by Jellicoe, Hamilton Memorandum, Hamilton Mss 124; Churchill to Battenberg, 11 Jul 14, *YS,* c3, 1986.

219. Churchill to Borden, 6 Mar 14, MG26H (microfilm reel C4349), p. 68016, Borden Mss.

220. Telegram, Churchill to Borden, 8 Jul 14, p. 68057, ibid.

221. Adm. Sir Percy Scott, the *Times,* 5 Jun 14.

222. Kennedy, "Two Interpretations of British Seapower," 54–55.

223. Churchill, first Draft "World Crisis," f.28, Chart 8/61.

224. Fisher to Churchill, 7 Jul 14, f.24, Chart 13/43.

225. Fisher to Corbett, 22 Jun 14, *FGDN*, II, 507.

226. Churchill to Battenberg, 12 Jul 14, enclosing memorandum (f.117) and Churchill to Harcourt, 13 Jul 14, f.115–122, CAB 1/34; also Churchill to Battenberg, 11 Jul 14, *YS,* c3, 1986 (not sent).

227. Admiralty to Coventry Ordnance, and Admiralty to Armstrongs, both 29 Jul 14, Ships Covers 325 (HMS *Resistance*).

Selected Bibliography

Manuscript Collections

U.K. Institutions

Admiralty Papers (ADM), PRO, Kew
Cabinet Papers (CAB), PRO, Kew
Colonial Defence Committee Papers (CAB), PRO, Kew
Colonial Office Papers (CO), PRO, Kew
Committee of Imperial Defence Papers (CAB), PRO, Kew
Foreign Office Papers (FO), PRO, Kew
India Office Papers (IO), India Office Library, London
Intelligence Services (HD), PRO, Kew
Ministry of Supply Papers (SUP), PRO, Kew
Royal Navy Controller's Department (Ships Covers), Brass Foundry, National
    Maritime Museum
Treasury Papers (T), PRO, Kew
War Office Papers (WO), PRO, Kew
Other official papers are held at:
    HMS *Dolphin,* RN Submarine Museum, Gosport, Hampshire
    HMS *Excellent,* RN Gunnery Museum, Whale Island, Portsmouth
    Ministry of Defence Admiralty Library, Whitehall, London
    Ministry of Defence Naval Historical Branch, Whitehall, London
    Portsmouth Naval Museum, Portsmouth Dockyard Heritage Area
    Priddy's Hard Ordnance Collection, Winchester Record Office
    The Royal Archives, Windsor Castle

U.S. Institutions

United States Department of the Navy Papers, National Archives Records
    Administration, Washington, D.C.
United States House Naval Committee (bill files), National Archives Records
    Administration, Washington, D.C.
United States Naval War College Papers, Newport, R.I.

French Institution

Archives du Ministère de la Marine, Service Historique de la Marine, Chateau de
    Vincennes, Paris, France

Individuals

H. Oakley Arnold-Forster, British Library, London
Rear Adm. Frank D. Arnold-Forster, HMS *Dolphin*
Henry H. Asquith, Bodleian Library, Oxford
Arthur J. Balfour, British Library, London
Adm. Prince Louis of Battenberg, Southampton University
Adm. David Beatty, NMM
Cmdr. Carlyton Bellairs, Admiralty Library
Adm. Hon. Sir Alexander Bethell, King's College, London
Sir Robert Borden, Canadian National Archives, Ottawa, Ontario
Adm. Cyprian Bridge, NMM
John Burns, British Library, London
Frederick Campbell, 3d Earl Cawdor, Admiralty Library (another collection of
    Cawdor Papers is held at the Carmathen County Record Office)
Sir Henry Campbell-Bannermann, British Library, London
Sir Ernest Cassell, Southampton University Library
Austen Chamberlain Papers, Birmingham University Library
Joseph Chamberlain Papers, Birmingham University Library
Sir Winston S. Churchill (Chartwell Collection), Churchill College, Cambridge
    University
Sir George Clarke (Baron Sydenham), British Library, London
Sir Julian Corbett, both NMM and Admiralty Library
Capt. Thomas E. Crease, Admiralty Library
Adm. Kenneth Dewar, NMM
Maj. Adrian Grant Duff, Imperial War Museum
Adm. Martin E. Dunbar-Nasmith VC, private collection
Eustace W. Tenneyson d'Encourt, NMM
Viscount Lord Esher, Churchill College, Cambridge University
Adm. John A. Fisher, Churchill College, Cambridge University
David Lloyd George, House of Lords Record Office, London
Cmdr. David Graham-Brown, HMS *Excellent,* Whale Island
Sir William G. Greene, NMM
Sir Edward Grey, PRO (FO 800)
Howell A. Gwynne, Bodleian Library
Richard B. Haldane, National Library of Scotland, Edinburgh
Maurice Hankey (Lord Hankey), Churchill College, Cambridge University
Lewis Harcourt, Bodleian Library, Oxford
Adm. Frederick T. Hamilton, NMM
Adm. William Henderson, NMM
Sir Michael E. Hicks-Beech (Lord St. Aldwyn), Gloucester Record Office
Charles Hobhouse, British Library, London
Adm. John R. Jellicoe, British Library, London
Adm. Roger Keyes, British Library, London
Adm. George King-Hall (Private Collection)

Francis Knollys, Lord Knollys, Royal Archives, Windsor Castle
Andrew Bonar Law, House of Lords Record Office, London
Adm. Noel Laurence, HMS *Dolphin*
Walter Long, British Library, London
Adm. Charles E. Madden, NMM
Edward Marjoribanks, Earl Tweedmouth, Admiralty Library
Adm. William H. May, NMM and private collection
Reginald McKenna, Churchill College, Cambridge University
John Morley (Lord Morley of Blackburn), India Office Library
Adm. Gerald Noel, NMM
Adm. Geoffrey Phipps-Hornsby, NMM
Adm. Reginald Plunkett-Ernle-Erle-Drax, Churchill College, Cambridge University
Adm. Herbert Richmond, NMM
George A. Riddle (Lord Riddle), British Library, London
Adm. John de Robeck, Churchill College, Cambridge University
John S. Sandars, Bodleian Library, Oxford
John E. B. Seely (Lord Mottistone), Nuffield College, Oxford
William Palmer, 2d earl of Selborne, Bodleian Library, Oxford
Sir John Simon, Bodleian Library, Oxford
Adm. Edmond Slade, Queens University, Kingston, Canada
James Masterton-Smith, PRO (CAB 1)
James A. Spender, British Library, London
J. T. Stead, Churchill College, Cambridge University
Admiral Frederick D. Sturdee Papers, Churchill College Cambrige
Adm. Cecil Talbot, Imperial War Museum, London
Vosper-Thorneycroft Ltd., NMM
Henry G. Thursfield, NMM
Adm. Ernest Troubridge, NMM and Imperial War Museum, London
Adm. Reginald Tupper, Portsmouth Naval Museum
Vickers–Armstrongs Ltd., Cambridge University Library
Adm. Rosslyn E. Wemyss, Churchill College, Cambridge University
Arnold White, NMM
Henry Spencer Wilkinson, All Soul's College, Oxford

Printed Sources

Dictionary of National Biography.
G. P. Gooch and H. Temperley, ed., *British Documents on the Origins of the War, 1898–1914.* (HMSO, London, 1926–38).
Journal Officiel, Chambre des Députés, débats parlementaires, French Government Printing Office.
Navy Lists, HMSO, London.
Parliamentary Debates Official Report 4th and 5th Series, Wyman & Sons and HMSO, London.

Newspapers and Periodicals

Brassey's Naval Annual
Economic History Review
English Historical Review
Engineering
Historical Journal
Historical Research
History
International History Review
International Security
Journal of Military History
Journal of Modern History
Journal of Royal United Services Institution
Journal of Strategic Studies
La Marine Française
Le Yacht
Mariner's Mirror
Military Affairs
Naval Review
Naval War College Review
Navy League Journal
Observor
Revue Maritime
Times (London)
Times (New York)
Transactions of the Institute of Naval Architects
United States Naval Institute: Proceedings

Doctoral Theses

Michael W. Dash. "British Submarine Policy, 1853–1918." University of London, 1990.
Nicholas d'Ombrain. "The Military Departments and the Committee of Imperial Defence." Oxford University, 1969.
Nicholas A. Lambert. "The Influence of the Submarine upon Naval Strategic Thought, 1896–1914." Oxford University, 1992.
Ian D. Packer. "The Liberal Land campaign and the Land Issue, 1906–14." Oxford University, 1995.
Neil Summerton. "The Development of British Military Planning for a War against Germany, 1904–1914." University of London, 1970.
John R. Walser. "France's Search for a Battlefleet French Naval Policy, 1898–1914." University of North Carolina at Chapel Hill, 1976.

Books Cited

H.O. Arnold-Forster. *The Army in 1906 A Policy and a Vindication* (New York: E.P. Dutton, 1906).

Adm. Reginald H. Bacon. *From 1900 Onwards* (London: Hutchinson, 1940).

————. *The Life of Lord Fisher of Kilverstone* (London: Hodder & Stoughton, 1929).

Geoffrey Bennett. *Charlie B: A Biography of Admiral Lord Charles Beresford of Metemmeh and Curraghmore* (London: Peter Downey Ltd., 1968).

Michael Bentley. *The Climax of Liberal Politics: British Liberalism in Theory and Practice* (London: Edward Arnold, 1987).

D. G. Boyce. *The Crisis of British Power: The Imperial and Naval Papers of the Second Earl of Selborne, 1895–1910* (London: Historians Press, 1990).

Edward E. Bradford. *The Life of Admiral of the Fleet Sir Arthur Knyvett-Wilson* (London: John Murray, 1923).

Sir Thomas Brassey. *The British Navy: Its Strength, Resources, and Administration,* Five parts in five vols. (London: Hodder and Stoughton, 1882).

Maurice V. Brett. *Journals and Letters of Reginald Viscount Esher* (London: Nicholson & Watson, 1934–38).

Michael and Eleanor Brock, eds. *H. H. Asquith: Letters to Venetia Stanley* (Oxford: Oxford University Press, 1982).

Paul J. Cain and Anthony G. Hopkins. *British Imperialism: Innovation and Expansion, 1688–1914* (New York: Longmans, 1993).

Randolph S. Churchill. *Winston S. Churchill: Young Statesman* (London: Heineman, 1967).

Winston S. Churchill. *The World Crisis 1914–19.* 6 vols. (London: Thornton-Butterworth, 1923–29).

Peter Clarke. *Lancashire and the New Liberalism* (London: Greenman, 1971).

Julian S. Corbett. *Some Principles of Maritime Strategy* (London, 1911).

John Cowie. *Mines, Minelayers and Minelaying* (Oxford: Oxford University Press, 1949).

Edward David. *Inside Asquith's Cabinet: From the Diaries of Edward Hobhouse* (London: John Murray, 1977).

Nicholas d'Ombrain. *War Machinery and High Policy: Defence Administration in Peace-time Britain, 1902–1914* (Oxford: Oxford University Press, 1973).

John A. Fisher. *Memoirs and Records* (London: Hodder & Stoughton, 1921).

François Fournier. *La Politique navale et la flotte française* (Paris, 1910).

————. *Notre marine de guerre, reformes essentielles, par un marin* (Paris, 1904).

————. *La Flotte nécessaire, ses advantages stratégiques, tactiques, et économiques* (Paris, 1896).

David French. *British Economic and Strategic Planning, 1905–15* (London: Allen & Unwin, 1982).

————. *British Strategy and War Aims, 1914–16* (London, 1986).

Aaron Friedberg. *The Weary Titan: Britain and the Experience of Relative Decline* (Princeton: Princeton University Press, 1988).

Norman Friedman. *Submarine Design and Development* (Annapolis: Naval Institute Press, 1984).

————. *U.S. Submarines through 1945* (Annapolis: Naval Institute Press, 1995).

Peter Gatrell. *Government, Industry, and Rearmament in Russia, 1900–1914* (Cambridge: Cambridge University Press, 1994).

Bentley B. Gilbert. *Lloyd George: Organiser of Victory* (London: Batsford, 1992).

Andrew Gordon. *The Rules of the Game: Jutland and British Naval Command* (London: John Murray, 1996).

Donald C. Gordon. *The Dominion Partnership in Imperial Defence, 1870–1914* (Baltimore: Johns Hopkins University Press, 1965).

Alfred Gollin. *No Longer an Island: Britain and the Wright Brothers, 1902–08* (London: Heinemann, 1984).

———. *The Observer and J. L. Garvin, 1908–1914* (Oxford: Oxford University Press, 1960).

Paul G. Halpern. *The Mediterranean Naval Situation, 1908–1914* (Cambridge: Harvard University Press, 1971).

Lord Hankey. *The Supreme Command, 1914–1918.* 2 vols. (London: Allen & Unwin, 1961).

David Hermann. *The Arming of Europe and the Making of the First World War* (Princeton: Princeton University Press, 1996).

Richard Hough. *First Sea Lord: An Authorised Biography of Admiral Lord Fisher* (London: Allen & Unwin, 1969).

Peter Kemp. *The Fisher Papers.* 2 vols. (London: Naval Records Society, 1960–64).

Paul Kennedy. *Grand Strategies in War and Peace* (New Haven:Yale University Press, 1991).

———. *The Rise and Fall of British Naval Mastery* (London: Allen Lane, 1976).

———. *The Rise and Fall of Great Powers* (London: Random House, 1987).

———. *The Rise of the Anglo-German Antagonism, 1860–1914* (London: Allen & Unwin, 1980).

———. *The Realities behind Diplomacy: Background Influences on British External Policy, 1865–1980* (London: Allen & Unwin, 1987).

Paul Kennedy, ed. *The War Plans of the Great Powers, 1880–1914* (London: Allen & Unwin, 1979).

Mark Kerr. *Prince Louis of Battenberg* (London: Longmans, Green, & Co., 1934).

Roger J. Keyes. *The Naval Memoirs of Sir Roger Keyes* (London: Thorton-Butterworth,1934).

William L. Langer. *The Diplomacy of Imperialism* (Cambridge: Harvard University Press, 1935).

Henri Le Masson. *Du Nautilus au redoutable: histoire critique du sous-marin de la marine française* (Paris, 1969).

Edouard Lockroy. *La Défense navale* (Paris, 1899).

———. *La Marine de guerre: six mois rue royale* (Paris, 1897).

Ruddock F. Mackay. *Fisher of Kilverstone* (Oxford: Oxford University Press, 1971).

Alfred T. Mahan. *The Influence of Sea-power upon History* (Boston: Little Brown, 1890).

Bernard Mallett. *British Budgets: 1887/88–1912/13* (London: Macmillan, 1913).

Frederick Manning. *The Life of Sir William White* (London: John Murray, 1923).

Edgar March. *British Destroyers* (London: Seely Service, 1967).

Arthur J. Marder. *Fear God and Dread Nought: The Correspondence of Admiral of the Fleet Lord Fisher of Kilverstone.* 3 vols. (Boston: Harvard University Press and London: Johnathan Cape, 1952–1959).

———. *From the Dreadnought to Scapa Flow.* 5 vols. (Oxford: Oxford University Press, 1961–1970).

———. *A History of British Naval Policy in the Pre-Dreadnought Era, 1880–1905.* Also published under the title of *The Anatomy of British Sea-power, 1885–1905* (London and New York: Alfred A. Knopf Inc., 1940) (rpt., London: Frank Cass, 1964) (rpt., Hamden, Conn.: Octagon Books, 1976).

William McNeill. *The Pursuit of Power* (Chicago: University of Chicago Press, 1982).

Ester Meynell. *A Woman Talking* (London: Chapman & Moore, 1940).

George Monger. *The End of Isolation: British Foreign Policy, 1900–1907* (London: Nelson, 1963).

J. E. Morpurgo. *Barnes Wallis—A Biography* (London: Penguin Books, 1973).

A. J. A. Morris. *Radicalism against War, 1906–1914: The Advocacy of Peace and Retrenchment* (London: Longman, 1972).

Jan Morris. *Fisher's Face* (London: Viking-Penguin Press, 1996).

Bruce Murray, *The Peoples Budget 1909/10: Lloyd-George and Liberal Politics* (Oxford: Clarendon Press, 1980).

Keith Neilson. *Britain and the Last Tsar: British Policy and Russia, 1894–1917* (Oxford: Oxford University Press, 1996).

Avner Offer. *The First World War: An Agrarian Interpretation* (Oxford: Oxford University Press, 1989).

Richard Ollard. *Fisher and Cunningham: A Study of Personalities of the Churchill Era* (London: Constable Press, 1991).

Peter Padfield. *Aim Straight* (London: Hodder & Stoughton, 1966).

Oscar Parkes. *British Battleships* (London: Seely Service, 1957).

A. Temple Patterson. *The Jellicoe Papers.* 2 vols. (London: Naval Records Society, 1966–68).

Hugh Peebles. *Warship Building on the Clyde: Naval Orders and the Prosperity of the Clyde Shipbuilding Industry, 1889–1939* (Edinburgh: John Donald, 1987).

Brian Ranft. *The Beatty Papers.* 2 vols. (London: Naval Records Society, 1990–1994).

Brian Ranft, ed. *Technical Change and British Naval Policy, 1860–1939* (London: Hodder & Stoughton, 1977).

Richard Rempel. *Unionists Divided: Arthur Balfour, Joseph Chamberlain & the Unionist Free Traders* (Dorset: Newton Abbot, 1972).

Theodore Ropp. *The Development of a Modern Navy: French Naval Policy, 1871–1904* (Annapolis: Naval Institute Press, 1987).

Stephen Roskill. *Churchill and the Admirals* (London: Collins, 1977).

———. *Hankey: Man of Secrets* (London: Collins, 1970).

Alex Rowland. *Underwater Warfare in the Age of Sail* (Bloomington: Indiana University Press, 1978).

Donald M. Schurman. *The Education of a Navy: The Development of British Naval Strategic Thought, 1867–1914* (London: Cassel, 1965).

———. *Julian S. Corbett, 1854–1922* (London: Royal Historical Society, 1981).

J. D. Scott. *Vickers: A History* (London: Weinfield & Nicholson, 1962).

Gaddis Smith. *Britain's Clandestine Submarines* (New Haven: Yale University Press, 1964).

Edward Spiers. *The Army and Society,1815–1914* (London: Edinburgh University Press, 1980).

———. *Haldane: An Army Reformer* (Edinburgh: Edinburgh University Press, 1980).

Johnathon Steinberg. *Yesterday's Deterrent: Tirpitz and the Birth of the German Battle Fleet* (London: Macmillan, 1965).

Murrary F. Sueter. *The Evolution of the Submarine* (Portsmouth: J. Griffin & Co., 1907).

Zara Steiner. *Britain and the Origins of the First World War* (London: Macmillan, 1977).

———. *The Foreign Office and Foreign Policy, 1898–1914* (Cambridge: Cambridge University Press, 1969).

Jon T. Sumida. *In Defence of Naval Supremacy: Finance, Technology and Naval Policy, 1889–1914* (London: Unwin Hyman, 1989).

———. *The Pollen Papers* (London: Naval Records Society, 1987).

Alan Sykes. *Tariff Reform in British Politics, 1903–1913* (Oxford: Clarendon Press, 1979).

Clive Trebilcock. *The Vickers Brothers* (London: Europa, 1977).

Sir Charles Walker. *Thirty-Six Years at the Admiralty* (London: Lincoln Williams Ltd., 1933).

Gary E. Weir. *Building American Submarines: 1914–1940* (Washington; D.C.: Department of the Navy, 1991).

Rhodri Williams. *Defending the Empire: The Conservative Party and British Defence Policy, 1899–1915* (New Haven: Yale University Press, 1991).

Samual R. Williamson. *The Politics of Grand Strategy: Britain and France Prepare for War* (Cambridge: Harvard University Press, 1969; pbk. ed., 1990).

John Wilson. *CB—A life of Sir Henry Campbell-Bannerman* (London: Constable, 1973).

Keith M. Wilson. *The Policy of Entente: Essays on the Determinants of British Foreign Policy, 1904–1914* (Cambridge: Cambridge University Press, 1985).

Articles and Essays

Robert Angevine. "The Rise and Fall of the Office of Naval Intelligence, 1882–1892: A Technological Perspective." *The Journal of Military History.* 62 (April 1998) 271–312.

William Ashworth. "Economic Aspects of Late Victorian Naval Administration." *Economic History Review.* 22 (1969) 491–505.

Nicholas d'Ombrain. "The Imperial General Staff and the Military Policy of a Continental Strategy during the 1911 International Crisis." *Military Affairs.* (October 1970): 88–93.

Charles H. Fairbanks. "The Origins of the Dreadnought Revolution: A Historiographical Essay." *The International History Review.* 13/2 (May 1991): 246–72.

Paul Hayes. "Britain, Germany, and the Admiralty's Plans for Attacking German Territory, 1906–1916." In *Strategy and International Politics: Essays in Honour of Sir Michael Howard*, ed. Robert O'Neill (Oxford: Oxford University Press, 1992).

Gerald Jordan. "Pensions not Dreadnoughts." In *Edwardian Radicalism*, ed. A. J. A. Morris, (London: Routledge, 1974).

Paul M. Kennedy. "The Development of German Naval Operational Plans versus England." *English Historical Review*. 86 (1971).

———. "The Relevance of the Pre-War British and American Maritime Strategies to the First World War and its Aftermath, 1898–1920. In *Maritime Strategy and the Balance of Power*, ed. John Hattendorf and Robert Jordan (London: Macmillan, 1989).

———. "Strategy versus Finance in Twentieth Century Great Britain." *International History Review*. 3 (1981): 45–52.

Nicholas Lambert. "Admiral of the Fleet Sir Arthur Wilson VC." In *The First Sea Lords: From Fisher to Mountbatten*, ed. Malcolm Murfett (Westport: Praegers, 1995): 35–53.

———. "Admiral Sir Francis Bridgeman." In *The First Sea Lords: From Fisher to Mountbatten*, ed. Malcolm Murfett (Westport: Praegers, 1995): 55–74.

———. "Admiral Sir John Fisher and the Concept of Flotilla Defence, 1904–1910." *The Journal of Military History*. 59 (October, 1995): 639–60.

———. "British Naval Policy 1913/14: Financial Limitation and Strategic Revolution." *The Journal of Modern History*. 67:3 (September 1995): 595–626.

———. "Economy or Empire: The Quest for Collective Security in the Pacific, 1909–1914." In *Far Flung Lines: Essays in Honour of Donald Mackenzie Shurman*, ed. Keith Neilson and Greg Kennedy (Frank Cass: London, 1996), 55–83.

———. "The Opportunities of Technology: British and French Strategy in the Pacific, 1905–09." In *The Perimeters of Naval Power*, ed. Nicholas Rodger (London: Macmillan, 1996).

Ruddock F. Mackay. "The Admiralty, the German Navy and the Redistribution of the British Fleet, 1904–08." *Mariner's Mirror*. (August 1970): 341–46.

John McDermott. "The British Army's Turn to Europe." In *The War Plans of the Great Powers*, ed. Paul Kennedy (London: Allen & Unwin, 1979. Rpt., 1985).

Bruce Murray. "Battered and Shattered: Lloyd-George and the 1914 Budget Fiasco." *Albion*. 23/3 (Fall 1991): 483–507.

Michael S. Partridge. "The Royal Navy and the End of the Close Blockade, 1885–1905." *Mariner's Mirror*. (May 1989): 119–30.

A. N. Porter. "Lord Salisbury, Foreign Policy and Domestic Finance, 1860–1900." In *Salisbury: The Man and His Policies*, ed. Lord Blake and Hugh Cecil, 148–84 (London: Macmillan, 1987).

Brian Ranft. "The Protection of British Seaborne Trade and the Development of Systematic Planning for War, 1860–1906." In *Technical Change and British Naval Policy*, ed. Brian Ranft (London: Hodder & Stoughton, 1977).

Charles Repington. "Imperial Strategy by the Military Correspondent of *The Times*." (London: John Murray, 1906)

Jon Sumida. "British Naval Administration and Policy in the Age of Fisher." *The Journal of Military History.* 54 (January 1990): 1–26.

Jon Sumida. "Churchill and British Sea Power: The Politician and Statesman as an Advocate and Antagonist of Royal Navy Expansion, 1908–1929" In *Sir Winston Churchill, Europe the Empire, and the United States,* ed. Alister Parker (London: Brassey's, 1995).

——. "The Historian as a Contemporary Analyst: Sir Julian Corbett and Sir John Fisher." In *Mahan Is Not Enough: The Proceedings of a Conference on the Works of Sir Julian Corbett and Admiral Sir Herbert Richmond,* ed. James Goldrick and John Hattendorf (Newport: Naval War College Press, 1993).

——. "The Quest for Reach: The Development of Long-range Gunnery in the Royal Navy, 1901–1912." In *Tooling for War: Military Transformation in the Industrial Age,* ed. Stephen D. Chiabotti, 49–97 (Chicago: Imprint Publications, 1996).

——. "Sir John Fisher and the Dreadnought: The Sources of Naval Mythology." *The Journal of Military History.* 59 (October 1995): 619–38.

Jon Sumida and David Rosenberg. "Machines, Men, Manufacturing, Management and Money: The Study of Navies as Complex Organisations and the Transformation of Twentieth Century Naval History." In *Doing Naval History: Essays Towards Improvement,* ed. John Hattendorf (Newport: Naval War College Press, 1995).

Clive Trebilcock. "Spin-Off in British Economic History: Armaments and Industry, 1760–1914." *Economic History Review.* 22 (1969), 474–91.

H. Weinroth. "Left Wing opposition to naval armaments in Britain before 1914." *Journal of Contemporary History.* 6 (1971).

F. W. Wiemann. "Lloyd George and the Struggle for the Navy Estimates of 1914." In *Lloyd George: Twelve Essays,* ed. A. J. P. Taylor, 71–91 (New York: Atheneum, 1971).

Keith M. Wilson. "The Question of anti-Germanism at the British Foreign Office before the First World War." *Canadian Journal of History.* 18 (1983): 23–42.

Index